The Nuremberg Trials
International Criminal Law Since 1945

Die Nürnberger Prozesse
Völkerstrafrecht seit 1945

The Nuremberg Trials
International Criminal Law Since 1945

60th Anniversary International Conference

On behalf of
Touro College Jacob D. Fuchsberg Law Center

edited by
Herbert R. Reginbogin
Christoph J. M. Safferling

in collaboration with
Walter R. Hippel

K · G · Saur München 2006

Die Nürnberger Prozesse
Völkerstrafrecht seit 1945

Internationale Konferenz zum 60. Jahrestag

Im Auftrag des
Touro College Jacob D. Fuchsberg Law Center

herausgegeben von
Herbert R. Reginbogin
Christoph J. M. Safferling

unter Mitwirkung von
Walter R. Hippel

K · G · Saur München 2006

Bibliographic information published by Die Deutsche Nationalbibliothek
Die Deutsche Nationalbibliothek lists this publication
in the Deutsche Nationalbibliografie; detailed bibliographic data
is available in the internet at *http://dnb.d-nb.de*.

Bibliografische Information Der Deutschen Nationalbibliothek
Die Deutsche Nationalbibliothek verzeichnet diese Publikation
in der Deutschen Nationalbibliografie; detaillierte bibliografische Daten
sind im Internet über *http://dnb.d-nb.de* abrufbar.

Cover photo / Umschlagfoto:
Courtroom 600 at the Palace of Justice in Nuremberg /
Gerichtssaal 600 im Nürnberger Justizpalast.
USHMM, courtesy of John W. Mosenthal

∞

Printed on acid-free paper / Gedruckt auf säurefreiem Papier

© 2006 by K. G. Saur Verlag GmbH, München
Printed in Germany
All Rights Strictly Reserved / Alle Rechte vorbehalten
Printed and Bound by / Druck und Bindung: Strauss GmbH, Mörlenbach
ISBN-13: 978-3-598-11756-5
ISBN-10: 3-598-11756-6

Contents/Inhaltsverzeichnis

Acknowledgements/Danksagung 8

Introduction/Einführung – Lessons of Nuremberg: Returning to Courtroom 600 on the
60th Anniversary of the Nuremberg Trial against the Major German War Criminals/
Lehren von Nürnberg: Rückkehr in den Saal 600 zum 60. Jahrestag des Nürnberger Prozesses
gegen die deutschen Hauptkriegsverbrecher 11

I. History and National Perspectives of the IMT at Nuremberg/
Historische und nationale Aspekte des IMT von Nürnberg

Raymond M. Brown: The American Perspective on Nuremberg: A Case of Cascading Ironies/
Die amerikanische Sicht auf Nürnberg: Ein Fall wechselnder Ironien 21

David Cesarani: The International Military Tribunal at Nuremberg: British Perspectives/
Das Internationale Militärtribunal von Nürnberg: Britische Perspektiven 31

Hervé Ascensio: The French Perspective/Die französische Perspektive 39

Michael J. Bazyler: The Role of the Soviet Union in the International Military Tribunal at
Nuremberg/Die Rolle der Sowjetunion vor dem Internationalen Militärtribunal in Nürnberg 45

Albin Eser: Das Internationale Militärtribunal von Nürnberg aus deutscher Perspektive/
The International Military Tribunal at Nuremberg from a German Perspective 53

II. Different Perspectives on the Nuremberg Trials/
Die Nürnberger Prozesse aus verschiedenen Perspektiven

Michael R. Marrus: A Jewish Lobby at Nuremberg: Jacob Robinson and the Institute of
Jewish Affairs, 1945-46/Eine jüdische Interessenvertretung in Nürnberg: Jacob Robinson
und das Institut für jüdische Angelegenheiten, 1945-46 63

Donald Bloxham: Genocide on Trial: Law and Collective Memory/Völkermord vor Gericht:
Recht und kollektives Gedächtnis 73

Sam Garkawe: The Role and Rights of Victims at the Nuremberg International Military Tribunal/
Rolle und Rechte der Opfer vor dem Nürnberger Internationalen Militärtribunal 86

Lawrence Douglas: History and Memory in the Courtroom: Reflections on Perpetrator
Trials/Geschichte und Erinnerung im Gerichtssaal: Reflektionen über Kriegsverbrecherprozesse 95

Whitney R. Harris: Tyranny on Trial – Trial of Major German War Criminals at Nuremberg,
Germany, 1945-1946/Tyrannen vor Gericht – Das Strafverfahren gegen die NS-Hauptkriegs-
verbrecher in Nürnberg, 1945-1946 106

III. Civilized People – Heinous Crimes, Philosophical-Historical Perspectives/ Zivilisierte Menschen – grauenhafte Verbrechen, historisch-philosophische Perspektiven

Herbert R. Reginbogin: Confronting "Crimes Against Humanity", from Leipzig to the Nuremberg Trials/„Verbrechen gegen die Menschlichkeit", von Leipzig nach Nürnberg 115

Klaus Kastner: Rückblick: NSDAP, Reichsparteitage, Rassengesetze/In Retrospect: Nazi Party, the Rallies, the Racial Laws 123

John Q. Barrett: "One Good Man": The Jacksonian Shape of Nuremberg/„Ein guter Mann": Jacksons Einfluss auf Nürnberg 129

Rodger D. Citron: The Nuremberg Trials and American Jurisprudence: The Decline of Legal Realism and the Revival of Natural Law/Die Nürnberger Prozesse und die amerikanische Rechtswissenschaft: Der Niedergang des Rechtsrealismus und die Wiedererstehung des Naturrechts 139

IV. The Later Nuremberg Trials/Die Nürnberger Folgeprozesse

Benjamin Ferencz: The Einsatzgruppen Trial/Der Einsatzgruppen-Prozess 153

Louise Harmon: The Doctors' Trial at Nuremberg/Der Mediziner-Prozess in Nürnberg 164

Harry Reicher: The Jurists' Trial and Lessons for the Rule of Law/Der Juristenprozess und die Lehren für den Rechtsstaat 175

Roland Bank: The Role of German Industry: From Individual Criminal Responsibility of Some to a Broadly Shared Responsibility for Compensatory Payments/Die Rolle der deutschen Industrie: Von individueller strafrechtlicher Verantwortung zur gemeinsamen Verantwortung für Entschädigungszahlung 182

Lisa Yavnai: Military Justice: War Crimes Trials in the American Zone of Occupation in Germany, 1945-1947/Militärjustiz: Kriegsverbrecherprozesse in der amerikanisch besetzten Zone in Deutschland, 1945-1947 191

V. National Prosecution in Germany, Israel, Australia and Other Nations/ Nationale Strafverfolgung in Deutschland, Israel, Australien und anderen Ländern

Hinrich Rüping: Zwischen Recht und Politik: Die Ahndung von NS-Taten in beiden deutschen Staaten nach 1945/Between Law and Politics: The Prosecution of NS-Criminals in the Two German States after 1945 199

Rebecca Wittmann: The Normalization of Nazi Crime in Postwar West German Trials/Die Normalisierung von NS-Kriegsverbrechen in den Nachkriegs-Prozessen der Bundesrepublik Deutschland 209

Gabriel Bach: Genocide (Holocaust) Trials in Israel/Völkermord (Holocaust)-Verfahren in Israel 216

Greg James: A Summary of the History of Nazi War Crime Trials in Australia/ Eine Zusammenfassung der Geschichte der Nazi-Kriegsverbrecherprozesse in Australien 224

VI. Germany's Attitude towards International Criminal Law/Deutschlands Haltung zum Völkerstrafrecht

Claus Kress: Germany and International Criminal Law: Continuity or Change?/Deutschland und das Völkerstrafrecht – Kontinuität oder Wandel?...235

VII. The Legacy of Nuremberg/Das Vermächtnis von Nürnberg

Hans-Peter Kaul: The International Criminal Court: Key Features and Current Challenges/Der Internationale Strafgerichtshof: Hauptmerkmale und künftige Herausforderungen 245

Anne Bayefsky: The Legacy of Nuremberg/Das Vermächtnis von Nürnberg...251

Wanda M. Akin: Nuremberg, Justice and the Beast of Impunity/Nürnberg, Gerechtigkeit und das Schreckgespenst der Straflosigkeit 257

Andreas Zimmermann: Das juristische Erbe von Nürnberg – Das Statut des Nürnberger Internationalen Militärtribunals und der Internationale Strafgerichtshof/The Judicial Legacy of Nuremberg – The Statute of the International Military Tribunal of Nuremberg and the International Criminal Court 266

Dan Derby: Enforcement of Nuremberg Norms: The Role for Mechanisms other than the ICC/Durchsetzung der Normen von Nürnberg: Strafverfolgungsmechanismen jenseits des Internationalen Strafgerichtshofs..278

Roger P. Alford: War Reparations, the Holocaust, and the ICC/Kriegsentschädigung, der Holocaust und der ICC 284

VIII. Totalitarianism and German Resistance/Totalitarismus und deutsche Widerstandsbewegungen

Winfried Heinemann: Das Attentat auf Hitler: 20. Juli 1944 und die Geschichte des deutschen Widerstands/The Plot to Kill Hitler: July 20, 1944 and the Story of the German Resistance Movement 293

Joachim Gauck: Totalitarismus im 3. Reich und in der DDR – eine vergleichende Analyse/Under Totalitarian Regimes: A Comparative Analysis of National Socialism and the German Democratic Republic 301

IX. A Different Story/Eine andere Geschichte

Robert Wolfson: Liberating Perspectives/Eine andere Geschichte 311

List of Authors/Autorenverzeichnis 319

ACKNOWLEDGEMENTS

As editors of the "Gedächtnisschrift" in commemoration of the Nuremberg trials 60 years ago, we take great pride and pleasure in thanking the authors for their outstanding presentations. They were presented in Nuremberg during a four-day international conference in the summer of 2005 called "Judging Nuremberg: The Laws, The Rallies, The Trials: Returning to Courtroom 600 on the 60th Anniversary of the Nuremberg Trials". This conference was made possible through the generous logistical and financial support of the following major sponsors

Touro College Jacob D. Fuchsberg Law Center,
Superior Court Nuremberg,
Foundation "Remembrance, Responsibility and Future", "Remembrance and Future" Fund,
Faculty of Law at the University Erlangen-Nuremberg,
German-American Lawyers' Association, Bonn,
The State of New York

as well as many other German and American sponsors listed below.

The "Gedächtnisschrift" provides an opportunity to read the presentations made at the conference last year and is dedicated to the many victims of World War II and those who have sought justice through international law in the 60 years since the Nuremberg trial.

We would also like to express our sincere appreciation to all the speakers and especially to the following colleagues:

Dean Professor Lawrence Raful, Touro College Jacob D. Fuchsberg Law Center for giving us the opportunity to edit this book; President and Vice-President of the Superior Court Nuremberg, Dr. Stefan Franke and Ewald Behrschmidt; Dean Professor Dr. Mathias Rohe, Faculty of Law at the University of Erlangen-Nuremberg, for unbureaucratic help in so many regards; Attorney at Law Walter R. Hippel, Member of the Board of the GALA, without whose assistance in editing and so many other ways, this book would (probably) not exist. We are also grateful to K. G. Saur Verlag for publishing the book.

Naturally, a book of this scope includes the efforts of many others than those already mentioned. We are grateful to all them and can only say, thank you: Brigitte Gräßl, Ulrike Seeberger, Dagmar Schwarzbach, Sabine Trippmacher, and the always helpful students from Erlangen University Louisa Brennecke, Laura Wevelsiep, Alexander Horlamus and Werner Thienemann.

Finally we would like to thank each other for the cooperation and exceptionally pleasant work in editing and writing this book together.

June 2006

Herbert R. Reginbogin   Christoph J.M. Safferling

DANKSAGUNG

Als Herausgeber dieser „Gedächtnisschrift" zum 60. Jahrestag der Nürnberger Prozesse ist es uns eine besondere Ehre und Freude, den Autoren für die herausragende Qualität ihrer Beiträge zu danken. Die Referate wurden in Nürnberg im Sommer 2005 im Rahmen der viertägigen internationalen „Nürnberger Konferenz: Rückkehr in den Gerichtssaal 600 zum 60. Jahrestag der Nürnberger Prozesse" gehalten. Die Durchführung dieser Konferenz war nur durch die großzügige finanzielle wie auch logistische Unterstützung von

Touro College Jacob D. Fuchsberg Law Center,
Oberlandesgericht Nürnberg,
Stiftung „Erinnerung, Verantwortung und Zukunft", Fonds „Erinnerung und Zukunft",
Juristische Fakultät der Friedrich-Alexander-Universität Erlangen-Nürnberg,
Deutsch-Amerikanische Juristen-Vereinigung e.V., Bonn,
dem Bundesstaat New York

sowie vielen anderen nachstehend aufgeführten deutschen und amerikanischen Sponsoren möglich.

Mit der vorliegenden „Gedächtnisschrift" können die Referate auch nach Abschluss der Konferenz dem interessierten Leser zur Verfügung gestellt werden. Die „Gedächtnisschrift" ist den vielen Opfern des Zweiten Weltkrieges gewidmet und denen, die in den 60 Jahren seit Nürnberg durch das Völkerrecht Gerechtigkeit einforderten.

Unser tiefer Dank gilt allen Rednern für ihre Präsentation. In ganz besonderer Weise möchten wir die Verdienste hervorheben von

Dekan Professor Lawrence Raful, Touro College Jacob D. Fuchsberg Law Center, der uns die Möglichkeit zur Herausgabe dieses Buches geboten hat; Präsident und Vize-Präsident des Oberlandesgerichts Nürnberg, Dr. Stefan Franke und Ewald Behrschmidt; Dekan Professor Dr. Mathias Rohe, Juristische Fakultät der Friedrich-Alexander-Universität Erlangen-Nürnberg, für seine unbürokratische Unterstützung in vielen Fällen; Rechtsanwalt Walter R. Hippel, Regionalvorstand der DAJV, dessen unschätzbare Hilfe das Zustandekommen dieser Gedächtnisschrift ermöglicht hat; dem K.G. Saur Verlag für die Veröffentlichung dieser Gedächtnisschrift.

Es steht außer Zweifel, dass ein Buch dieser Art seine Existenz noch vielen Anderen als den bereits Erwähnten verdankt. Wir bedanken uns außerdem für Hilfe und Beistand in verschiedener Weise bei Brigitte Gräßl, Ulrike Seeberger, Dagmar Schwarzbach und Sabine Trippmacher und bei den stets hilfreichen Erlanger Studierenden Louisa Brennecke, Laura Wevelsiep, Alexander Horlamus und Werner Thienemann.

Schlussendlich möchten wir uns gegenseitig für die Kooperation und außerordentlich angenehme Zusammenarbeit bei der gemeinsamen Erstellung und Herausgabe dieses Buches bedanken.

Juni 2006

Herbert R. Reginbogin   Christoph J.M. Safferling

German and American Sponsors/Deutsche und U.S.-amerikanische Sponsoren:

Universität Karlsruhe (TH) Institut für Geschichte Forschungsstelle „Widerstand gegen den Nationalsozialismus im deutschen Südwesten"
German-American Institute Nuremberg/Germany
Documentation Centre Nazi Party Rally Grounds
The International Association of Genocide Scholars
Faber-Castell, Stein/Nürnberg
VAG Verkehrs-Aktiengesellschaft Nürnberg

With Underwriting Support from/Mit finanzieller Unterstützung durch
The New York State Assembly; Hon. Sol Wachtler; Melvyn Weiss/Milberg Weiss Bershad & Schulman, LLP; United States Department of State, US Embassy Berlin and The Ethel and Alexander Nichoson Foundation

Initiated by/Initiiert von
Professor Michael J. Bazyler
Whittier Law School
Professor Herbert R. Reginbogin
Touro College, Potsdam Germany Law Program, University of Potsdam, and Bogazici University, Istanbul
Professor Lawrence Raful
Dean, Touro College Jacob D. Fuchsberg Law Center

With Special Thanks to/Besonderer Dank an
Hon. Sol Wachtler
Chief Judge of the New York State Court of Appeals (ret.)
Professor Howard A. Glickstein
Dean Emeritus, Touro College Jacob D. Fuchsberg Law Center

Conference Organizational Committee/Organisationsleitung
Dr. Stefan Franke, *President, Superior Court Nuremberg*; Ewald Behrschmidt, *Vice President, Superior Court Nuremberg*; Prof. Dr. Klaus Kastner, *former President, Regional Court Nürnberg-Fürth*; Walter R. Hippel, *Attorney at Law, Member of the Board of the German-American Lawyers' Association*; Monika Müller-Rieger, *Büro Müller-Rieger GbR*, Prof. Herbert R. Reginbogin, *Touro College, Potsdam Germany Law Program, University of Potsdam, and Bogazici University Istanbul*; Dr. Christoph J.M. Safferling, *Friedrich-Alexander-University Erlangen-Nuremberg*; Mario Schaffer, *Superior Court Nuremberg*; Hans-Christian Taubrich, *Director of the Documentation Centre, Nuremberg*; Linda Howard Weissman, *Assistant Dean, Touro College Jacob D. Fuchsberg Law Center*

Staff Organization/Sekretariat
Allison Flor and Carol Howell, *Touro College Jacob D. Fuchsberg Law Center*

Sponsors/weitere Sponsoren:
Siemens AG, OBI Baumarkt Franken, Stadtsparkasse Nürnberg, Eckart GmbH, Alpha Projektentwicklung, City West, Nuremberg; Weiß Glimm & Kollegen, Erlangen; Hildmann, Langenwalder, Lüders, Hoffmann, Erlangen; Dr. Beck & Partner, Nuremberg; Beiten Burkhardt, Nuremberg; Salleck und Partner, Erlangen; Alumni Association of the Law Faculty of the University of Erlangen-Nuremberg, the Vinzl-Foundation, Erlangen.

Introduction – Lessons of Nuremberg
Returning to Courtroom 600 on the 60th Anniversary of the Nuremberg Trial against the Major German War Criminals

Herbert R. Reginbogin & Christoph J.M. Safferling

I.

On November 20, 1945, the English President of the International Military Tribunal, Sir Geoffrey Lawrence, opened trial proceedings to try twenty-one war criminals sitting in Courtroom 600 at the Palace of Justice at Nuremberg.[1] The next day, Chief Counsel of the United States of America, Justice Robert Jackson, presented the case for the prosecution pointing out the abominable acts of cruelty and unmistakably confronted the world with the horrors of the German concentration camps. For the first time in history, an international tribunal took on the grave responsibility of hearing a case against economic, political and military leaders charged with crimes involving the commission of conspiracy, crimes against the peace, war crimes, and 'crimes against humanity' (involving persecution, mass deportation, and extermination on political, racial, or religious grounds). Although the Nuremberg trial was an attempt to reconcile justice by punishing Nazi leaders, it has been difficult for people and nations to live as neighbors with Germany again due to the amount of cruelty exhibited through the awesome brutality and meticulousness with which Germans killed millions of harmless people. While the mere shock of the Holocaust continues to leave a void in international affairs even sixty years after World War II, attempts have been made to heal the wounds of the past by calling for the establishment of an international system of justice modeled after the Nuremberg trials, which has met a good deal of opposition. "We must never forget," Jackson declared in his opening address "that the record on which we judge these defendants today is the record on which history will judge us tomorrow." This book will examine a range of aspects surrounding the trials' legacy.

II.

The collection of papers in this book contains 33 different expert opinions and eyewitness accounts of the Nuremberg trials, which were presented during a four-day-conference held in Nuremberg last summer in July, 2005. A broad range of historical and contemporary topics are offered about the historical pretext of the Nuremberg trials and impact on modern international criminal law. Papers presented in this book were submitted in form of a manuscript for oral presentation, or transcripts of the spoken word, or as an academic publication. Each paper includes an abstract in either German or English to allow scholars, students and other interested readers greater accessibility to the valuable contributions held at the conference and important references made in the papers.

At the outset of the conference, five scholars represented each of the countries that convened at the International Military Tribunal (IMT) in Nuremberg, which constituted the four presiding allied nations (the United States of America, the United Kingdom, the Soviet Union and France) over Germany's war crimes. In this session we are told of the dominant role played by the American prosecution team in planning and organizing the trial through Chief Prosecutor Robert H. Jackson, whose predominant aim focused mainly to incriminate the Nazi defendants on conspiring to wage an aggressive war and not on account of the Holocaust (*Raymond Brown*). In contrast the UK (*David Cesarani*) was at first skeptical about holding a trial, but due to the enormous pressure exerted by the many exiled European governments headquartered in London and the U.S. position, the UK decided to participate. France (*Hervé Ascensio*), the last to join the IMT, was particularly interested in punitive justice for the

---

[1] The Tribunal had originally planned to try twenty-four Nazi leaders, but Robert Ley committed suicide on October 25, 1945 and the trial of Gustav Krupp von Bohlen und Hallbach had been postponed indefinitely owing to a serious health condition. Martin Borman was not in the custody of the court and tried *in absentia*, who was officially proclaimed dead by a German court almost ten years later, declaring he was killed on May 1 or 2, 1945.

atrocities that occurred within its borders. The same held true for the Soviet Union (*Michael Bazyler*), which suffered the greatest losses among the Allies in the 2nd World War with as many as 20 million killed Soviet civilians, but had at the same time tried to cloud the issue that Stalin had ordered mass atrocities. Finally, many in the German legal profession at the time viewed the trial (*Albin Eser*) as nothing more than a piece of "victor's justice" and invalidation of retroactive lawmaking.

When reviewing the procedures of Nuremberg, discrepancies and flaws can be found as a result of the challenges between the aims of criminal prosecution and history. Specifically, it is striking to note that the Holocaust did not play the decisive role we would expect today in the prosecution of the Nazi leaders. Even if Jewish organizations had considerable influence on the US prosecution (*Michael Marrus*), the Nuremberg trial did little to enhance a collective understanding or consciousness of the Holocaust (*Donald Bloxham*). The victims did not play the role at Nuremberg that they could and should have (*Sam Garkawe*), as in any criminal trial, where victim's testimony is heard as evidence giving survivors the opportunity to describe the life experiences and stories of cruelty they endured. This would have made the trial much more dramatic and memorable to the public, and lent substantial weight to the "guilty" verdict (*Lawrence Douglas*). The address of the former member of the US prosecuting team, *Whitney R. Harris*, recalled the Nuremberg trial as a remarkable event.

Nuremberg was, however, not the first time ever that war crimes were prosecuted. In fact, after World War I, Germany put hundreds of its own people on trial before national courts for committing war crimes (*Herbert Reginbogin*), almost all of whom were acquitted. The city of Nuremberg was not only the venue for the trial; it played quite an extraordinary role during the time of the Nazi regime (*Klaus Kastner*). However, Justice Robert Jackson had different reasons to choose Nuremberg in preparation of the IMT in 1945 other than the city's notorious Nazi past. (*John Barrett*). The legal difficulties in prosecuting the Nazi criminals in Nuremberg had an impact on American jurisprudence, which led to a revival of theories about natural law (*Rodger Citron*).

After the IMT in Nuremberg rendered its verdicts against the 21 accused Nazi leaders present and one *in absentia*, it concluded its assignment in October 1946. Twelve more trials were held in Nuremberg under the sole jurisdiction of the USA as the occupying power in this sector of Germany. The trial against members of the Nazi extermination squads (Einsatzgruppen) was presented by the former Chief prosecutor, Benjamin Ferencz. Other trials were conducted against Nazi doctors (*Louise Harmon*), against Nazi jurists (*Harry Reicher*) and against the Nazi-supporting German industry, whereas the matter of compensation for forced labour was settled only in 2001 (*Roland Bank*). Also after the end of World War II, several war criminals were prosecuted in the different German occupied zones. The US administration conducted besides the trials at Nuremberg also special proceedings in Dachau (*Elisabeth Yavnai*).

It is a different story about the national prosecution of Nazi criminals. After West Germany regained its sovereignty, it retained the full responsibility to put former Nazis on trial. The record of both the West- and East-German legal systems in prosecuting former Nazi collaborators is actually quite shameful (*Hinrich Rüping*), and Germany's civil servants and judges were either not inclined or unable to enforce existing laws to bring Nazi criminals to justice (*Rebecca Wittmann*). Maybe the most spectacular and debated national crime against a former Nazi was the trial against Adolf Eichmann in Jerusalem. The former prosecutor of Eichmann in Israel, Gabriel Bach, presented this and other cases in Israel. A final presentation was made by (*Greg James*) about Australia and ist country's effort to prosecute accused Nazi war criminals.

Before turning to the latest developments in international criminal law, one presentation (*Claus Kress*) describes the German attitude towards international criminal law and finds that it has changed considerably since Nuremberg. Today, Germany is a member of the International Criminal Court (ICC) and a report was presented on the latest achievements at the ICC by one of its judges (*Hans-Peter Kaul*). A quite different view was expressed by (*Anne Bayefsky*), who sees clearly an anti-Israeli bias in decisions rendered by both the ICC and the United Nations. Several tribunals have been created to protect human rights and prosecute crimes against humanity like the UN backed Special Court for Sierra Leone (*Wanda Akin*). Although the ICC is still a fairly young institution, it is considered by the Security Council of the United Nations to have the legal authority to bring war criminals to justice. The origins of the ICC can be traced back to the Nuremberg trials although many things have changed in terms of enhancing both the efficiency of the proceedings and protecting the rights of the victim as well as those of the accused (*Andreas Zimmermann*). Despite this international institution, international criminal law depends on national, i.e. indirect enforcement; the ICC's jurisdiction is after all supposed to be complementary to national jurisdictions (*Dan Derby*). Finally the role and the rights of the victim deserve attention. The ICC has found quite an interesting and promising way to integrate the victim into the overall procedure of the court (*Roger Alford*).

When looking at the history of Nazi Germany it cannot be overlooked that there were resistance movements against Hitler, which included high profiled military and political leaders involved in unsuccessful plots to kill Hitler (*Winfried Heinemann*).

Germany's fate was dramatically shaken as its eastern territory was occupied by the Soviet Union, which set-up a socialist regime. This second totalitarian regime continued to exist until the end of the Cold War marked by the fall of the Berlin Wall and the reunification of Germany. Many people which had lived through both regimes, experienced similar forms of suppression (*Joachim Gauck*).

At the very end of the conference, a paper was presented, which portrayed quite a different story, the story of a photograph. Memories and pictures of Dachau's liberation, so horrible, one would never be able to forget (*Robert Wolfson*).

III.

A thread of international human rights law did exist even before World War I. Yet the idea of inalienable right of human beings and humanity materialized in 1945 at the Nuremberg trials. While human rights were promoted around the world and the United Nations embraced the Nuremberg principles by adopting and codifying provisions of humanitarian law, the ideals of Nuremberg to internationally prosecute crimes against humanity were put on ice during the Cold War. Yet the thread of international criminal law was never completely forgotten as the United Nations, some national states and the international civil society represented by a number of NGOs kept the fire burning to create a permanent international criminal court. The UN International Law Commission continued drafting codifications of international criminal law and statutes for an International Criminal Court, while some countries never ceased to try bring former Nazi criminals to justice as in the case of the Eichmann Trial in Israel. However, it would not be before the fall of the Berlin Wall that the thread of international criminal prosecution would finally reappear as a means to respond to the ethnic cleansing and massacres on the Balkans. Since then, international criminal law has been seen as a political tool serving international peace and security while used sporadically to seek justice. At the moment, the International Criminal Court is the knot at the end of the thread, which is heavily disputed currently as a tool of "judicial intervention" and political agendas, which need to be rectified.

The "Gedächtnisschrift" attempts to shed light on some of the inconsistencies and complexities by Judging Nuremberg: the Rallies, the Laws and the Trials sixty years after the proceedings began against some of the major German war criminals. We are still mid-way upstream as reports are filed about atrocities from around the world pointing out the need to develop a system of international justice. As we turn to Nuremberg and its legacy, we can only hope that the papers in this volume will contribute in finding an answers to enforce laws against war criminals how to effectively bring them to justice.

Einführung – Lehren von Nürnberg
Rückkehr in den Saal 600 zum 60. Jahrestag des Nürnberger Prozesses gegen die deutschen Hauptkriegsverbrecher

Herbert R. Reginbogin & Christoph J.M. Safferling

I.

Am 20. November 1945 eröffnete der englische Vorsitzende des Internationalen Militärtribunals, Sir Geoffrey Lawrence, die Hauptverhandlung im Strafverfahren gegen 21 anwesende Angeklagte im Gerichtssaal 600 des Nürnberger Justizpalastes.[1] Am darauf folgenden Tag trug der Chefankläger der Vereinigten Staaten von Amerika, der Bundesrichter Robert Jackson, die Anklage vor. Darin beschrieb er die ungeheuerlichen Grausamkeiten des NS-Regimes und konfrontierte die Weltöffentlichkeit mit dem Horror der Konzentrationslager. Zum ersten Mal in der Geschichte der Menschheit wurde wirtschaftlichen, politischen und militärischen Führern vor einem internationalen Tribunal wegen des Verbrechens der Verschwörung, Verbrechen gegen den Frieden, Kriegsverbrechen und „Verbrechen gegen die Menschlichkeit" (darunter Verfolgung, Massendeportationen, Vernichtung wegen politischer, rassischer oder religiöser Gründe) der Prozess gemacht. Mit diesem so genannten Nürnberger Prozess wurde der Versuch unternommen, durch die strafrechtliche Verfolgung von wichtigen Nazi-Führern ein Zusammenleben der Völker und Nationen als Nachbarn Deutschlands, das Millionen unschuldiger Menschen mit erschreckender Brutalität und Perfektion ermordet hatte, wieder zu ermöglichen. Der durch die Bekanntmachung des Holocaust ausgelöste Schock hat sich selbst 60 Jahre nach den furchtbaren Ereignissen des 2. Weltkrieges noch nicht völlig verflüchtigt und überschattet auch heute noch die internationalen Beziehungen. Nach Beendigung des Nürnberger Prozesses sind immer wieder Versuche unternommen worden, internationale Strafgerechtigkeit nach dem Nürnberger Modell zu etablieren, nicht ohne dabei auf erhebliche Opposition zu stoßen.

„Wir dürfen nie vergessen", betonte Jackson in seinem Eröffnungsplädoyer, „dass der Maßstab, mit dem wir diese Angeklagten heute beurteilen, derselbe ist, mit dem die Geschichte uns morgen beurteilen wird." In diesem Buch werden verschiedene Aspekte im Zusammenhang mit dem Vermächtnis des Nürnberger Prozesses untersucht.

II.

Die hier vorgelegte Aufsatzsammlung enthält 33 Beiträge von Augenzeugen und Wissenschaftlern der Nürnberger Prozesse, die anlässlich einer viertägigen Konferenz im Juli 2005 in Nürnberg präsentiert wurden. Die Spannbreite des Buches umfasst historische und aktuelle Themen, ausgehend von der geschichtlichen Entwicklung hin zum Nürnberger Prozess bis zu dessen Auswirkungen auf das moderne Völkerstrafrecht. Die Beiträge liegen teilweise in Form eines Redemanuskripts, als Niederschrift des gesprochenen Wortes, oder als wissenschaftliche Ausarbeitung vor. Um Wissenschaftlern, Studierenden und anderen interessierten Lesern den Zugang zu den Vorträgen der zweisprachigen Konferenz zu erleichtern, umfasst jeder Beitrag entweder eine deutsche oder englische Zusammenfassung.

Zu Beginn der Konferenz stellten fünf Wissenschaftler, stellvertretend für die am Internationalen Militärtribunal (IMT) in Nürnberg beteiligten Nationen (die Vereinigten Staaten von Amerika, das Vereinigte Königreich, die Sowjetunion und Frankreich als Richternationen und Deutschland als Heimatstaat der Angeklagten) die Interessen ihres Landes an dem Prozess dar. Dabei wurde die herausragende Rolle des US-amerikanischen Anklageteams um den Chefankläger Robert Jackson bei der Planung und Durchführung des Verfahrens deutlich, dessen primäres Interesse darin bestand, die

---

[1] Ursprünglich waren 24 ehemalige NS-Größen angeklagt. Robert Ley nahm sich am 25 Oktober 1945 das Leben; das Verfahren gegen Gustav Krupp von Bohlen und Hallbach wurde wegen Verhandlungsunfähigkeit auf unbestimmte Zeit vertagt; gegen Martin Bormann wurde in Abwesenheit verhandelt. Zehn Jahre später wurde Bormann von einem deutschen Gericht für tot erklärt, wobei festgestellt wurde, dass er am 1. oder 2. Mai 1945 umgekommen war.

Angeklagten für den Angriffskrieg und weniger für den Holocaust strafrechtlich zur Verantwortung zu ziehen (*Raymond Brown*). Im Vergleich dazu war England (*David Cesarani*) zunächst skeptisch, was die Durchführung von Strafverfahren insgesamt anbelangte, entschloss sich schließlich aber auf Grund des enormen Drucks seitens der vielen in London anwesenden europäischen Exilregierungen und den USA doch zur Kooperation. Frankreich (*Hervé Ascensio*) kam als letzte Nation zur Teilnahme am IMT und war besonders daran interessiert, die auf französischem Territorium verübten Verbrechen zu sühnen. Das Gleiche gilt für die Sowjetunion (*Michael Bazyler*), die mit fast 20 Millionen toten Zivilisten die höchsten Verluste unter den Alliierten zu beklagen hatte, zugleich aber darauf bedacht war, die von Stalin befohlenen Massenverbrechen zu verschleiern. In Deutschland schließlich (*Albin Eser*) war die Ansicht weit verbreitet, dass „Nürnberg" nichts als blanke „Siegerjustiz" war und ein Verstoß gegen das Rückwirkungsverbot darstellte.

Das Verfahren in Nürnberg bringt die Schwierigkeiten zu Tage, die entstehen, wenn Strafverfahren zugleich einer geschichtlichen Aufarbeitung gerecht werden sollen. Im Speziellen ist es erstaunlich, dass der Holocaust im Nürnberger Prozess bei weitem nicht die Rolle gespielt hat, die wir heute erwarten würden. Trotz des nicht unerheblichen Einflusses jüdischer Organisationen vor allem auf das Anklageteam der USA (*Michael Marrus*) ist unser kollektives Verständnis des Holocausts wenig vom Nürnberger Prozess geprägt (*Donald Bloxham*). Opfer fanden dort nicht das Podium, das ihnen zugestanden hätte, um als Überlebende ihre Erfahrungen der unsagbaren Grausamkeiten öffentlich zu formulieren (*Sam Garkawe*). Das Nürnberger Verfahren wäre durch eine breitere Opferbeteiligung für die Öffentlichkeit um einiges dramatischer und einprägsamer gewesen; zugleich hätte der Schuldspruch dadurch eine höhere Legitimität erhalten (*Lawrence Douglas*). Der Vortrag des früheren Mitglieds des Anklageteams der USA, *Whitney R. Harris*, brachte die damaligen Vorgänge im Gerichtssaal 600 neuerlich lebendig vor Augen.

Grundsätzlich stellte Nürnberg für die strafrechtliche Verfolgung von Kriegsverbrechen kein Novum dar. Tatsächlich waren in Deutschland nach Ende des 1. Weltkrigs gegen Hunderte von Deutschen vor nationalen Gerichten Anklagen erhoben worden; die Verfahren endeten jedoch fast alle mit einem Freispruch (*Herbert Reginbogin*). Nürnberg war nicht nur der Ort, an dem die Prozesse abgehalten wurden; die Stadt spielte auch eine besondere Rolle in der Geschichte des NS-Regimes (*Klaus Kastner*). Trotz dieser NS-Vergangenheit Nürnbergs standen für Robert Jackson 1945 andere Gründe für die Standortwahl im Vordergrund (*John Barrett*). Die rechtlichen Schwierigkeiten mit der strafrechtlichen Ahndung der NS-Verbrecher blieben auch in den USA nicht ohne Wirkung und führten zu einer Wiederbelebung von Naturrechtstheorien (*Rodger Citron*).

Nach der Urteilsverkündung gegen die 21 anwesenden und einen abwesenden Angeklagten schloss das IMT in Nürnberg im Oktober 1946 seine Tore. Zwölf weitere Verfahren fanden im Schwurgerichtssaal in Nürnberg statt, allerdings unter der alleinigen Kompetenz der amerikanischen Besatzungsmacht (sog. Nürnberger Nachfolgeprozesse). Im Verfahren gegen Mitglieder der „Einsatzgruppen" vertrat *Benjamin Ferencz* die Anklage. Es wurden noch weitere Verfahren gegen Nazi-Ärzte (*Louise Harmon*), gegen Juristen (*Harry Reicher*) und gegen die deutsche Industrie durchgeführt, wobei die Frage der Entschädigung für Zwangsarbeit erst im Jahr 2001 geklärt wurde (*Roland Bank*). Es wurden nach Ende des 2. Weltkriegs in den individuellen Besatzungszonen verschiedene Prozesse gegen deutsche Kriegsverbrecher durchgeführt. So fanden auch in Dachau neben den Nürnberger Nachfolgeprozessen Kriegsverbrecherverfahren statt (*Elisabeth Yavnai*).

Auf der Konferenz wurden auch die nationalen Verfahren gegen Nazi-Verbrecher angesprochen, die sehr unterschiedlich verlaufen sind. Nach der Wiedererlangung staatlicher Souveränität war Deutschland für die Strafverfolgung der eigenen Nazi-Verbrecher verantwortlich. Im Rückblick muss man allerdings feststellen, dass die Geschichte der west- wie ostdeutschen gerichtlichen Aufarbeitung eher beschämend ist (*Hinrich Rüping*) und dass die deutschen Beamten und Richter nicht willens oder unfähig waren, die bestehenden Gesetze des Landes anzuwenden, um die NS-Verbrechen zu ahnden (*Rebecca Wittmann*). Vielleicht der spektakulärste und umstrittenste nationale Prozess gegen einen früheren Nazi-Verbrecher war der Prozess gegen Adolf Eichmann in Jerusalem. Der frühere Ankläger Eichmanns in Israel, *Gabriel Bach*, berichtet von diesem und anderen Prozessen in Israel. Zuletzt wurde noch ein Blick auf Kriegsverbrecherprozesse in Australien geworfen (*Greg James*).

Vor verschiedenen Beiträgen zu jüngsten Entwicklungen im Völkerstrafrecht, wird die Haltung Deutschlands zum Völkerstrafrecht betrachtet, die seit dem Nürnberger Verfahren erstaunliche Wendungen genommen hat (*Claus Kress*). Heute ist Deutschland ein wichtiges Mitglied des Internationalen Strafgerichtshofs (ICC). Über den dortigen aktuellen Stand berichtete der deutsche Richter am ICC (*Hans-Peter Kaul*). Die nächste Rednerin erhob sowohl gegen den ICC als auch die Vereinten Nationen den Vorwurf einer insgesamt offenkundig anti-israelischen Haltung (*Anne Bayefsky*). In den letzten Jahren wurden verschiedene Tribunale zum Schutz der Menschenrechte und der strafrechtlichen Ahndung von Verbrechen gegen die Menschlichkeit eingerichtet, wie das von den Vereinten Nationen unterstützte Sondergericht für Sierra Leone (*Wanda Akin*). Trotz seines jungen Alters wird nun der ICC vom Sicherheitsrat der Vereinten Nationen mit der Verfolgung von Kriegsverbrechen beauftragt. Er entwickelt sich so zur wichtigsten Institution der Durchsetzung von Völkerstrafrecht. Die Ursprünge des ICC können zum Nürnberger Tribunal zurückverfolgt werden, auch wenn sich zwischenzeitlich viele Dinge verändert haben, um die Effizienz des Gerichts zu erhöhen und die Rechte der Opfer sowie der Angeklagten zu verbessern (*Andreas Zimmermann*). Trotz der Existenz dieser internationalen Institution hängt die Durchsetzung von Völkerstrafrecht von nationaler Strafverfolgung, d.h. indirekter Durchsetzung, ab. Schließlich ist die Kompetenz des ICC komplementär zur Zuständigkeit nationaler Behörden (*Dan Derby*). Zuletzt verdienen die Rolle und Rechte der Opfer gesonderte Aufmerksamkeit. Beim ICC wurde ein interessanter und viel versprechender Weg gefunden, Opfer in das Strafverfahren zu integrieren (*Roger Alford*).

Die Nazi-Geschichte in Deutschland wäre nicht vollständig, würde man nicht auch den Aktivitäten der innerdeutschen Widerstandsbewegungen Beachtung schenken. Eine davon bestand in dem von hohen militärischen und politischen Persönlichkeiten initiierten, allerdings missglückten Attentat auf Hitler (*Winfried Heinemann*).

Das Schicksal Deutschlands wurde nach dem Krieg auf dramatische Art und Weise durch den Umstand beeinflusst, dass in der sowjetischen Besatzungszone ein „sozialistisches" Regime nach kommunistischem Vorbild errichtet wurde. Dieses im Anschluss an den Nationalsozialismus zweite totalitäre System auf deutschem Boden mit ähnlichen Formen der Unterdrückung konnte sich bis zum Ende des Kalten Krieges halten. Der Fall der Berliner Mauer und die Vereinigung der beiden Teile Deutschlands stehen gleichsam als Symbol für das Ende der Blockbildung (*Joachim Gauck*).

Das Ende der Konferenz bestand in einem etwas anderen Vortrag. Es handelte sich dabei um die Geschichte eines Fotografen, der mit erschütternden Bildern und Erinnerungen, die man niemals wird vergessen können, die Befreiung des Konzentrationslagers Dachau schilderte (*Robert Wolfson*).

III.

Hinweise auf ein universelles Konzept von Menschenrechten waren schon vor dem 1. Weltkrieg existent. Im Nürnberger Prozess allerdings hat sich die Idee unveräußerlicher Rechte der Menschen und der Menschheit auf wundersame Weise materialisiert. Daran anschließend wurden Menschenrechte auf dem gesamten Globus publik gemacht und die Vereinten Nationen verabschiedeten neben den „Nürnberger Prinzipien" verschiedene Menschenrechtspakte, das Ideal von Nürnberg aber, nämlich die internationale strafrechtliche Verfolgung von Verbrechen gegen die Menschlichkeit, wurde während des Kalten Kriegs auf Eis gelegt. Trotzdem erlitt die Idee eines Völkerstrafrechts niemals eine völlige Niederlage; im Gegenteil: die Vereinten Nationen, verschiedene Nationalstaaten und nicht zuletzt eine internationale Zivilgesellschaft vertreten durch eine Reihe von Nichtregierungsorganisationen, fachten die Flamme für einen ständigen Internationalen Strafgerichtshof immer wieder an. Der Rechtsausschuss der Vereinten Nationen formulierte in regelmäßigen Abständen Entwürfe sowohl für eine Kodifikation von Völkerstrafrecht sowie für Statuten eines internationalen Strafgerichts. Einige Nationalstaaten ließen nicht in ihrem Eifer nach, Nazi-Verbrecher zu verfolgen und vor Gericht zu bringen, wie Israel im Fall Eichmann. Die Idee eines internationalen Strafgerichtshofs kehrte erst nach dem Fall der Berliner Mauer auf die politische Agenda zurück, um damit auf ethnische Säuberungen und Massaker auf dem Balkan reagieren zu können. Seitdem wird Völkerstrafrecht als ein politisches Mittel zur Erhaltung und Wiederherstellung von internationalem Frieden und Sicherheit eingesetzt. Am Ende dieser Entwicklung steht zum jetzigen Zeitpunkt der ICC, der zwar zur „juristischen Intervention" herangezogen wird, aber politisch international hoch umstritten ist.

60 Jahre nach dem Verfahren gegen die deutschen Hauptkriegsverbrecher versucht dieses Buch, den Nürnberger Prozess zu bewerten und dabei Zusammenhänge und Widersprüche aufzuzeigen. Angesichts stetig wiederkehrender Berichte über Massenverbrechen in der Welt befinden wir uns erst auf halbem Weg hin zu einem effektiven System internationaler Strafgerechtigkeit. Mit dem Blick auf das Vermächtnis von Nürnberg hoffen wir, dass dieser Band dazu beiträgt, Antworten auf die Fragen zu finden, wie Recht durchgesetzt werden kann und Menschenrechtsverbrecher wirkungsvoll für ihre Taten zur Verantwortung gezogen werden können.

I. History and National Perspectives of the IMT at Nuremberg/ Historische und nationale Aspekte des IMT von Nürnberg

Raymond M. Brown

The American Perspective on Nuremberg: A Case of Cascading Ironies

It is an honor to attend this 60th Anniversary Nuremberg conference and to explore the American perspective on the Nuremberg trials. There are many states of mind appropriate to examining the US point of view. At this moment in history, however, the most appropriate mental state is a healthy taste of irony.[1] I would like to explore three of these ironies.

The first emanates from the contrast between the profound impact the Nuremberg trials have had on international law, and the fact that the United States, a prime moving force behind the trials came close to neither fostering nor participating in them. A second flows from the fact that the paramount legal principle motivating US participation at Nuremberg, criminalizing aggression, has been the least durable of the Nuremberg principles. The final, and most dramatic irony lies in the efforts of the current American Administration to advocate new norms governing the use of force and to foster new attitudes suggesting US unwillingness to adhere to international law. These efforts could nullify much of the meaning of Nuremberg for the US.

However, before examining these ironies let me suggest a framework for analyzing the American role at Nuremberg. Professor Richard Falk has described a post war "normative architecture"[2] which rejects "genocide, crimes against humanity" and other violations of human rights and humanitarian law. The foundation for this architecture can be found in a trilogy[3] of documents, the London Charter, the Universal Declaration of Human Rights, and the UN Charter. This trilogy and the resulting normative architecture has provided a quantum leap in the protections afforded to two vulnerable groups: (1) non-combatants during armed conflict and (2) all human beings subject to persecution by government authorities. Those protections include establishing and confirming norms, criminalizing violations of many of those norms and, where necessary, conferring jurisdiction on international courts and tribunals to adjudicate major norm violations.

Within this trilogy of documents and the resulting normative architecture, the London Charter is unique in providing all these forms of protection. It assessed individual criminal responsibility before a multinational tribunal, established new norms and reaffirmed aspects of customary law. Additionally, in charging violations of "crimes against humanity" the Charter challenged the idea that Westphalian

---

[1] It is not suggested that this paper constitutes an exhaustive or comprehensive exploration of the US contribution to Nuremberg. See for example Evan J. Wallach, *'The Procedural And Evidentiary Rules of the Post-World War II War Crimes Trials: Did They Provide An Outline For International Legal Procedure?'* 37 COLUMB. J. TRANSNAT'L L. 851 (1999) on the US contribution to the Rules of Procedure and Evidence at the trial.

[2] Richard Falk has explained the term in the following way: "There has been the remarkable emergence of what I would call a normative architecture that repudiates genocide and crimes against humanity that has been erected in the half century since World War II." Keynote Speech, *Remembering the Holocaust and the Geopolitical Persistence of Indifference*, Conference on Law and the Humanities: Representation of the Holocaust, Genocide, and Other Human Rights Violations at Thomas Jefferson School of Law (Jan. 17, 2005). For those who might see the "normative architecture" as an ideological construct, *see* the view from a career military officer, *Lt* Col. Schmitt.

[f]or nearly as long as humans have engaged in organized violence, there have been attempts to fashion normative architectures to constrain and limit it. Such architectures – labeled the law of armed conflict in late Twentieth century parlance – are the product of a symbiotic relationship between law and war.

Michael N. Schmitt, *'Bellum Americanum: The U.S. View of Twenty-First Century War and its Possible Implications for the Law of Armed Conflict'*, 19 MICH. J. INT'L L. 1051, 1051 (1998). The "Deep Concerns" expressed by twelve senior Flag and General Officers about the nomination of Alberto Gonzales as Attorney General because of his characterization of Geneva Convention protections of POWs from torture as "quaint" further reflects the legal rather than political nature of the normative architecture. An Open Letter to the Senate Judiciary Committee, (available at http://www.humanrightsfirst.org/us_law/etn/gonzales/statements/gonz_military_010405.pdf.

[3] I note with interest Professor Rebecca Witmann's observation that one of the prosecutors at the Auschwitz Trial conducted in the German municipal court system in 1967 "sought to place his efforts in the context of the worldwide human rights movement that had begun with the creation of the United Nations and been solidified with the human rights convention." See comment on closing argument of Hans Grofmann BEYOND JUSTICE: THE AUSCHWITZ TRIAL, 195 (2005).

sovereignty was absolute and laid the groundwork for extending international jurisdiction to humanitarian law (and ultimately human rights) violations even during peacetime.[4]

The notable contributions of the United States to this process include its role in spawning the Nuremberg trials, its determination, to reinforce existing norms governing the use of force, and its desire to criminalize violations of the norm prohibiting aggressive war. (Additionally, the United States supported, albeit inconsistently, evolution of much of the balance of the normative architecture.)

Trial, "Punishment" or Both

The initial irony surrounding American participation in Nuremberg springs from the very existence of multinational postwar trials for "major war criminals of the European Axis counties." Despite the huge shadow that the trials have cast in retrospect, judicial proceedings for leading Nazis and alleged German war criminals were not a foregone conclusion for most of the war. Both the US and Great Britain were undecided about non-judicial punishment for Senior Nazi's as late as 1944.

The 1943 Moscow Declaration's[5] Statement of Atrocities noted that most offending German military personnel and Nazis would face legal process. The Statement warned that those who took "consenting part" in

"...atrocities, massacres and executions will be sent back to the countries in which their abominable deeds were done in order that they may be judged and punished according to the laws of these liberated countries and of free governments which will be erected therein."[6]

However, the major potential offenders, "German criminals whose offenses have no particular geographical localization,"[7] faced the calculatedly ambiguous promise of being "punished" by joint decision of the government of the Allies."[8]

At the Quebec Conference of 1944 Roosevelt and Churchill endorsed both the "Napoleonic Precedent" (punishment without trials) and the Morgenthau Plan (Germany reduced to an agrarian non industrial society and summary executions of leading Nazis).[9]

The draconian nature of Morgenthau's proposal left little room for trials for major violators. It advocated the following:

APPENDIX B
PUNISHMENT OF CERTAIN WAR CRIMES AND TREATMENT OF SPECIAL GROUPS.
A.   *Punishment of Certain War Criminals*
(1)   Arch-Criminals.

A list of the Arch criminals of this war whose obvious guilt has been recognized by the United Nations shall be drawn up as soon as possible and transmitted to the appropriate military authorities. The military authorities shall be instructed with respect to all persons who are on such list as follows:

(a) They shall be apprehended as soon as possible and identified as soon as possible after apprehension, the identification to be approved by an officer of the General rank.

(b) **When such identification has been made, the person identified shall be put to death forthwith by firing squads made up of soldiers of the United Nations.**[10]

---

[4] See, e.g. Telford Taylor FINAL REPORT TO THE SECRETARY OF THE ARMY ON THE NUREMBERG WAR CRIMES TRIALS UNDER CONTROL COUNCIL LAW NO. 10, at 64-5, 69, 224-229 (1949).

[5] See Declaration of Four Nations on General Security, 9 DEP'T ST. BULL. 308 (1943), reprinted in 38 AM. J. INT'L L. 5 (1944) (Hereafter Moscow Declaration).

[6] Moscow Declaration, Statement of Atrocities.

[7] Ibid.

[8] Ibid.

[9] Ibid. There does appear to be a subordinate irony that on September 15th, the day the President "initialed" the Morgenthau Plan in Quebec, that Col Murray Bernays, assigned to G-1 in the War Department distributed a memorandum in which the beginnings of the "Nuremberg ideas" were to be found Telford Taylor THE ANATOMY OF THE NUREMBERG TRIALS (Hereafter ANATOMY) at 35 (1992).

The first official indication that the US position would change came on January 3, 1945. Roosevelt sent a brief note to Secretary of State Stettinius which constituted the President's first and only written communication on the subject. Please send me a brief report on the state of the proceedings before the War Crimes Commission, and particularly the attitude of the US representative on offenses to be brought against Hitler and the chief Nazi war criminals. The charges against the top Nazis should include an indictment for waging aggressive warfare, in violation of the Kellogg[-Briand] Pact. Perhaps these and other charges might be joined in a conspiracy indictment.[11]

Of course this memo did not spring without prompting from the President's pen. Both Nuremberg participants[12] and subsequent scholars[13] believe that Roosevelt was heavily influenced by the work of Colonel William Chandler of the War Department, one of the moving forces shaping American perspectives on the eventual trials and an advocate of prosecuting the crime against peace. However, even Chandler and other War Department lawyers did not begin actively working on the legal foundations for post war trials until the fall of 1944.

The broader American consensus for trials developed slowly as well. In April of 1945, just weeks before President Truman appointed Associate Supreme Court Justice Robert Jackson as the US Chief Counsel for war crimes, Jackson had suggested in his famous "Rule of Law Among Nations" speech[14] that he would not enter into the "controversy" about the wisdom of a "military or political" decision to execute war criminals "high or humble."[15] (The speech has become better known for Jackson's warning that no man should be tried "if you are not willing to see him freed if proven not guilty"). Although Jackson accepted Truman's offer and was committed wholeheartedly to the notion of war crimes trials, he more than once threatened the British, Soviets and the French with the prospect of withdrawing from the London Charter negotiations and holding separate American proceedings.[16]

The substance of President Roosevelt's Note of January 1945 provides additional evidence of the late hour at which the US decided to conduct international post war trials. If the President had determined early in the war to focus primarily on "aggression" and "conspiracy" much of the legal analysis for the trials could have commenced as early as 1942. We now know that the Tribunal's verdict focused on Germany's long list of treaty violations in lieu of an element analysis of the crime against peace. These treaty violations were well known before 1944, as were the contents of *Mein Kampf*, cited in the Judgment's analysis of the German preparation for war. For example, the fate of Rudolf Hess hinged almost entirely on documents available early in the war. He was convicted on Counts 1 and 2 in large part on the basis of public speeches made and orders he had signed before his 1941 flight to the United Kingdom.

These observations do not denigrate the significant evidence accumulated by the prosecution during the occupation of Germany or suggest that prosecutors or pre-war planners could have known the

---

[10] Italics in original, bold text added for this paper. Memorandum from Henry Morgenthau Jr. to President Roosevelt (the Morgenthau Plan), September 5, 1944 Bradley F. Smith THE AMERICAN ROAD TO NUREMBERG, THE DOCUMENTARY RECORD, 27-8 1944-1945 (1982).

[11] Roosevelt Memorandum to Stettinius cited in ANATOMY at 37.

[12] ANATOMY at 38.

[13] Professor Jonathan A. Bush has observed that Roosevelt's note was a "milestone on the road to Nuremberg" and that Chandler's apparent involvement in inspiring it is "a humble reminder of a time when Pentagon lawyers were well in advance of activists and academics in formulating human rights theories," in: *"The Supreme ... Crime" And Its Origins: The Lost Legislative History of the Crime Of Aggressive War'* 102 COLUMB. L. REV. 2324, 2363-4 (2002) Hereafter *Lost Legislative History*.

[14] This section of the speech cited ANATOMY 44-5. The entire text can be found at *http://www.roberthjackson.org/Man/theman2-7-7-1/*.

[15] Jackson would later declaim in his opening statement at the trials "That four great nations, flushed with victory and stung with injury stay the hand of vengeance and voluntarily submit their captive enemies to the judgment of the law is one of the most significant tributes that Power ever has paid to Reason."

[16] In July of 1945, during the four power negotiations on the London Charter Jackson threatened to withdraw and hold separate American sponsored trials because he was not satisfied with the authority held by the other negotiators. (ANATOMY, 63). Subsequently Jackson issued the same threat in frustration at the substantive disagreement over the scope of the crime against peace. (ANATOMY, 66-7).

principle evidence on which the Judges would rely. However, it is clear that preparatory analysis for "conspiracy" and "aggression" could have begun earlier than the work on Counts 3 and 4 had there been a decision before 1945 to proceed with trials.

The possibility that there might not have been any Nuremberg trials becomes more dramatic when we acknowledge the belated endorsement of trials by the United Kingdom. The impact of two twentieth century wars involving Germany, and the conduct of the leaders of the insatiably bellicose[17] Third Reich, left the British war Cabinet still favoring summary executions as late as April of 1945.[18]

The more we value the trials' historic and legal impact, and closer we study the catalytic role of the US, the more pronounced is the ironic possibility that the trials could easily have been replaced by summary executions or by the exclusive use of national traditional military tribunals, processes that would have lacked Nuremberg's profound legacy.

Victor's Justice or Not

Some contemporary voices charged that the entire Nuremberg effort was fatally flawed. All of those charges did not emanate from sources as tainted as Hermann Goering, who when he received his indictment, allegedly added to it the phrase, "The victor will always be the judge and the vanquished the accused."[19] The Chief Justice of the United States Supreme Court, Harlan F. Stone, (annoyed that he had not been consulted about Jackson's appointment to serve as war crimes prosecutor while remaining on the Supreme Court) opined,

"Jackson is away conducting his high-grade lynching party in Nuremberg. I don't mind what he does to the Nazis, but I hate to see the pretense that he is running a court and proceeding according to common law. This is a little too sanctimonious a fraud to meet my old-fashioned ideas."[20]

Immediately after the trials, Senator Robert Taft used the criticism of crimes against peace to condemn both the Nuremberg and Tokyo trials.

"I believe that most Americans view with discomfort the war trials which have just been concluded in Germany and are proceeding in Japan. They violate that fundamental principle of American law that a man cannot be tried under an ex post facto statute. The trial of the vanquished by the victors cannot be impartial, no matter how it is hedged about with the forms of justice. I question whether the hanging of those who, however despicable, were the leaders of the German people will ever discourage the making of aggressive war, for no one makes aggressive war unless he expects to win. About this whole judgment there is the spirit of vengeance, and vengeance is seldom justice. The hangings of the eleven men convicted will be a blot on the American record which we shall long regret."[21]

Over the ensuing 60 years that broad criticism of Nuremberg has receded[22] even as uncertainty about the viability of the crime against peace has remained. The establishment during the post cold war years of the Ad Hoc Tribunals for the former Yugoslavia and Rwanda, the Special Court for Sierra Leone and the entering into force of the Rome Treaty for the International Criminal Court have built on the legal precedents, the political example, and the spirit of Nuremberg. As a lawyer practicing as co-

---

[17] For an excellent synthesis of the relationship of Hitler's regime and military Aggression see Richard Bessel NAZISM AND WAR (2004).

[18] ANATOMY at 35.

[19] Lieutenant Colonel Michael A. Newton, '*Comparative Complementarily: Domestic Jurisdiction Consistent with the Rome Statute of the International Criminal Court*', 167 MIL. L. REV. 20, 23 (2001).

[20] Graeme A. Barry, *'"The Gifted Judge": An Analysis of the Judicial Career of Robert H. Jackson'*, 38 ALBERTA L. REV. 880, 883 (2000).

[21] See Mary Margaret Penrose, '*Lest We Fail: The Importance of Enforcement in International Criminal Law*', 15 AM. U. INT'L L. REV. 321, 330 fn 34 (2000).

[22] But see, Istvan Deak, *The Thinkable*, "Acting on the basis of [the Llandovery Castle case at Leipzig], the Nuremberg Court and the postwar German courts, at least in my own view, could have tried and severely punished all the Nazi mass murderers. Instead the courts chose to create legally doubtful ex-post-facto laws so as to punish the defendants." [Review essay] The New Republic, February 18, 2002.

counsel for an accused[23] at the Special Court for Sierra Leone during 2004, I was continuously impressed at the frequency and vigor with which Nuremberg was cited as a precedent by Judges, Prosecutors, and Defense Counsel.[24] In fact some observers maintain that "contemporary international criminal courts typically treat Nuremberg precedent as canonical."[25]

The American commitments to "aggression" and "conspiracy" found the US pressing against the boundaries of existing international law. Although conspiracy, has gained traction[26] since Nuremberg, in 1945 and 1946 it endured vigorous attacks. The French and Soviet delegates were confounded by the concept during the Charter negotiations. During deliberations, the French Judge Donnedieu de Vabres believed that the charge was "ex post facto"[27] and would likely lead to a revised version of the German "stab in the back-legend."[28]

Despite the Judges' ultimate acceptance of conspiracy to wage aggressive war, their sentencing calculus suggests it was a less than wholehearted embrace. Only defendants convicted of war crimes and crimes against humanity were executed.[29] Hess, convicted only on Counts 1 and 2 was sentenced to Spandau. An intellectual fault line existed between the conspiracy and the crime against peace on one hand, and war crimes and crimes against humanity on the other.

Despite this skepticism, conspiracy has continued to remain a viable part of international criminal law. A much less favorable view can be taken of the charge most important to the US and to Robert Jackson, the crime against peace. Once the US was committed to holding the trials, (or at least to negotiating the London Charter) it was primarily motivated by a desire to solidify legal norms governing aggression and to criminalize the violation of those norms.

This highlights the irony that this objective was only partially achieved and is now being challenged by the United States. The UN's ratification of the Nuremberg judgments[30] and the adoption of Article 51 of the UN Charter[31] reflect the rapid acceptance of the prohibition of aggression in international law. However, the criminalizing of the violation of this norm has been the most heavily and trenchantly resisted aspect of the Nuremberg experience.

This negative reaction has not been restricted to legal scholars or critics with questionable anti-Nazi credentials. General Matthew Ridgeway, wartime commander of the 82nd Airborne Division and ultimately President Eisenhower's Army Chief of Staff believed that,[32]

---

[23] There were nine detainees in the Special Court Detention Facility. (No accused had been granted bail.) Except for the Sierra Leonean Army, each of the main military forces active during the conflict was represented. Three accused were from the Revolutionary United Front, RUF, three from the Civilian Defense Force, CDF, and three from the Armed Forces Revolutionary Council, AFRC. Although prosecutors originally sought a joint trial, the Special Court severed the proceeding into three different trials. The three RUF accused were Issa Sesay, Augustine Gbao, and Morris Kallon; they faced indictment SCSL-04-15-T. I was co-counsel to Kallon.

[24] This was especially intense in citations to the High Command Case in disputes over distinctions between "staff" and "command" functions during arguments about the scope of command responsibility, and in citations to the Nuremberg Judgment over the nature of "criminal enterprise," a critical theory of liability in the AFRC and RUF indictments.

[25] See Allison Marston Danner and Jenny S. Martinez, *'Guilty Associations: Joint Criminal Enterprise, Command Responsibility, and the Development of International Criminal Law Guilty Associations: Joint Criminal Enterprise, Command Responsibility, and the Development of International Criminal Law'*, 93 CALIF. L. REV. 75, 118 (2005).

[26] Id.

[27] Bradley F. Smith, REACHING JUDGMENT AT NUREMBERG, 122 (1977).

[28] Id., at 1256.

[29] Except for the frequently criticized Streicher verdict.

[30] Affirmation of the Principles of International Law recognized by the Charter of the Nuremberg Tribunal. Resolution 95 (I) of the United Nations General Assembly, 11 December 1946.

[31] All Members shall refrain in their international relations from the threat or use of force against the territorial integrity or political independence of any state, or in any other manner inconsistent with the Purposes of the United Nations.

[32] Cited in THE LAWS OF WAR: A COMPREHENSIVE COLLECTION OF PRIMARY DOCUMENTS ON INTERNATIONAL LAWS GOVERNING ARMED CONFLICT (W. Michael Reisman and Chris T. Antoniou eds. 1994), 334 citing, DOENITZ AT NUERMBERG: A REAPPRAISAL; WAR CRIMES AND THE MILITARY PROFESSIONAL (H.K., Thompson Jr. and Henry Sturtz eds. 1975) 181, 194.

"[t]o apprehend, arraign and try an individual for the wanton killing – murder, if you please, – of prisoners of war, for example, is one thing. To do likewise to individuals who waged war in the uniform of their nation and under the orders or directives of their superiors is another and quite different thing. I believe the former is fully justified. I believe the latter is unjustified and repugnant to the code of enlightened governments. ... Until such distant date, if this ever transpires, as nations can and will agree on a world political organization with judicial tribunals whose jurisdiction is acknowledged and whose judgments are accepted, I think trials in the second category described above, are steps backwards to the instant past when the fate of a defeated people was determined at the whim of a victor."

Raymond Aron who edited *France Libre,* newspaper of the Free French forces and became a prominent post-war intellectual [33] held a similar view.

Interestingly, two of Jackson's Nuremberg assistant's abandoned their defense of the crime against peace against the ex post facto charge in their later years. Telford Taylor's 1992 memoir recites his own 1945 memorandum evaluating the draft executive agreement for the London Charter. In his memorandum he offered the elegant but unpersuasive argument that the aggressive war charge survives the ex post facto attack,[34] because "this is a political *decision* to declare and apply a principle of international law."[35]. However, in the memoir's final chapter, *Epilogue and Assessment,* Taylor conceded that,

"Arguments in support of punishing individuals ex post facto for violation of the crime against peace can be made, but, if conducted on a plane devoid of political and emotion factors will be won by the defense. But in 1945 those very factor were overwhelming. Peoples whose nations had been attacked and dismembered without warning, wanted legal retribution whether or not this was a 'first time.' The inclusion of the crime against peace vastly enhanced the world's interest in a support to the trials at Nuremberg."[36]

Professor Bernard Meltzer, who served under Jackson at Nuremberg, also expressed a change of heart concerning the ex post facto criticism of the crime against peace.

"The international formulations relied on by Justice Jackson were silent about individual responsibility for aggressive war. Indeed, such responsibility was disclaimed during the confirmation discussions in the United States Senate of the Kellogg-Briand Pact, a pact on which Jackson heavily relied. Thus, Senator Borah, the chairman of the Senate Foreign Relations Committee, had declared that the pact was an appeal solely to the conscience of the world and that its breach was not to lead to any punitive consequences."[37]

Although the International Military Tribunal convicted twelve defendants of the crime against peace and generally defended the Charter, this aspect of the trial and verdict has been the most heavily

---

[33] ...There is no international court. To that you will retort that after the last war, there was the Nuremberg court. But we know now – and I think I wrote at the time – that any nation losing a war will be subjected to the decisions of a Court like that of Nuremberg. But it is sure that the country subjected to a Nuremberg court will be the guilty country; it will certainly be the country that has been conquered. In the case at hand, the conquered nation was also the guiltiest one that is Nazi Germany. But as soon as we begin condemning 'crimes against peace,' for example, I am sure the country that wins a war will demonstrate that the vanquished was responsible for it." Raymond Aron FROM THE COMMITTED OBSERVER *LE SPECTATEUR ENGAGÉ* – CONVERSATIONS WITH JEAN-LOUIS MISSIKA AND DOMINIQUE WOLTON, 247 (1983).

[34] Taylor regarded the arraignment of the Kaiser in Article 227 of the Treaty of Versailles as lacking precedential value because the language of Versailles was "opaque" and "had no roots in international legal doctrine." ANATOMY 16. Professor Bush is slightly more open to Versailles as precedent but regards the language of Article 227 as "loose" and "never put to the test." *Lost Legislative History* at 2332. See Treaty of Versailles, June 28, 1919, art. 227, 2 Bevans 43, 136.

[35] ANATOMY at 51 (emphasis Taylor's).

[36] ANATOMY at 629.

[37] Bernard D. Meltzer, *'TRIBUTE: Robert H. Jackson: Nuremberg's Architect and Advocate'*, 68 ALB. L. REV. 55, 60 (2004).

criticized.[38] The inability of the international community after years of debate and a concerted effort at the Rome Conference for the International Criminal Court to arrive at a suitable definition of aggression are signs that a principle American Nuremberg objective, to criminalize aggression, has still not been achieved.[39]

Supreme Irony or Reasoned Response to Latent Threats

Technical difficulties offer a partial explanation for the lack of a post-Nuremberg treaty banning aggressive war. However, no such ambiguity surrounds the underlying norm governing the use of force. The United States currently asserts that it will use force to pre-empt "emerging" threats as well as those which are imminent. It argues that changing circumstances warrant new strategies. On its face, this suggests movement away from the accepted norm embodied in Article 51 of the UN Charter. Although there is a rich and growing literature debating this point, it would be ironic if the US were deemed to be taking the lead in changing a norm it sought to criminalize at Nuremberg, even if it does so in response to new technological and geopolitical threats.

However, a larger irony would surface if as some suspect, the US is asserting that the world's "hyperpower" is not bound by any international norms governing the use of force. Such a position would be in dramatic contrast to the position asserted by the US at Nuremberg and supported in the UN Charter.

The Bush Doctrine, articulated shortly after the attacks of September 11th announced that the US would use force to "to preempt emerging threats."[40] This doctrine was ultimately employed to justify the US invasion of Iraq in 2003. As the British and American publics learned during the May 2005 British Parliamentary election, even America's staunchest ally had reservations about this extension of the parameters governing the use of force. The now famous "Goldsmith Memorandum" submitted by the United Kingdom's Attorney General to British PM Tony Blair[41] March 7, 2003, set forth the following view:

"...It is now widely accepted that an imminent armed attack will justify the use of force if the other conditions are met.... However, in my opinion there must be some degree of immanence. I am aware that the USA has been arguing for recognition of a broad doctrine of a right to use force to pre-empt danger in the future. If this means more than a right to respond proportionately to an imminent attack (and I understand that the doctrine is intended to carry that connotation) this is not a doctrine which, in my opinion, exists or is recognized in international law."

In response to the controversy surrounding the United States' articulation of this new doctrine the UN Secretary General has announced the need for a "consensus" on "when and how force can be used to defend international peace and security..." specifically focusing on whether states "may use force against 'latent' or non-imminent threats...."[42] However, there remains a large gap between much of the

---

[38] Despite the principle of *tu quoque,* certain factual discrepancies between the wartime conduct of victor nations and the factual bases of the convictions of the leading Nazi's on the crime against peace created embarrassment and broadly raised questions about the Tribunal's credibility. The Soviet invasion of Poland and the fact that the allegation of Nazi aggression against the USSR hinges on the German violation of Nazi – Soviet Non-Aggression Pact of 1939 was embarrassing at the time the verdict was rendered. Serious questions about whether the German Invasion of Norway was a response to earlier British invasion plans also raises difficult questions. Bradley F. Smith, REACHING JUDGMENT AT NUREMBERG 144-150.

[39] ICC Article 5 which defines "Crimes within the Jurisdiction of the Court" provides that "The Court shall exercise jurisdiction over the crime of aggression once a provision is adopted in accordance with articles 121 and 123 defining the crime and setting out the conditions under which the Court shall exercise jurisdiction with respect to this crime. Such a provision shall be consistent with the relevant provisions of the Charter of the United Nations."

[40] See National Security Strategy of the United States of America (2002), available at www.whitehouse.gov/nsc/nss.pdf.

[41] First made public on in May of 2005.

[42] Report of the Secretary-General, In Larger Freedom: Towards Development, Security and Human Rights for All, U.N. GAOR, 59th Sess., Agenda Items 45 and 55, U.N. Doc. A/59/2005 (2005) para 122.

world and the US on whether the new "consensus" will endorse unilateral action or find that the prevailing norms require action by the Security Council.

Underlying this serious debate about whether the "war on terror" will be a catalyst for a new international consensus on the use of force is the suspicion that the US is rejecting the idea that it is bound by international norms governing force. The controversial Downing Street Memorandum[43] hints at the possibility that the Bush Administration attempted to "fix" the evidence that Saddam Hussein was a latent threat possessing Weapons of Mass Destruction. If the United States employed a pretext in order to bring its Iraq invasion within the parameters of its new use of force doctrine such conduct would constitute a flagrant affront to the rule of law. It would also suggest that America's UN Ambassador Bolton[44] should be taken literally when he says,

*"It is a big mistake for us to grant any **validity to international law** even when it may seem in our short-term interest to do so, because over the long term, the goal of those who think that international law really means anything are those who want to constrict the United States."*[45]

Eventually, participants at this Conference, diplomats, scholars, NGO and rights activist will be forced to explore in the future a <u>supreme Nuremberg irony</u>. This controversial irony will center around the questions of whether the American responses to the terrorist[46] attacks of September 11, 2001, the promulgation of the Bush Doctrine and the invasion of Iraq without unambiguous Security Council support, have neutralized the American contributions to Nuremberg. In fact the debate will extend to whether the current US position is in derogation of the use of force principles articulated throughout the normative architecture. One American "realist" has already announced that,

"The effort to subject the use of force to the rule of law was the monumental internationalist experiment of the 20th century; the fact is that that experiment has failed."[47]

Another American "realist" has announced that US legitimacy in the world stems from military power not from commitment to international law.[48] While realists can make valuable contributions to debates about the rule of law their contributions often warrant close scrutiny. Had the realist plans of Secretary Morgenthau been embraced in 1945, 2500[49] "arch criminals"[50] would have been "summarily

---

[43] See http://www.timesonline.co.uk/article/0,,2087-1593607,00.html.

[44] At the time of the Judging Nuremberg Conference, John Bolton was the UN Ambassador Designate. He subsequently received a recess appointment on August 1, 2005. Bush Names Bolton U.N. Ambassador in Recess Appointment, *Jim VandeHei and Colum Lynch, Washington Post August 2, 2005*.

[45] *Nomination of John R. Bolton: Hearing Before the Senate Foreign Relations Committee*, 109th Cong. (April 12, 2005) (testimony of John R. Bolton, then nominee for U.S. Ambassador to the United Nations). It should be acknowledged however, that there is a school of thought that argues that during its pre-war diplomatic efforts the Bush Administration believed it was "acting on behalf of international, and not exclusively national, interest " see Jonathan Monten, *'The Roots of the Bush Doctrine: Power, Nationalism and Democracy Promotion in U.S. Strategy'*, INTERNATIONAL SECURITY 29:4, 112, 146 (2005).

[46] For purposes of this article "terrorism" describes ideologically motivated violence against civilian targets. This is not the forum for an extended discussion of "terrorism" or the lack of a universally accepted definition but see the acknowledgment of the UN's High Level Threat Panel that "The United Nations ability to develop a comprehensive strategy has been constrained by the inability of Member States to agree on an anti-terrorism convention including a definition of terrorism," UNITED NATIONS, A MORE SECURE WORLD: OUR SHARED RESPONSIBILITY, REPORT OF THE SECRETARY-GENERAL'S HIGH-LEVEL PANEL ON THREATS, CHALLENGES AND CHANGE, UN Doc. A/59/565, para. 157 (2004) See also Johnathan Weinberger, *'Defining Terror'*, 4 SETON HALL JOURNAL OF DIPLOMACY AND INTERNATIONAL RELATIONS, 63 (2003) and for an earlier exploration of this definitional problem from a widely respected scholar of international law currently serving as an advisor to the Iraqi Special Court see M. Cherif Bassiouni *Crimes of Terror Violence* in INTERNATIONAL CRIMINAL LAW 2ED. 777 et seq. (M. Cherif Bassiouni ed. 1999).

[47] *See* Michael J. Glennon, *'Why the Security Council Failed'*, FOREIGN AFFAIRS, May/June 2003 at 24.

[48] *See* Robert Kagan, *'America's Crisis of Legitimacy'*, FOREIGN AFFAIRS, March/April 2004, at 65. Kagan maintains that American legitimacy since World War II stems from its ability to contain the Soviets during the cold war, not from its commitment to emerging international legal norms.

[49] Howard Ball PROSECUTING WAR CRIMES AND GENOCIDE: THE TWENTIETH CENTURY EXPERIENCE. 46 (1999).

executed" and the normative architecture to which Nuremberg has made such a significant contribution might never have been constructed.

In fact, these departures from Nuremberg's legacy suggest the possibility of a US retreat from the normative architecture itself. There has been a strong, though not unanimous consensus[51] among speakers at this Conference that the establishment of the International Criminal Court is an effort to extend Nuremberg's legacy.[52] If history confirms this view, the United States' rejection of the Rome Treaty provides further evidence of the Bush Administration's abandonment of a set of human rights, and humanitarian law principles the US has championed since the Second World War. Even more troubling is the enthusiasm which has accompanied this repositioning. It is difficult to misinterpret the ironic portent of the comments of Ambassador Bolton who described the signing of the Rome Treaty as "the happiest moment in my government service."[53]

---

[50] Bradley F. Smith THE AMERICAN ROAD TO NUREMBERG, THE DOCUMENTARY RECORD, 27-8 1944-1945 (1982).

[51] See for example the comments of Benjamin Ferencz, Whitney Harris, and Judge Hans-Peter Kaul.

[52] Interestingly, the criticisms by General Ridgway and Raymond Aron of the employment of the crime against peace at Nuremberg disappear with the creation of an "international court" See Notes 32-3 above.

[53] *UN will refer Darfur crimes to court in Hague. U.S. decides not to oppose resolution,* Warren Hoge, International Herald Tribune, April 2, 2005, 6.

Raymond M. Brown

Die amerikanische Sicht auf Nürnberg: Ein Fall wechselnder Ironien

Dieser Beitrag beschäftigt sich mit der Haltung der USA zu den Nürnberger Prozessen. Die Vielschichtigkeit der amerikanischen Perspektiven vor und nach den Verfahren vor dem IMT in Nürnberg lässt sich zum jetzigen Zeitpunkt – nach Meinung des Autors – am ehesten mit einem gesunden Schuss Ironie beschreiben. Dabei ist zunächst festzustellen, dass die USA maßgeblichen Anteil an der Erstellung der „normativen Architektur" des nach dem Zweiten Weltkrieg geschaffenen Menschenrechtssystems hatten, das insbesondere auf der Trias Londoner IMT Statut, Allgemeine Erklärung der Menschenrechte und UN Charta fußt.

Die erste Ironie besteht darin, dass die USA die durch Nürnberg gerade auf Grund des kompromisslosen Engagements der USA im Vorfeld und während der Prozesse teilweise gegen den Widerstand der anderen Alliierten erreichte Fortentwicklung des Völkerrechts in der Folgezeit weder nährten noch überhaupt mittrugen. Eine zweite Ironie zeigt sich darin, dass das primäre Interesse der USA bei der strafrechtlichen Verfolgung von NS-Verbrechen, die Ächtung des Angriffskriegs, von allen Errungenschaften in Nürnberg von kürzester Dauer war. Auch wenn das Gewaltverbot in Art. 51 der UN Charta unmittelbar nach Nürnberg völkerrechtliche Normierung erfuhr, bleibt doch die völkerstrafrechtliche Ahndung der Aggression bis heute, bis hin zum Statut des Internationalen Strafgerichtshof umstritten.

Die dritte, letzte und zugleich größte Ironie liegt in dem Umgang der derzeitigen amerikanischen Regierung mit Völkerrecht insgesamt und Völkerstrafrecht im Besonderen. Nicht nur das in Nürnberg vehement geforderte internationale Gewaltverbot scheint für die heutige USA selbst keine Bindung zu besitzen; die Relevanz der völkerrechtlichen Ordnung wird insgesamt jedenfalls dann abgelehnt, wenn diese mit politischen Interessen der USA in Konflikt gerät. Die Größe der USA basiert, so heißt es aus „realistischer" Sicht, nicht auf internationalem Recht, sondern auf militärischer Macht. Der Unwillen, an der weiteren internationalen Entwicklung teilzuhaben, könnte indes die Bedeutung Nürnbergs für die USA zunichte machen und letztlich den Ausstieg aus der normativen Menschenrechtsarchitektur bedeuten.

David Cesarani

The International Military Tribunal at Nuremberg: British Perspectives

Sixty years after the International Military Tribunal in Nuremberg (IMT) sat in judgment on the surviving leaders of Nazi Germany its proceedings still cast a shadow over history. Since 1946 it has informed the ways in which diplomats, politicians and lawyers have attempted to reckon with war crimes, atrocity, and the mass violation of human rights.[1] However, it was not self-evident that the IMT should have attained the salience it commands today. Nor has it necessarily served well as a beacon to jurisprudence, policy makers or public opinion.

In the public mind the IMT has been sanctified by time. It exercised an almost magical effect on the debates that raged during the 1990s when politicians approached the question of retribution for crimes of war and peace in such varied contexts as South Africa, the former Yugoslavia, Rwanda, and Iraq. Rather suddenly, the IMT became the point of reference and urgent precedent.[2] It was even given the Hollywood treatment in a major TV movie starring Alec Baldwin as Justice Robert Jackson.

This veneration hardly reflected its dubious origins, shaky legal foundation, controversial modus operandi, and highly equivocal results. In the post-war decade the judicial process for which the IMT formed the keystone was treated as something of an embarrassment. Time and effort was expended undoing the work of the subsequent trials, exercising pardons on those who had been convicted, reducing penal sentences, and placating West German opinion that had never accepted their validity.[3] Thanks to the Cold War the narrow application of justice against Nazi war crimes perpetrators, in particular, and the broader application of the international law developed for the IMT atrophied.[4]

In the light of this nemesis the British, who had never been keen on the trial of Nazi malefactors, could have been excused a feeling of smug self-satisfaction. Writing in 1996, Lord Annan, who had served as an officer in the Political Branch of the British element of the Control Commission, evoked the cautious pragmatism that governed Whitehall in all matters concerning de-Nazification. While making the ritual comment that "Die-hard Nazis, of course, should be removed, and if guilty of crimes put on trial" he did not conceal his scorn for those who had been prepared to pay a heavy price in real terms for the application of an abstract notion of justice.[5]

The success and failure of the IMT and the larger Nuremberg process can thus be observed with advantage through the optic of the British experience. Britain had fended off occupation during the war, but was the host to the governments-in-exile of less fortunate countries. When it came to deliberating on war crimes, debate in Whitehall was uncontaminated by the problems connected with defeat and collaboration. Britain was at the heart of policy making towards the treatment of Nazi war crimes and the Nazi elite. British jurists, notably Sir Hartley Shawcross, Sir David Maxwell-Fyfe, Sir Geoffrey

---

[1] From the extensive literature tracing the impact of the IMT see Geoffrey Robertson, *Crimes Against Humanity. The Struggle for Global Justice* (London: Allen Lane, 1999), Howard Ball, *Prosecuting War Crimes and Genocide. The Twentieth Century Experience* (Lawrence: University of Kansas Press, 1999); and Phillipe Sands ed., *From Nuremberg to the Hague* (Cambridge: Cambridge Univertsity Press, 2003).

[2] See, for example Richard Goldstone, *For Humanity* (New Haven: Yale University Press, 2000) passim, G J Bass, *Stay the Hand of Vengeance, The Politics of War Crimes Tribunals* (Princeton: Princeton University Press, 2002 revised edition) and Geoffrey Robertson, *Crimes Against Humanity* (London: Penguin, 2002 edn), xxii-xxvi, 218-36.

[3] Frank Buscher, *The US War Crimes Trial Programme in Germany 1946-1955* (Westport, CONN., Greenwood: 1989). Airy Neave, *Nuremberg. A Personal Record of the Trial of the Major Nazi War Criminals in 1945-6* (London: Hodder and Stoughton, 1979), 319-330,reflects defensively on the tarnished reputation of the IMT from the point of view of a member of the British prosecution team.

[4] See Robertson *Crimes Against Humanity*, 236-44 for one lament. Whitney R Harris, *Tyranny On Trial. The Trial of the Major German War Criminals At the End of World War II At Nuremberg, Germany, 1945-1946* (Dallas: Southern Methodist University Press, 1999 edn. [first published in 1954]), 571-78, expresses the early hopes, disappointment, and ultimate triumph of an American participant in the IMT who held a candle for the creation of a permanent international criminal court.

[5] Noel Annan, *Changing Enemies* (London: Harper Collins, 1996), 202-12. Also, Frank Roberts, *Dealing With Dictators* (London: Weidenfeld and Nicolson, 1991), 155.

Lawrence and Justice Norman Birkett played a leading part in the proceedings. The response of the British public to the work of the IMT exemplifies its contemporary impact.

Although Britain's role in the prosecution of the major Nazi war criminals is now celebrated in British memory of the war and its aftermath, it was never a foregone conclusion that Britain would support such trials. From 1939 to 1942 the Foreign Office [FO] was adamantly opposed to any form of judicial retribution against either the civil or military echelons in Germany except in the case of war crimes, as conventionally defined, and committed only against British and Allied nationals.[6]

In the first half of the war, pressure for a pledge to try German war criminals came from the governments-in-exile that were established in London. The Poles, Czechs, and French, especially, were in regular receipt of intelligence recording depredations against their civilian populations. The victims of Nazi occupation included Jews, although their specific experience featured only intermittently in the reports of the exile regimes. In the course of 1942, however, the deportation and mass murder of the Jews across Europe climbed the agenda of the governments-in-exile. Specific appeals were now also made by the representatives of Jewish organisations in London and Washington who sought a pledge of Allied retribution in the hope of dissuading the Nazis from following the policy of extermination.[7]

However, such requests met a chilly response. The FO had bad institutional memories of war crimes trials. Officials were haunted by the farcical experience of the trials conducted by the Germans in Leipzig after the Great War (1914-18). The failure to apprehend the fugitive Kaiser, despite assurances given to a vengeful public who wanted him hung, added to the memory of embarrassment. In April 1940, when the Polish Government-in-Exile pressed London for a declaration in favour of trials against Germans responsible for perpetrating atrocities in occupied Poland, Sir Alexander Cadogan, Permanent Under Secretary of State at the Foreign Office, remarked in a withering understatement that similar pronouncements "had led us into a certain amount of trouble after the last war."[8]

The Foreign Secretary, Anthony Eden, was wholly in agreement with his officials. During 1941, he effectively countered those in the War Cabinet, notably Hugh Dalton, who sympathised with the aspirations of the exiled governments. Eden had more difficulty coping with his effusive Prime Minister. In a speech in June 1941, shortly after the German invasion of the Soviet Union, Churchill said that the Allies would bring "quislings" to justice if no one in their own countries was willing to do so. Four months later, he publicly associated himself with a statement by Franklin D Roosevelt, the American President, promising "retribution" for acts such as the shooting of hostages. Nevertheless, Churchill always avoided any specific commitments. Sir Orme Sargent, Deputy Undersecretary of State at the FO, commented in a memorandum, that the government "must at all costs avoid saying anything which would commit us to the policy of making lists of war criminals for subsequent trial." Consequently, the British Government declined to be a signatory to a declaration by the combined governments-in-exile on 13 January 1942 promising legal punishment of those guilty of war crimes.[9]

It became harder to hold the line during 1942. In response to the inter-allied declaration, Eden solicited a view of war crimes policy from the government's law officers. On 19 April 1942, the Attorney General Sir Donald Somervell and the Solicitor General Sir David Maxwell Fyfe, recommended that the UK Government should adhere to existing international law, seek the prosecution of war crimes only, and exclusively when committed against British and Allied nationals, and use

---

[6] Bradley F Smith, *Reaching Judgment at Nuremberg* (New York: Basic Books, 1977). See also, John and Ann Tusa, *The Nuremberg Trial* (London: Macmillan, 1983).

[7] See Priscilla Dale Jones, 'British Policy Towards German Crimes Against German Jews,' *Leo Baeck Institute Yearbook* 36 (1991), reproduced in David Cesarani ed. *Holocaust. Critical Concepts in Historical Studies* (London: Routledge, 2004), vol 6, 95-128, here 95-103; David Engel, *In the Shadow of Auschwitz: The Polish Government-in Exile and the Jews, 1939-1942* (Chapel Hill, NC: University of North Carolina Press, 1987); Bernard Wasserstein, *Britain and the Jews of Europe, 1939-1945* (Oxford: Clarendon Press, 1979); David Wyman, *The Abandonment of the Jews* (New York: Pantheon, 1984).

[8] Arieh Kochavi, *Prelude To Nuremberg* (Chapel Hill, NC: University of North Carolina Press, 1998), 8.

[9] Dale Jones, 'British Policy Towards German Crimes Against German Jews,' 101; Kochavi, *Prelude To Nuremberg*, 10-16.

military tribunals for the purpose. This policy would forbid consideration of acts before 1939 and, crucially, exclude crimes perpetrated by the Germans against their own nationals and stateless persons.[10]

Yet it was precisely crimes of this nature that bulked increasingly large. When Churchill and Roosevelt met in Washington in June 1942 they were both under pressure from the exiled governments and public opinion in their own countries to respond to atrocities such as the Lidice massacre. Meanwhile, information about the systematic mass murder of the Jews accumulated and by the autumn the scepticism of British officials regarding this information was overcome. However, at this stage of the war the British had another reason for inaction. The Germans now held many thousand British POWs. The Foreign Office and, critically, the War Office and the army, feared that threats of retribution would lead the Nazis to use POWs as hostages or even retaliate against them.[11]

During the summer of 1942, Whitehall looked for a policy that would enable Churchill to satisfy those calling for action. Eden favoured administrative justice against the top political and military leadership and quick trials, in situ, of middle and lower level perpetrators. Provision for such measures should be written into the armistice agreement with the vanquished enemy. The government's law officers, led by Lord Simon, the Lord Chancellor, disagreed. It would be wrong, they argued, to try those who followed orders while those who gave them were summarily treated. The War Office was content with the punishment of war crimes, as traditionally defined, but this would exclude proceedings against the civil echelon and would not easily cover atrocities carried out for religious, racial or political motives. In order to appear to be doing something and in a genuine search for a device to break the deadlock, on 6 July 1942 the War Cabinet agreed to promote a UN commission for the investigation of war crimes. A Cabinet Committee on the Treatment of War Criminals was set up and this, in turn, invited the governments-in-exile to appoint representatives to the UN body.[12]

London provided the base for the UN war crimes commission, inaugurated on 20 October 1943. Its initial mission was to collect information on alleged war crimes, the names of perpetrators, and to report this data to the seventeen member states. The USSR, which felt snubbed and wanted trials during the war, refused to participate. The United States was less than keen, either. In English eyes this was no bad thing. According to Arieh Kochavi, "The FO viewed the establishment of the commission largely as a means of neutralising calls for acts of retribution against the Germans and of creating the impression that the war crimes issue was being handled."[13]

Contrary to the view propounded in the 1970s by John Fox, that the Allies were responding in earnest to the mounting evidence of crimes against the Jews, it is more likely that the creation of the commission was merely coincidental with the evolution of the Allied statement on the extermination of the Jews that eventuated on 17 December 1942.[14]

The FO rejected all efforts by Jewish organisations to achieve recognition that the Jews were suffering from a specific onslaught or that the Allies should empower themselves to try Germans and their collaborators for crimes against their own nationals or crimes against stateless persons carried out on German territory. The negative response of FO officials is sometimes attributed to actual or latent anti-Semitism, but the demand that the Allies should try Germans for crimes committed against their own nationals or against stateless persons on Axis territory was to seek something unprecedented and, indeed, taboo.[15] Furthermore, it could feed Nazi paranoia about Jewish influence in the Allied capitals and incite a reaction. This is, put charitably, what Frank Roberts, at the FO Central Department, meant when he said that it "seems to me unnecessary to irritate him [Hitler] more than is necessary,

---

[10] Dale Jones, 'British Policy Towards German Crimes Against German Jews,' 102.
[11] Kochavi, *Prelude To Nuremberg*, 27-8, 59-60, 71-2 and Arieh Kochavi, 'Britain and the War Crimes Question at the Conclusion of the Second World War: The Military Dimension', *Journal of Holocaust Education*, 2:2 (1993), 123-48.
[12] Kochavi, *Prelude To Nuremberg*, 28-54.
[13] Kochavi, *Prelude To Nuremberg*, 59-60.
[14] John Fox, 'The Jewish Factor in British War Crimes policy in 1942', *English Historical Review*, 92 (1977), 82-106.
[15] Dale Jones, 'British Policy Towards German Crimes Against German Jews,' 104-9.

particularly on the Jewish issue". In any case, as Kochavi maintains, "Knowledge of the massacre of European Jews had an insignificant effect on either British or American officials who dealt with the issue of Axis crimes."[16]

As often happens in international bureaucracies with a remit over a conflicted area of policy, the UN war crimes commission experienced "mission creep". Under the guidance of Cecil Hurst, the British delegate and Herbert Pell, from the US, it went much further than Whitehall had intended. Hurst and Pell initiated a debate over the definition of war crimes, seeking to extend the commission's scope to include offences committed on a religious, racial or political basis. They further innovated by coming up with a category of "waging aggressive war". And they sought to invest the UN with jurisdiction over such offences committed by Germans from the humblest to the highest rank.[17]

In the long term, this was valuable work. But in the short term it set the commission on a collision course with both Downing Street and the White House. As far as Churchill and Roosevelt were concerned the fate of any surviving Nazi leaders would lie in their hands and they would not be tied by any judicial process. The Moscow Declaration of 1 November 1943, to which they and Stalin were signatories, promised retribution against Germans responsible for "atrocities, massacres and executions' (it is notable how restrictive the categories were: they did not include forced labour, expulsion etc). But it specifically excluded the "major war criminals whose offences have no particular geographical location and who will be punished by a joint decision of the Government of the Allies".[18]

Churchill and Roosevelt notoriously concurred that the best policy with regard to the leading Nazis was summary execution. At the same time as the UN war crimes commission was drawing up lists of war criminals for prosecution, Churchill was ordering his law officers to provide a roster of "outlaws" whose culpability was held to be beyond any doubt, who would be shot by the military after a commission of inquiry had established their identity. In fact, by June 1944 British policy had reached an impasse. Churchill and Eden favoured quick executive action against the Nazi leadership, Like Victor Cavendish-Bentinck, head of the Joint Intelligence Committee, they deplored the idea that men like Hitler and Göring should be allowed to defend themselves before a court and the bar of international public opinion in the course of a protracted legal process. However, the FO was wary of summary justice, could not produce a list of candidates for execution, and was sensitive to what other arms of government thought about such a proposal. The War Office [WO] and the army, for example, were appalled at the notion that members of the German general staff might be shot like dogs once their identity was known. As a compromise, the FO and WO suggested passing these hot potatoes to the UN.[19]

In the autumn of 1944, Churchill and Roosevelt were forced to draw back from their drastic, not to say vengeful and savage, policy. Their volte-face is usually attributed to a combination of Stalin's rather surprising insistence on trials and the outcry against the vindictive Morgenthau plan for post-war Germany. However, their thinking was also influenced by the nagging fear about the fate of Allied POWs. Thousands of additional British and US airmen were now in German captivity as a result of the intensification of the air war in 1943-44. Goebbels routinely referred to the actions of the RAF and USAAF as "terror bombing" and airman who bailed out over Germany were at risk of lynching until they were taken into custody. Even then, as they showed in the treatment of the escapees from Stalug Luft III, the Germans demonstrated a willingness to massacre Allied POWs on the flimsiest of pretexts.[20]

---

[16] Kochavi, *Prelude To Nuremberg*, 139-52. C. F. Roberts, *Dealing With Dictators*, pp. 46-8.

[17] Kochavi, *Prelude To Nuremberg*, 92-103.

[18] Michael Marrus, *The Nuremberg War Crimes Trial 1945-46. A Documentary History* (New York: St Martin's Press, 1997), 20-21.

[19] Kochavi, *Prelude To Nuremberg*, 73-76.

[20] Priscilla Dale Jones, 'Nazi Atrocities Against Allied Airmen: Stalag Luft III and the End of British War Crimes Trials, *Historical Journal*, 41 (1998), 543-65.

By early 1945, the British did not have a comprehensive policy on the treatment of German war criminals. Churchill and Eden had been checked. But there was no obvious alternative after the Foreign Office had successfully undermined the UN war crimes commission. While FO officials publicly decried the tardiness of the commission, in private, Sir William Malkin, the FO legal adviser, along with Denis Allan of the FO, assembled a compelling armoury of reasons why the commission was over-reaching itself. The commission had suggested an international court to try German war criminals, but this was an objectionable form of "universal retrospective justice". It would take so long to set up and operate such a court that the victims of Nazi persecution would resort to their own means. Which legal system would it use, anyway? And who would it try if the major war criminals were to be excluded? They preferred to leave the thorny matter of crimes by Germans against German nationals and stateless persons in Germany to German courts, a notion that the Lord Chancellor could see was full of holes. But the law officers had fared no better. Lord Simon had attempted to introduce into Parliament a War Crimes Bill to enable the prosecution of Germans for the most narrowly defined offences, but he was stymied by the War Cabinet which feared German retaliation.[21]

Such a situation could not continue. By March 1945 it was clear that German military resistance was collapsing. In April the first concentration camps in western Germany were overrun, leading to publicity that generated an enormous head of steam for justice or revenge against the perpetrators. To some extent London was saved by the advent of the Americans with the first comprehensive plan for dealing with German war criminals. But it also implemented its own preparations for a limited war crimes trial programme.

In November 1943, following the Moscow Declaration, the War Cabinet resolved that war crimes, in the strict sense of the term, committed against British nationals between September 1939 and the end of hostilities, should be tried by military courts under a Royal Warrant. On 14 June 1945, the terms of the Royal Warrant were published. By focussing narrowly on war crimes and limiting jurisdiction to Allied nationals, the British essentially abdicated responsibility for the nightmarish problem of holding Germans to account for a European-wide genocide, the epicentre of which was the former territory of Greater Germany, that involved the systematic murder of German nationals by their own government and the deportation of persons for religious and racial reasons from Axis states to other Axis territory for the purpose of murdering them there or abusing them.[22]

Here was the crux of the problem as the British saw it. Precisely because Nazi crimes were unprecedented there was no legal mechanism for coping with them. The traditional category of war crimes evidently excluded crimes committed before September 1939, could not encompass acts against German or Axis nationals, and did not fit many of the atrocities perpetrated by the Nazis. Never before had a government turned on its nationals in such a fashion or inflicted mass murder on the populations of its allies. Nor was there any accumulated experience of dealing with such crimes against vast numbers of stateless persons. While it was conceivable to hold Germans to account on the territory of Allied countries in the case of atrocities committed against Allied nationals, even if they were from a third country, there was simply no means of prosecuting Germans for acts against Axis nationals or stateless persons carried out on German soil. To encompass such acts required judicial innovation and as good lawyers, the British Government law officers and the legal advisors in other departments were leery of any such moves.

However, as in the conduct of so many other aspects of policy at this stage of the war and the Anglo-American relationship, the British essentially came into line with the US perspective. At a meeting in London with US Judge Rosenman in April 1945, Lord Simon attempted to preserve the minimalist British position of quick trials of a small number of Nazi leaders, with the sentencing left to governments to decide. Simon did not have authority for such a proposal and his effort was negated first

---

[21] Kochavi, *Prelude To Nuremberg*, 110-37, 203-4.

[22] Donald Bloxham, *Genocide on Trial* (Oxford: Oxford University Press, 2001), 34-5, 55-56. See also, Anthony Glees, 'The Making of British Policy on War Crimes History as Politics in the UK', *Contemporary European History*, 1:2 (1992), 172-79.

by the War Cabinet and second by the death of Roosevelt. When London and Washington resumed negotiations in the summer of 1945, the personnel on both sides had changed. Sir William Jowitt, the new Lord Chancellor, broadly went along with the American conception of the IMT with the full consent of the new Labour Government.[23]

At the London Conference in July–August 1945, held to draft the Charter of the IMT, the British delegation was led by the new Attorney General Hartley Shawcross, also head of the British War Crimes Executive, and his predecessor, Sir David Maxwell Fyfe, as his deputy. They were supportive of American aims, but with reservations. First, they could not comprehend the American plan to install conspiracy at the heart of the indictment. This reservation was based on both legal grounds and a shrewd understanding of the Third Reich. An official at the FO commented on the draft American indictment that: "The Nazis, and Hitler in particular, were supreme opportunists and, whilst they had almost certainly aggressive designs from the beginning, it is very probable that their aggressive plans only gradually took the shape in which they were carried through." The FO Research Department scorned the idea that "Mein Kampf" could be used in evidence against the defendants. It "does not reveal the Nazi aims of conquest and domination fully and explicitly"[24] Nor did the British understand the concept of prosecuting organisations. Maxwell Fyfe worried that the trial would diverge in two separate directions: war crimes and waging aggressive war. Above all, the British wanted to limit the scope of the trial, the number of the defendants, and the volume of evidence. All these anxieties were manifested in the draft indictment they produced, only to see it re-written by the American team.[25]

Shawcross feared an "exceedingly long and elaborate" process that would be perceived as a show trial or serve as a platform for the accused to defend Nazi ideology and actions. The danger was all the greater because of the legal innovation employed by the Tribunal. It was heightened also by awareness that the defendants were being accused of deeds that were not alien to those who were judging them. For example, when accusing the Germans of conspiring to wage aggressive war the British could only reflect uncomfortably on their part in the dismemberment of Czechoslovakia in 1938.[26] For a connected reason, the British were always queasy about the participation of the Soviet Union but they knew there was nothing they could do to prevent it. Indeed, Jowitt and Maxwell Fyfe spent a lot of time mediating between the Americans and the Soviets to keep the show on the road.[27]

In the end, it is fair to say that the British were vindicated. The force of the IMT was dissipated by its extraordinary duration. On 26 March 1946, Earl Birkenhead, asked in the Daily Telegraph, "why is it dragging on month after month?" The charge of conspiracy was unprecedented, unwieldy, and hard to prove. The evidence of crimes against humanity was diluted both by the structure imposed on the trial by the need to demonstrate conspiracy and the salience afforded to the charge of waging aggressive war. Jackson's insistence on bringing to bear a mass of documents as evidence slowed the proceedings and made them intolerably dull. The journalist Rebecca West reported that the Tribunal was "boredom on a huge, historic scale". She praised Nuremberg for documenting Nazi crimes, but "For the rest the Nuremberg trial must be admitted as a betrayal of the hopes which it engendered".[28]

Tedium, however, was a trivial complaint and hardly avoidable in matters to do with the law. Many more serious objections to the Tribunal were aired in Britain during its course and afterwards. In May 1946, Gilbert Murray, once a leading supporter of the League of Nations, attacked the Tribunal for systematic double standards. "I doubt if these trials will produce in history that moral effect which is claimed to be their main justification. A soldier judged and hanged by his enemies is to his own people

---

[23] Kochavi, *Prelude To Nuremberg*, 163-71, 216-27.
[24] Richard Overy, *Interrogations* (London: Allen Lane, 2001), 48-52.
[25] Bradley F. Smith, *Reaching Judgment at Nuremberg*, 41-2, 48-49, 55-6, 62, 72. Telford Taylor, *The Anatomy of the Nuremberg Trials* (London: Bloomsbury, 1993), 58-77.
[26] Hartley Shawcross, *Life Sentence. The Memoirs of Hartley Shawcross* (London: Constable, 1995), 90-2.
[27] Hartley Shawcross, *Life Sentence*, 103.
[28] Reports for the *Daily Telegraph*, 1946, reprinted in Rebecca West, *A Train of Powder* (London: Virago, 1984), 254-5. Shawcross, *Life Sentence*, p. 115.

an object of sympathy rather than horror."[29] George Bernard Shaw wrote to the press after the verdicts were announced to protest that, given the dropping of the atomic bombs on Japan, none of the Allied powers was in a position to hang Göring.[30] To Lord Hankey, a minister in Churchill's war cabinet in 1940-1, the IMT was a travesty of justice. War, he maintained, is an instrument of policy and not a crime. If it was a crime, then the countries sitting in judgement were equally guilty of aggressive war at one time or another over the previous six years. In this respect, alone, the participation of the USSR made a mockery of the proceedings and gave them every appearance of "victors' justice".[31]

Perhaps the last word, however, should be left to Lord Shawcross. Fifty years after the Tribunal he reflected that: "For my part, while not excusing the imperfections and deficiencies of the trial, I still feel satisfied that it has laid down the law for the future, even if that law is imperfectly applied and still often disregarded."[32]

---

[29] *The Times*, 2 May 1946.
[30] Letter, *Daily Express*, 10 September 1946.
[31] The Rt Hon Lord Hankey, *Politics, Trials and Errors* (Oxford; Oxford University Press, 1950), 10-27 59-65, 125-30.
[32] Shawcross, *Life Sentence,* 136-7.

David Cesarani

Das Internationale Militärtribunal von Nürnberg: Britische Perspektiven

Das Nürnberger Tribunal von 1945-46 legte einen Grundstein für den nachfolgenden Umgang mit Kriegsverbrechen, Genozid und der Massenverletzung von Menschenrechten. Das Tribunal hatte jedoch einen schwierigen Start und wurde für seine Arbeit weithin kritisiert.

In den 60 Jahren nach dem Zweiten Weltkrieg diente das Tribunal nicht unbedingt als ein leuchtendes Beispiel für Justiz, Politik und öffentliche Meinung. Die nähere Betrachtung der Konflikte, die nicht nur seine Entstehung, sondern auch seine Arbeit begleitet haben, lässt es aus britischer Perspektive deshalb geraten erscheinen, das Tribunal nicht auf einen zu hohen Sockel zu stellen.

Zu Beginn zeigten sich die Briten gegenüber Nazi-Kriegsverbrecherprozessen nicht sehr aufgeschlossen, was nicht zuletzt in der Ergebnislosigkeit der Leipziger Kriegsverbrecherprozesse nach dem 1. Weltkrieg wurzelte. Außerdem war die britische Regierung darauf bedacht, die nicht unerhebliche Zahl der britischen Soldaten zu schützen, die sich in deutscher Kriegsgefangenschaft befand. Zugleich stand sie unter erheblichem Druck seitens der Exilregierungen der von den Nazis besetzten europäischen Staaten, die sich für eine strafrechtliche Verfolgung der Aggressoren aussprachen.

Die Erfahrungen der Nürnberger Prozesse hatten speziell in den 1990er Jahren einen beinahe magischen Effekt auf die heftigen Debatten, die aus der Annäherung der Politik an Fragen des Umgangs mit Verbrechen in Krieg und Frieden mit so unterschiedlichen Konflikten wie in Südafrika, dem früheren Jugoslawien, Ruanda und Irak entstanden.

Diese „Verehrung" reflektiert kaum noch die zweifelhafte Herkunft, die unsichere rechtliche Basis, die umstrittene Verfahrensweise und die fragwürdigen Resultate der Prozesse in Nürnberg und die Tatsache, dass in der Nachkriegszeit die auf den IMT basierenden juristischen Prozesse als eher lästig und unangenehm angesehen wurden. Viel Zeit und Anstrengung waren notwendig, um die Verurteilungen der Nachfolgeprozesse zu relativieren, jenen, die verurteilt worden waren, gänzlichen Erlass oder Reduzierung ihrer Freiheitsstrafe zu gewähren, und die westdeutsche Bevölkerung zu beschwichtigen, die niemals die Gültigkeit der Nürnberger Prozesse wirklich anerkannt hatte. Die britische Intelligenzia zweifelte außerdem die Legitimität durch die eigenen ungesühnten Verbrechen der Alliierten während des Krieges an. Dennoch sah beispielsweise der britische Chefankläger Shawcross den Wert des Nürnberger Prozesses trotz seiner Mängel darin, dass internationales Recht für die Zukunft geschaffen wurde.

Hervé Ascensio

The French Perspective

There may be no such thing as one French perspective. The idea, in itself, is contradictory to the spirit of Nuremberg, which is about the deconstruction of the State and deconstruction of the nation as collective entities to determine the specific role individuals played in Germany's moral decay. Individuals make history, and not the opposite: this is the lesson the promoters of the trial intended to teach. This is also the lesson lawyers usually teach, as responsibility is a central concept for them, unlike historians or sociologists. If one wishes to remain faithful to this spirit, it would be inappropriate to refer to the 'perspective of France' when trying to understand the 'French perspective'. It is about asking questions such as: What were the interests of the members of the French government? What were the reactions of the French media of that time? What were the expectations of the French victims of war crimes? What role played French actors during the trial? How is Nuremberg perceived today by lawyers, by politicians, by French citizens? But as I have only limited time, I need to concentrate on some specific themes. The first one will be the contextual creation of the tribunal, which provides a response to the call for justice emanating from different parts of French society. The second theme appears to me to be also the central question about the Nuremberg trial, and a very legal one indeed: the invention of criminal responsibility in international law. The third theme will be the heritage of Nuremberg in French law, a paradoxical heritage indeed, as it concerns mostly the crime against humanity.

1. The Context: A Call for Justice

The interest of some French politicians for a trial comes from far away. One of the first political reactions against the crimes committed by the Germans in the occupied countries of Europe was a declaration by the governments in exile (Inter-Allied Declaration) on 13 January 1942, at the end of a conference at St-James Palace. The "Comité national de la France libre", led by General de Gaulle, was one of the signatories. Paragraph 3 of the declaration mentions that amongst the main goals of the war is the punishment of those persons responsible for war crimes by way of organised justice. A joint allied committee for the repression of war crimes was created to put pressure on the Three Allied Powers (UK, USA, and USSR). In this framework, the French transmitted an oral note to the Soviet representative in London in July 1942. On 3 October 1942, the English government proposed the creation of a fact-finding commission to the signatories of the Saint-James Declaration. But it was a year later that on 20 October 1943 this commission on war crimes first met with French representatives attending. All these efforts prepared the way for the famous Moscow Declaration of 1 November 1943 signed by the Three Allied Powers.

After the liberation of the French territory, the French exile-government had, of course, a clear interest to appear as one of the victorious nations. It is mentioned as such in the London Agreements of 8 August 1945. In a way, speaking about a "victor's justice" is not so problematic from the French perspective, as France is thus recognized as one of the victors of World War II, despite the shaming political episode of the Vichy regime. The official discourse, and not only just after the liberation, but at least until the 1980's, was that France – *i.e.* the French spirit – was represented during the war by "*La France libre*" in London. But this political motive is not the only one. It cannot be dissociated from another motive, probably a more important one, which constitutes at the same time a legitimating factor for the new government in France.

The high number of crimes committed on French territory explains the strong public opinion in support of a trial against those, who were mostly responsible for them. The idea was broadly sustained in legal doctrine.[1] The name of Oradour-sur-Glane, a French village where crimes were committed by

---

[1] See the article published by *Rey* at the end of the war in the *Revue générale de droit international public* (reference in the bibliography).

Nazis on 10 June 1944, became the symbol of this call for justice. During the proceedings, the French Prosecutor, M. de Menthon, was in charge of presenting crimes committed in France, and also in the other occupied countries of Western Europe: Belgium, Luxemburg and the Netherlands. He especially stressed the deportation and internment of Jews as well as resistance fighters in concentration camps. The absence of making any distinction between Jews and non-Jews was conform with the French concepts of nation and equality based on the principles of the French revolutionary ideology, which was rejected by the reactionary Vichy-regime. For the purpose of reaffirming these concepts, the voices of all kinds of victims needed to be heard at once. All of them called for justice, as in the case of Champetier de Ribes, one of the French deputy-prosecutors in Nuremberg, in his closing statement, when he addressed very directly the judges: "*C'est à vous d'entendre maintenant dans les silences de vos délibérés, le sang des innocents qui réclame justice*" (It is up to you now, in the silence of your deliberation, to hear the blood of innocents which call for justice).

Moreover, all French actors of the trial agreed to a conception of justice stemming from the conscience of mankind, which constitutes a rejection of rigid legal positivism. This concurred entirely with French legal doctrine of the 1930s, especially in public law, considering law as the by-product of social circumstances and common sense of justice.[2] Justice is conceived as an alliance between force and ethics. On the one hand, force is always a pre-condition for the establishment of criminal justice; thus, the establishment of the Nuremberg trial by the Allied was a logical necessity in order to prosecute, considering the under-institutionalisation of the society of nations. On the other hand, the law applied in Nuremberg is justified by the evolution of international law in the first part of the 20th century and consolidated by the public indignation at the crimes committed during the war. Thus, Menthon, the French Chief Prosecutor, affirms the existence of a "*droit international commun*", which means an international *jus commune* (and not an international common law), constituted by minimum legal standards common to all civilized nations and at the roots of international customary law. The French Deputy-Prosecutor, Charles Dubost, mentions in length the conscience of mankind, and, with a probable allusion to the Shoah, insists on the fact that the sense of good and evil cannot be ignored, even by the Heads of States, in the name of the legal methodology and by legal methodology. Such a theory of law is echoed in the judgement itself, when stated "often, treaties only express principles of law already in force" (p. 231) and "the conscience of the world, far from being offended if he [the criminal] were punished, would be shocked if he were not" (p. 233).[3]

2. The Central Question: Thinking on Responsibility

In writing the Statute of the Nuremberg Tribunal, French influence was probably low, as the procedure was modelled on traditions of *common law*. Crimes resulted from previous efforts made by so-called "civilised nations", including France, to develop international law. We need here to mention especially a pact drafted in Paris in 1928 ("Kellog-Briand" Pact for the American, and "Pacte Briand-Kellog" for the French!), which prohibited wagging an aggressive war and thus enabled the Allies to prosecute crimes against peace at Nuremberg. But during the trial, it seems that the specific French contribution was mostly concerned with the subject of responsibility.

Among French actors, the major character was certainly Judge Henri Donnedieu de Vabres, whose role is sometimes underestimated or down played in English-speaking literature. In his famous book on the Nuremberg trial, Telford Taylor describes him as hesitant and weak because among other reasons he opposed the death penalty for some of the accused. Moreover, in the series of lectures he gave at the The Hague Academy of International Law in 1947, Donnedieu de Vabres justified the judgments of acquittal and also expressed doubts about Dönitz's culpability. These opinions were clearly in

---

[2] See a.o., in the English-speaking literature, Martti KOSKENNIEMI, *The Gentle Civilizer of Nations. The Rise and Fall of International Law 1870-1960*, Cambridge University Press, 2003, at 266. For the French-speaking literature, see the bibliography.

[3] We quote from the French version of the judgement (*Procès des grands criminels de guerre devant le tribunal militaire international, textes officiels en langue française*, tome I, *Documents officiels*, Nuremberg, 1947) (our translation).

contradiction with the general feeling of the time: death penalty was expressly called for against all the accused by the French Deputy-Prosecutor, Champetier de Ribes in his closing speech, and acquittals were strongly criticized after the trials. A reappraisal of the acquittals as well – I hope! – as to the death penalty, this would probably lead to a different result, much more incline with Donnedieu de Vabres' view. But the real reason for the misunderstanding was the position he took against the judicial strategy of Chief Prosecutor Robert Jackson. The legal dispute was about the appraisal of individual responsibility in the context of collective crimes, and it had a major impact on the future development of international criminal law.

The political organization, which is necessary to commit crimes such as aggression or crime against humanity, makes the distinction between collective and individual responsibility rather unclear. Of course, some remarks of the French actors reveal resentment against Germany and Germans altogether. But despite this, all of them tried to encompass crimes in the legal framework of classical criminal responsibility. As Donnedieu de Vabres explained in his Hague's lectures, even if these crimes were political crimes because they were committed by individuals using the political structure of the State, it was necessary to individualize the punishment. For him, this was "new international law"[4], an expression by which he meant international law having individuals and not only States as subjects. That is why he criticizes strongly the insistence of the prosecution on notions like "conspiracy" or "criminal organisations", because they fall too short from collective responsibility[5]. They give to the Hitler enterprise a kind of "romantic prestige"[6], whereas, according to him, Hitler's individual responsibility was the main one, and complicity would have been more appropriate for most of the trial accused.

What appears here seem to be two opposing concepts of criminal responsibility for crimes committed jointly by two or more individuals. The French legal tradition of that time insisted more on the subjective element of the crime (criminal intention), whereas the English tradition insisted on the objective element (criminal act). Donnedieu de Vabres – not unexpectedly – preferred the French tradition, because it concurred with modern legal doctrine, which recommend individualized prosecution.[7] The analysis of the French prosecutor Dubost was not different, but more balanced: he tried to demonstrate that the accused were not only accomplices but direct authors of the crimes. He underlined the existence of a "criminal policy" as an element of the crime against peace, rather than that of a "criminal enterprise" as a technique of responsibility.

As a result of this implicit legal debate between the different prosecutors and between the prosecution and the judges, count n°1, conspiracy, was completely dismissed; instead, the judgment concentrates on the planning of the crimes. For the same reason, the crime of participating in a criminal organization was seriously limited by way of interpretation. The International Tribunal recognized the criminal character of some organizations, but it addressed recommendations to courts, which would implement international criminal law in the future. The criminal intention of each individual member of these organizations should be demonstrated at trial, as a constitutive element of the crime.

It should be noticed that this central debate still continues today before international criminal courts. The notion of "joined criminal enterprise", used in the *Milosevic* case for instance, seems to be close to conspiracy. Its extensive use is now criticised by defense counsels, and even by some of the judges in other cases before the ICTY. It seems more appropriate to require not only complicity, but co-action in order to determine the role of the individual in collective crimes, while giving the highest regard to protecting the rights of the accused.

---

[4] at 526 (reference in bibliography).

[5] at 528 : « Il a plu à l'accusation de présenter l'épopée nationale-socialiste comme une entreprise dont le but immédiat fut le déclenchement des guerres d'agression, et la conséquence indirecte la commission de crimes de guerre et de crimes de lèse-humanité. L'acte d'accusation et les réquisitoires qui l'ont suivi sont échafaudés sur cette hypothèse ».

[6] at 530 : « L'imputation d'un complot pare l'entreprise hitlérienne d'un prestige romantique qui n'est pas sans séduire les imaginations ».

[7] Apparently, this legal thinking is no more firmly established in France, as is demonstrated by the well-known crime of participation in a terrorist enterprise!

3. The Paradoxical Heritage: Crimes against Humanity

Crime against peace was the main count, the one which encompassed all the others. War crimes were also important, but they were presented as a consequence of the Nazi-ideology, following the wagging of aggressive wars. Crime against humanity came as a subsidiary count, and not as an autonomous one. However, it was considered by the French Deputy Prosecutor Charles Dubost as the node of the process. But the French prosecution as well as the French judge seemed reluctant towards the use of this count. In his lectures in The Hague, Donnedieu de Vabres took position in favour of a flexible conception of the principle *nullum crimen sine lege*. According to him, it would be absurd to deny its presence in international law, but absurd as well to apply it strictly, because the international legal order is not yet a complete one, and a strict application of the principle would result in an attack on the principle of justice. This line of reasoning applied for the crime against peace, but not for the crime against humanity. He thought the definition of the last one was too obviously posterior to the facts and, then, contrary to the principle on non-retroactivity. Probably reluctant to criticize the Nuremberg process, Donnedieu de Vabres perpetuated the idea that crime against humanity almost vanished in the Nuremberg judgment,[8] which is almost true – it applied for German victims instead of war crimes.

Considering the lack of concern for "crimes against humanity" in the judgement, it is all the more surprising that this crime became the major legacy of Nuremberg in French law. Until 1 March 1994, which was the enforcement date of the new criminal code, the Nuremberg statute was the sole legal basis for the prosecution of crimes against humanity before French courts. In 1975, in the *Touvier* case, the French *Cour de cassation* (last degree court in civil and criminal matters) decided that the Nuremberg Statute was directly applicable in the French legal order. Consequently, individuals could be prosecuted before French courts, without any definition other than the one of Nuremberg, with some details added by French case-law (see especially Cour de cassation, criminal chamber, *Barbie* case, 20 December 1985). Moreover, the reference to the Nuremberg statute allowed the retroactive application of the 1964 law for imprescriptibility of crimes against humanity. It was then possible, forty years after the end of the war, to prosecute the SS-Hauptsturmführer Klaus Barbie, but also, ten years later, French collaborators like Touvier, Bousquet, Papon (for complicity in crime against humanity). This is the best part of the heritage: Nuremberg evolved as a German mirror for French duality, *i.e.* French complicity in crimes against humanity committed in France during World War II.

However, there are still problems with this heritage. The definition of crimes against humanity before 1994 was strictly designed for crimes committed by the Nazis during World War II requiring a "criminal policy", a State "ideology", and a necessary link with World War II. This last element of the crime has disappeared with the definition adopted in the criminal code of 1992 (in force since 1994). But the new definition is not applicable to previous acts. It is then completely impossible to use crimes against humanity for acts committed during decolonisation; and for war crimes, there are amnesty laws as well as statutory limitations. The new definition applies for acts committed after 1 March 1994, and for crimes committed in the former Yugoslavia since 1991 and in Rwanda in 1994, because of specific laws of cooperation with the ICTY and ICTR. French courts may then be seized, for instance, in the hypothesis that some French citizens would have been accomplice in the genocide committed in Rwanda.[9] As you see, the German mirror could be of use again.

---

[8] at 526-527.
[9] Genocide is conceived in French law as the gravest form of the crime against humanity; it appears as an autonomous crime in the new criminal code.

Bibliography:

Louis RENAULT, « De l'application du droit pénal aux faits de guerre », *Revue générale de droit international public*, 1918, 5;

Vespasien V. PELLA, *La criminalité collective des Etats et le droit pénal de l'avenir*, 2ème éd., Imprimerie de l'Etat, Bucarest, 1926;

Henri DONNEDIEU DE VABRES, *Les principes modernes du droit pénal international*, Recueil Sirey, Paris, 1928 (rééd. Editions Panthéon Assas, Paris, 2004);

REY, « Les violations du droit international commises par les Allemands en France dans la guerre de 1939 », *Revue générale de droit international public*, t. XVI, 1941-1945, vol. II, 1;

CENTRE DE DOCUMENTATION JUIVE CONTEMPORAINE, *La persécution des Juifs en France et dans les autres pays de l'Ouest : présentée par la France à Nuremberg. Recueil de documents*, publié sous la direction de Henri MONNERAY, préface de René CASSIN, introduction d'Edgar FAURE, série « Documents » 2, Editions du Centre, Paris, 1947;

Jacques DESCHEEMAEKER, *Le Tribunal militaire international des grands criminels de guerre*, préface de V.-V. PELLA, Pedone, Paris, 1947;

Henri DONNEDIEU DE VABRES, « Le jugement de Nuremberg et le principe de légalité des délits et des peines », *Revue de droit pénal et de criminologie*, 1946-1947, 813;

et « Le procès de Nuremberg devant les principes modernes du droit pénal international », *Recueil des cours de l'Académie de droit international de La Haye*, 1947-I, tome 70, 477;

Marcel MERLE, *Le procès de Nuremberg et le châtiment des criminels de guerre*, préface de H. DONNEDIEU DE VABRES, Pedone, Paris, 1949;

Georges SCELLE, « Quelques réflexions sur l'abolition de la compétence de guerre », *Revue générale de droit international public*, 1954, 5;

Claude LOMBOIS, *Droit pénal international*, 2ème éd., Dalloz, Paris, 1979;

Sandra SZUREK, « Historique de la formation du droit international pénal », *in* H. ASCENSIO, E. DECAUX ET A. PELLET (dir.), *Droit international pénal*, Pedone, Paris, 2000, 7;

Jean-Paul JEAN et Denis SALAS (dir.), *Barbie, Touvier, Papon. Des procès pour la mémoire*, Editions autrement, Paris, 2002;

Géraud de LA PRADELLE, *Imprescriptible. L'implication française dans le génocide tutsi portée devant les tribunaux*, Les arènes, Paris, 2005.

Hervé Ascensio
Die französische Perspektive

Es ist schwierig, umfassend von einer „französischen Perspektive" auf die Nürnberger Prozesse zu sprechen. An drei konkreten Punkten erläutert der Autor daher, welche Rolle Frankreich in der strafrechtlichen Verfolgung von NS-Verbrechen gespielt hat.

Zunächst wirft Ascensio einen Blick auf das politische Umfeld gegen Ende des 2. Weltkriegs. „La France libre" unter General De Gaulle war bereits 1942 an den Verhandlungen der Alliierten im St. James Palast in London beteiligt. Nach der Befreiung des gesamten französischen Staatsgebiets von der Nazi-Besetzung war es der Regierung besonders wichtig, zu den „Siegern" des Krieges zu gehören, trotz der beschämenden Kollaboration der Vichy-Regierung mit dem NS-Regime. Für die französische Öffentlichkeit war eine strafrechtliche Verfolgung der Nazi-Kriegsverbrecher wegen der in Frankreich begangenen Grausamkeiten von herausragender Bedeutung. Ebenso wurde von den französischen Juristen die Gerechtigkeit in den Mittelpunkt gestellt und zugleich einem rigiden Rechtspositivismus eine Absage erteilt.

In einem zweiten Punkt diskutiert er die strafrechtliche Verantwortung. Der französische Einfluss auf das Statut des IMT war unter der Dominanz der angloamerikanischen Juristen eher gering. Ebenso wird der Einfluss des französischen Richters, Henri Donnedieu de Vabres, in der Rezeptionsgeschichte des Nürnberger Prozesses vielleicht zu Unrecht heruntergespielt, da seine Kritik an den – im Übrigen auch heute z.B. im Milosevic-Prozess vor dem Jugoslawientribunal umstrittenen – Ideen des US-amerikanischen Chefanklägers Jackson zur Strafbarkeit wegen Verschwörung und Kriminalisierung von Organisationen, an der restriktiven Handhabe im Nürnberger Urteil mit verantwortlich ist.

Schließlich macht Ascensio auf einen Anachronismus in der französischen Rezeption der Verbrechen gegen die Menschlichkeit aufmerksam. Während des Nürnberger Prozesses waren die französischen Beteiligten eher darauf bedacht, den Tatbestand der Verbrechen gegen die Menschlichkeit zu marginalisieren, da sie in dessen Verfolgung einen Verstoß gegen das Rückwirkungsverbot sahen. Eine Transformation von Menschlichkeitsverbrechen in französisches Recht gelang allerdings erst in der Strafrechtsreform von 1992, die 1994 in Kraft trat. In den bekannten Verfahren gegen Barbie, Touvier, Bousquet oder Papon, vor Einführung des neuen Strafgesetzes, mussten die französischen Gerichte auf das Statut des IMT zurückgreifen. Die französischen Kollaborateure konnten daher nur wegen Nürnberg und auf der gleichen rechtlichen Grundlage wie die Nazi-Verbrecher selbst strafrechtlich verfolgt werden. Auch nach der Strafrechtsreform können Verfolgungslücken nur durch den Rückgriff auf das Nürnberger Verfahren geschlossen werden. Das ist vermutlich für das französische Recht das wichtigste Vermächtnis von Nürnberg.

Michael J. Bazyler

The Role of the Soviet Union in the International Military Tribunal at Nuremberg*

I. The Soviet Role in the International Military Tribunal Trial

The nation first to announce their preference for a judicial process for the crimes of the Nazis was the Soviet Union. This was in 1944, even before the war ended, and was in opposition to the Americans, who at that time were favoring the plan of U.S. Treasury Secretary Henry Morgethau Jr. The so-called Morgenthau-Plan aimed for the total denazification of Germany and severe economic reparations to make Germany into a weak agricultural state. As for individual criminal responsibility, "Morgenthau's eye-for-an-eye proposal suggested summarily shooting many prominent Nazi leaders at the time of capture and banishing others to far off corners of the world. Under Morgenthau's plan, German POWs would be forced to rebuild Europe."[1] The British also were not keen on setting up a court to judge the Nazis. Winston Churchill likewise favored execution by firing squad of the major Nazi war criminals.[2]

Of course, the Soviet understanding of the concept of judicial process was quite different than its meaning in the West. To the Soviets, the judicial proceedings – which they wanted to hold in Berlin – were going to be "show trials" of the kind they were quite used to under Joseph Stalin. In fact, Major General I.T. Nikitchenko, the judge appointed by the Soviet Union to the IMT, had earlier presided over some of the most notorious of Stalin's show trials during the purges of 1936-1938. Nikitchenko publicly pronounced his view that all of the defendants were guilty even prior to the start of the IMT proceedings:

"We are dealing here with the chief war criminals who have already been convicted and whose conviction has been already announced by both the Moscow and Crimea [referring to Yalta] declarations by the heads of the governments.... The whole idea is to secure quick and just punishment for the crime."[3]

He then famously added: *"If... the judge is supposed to be impartial [at Nuremberg], it would only lead to unnecessary delays."*[4]

When it came time to render judgment, Nikitchenko dissented against the three acquittals issued by the other three judges, and also argued that Rudolf Hess, the great enemy of the Soviet Union for his effort to create a separate peace with the British when he parachuted into England and was captured there, should also receive a death sentence. Nikitchenko also resisted French efforts to have the judgment against the defendants receiving a death sentence to be carried out by a firing squad – considered the more honorable way to die – than death by hanging, reserved for common criminals.[5]

---

* The author wishes to express his gratitude for the assistance of Natalie Saadian (05 Chapman University School of Law).

[1] Douglas Linder, "The Nuremberg Trials", http://jurist.law.pitt.edu/trials12.htm (author is law professor at University of Missouri-Kansas City School of Law (accessed July 15, 2005).

[2] As Linder explains, "Churchill reportedly told Stalin that he favored execution of captured Nazi leaders. Stalin answered, 'In the Soviet Union, we never execute anyone without a trial.' Churchill agreed saying, 'Of course, of course. We shall give them a trial first.'" Linder, *Id.*

[3] Whitney R. Harris, *Tyranny on Trial: The Evidence at Nuremberg Trials* (Dallas: SMU Press, 1954), 16-17. See also Robert E. Conot, *Justice at Nuremberg* (New York: Harper & Row, 1994), 18.

[4] *Id.* Nikitchenko's views were also rooted in a different understanding of the role that a judge plays in a criminal proceeding. The Soviet legal system was modeled on Continental Europe's view of criminal procedure. As Conot explains, "Unlike procedure in Anglo-American law, where the prosecutor and defense counsel are adversaries, with the judge sitting as arbiter, in continental law[,] prosecutor, defense counsel and judge are all charged with the task of arriving at the truth. Thus, Nikitchenko did not really understand what Jackson meant when he emphasized that the judges must be independent and impartial...." Conot, *supra*, 18.

[5] Goering, in his suicide note, explained the importance of this distinction. "I would have had no objection to being shot. However, I will not facilitate execution of Germany's Reichsmarshall by hanging! For the sake of Germany, I cannot permit this." Linden, *supra*.

The Soviet Union played an active role in the London Conference, in which Britain, France, the United States, together with the U.S.S.R. in 1945 mapped out their plan to establish the IMT. The Soviets played a major role not only in drafting the procedural rules of the tribunal,[6] but also in defining the legal theories under which the defendants would ultimately be tried.[7] For example, the notions of criminal organizations "proved a major bone of contention from the start."[8] The Soviets maintained that the IMT should focus on the leaders and members of the Nazi organizations, with the authority to rule after each case whether the entire organization – for example, the Gestapo – constituted a criminal enterprise. This procedural move would thereby "eliminat[e] the need to prove the criminality of the organization in each subsequent case of prosecution of a member of the organization."[9] In the end, the Soviet position prevailed, and became an important prosecutorial tool during the trial.[10] Additionally, the Soviets were responsible for the clause in the London Charter stating that the IMT "may require to be informed of the nature of any evidence before it is offered so that it may rule on the relevance thereof."[11] Moreover, the Soviets directed that the tribunal take judicial notice of facts of common knowledge instead of requiring their proof. They also attempted to have the judges agree – not always successfully, though – to take judicial notice of, among other things, the evidence propounded by committees established by the allies for the investigation of war crimes (such as the Soviet Extraordinary State Commission, discussed below).[12]

The Soviets and the Americans agreed that the tribunal need not be bound by the technical rules of evidence, allowing for introduction of any evidence considered to have probative value.[13] In addition, the Soviets and Americans wholeheartedly agreed that waging an aggressive war constituted an international crime deserving of sanctions.[14] Moreover, the Soviet terminology eventually used in the indictment, that of "crimes against peace", prevailed over the then-existing draft by the United States of "crimes of war."[15] The Soviet insistence on the aforementioned terms of the IMT was not intended to cause conflict between the Soviets and the three other prosecuting nations, but was meant to encourage a "court drama that would lay bare all the evilness of the Nazi system by detailing in public the criminal career of its leading personages".[16]

One of the criticisms made of the IMT trial is that the accusers were also victims of the Nazis and acted as prosecutors, judges and executioners. Therefore, the argument runs, the defendants could not and did not obtain a fair trial. The general proposition that the victims (and here also the victors) cannot also be the adjudicators of guilt, while superficially appealing, is not correct. As Professor A.L. Goodheart of Oxford explained soon after the conclusion of the trials in an article entitled "The Legality of the Nuremberg Trials",

"Attractive as this argument may sound in theory, it ignores the fact that it runs counter to the administration of law in every country. It if were true, then no spy could be given a legal trial, because his case is always heard by judges representing the enemy country. Yet no one has ever argued that in such cases it was necessary to call on neutral judges. The prisoner has the right to demand that his judges shall be fair, but not that they shall be neutral. As Lord Witt has pointed out, the same principle

---

[6] George Ginsburgs, *Moscow's Road to Nuremberg*, (New York: Kluwer Law International, 1996), 97-8.
[7] *Id.* at 98.
[8] *Id.*
[9] *Id.*
[10] *Id.*
[11] *Id.* at 102.
[12] *Id.*
[13] *Id.* at 103.
[14] *Id.* at 104.
[15] *Id.* at 105.
[16] *Id.* at 107. Indeed, it has also been argued that Soviet judge Nikitchenko raised objections to several American proposals in order to display "Moscow's determination not to serve as a rubber stamp." Arie Kochavi, *Prelude to Nuremberg: Allied War Crimes Policy and the Question of Punishment* (Chapel Hill and London: University of North Carolina Press, 1998), 240.

is applicable to ordinary criminal law because 'a burglar cannot complain that he is being tried by a jury of honest citizens."[17]

The same argument was made by Adolf Eichmann, who argued that it would be unfair for him to be adjudged by a Jewish judge. The three-judge Israeli court rejected the argument. As explained by Presiding Judge Moshe Landau,

"Will the memory of the Holocaust prevent the judges from carrying out their considered intention to conduct a fair trial? No....[W]e shall have no difficulty adhering to the guarantees given all defendants under our criminal code, to be considered innocent until proven guilty and to be judged solely according to evidence presented before the court....The judge, in his capacity as adjudicator, does not cease to be a creature of flesh and blood, with feelings and urges[,] but he is required by law to control them. We shall abide by this requirement."[18]

It is clear from Nikitenko's statements quoted above that he did not abide by this proposition as a judge at the IMT. Of course, this is not surprising, since the Soviet view of trials was not of a proceeding before finders of fact who aim to put their prejudices aside and decide culpability solely on the basis of facts presented to them. If the remaining three judges were also Soviet, or followed Nikitenko's view, it is likely that today the legacy of Nuremberg would be quite poor.

The Soviet aim to make Nuremberg a "show trial" by putting forth mounds of evidence of Nazi atrocities, especially those committed after the Nazi invasion of the Soviet Union, ironically had the effect of making the Nuremberg proceedings more legally effective. The chief Soviet prosecutor R. A. Rudenko and his staff were in many ways the most prepared prosecuting team of the four Allied prosecutorial teams. Moreover, the Soviet presentation of their case through extensive documentary evidence played a critical role in the thorough documentation of Nazi crimes and the exposure to the world of the brutality of the Nazi regime. Rudenko offered vast amounts of paper evidence to support the counts of conspiracy and crimes against peace.[19] Such evidence included not only the official documents of the defendants and their associates, but also transcripts of speeches at congresses and Reichstag sessions, books, maps, private correspondence, diaries, and memoirs.[20] Rudenko also presented material proof such as written depositions and statements of victims and witnesses, including those of the Germans.[21] The Soviets "claimed credit for convincing their partners not to build the proceedings around documentary evidence alone", for the offering of live evidence would produce "a dramatic effect on the atmosphere in the court-room".[22]

Much of the Soviet evidence came from the work of their "Extraordinary State Commission for Ascertaining and Investigating Crimes Perpetrated by the German-Fascist Invaders and their Accomplices". Created in November 1942, its task was to

"...keep complete records of the vile crimes perpetrated by the Germans and their accomplices and the damage inflicted by them on Soviet citizens and the socialist state; establish wherever possible the identity of the German-Fascist criminals guilty of the organization or execution of the crimes in occupied Soviet territories, so that they might be handed over to the courts for severe punishment; [and] unify and coordinate the work already performed by Soviet state organs in this area."[23]

Among the detailed and massive work performed by the Commission was inspection of graves and corpses, gathering of witness accounts, forensic examinations, and interrogations of captured Germans.[24] The records contained "the most complete description possible of the crimes committed, the full name and place of residence of the individuals furnishing the evidence", and "all the relevant

---

[17] A.L. Goodheart, "The Legality of the Nuremberg Trials," Juridicial Review (April 1946).
[18] Haim Goury, *Facing the Glass Booth: The Jerusalem Trial of Adolf Eichmann* (Michael Swirsky, transl.) (Detroit: Wayne State U. Press, 2004), 6-7.
[19] Ginsburgs, *supra*, p. 111.
[20] *Id.*
[21] *Id.* at 112.
[22] *Id.*
[23] *Id.* at 37–8.
[24] *Id.* at 39.

documents" such as minutes of the interrogations, medical expert conclusions, German documents, and films.[25] The Commission's extraordinary efforts resulted in an impressive list of "hundreds of Germans, from generals to humble privates", and a "specific and detailed enumeration of the crimes of which they stood accused".[26] These records proved indispensable at the IMT.

The Soviets also had the earliest experience in trying Nazis. In Kharkov in December 1943, the Soviets conducted the first domestic trial of Germans accused of atrocities.[27] The defendants consisted of a military intelligence captain, an SS lieutenant, a police private, and a Russian collaborator who chauffeured the Kharkov Gestapo.[28] The Soviet prosecution in the Kharkov trial invoked the theme of collective complicity in that the atrocities committed by the defendants were "links in a long chain of crimes...committed by the German invaders on the direct instructions of the German Government and of the Supreme Command of the German Army".[29] The Kharkov indictment "sounded vaguely like a medium for indicting a criminal gang and so anticipated the novel concept of 'criminal organization' later consecrated in the Charter of the Nuremberg Tribunal".[30] The Kharkov defendants admitted that the orders for atrocities for which they stood accused "emanated from the German government".[31] In its closing argument, the prosecution de-legitimized the defense of superior orders and "insisted that the accused be personally and individually held to account for their actions".[32]

At the same time, the prosecution did not hesitate to take advantage of the plea of *respondeat superior* in order to "trac[e] the responsibility to the men at the top of the Nazi pyramid", thus again emphasizing the notion of collective responsibility for the German atrocities.[33] Thus, the importance of domestic war crimes trials such as the Kharkov trial lies not only in their bringing of Nazi war criminals to justice, but also their effect, as put by Professor George Ginsburgs, of "point[ing] the way toward the grand finale at Nuremberg".[34]

Last, the Soviet evidence at the IMT did not focus only on crimes against its own citizens. In total, the evidence presented by the Soviets

"*...recorded the systematic execution by firing squads, torture, and abuse of Soviet, Polish, French, and English prisoners of war, the extermination and enslavement of peaceful population in "death camps" and in Jewish ghettos, the senseless destruction of towns and villages, the plunder of both public and private property, as well as historical and cultural treasures in Yugoslavia, Poland, Greece, and the U.S.S.R.*"[35]

---

[25] *Id.*

[26] *Id.* at 40.

[27] *Id.* In addition, in July 1943, the Soviets prosecuted eleven Soviet citizens for treason and collaboration with the German authorities in what came to be known as the Krasnodar trials. These trials, because they were based upon the Soviet Criminal Code, were inapplicable to and thus could not serve as a judicial precedent for any subsequent proceedings against the Gestapo or German army. Still, they reinforced the notion that "responsibility...ultimately attached to the German government and High Command", and that the "atrocities were lengthily and convincingly depicted as an integral part of a total and premeditated plan basic to the whole Fascist way of life". George Ginsburgs, "*The Nuremberg Trial: Background,*" in George Ginsburgs & V.N. Kudriavtsev, *The Nuremberg Trial and International Law*, 5 (Leiden, Netherlands: Martinus Nijhoff Publishers, 1990), 19–21.

Furthermore, the Krasnodar trials, in addition to the Kharkov trials, were the "first judicial record of cases on the crimes and criminal responsibility of the Hitlerites which served as the original introduction to the Nuremberg Trial, paving the way for the application and effectuation of many norms and principles which later constituted the basis of Nuremberg law." The evidence presented at the Krasnodar trials revealed that tens of thousands of peaceful Soviets were killed or tortured by the Germans, including many children, the elderly, women, prisoners of war, and all patients in hospitals. I.A. Lediakh, "*The Application of the Nuremberg Principles by Other Military Tribunals and National Courts,*" in Ginsburgs & Kudriavtsev, *supra*, 263–4.

[28] Ginsburgs, *Moscow's Road to Nuremberg*, *supra*, 52.

[29] *Id.*

[30] *Id.* at 53.

[31] *Id.* at 53.

[32] *Id.* at 54.

[33] *Id.*

[34] *Id.* at 56.

[35] A. M. Larin, "The Trial of the Major War Criminals," *in* Ginsburgs & Kudriavtsev *supra*, 78.

II. *Tu Quoque*: The Crimes Committed by the Soviet Union During World War II Under the IMT Charter

The criticisms made of the IMT trial that the accusers and adjudicators were also victims must be distinguished from another criticism: that the Allied Powers judging the individual German defendants at the dock also committed some of the same crimes for which the German defendants were being charged.

First on the list, of course, was the Soviet Union. It seems obvious that the Soviet Union also committed the crime of waging an aggressive war, its leaders – foremost Joseph Stalin – could be considered conspirators in that crime, and that the Soviets during the war committed both war crimes and crimes against humanity. At the same time, it must be remembered that the Soviets – among the Allies – were not only the greatest perpetrators of the crimes enumerated in the IMT Charter but also were the greatest victims of Nazi atrocities. Twenty million Soviet civilians and eight million Soviet soldiers perished at the hands of the Nazis.[36]

A. Crimes Against Peace: The German-Soviet Non-Aggression Pact and Soviet Conquest of the Baltic Republics and Eastern Poland

At the outbreak of World War II in September 1939, the official position of the U.S.S.R. was that of neutrality.[37] Just a few weeks earlier, on August 23, 1939, the U.S.S.R. signed a treaty of non-aggression with Germany. This pact contained a secret additional protocol[38] wherein in exchange for agreeing not to join the future war, Germany promised the Soviets the Baltic states of Lithuania, Estonia, and Latvia. By signing the non-aggression pact with Germany and including the secret provisions, Stalin and his cohorts actively collaborated with the Nazis in Germany's invasion of Poland on September 1, 1939. On September 17, 1939, despite their "neutral" status, the Soviets marched into Eastern Poland, with the explanation of protecting the "ethnic brothers of [their] Ukrainian and White Russian populations".[39] As Bradley Smith explains,

"[I]f the Nuremberg prosecutors were correct that there was conspiracy in the planning of aggression against Poland in 1939, then Stalin was one of the parties to the conspiracy."[40]

Indeed, the "most troublesome problem" facing the Nuremberg judges was that:

"Stalin's signature on the Nazi-Soviet Pact had left Hitler free to move against Poland. Once the secret clauses of that pact appeared in evidence, even in summary form, it was difficult to avoid the conclusion that Stalin, like some of the defendants in the dock, had continued to "cooperate" with Hitler after he knew of the Nazi attack plans. If this kind of conduct would earn defendants such as Wilhelm Frick prison sentences or death, what was the Court to say about the actions of the Soviet Union?"[41]

As put by another author, if the participants at Nuremberg believed the "'rape of Poland' to be an international crime 'then there follows an irrefutable implication that Soviet Russia and its officials were *participes criminis.*'"[42]

---

[36] During the course of the IMT trial, the Soviets failed to recognize that the largest proportion of those murdered by the Nazis in their territory were Jews. Rather, these Jewish murders were noted by the Soviet prosecutors as murders of Soviet citizens.

[37] Ginsburgs, *supra*, 129.

[38] *Id.*

[39] Ginsburgs, *supra*, 142.

[40] Bradley Smith, *Reaching Judgment at Nuremberg* (New York: Basic Books, 1977), 105.

[41] *Id.* at 147.

[42] William Bosch, *Judgment on Nuremberg: American Attitudes Toward the Major German War-Crime Trials* (Durham, N.C: University of North Carolina Press, 1970) p.44. Alfred Seidl, attorney for Rudolf Hess, was most insistent in raising this argument during the course of the IMT proceedings. As Conot explains, "By revealing to the world that Germany and the Soviet Union had agreed to divide Eastern Europe between them in 1939, Seidl aimed to blow Count One, the Conspiracy to Wage Aggressive War, right out of the trial: For if there had been a conspiracy, then one of the conspirators, the Soviet Union, was in violation of all legal standards, participating in the prosecution and the judging of the

B. War Crimes and Crimes Against Humanity: The Katyn Massacre

One of the most embarrassing events at the IMT was the attempt by the Soviets to pin the massacre of 15,000 Polish officers, a proportion of whose bodies were discovered by the Germans in 1942 at the Katyn Forest near Smolensk, upon Germany. In the course of the IMT proceedings, Soviet assistant prosecutor Y.V.Porkovsky brazenly asserted,

"[O]ne of the most important criminal acts for which the major war criminals are responsible was the mass execution of Polish prisoners of war shot in the Katyn forest near Smolensk by the German fascist invaders."[43]

The United States and the United Kingdom refused to support the charge, and Justice Jackson, the American prosecutor, tried, but was unsuccessful, in convincing the Soviets to drop the Katyn matter. Unable to dissuade the Soviet prosecutors, the Soviets were given the opportunity to to go forward and prove German culpability. This proved to be a disaster for the Soviets. German defense lawyers had a field day with this accusation by mounting an effective defense. As Conot explains, "Katyn consequently had become an albatross hung around their own neck by the Russians...."[44] After much embarrassment, the Soviet prosecutors eventually agreed to drop the Katyn incident from the proceedings, and there is no mention of Katyn in the Nuremberg final judgments.

In 1990, Soviet President Mikhail Gorbachev acknowledged that the Soviets were indeed the ones who carried out the massacre, under the direct orders of Stalin.[45] While one scholar commented that, technically, "the killing of Polish officers...at Katyn and elsewhere on Soviet soil would not qualify as a war crime or even a crime against humanity on the Nuremberg model," he admits that the massacre would "still leave the Stalin regime guilty of...the common crime of mass murder, notwithstanding today's preference...for calling the case a war crime".[46] Thus, although the Katyn episode "raised few side questions" at Nuremberg, it succeeded in demonstrating that the "Nazis might not have a monopoly on atrocities."[47]

III. The Legal and Moral Implications of the Soviet Role as Prosecutors at Nuremberg

The culpability of the Soviet Union in committing similar offenses, and worse, its complicity in the commission of some of the crimes charged, arguably de-legitimizes the authority of the IMT to "judge and condemn their fellow criminals and accomplices."[48]

From a purely legal point of view, however, any accusations of crimes committed by the Allies during World War II could not be adjudged by the IMT tribunal. The London Charter, issued on August 8, 1945, specifically pronounced that the proceedings were restricted to the "trial and punishment of the major war criminals of the European Axis countries." If Stalin was a major war criminal, Nuremberg was not the place where his crimes would be adjudged. As Linder explains,

"The indictments against the defendants would prohibit defenses based on superior orders, as well as tu quoque (the "so-did-you") defense. Delegates [to the London Conference] were determined not to let the defendants and their German lawyers turn the trial into one that would expose questionable war conduct by Allied forces."[49]

---

case. If, on the other hand, the Moscow Pact had not constituted a conspiracy, then the Germans could be no more guilty than the Soviets." Conot, *supra*, 350-1.

[43] IMT Proceedings, v. VII.
[44] Conot, *supra*, 452.
[45] To Poland's great displeasure, an official Russian commission examining events at Katyn decided that the massacre was not a crime against humanity or a war crime, but an ordinary criminal act. The Russian government also refused to open their archives on the matter to a Polish commission of inquiry. For this reason, 65 years after the event, the Katyn massacre remains a sore point in Polish-Russian relations.
[46] Ginsburgs, *supra*, 128, fn. 3
[47] Smith, *supra*, 104.
[48] Bosch, *supra*, 18.
[49] Linder, *supra*.

When the German defense attorneys attempted during the course of the IMT trial to introduce the behavior of the Soviet Union as a defense to their clients' actions, Soviet prosecutor Rudenko correctly objected: "We are examining the matter of the crimes of the major German war criminals. We are not investigating the foreign policies of other states."[50] Moreover, in any trial the adjudicators need not be completely innocent to be able to fairly judge the accused. William Shakespeare, in his play *Measure for Measure,* pointed out this reality: "The jury, passing on the prisoner's life, /May in the sworn twelve have a thief or two/ Guiltier than him they try."[51]

Benjamin Ferencz, the chief prosecutor in the Einzatzgruppen trial at the subsequent Nuremberg zonal trials, similarly countered this argument in a Court TV interview on the Nuremberg Trials, by noting that the individuals defendants were on trial for the acts they themselves committed, and their "You too" or "You also" argument bears no relevance on their individual guilt or innocence for such acts.[52] From a moral or ethical point of view, the *Tu Quoque* [You Also/You Too] argument is also not recognized as a valid excuse. As the *Encyclopedia of Fallacies* explains,

"[Tu Quoque] is a fallacy regardless of whether you really did it or not. . . .For example, when one is arguing "Jack is a murderer", Jack's defendant says "You're a murderer too". The response is only blaming the claimer for the same thing he/she did as well. This doesn't refute the fact that Jack is a murderer, but only draws away the attention by involving another person."[53]

As with children, therefore, the cry of "Everyone else is doing it," should have no consequence.

IV. Conclusion

The Soviet Union's suitability to play prosecutor and judge at Nuremberg understandably diminishes the legacy of the IMT. The secret collaborations with Germany makes the Soviets appear more as accomplices to some of Germany's crimes than the neutral bystanders or pure victims they held themselves out to be. In addition, the Soviets themselves were guilty of direct perpetration of atrocities not only against their "enemies", but also against their own people.

Nevertheless, the Soviets did not play a passive role in the development of the trials. Because of the enormity of the atrocities committed on Soviet soil by the Germans, the Soviets had a legitimate stake in the outcome of the trial of the perpetrators, and in that sense, were no different from the other prosecuting teams who were also directly impacted by the war. Indeed, Soviet contributions to the trials were numerous; from their scrupulous gathering of evidence, to the precedents set by their domestic trials of war criminals, to their substantial hand in the drafting of the London Charter, and to their presentation of the records of massive Nazi atrocities on Soviet and foreign soil alike. Such contributions cannot be underestimated and lends credence to the legitimacy of the trials as a whole.

---

[50] Conot, *supra*, 421.
[51] William Shakespeare, *Measure for Measure*, Act II, Scene 1.
[52] Interview of Benjamin Ferencz by Terry Moran, Court TV Program "The Nuremberg Trials," November 13, 1995.
[53] <http:wiki.coth.net/index.php/Tu_quoque> (accessed July 15, 2005).

Michael J. Bazyler

Die Rolle der Sowjetunion vor dem Internationalen Militärtribunal in Nürnberg

Dieser Beitrag setzt sich mit der Rolle der Sowjetunion im Rahmen des Verfahrens vor dem Internationalen Militärtribunal in Nürnberg (IMT) auseinander. Stalin stand von vorneherein der Idee eines Strafverfahrens gegen die Hauptkriegsverbrecher recht aufgeschlossen gegenüber. Ihm lag allerdings weniger an einem ergebnisoffenen, rechtsstaatlichen Strafverfahren als an einer formalen Scheinerlaubnis für eine Massenexekution. Während der Statuts-Verhandlungen in London war die sowjetische Verhandlungsdelegation unter Führung des späteren IMT-Richters Nikitchenko nicht ohne Einfluss auf die Ausgestaltung des IMT; so setzte sich beispielsweise die sowjetische Stellung zur Frage der kriminellen Organisation durch. Auch der Begriff „crime against peace" stammt von der sowjetischen Delegation. Schließlich konnte auch während des Prozesses der sowjetische Ankläger Rudenko erhebliches Beweismaterial zur Verurteilung beisteuern.

Allerdings bereitete das völkerrechtliche Prinzip des „tu quoque" während des Prozesses Schwierigkeiten. So wurde gerade der sowjetischen Seite immer wieder entgegengehalten, Stalin habe seinerseits sowohl den Angriffskrieg als auch Verbrechen gegen die Menschlichkeit zu verantworten. So machte sich Stalin durch die Unterzeichnung des geheimen Zusatzprotokolls zum Nichtsangriffspakt mit Hitler am 23. August 1939 der Verschwörung gegen den Frieden schuldig, indem er dem Angriff auf Polen zustimmte. Das im Nürnberger Prozess angesprochene, schließlich wegen erheblicher Zweifel an der Verantwortlichkeit der Deutschen nicht weiter verfolgte Massaker von Katyn war – wie der spätere Präsident der U.d.S.S.R. Michael Gorbatschow 1990 offenlegte – eine von Stalin befohlene Hinrichtung polnischer Offiziere.

Trotz dieser von den Sowjets begangenen Völkerstraftaten schwindet die Legitimität des IMT insgesamt nicht, wenn auch die moralische Autorität des IMT darunter leidet. Das Verfahren gegen die deutschen Hauptkriegsverbrecher ist rechtlich weder der Ort noch der Zeitpunkt, um gleichartige Verbrechen der Gegenseite vorzutragen oder gar die Angeklagten zu entlasten.

Albin Eser

Das Internationale Militärtribunal von Nürnberg aus deutscher Perspektive*

Lassen Sie mich mit einem Bekenntnis beginnen: Ich sitze hier mit sehr gemischten Gefühlen. Auf der einen Seite bewegen mich Ehre und Dankbarkeit, an einer Erinnerungsveranstaltung von einem Tisch aus mitwirken zu dürfen, der als Richtertisch für das Nürnberger Internationale Militärtribunal diente. Zwar hat er historisch seinerzeit auf der linken, damals verhüllten, Fensterfront gestanden, während diese Stelle hier für die Dolmetscher reserviert war. Gleichwohl sitzen wir hier gleichsam symbolisch an dem Richtertisch, von dem aus Urteile gesprochen wurden, die für die Entwicklung des Internationalen Strafrechts von ganz besonderer Bedeutung geworden sind. Aufgrund meiner derzeitigen Tätigkeit als Richter am Internationalen Strafgerichtshof für das ehemalige Jugoslawien in Den Haag kann ich Ihnen versichern, dass eigentlich fast kein Tag vergeht, an dem man nicht – wenn auch nicht wörtlich, so doch gedanklich – auf Prinzipien und Rechtsfiguren zurückgreifen würde, die in den hier gefällten Urteilen ausgesprochen wurden, seit damals lebendig geblieben sind und weiterhin die Entwicklung des Völkerstrafrechts bestimmen.

Andererseits drückt mich aber auch eine Bürde, nämlich auf diesem Panel neben den Vertretern von Ländern, von denen damals hier jeweils ein Richter fungierte, ein einzelnes Land und dabei jenes Land vertreten zu sollen, von dem die schlimmsten Verbrechen des letzten Jahrhunderts ausgegangen sind. Diese Verantwortung muss unser Land auch dann übernehmen, wenn in diesem Saal der berühmt gewordene Satz gesprochen worden ist, dass „international crimes are not committed by states but by individuals". Auch wenn damit die individuelle Verantwortlichkeit bestimmter Einzelpersonen konstatiert wurde, vermag dies nichts daran zu ändern, dass dabei auch das Volk, auf dessen Territorium jene Verbrechen begangen wurden und ohne dessen Tolerierung nicht hätten begangen werden können, mitverantwortlich bleibt. Deshalb bin ich sehr dankbar dafür, dass sowohl Herr Oberlandesgerichtspräsident Dr. Franke wie auch Herr Dekan Rohe von der Juristischen Fakultät der Universität Erlangen-Nürnberg den Gedanken dauerhafter Verantwortlichkeit Deutschlands und des deutschen Volkes und nicht zuletzt auch seines Rechts betont und an unsere besondere Verpflichtung erinnert haben, mit allen Mitteln zu verhindern, dass Ähnliches auf deutschem Boden oder von diesem aus wieder geschieht.

Ein weiteres Gefühl ist das der Erleichterung, hatte ich doch befürchtet, hier als Einzelner gegen eine Front von „Alliierten" zu sitzen und eine bestimmte Position verteidigen zu müssen, die von anderen nicht geteilt wird. Wie sich jedoch herausgestellt hat, ist auch die Sicht der Vertreter der damaligen Richterstaaten eine sehr unterschiedliche, indem die Nürnberger Verfahren sowohl Bestätigung gefunden haben, aber auch immer wieder Kritik laut geworden ist, damit ähnlich unterschiedlich wie auch aus deutscher Sicht. Somit ist international gesehen die Einstellung gegenüber den Nürnberger Urteilen keineswegs einseitig homogen im Sinne von Ablehnung oder Zustimmung, sondern durchaus differenziert. In diesem Sinne möchte ich nachfolgend einige Aspekte dieser differenzierten Sicht aus deutscher Perspektive aufzeigen, wobei dies in drei Frageschritten geschehen soll:

Erstens: Nürnberg als Rechtsfrage? Kritischer Rückblick aus juristischer Sicht.
Zweitens: Nürnberg als eine nicht nur rechtliche, sondern auch politische Frage? Unterschiedliche Einstellungen zu den Nürnberger Urteilen.
Drittens: Nürnberg als rechtspolitische und moralische Frage? Einige Schlussgedanken.

---

* Für seine Mitarbeit bei Sammlung und Sondierung des diesem Vortrag zugrundeliegenden Materials bin ich Herrn Referendar Christoph Burchard zu besonderem Dank verpflichtet.

I. Nürnberg als Rechtsfrage. Diese Frage findet sich vor allem aus zwei Blickwinkeln gestellt:

1) Da ist zum einen die Frage, inwieweit es sich beim Nürnberger Militärtribunal um bloße „Siegerjustiz" gehandelt hat oder darin nicht doch vielleicht ein Triumph internationaler Strafjustiz im Sinne einer humanitären, in die Zukunft gerichteten Gerechtigkeit zu erblicken wäre. Um die deutsche Position verstehen zu können, empfiehlt es sich, kurz einige der Stichworte zu nennen, die mit Nürnberg als „Siegerjustiz" verbunden werden.

a) Am häufigsten findet sich moniert, dass hier ausschließlich Richter aus den Reihen der alliierten Siegermächte England, Frankreich, Russland und der Vereinigten Staaten von Amerika saßen. Demgegenüber wird gefragt, ob man nicht schon damals hätte überlegen können, warum nicht auch Richter aus neutralen Staaten – wie etwa der Schweiz oder aus Lateinamerika, wenn nicht schon Richter aus Deutschland – auf der Richterbank hätten sitzen können. Wenn man etwa heute miterleben muss, wie beispielsweise von amerikanischer Seite gegen den Internationalen Strafgerichtshof unter anderem auch damit argumentiert wird, dass amerikanische Staatsbürger Gefahr liefen, „not to be judged by their own peers", mag die Frage erlaubt sein, warum man nicht schon vor 60 Jahren auf diese Idee gekommen ist oder sie besser auch heute nicht ins Feld führen sollte.

b) Des Weiteren stört man sich als Anzeichen von „Siegerjustiz" daran, dass das Nürnberger Gerichtsstatut zum Teil von Juristen entworfen worden war, die später als Ankläger (wie insbesondere Robert H. Jackson) oder gar als Richter (wie der sowjetische Generalmajor Nikitchenko) fungierten. Diese Überlappung von Rechtsschöpfung und Rechtsanwendung fand sich beispielsweise kritisiert durch ein „Joint Defence Motion", als es feststellte: „all in one: creator of the statute of the tribunal and of the rules of law, prosecutor and judge". Dadurch sah man nicht nur das Prinzip der Gewaltenteilung missachtet, sondern auch die Gefahr einer vorurteilsbehafteten Führung des Prozesses. Angesichts einer solchen Dominanz der Siegermächte konnte es nicht ausbleiben, dass das Internationale Militärtribunal weniger als eine wahrhaft supranationale Instanz internationaler Gerechtigkeit, sondern mehr als ein Besatzungsgericht siegreicher Mächte erscheinen konnte und das hehre Bild unbefangener internationaler Strafgerechtigkeit durch das Zerrbild vermeintlich voreingenommener Siegerjustiz verstellt wurde.

Ohne mir diese Einwände ohne weiteres zu eigen machen zu wollen, wurde der Eindruck von Einseitigkeit der Nürnberger Prozesse noch durch weitere Faktoren verschärft, wobei hier lediglich drei kurz erwähnt seien:

c) Ein erster Vorwurf rügt die mangelnde Waffengleichheit zwischen Anklage und Verteidigung, weil letztere von der Anklage vorgelegte Urkundenbeweise nicht angreifen durfte. Wenn ich das etwa mit den heutigen Möglichkeiten der Defence vor dem Internationalen Strafgerichtshof für das ehemalige Jugoslawien vergleiche, so kann man nur positiv beeindruckt sein von den verschiedenen disclosure rules, nach denen die Prosecution schon Monate vor Prozessbeginn ihre exhibits offenlegen muss, um der Defence eine entsprechende Vorbereitung zu ermöglichen. Aus heutigem Blickwinkel wird man daher in der Tat bezweifeln können, ob seinerzeit wirklich schon eine Waffengleichheit zwischen Anklage und Verteidigung gewährleistet war. Umso mehr mag es überraschen, dass damals der Prozess vor dem Nürnberger Tribunal von deutschen Verteidigern als durchaus „fair" bezeichnet wurde.

d) Ein zweiter Vorwurf rügt die Nicht-Erwähnung der deutschen Opfer des NS-Regimes in der Anklage beziehungsweise im Urteil von Nürnberg. Dieser Vorwurf beruht auf der engen Auslegung der „crimes against humanity" durch das IMT, derzufolge – unter anderem – nicht über innerdeutsche Verfolgungen, denen Opfer vor Kriegsbeginn ausgesetzt waren, zu befinden war. Damit stellte sich schon damals das Problem, dass sich der Gerichtshof – wie heute auch das Jugoslawien- und das Ruanda-Tribunal und nicht zuletzt auch der künftige Internationale Strafgerichtshof – nur mit zeitlich und örtlich begrenzten Teilausschnitten von Völkerrechtsverbrechen befassen dürfen und solche zeitlichen Schnitte für jene Opfer schmerzhaft sein müssen, die nicht die Genugtuung irgendeiner Art von Gerechtigkeit erfahren dürfen.

e) Ein dritter Vorwurf rügt die Nichtzulassung des tu quoque-Einwands, von dem bereits Herr Kollege Bazyler gesprochen hat – der Einwand also, dass die gegnerische Seite ja bereits ähnliche

Verbrechen begangen habe und man deshalb gleichsam „quitt" sei. Obwohl dies auf den ersten Blick eine menschlich verständliche Reaktion sein mag, kann ich mich gerade aus meiner Erfahrung als Richter am Jugoslawien-Tribunal darin bestätigt sehen, dass es in vielen Fällen das Ende internationaler Strafjustiz bedeuten müsste, wenn man den tu quoque-Einwand zuließe. Wenn man etwa an die – wie ich, solange kein Urteil gesprochen ist, vorsorglich sagen muss: angeblichen – Greueltaten auf dem Balkan denkt, wo sich die Serben auf Übergriffe von Moslems und diese wiederum auf vorangegangene Übeltaten von Serben berufen, so könnte man rückwärts ad infinitum immer wieder einen Grund finden, mit dem man seine eigenen Untaten meint rechtfertigen zu können. Dem bleibt entgegenzuhalten, dass Morden der einen Seite keine Rechtfertigung für das Morden auf der anderen Seite sein kann. Sicherlich muss die Justiz immer bestrebt sein, beiden Seiten gerecht zu werden: dies jedoch nicht im Sinne von Nichtverfolgung, sondern vielmehr im Sinne des Bemühens um Strafverfolgung beider Seiten!

2) Lassen Sie mich zum zweiten Rechtsaspekt kommen, der auf den ersten Blick ebenfalls als „nürnbergkritisch" erscheint, in einem Weitblick jedoch auch als zukunftsweisend gewürdigt werden kann. Ich meine den häufig geäußerten Vorwurf, dass mangels einer zum Zeitpunkt der angeklagten Verbrechen fehlenden formellen Strafandrohung der Grundsatz von „nullum crimen sine lege" verletzt worden sei. Teils meinte man dieses Problem schon damit erledigen zu können, dass es sich bei den Nürnberger Angeklagten um Mitglieder des nationalsozialistischen Regimes gehandelt habe, das den „Gesetzlichkeitsgrundsatz" aus dem Strafgesetzbuch hatte streichen lassen, und dass demzufolge diese angeklagten Parteigenossen ihr Recht verwirkten, eine ex post-Sanktionierung zu rügen. Dem wird in der deutschen Debatte regelmäßig entgegengehalten, dass es eine Verwirkung nicht gebe, dass sich vielmehr jeder Verbrecher auf das „nullum crimen sine lege"-Prinzip berufen dürfe. Gleichwohl wird noch zu fragen sein, ob diesem Einwand nicht besser durch Rückbesinnung auf die Funktion von „nullum crimen sine lege" als Respektierung „legitimen Vertrauens" beizukommen wäre.

In der Sache selbst ist Folgendes im Auge zu behalten: Soweit man den „nullum crimen sine lege"-Grundsatz überhaupt als tangiert ansehen konnte, galt das keineswegs für alle Anklagepunkte, vielmehr war folgendermaßen zu unterscheiden:

a) Soweit es um „crimes against humanity" geht, finden sich zur Vereinbarkeit mit dem „nullum crimen sine lege"-Prinzip zwei unterschiedliche Begründungsstränge: Zum einen – vielleicht für manche überraschend – bei Carl Schmitt, wonach die Außerordentlichkeit dieser Verbrechen den „nullum crimen"-Einwand abschneide. Zum anderen das von meinem Amtsvorgänger am Max-Planck-Institut für ausländisches und internationales Strafrecht Hans-Heinrich Jescheck vorgetragene Argument, dass diese Verbrechen nichts anderes als politisch motivierte und systematisch begangene „normale" Straftaten seien, wie sie sich bereits in den nationalen Strafgesetzbüchern als inkriminiert finden.

b) Weitaus kontroverser war jedoch die Vereinbarkeit des Straftatbestandes von Verbrechen gegen den Frieden mit dem „nullum crime sine lege"-Prinzip. Dazu wurden folgende Fragen gestellt: Soweit es um die grundsätzliche Ächtung des Krieges schon vor dem Zweiten Weltkrieg ging, bestand breiter Konsens, dass bereits der Kellogg-Briand-Pakt zu einer Kriegsächtung geführt hatte. Ob sich aber daraus auch eine schon vor dem Zweiten Weltkrieg vorfindbare individuelle Strafbarkeit für das Führen eines Angriffskriegs begründen lasse, wurde unterschiedlich gesehen: Auch wenn auf zwischenstaatlicher Ebene das Führen eines Angriffkrieges völkerrechtswidrig sei, lasse sich daraus noch keine individuelle Strafbarkeit für das Führen eines rechtswidrigen Krieges ableiten. Auch die weitere Frage, ob dann nicht die Verletzung des „nullum crimen"-Grundsatzes wenigstens ausnahmsweise hingenommen werden dürfe, wurde unterschiedlich beantwortet: meist negativ mit dem Argument, dass die Schutzgewähr des „nullum crimen"-Grundsatzes nicht durch normative Erwägungen ausgehöhlt werden dürfe, andererseits aber auch positiv, weil der Schutz der menschlichen Zivilisation ausnahmsweise Vorrang gegenüber dem Formalprinzip des „nullum crimen"-Grundsatzes haben müsse. Dieser neue zukunftsweisende, auf den Vorrang höherer Gerechtigkeit hinweisende Gedanke hätte kaum besser als durch die Worte des British Chief Prosecutor zum Ausdruck gebracht werden können:

„*If this be an innovation, it is an innovation long overdue – a desirable and beneficent innovation fully consistent with justice, fully consistent with common sense and with the abiding purposes of the law of nations.*"

Dass diese Sicht heute selbst von Rechtskollegen vertreten wird, die dem Nürnberger Prozess ansonsten eher kritisch gegenüber stehen, mag durch die Einschätzung von Reinhard Merkel (1996) belegt sein:

„*Am Ende des furchtbarsten Krieges der Menschheitsgeschichte war die Zeit reif für die Feststellung, dass es zur Kriminalisierung seiner Urheber (und der aller künftigen Kriege) keine moralische, keine rechtliche und keine politische Alternative mehr gab. Auch in diesem Fall wäre eine notstandsähnliche Abwägung zwischen den Prinzipien des Rückwirkungsverbots einerseits und des strafrechtlichen Schutzes für die Fundamente der Zivilisation andererseits notwendig und entscheidbar gewesen: zugunsten des letzteren.*"

Kurzum: Selbst wenn die Nürnberger Prozesse aus „Siegerjustiz" hervorgegangen sein mögen, führten sie schließlich doch zu einem Triumph internationaler Strafgerichtsbarkeit.

II. Bisher ging es um rein juristische Einschätzungen. Aber war Nürnberg wirklich nur eine Rechtsfrage? Oder haben dabei auch politische Einstellungen eine Rolle gespielt? Das ist in der Tat nicht zu übersehen, wobei vor allem zwei Zeiträume zu unterscheiden sind, und zwar die Zeit bis Ende der 40er und ab Beginn der 50er Jahre.

1) Bis in die späten 40er Jahre wurde es offenbar nicht für opportun angesehen, mit Kritik an den Nürnberger Prozessen hervorzutreten, so dass sich auch kaum Auseinandersetzungen dazu finden lassen. Dies könnte folgende Gründe gehabt haben:

a) Soweit es etwa die alliierte Zusammensetzung des Tribunals und die Rechtsnatur des Gerichts betraf, hat man darin offenbar eine akademische Frage gesehen, deren Beantwortung kein praktischer Nutzen zukam.

b) Soweit eine Verletzung des „nullum crimen sine lege"-Grundsatzes diskutiert wurde, wurde darin eine primär völkerrechtliche Fragen erblickt, deren Bedeutung für die deutschen Völkerrechtler nur von sekundärem Interesse war, weil das Hauptaugenmerk auf dem völkerrechtlichen Status des besetzten Deutschland lag. Auch in den Augen der allgemeinen Bevölkerung scheinen die Nürnberger Prozesse keine besondere Rolle gespielt zu haben. Was meine eigenen Erfahrungen betrifft, so war ich im Jahre 1945 gerade zehn Jahre alt, und obwohl ich danach in einer Internatsschule aufgewachsen bin, die als politisch durchaus aufgeschlossen angesehen werden konnte, kann ich mich nicht erinnern, dass die Nürnberger Prozesse als ein deutsches Problem diskutiert worden wären: Das war offenbar Sache der Alliierten.

2) Ein deutlicher Umschwung zeigte sich zu Beginn der 50er Jahre. Plötzlich gewannen Rechtsfragen eine praktische Bedeutung.

a) So zum einen hinsichtlich der Rechtsnatur der Kriegsverbrecherprozesse, soweit sie als Nachfolgeprozesse in der US-Besatzungszone stattfanden. Da das Kontrollratsgesetz Nr. 10 kein Berufungsrecht der Angeklagten vorsah, wollten sich diese ein solches mit dem Argument erstreiten, dass die Nachfolgeprozesse gleichsam vor nationalen US-Gerichten stattfänden, sodass man eine Nachprüfung vor US-Bundesgerichten durch so genannte habeas corpus motions erreichen könnte. Eine solche Zuflucht bei der Verfassung der USA wurde jedoch schon damals mit ähnlichen Extraterritorialitätserwägungen abgelehnt, wie sie heute wiederum im Zusammenhang mit Rechtsbehelfen der in Guantanamo festgehaltenen Gefangenen vorgebracht werden.

b) Zum anderen wurde plötzlich auch für die deutsche Justiz das Nürnberger Statut bedeutsam, nachdem diese ebenfalls zur Verfolgung von NS-Verbrechen nach dem Kontrollratsgesetz Nr. 10 berufen war. Auf dieser Ebene schlugen dann unter anderem auch die Bedenken hinsichtlich einer Verletzung des „nullum crimen sine lege"-Grundsatzes durch, wobei die deutsche Strafverfolgung mit Beginn der 1950er Jahre fast vollständig zum Erliegen kam.

c) Zudem machte sich auch allgemeinpolitisch eine Änderung des Klimas bemerkbar, nachdem inzwischen eine zunehmende Entnazifizierungsmüdigkeit eingetreten war: Man wollte von den NS-

Greueltaten nichts mehr wissen. Diese Verdrängung der eigenen NS-Vergangenheit und die Verweigerung einer echten Vergangenheitsbewältigung wurden von meinem ehemaligen Tübinger Strafrechtskollegen Jürgen Baumann, der sich als einer von wenigen der deutschen Vergangenheit gestellt hat, in seinem Buch „Der Aufstand des schlechten Gewissens" (1965) folgendermaßen charakterisiert:

„*Jahrelang haben die meisten Bürger der Bundesrepublik keine Anstrengung gescheut zu vergessen, was in zwölf unseligen Jahren geschehen ist. Sie haben ihre Gedächtnislückenhaftigkeit zum System und die Handhabung dieser wohltätigen Lückenhaftigkeit zur Perfektion entwickelt... Nur grässliche Nestbeschmutzer waren einsame Rufer in einer Zeit, die vornehmlich gegenwärtigem und zukünftigem Wohlstand zustrebte und endlich vom Ballast der Vergangenheit befreit sein wollte.*"

Diese Klimaveränderung schlug sich auch in empirischen Umfragen über die gesellschaftliche Wahrnehmung des Internationalen Militärtribunals in Deutschland nieder: Während unmittelbar nach dem Nürnberger Prozess ermittelt worden war, dass 80 % der Befragten den Prozess für fair erachteten, eine Mehrheit, die Hauptkriegsverbrecher für schuldig hielten, nur 9 % die Urteile als zu hart ansahen und sich lediglich 6 % kritisch äußerten, sehen zu Beginn der Fünfziger Jahre die Vergleichszahlen ganz anders aus: Nun erachteten 30 % der Befragten den Prozess für unfair, 40 % sahen das Urteil als zu hart an und 50 % lehnten es ab, wie die Alliierten das Problem der deutschen Kriegsverbrecher gelöst hatten. Über die Gründe für diese Meinungsänderung lässt sich spekulieren. Auf jeden Fall dürfte dabei eine Rolle gespielt haben, dass man in Deutschland hoffte, es würden nicht nur Kriegsverbrechen, die auf deutscher Seite begangen wurden, gerichtlich aufgearbeitet, sondern auch Verbrechen, die von Seiten anderer Länder begangen worden sein könnten.

III. Mit dem letztgenannten Aspekt ist bereits meine dritte Hauptfrage angesprochen, nämlich „Nürnberg als rechtspolitische und moralische Frage", wobei es um einige Aspekte geht, die über die deutsche Rechtsdiskussion hinaus eine weithin noch zu bewältigende Herausforderung darstellen.

1) Das betrifft zum einen das Problem, das sich im Grunde bei jedem Wechsel von einem Unrechts- zu einem rechtsstaatlichen System stellt, nämlich wie mit der unterschiedlichen Viktimisierung umzugehen ist, und wer dabei die eigentlichen Opfer oder die Unterdrücker waren. Wenn etwa moniert wird, dass in den Nürnberger Prozessen deutsche Opfer des NS-Regimes nicht ausreichend berücksichtigt worden seien, drängt sich die Frage auf, inwieweit es sich dabei lediglich um die (echte) Viktimisierung von deutschen Minderheiten oder nicht eher um (erschlichene) Selbst-Viktimisierung der deutschen Mehrheit handelt. Auf der einen Seite kann natürlich in der Nichterwähnung der von den Nazis verfolgten Minderheiten in den Nürnberg-Urteilen in der Tat eine erneute Viktimisierung dieser damaligen Opfer gesehen werden. Soweit jedoch diese „Opferrhetorik" von Nichtbetroffenen betrieben wird, muss man sich fragen, ob dies wirklich aus Fürsorge für die tatsächlich durch die Nazis verfolgten deutschen Minderheiten geschieht oder ob nicht eher eine Art von Selbst-Viktimisierung dahintersteht. Bemerkenswerterweise ist ja der Sieg der Alliierten nicht von Anfang an als eine „Befreiung" empfunden worden, sondern erst als man eine Dichotomie zwischen Siegern und Verlierern herzustellen begann und zu den „Siegern" gewissermaßen auch die deutsche Bevölkerung gezählt wurde, während „Verlierer" nur die Unterdrücker gewesen seien. Auf diesem Wege war es dann auch leichter, die vielen deutschen Gehilfen aus der allgemeinen Bevölkerung, ohne deren Ausführung der Befehle von oben ja auch die Konzentrationslager nicht hätten betrieben werden können, ihrerseits zu „Opfern" der Unterdrücker gemacht hat. Eine weitere unbeabsichtigte Nebenwirkung, die durch die Individualisierung von Humanitätsverbrechen ausgelöst werden kann, ist darin zu sehen, dass im Wege einer „Schuldabladung" alle Verantwortlichkeit auf die Angeklagten verlagert wird. Auch damit wird es leichter, sich von irgendeiner Mitverantwortung freizuzeichnen.

Was man daraus lernen könnte – und das ist auch eine Erfahrung in Den Haag – ist das Bedürfnis nach einer stärkeren Einbeziehung der tatsächlichen Opfer. Das „adversatorische" Prozesssystem, wie es gegenwärtig in den internationalen Strafverfahren vorherrscht, hat – neben manch anderem – auch den großen Nachteil, dass das Opfer praktisch keine Rolle spielt oder allenfalls sich durch den Prosecutor vertreten sehen kann, mit der Folge, dass sich im Grunde nur der Staat und der Angeklagte gegenüberstehen, während das Opfer allenfalls eine Zeugenrolle spielt. Das wird von nicht wenigen Opferzeugen als schmerzlich und enttäuschend empfunden, wenn sie sich lediglich als Beweismittel gefragt sehen und im Grunde gar nicht das zum Ausdruck bringen können, was sie im Innersten bewegt. In solchen Fällen muss das Gericht dann auch einmal die Möglichkeit einräumen können, nach Abschluss der Beweisaufnahme dem Zeugen Gelegenheit zu geben, alle Opfer zu nennen, deren man sich in der Öffentlichkeit erinnern sollte. Ich muss gestehen, dass es für mich immer zu den bewegendsten Augenblicken gehört, wenn Menschen auf diese Weise zum Ausdruck bringen dürfen, was für sie Gerechtigkeit bedeuten könnte. In dieser Hinsicht wäre nicht zuletzt in der internationalen Strafjustiz noch manches nachzuholen.

2) Schließlich wäre noch auf einen Punkt aufmerksam zu machen, bei dem sich kontinentale Sichtweisen und common law-Perspektiven offenbar nicht decken, weswegen es zu unterschiedlichen Einschätzungen kommen kann. Das betrifft vor allem das Verständnis des Grundsatzes „nullum crimen sine lege", der schon sprachlich im Englischen anders zum Ausdruck gebracht wird als in anderen Sprachen – wie insbesondere der deutschen. Während man im Deutschen von „keine Strafe ohne Gesetz" spricht, heißt es im Englischen „no crime without law", nicht aber „no crime without statute", sodass man dementsprechend nicht von „nullum crimen sine lege", sondern von „nullum crimen sine iure" sprechen müsste. Während also in der deutschen Sprache zwischen Recht und Gesetz unterschieden wird, steht im Englischen – jedenfalls im Zusammenhang mit dem „nullum crimen sine lege"-Grundsatz für beides „law". Deshalb ist es für den common law approach viel leichter, auch ungeschriebenes customary law als Strafrechtsgrundlage zu akzeptieren, während der kontinentale Jurist eine gesetzliche Grundlage erwartet und sich daher auch im Völkerstrafrecht mit ungeschriebenem customary law schwer tut.

Die damit vebundenen Verständigungsschwierigkeiten werden noch größer, wenn man auch noch unterschiedliche Funktionen des „nullum crimen sine lege"-Grundsatzes mitbedenkt.

a) Versteht man diesen – von der Französischen Revolution herkommend – vornehmlich als einen Schutz vor Willkür – zunächst gegenüber dem König, dann gegenüber jeder staatlichen Macht – so wäre im Hinblick auf die Nürnberger Prozesse lediglich zu prüfen, ob es sich dabei um einen Akt der Willkür gehandelt hat – was man angesichts der Ungeheuerlichkeit der NS-Verbrechen wird leicht verneinen können.

b) Sieht man in „nullum crimen sine lege" hingegen einen Vertrauensgrundsatz (im Sinne von Feuerbach), wonach der Bürger darauf soll vertrauen dürfen, dass sein Verhalten nicht im Nachhinein für strafbar erklärt wird, so könnten sich die NS-Verbrecher in der Tat sichergefühlt haben, für ihre Untaten nicht zur Verantwortung gezogen zu werden. Da es jedoch wohl nicht um den Schutz von Vertrauen jedweder Art und Herkunft, sondern lediglich um den Schutz „legitimen Vertrauens" gehen kann, wird man den NS-Verbrechern die Legitimität ihres Vertrauens auf offensichtliches Unrecht absprechen können.

IV. So wie ich mit gemischten Gefühlen begonnen habe, muss ich mit solchen auch zum Schluss kommen. Vieles Wichtige musste ungesagt bleiben und manches kritisch Gesagte könnte als Abwertung der Nürnberger Strafjustiz missverstanden werden. Das Gegenteil ist der Fall. Meines Erachtens ist die zukunftsweisende Rolle der Nürnberger Prozesse in der Entwicklung der internationalen Strafjustiz gar nicht hoch genug zu veranschlagen. In diesem Sinne einer kritischen Hochschätzung ergeht es mir wie dem bereits genannten Reinhard Merkel, dessen Einschätzung der moralischen Wirkung des Nürnberger Prozesses ich mir – trotz aller vorgenannten Einwände – zu eigen machen darf:

„Nürnberg hat jene Revolution im Völkerrecht, die 1919 noch gescheitert war, in einem exemplarischen Akt vollzogen. Keine gegenläufige, spurenverwischende Praxis der Staaten in der nachfolgenden Ära des Kalten Krieges hat die Grundidee des Prozesses zerstören können: dass die Selbstlegitimation aller staatlichen Macht ihre Grenze findet in einem Recht der Menschheit; und dass der Täter, der diese Grenze missachtet, als einzelner zur Verantwortung gezogen wird, vor der ihn keine staatliche Deckung seiner Taten schützen kann. Nürnberg war der weltgeschichtlich erste Versuch, auf ungekannte Exzesse der Macht gleichwohl in den Formen des Rechts zu antworten."

Albin Eser

The International Military Tribunal at Nuremberg from a German Perspective

Delivering the German perspective of the Nuremberg trials at this conference carries a special burden due to the fact that this country caused the most heinous crimes of the last century. It is our responsibility to ensure that never again similar atrocities happen on German soil or originate from Germany. I'm relieved to know that I'm not standing alone against an "Allied" front; but instead next to me on the panel are critical voices with regard to Nuremberg just as in Germany.

At first I want to address legal issues. The International Military Tribunal (IMT) has been criticised for being a piece of "victors' justice". There are several reasons for this argument: First, there have been only allied judges on the bench and no German ones, second, the same people have created the Statute and then served as prosecutors (as did Robert Jackson) or even as judges (as did Nikitschenko), third, there has been no equity of arms between prosecutor and defence, and finally, the "victors" had committed war crimes just the same. Likewise German victims were not mentioned at the trial due to a restrictive interpretation of crimes against humanity. It is often heard that the IMT violated the principle *nullum crimen sine lege*. While such a violation can be denied as regards crimes against humanity and war crimes, the argument is more difficult to counter as regards the crime of aggression; however, the purely formalistic view on the *nullum crimen*-principle is receding.

Nuremberg is also a political issue. In the immediate aftermath of the IMT-trial there was hardly any discussion on these subjects, which were mentioned above. This changed in the 1950s, when the German judicial system took over the responsibility to prosecute former Nazis. There was also a change in the political climate: While at first 80 % of the German population thought that the IMT-trial was fair and the accused deserved the sentences, and only 9 % stated that the sentences were too harsh and merely 6 % raised general criticism, this changed in the 1950s. Now, 30 % thought the trial was unfair, 40 % said the judgments were too harsh and 50 % criticised the way, the Allies dealt with the Nazi criminals, in principal. Germans at this time wanted to forget about the past and set aside the horrible crimes.

Nuremberg implies also moral questions. The fact that German victims were left out of the IMT-trial, made it possible for certain victim rhetoric to come about in Germany. The real minority of victims was absorbed by a general (hypocritical) sentiment of victimisation of the German majority, by which helpers and abettors in Nazi-crimes called themselves victims of the suppressive system.

Despite all these critical points it has to be emphasized that Nuremberg is the blatant sign, that it is possible to answer with the rule of law to incredible state-ordered atrocities.

II. Different Perspectives on the Nuremberg Trials/ Die Nürnberger Prozesse aus verschiedenen Perspektiven

Michael R. Marrus

A Jewish Lobby at Nuremberg: Jacob Robinson and the Institute of Jewish Affairs, 1945-46

"[W]e have been working in this field for four and a half years," insisted Dr. Jacob Robinson in June 1945, referring to the Holocaust and speaking authoritatively to United States Supreme Court Justice Robert H. Jackson, the newly appointed American Chief Prosecutor for the Nuremberg War Crimes Tribunal.[1] This article takes up the disputed question of how the Holocaust was perceived in the immediate wake of the Second World War from the vantage point of a Jewish lobby at the Trial of the Major War Criminals at Nuremberg – the New York based Institute of Jewish Affairs (IJA), directed by Robinson, a committed researcher and lobbyist as well as a learned international lawyer. It explores the Institute's case made to Jackson and his team, looking at how Jewish professionals, consumed by evidence of the destruction of the European Jews, understood the Jewish calamity and tried to relay their concerns to a wider public.

Historians continue to debate how the Holocaust appeared at this most famous of the postwar trials of Nazi leaders. I have myself argued that, notwithstanding the centrality of other issues in the American trial plan, the varied objectives of the Allied powers and the eventual outcome of the proceeding, Nuremberg was a major landmark in the presentation of the dreadful fate of the Jewish people at the hands of the Nazis.[2] Although the Holocaust was not, to be sure, described at Nuremberg quite as we would today, the trial provided the first validation, before an international body, of the death toll of six million; it provided major elements of the history of the Holocaust such as the role of Adolf Hitler and his immediate entourage, especially the SS; prewar persecutions; the mass shootings of the *Einsatzgruppen*; the Wannsee Conference of 1942; ghettoization; the death camps of the East, especially Auschwitz; the uprising of the Warsaw Ghetto; the Hungarian Jewish deportations, and so on. Others have focused on the trial's shortcomings: how the emphasis on conspiracy tilted Nuremberg in the direction of an overly "intentionalist" interpretation of the Holocaust; how the American obsession with crimes against peace distracted attention from the assault on European Jewry; how the trial's privileging of documentary evidence meant that Jewish voices were scarcely heard before the tribunal; and how the framing of the case meant inattention to prewar crimes and, more importantly, prevented the presentation of the Holocaust as a distinctive element of Nazi criminality. In what follows, I revisit this debate from the perspective of those with "four and a half years" of painful accumulation of information, frustration, and appeals on behalf of the Jewish victims of the Nazi onslaught.

The Institute of Jewish Affairs was not, to be sure, the only Jewish presence in the lobbying on behalf of a trial of major German war criminals or the only organized effort to bring the destruction of European Jewry to the attention of those who scrambled, at the end of the war, to organize an international proceeding. In England, among others, the great Cambridge University authority on international law, Professor Hersch Lauterpacht, made the case for a war crimes trial and he may have been the first to recommend applying to the Holocaust the category of "crimes against humanity". In the United States, drawing on his understanding of the slaughter, which included that of his own family, Raphael Lemkin lobbied single-mindedly for the recognition of a new crime of genocide, a term that he coined in his 1944 book *Axis Rule in Occupied Europe*. And, in the American Office of Strategic Services (OSS), the forerunner of the Central Intelligence Agency, a junior official in the Research and Analysis Section named Charles Irving Dwork, with a Ph.D. in Judaic Studies from the University of Southern California, was for a time responsible for gathering information on the Holocaust with a view

---

[1] Minutes, meeting of the World Jewish Congress with Robert H. Jackson in New York City, June 12, 1945, Records of the World Jewish Congress, Jacob Radler Marcus Center of the American Jewish Archives, (hereinafter WJC Archives), Truman Presidential Museum & Library (hereinafte TPML), http://www.trumanlibrary.org/whistlestop/study_collections/nuremberg/index.php?action=docs#1945. Retrieved, September 6, 2005.

[2] Michael R. Marrus, 'The Holocaust at Nuremberg', 26 YAD VASHEM STUDIES 4-45 (1998).

to assisting American prosecutors.[3]

But so far as I have found there was only one explicitly Jewish lobby – constituting what we would now call a Non-Governmental Organization or NGO – organized to concern itself specifically with the Jewish issue and which made its case insistently to the American prosecution team.[4] Founded in New York in 1941 as a joint project of the American Jewish Congress and the World Jewish Congress, the Institute grouped together specialists on Jewish matters committed to documenting and exploring what one might call the "big picture" for World Jewry: the course and direction of Jewish life in the modern period, Jewish minority rights, the Jewish fate at the hands of Nazism, and the fortification of Jewish rights in the postwar period.

Robinson was unquestionably the key figure. A distinguished jurist born in 1889 in the Lithuanian town of Seirijai (pronounced "Saray"), Robinson was a tireless crusader who brought a broad European perspective to the task. After his legal training at the University of Warsaw, Robinson had a double career in Lithuania, both as a Jewish educator and founder of a Hebrew *Gymnasium* in Virbalis, and as a Zionist legislator, representing the Jewish faction in the Lithuanian parliament and later serving the Lithuanian government both a legal advisor and its representative at the International Court in The Hague. Fleeing to the United States in 1940, he lectured at Columbia University as well as heading the Institute when it was formed in 1941. Widely acknowledged for his expertise in international law, and working closely with his brother Nehemiah, Robinson continued to formulate Jewish positions on such matters as Nazi war crimes and Nazi reparations. Fifteen years later he assisted the Israeli prosecution in formulating its case against Adolf Eichmann. Robinson is perhaps most widely remembered today for his detailed polemic against Hannah Arendt's reportage of that trial, *When the Crooked Shall Be Made Straight*.

The Jewish Perspective and the American Trial Plan

In Robinson's first encounter with Justice Jackson he conveyed the substance of the Jewish case for the prospective Nuremberg trial. Accompanied by New York state Judge Nathan Perlman and Dr. Alexander Kohanski, Robinson met Jackson at the Federal Court House in New York for an hour and a half on June 12, 1945, just over a month after the latter's appointment by President Harry Truman, to head the United States prosecution team.

At their meeting on the 12th, understood as strictly confidential, Robinson made a wide-ranging claim for a hearing to the powerful architect of the American case, and indeed of the Charter of the Nuremberg Trial, to be negotiated by the Allied powers in the succeeding weeks. Robinson praised Jackson's report to Truman (released on the 7th), with its public outline of the American trial plan, calling it a "historic document" and noting that "it meets some of our aspirations in this matter."[5] From the report Robinson knew that the centre piece of the American case would be "the establishment of a well-documented history of what we are convinced was a grand, concerted pattern to incite and commit

---

[3] Shlomo Aronson, *'Preparations for the Nuremberg Trial: The O.S.S., Charles Dwork, and the Holocaust'*, 12 HOLOCAUST AND GENOCIDE STUDIES 257-81 (1998).

[4] According to Robinson himself, "the matter of war crimes is one of the very few in which our group is the only Jewish group that made a contribution and remained active in to the end (sic)." Minutes, meeting of the World Jewish Congress with Robert H. Jackson in New York City, June 12, 1945, Records of the World Jewish Congress, Jacob Radler Marcus Center of the American Jewish Archives, (hereinafter WJC Archives), Truman Presidential Museum & Library (hereinafter TPML), http://www.trumanlibrary.org/whistlestop/study_collections/nuremberg/index.php?action=docs#1945. Retrieved, September 6, 2005. Robinson's English was imperfect, leading to formulations such as this and an occasional corresponding lack of clarity.

[5] Minutes, meeting of the World Jewish Congress with Robert H. Jackson in New York City, June 12, 1945, WJC Archives,TPML http://www.trumanlibrary.org/whistlestop/study_collections/nuremberg/index.php?action=docs#1945. Retrieved, September 6, 2005. First among the documents submitted to Jackson on the 18th were the minutes of their meeting of the 12th, from which we draw the account in this paper. See List of Documents, Evidence, Jacob Robinson to Robert H. Jackson, June 18, 1945. WJC Archives, TPML, http://www.trumanlibrary.org/whistlestop/study_collections/nuremberg/index.php?action=docs#1945. Retrieved, September 6, 2005.

the aggressions and barbarities which have shocked the world."[6] Without additional fanfare, Robinson came quickly to the point, asserting a central Jewish interest in the forthcoming trial. "The Jewish people is the greatest sufferer of this war," he said, "if not in absolute number of its casualties ... [then] certainly in relative numbers (the ration of surviving Jews in Europe to their pre-war total in the same areas. It therefore has a case of its own against the master Nazi criminals and their accomplices." Robinson embraced the idea of a Nazi "master plan" – a conspiracy that embraced both the Nazi leaders and their organizations. And, lest the point was lost, Robinson insisted that it was the Jewish *people* which was at issue – not just Jews who happened to be the victims. "The Jewish casualties ... are not a pure incident of the war or its preparatory stage, but the result of a well-conceived, deliberately plotted and meticulously carried out conspiracy." This conspiracy, moreover, "was directed not only against the Jews under their control, but also against those beyond their reach."[7]

Robinson took pains to emphasize that the anti-Jewish objectives of the Hitlerian regime were at the very core of the conspiracy. Referring to the "motives of the Nazi plot," he argued that attacking Jews was "dynamite to explode democratic society." Even after the German defeat, Europe remained infested "…with anti-Jewish feeling." Pressing his case, Robinson felt that "a specific indictment for the crime committed against our people will clear the atmosphere in Europe and make it easier for the survivors to reestablish themselves there." "Jewish survivors [were] entitled to have someone represent them at the trials," Robinson said. There should, he argued, be some *amicus curiae* presence of Jewish survivors that would "bring to the fore more clearly the moral implications of punishing the conspirators against an entire people." Jackson, for his part, listened intently to Robinson's presentation, asking at several points for supportive documentation – in particular on the numbers of Jewish victims and the original sources for incriminating Nazi statements. Gently, he pushed back on the matter of a specific charge of anti-Jewish activity and specific Jewish representation. Jackson "explained that it is intended to have one military trial embracing the whole conspiracy of the Nazis against the world, in which the Jewish count should have its place." As to more general Jewish representation, "the international military tribunal might not be well disposed towards such an idea," he said. "[O]ther groups might also ask for the same consideration, which would complicate matters."

The minutes of the June 12th meeting suggest that the matter of Jewish representation was not definitively settled, and indeed the issue was discussed within Jewish circles in the weeks and months that followed. Jackson was not opposed in principle, although he had reservations. In London, in August, possibly through the good offices of Lauterpacht, he proposed to call Chaim Weizmann, the revered president of the World Zionist Organization, to testify as "an authority on the total picture of the Holocaust," as Robinson later put it.[8] The British opposed the idea, fearing that the testimony would fuel support for the Jewish case in Palestine.[9] For their own reasons, Robinson and his staff were ambivalent. On the one hand, they recognized the "unique opportunity of pronouncing an earth-shaking *j'accuse*" on the crimes against world Jewry, as an internal memorandum put it. This would be a "historic occasion," not unlike Weizmann's appearance before the Peel Commission ten years before, appealing "to the emotions and reason of mankind."[10] On the other hand, "We have to expect a severe cross-examination," and the result could be to focus guilt not on the Nazi accused, but on the

---

[6] Report of Robert H. Jackson, United States Representative to the International Conference on Miliatary Trials, London 1945 (Washington, D.C.: Department of State, 1949), 46-50.

[7] Minutes, meeting of the World Jewish Congress with Robert H. Jackson in New York City, June 12, 1945, WJC Archives, TPML http://www.trumanlibrary.org/whistlestop/study_collections/nuremberg/index.php?action=docs#1945. Retrieved, September 6, 2005.

[8] Jacob Robinson, "The International Military Tribunal and the Holocaust: Some Legal Reflections," 7 ISRAEL LAW REVIEW 3 (1972).

[9] Leonard Stein to Chaim Weizmann, August 28, 1945. Rehovot, Israel: Weizmann Archives, Weizmann Papers, File 2600; Robinson, *'International Military Tribunal and the Holocaust'*, 3.

[10] Report, "Some Basic Ideas with Regard to the Appearance of a Jewish Witness at the International Military Tribunal", September 5, 1945. WJC Archives, TPML. http://www.trumanlibrary.org/whistlestop/study_collections/nuremberg/index.php?action=docs#1945. Retrieved, September 6, 2005.

bystanding nations. Weizmann, his close associates knew, was in frail health and might not be up to the challenge. "[U]nless skillfully handled," an IJA memorandum put it, "... the whole appearance [might] boomerang."

Israeli political scientist Shlomo Aronson is probably right to observe that given the conceptions of the day, Robinson's accent on the crimes against the "Jewish people" "may have grated on Jackson's ear," observing that throughout the trial the American prosecutor referred to the Jews as a "race" – "albeit in a culturally neutral sense."[11] In 1945, the Jewish collectivity was far from clearly defined in ethno-cultural terms as it is today. Non-Jews in particular were sometimes reluctant to think of the Jews in collective terms at all, except as a religion, arguing that doing so implicitly cast some sort of aspersion on them, or even involved playing the game of anti-Semites and Hitler. Important as this issue is to us, however, what is apparent from the presentation of the Jewish case to Jackson, at this early point in the preparation of the Nuremberg Trial, is the degree to which he and Robinson agreed on the essentials and were set to cooperate. Robinson understood the importance of fitting the Jewish case within the wider American project for Nuremberg. And Jackson, for his part, knew he needed help, and that Robinson and his team were well placed to provide it.

Jewish Assistance in the Preparation of the American Case

Toward the end of their meeting on June 12th, Robinson and Jackson discussed how they would work together: Robinson wanted Jackson to appoint someone on his team to deal with the Jewish issue; Jackson seemed more inclined to rely on the IJA for documentary assistance, both for legal and other matters. As the Institute's minutes noted, "Justice Jackson expressed interest in receiving from us all pertinent material we may be able to submit." Helpfully, Jackson noted that "he does not expect perfection in the preparation of such material, as he realizes the need for speedy action."[12] A week later Robinson appeared in Washington to hand deliver his first installment – about a dozen studies, including a paper on the "Armenian Massacres," surveys of anti-Jewish laws, statistical analyses, legal briefs on particular topics, and so on.[13]

Robinson's involvement continued throughout the summer of 1945, as the Americans prepared their case, and as Jackson negotiated with Allied representatives in London on the shape of the Nuremberg proceedings. As requested, the Jewish researchers worked on both legal and substantive matters. In July, for example, Robinson wrote to Jackson directly, recommending that one important defendant be added to the list – "SS Obersturmfuehrer Adolf Aichman ... sometimes spelled Eichmann," referred to as "a man who is probably more directly responsible for the destruction of the Jews than any other single Nazi" (sic).[14] Material in the archives of the Institute shows that the Jewish team also worked on German legal theory, problems associated with defining aggressive war, and so on.[15]

Jackson's Office of Chief Counsel expanded to include several hundred people, with a shifting organizational structure that included extensive involvement in Jewish matters, both in a Section IV, Crimes Against Humanity, but also elsewhere. Robinson had a stream of communications with this office and with Dwork, both of whose abilities to deal with the material he came to question. Dwork

---

[11] Aronson, *'Preparations for the Nuremberg Trial'*, 265.

[12] Minutes, meeting of the World Jewish Congress with Robert H. Jackson in New York City, June 12, 1945, WJC Archives, TPML http://www.trumanlibrary.org/whistlestop/study_collections/nuremberg/index.php?action=docs#1945. Retrieved, September 6, 2005.

[13] List of Documents, Evidence, Jacob Robinson to Robert H. Jackson, June 18, 1945. WJC Archives,TPML, http://www.trumanlibrary.org/whistlestop/study_collections/nuremberg/index.php?action=docs#1945. Retrieved, September 6, 2005.

[14] Robinson to Jackson, July 27, 1945. WJC Archives, TPML, http://www.trumanlibrary.org/whistlestop/study_collections/nuremberg/documents/index.php?documentdate=1945-07-27&documentid=C106-16-2&studycollectionid=&pagenumber=1 Retrieved, September 6, 2005.

[15] Draft of Letter, World Jewish Congress to Robert H. Jackson, July 1945. WJC Archives, TPML, http://www.trumanlibrary.org/whistlestop/study_collections/nuremberg/documents/index.php?documentdate=1945-07-00&documentid=C106-16-4&studycollectionid=&pagenumber=1 Retrieved, September 6, 2005.

never left Washington to join the prosecutors in Europe, and his OSS unit seems to have dropped out of involvement in the trial's preparation. Robinson later described Section IV in particular as "a group of men of good will but who lack competence in Jewish affairs." "The deeper reasons for this state of affairs," he concluded, were three-fold: "(1) American unpreparedness; (2) the assumption that a military man (and a lawyer, to boot) must know everything, especially how to execute any orders she may receive; (3) over-simplification of the whole Jewish matter."[16]

While maintaining their role as lobbyists, Robinson and the IJA never felt frozen out. In his succinct view, "we, those who are competent, are on the outside, and those who are on the inside are incompetent. The solution was either to bring the outsiders in, or to educate the insiders. The former was deemed more expedient, and that's what was done."[17] Bringing the outsiders in meant continued involvement as the American prosecution took shape. Robinson flew to London in late August – apparently to help prepare the then expected testimony at the trial of Chaim Weizmann, but he remained in active contact with Jackson's Office. In London during the preparation of the indictment, he was summoned to Nuremberg in the autumn – at first, in order to give evidence to support the allegation, in the indictment, of 5.7 million Jewish victims, and later to assist the American prosecutors, both with respect to the presentation of the Jewish case by Major William F. Walsh, the use of captured German films of Jewish ghettos, and in the interrogation of at least one of the German witnesses, SS Captain and Eichmann deputy Dieter Wisliceny, conducted by Lieutenant Colonel Smith W. Brookhart.[18]

Robinson's Evaluation of the Presentation of the Holocaust at Nuremberg

How did Robinson and his colleagues at the IJA evaluate the presentation of the Holocaust at Nuremberg? While by no means fully satisfied, and with reservations that perhaps grew in significance as the years passed, the Jewish lobby that is at the centre of this paper understood the momentous significance of the trial and the Jewish contribution to it. Nuremberg, Robinson was already stating in December 1945, created a revolution in legal thinking on war crimes, and the Jewish contribution had been "instrumental" in the resulting transformation.[19]

Strikingly, given his own European background and international experience, Robinson's perspective was utterly American. Like many of the American participants in the trial, Robinson ascribed important shortcomings to the exigencies of international cooperation. He attributed the insufficient attention or focus on Jewish matters in the indictment of the accused to "the system of division of labor among the four governments, resulting in four different styles which are not strongly unified." In what turned out to be a momentous decision, the clarification of the four-power Charter of the Nuremberg Trial in the Protocol of October 6, 1945 resulted in a restrictive interpretation of "crimes against humanity," rendering these "accompanying" or "accessory" crimes by requiring them to have been committed in connection with or in execution of war crimes or crimes against peace. As a result, Robinson noted, crimes against the Jews before the war did not fall within what constituted crimes against humanity at Nuremberg; and perhaps even more damagingly, the Holocaust was never highlighted as a distinct crime as Jewish lobbyists hoped it would be when they began work in the summer of 1945. In Robinson's own phrase, describing the International Military Tribunal's deductions

---

[16] General Report to the Combined Staffs of the Office by Dr. Jacob Robinson on the Nuremberg War Criminals Trial, Thursday, December 6, 1945. WJC Archives, TPML, http://www.trumanlibrary.org/whistlestop/study_collections/nuremberg/documents/index.php?documentdate=1945-12-06&documentid=C14-16-1&studycollectionid=&pagenumber=1 Retrieved, September 6, 2005.

[17] Ibid.

[18] "Col. Brookart (sic), a good American criminal lawyer, is conducting Wisliczeny's (sic) interrogation: It was impossible for me, a civilian without status, to get the permit necessary to interrogate him. So the following procedure was adopted: I would prepare the questions, Col. Brookart would go to see Wisliczeny and put these questions to him, get his replies, and bring them to me. I would write these answers up and Brookart would take them back to Wisliczeny for his approval, etc." Ibid.

[19] Ibid.

from this formulation, the Holocaust did not emerge "as a unit in fact and in law."[20]

In a key passage in Robinson's confidential report to Jewish leaders in New York in December 1945, he balanced these shortcomings with effusive appreciation of the American role in formulating the Jewish case. "If there is any group that took the Jewish case seriously," he said, "it is only the Americans" (sic). It was the United States which drove home the case for "Crimes against Humanity," he contended. Neither the British, nor the French nor the Soviets provided a framework for the integration of Jewish concerns into the prosecution's case. "It is the self assertion of American leadership in world affairs on the moral plane which has proved of tremendous importance. The others missed the bus." Robinson was unreserved in his praise of Jackson, particularly for the latter's opening speech for the American prosecution. Robinson reminded his listeners of how Jackson described the goal of the Holocaust: "It is my purpose to show a plan and design, to which all Nazis were fanatically committed, to annihilate all Jewish people ... . The persecution of the Jews was a continuous and deliberate policy." "[H]ow could it have been better said than that?" Robinson asked his Jewish audience rhetorically, then making a point of how this impacted on the trial. "At this point the defendants were at their lowest ebb, completely crushed. This situation gave rise to a certain competition among the four prosecutors in their desire to speak on the Jewish case ... ."[21]

What Robinson appreciated about Jackson's presentation was the authoritative acknowledgement, from the highest perch of prosecutorial authority, of the comprehensive, murderous anti-Jewish objective at the core of Nazi criminality – a theme to which all four prosecuting powers were, in the end, formally committed. Documenting the existence of a policy of deliberate, comprehensive mass murder was considered a major achievement. "[T]he ultimate goal of Nazi-German policies with regard to the Jewish people was nothing short of complete physical annihilation," was one typical IJA formulation, among many similar observations in 1945.[22] Assessing the judgment of the court the following year, Robinson wrote that it was "important to emphasize that time and again the Court underlines the connection between the initial stage of persecution and the so-called 'final solution.'"[23]

Over and over again, in memoranda describing the prosecution, the IJA took note whenever there was "prominent place" devoted to describing the murder of the Jews and whenever there was clear evidence of the Nazis' murderous objectives. Tracking how this was done was one of the few discussions in which IJA material ventured outside an American perimeter: "The case presented by the British Prosecutors also made frequent references to the Jews as victims of Nazi oppression," noted one report. "The French and the Russians, dealing with war crimes in the narrower sense of the word, also dealt with the crimes against the Jews."[24] Were the Jewish lobbyists of 1945 gratified by too little? Fully to appreciate Jewish perceptions of how their wartime ordeal was treated in 1945-46 one must imagine a time before "Holocaust" was an established category, before Raphael Lemkin's "genocide" was an established term which could be applied to the Nazis' assault on Jews or anyone else, and when anti-Semitism not only maintained a place in respectable opinion but was even resurgent in many parts of liberated Europe. As the evidence accumulated – with reference to what are for us indelible landmarks such as Wannsee, the *Einsatzgruppen*, ghettos, Auschwitz, the Warsaw Ghetto, Robinson

---

[20] Robinson, *'International Military Tribunal and the Holocaust'*, 7.

[21] General Report to the Combined Staffs of the Office by Dr. Jacob Robinson on the Nuremberg War Criminals Trial, Thursday, December 6, 1945. WJC Archives, TPML, http://www.trumanlibrary.org/whistlestop/study_collections/nuremberg/documents/index.php?documentdate=1945-12-06&documentid=C14-16-1&studycollectionid=&pagenumber=1 Retrieved, September 6, 2005.

[22] Report, "Criminal Conspiracy Against the Jews, Part Two: Successive Stages of the Crimes Committed Against the Jewish People," n.d., WJC Archives, TPML, http://www.trumanlibrary.org/whistlestop/study_collections/nuremberg/documents/index.php?documentdate=1945-00-00&documentid=C192-2-3&studycollectionid=&pagenumber=1 Retrieved, September 7, 2005.

[23] Jacob Robinson, *'The Nuremberg Judgment'*, CONGRESS WEEKLY: A REVIEW OF JEWISH INTERESTS, October 25, 1946, 8.

[24] Report, "The Legal Problems of the Crimes Against Humanity with Special Consideration of the Anti-Jewish Crimes", n.d. http://www.trumanlibrary.org/whistlestop/study_collections/nuremberg/documents/index.php?documentdate=1945-00-00&documentid=C107-9-1&studycollectionid=&pagenumber=1 Retrieved, September 7, 2005.

must have felt that his essential goals were achieved. "The evidence submitted to the IMT in the Jewish case was overwhelming," he wrote a dozen years later, "more than eight hundred Nazi self-accusing documents (in whole or in part) were presented and thirty-three witnesses were heard in addition to all the defendants present."[25]

Did the failure of the Jewish lobby to get a separate Jewish presence at Nuremberg as an *amicus curiae* rank as a shortcoming in Robinson's evaluation? Definitely not. Speaking confidentially in December 1945, Robinson told his Jewish listeners that in the context of the actual conduct of the trial, and in particular the arrangement of the courtroom, this demand did not make sense. "Far away from Nuremberg, the idea of our 'representation' or 'observers' being officially admitted to the trials sounded like a good idea. But the fact is that there are no 'representatives' at Nuremberg at all. The court consists of the floor and the gallery. The 'representatives' of the countries not represented on the bench are in the gallery, and so is everybody else, and there is no place for 'observers.'" Fifteen governments that adhered to the Four Power Agreement for the trial were accommodated there with great difficulty, but in practical terms there was no real point in being there. Not only was it difficult to see from the gallery, the proceedings themselves were tedious – Robinson was not the first to have noticed it – and consisted mainly in the reading aloud of documents that could be easily read elsewhere.[26]

Conclusions

Remarkably I think, given the responsibilities American Jewish leaders assumed in making the case for a shattered people, their perspective and that of the Institute of Jewish Affairs were resolutely internationalist and sought energetically to expand the scope of international criminal jurisdiction. Responding to Justice Jackson's Report to President Truman of June 1945, Rabbi Stephen Wise, speaking as president of the World Jewish Congress, heaped praise upon the American Chief Prosecutor for having "gone to the root of the war crimes problem." Jackson's approach, Wise said, was "undeterred by 'sterile legalisms,'" but sought to find a solution "in conformity with the highest traditions of justice, the laws of humanity and the ideals for which this war has been fought."[27] Following suit, the director of the Institute of Jewish Affairs, an international lawyer who had served at the International Court at the Hague and who was fully at home with the idioms of international humanitarian law, saw his role as seeking "an extension in time and space of the orthodox definition of war crimes."[28]

To these Jewish campaigners, crimes against humanity were always at the centre of their attention, and while many crimes against Jews fell within the definition of war crimes the lobbyists devoted most of their legal analysis to the former, seeing in them a means to punish anti-Jewish activity for which there were otherwise no legal remedies. Outlined in Article 6(c) of the Nuremberg Charter, Robinson later noted, these charges "had gone a long way from some traditional taboos of public international law."[29] By this he meant three things: first, that accused persons could be convicted of crimes against the Jews "whether or not in violation of the domestic law of the country where perpetrated"; second, that prosecution could be for crimes against "any civilian population," meaning subjects of Germany

---

[25] Robinson, *'International Military Tribunal and the Holocaust'*, 6.
[26] General Report to the Combined Staffs of the Office by Dr. Jacob Robinson on the Nuremberg War Criminals Trial, Thursday, December 6, 1945. WJC Archives, TPML, http://www.trumanlibrary.org/whistlestop/study_collections/nuremberg/documents/index.php?documentdate=1945-12-06&documentid=C14-16-1&studycollectionid=&pagenumber=1 Retrieved, September 6, 2005.
[27] Press Release, Statement from Stephen S. Wise, World Jewish Congress, June 9, 1945. WJC Archives, TPML, http://www.trumanlibrary.org/whistlestop/study_collections/nuremberg/documents/index.php?documentdate=1945-06-09&documentid=C106-15-4&studycollectionid=&pagenumber=1 Retrieved, September 8, 2005.
[28] General Report to the Combined Staffs of the Office by Dr. Jacob Robinson on the Nuremberg War Criminals Trial, Thursday, December 6, 1945. WJC Archives, TPML, http://www.trumanlibrary.org/whistlestop/study_collections/nuremberg/documents/index.php?documentdate=1945-12-06&documentid=C14-16-1&studycollectionid=&pagenumber=1 Retrieved, September 6, 2005.
[29] Robinson, "International Military Tribunal and the Holocaust," 4.

and its satellites; and third, that prosecution could be for crimes committed "before or during the war" – all three cases, to be sure, being subject important limitations we will come to in a moment.

Of course, Robinson knew well that with the introduction of crimes against humanity the walls of national sovereignty had not come crashing down. But Nuremberg, he seemed to be saying to a Jewish audience, took a commendable step forward in the development of international law: "The theory of humanitarian intervention, the protection of minorities, the recently established duty of the United Nations to promote human rights and fundamental freedoms notwithstanding, sovereignty is still generally understood as absolute freedom in treating its own nationals. The Tribunal did not discuss this problem, but the answer is certainly clear that crimes committed by Germans against German nationals are within the general scope of crimes against humanity."[30]

Robinson and his colleagues were acutely aware of the limitations placed upon the newly defined crimes against humanity and the resulting scope of the judgment that was announced by the Nuremberg court in October 1946. He identified two problems, from the Jewish point of view. First, having had to accept that crimes against humanity were to be "in execution of or in connection with" war crimes or cries against peace, the Jewish lobby had to bow to the court's view that the persecution of the Jews before the war were not so connected and thus did not constitute crimes against humanity. Second, since the Tribunal did not find in favor of the existence of a "common plan or conspiracy" to commit war crimes or crimes against humanity, there was an additional reason not to extend criminal culpability backwards in time to cover acts against German Jews in the prewar period. Crimes against humanity were therefore by no means a generous category of criminality that would satisfy all of the Jewish concerns about Holocaust prosecutions in the 1945. Robinson and his colleagues knew, particularly after the restrictive interpretations agreed to by the Allies in October 1945, that they had to work with imperfect legal instruments.

Accepting these restrictions and having embraced the American trial plan, Robinson expended much effort to impress upon the American prosecutors, and thus the Nuremberg court, that the crimes against the Jews flowed from a coherently articulated plan – the kind of conspiracy so favored by the American conception of Nazi criminality. "According to our theory," he told his Jewish listeners in 1945, "these killings must be tied up with previous stages of the crime, constituting the last link in a chain of criminal acts of the conspiracy to destroy the Jewish people."[31] In addition to providing an explanation for the Holocaust and a strategy congenial to the Americans, this approach to understanding what had transpired made it more likely, Robinson felt, that the Holocaust would be considered "a unit in fact and in law" – a standing, he undoubtedly felt, that was in keeping with the unprecedented scale and nature of the massacre of European Jewry.[32] Robinson was, of course, disappointed in the finding of the court in this regard – and it is interesting to observe, in response to the charges that Nuremberg encouraged a conspiratorial understanding of the Holocaust, that in this case the court's judgment sought precisely to do the reverse.[33]

Was Robinson unhappy about the scarcity of Jewish witnesses, the relative absence of survivor testimony? This is doubtful. Certainly he said not a word about this – neither in his confidential briefing of Jewish leaders in New York in December 1945, nor in the articles he wrote at the time of the trial, nor even in his overview in an Israeli law journal in 1972, a decade after the Eichmann trial in which he had actively participated and in which survivor testimony was a cornerstone of the prosecution's case.

---

[30] Robinson, 'The Nuremberg Judgment', 7.

[31] General Report to the Combined Staffs of the Office by Dr. Jacob Robinson on the Nuremberg War Criminals Trial, Thursday, December 6, 1945. WJC Archives, TPML, http://www.trumanlibrary.org/whistlestop/study_collections/nuremberg/documents/index.php?documentdate=1945-12-06&documentid=C14-16-1&studycollectionid=&pagenumber=1 Retrieved, September 6, 2005.

[32] See Robinson, "International Military Tribunal and the Holocaust," 7.

[33] On the links between Nuremberg and the "intentionalist" line of Holocaust interpretation, see Michael R. Marrus, THE HOLOCAUST IN HISTORY 36 (Hanover and London: University Press of New England, 1987) and Donald Bloxham, GENOCIDE ON TRIAL: WAR CRIMES TRIALS AND THE FORMATION OF HOLOCAUST MEMORY 204-5 (Oxford: Oxford University Press, 2001).

And the explanation is simple: Not only did the legal culture of the day not privilege victims' testimony in the manner that is so favored today, but Robinson and the IJA seem to have agreed unspokenly with the determination of Robert Jackson and his colleagues to anchor their case against the Nazis in the latter's own words, recorded in the avalanche of paper that was submitted to the court, and which Robinson and his colleagues had so painstakingly and professionally assembled on the persecution and murder of the Jews. "[M]ore than eight hundred Nazi self-accusing documents" Robinson reminded his readers. A seasoned lawyer himself, and like many Jews preoccupied with defining an as yet ill-understood and unprecedented catastrophe, this was what he considered the surest way to do so.

Finally, and to put this sometimes detailed assessment into broader perspective, my sense is that Robinson and the IJA came away from Nuremberg gratified by the achievement of what was to them a core objective: formal recognition, by an internationally authorized body, of the modern catastrophe of the Jewish people. Disappointing as were the shortcomings in crimes against humanity and the legal ramifications of the judgment, the essential was otherwise – what Robinson referred to in December 1945 as "our struggle in securing the recognition for the *Jewish people* as the victim of the Nazi fury" (emphasis in original).[34] At the heart of it all was the campaign in a relatively unfamiliar non-Jewish environment for the notion of a grievously victimized Jewish collectivity – a new idea, for many, in 1945-46. Years after the trial, Robinson praised the "valiant effort to lead the IMT towards a proper definition of the crime committed by the Nazis against the Jewish people" by Robert Jackson and his associate, Major Walsh. And despite the findings of the tribunal, as we have already noted, Robinson felt that the evidence presented in support of this case was "overwhelming," the more so for its having been assembled in documentary form. "A careful analysis of this documentation leads inexorably to the conclusion of the existence of a conspiracy to destroy the Jewish people and its ruthless implementation, resulting in the death of some six million Jews, which constituted 75% of the Jewish population in Europe" (sic). To its conclusion, the Nuremberg Trial highlighted the inescapable facts of the disaster that had befallen world Jewry. In sentencing, Robinson noted, practically all of those who had been actively involved in committing crimes against humanity received the death penalty. This illustrated how the Nuremberg court "was consistently aware of the Jewish element in the trial." To us, this is a banal observation, for we would expect nothing less. But to many Jews at the time, and to their spokesmen at Nuremberg, hungry as they were for the sort of recognition the American prosecutors offered them, this was an achievement that they had worked for years with almost frantic, if highly professional, determination.

---

[34] General Report to the Combined Staffs of the Office by Dr. Jacob Robinson on the Nuremberg War Criminals Trial, Thursday, December 6, 1945. WJC Archives, TPML, http://www.trumanlibrary.org/whistlestop/study_collections/nuremberg/documents/index.php?documentdate=1945-12-06&documentid=C14-16-1&studycollectionid=&pagenumber=1 Retrieved, September 6, 2005.

Michael R. Marrus

Eine jüdische Interessenvertretung in Nürnberg: Jacob Robinson und das Institut für jüdischen Angelegenheiten, 1945-46

Welche Relevanz wurde dem Holocaust bei den Hauptkriegsverbrecherprozessen des Internationalen Militärtribunals in Nürnberg eingeräumt? Mit der Beantwortung dieser Frage setzen sich Historiker bis zum heutigen Tage auseinander. Bei Betrachtung dieser Debatte aus der Perspektive jener, die während der Kriegsjahre durch ihre Anteilnahme an den jüdischen Opfern der Nazi-Schlächterei schmerzvolle Erfahrungen machten, hat Michael Marrus die Umstände der Nürnberger Prozesse und des Holocaust porträtiert. Wenn man die „Jüdische Lobby" jener Zeit betrachtet, tritt besonders eine Organisation, genannt „Institut für Jüdische Angelegenheiten", unter der Leitung ihres Direktors Dr. Jacob Robinson hervor. Gegründet in New York im Jahr 1941 als ein Gemeinschaftsprojekt des American Jewish Congress und des World Jewish Congress, brachte das Institut für Jüdische Angelegenheiten seinen Fall beharrlich dem amerikanischen Anklägerteam zur Kenntnis.

In seinem ersten Treffen mit Richter Jackson, dem von Präsident Harry Truman ernannten Leiter des Anklägerteams, übermittelte Robinson diesem die jüdische Sicht auf die bevorstehenden Nürnberger Prozesse und betonte ausdrücklich das zentrale jüdische Interesse an einer Thematisierung der anti-jüdischen Exzesse und an einer speziellen jüdischen Vertretung. Jackson war trotz gewisser Vorbehalte nicht grundsätzlich gegen diese Forderung. Es gab schließlich noch andere zentrale Fragen im amerikanischen Anklageplan zu berücksichtigen, einschließlich der unterschiedlichen Ziele der alliierten Mächte. Als Konsequenz konnte Robinson seinen Wunsch nach einer separaten Vertretung bei den Nürnberger Prozessen nicht durchsetzen. Trotzdem war Nürnberg ein wichtiger Markstein in der Darstellung des schrecklichen Schicksals, das Menschen jüdischen Glaubens durch die Nazis zugefügt worden war.

Nach Ansicht von Michael Marrus wurde der Holocaust in Nürnberg sicherlich nicht in derselben Weise dargestellt, wie das heutzutage geschehen würde. Immerhin erfolgte hier erstmalig eine Erklärung zu der Ermordung von sechs Millionen Menschen, die vor einem internationalen Gremium öffentlich abgegeben wurde. Dazu zählten bereits die Hauptelemente des Holocaust wie die Vorkriegsverfolgungen, die Massenerschießungen durch die Einsatzgruppen, die Wannseekonferenz von 1942, der Aufstand im Warschauer Ghetto, die Deportation ungarischer Juden und, schlussendlich, die Todeslager Auschwitz, Buchenwald und viele andere.

Unter Historikern gab es kontroverse Meinungen über die Behauptung, der Holocaust habe nicht die angemessene Aufmerksamkeit erhalten oder – noch schlimmer – die Nürnberger Prozesse hätten in schwerwiegender Weise die geschichtlichen Tatsachen verdreht. Die Kritik bezog sich auf die Unzulänglichkeit der Prozesse. So beispielsweise, dass die Betonung der Verschwörung oder die amerikanische Besessenheit im Hinblick auf Verbrechen gegen den Frieden die Aufmerksamkeit von dem Angriff auf die Juden Europas ablenkte; ebenso, dass als Folge des Privilegs der dokumentarischen Beweise jüdische Stimmen kaum vor dem Tribunal zu hören waren und nicht zuletzt die Rahmenbedingungen des Falles eine Vernachlässigung der Vorkriegsverbrechen verursachten und – noch bedeutender – die Präsentation des Holocaust als ein spezifisches Element der Nazi-Kriminalität verhinderten.

Donald Bloxham

Genocide on Trial: Law and Collective Memory

Introduction: (Mis-)Remembering Nuremberg

Assessing the impact of the Nuremberg trials on something as amorphous as 'collective memory' will inevitably be a subjective exercise, coloured strongly by the indicators one selects. While the trial records themselves provide an indelible record of what was said at Nuremberg, and thus a fixed point for the historian of the trials per se, ideas of what 'Nuremberg' as a whole meant and means are far from fixed. At the most basic level, there is confusion as to what is meant by 'the Nuremberg trials', since some use that formula to refer exclusively to the quadripartite International Military Tribunal (IMT) 'trial of the major war criminals' of 1945-6, and some more inclusively to refer to both the IMT trial and the twelve subsequent Nuremberg trials conducted under solely American auspices. The distinction between these categories is not just academic: while the subsequent trials went into much greater detail than the IMT proceedings on specific aspects of Nazi criminality, they were simultaneously much less significant in the process of popular memory-formation in the 1940s and 1950s. General comprehension has not been aided by the single most important popular representation of 'Nuremberg', Abby Mann's Judgment at Nuremberg. This Hollywood production spliced together with considerable artistic license episodes from both the IMT trial and some of the subsequent proceedings.

Perceptions of 'Nuremberg' continue to change to this day. The introductory notes to this panel in the present conference programme, for instance, tell us that the trials 'aimed to restore justice both to the defendants and to the history and memory of the Holocaust.' This is strongly reminiscent of a conference held at the Benjamin B. Cardozo Law School in New York in March 2005, 'The Nuremberg Trials: A Reappraisal and their Legacy'. There, the introductory sessions were filled with depictions of the Nuremberg confrontation with perpetrators of genocide, disregarding the fact that the primary thrust of the trials, from the dominant American perspective at least, was the aggressive war making of the Nazi regime. We were told in that conference programme that the gathering sought 'to recall and reaffirm the lessons – the legacy – of Nuremberg that underlay the trials' deliberations: that the Nazi regime almost succeeded because of the pathologies of hate and evil, as well as the crimes of indifference and silence.' It is almost as if these pronouncements too were influenced by Judgment at Nuremberg, which was, in relation to the proceedings it purported to represent, disproportionately concerned with crimes against humanity as opposed to the crime of aggressive war. Such genocide-centric conceptions of 'Nuremberg' may tell us much about the way that we in a most Holocaust-conscious world would like to think the trials were conducted; they tell us less about the priorities of the Allied law-makers and trial participants, or about the balance of everyday practice and discussion in courtroom 600 in 1945-6.

At Nuremberg addressing crimes against humanity as a whole was an important but ultimately subsidiary end to the primary goal of tackling 'crimes against peace'; addressing what we now know as the Holocaust was subsidiary even to that subsidiary end. For the most part, when they were considered at the IMT trial, crimes against Jews qua Jews tended to be subsumed within the larger whole of Nazi atrocity, left ill-defined within the mass of murder, enslavement and war-related destruction affecting other groups in Europe. It is possible to argue, by piecing together disparate pieces of evidence marshalled in the Nuremberg courtroom, that the IMT trial presented a more-or-less representative if rudimentary outline of the 'final solution of the Jewish question'. This, however is a far different matter to attributing a conscious plan for such an outcome to the Allied prosecutors (left to his own devices US chief prosecutor Robert Jackson would not have had Einsatzgruppe leader Otto Ohlendorf testify at Nuremberg, while the other witness who did something to animate the 'final solution', former Auschwitz commandant Rudolf Höß, was actually brought to the stand by the defence rather then the prosecution). It is also a world away from proving anything at all about the effect of such a representation on audiences then or latterly. More importantly, it is probably to fall into the trap of finding what one wants to find in the historical record.[1]

Writing about the exaggeration in some recent scholarship on the British Empire of the impact that the imperial experience had on domestic British society, Bernard Porter has observed that it is imperative to look at the empire's impact on British society in context; to survey … the whole site. It will not do simply to look for 'imperial' evidence without being aware of what lies around it; or even, perhaps, to look for imperial evidence at all. People who look for things sometimes find them when they are not there; especially – in this case – if they are looking through distorting lenses. Even when you can avoid that, there is still the temptation to exaggerate the significance of what you have found. There is a lot of genuinely 'imperialist' material from this period, which if corralled together looks impressive, and even overwhelming, but which really needs to be viewed *in situ* and against the background of other kinds of evidence if its real importance and meaning are to be adjudged.[2] If we were to substitute 'the Holocaust' for 'the Empire' in the first sentence, and likewise 'the trial of the major war criminals' for 'British society', and read the rest of the paragraph around those two new referents, we have the basis for a trenchant critique of the idea that the trial of the major war criminals did 'justice' to the Holocaust or any other Nazi genocide.

For present purposes, any discussion of the relationship between collective memory and the trials must recognise that the very fact and the shape of the trials, as well as the profile of the tried, were at least as significant as was the actual substance of the trials in terms of the day-to-day proceedings and the evidence adduced there. This may even be truer in the IMT case than in other instances, owing on one hand to the contentious, ex post facto nature of the laws applied and, on the other hand to the dry, tedious documentary approach favoured by the dominant US prosecution team, OCCPAC (Office, Chief of Counsel for the Prosecution of Axis Criminality). The crux of my argument hereafter is that whatever hugely significant things they achieved as a precedent for trying leaders of state for international crimes, in creating a huge documentary database for future historians of Nazism, and tempering vengeance with a measure of justice, the Nuremberg trials did little by way of influencing a collective memory of Nazi criminality. Other instructional media and propaganda forms were more significant than the courtroom. Moreover, the victim groups of the war era that most preoccupied most countries either conducting or on the receiving end of trials tended not to be the main target-groups of Nazi genocide, but instead whichever groups best served national agendas. Already by the 1950s, in those places where there was still the remotest interest in 'Nuremberg', for which we can read primarily Germany, these more powerful influences had successfully occluded what the trials had endeavoured to transmit. Subsequent 'rediscoveries' of Nuremberg, and reassessments of its 'true' lessons and legacies have had as much to do with the values of the time of the reassessments as with what 'Nuremberg' itself actually was.

National agendas and international crimes

Martin Conway has observed that the shape and character of the various purges and prosecutions provide an excellent means of analyzing the dynamics of European societies in the immediate post-war

---

[1] Donald Bloxham, Genocide on Trial: War Crimes Trials and the Formation of Holocaust History and Memory (Oxford: Oxford University Press, 2001), chs. 1, 2 and 3; contrary views about the effectiveness of the Nuremberg trial in informing about the Holocaust are held in Michael Marrus, 'The Holocaust at Nuremberg', Yad Vashem Studies, vol. 26 (1998), 5-41; Jürgen Wilke et al, Holocaust und NS-Prozesse (Cologne: Böhlau, 1995); Jürgen Wilke, "Ein früher Beginn der 'Vergangenheitsbewältigung': der Nürnberger Prozess und wie darüber berichtet wurde", Frankfurter Allgemeine Zeitung 15 November 1995; and, with much more nuance, and a different focus, Lawrence Douglas, The Memory of Judgment: Making Law and History in the Trials of the Holocaust (New Haven, Conn.: Yale University Press, 2001), part one. For analysis of the idea of 'crimes against peace' as the supreme crime, see Jonathan A Bush, "'The Supreme … Crime' and its Origins: The Lost Legislative History of the Crime of Aggressive War", Columbia Law Review, vol. 12, no. 8 (December 2002), 2324-2423. On the testimony of the Nazi perpetrators mentioned, see Bloxham, Genocide on Trial, pp. 61-2, 105-6.

[2] Bernard Porter, The Absent-Minded Imperialists (Oxford: Oxford University Press, 2004), p. 13.

years. The devising and implementation of the structures of justice constituted a highly politicised arena in which mass pressures and elite concerns were focused with a rare intensity.[3] In other words, the trials of the post-war years provide an insight into the societies bringing trial as much as into the actions of the accused. In the post-war era, the trial programmes of the victorious Allies and the liberated Europeans reveal a series of concerns related primarily to the reformation of national communities of identity and the writing of 'usable' historical records.[4] These tendencies were all influenced, if often simply reinforced, by the developing cold war environment.

By far the greatest concentration of prosecutions of war and Nazi occupation-related offences occurred in the five years following the end of the war. In that time the British authorities in Europe tried more than a thousand Axis nationals, primarily Germans, for war crimes, and the USA tried more than 1,800. Neither would convict another war criminal until the London trial of the Belorussian collaborator-murderer Anthony Sawoniuk in 1999. Soviet figures are imprecise but we know that in May 1950, Soviet camps held 13,532 inmates convicted of war-related offences. In the same five-year period, in the Soviet zone of Germany, later the DDR, there were 12,177 convictions for Nazi- and war-related crimes; thereafter, there were only 630 such convictions up to 1964, and thence only 54 convictions to 1978. The French authorities in occupied Germany and in French military courts tried more than 2,000 individuals for war crimes and crimes against humanity from 1945-54, the majority in the first half of the period; the gauntlet was only picked-up again in 1987, with the trial of the Gestapo officer Klaus Barbie in Lyons. In Austria, 1945-55 saw 13,607 convictions, to be followed in the succeeding 17 years by only a further 18.

It is entirely natural that the immediate aftermath of war should have seen such a reckoning, as passions for retribution ran high and suspects were more easily identified. But what precisely were these suspects tried for? As Adalbert Rückerl observes, where figures are available, they indicate that the scale of trials for collaborators is of a different order to that of trials of war criminals proper.[5] In Poland, the ratio was approximately 2:1; in Western Europe, collaboration trials accounted for thousands and tens of thousands rather than tens or hundreds as was the case with war criminals. The countries that had been under occupation by Germany seemed more interested in purging themselves of fascists and collaborators – or at least in some cases merely giving the appearance of a purge – then they were with charting substantive war crimes.[6] In the immediate aftermath of the liberation of the Netherlands, for instance, a staggering 450,000 Dutch citizens were arrested. And 'the purification' – 'l'épuration' – of collaborators in France was much more important symbolically to the French people than the trials of German war criminals, quantitatively much more significant, and touched the lives of many more people. Before the establishment of the post-liberation French government after August 1944, some 9,000 French citizens were executed summarily or after 'kangaroo' trials. From 1945 onwards properly-constituted French courts passed another 1,500 death sentences, and 40,000 prison sentences.[7]

There was a fundamental dissonance between the national cleavage of the various trial programmes in existence and the international nature of Nazi criminality in terms of both the locus of the crimes and the profile of the victims. This particularly affected the confrontation with crimes against Europe's Romanies and Jews. As diaspora communities, who was to take up the cause of Jewish and Romany suffering in a world in which the emphasis was on the restoration of state boundaries and sovereignty, and on, to put it colloquially, sorting out one's own backyard? (This question still remains to be answered in the case of the Romanies, for neither at Nuremberg nor any national legal forum was that

---

[3] Martin Conway in Istvan Deak, Jan T. Gross and Tony Judt (eds.), The Politics of Retribution in Europe: World War II and its Aftermath (Princeton, NJ: Princeton University Press, 2000), p. 134.

[4] On the notion of a 'usable past', see Robert G. Moeller, War Stories: the Search for a Usable Past in the Federal Republic of Germany (Berkeley, Calif.: University of California Press, 2001).

[5] Adalbert Rückerl, NS-Verbrechen vor Gericht (Heidelberg: CF Müller, 1982), pp. 102-4.

[6] Deak, Gross and Judt (eds.), The Politics of Retibution in Europe.

[7] Henry Rousso, The Vichy Syndrome: History and Memory in France since 1944 (Cambridge, MA: Harvard University Press, 1991); Michael Fabreguet, "Frankreichs Historiker und der Völkermord an den Juden 1945-1993", in Rolf Steininger (ed.), Der Umgang mit der Holocaust: Europa – USA – Israel (Cologne: Böhlau, 1994), 317-28.

case of genocide addressed either in the post-war years or since, illustrating again the influence of prevailing national and cultural norms – in this case, clearly chauvinist norms – in shaping the legal confrontation with the past.) Further, in states that had colluded by omission or commission in the 'final solution of the Jewish question', proper confrontation with that crime was a victim of the logic of state re-formation based on the myth of opposition to Nazism and its crimes. The latter imperative would only be reinforced as, approximately from mid-1947, the cold war began to descend on Europe, as we shall see shortly.

Aspects of the IMT trial itself were marked by the national and ideological agendas of each of the 'big four' Allied powers. In a sense, despite its eponymous aspiration to be an 'international' forum, it remained in significant ways quadripartite. This was certainly how it was regarded by many of the governments and former governments-in-exile that had been involved in the United Nations War Crimes Commission and that pressed in vain in 1945 for separate national representation at the trial, feeling that their interests could only be represented in such an environment by their own delegates. The same went for those Jewish organisations that petitioned the USA and the UK for a representative presence on the prosecution. Let us briefly consider as illustration of the influence of national agendas some aspects of the Soviet and French presentations at the IMT trial.

In the official Marxist-Leninist Soviet comprehension of Nazism, Auschwitz, like the Majdanek concentration camp, was promoted as a symbol of the 'martyrdom' of the international 'victims of fascism' rather than any particular ethnic group. In evidence at the trial a Soviet extraordinary state commission report concluded that the camp had consumed 'four million [sic] citizens of the USSR, Poland, France, Yugoslavia, Czechoslovakia, Romania, Hungary, Bulgaria, Holland, Belgium and other countries'. The failure to mention Jews as victims was duplicated in the Soviet prosecution's courtroom references to Treblinka and, uniquely in the Allied presentations, Chelmno.[8]

Characteristic of a post-war regime that sought to locate all of the blame for the chequered French war record on the Nazis, and exaggerated the part of the French resistance, heroes of the resistance were prominent on the French section of the IMT bench and amongst the French prosecutors.[9] In the French prosecution case on war crimes and crimes against humanity in Western Europe, Jews were for the most part notable by their absence, most starkly so in the closing address of the French chief prosecutor François de Menthon.[10] Even the one French witness who shed as much light at Nuremberg as any victim on the fate of the Jews at the largest Nazi extermination centre was representationally problematic. Marie-Claude Vaillant-Couturier had been transported from Ravensbrück to Auschwitz, there to witness the selection process for the gas chambers. The memory of this formidable witness proved accurate in every respect except those on which she could only speculate.[11] But in addition to her strength of character and memory, Vaillant-Couturier had one quality as a witness that made her attractive to the French, so much so that the French authorities used her in other contexts beyond the trial.[12] She had been deported to Auschwitz as a member of the resistance.

The case of Britain was slightly different. Britain had been a classic 'bystander' state to genocide, but, uniquely in Europe, had neither been militarily occupied or defeated. Nevertheless, Britain followed the rest of Europe in being heavily concerned in its war crimes trial programme with crimes committed against British servicemen. Like the other powers occupying Germany, it also acquired a responsibility for reckoning with offences committed within its zone of occupation. This zone

---

[8] Trial of the Major War Criminals before the International Military Tribunal, 42 vols. (Nuremberg: IMT, 1947) (hereafter 'IMT'), vol. 8, p. 322. Emphasis added. See Alexander Victor Prusin, '"Fascist Criminals to the Gallows!": The Holocaust and Soviet War Crimes Trials, December 1945-February 1946', Holocaust and Genocide Studies, vol. 17, no. 1 (2003), 1-30, on the way that crimes against Jews were represented in Soviet courts.

[9] Robert H. Jackson papers, Library of Congress, Washington, D.C., container 191, 'Justice Jackson's Story', fols. 1345-7. On French attitudes, see the literature cited in note 7 above.

[10] IMT, vol. 5, pp. 368-426.

[11] IMT, vol. 6, pp. 203-27.

[12] On the uses of Vaillant-Couturier, Annette Wieviorka, "La construction de la mémoire du génocide en France", Le Monde Juif, no. 149 (1993), pp. 24-6.

effectively became part of Britain's 'backyard', and the trials of various concentration, labour and prison camps constituted the other major component of the British trial programme.[13]

British perceptions of Nazi criminality were shaped, and remained so for decades, by the institutions that British troops encountered as they occupied German territory. In much the same way that Buchenwald and Dachau were to colour American perceptions, the Bergen-Belsen concentration camp came to symbolise German perfidy. However the Belsen that the British media described to the domestic audience was not the same as that remembered today, primarily because of the silence surrounding the preponderance of Jewish inmates; a silence stemming, it seems, from the prevailing British institutional determination not to be seen to be fighting a war on behalf of the Jews.[14] Moreover, Belsen was clearly not representative of the extremes of Nazi population policy in that it was not the same as the Polish extermination centres of the 'final solution'. The rather partial picture of Nazi criminality presented by the western concentration camps liberated by the western Allies was also widely disseminated in Germany through occupation films, newspapers, newsreels and inmate memoirs licensed for publication, and through forcing the German public to visit the camps.[15]

If Britain effectively domesticated a German institution of atrocity for its own war memory, Germany itself remained entirely insular in its preoccupations. Given the extent of German criminality in WWII it is perhaps understandable that many latter-day historians have seen in German self-pity only a cynical diversionary tactic. However, not only did the concern with the national fate mirror such concerns elsewhere, the sheer dimensions of German suffering at the close of the war and the rather sudden onset of such suffering within national boundaries were inevitably to colour any German perception. The influx of millions of 'Volksdeutsche' refugees and expellees from eastern- and southern-central Europe, the experience of increasingly massive area bombing, and the loss of further millions of menfolk either on the battlefield or to Soviet POW camps, combined with the effect of military defeat and occupation had a traumatic effect that was not diminished in German eyes by the objective fact that its cause lay in the Nazi campaigns of aggression.[16] As for the Nuremberg and other trials, these were seen by many Germans – however perversely – as another form of victimisation, a simple extension of the punitive occupation of the country.

The other popular German reaction to the trial of the major war criminals – besides ignorance and nigh ubiquitous boredom – was to place all of the blame for Germany's misfortunes on the men in the dock, and thus to exculpate the German masses and, indeed, anyone below the very highest rank of perpetrators. There was a particular enthusiasm in this connection to protest against any indictment of German servicemen. Ultimately the concept of the serviceman was extended not just to all of the military and indeed paramilitary forces of the Third Reich, but also to the majority of state functionaries – hence the enduring popularity of the flawed defence that Germans were only obeying senior orders. Moreover, Germans were not slow to point out that the German concentration camps that the Allies were so keen to highlight contained many Germans targeted by the Nazi regime, thus providing another spurious defence concerning the distance between the Nazi leadership and the people.[17] The commonality between these varying responses was that in none of them were Germans really interested in courtroom information about Nazi atrocities, but simply in distancing themselves from such deeds either by focusing upon the perceived inequities of the trial medium – as ex post facto justice, or 'victor's justice', or whatever – or by averring that the trials and their subject-matter had nothing to do with them anyway.

---

[13] Donald Bloxham, "British War Crimes Trial Policy in Germany, 1945-1957: Implementation and Collapse", Journal of British Studies, vol. 42, no. 1 (2003), 91-118.

[14] Tony Kushner, The Holocaust and the Liberal Imagination: a Social and Cultural History (Oxford: Blackwell, 1994).

[15] Bloxham, Genocide on Trial, pp. 80-90.

[16] Moeller, War Stories; Norbert Frei, Vergangenheitspolitik: Die Anfänge der Bundesrepublik und die NS-Vergangenheit (Munich: C.H. Beck, 1996).; Neil Gregor, "'Is he still alive, or long since dead?': Loss, Absence and Remembrance in Nuremberg, 1945-1956', German History, vol. 21, no. 2 (2003), 183-203; Michael L. Hughes, "'Through No Fault of Our Own': West Germans Remember Their War Losses", German History, vol. 18, no. 2 (2000), 193-213.

[17] On German responses to the IMT trial and the occupation, see Bloxham, Genocide on Trial, pp. 80-88, 137-53.

There is one clear exception to the generalisation about narrow national interest amongst all parties. The American agenda at Nuremberg, as opposed to the US Dachau trial programme, and irrespective of any inconsistencies of problems that we might identify with it, was quite consciously intended as a universalistic exercise with genuinely international ramifications and aspirations for the regulation of international affairs in future. One suspects that it was easier for American representatives to take a broader view at this time since of all the big four powers the USA had been by far the least affected by the hardships of war, and therefore was least concerned with a 'national' reckoning; at the same time, the 'big idea' of Nuremberg was consistent with certain traditions of American optimism about the regulatory role that law might play in international affairs as in domestic, constitution-bound life. Whatever the precise combination of reasons, the American approach to Nuremberg stands in sharp contrast, for example, to the initial British refusal to engage with the idea of an international court for international crimes, and indeed the legal conservatism of the British in everything they did outside of their association with the USA at Nuremberg.[18] Moreover, the American commitment to the goals of the IMT prosecution was strong enough to ensure the single-handed extension of the effort through the subsequent proceedings programme.

Paradoxically, it was the very universalism of American intentions that prevented a more extensive focus on the 'final solution' in the US prosecution effort. The 'final solution' and contingent parts thereof were to be used simply as illustrations of the crimes emerging from the 'supreme crime' of aggressive war; indeed, they would be used more-or-less interchangeably with what were in US Chief Prosecutor Robert Jackson's lexicon called 'representative examples' of atrocity selected from across the full spectrum of Nazi criminality.[19] This notion of 'representative examples' actually provided leeway for the use by France and the USSR of instances favourable to their own agendas, while the Anglo-Saxons continued as a rule to prefer evidence from German concentration camps rather than eastern extermination centres. More than this, some of the (Anglo-)American ambivalences evinced in responses to the 'final solution' during the war were also manifest in an apparent reluctance to give the Jewish fate in its specificity too great a proportion of attention at the trial.

When confronted with Jewish organisations requesting representation on the prosecution this was refused by Jackson, but not on the grounds given in reply to a similar request by the Polish Government, namely that it was logistically impossible to give time and space to all interested parties.[20] Rather, as Jackson recalled, he had wished to 'get away from the racial aspects of the situation': 'we didn't want to exaggerate racial tensions'. 'The only thing to do about that was to avoid making [Nuremberg] a vengeance trial',[21] he claimed, thus playing unfortunately into the stereotype of the vengeful Jew. Jackson was prepared to admit Chaim Weizmann as an expert witness for the prosecution on the murder of the Jews, but only on the condition of prior presentation of a statement carefully prepared in advance; Weizmann demurred. (The British remained faithful to their perennial line in insisting that it would be preferable to have non-Jews testify.)[22] Colonel Murray Bernays, the inventor of the 'conspiracy – criminal organisation plan' had earlier gone a little further still, and suggested that it would give 'added authority' to the American case if 'the Jewish problem [was] assigned to a group of high churchmen' for presentation in court.[23]

Tied into knots by his strategic-cum-ideological dilemma, Jackson was happy to have Jewish lawyers on his team, as long as they were not involved in presenting the Jewish case. As he said, "we

---

[18] Priscilla Dale Jones, "British Policy towards German Crimes against German Jews, 1939-45", Leo Baeck Institute Yearbook, vol. 36 (1991), 339-66.

[19] Bloxham, Genocide on Trial, pp. 62-3.

[20] Ann Tusa and John Tusa, The Nuremburg Trial (London: Atheneum, 1983), pp. 103-4.

[21] 'Justice Jackson's story', fols. 1075-7.

[22] Ibid, fols. 1076-7; Jacob Robinson, 'The International Military Tribunal and the Holocaust: Some Legal Reflections', in Michael R. Marrus (ed.), The Nazi Holocaust, 9 parts (London: Meckler, 1989), part 9, p. 610; Marrus, "The Holocaust at Nuremberg", p. 13.

[23] Jackson Papers, container 107, "Office files, US Chief-of-Counsel: pre-trial planning", Bernays to Jackson, 3 July 1945.

thought it would be just as bad not to let any appear as it would be to let too many appear."[24] Likewise, both Jackson and the British were prepared to seek information pertaining to the Holocaust from Jewish sources, provided, as the British put it, they were 'reliable' conduits (which presumably implied them not being stridently Zionist).[25] But Jews could not be allowed to be seen to describe the fate of their kin either as prosecutors or witnesses; this was the task of 'objective' Nazi documentation on the one hand, and the voice of 'universal' opinion – personified in US Supreme Court Justice Jackson – on the other. By the same token, no individual crime against a specific group, however vast, could be allowed to supplant the quasi-universalist focus on prosecuting the waging of aggressive warfare. But irrespective of the precise balance of representation in the IMT's proceedings, the key point to bear in mind in terms of collective memory-formation is that for aforementioned reasons the courtroom discussions fell largely on deaf ears.

The subsequent Nuremberg trials continued the titanic American effort, and their main thrust was to try to reinforce what had only tentatively been established by the IMT about the scope of German military and industrial responsibility for the Nazi campaigns of aggressive war. Nevertheless, other criminal complexes were also examined, including some of the primary agencies of the 'final solution' (if the most obviously relevant case, that of Ohlendorf and other Einsatzgruppen leaders, was only brought, despite it being a relatively lowly priority, because the surviving Nazi documentation promised a swift, open-and-shut case)[26]. Yet it is a sad truth that public attention and media coverage dwindled almost in inverse relation to the degree to which the detail and extent of Nazi criminality was being laid bare in court. Most of the subsequent trials were conducted amid virtual press silence, and when the trials were made the focus of public discourse this was to criticise the trial medium rather than the message.

In a more unambiguous fashion than in 1945-6 with the IMT trial, the subsequent Nuremberg trials became the focus of a revisionist nationalism whose concerns were re-establishing German sovereignty and removing the taint on the German name that war crimes trials represented. In October 1950, the reactions analysis staff of the US High Commission encountered the greatest shift in German societal attitudes ever recorded to that time. Only thirty-eight percent of a sample of 2,000 people regarded the IMT trial as having been conducted fairly, compared to the seventy-eight percent registered four years earlier.[27]

The increasingly strident West German rejection of the Allied trial programmes was, like the German attitude to the wartime atrocities themselves, not as exceptional as it might at first glance appear. If each country had its own concerns to highlight or downplay in the post-war years, the development of these national agendas was, equally, bound together in a series of temporal waves. 'Mastering the past' – 'Vergangenheitsbewältigung' – was everywhere aided by the cold war.

The rhythms of the 'post-war decade'

Across the European board, among the countries liberated from Nazi rule in the period, the years 1944-5 saw the aforementioned purges, where rough justice and political solutions frequently preceded

---

[24] Justice Jackson's story, fol. 1077.
[25] Public Record Office, Kew, London (hereafter, 'PRO'), WO 311/39, British War Crimes Executive to Foreign Office, 8 April 1946, requesting details of estimated numbers of Jewish dead, to be used in the cross-examination of Julius Streicher. The statistics were to be provided by the Board of Deputies of British Jews or "other reliable Jewish organisations." For further comments as to the relative merits of different Jewish organisations, see PRO, FO 371/ 57561, Henderson to FO, 10 January 1946. Herein, the author favours representation at the IMT trial of the Board of Deputies over that of "the more extreme bodies such as the [World Jewish] Congress".
[26] Bloxham, Genocide on Trial, pp. 72-3.
[27] Anna J. Merritt and Richard L. Merritt (eds.), Public Opinion in Semisovereign Germany: the HICOG Surveys, 1949-1955 (Chicago, Illinois: University of Illinois Press, 1980), p. 101, HiCOG report no.57. Indeed, in August 1949, a cross section of West German university students – the potential leaders of that nation – rejected in the ratio of seven to one the right of the Allies to judge war criminals; George Gallup (ed.), The Gallup Poll: Public Opinion 1935-1971, vol.1, 1935-1948 (New York, NY: Random House, 1972), p. 842.

any formal legal reckoning. Thereafter for perhaps another year – the period that Jeffrey Herf labels the 'Nuremberg interregnum', but which might better be characterised by the epithet the last year of the 'antifascist consensus'[28] – the determination for a reckoning with the past was clearly still evident, despite early signs of a rift between Western and Eastern Allies. The IMT trial, the high watermark of judicial process at a point shortly succeeding the open bloodletting, therefore also occurred within this time-frame.

In Germany, the years 1945-6 were the harshest occupation years, with non-fraternization regulations strictly enforced in the spirit of the earlier demand for unconditional surrender, and denazification in full force. While British and American domestic constituencies were rapidly losing interest in issues of trial and occupation, and starting to address the needs of demobilisation and reconstruction, so much so that midway through the IMT trial the British chief prosecutor Hartley Shawcross had to plead with the press magnate Lord Beaverbrook to devote more column inches to the case in his newspapers, and that the BBC had withdrawn its reporter by the beginning of 1946,[29] the Allied 're-education' programmes continued to focus on the issues of complicity in Nazism, and the aforementioned concentration camp imagery was used extensively both to shame the populace and ram home the justification for occupation.

The decline and fall of the anti-fascist consensus was also the beginning of the cold war proper. The year 1947 brought with it serious schisms in the council of foreign ministers of the 'big four' powers; the announcement of the Truman Doctrine; intensified Stalinization in eastern Germany and throughout the Soviet sphere; and the eviction of socialists from a number of coalition governments in the west. Even earlier than this, during the course of 1946, the British government had decided for good realpolitik reasons that there was no utility in proceeding with a mooted second quadripartite trial of major war criminals, and was accordingly instrumental in scuppering French and Soviet plans for the trial.[30] In the changed international environment of 1947, purges and war crimes trials programmes everywhere were being wound down, their focuses ever more narrowly brought to bear on matters of solely national interest before they were closed down altogether in the succeeding months and, at most, very few years. States in the west were now 'allowed', if not encouraged, to put aside awkward wartime memories while emphasizing their anticommunist credentials; states in the communist east were encouraged to overplay wartime antifascism and resistance. On both sides many state functionaries compromised in the war years were kept in post, illustrating the limits of denazification across the board.[31]

As the cold war set in, so too did an increasingly explicit tendency on either side of the iron curtain to use and abuse for political ends the record of Nazi atrocity. Whereas in 1945-6 there had been a certain plurality of victim voices in both East and West Germany, these were rendered increasingly uniform thereafter. Thus, for instance, we see the promotion in the Soviet-controlled media of the East German zone of individuals like Walter Bartel, the former head of Buchenwald's International Resistance Committee, a communist with distinctly anti-western leanings.[32] Owing to the leftist-dominated prisoner rising in Buchenwald, that camp became a particular focus of eastern German remembrance, but at Sachsenhausen too political prisoners were prioritised in memory by the large memorial obelisk bedecked with a red triangle alone, while the ruins of the crematoria mentioned only the Soviet POWs murdered there (in an interesting inversion of the pattern of memory in the west, where the massive tragedy of millions of POW deaths has long been ignored). Corresponding to the

---

[28] Jeffrey Herf, Divided Memory: the Nazi Past in the Two Germanies (Cambridge, Mass: Harvard University Press, 1997), cf. Geoff Eley, Forging Democracy: the History of the Left in Europe, 1850-2000 (New York, NY: Oxford University Press, 2002).
[29] Bloxham, Genocide on Trial, p. 147.
[30] Donald Bloxham, "'The Trial That Never Was': Why there was no Second International Trial of Major War Criminals at Nuremberg?", History, vol. 87, no. 285 (2002), 41-60.
[31] Deak, Gross and Judt (eds.), The Politics of Retribution; Frei, Vergangenheitspolitik.
[32] Christoph Classen, Faschismus und Antifaschismus. Die nationalsozialistische Vergangenheit im ostdeutschen Hörfunk (Cologne: Böhlau Verlag, 2004), pp. 228-9.

grossly disproportional emphasis on the resistance movements within these camps and within the Soviet sphere as a whole, there was little emphasis on other camp inmates, be they homosexuals, Romanies or Jews.[33]

The symbolic significance of individual survivor-witnesses and institutions was not lost on the British and the American occupiers either. Indeed, contrary to stock generalisations about the difficulties the Allies had in getting to grips with the scale and complexity of Nazi criminality, the Allied authorities in Germany showed themselves aware about and adept at selecting from the range of Nazi crimes. A report produced in April 1945 by the influential Psychological Warfare Department (PWD) of the joint Allied supreme command SHAEF[34] on the making of a documentary on the concentration camps aimed to 'promote German acceptance of the justice of the Allied occupiers by reminding Germans of their past acquiescence' and therefore, their 'responsibility'. However it also aimed to show specific crimes committed in the German name to rouse the populace against the Nazis. The latter was to be accomplished specifically by focusing upon German victims of atrocities, and if possible, personalising them by establishing their individual identities.[35]

Finding iconic 'good' Germans who had been mistreated by the Nazis was naturally an important part of leading the country towards democracy in illustrating by example the existence of political alternatives and moral choice. Yet the straightforward message could and would be subverted, notably in the case of the military 'resistance' in Germany, whose most ostentatious act was the bomb plot on their leader's life on 20 July 1944. Their actions, as recorded in 1946 in Schlabrendorff's *Offiziere gegen Hitler* and in 1947-8 in Allen Dulles's *Germany's Underground*[36] and Hans Bernd Gisevius's *Bis zum bitteren Ende*[37] provided apparent testimony to both Germany and the west[38] to the rift between the established order and Nazism, and 20 July remains a touchstone of all those wishing to mitigate German guilt, regardless of the true and often tainted motives and characters of the resistors.[39]

Once again, the institutions in which iconic Germans such as some of the aforementioned, and the likes of the prominent Christian Martin Niemöller, had been incarcerated were orthodox concentration camps. PWD consciously deployed these camps in its metamorphosing propaganda campaign, as for instance in its sponsorship of the writing of a treatise on the camp system by the survivor of Buchenwald (and another prominent Christian) Eugen Kogon. Interestingly, the final chapters of the second (German) edition of Kogon's *Der SS-Staat* and the first edition in English translation, *The Theory and Practice of Hell* (1948), are given over to a comparative examination of the use of prison camps in the USSR under Stalin. This nourished the parallel Allied trend towards using the concentration camps as generic symbols of totalitarian domination rather than specific manifestations of Nazism - an approach adopted in British information policy in May 1948 when it was decided for anti-communist reasons to broadcast information on Soviet camps and Stalinist deportations.[40] There was certainly no place now for the depiction of Soviet citizens as victims of Germany.

---

[33] Mary Fulbrook, German National Identity after the Holocaust (Cambridge: Polity Press, 1999), pp. 28-35. See also Peter Reichel, Politik mit der Erinnerung. Gedächtnisorte im Streit um die nationalsozialistische Vergangenheit (Munich: Hanser, 1995).

[34] On the PWD, Kurt Koszyk, Pressepolitik für Deutsche 1945-49. Geschichte der deutschen Presse Teil IV (Berlin: Colloquium, 1986), pp. 21-3.

[35] University of Warwick, Modern Records Centre, Crossman papers, MSS.154/3/PW/1/1-211. SHAEF PWD report, 25 April 1945.

[36] New York, 1947.

[37] Vols. 1 and 2, Darmstadt, 1947/8.

[38] Thomas Alan Schwartz, America's Germany (Cambridge, Mass, 1991), p. 158, on the influence of Dulles's (highly propagandist) work on moderating western opinion; Helmut Peitsch, 'Deutsche Gedächtnis an seine dunkelste Zeit'. Zur Funktion der Autobiographik in den Westzonen Deutschlands und den Westsektoren von Berlin 1945 bis 1949 (Berlin: edition Sigma, 1990), pp. 48-9 on Gisevius's work.

[39] David Clay Large, "A Beacon in the German Darkness: The Anti-Nazi Resistance Legacy in West German Politics," Journal of Modern History, vol. 164 (1992), supplement, 173-86.

[40] Koszyk, Pressepolitik für Deutsche, 233.

While 'western' atrocity propaganda policies never went as far as its 'eastern' counterpart in suggesting that the legacy of Nazism had been fully dealt with, the 'western' focus on German icons of suffering and its increasing anticommunism was ever less well equipped to counteract the German nationalist propaganda of the time. One thing, though, is for certain: despite their differences in focus, one hugely significant commonality in both propaganda approaches was the substantial omission of reference to Jews, the 'final solution', and the eastern extermination centres.

Again, the major exception to these generalisations about the cold war and changing depictions of Nazi criminality is the subsequent Nuremberg trials. That the American trial structures survived into 1950 despite significant political and (thus) budgetary pressure from within Congress, and despite the 1947 shift in US occupation policy from 're-education' to the milder 're-orientation', is testament to the huge commitment of Telford Taylor and his liberal, Harvard Law School-oriented staff, and of the US zonal military governor, Lucius Clay. As I have argued elsewhere, however, had Clay had less autonomy in his sphere and been subject to the same sort of close control by the State Department as the British representatives in Germany had been by the Foreign Office, it is not at all clear that the subsequent proceedings venture would long have survived 1947.[41] Less hypothetically, the wider changes in US occupation policy meant that the subsequent proceedings were left increasingly exposed to German nationalist – and right-wing American – attack as an 'unnecessary' vestige of early occupation policy. Once again, whatever was said in the courtrooms of the subsequent proceedings was drowned-out in the wave of nationalist rhetoric that was primarily concerned with German interests and victimhood.[42]

The swift disintegration of the Nuremberg edifice from the early 1950s on the watch of High Commissioner John J. McCloy and in the succeeding years was all the more spectacular for the surprising length of time that it had survived in the late 1940s. This collapse was, in the eyes of political contemporaries (if not their legal counterparts, who could still point to the legal record as history and as precedent), complete by 1958. By that point, all of the convicted war criminals incarcerated in the American zone jail at Landsberg – including prominent Einsatzgruppen leaders and leading members of the concentration camp administration – had been released, and many of them well before the exhaustion of their original sentences, as the result of a series of politically-related measures of clemency and sentence review designed to appease German nationalist sentiment in a cold war context of prospective German rearmament.[43] The British jails at Werl and Wittlich were emptied a year earlier. The timetable of releases brought the hitherto exceptional American trial venture back into synchronisation with other national trial and purge programmes as what Tony Judt has called the 'post-war decade' of approximately 1945-56 drew to a close.[44] The only prisoners not to benefit from this chronic bout of leniency were those major war criminals still serving sentences passed down by the IMT: under quadripartite control in Spandau jail, they could not be released without gaining a near-impossible four power consensus.

The context of remilitarisation in the 1950s explains why McCloy was at pains to point out that the honour of the German army had not been brought into question by the earlier American prosecution of a number of its most prominent soldiers.[45] On the back of the manipulation of national memory by the Adenauer government, and the prevalent focus on German wartime and post-war suffering, this reversal of American priorities and the undermining of Telford Taylor's work[46] served simply to reinforce the

---

[41] Bloxham, Genocide on Trial, pp. 54-5.
[42] Frank Buscher, The US War Crimes Trial Programme in Germany, 1946-1955 (Westport, CT: Greenwood Press, 1989).
[43] Ibid; Thomas Alan Schwartz, "Die Begnadigung deutscher Kriegsverbrecher: John J. McCloy und die Häftlinge von Landsberg", Vierteljahreshefte für Zeitgeschichte, vol. 38 (1990), 375-414; Peter Maguire, Law and War: An American Story (New York, NY: Columbia University Press, 2001).
[44] See Judt's preface to Judt, Deak and Gross (eds.), The Politics of Retribution in Europe, p. ix.
[45] PRO, LCO 2/4428, HiCoG Public Relations Division APO 757-A, p. 6.
[46] Telford Taylor, "The Nazis go Free", Nation, 24 February 1951, pp. 170-172.

popular west German wisdom that the Nuremberg trials could be disposed of as merely a form of victor's justice.

Aftermaths

Much has changed since the 1950s in German attitudes towards Nuremberg and the crimes addressed – at least in part – there. Germany today has some of the most enthusiastic proponents of the International Criminal Court and of the international prosecution of the perpetrators not just of war crimes and of crimes against humanity but also of aggressive war. It would, however, be a mistake to infer from these self-evident facts that the Nuremberg trials were somehow ultimately responsible for such shifts in opinion. This would be to confuse cause and effect. Rather, the re-evaluation of 'Nuremberg' has been a mere function of the changing German attitudes towards the Nazi past as a whole.

In the 1960s and 1970s the Nuremberg trials served in West Germany as a dual-faceted symbol of guilt and the imposition of punishment by alien powers. They also became a stick with which to beat other states in way that was partly founded on legitimate criticism but was also partly an extension of the *tu quoque* charge. During the Vietnam War, evidence of American atrocities and the suspicion of imperialist ends elicited criticism of the American hypocrisy in the conduct of international affairs and a comparison of American guilt with that of the Nazis. Manifestly symbolic also was the inauguration by the German Greens of a 'war crimes' tribunal in Nuremberg at the height of the arms race, designed to draw attention to American nuclear strategy.[47] A less defensive engagement with the trials gradually developed in relation to a growing acquaintance with the Holocaust and other Nazi crimes in the final decades of the Federal Republic. This was primarily an outcome of a generational shift in values and perspectives.

Germany's present confrontation with its past is more extensive and intensive than any equivalent commitment by a former perpetrator state anywhere in the world. This is testament to the success of educational initiatives in an atmosphere of strong civic responsibility. Of the key moments in the development of 'Holocaust-awareness', however, the Nuremberg trials are notable by their absence. The popularisation of the story of Anne Frank was vital,[48] though it was surpassed by the screening in 1979 on national television of the American mini-series Holocaust;[49] but these in turn would not have had such an impact had not the ground been prepared by the student movement of the late 1960s, in which the 'guilt of the fathers' was brought to the fore by a German youth that implicitly felt itself to be innocent. And since Germans born in the decades after the war could clearly have no personal responsibility for Germany's crimes of aggression and murder, they also saw less need than their 'fathers' and 'mothers' to reject the accusations of criminality launched at the latter in Nuremberg.

In other words, cultural changes have influenced as a by-product the way the legal event is viewed in Germany (and elsewhere); the legal event did not shape the cultural change. This observation is of contemporary importance, since, alongside the popular but unproven and probably unprovable assertion of the deterrent effect of war crimes trials, they are also commonly promoted as re-educational media, a contention that the experience of the Nuremberg trials does not support. The other relevant part of a burgeoning 'Nuremberg hagiography' is the notion, addressed at the outset of this paper, that the IMT trial had as one of its primary foci the Nazi genocide of the Jews and its perpetrators. It may well be that this is simply how collective memory works, that in a Holocaust-conscious world we will see the Holocaust where we wish to see it, and where better than at Nuremberg, in that now-idealised forum of

---

[47] Dan Diner, Verkehrte Welten: Antiamerikanismus in Deutschland: Eine historischer Essay (Frankfurt am Main: Eichborn, 1993), pp. 141-2, 147-8; Werner Jochmann, Gesellschaftskrise und Judenfeindschaft in Deutschland 1870-1945 (Hamburg: Hans Christians Verlag, 1988), p. 337.

[48] Werner Bergmann, "Die Reaktion auf den Holocaust in Westdeutschland von 1945 bis 1989",Geschichte in Wissenschaft und Unterricht, 43 (1992), 327-50, here pp. 329, 332, 350.

[49] Henryk M.Broder, Volk und Wahn (Hamburg: Spiegel Buchverlag, 1996), 215-16.

American-inspired reckoning with Nazism?[50] And better still that this Holocaust-conscious representation of the past ties in with current agendas for 'humanitarian intervention' in genocidal states. Yet above all others, scholars of the Holocaust should be aware of the perils of allowing the historical record to be distorted by ex post facto considerations, however these may support our designs to regulate the affairs of today's turbulent world.

---

[50] The recent rise of a much less critical overall approach to the Nuremberg trial – less critical, that is, than approaches that pointed out firstly technical, legal and procedural problems with the trial, secondly the issues of Anglo-French-American collaboration with prosecutors from a genocidal regime (in the USSR), and thirdly the elision of such issues as area bombing that would have been susceptible to the *tu quoque* charge – is presumably in part a function of the end of the Cold War. With the end of overarching bi-polar superpower politics and the pure geopolitical 'realism' that accompanied foreign policy decision-making on both sides in that era, it has become possible again to pay lip-service to the rule of law in international affairs and the principle of universal jurisdiction that Nuremberg did so much too establish – always allowing, of course, that the current world hegemon, the USA, reserves the right not to play by the rules it is happy to insist on selectively elsewhere, as illustrated by its recent illegal invasion of Iraq and opposition to the Rome Treaty for the International Criminal Court. (On which, see Michael P. Scharf, "The ICC's Jurisdiction over the Nationals of Non-Party States: a Critique of the US Position", Law and Contemporary Problems, vol. 64, no. 1 (2001), 67-117.).

Donald Bloxham

Völkermord vor Gericht: Recht und kollektives Gedächtnis

Dieser Beitrag befasst sich mit dem Einfluss der Hauptkriegsverbrecherprozesse und anderer Fälle auf die Entstehung einer kollektiven Erinnerung an Nazi-Verbrechen. Es werden die Nachkriegsjahre in Europa insgesamt untersucht, bevor sich der Fokus auf Westdeutschland richtet, den eigentlichen Mittelpunkt der alliierten „Umerziehungs"-Anstrengungen, bei denen die Nürnberger Prozesse einen essentiellen Bestandteil bildeten. Das Ergebnis der Untersuchung ist, dass die Prozesse wenig zur Entwicklung eines kollektiven Verstehens oder Bewusstseins im Hinblick auf den Holocaust oder andere NS-Völkermorde beigetragen haben. Im Prozess gegen die Hauptkriegsverbrecher spielte die „Endlösung" eine relativ geringe Rolle, zumal die Aufmerksamkeit in jedem europäischen Land, Deutschland eingeschlossen, zu diesem Zeitpunkt auf die eigenen Sorgen und auf die Bildung einer Mythologie gerichtet war, um die Wiederherstellung der jeweils eigenen nationalen Identität zu unterstützen. Der sich entwickelnde Kalte Krieg verstärkte noch die Tendenz, die Verbrechen des Zweiten Weltkrieges zu ignorieren und sich den „Lektionen" von Nürnberg zu entziehen. Die positivere deutsche Haltung gegenüber den Nürnberger Prozessen in jüngerer Zeit ist hingegen das Resultat einer mit dem Generationenwechsel verbundenen vertieften Auseinandersetzung mit der NS-Vergangenheit ganz allgemein. Die Umerziehungseffekte der Prozesse an sich waren unwesentlich.

Sam Garkawe

The Role and Rights of Victims at the Nuremberg International Military Tribunal

I. Introduction

One of the least analysed and discussed aspect of the Nuremberg IMT is the relatively small emphasis that was placed on role and rights of the victims[1] and survivors[2] of Nazi policies during the Tribunal's proceedings. This may come as a surprise to many people, given that one of the main perceived purposes of the trial was to provide a sense of justice and vindication for the millions of victims of Nazi policies. However, the American and British prosecutors failed to call any survivors to testify. Although French and Soviet prosecutors did call a number of survivors to provide evidence during the trial,[3] the reality was that these survivor witnesses were peripheral to the proceedings given that the trial was very much dominated by the American prosecution case and approach. The overall conclusion that one draws in examining the trial from the perspective of victims and survivors is that it was a disappointment. This was not just because the American (and British) prosecutors failed to call any survivors to testify, thus largely excluding survivors from the proceedings,[4] but was also due to the founding Statute of the IMT making no mention of the words 'victim' or 'survivor'. This meant that the IMT did not foresee that survivors might testify or otherwise have some role in proceedings, and would thus need to have rights to protection and support before, during and after their testimony. Furthermore, the possibility of victims and survivors receiving or being awarded some form of reparations was never discussed before or during the IMT proceedings.

This situation should be compared and contrasted to recent international criminal courts, where I would argue that the trend towards enhanced victim awareness, support, protection, reparation and participation has been one of the greatest innovations of modern international criminal justice. After a considerable hiatus in the formation of international criminal courts during the Cold War period, the International Criminal Tribunal for the former Yugoslavia (the 'ICTY') was established by the UN Security Council in 1993.[5] The Statute of the ICTY introduced a number of innovative and progressive measures to assist and protect victims that represented a great advance for the rights and concerns of victims internationally. These measures were largely replicated by the Statute of the International Criminal Tribunal for Rwanda (the 'ICTR') formed in the following year.[6] These measures included,

---

[1] Defining the word 'victim' is often fraught with difficulties and in many cases will depend on the context in which it is used. For the purposes of this article, a 'victim' will be broadly defined as someone who had been killed, injured, imprisoned, denied their liberty or otherwise suffered harm as a direct result of Nazi racial and other repressive policies. These victims of the Nazis or their allies included a wide variety of minorities, the most prominent being Jews, Gypsies, disabled persons, gays and lesbians, Slavs, other religious minorities, and people of colour. The definition includes people whom, although not direct victims of Nazi policies in the above sense, nevertheless were in a close relationship with someone who suffered from any of these types of harms.

[2] A 'survivor' in the sense used in this article will be someone, who lived through imprisonment or other forms of denial of liberty, torture, or other forms of harm as a direct result of Nazi racial policies or policies of repression. Thus for the purposes of this article all survivors were also victims.

[3] For example, evidence of the conditions at Auschwitz was provided by a French survivor Marie Vaillant-Couturier, and by a Soviet survivor Severina Shmaglerskaya. See Conot R, *Justice at Nuremberg*, Harper & Row Publishers, 1983, at 300 and 304 respectively. The Russians also called Abram Suzkever (testified on the liquidation of the Vilna ghetto) and Samuel Rajzman (testified on Treblinka). Lawrence Douglas makes the interesting point that the three Russian witnesses were presented in a way to the IMT that seemed to obscure the fact that they were Jewish. See Douglas L, *The Memory of Judgment: Making Law and History in the Trials of the Holocaust*, Yale University Press, 2001, at 78-79.

[4] It is true that a number of American Jewish organisations attempted to influence the American government in their approach to the Tribunal. However, such organisations did not generally represent survivors (who were principally the remnants of *European* Jewry), and the influence of these organisations did not appear to have been great anyway.

[5] See Resolution 827, which was passed by the Security Council on the 25 May 1993. It is significant that the Security Council acted under Part VII of the UN Charter as this means that all member States of the UN are bound to cooperate with the ICTY.

[6] The ICTR was established by Security Council Resolution 955, passed in November 1994.

first, the establishment of Victims and Witness Units or Sections[7] to assist and support victims in their dealings with the respective Tribunals.[8] Secondly, the Tribunals were given the power to develop special procedural rules or measures of protection for victims and witnesses.[9] Thirdly, special 'vulnerable' victims, particularly women and children, were given special consideration in the rules developed by the ICTY and ICTR.[10] The final feature of the ICTY was that for the first time an international criminal court made an attempt to facilitate victim reparation or compensation.[11] The Statute of the International Criminal Court (ICC) agreed to at Rome in 1998 not only replicates these measures, but also introduces a number of further innovations in favour of victims. For the first time in international criminal justice the ICC Statute allows for the possibility of victims having their own legal representation, and thus playing an active part in the proceedings.[12] This is very much in line with the Continental European criminal justice model.[13] The ICC Statute also provides for a much more serious attempt to ensure victims receive reparation. This includes the ability of the ICC to make orders for 'appropriate' reparations directly against convicted offenders in favour of victims,[14] and the establishment of a victims' Trust Fund that can also be utilised to satisfy any orders for victim reparations.[15]

In a previous article I set out what I perceived to be the main reasons *why* there has been this large turnaround in concern for and in the rights of victims and survivors in modern international criminal courts as compared to the IMT.[16] I do not wish to repeat what I said there, but what I intend to do in this article is to first make the argument in Part II as to why more survivors *should* have testified and generally have been more involved in the proceedings of the IMT. Part III will then examine the reasons why victims played such a relatively small role in the IMT. It will be seen that many of these reasons were genuine ones. However, it will be the major contention of this article that none of these reasons should have precluded more survivors from testifying and being involved in the IMT proceedings. Consequently, each of these reasons for the lack of survivor involvement will be analysed in Part IV in order to see how the genuine concerns against survivor testimony could have been overcome or at least

---

[7] The ICTY's Unit has been described as "the first of its kind in any international context". See Rydberg A, 'The Protection of the Interests of Witnesses – The ICTY in Comparison to the Future ICC' (1999) 12 *Leiden Journal of International Law* 455 at 462

[8] This includes administrative, financial and other practical arrangements to bring a witness from their country to The Hague or Arusha, and providing basic information to witnesses regarding the work of the Tribunals and trial procedures. The Units also offer emotional support and counselling and arranges medical and psychological care where needed, as well as provides protection to witnesses during their stay at The Hague or Arusha. Another important task of the Units is to make recommendations to the Tribunals regarding what special protection measures for witnesses might be needed. See Rydberg A, ibid.

[9] See Article 22 of the ICTY Statute ('The International Tribunal shall provide in its rules of procedure and evidence for the protection of victims and witnesses. ....'). See also Garkawe S, 'Victims and the International Criminal Court: Three major issues' (2003) 3 *International Criminal Law Review* 345 at 353-354 for a list of the special measures that were developed by the ICTY.

[10] For example, Rule 96 of the ICTY's *Rules of Procedure and Evidence* specifies, *inter alia*, that in cases of sexual assault no corroboration of the victim's testimony shall be required, the defence of consent is to be limited, and that a victim's prior sexual history shall not be admitted in evidence.

[11] See Rules 98(B), 105 and 106 of the ICTY's *Rules of Procedure and Evidence*. These are considered to be weak provisions and unlikely 'to produce concrete results' as they require the ICTY to refer their judgment for an award of compensation to the offender's national legal system, and it is unlikely that victims will find satisfaction in this legal system. See van Boven T, 'The Position of the Victim in the Statute of the International Criminal Court', in von Hebel J, Lammers G & Schukking J (eds), *Reflections on the International Criminal Court: Essays in Honour of Adriaan Bos*, T.M.C. Asser Press, The Hague, 1999, 77-89 at 81-82.

[12] See article 68(3) of the ICC Statute. The appointment and participation of victims' legal representatives is at the discretion of the ICC. See Garkawe, note 9, at 359-362.

[13] See Joutsen M, 'Listening to the Victim: The Victim's Role in European Criminal Justice Systems' (1987) 34 (1) *Wayne Law Review* 95

[14] Article 75(2) of the ICC Statute.

[15] Article 79 of the ICC Statute.

[16] See Garkawe, note 9, at 349-351.

minimised. It will thus be shown that survivors and victims could have played a much greater role in the IMT and this would not only have enhanced the proceedings, but also provided a greater sense of justice to the most effected victim communities of the Nazi regime.

II. The arguments in favour of greater survivor involvement and testimony during the IMT proceedings

In this part I want to suggest four important reasons why survivors should have had more of a role and more involvement with the IMT proceedings. The first reason is that this would have highlighted the aspect of the trial that dealt with what many now view as the essential feature of World War II and the IMT itself – namely the Holocaust and the Nazi's crimes against other minorities. It may seem surprising to many that the IMT was not primarily about this. The American prosecution case (which, as stated above, dominated the proceedings) focused mainly on the waging of, and conspiring to, wage aggressive war. These were seen as the major crimes of the Nuremberg defendants,[17] and not the Holocaust and the Nazi crimes against other minorities.

Evidence for this is found in the dramatic screening by the American prosecution of the documentary film entitled 'Nazi Concentration Camps'. Given the lack of survivor testimony during the American (and British) prosecution case, this happened to be one of the very few times that victims' suffering was actually shown during the course of the trial. However, even this film was problematic from the perspective of victims and survivors. In an important article Lawrence Douglas points out that not only was the word 'Jew' mentioned only one time during the film, but what the film was really about was

"... political terror and the excesses of war. It documents a barbaric campaign to exterminate political enemies of a brutal regime. ... It does so, however, in a manner that understands extermination in terms of the perverted logic of political control and military conquest. The film understands the crimes to be the consequences of aggressive militarism rather than genocide."[18]

A second major and related reason why survivor evidence would have enhanced the IMT was that it would have injected real life experiences and stories into the proceedings, thereby making the trial much more dramatic and memorable. It seems incongruous to suggest that while many (including this writer) regard the IMT as the most important criminal trial in history, the reality of the trial was anything but dramatic and memorable. Apart from some moments of particular interest and drama, the trial was actually quite a lacklustre one for the majority of the time.[19] This was because most of the duration of the IMT proceedings was spent on rather technical and routine arguments concerning the voluminous and detailed documentary evidence that the Nazis themselves had compiled, particularly the issues of whether this evidence was admissible, and if so, the significance of such evidence. This documentary evidence was the main thrust of the proof of the Nazi crimes that the prosecution

---

[17] Count One of the indictment referred to conspiracy, whereas Count Two referred to 'crimes against the peace', the then equivalent to the modern crime of aggression. Robert Jackson, the Chief American Prosecutor, stated in his opening address on November 21, 1945: 'My emphasis will not be on individual barbarities and perversions which may have occurred independently of any central plan.' Quoted in Marrus M, *The Nuremberg War Crimes Trial 1945-46: A Documentary History*, Bedford Books, 1997, at 83. Jackson's assistant, Sidney Alderman, addressed the Tribunal two days later in the following terms: 'After all, everything else in this case, however dramatic, however sordid, however shocking and revolting to the common instincts of civilized peoples, is incidental to, or subordinate to, the aggressive war aspect of the case. All the dramatic story of what went on in Germany ... even the concentration camps and the Crimes against Humanity, the persecutions, tortures, and murders committed – all these things would have little juridical international significance except for the fact that they were the preparation for the commission of aggression against a peaceful neighbouring peoples'. Quoted in Marrus, op cit, at 123-124.

[18] See Douglas L, 'Film as witness: Screening Nazi Concentration Camps before the Nuremberg Tribunal' (1995) 105 (2) *Yale Law Journal* 449 at 477.

[19] Bloxham remarks that '[i]t took considerable pressure from several [prosecution] staff, as well as from a body of journalists bored by the relentless documentary barrage which the prosecution case had become, to persuade Jackson to put on the stand even the few witnesses [the prosecution] did call'. See Bloxham D, *Genocide on Trial: War Crimes Trials and the Formation of Holocaust History and Memory*, Oxford University Press, 2001, at 61-62.

provided[20], although of course they also relied upon the defendants' own admissions and evidence from their own key witnesses, such as Dieter Wisliceny,[21] Otto Ohlendorf[22], Rudolf Höss[23] and Erich von dem Bach-Zelewsky.[24] The exceptions to the otherwise technical proceedings occurred during the screening of 'Nazi Concentration Camps', and perhaps most dramatically, the examination, cross-examination and final statements of the defendants themselves. Given this history, it is submitted that having more actual survivors of Nazi persecution testify and be involved in proceedings (as the Statute of the ICC now contemplates) would have added an extra dimension and drama to the proceedings. This would have also had the effect of improving the IMT's legitimacy in front of the world community and particularly in front of a sceptical German public. It would further have personalised the crimes of the Nazis and their allies, thus not making their crimes seem like an endless list of gruesome statistics contained within voluminous, bureaucratic and seemingly repetitive documentation.

The third reason for greater victim and survivor involvement was that testifying would have been a cathartic experience for survivors themselves. While this might have not been well-known at the time, there is much evidence today from psychologists and others that there is therapeutic value for survivors of traumatic events being able to tell their story in a publicly recognised process. For example, Brendon Hamber, a psychologist who did a lot of work with victims and survivors during the South African Truth and Reconciliation Commission hearings stated:

"Providing space for victims to tell their stories, particularly in public forums, has been of use to many. It is indisputable that many survivors and relatives of victims have found the public hearing process psychologically beneficial."[25]

The need for the survivors of Nazi oppression to be able to tell their side of the story was shown by the overwhelming desire of many survivors to give evidence some 15 years after the IMT proceedings in the *Eichmann* trial.[26] It was during this trial in Israel that survivors were strongly encouraged to testify. History shows that many took this opportunity to pour their heart out in describing what happened to them. In a sense, the *Eichmann* trial became the counter-balance for the lack of survivor testimony during the IMT proceedings,[27] and clearly showed the possible benefits for survivors in having the chance to tell of their experiences and to thus feel listened to in a publicly sanctioned process.

The final reason in favour of greater survivor testimony and involvement is that it is a matter of justice. Survivors were the actual people harmed by the crimes of the Nazis and their allies, and yet did not seem to have the opportunity to testify or otherwise become involved in the IMT proceedings. This stands in direct contrast to the fact that all the defendants were able to testify and make final statements. While I am not suggesting that every survivor who wanted to testify should have been allowed to do so (see later), it is clear that denying the right of all survivors to testify was unjust.

---

[20] Robert Jackson stated in his opening address of November 21, 1945 that 'We will not ask you to convict these men on the testimony of their foes. There is no count in the Indictment that cannot be proved by books and records. The Germans were meticulous record keepers …' Quoted in Marrus, note 17, at 82.

[21] Eichmann's deputy, whose testimony accounted for the murder of about 5,200,000 Jews in the East.

[22] He led mobile SS killing squad, Einsatzgruppe D, and his evidence included the admission that about 90,000 Jews were killed under his command.

[23] The commandant of Auschwitz, who was able to testify to 3,000,000 people dying at Auschwitz.

[24] Chief of the anti-partisan forces, whose evidence affirmed the indiscriminate extermination of innocent civilians during anti-partisan operations or reprisals.

[25] Hamber B, 'The Burdens of Truth: An Evaluation of the Psychological Support Services and Initiatives Undertaken by the South African [TRC]' (1998) 55(1) *American Image* 9 at 18.

[26] *Attorney-General of the Government of Israel v Adolf Eichmann* (1961) 36 I.L.R. 5.

[27] Douglas states that 'survivor testimony enjoyed pride of place at the Eichmann trial …; at Nuremberg, by contrast, testimony of the final solution was most importantly provided by non-Jews.' Douglas, note 3, at 78. Douglas also provides a critical analysis of the issue of non-Jews speaking for Jews at Nuremberg. While this is an important issue, it is beyond the scope of this article.

III. The reasons why victims and survivors played a relatively small role during the IMT proceedings

Having established that there are strong reasons as to why survivors *should* have played a greater role in the American and British prosecution cases, in this part I want to examine the main reasons why survivors played such a small role. These reasons are numerous and inter-related, and as stated above, most of them were genuine.

The first reason for the lack of victim testimony and involvement was that as the IMT was designed to deal only with defendants, who were at the highest levels of the Nazi establishment. It would have been unlikely for a survivor to have specific information about the criminal culpability of these defendants, such as copies or proof of the orders they gave or the policies they promulgated. Their experiences were more likely to have been with perpetrators who were much lower down the chain of command. These were generally not those indicted at the IMT.

Very much related to this reason was a second reason – the Allies already had in their possession voluminous and detailed documentary evidence that the Nazis themselves had compiled.[28] This self-incriminating evidence, combined with the confessions of the defendants themselves and the information provided by important other prosecution witnesses,[29] made survivor testimony largely unnecessary for convictions to be achieved.[30] In relation to the possibility of some survivors testifying (as occurred with the French and Soviet prosecutions), there was also no need to specifically provide for protection for victims in the IMT Charter because the Nazi regime no longer posed any threat to witnesses as it had been comprehensively defeated. This can be compared to the situation that, for example, confronted the ICTY where the warring parties in the former Yugoslavia still retained much power and thus the ability to exact revenge and intimidate prosecution witnesses. This thus required specific and concrete measures of protection and support in order to encourage witnesses (including victims and survivors) to come to The Hague to give evidence.

A third reason for the lack of victim involvement and testimony was that at the time of the IMT there was a general lack of awareness and/or disbelief of the full extent of the Nazi crimes, including the Holocaust and other atrocities. It took some time before the international community was able to fully comprehend the extent of the criminal culpability of the Nazi regime.

A fourth and important reason for the lack of survivor testimony was the perception that they were psychologically unable to be useful as witnesses due to the terrible experiences they had endured. Directly following the Holocaust and World War II there was a sense that the horrors experienced by victims and survivors was so great that little could be done to help them, and clearly this did not bode well for them being perceived to be useful witnesses during the IMT. It was really only until well after the IMT, with much more research of the psychological effects of war and living through the horror of concentration and extermination camps becoming known[31], that the assumption that survivors were psychologically unable to provide testimony might be questioned.

A related fifth reason was the common perception that survivors would make very biased witnesses given the extreme nature of the persecution they had endured.[32] Thus, even if they could have been able psychologically to testify, they were still perceived as being too emotional and thus not capable of providing objective and factual evidence. It is submitted that this would have led to prosecution concerns that such witnesses would end up being counter-productive for the prosecution case.

---

[28] Bloxham states: 'The treasure trove of documents preserved for the prosecution had convinced the trial planners, and Jackson in particular, that everything they needed to illuminate the darkest corners of the Nazi era was in printed form'. Bloxham, note 19, at 60. Another way of putting this is that the documentary approach 'favored paper over people'. Douglas, note 3, at 78.

[29] See the witnesses referred to above in notes 21 to 24.

[30] Robert Jackson takes this position in his opening statement to the IMT. See note 20.

[31] See, for example, Danieli Y et al (eds), *International Responses to Traumatic Stress*, New York: Bayward, 1996.

[32] Bloxham makes the point that 'with regard to the potential use of four witnesses, who had been involved to varying degrees with resistance movements in the Third Reich', the American Chief Prosecutor, Robert Jackson, objected to putting them on the witness stand on the basis that 'they had a strong bias against the Hitler regime[!]'. Bloxham, note 19 at 61.

There is a related sixth reason for excluding survivors from giving testimony that is in addition to the above perceptions concerning the possible lack of reliability and objectivity of their evidence. It seems likely that prosecutors would have held a genuine fear that having survivors testify would leave them liable to cross-examination from defence counsels, and this might further traumatise them and delay the possibility of their psychological recovery.

A very significant seventh reason for the lack of victim involvement related to the domination of proceedings by the American prosecutors. This has a number of dimensions. One of these related to the adversarial nature of American criminal trials in the Anglo-American common law tradition, where victims are excluded from being parties to the proceedings and thus lack any substantive rights. It is submitted that it is no coincidence that the two civil law allies, the French and the Soviet Union, did allow some victims to testify, whereas the two common law allies, America and Great Britain, did not. In civil law jurisdictions victims generally do have the right to be a party to criminal proceedings.[33] The other dimension of the domination of proceedings by the American prosecutors has already been referred to above. This was the emphasis placed by the Americans on the concept of conspiracy, particularly in relation to the Nazi decisions to wage aggressive war. The IMT in its judgment decided to confine the charge of conspiracy to crimes against the peace; it did not extend these to the war crimes or crimes against humanity charges. This meant that the first two charges, conspiracy and crimes against the peace, dominated the American prosecution case at the expense of the last two charges much more directly relevant to victims and survivors, namely, war crimes and crimes against humanity.

The final reason for the American and British prosecution cases not allowing survivors to testify or be involved in the proceedings was that the prosecution came under pressure of time and resources. The trial was already scheduled to last a long time due to the fact that there would be four different prosecuting powers[34], a massive indictment against a very large number of individual and organisational[35] defendants, and multiple and complex charges.[36] Furthermore, the trial concerned an unprecedented level, volume and scope of wrongdoing to be prosecuted in the one criminal trial. Such a vast and complex prosecution had previously never been attempted before in the history of criminal law.[37] Finally, the volume of the massive documentary evidence and their tabling and argument all took an enormous amount of time. It was thus not surprising that some months into the trial the prosecution found themselves under a large amount of pressure by Allied governments to wind up their case. In these circumstances where there was already more than sufficient evidence for convictions without any survivor testimony it was not unexpected that survivor evidence was not sought, and the prosecution did not seek to involve survivors and victims more in the trial. These matters were not priorities at the time.

IV. Some conclusions – what might have taken place during the IMT

It is now very easy to be critical of the American prosecutors when examining the Nuremberg IMT from a victim perspective. Hindsight is of course a wonderful thing when we are in the luxurious position of being able to look back at history. At the time of the IMT, the prosecutors were facing enormous pressures and conflicting duties towards international law, the historical record, their own

---

[33] See Joutsen, note 13.
[34] The conduct of the trial and its procedures had to be decided by agreement between the four powers, and often this was not easy as each country's legal system had its own norms and culture. Although the Americans generally got their way on most issues, some concessions to the inquisitorial type criminal justice systems of France and to a lessor extent, the Soviet Union, were granted. For example, the trial did not have a jury, defendants could be tried *in absentia*, and perhaps to a lesser extent judges were able to play a more interventionist role than what was customary in common law adversarial criminal trials.
[35] Along with the 22 individuals indicted by the IMT, seven organisations were also placed on trial.
[36] The charges were set out in Article 6 of the Charter. Most of these charges were also quite novel to criminal law at the time, such as the 'crimes against the peace' charge and the 'crimes against humanity' charge.
[37] Robert Jackson in his opening address of November 21, 1945 said that 'Never before in legal history has an effort been made to bring within the scope of a single litigation the developments of a decade, covering a whole continent, and involving a score of nations, countless individuals, and innumerable events'. Quoted in Marrus, note 17, at 80.

governments, a sceptical German public, their own legal systems, and from the other prosecuting nations. So I want to make clear and stress that this article is not intended to be a critique of prosecution approaches towards victims and survivors. In fact, many of the reasons for not involving victims and survivors in the IMT and not having more survivors testify, as set out in Part III, were very genuine and logical ones.

However, keeping these above considerations in mind, I still feel that more could and should have been done to involve victims and survivors in the IMT's proceedings. The analysis in Part II of this article did show that there were very good reasons why more survivors should have been able to testify. These included that it would have improved the IMT's proceedings and made them more personal, interesting and relevant, it would also have been a cathartic and beneficial experience for victims themselves, and finally, it was a simple matter of justice.

On the other hand, the analysis in Part III suggests that there were many genuine reasons for the relative lack of survivor testimony. I shall now examine each of these reasons in turn as they each may provide us with some lessons on what could have been done to encourage greater survivor testimony and involvement.

The first reason was that it was unlikely for a survivor to have specific information about the culpability of the indicted defendants at the IMT. The lesson to be learnt here is that any survivor chosen to provide evidence should have been carefully selected, so that they would have some useful knowledge and information for the IMT. While this may have precluded most survivors, I strongly believe some could have been found that would have provided relevant and useful testimony. A good example might have been Alfred Weczler and Rudolf Vrba, two Slovakian Jews who had escaped from Auschwitz on April 17, 1944, and found their way back to Bratislava. Robert Conot commences his landmark book on the IMT, *Justice at Nuremberg,*[38] with a brief mention of their story. The Jewish community in Slovakia at first doubted them, but after they had provided a large amount of detail they came to be believed, and the Rabbi of the community, Rabbi Weissmandel, wrote a Report based on their description of what they had been through. This Report, known as the Weczler/Vrba Report, became very influential and Conot points out that it was a significant factor in the eventual move towards a criminal trial that finally resulted in the IMT.[39] I am not sure what happened to these two individuals, but they did not give testimony during the IMT trial.[40] It seems to the writer that they would have been ideal witnesses as their evidence was the first eye witness account of the extermination camps made available to the Western world. Their testimony, even though it might not have been directly relevant to the culpability of any particular defendant, certainly would have added to the proceedings and the prosecution case in respect of the charge of crimes against humanity.

The second reason for the relative lack of survivor testimony was that it was largely unnecessary for convictions to be won. While this was an understandable and valid reason, I do not think it should have precluded such testimony. A simular conclusion can be drawn in respect of the third reason provided – that there was a general lack of awareness and/or disbelief of the full extent of the Nazi's crimes. Again, while this might have been understandable on some levels, by the time of the IMT proceedings there was knowledge of the extermination camps and the terrible persecution and extermination of minorities by the Nazis and their allies.

The fourth reason for the relative lack of survivor testimony was the perception that victims were psychologically unable to be useful as witnesses. This was also related to the fifth reason, namely, their alleged bias given their experiences, and the consequential perception that they would have been too emotional and thus incapable of providing objective and factual evidence. The sixth reason is also relevant here – the fear that having survivors testify would leave them liable to cross-examination from defence counsel, and this might further traumatise them. All these reasons have validity, but collectively

---

[38] Conot, note 3.
[39] Conot, note 3, at 3.
[40] The main evidence I have for this is after Conot's initial description of their story at the very start of his book, their names are no longer mentioned anywhere in his detailed descriptions of the IMT proceedings.

they can be countered by reiterating again that any survivors chosen to give evidence should have been carefully selected. Furthermore, most importantly, each survivor giving evidence should have been provided with the best of psychological and physical support and assistance before, during and after their testimony. The trial procedures should have been explained to them beforehand, as well as the possibility of cross-examination and how they needed to handle this. Overall, I believe that these genuine concerns embodied in these three reasons should not have precluded survivors from testifying, provided the above safeguards were put in place.

The seventh reason for the lack of survivor involvement and testimony, the dominance of the American prosecution case, is not a genuine one that should have precluded survivors and victims from testifying or otherwise being involved in proceedings.

The final reason for the American and British prosecutors not allowing survivors to testify was the issue of the pressure of time and resources. Again, while this reason does provide an explanation for the relative lack of survivor involvement in the trial, time and resources should not have been an excuse to exclude the involvement and testimony of survivors. The requirement of fundamental justice often means that time and resources must be expended in order for fairness to be achieved, and this is a good example.

In conclusion, while the IMT proceedings can be seen as largely a 'victim free' trial, it is hoped this article has shown that there are some good reasons why this should not necessarily have been the case. The article has also shown that there were some genuine reasons as to why survivors had so little input into the trial, but at the same time it has outlined some concrete ways in which more survivors could have given evidence and been more involved in proceedings. Given that the scene has been set for far greater victim involvement in future international criminal courts, the lessons to be learnt from the Nuremberg IMT, arguably the most important criminal trial in history, should not be lost.

Sam Garkawe

Rolle und Rechte der Opfer vor dem Nürnberger Internationalen Militärtribunal

Der Beitrag beschäftigt sich mit der Stellung der Opfer im Verfahren vor dem IMT in Nürnberg. Schon ein oberflächlicher Blick lässt erkennen, dass die Opfer eine untergeordnete Rolle gespielt haben. Das mag überraschen, war es doch Ziel des internationalen Strafverfahrens, gerade den Millionen von Opfern Gerechtigkeit zu Teil werden zu lassen.

Es wäre für den Prozess gegen die Hauptkriegsverbrecher aber aus mehreren Gründen erstrebenswert gewesen, Opfer als Zeugen anzuhören: Zum einen wäre das tatsächliche Leid der Verfolgten sichtbarer geworden. Die Aussage von Überlebenden im Gerichtssaal hätte außerdem das Verfahren dramatischer und damit einprägsamer gestaltet. Die wenigen zugelassenen Zeugenaussagen, wie die Otto von Ohlendorfs oder Rudolf Höss', bestätigen dies. Ansonsten basierte die Verfahrensführung neben Urkundsbeweis auf der Einvernahme der Angeklagten. Eine verstärkte Einbeziehung von Überlebenden hätte sicherlich die Legitimität des Verfahrens für die Weltöffentlichkeit, aber vor allem auch für die deutsche Bevölkerung erheblich gesteigert. Zum anderen hätte die Aussage von Überlebenden im Verfahren auch eine kathartische Wirkung für die Opfer gehabt. Diese moderne psychologische Erkenntnis war zwar zur Zeit des IMT noch nicht weit verbreitet, der Drang der überlebenden Opfer, ihr Leid zu bezeugen, zeigt sich indes eindrücklich in der Aussagebereitschaft von Zeugen im Eichmann-Verfahren in den 1960er Jahren in Israel. Schließlich ist es auch eine Frage der Gerechtigkeit, Opfer am Strafverfahren gegen die Täter zu beteiligen.

Der Grund für die restriktive Haltung hinsichtlich der Einbeziehung der Opfer lag aber vor allem in dem Bestreben der US-amerikanischen und britischen Ankläger begründet, eine Verurteilung auf der Basis von reichlich vorhandenem „hartem" Urkundenbeweis zu erreichen. Abgesehen davon war es unwahrscheinlich, dass die Opfer im Verfahren gegen die höchsten politischen und militärischen NS-Machthaber Substantielles hätten beitragen können, zumal der amerikanischen Ankläger intendierte, den Prozess auf „Verbrechen gegen den Frieden" zu konzentrieren. Außerdem war zum damaligen Zeitpunkt das wirkliche Ausmaß des Holocaust noch nicht überschaubar. Fraglich war schließlich die psychische Belastbarkeit der Opfer als Zeugen und die Wirkung der Aussage auf diese.

Im Nachhinein ist es einfach, das Vorgehen der Ankläger zu kritisieren. Bei genauerer Betrachtung gab es allerdings, wie hier gezeigt wird, gute Gründe, die Opfer nicht extensiv als Zeugen in den Prozess einzubeziehen. Für zukünftige internationale Strafverfahren sollten allerdings die Lehren aus Nürnberg gezogen und Opfer am Strafverfahren beteiligt werden, was sowohl bei den UN-Tribunalen als auch beim Internationalen Strafgerichtshof in den jeweiligen Statuten zugleich mit intensiver Vorsorge für die psychologische Betreuung der Opfer vorgesehen ist.

Lawrence Douglas

History and Memory in the Courtroom: Reflections on Perpetrator Trials

That the atrocities of perpetrators should describe legally recognized crimes, and that perpetrators should have to answer for their conduct in courts of criminal law are hardly controversial claims. Granted: one might argue about form, venue, and procedure – about whether, for example, domestic institutions are to be preferred over international tribunals; about whether it is proper to impose capital punishment upon those who grossly violate international humanitarian law; about whether Continental or Anglo-American norms of procedure better develop the aims of the trial; or about whether it is wise or fair to try an individual for crimes committed half a century before. One might even argue about the wisdom of trying perpetrators in light of specific conditions "on the ground" – whether, for example, the interests of transitional democracy or negotiated settlement counsel in favor of reliance on a South African style "Truth and Reconciliation Commission" over a perpetrator trial[1] – still, the deeper logic and normative appeal of trying perpetrators is generally accepted as self-evident.

At its most basic, the perpetrator trial is seen as a fundamental requirement of justice itself. The concept of justice, in turn, might be said to include at the very least: the idea that impunity is a wrong, both in itself – as a violation of the fundamental moral norm that no one should benefit from his or her wrongdoing – and instrumentally, inasmuch as unpunished crimes serve to destabilize the ever-precarious balance of domestic and international power. This latter idea often finds expression in the notion that criminal trials, as impersonal acts of state- or internationally-sanctioned retribution, serve to break the cycles of revenge that often erupt in spasms of mass atrocity. This notion, in turn, is related to the idea of reconciliation – the idea that criminal trials, by providing victims with a venue for expressing their pain, and by conferring public recognition upon the suppressed history of their victimization, serve to reconcile an afflicted people to the sufficiency of legal response to their woes.[2] This idea is closely related to the pedagogic aim of the trial, the idea that perpetrator proceedings can serve as tools of historical instruction. For example, Robert Kempner, a leading war crimes prosecutor, described the Nuremberg trials as "the greatest history seminar ever held."[3] The Eichmann, Barbie and Papon trials likewise aimed to use the courtroom both to clarify the historical record and to teach history lessons.

Broadly speaking, we can describe these multiple purposes of the high-level perpetrator trial as sharing a common feature: they are all didactic in nature; they push the trial in the direction of serving as a tool of instruction. In a sense, all criminal trials are didactic in two critical ways. First, they strive to demonstrate the truth of the charges brought against the accused. Second, they all seek to demonstrate the legitimacy of the process by which the first goal is pursued. The shibboleth, "justice must be seen to be done," captures this basic insight. All criminal trials, in this regard, can be seen as normative demonstrations of the efficacy and legitimacy of the rule of law.

---

[1] The literature on this subject is large. For a helpful overview, see Ruth Teitel, *Transitional Justice* (Oxford: Oxford University Press, 2000).

[2] Reconciliation is mentioned as a declared purpose of both the International Criminal Tribunal for the Former Yugoslavia, and for the International Criminal Court. To understand how the trial can further the end of reconciliation, it is important, I believe, to distinguish two possible meanings of the concept. First, "to reconcile" has a transitive meaning as captured in the expression, "the neighbors reconciled their differences." Here the idea is that two feuding or antagonistic parties have learned to put aside their past problems. This, I would argue, is the meaning of the term as it applies to the South African Truth and Reconciliation Commission. But "to reconcile" also has a second, call it intransitive, meaning, as in the phrase, "He became reconciled to his fate." It is this second, intransitive meaning that is at work in perpetrator trials. In this regard, such trials play a legally insular or even self-legitimating function: they serve to reconcile a people to the adequacy or sufficiency of a legal response to their sufferings.

[3] Quoted in Ian Buruma, *The Wages of Guilt: Memories of War in Germany and Japan* (New York, 1994), 142. Kempner was referring to both the trial of the major war criminals and the subsequent trials of Nazi criminals before American courts.

That said, I want to insist that the "perpetrator trial" defines its own specialized sub-breed of the criminal trial. Here the didactic function or quality of the trial is not an incidental feature of the inevitable process of proving charges or of upholding well-accepted and largely uncontested social norms. Instead, the didactic purpose of the trial lies at the very heart of the proceeding. Given that such trials invariably follow in the wake of episodes of mass atrocity, political upheaval, and horrific social dislocation, courts are invariably thrust in the position both of looking into the larger sweep of history and of making visible the efficacy of the law as a tool of such inquiry. If all trials are meant publicly to project the sober norms of the rule of law, perpetrator trials are burdened with the task of actively re-imposing such norms into spaces in which rule-based legality has been either radically evacuated or perverted. In part because of their explicitly didactic nature, in part because of the circumstances surrounding their staging, high-level perpetrator trials are by their very terms anomalous, unusual legal events, and as such, will invariably invite challenges to their legitimacy. They are, then, trials, which, by their very nature, place law –as a tool of deterrence, reconciliation, pedagogy and justice– on trial. If such a trial were staged in an international court, it may invite the charge of serving the ends of victor's justice or of having been orchestrated at the behest of a select group of powerful nations (such as NATO), or, alternatively, of being hopelessly removed from the region in which the crimes occurred. If a domestic national court was to conducted the trial, it may be attacked as a partisan tool, insufficiently removed from the crimes it is asked to judge.

Compounding these problems of legitimation is the fact that the multiple purposes of the didactic trial often pull courts in different directions. For example, the clarification of the historical record and the teaching of history lessons are obviously related, though importantly distinct: the former is largely descriptive and explanatory, while the latter is ineluctably normative. The distinction is important inasmuch as collective memory may have little to do with historical accuracy. The bombing of Hiroshima is remembered in the United States as a life-saving act born of military necessity, though the consensus among historians challenges this view. President Bush recently memorialized the victims of United Airlines Flight 93, recalling their heroic act of crashing their hijacked aircraft into a Pennsylvania field in order to save 1600 Pennsylvania Avenue – this notwithstanding the conclusion of the 9-11 Commission that the hijackers crashed the plane after the passengers mutinied. Trials, too, particularly those burdened with the legacy of traumatic history, often succeed at shaping the terms of collective memory precisely by demonstrating – intentionally or not – a relaxed fidelity to the historical record. By this, I do not mean to suggest that falsehoods are inserted into the historical narrative told at trial, though this, of course, may occur. Rather, the point is one of interpretation, nuance, emphasis, sympathetic imagination. Victims become, in the hagiography of the prosecution, exemplars of an unsustainable innocence, while perpetrators come to embody evil of mythic proportions. Over time, trials may find themselves subject to the very forces that they once contributed to. The Nuremberg trial, currently celebrating its sixtieth anniversary, has been hailed in many tributes as a path breaking proceeding about the Holocaust, notwithstanding the fact that the Nazis' crimes against the Jews of Europe played a largely ancillary role in the trial before the International Military Tribunal.

Or to take another example, the desire to make visible the workings of the rule of law may pull a court in a very different direction from, say, the impulse to teach history and to honor the memory of victims and survivors. The former impulse, I would argue, pushes the Court in the direction of sobriety, while the latter gestures toward spectacle. Writing about the Nuremberg trial, which she attended as a journalist, Rebecca West famously described the proceeding as a "citadel of boredom."[4] The Croatian journalist Slavenka Drakulic recently described the ICTY in similar terms – "painstakingly slow and boring."[5] Yet in a certain respect the very dullness of these proceedings can be seen as an achievement. If one of the purposes of the perpetrator trial is to reintroduce norms of legality into a radically lawless space, the very dryness of the proceeding can be construed as a triumph of legal sobriety over lawless

---

[4] Rebecca West, *A Train of Powder* (New York: Viking Press, 1955), 3.
[5] Slavenka Drakulic, *They Would Never Hurt a Fly: War Criminals on Trial in The Hague* (New York: Viking Press, 2004), 22.

chaos. Granted, the Nuremberg trial might have been characterized by a supererogatory dullness. Justice Robert Jackson, the chief Allied prosecutor, considered it essential for the Tribunal to establish an unassailable factual record of Nazi atrocities, and so the prosecution tactically limited the use of "soft evidence" – eyewitness testimony – in favor of "hard evidence": trial by document. By privileging historical document over personal testimony, Jackson aimed to "establish incredible events by credible evidence"; these written documents, however, had to be read into the record at trial, slowing the trial terribly.[6] Even Sir Norman Birkett, the British alternate judge on the Tribunal, bemoaned the "shocking waste of time."[7] In other respects, however, the dullness of the Nuremberg trial can be viewed as structural rather than idiosyncratic. Perpetrator trials – involving the adjudication of international crimes – will almost invariably have a multi-lingual complexion. The odd time-lags as faceless interpreters recast questions into another tongue and then retrieve and translate the answers; the stumbling to find proper equivalent terms; the mistimed interventions by judges and lawyers – these qualities cannot be viewed as passing or contingent qualities of perpetrator trials. On the contrary, they must be seen as structural elements of a proceeding characterized by its own peculiar and signature lugubrious tempo.

But if such trials raise novel topics for theoreticians of law – is it possible to speak of a *jurisprudence of boredom?*[8] – they also refocus attention on the meaning of the *spectacle* in law. If certain legal actors, principally judges, aspire to sobriety, others, in particular prosecutors, often push proceedings in the direction of drama. The prosecution at the Eichmann trial structured the State's case around survivor testimony in a conscious effort to rectify the missteps of Nuremberg and to inject drama into the proceeding. Thus the decision to rely on the voice and demeanor of the survivor witness was not, in the first instance, born out of an evidentiary strategy – Attorney General Hausner later openly acknowledged that the prosecution could easily have presented its case relying exclusively on written documents – but of a didactic ambition: to capture the imagination and conscience of a domestic Israeli and a world audience. That the trial took place in a municipal theater hastily retrofitted to serve as a courtroom perhaps only underscores the complex ways in which an explicitly didactic logic informed the trial's staging.

These tensions – between the teaching of history and the teaching of history lessons; between the longing for sobriety and the dramatic impulse – have led some to insist that the *just didactic* trial is something of an oxymoron. Hannah Arendt argued in her famous critique of the Eichmann trial that the "purpose of a trial is to render justice, and nothing else."[9] We must be wary, Arendt insisted, of subjecting the perpetrator trial to so-called "extra-legal" pressures, lest these pressures distort the solemn dictates of justice, and turn the trial into a legal sham, a show-trial in the old Stalinist sense. Clearly this concern is important, yet in my mind it is overstated. No one, I believe, would deny that the *core* responsibility of a criminal trial is to resolve the question of guilt in a procedurally fair manner. To insist, however, as Arendt does, that the *sole* purpose of a trial is to render justice, and nothing else, defends a crabbed and unnecessarily restrictive vision of the trial form. Especially in high-profile perpetrator trials – which by their very nature – will attract intense media attention, it is unrealistic to expect and silly to demand that the trial be conducted as an ordinary exercise of the criminal law. The question, then, is not whether the trial should be used for these larger ends, but how to do so responsibly.

This claim leads us to consider the arguments of other scholars, such as Martha Minow, Michael Marrus and Mark Osiel, who have leveled a critique that is the obverse of Arendt's.[10] Here the argument

---

[6] Robert Jackson, *The Nürnberg Case* (New York, 1947), 10.
[7] Quoted in Michael Marrus, *The Nuremberg War Crimes Trial 1945-46: A Documentary History* (Boston: Bedford Books, 1997), 117.
[8] For an insightful discussion, see Ravit Reichman, "Committed to Memory: Rebecca West's Nuremberg," in: A. Sarat, L. Douglas and M. Umphrey eds., *Law and Catastrophe* (Palo Alto: Stanford University Press, 2006).
[9] Hannah Arendt, *Eichmann in Jerusalem: A Report on the Banality of Evil* (New York, 1963), 254.
[10] Michael Marrus, "History and the Holocaust in the Courtroom," in: F. Brayard, ed., *Le Génocide des Juifs entre procès et histoire* (Paris, 2000), Mark Osiel, *Mass Atrocity, Collective Memory and the Law* (New Brunswick, 1997). See

is not that didactic trials fail to do justice to the accused. Rather, it is that didactic trials fail to do justice to history. The law, it is argued, fails to lead to a productive engagement with the most disturbing and foundational issues raised by traumatic history, issues more satisfactorily explored through discourses of history, philosophy, literature, theology, or psychoanalysis – or through alternative *fora*, such as truth commissions. This is a claim I find more pressing, and I am chiefly concerned with it in my own ongoing studies of perpetrator trials.[11] Yet at the same time that I am painfully aware of the limits of law, I also find myself appreciative of the creative labors of the legal imagination to master the problems of representation and judgment posed by episodes of mass atrocity and genocide. Let me briefly consider some of the structural constraints that scholars often say limit the usefulness of the didactic trial as a tool for exploring traumatic history. The first are procedural or evidentiary. Here it is argued that the formal procedures that constrain the production of knowledge in a criminal trial render this instrument a flawed tool for clarifying and comprehending traumatic history. Certainly I would agree that the rules of evidence and trial procedure limit the utility of the trial as a tool of historical representation. And the Nuremberg and Eichmann trials provide important examples of criminal proceedings that were governed by unusual rules of evidence designed to permit the use of hearsay and to embrace a more capacious notion of relevance. These unorthodoxies permitted survivor testimonies to assume a more fluid narrative form, quite different from the fractured, tutored testimony produced at standard adversarial trials. Did such an approach compromise the fairness of these trials? I would say no. These trials protected rights of confrontation of witnesses and other core procedures foundational to a concept of trial fairness. Bars against hearsay and rules controlling relevance, by contrast, can be seen as devices tailored for a jury system, and thus relaxing their application may serve the trial's didactic ends without eroding principles of fairness. In this regard, these trials came to look more like hybrid tribunals, combining elements of Anglo-American and Continental jurisprudence, anticipating some of the procedural arrangements that govern the International Criminal Tribunal for the Former Yugoslavia (ICTY) and the International Criminal Court (ICC).

This is not to deny that history and law are governed by differing epistemological and evidentiary conventions; still, it is easy to over-exaggerate the differences. After all, history and law remain deeply committed to the notion of reliable proof, even if what counts as reliable proof differs across the disciplines. Many historians, it should be noted, remain indebted to law's power as a fact-finding tool.[12] For example, many of the path-breaking early histories of the Holocaust, most notably Raul Hilberg's magisterial *The Destruction of the European Jews*, could not have been written without the astonishing documentary archive gathered at Nuremberg. More recently, Daniel Goldhagen's *Hitler's Willing Executioners* and Christopher Browning's *Ordinary Men* drew largely on depositions and other documents assembled through the labor of German prosecutors.

A second argument insists that didactic trials distort history inasmuch as a complex and refractory historical record must be encapsulated to fit legal categories. Thus one prominent historian has observed, "the shape of the stories told in trials ... follows the definition of the crimes with which the accused are charged, rather than an impartial assessment of the events themselves."[13] The famous trial of the Auschwitz guards that began in Frankfurt in 1963 provided a particularly vivid, if not egregious, example of this problem, as the atrocities committed by the defendants at Auschwitz had to be pigeonholed into the legal concept of simple "murder", the most serious criminal offense that the guards could be charged with under available German law at the time.[14] (Although the Federal Republic of

---

also, Donald Bloxham, *Genocide on Trial: War Crimes Trials and the Formation of Holocaust History and Memory* (Oxford, 2001).

[11] Lawrence Douglas, *The Memory of Judgment: Making Law and History in the Trials of the Holocaust* (New Haven, 2001).

[12] See Carlo Ginzburg, *The Judge and the Historian: Marginal Notes on a Late-Twentieth-Century Miscarriage of Justice* Anthony Shugaar, trans. (London, 1999).

[13] Marrus, "History and the Holocaust in the Courtroom," in: F. Brayard, ed., *Le Génocide des Juifs entre procès et histoire,* 48.

[14] Adalbert Rückerl, *NS-Verbrechen vor Gericht: Versuch einer Vergangenheitsbewältigung* (Heidelberg, 1984).

Germany had criminalized genocide in the early fifties, the application of the genocide law to Nazi crimes was held to run afoul of *ex post facto* prohibitions.)

The law of murder, however, was restrictively defined in German law – limited to killings born of "thirst of blood (*Mordlust*), satisfaction of…sexual desires, avarice or other base motives in a malicious or brutal manner." Inasmuch as German prosecutors had to prove that individual defendants had been motivated by such special factors as "*Mordlust*", this requirement had the regrettable consequence of transforming the everyday horrors and killings of Auschwitz into the "normal" against which the particularly malicious or brutal conduct of certain guards or functionaries could be measured.[15] But if the trial of the Auschwitz guards offers a particularly troubling example of law shoe-horning complex history to fit restrictive legal categories, other trials remind us of law's bold attempts to shape concepts of criminal wrongdoing adequate to the task of naming and condemning radical transgressions. In this regard, two critical legal innovations stand out, the concept of *genocide* and the concept of the *crime against humanity*. It is not within the scope of the present essay to review the evolution of the idea of genocide[16] and of crimes against humanity; nor do I mean to ignore the serious problems with the idea as it was first adumbrated in the Charter of the International Military Tribunal at Nuremberg.[17] These critical problems notwithstanding, the idea of genocide and the concept of crimes against humanity must be seen as attempts on the part of the law to shape novel concepts adequate to the task of naming and condemning unprecedented atrocities. These concepts have demonstrated their importance not simply as legal terms of art that have made possible the advent of the perpetrator trial; they have also proved their value as terms of cultural meaning. Admittedly, the clash between legal and cultural usages of these terms may make for confusion. For example, the refusal of the United Nations Commission of Inquiry to characterize the atrocities in the Darfur region of Sudan as genocide aroused considerable outrage among many commentators. Part of the problem, however, can be traced to the different registers of meaning of the concept of genocide. The term genocide has entered popular parlance as a powerful vehicle for expressing profound outrage at horrific atrocities. That such atrocities have been perpetrated in Darfur cannot be denied. The UN Commission of Inquiry, however, was concerned with the investigation of crimes, not with the expression of outrage; "genocide", for the Commission, referred to acts that satisfy the definition framed in the Genocide Convention of 1948, acts that could form the basis of international trials. This is not to suggest that the Commission was correct in withholding the designation; the Darfur controversy does, however, remind us of the power of legal terms to filter into popular consciousness. Thus, far from static or insular, we find legal discourse supplying a needed vernacular by which we may name and condemn horrific crimes. It is law that has delivered the terms and concepts that have helped fill the conceptual and representational vacuum left by acts of extreme atrocity.

Moreover, the concepts produced by law must be seen as highly plastic, adaptable, an observation that challenges a third common criticism of the didactic trial. A number of scholars argue that we should eschew justice as pedagogy, inasmuch as the picture of the past that emerges from a didactic trial threatens to become the Official History, fixed, refractory to the movement of historiography.[18] These scholars argue that "while judgments of courts are fixed, ... historiography moves."[19] By way of response, one should first note that the sense of fixedness – the closure of the trial – describes one of

---

[15] See Rebecca Wittmann, *Beyond Justice: The Auschwitz Trial* (Cambridge: Harvard University Press, 2005).

[16] For a useful discussion, see Samantha Power *"A Problem from Hell": America and the Age of Genocide* (New York: Basic Books, 2002).

[17] Suffice it to say that genocide was mentioned only fleetingly in the indictment, and then as a kind of war crime; and crimes against humanity was deemed justiciable only if committed by the Nazis in furtherance of their war aims. See Douglas, *Memory of Judgment*, 38-64.

[18] In addition to the important arguments of Marrus, also of interest are Martha Minow, *Between Vengeance and Forgiveness: Facing History after Genocide and Mass Violence* (Boston, 1998); and Tzvetan Todorov, "Letter from Paris: The Papon Trial", in: Richard Golsan, ed., *The Papon Affair: Memory and Justice on Trial* (New York, 2000).

[19] Marrus, "History and the Holocaust in the Courtroom," in: F. Brayard, ed., *Le Génocide des Juifs entre procès et histoire*, 45.

the most profound attractions for using the trial as a response to traumatic history. Trials *are* riveting cultural dramas because stories receive resolution in judgment and narratives find emphatic closure in juridically-sanctioned violence – an advantage that trials arguably hold over truth commissions.[20] The dramatic closure offered by trials thus frames and adds meaning to shared narrative, a process that was clearly at work in the Eichmann trial, where many witnesses testified that they were sustained by the hope that their bleak tale of survival might someday serve as legally probative evidence.

That said, it does not follow that the picture of history presented in any specific trial is fixed by the fact that a trial court must render an unequivocal verdict. On the most obvious level, legal judgment can be set aside by appeal, thus changing our understanding of the past enshrined at trial.[21] On a deeper and more interesting level, legal judgment can be revised through a complex process of renegotiation. Particularly in the case of traumatic or sensational history, it seems the law often only reaches a satisfactory result and understanding through a processing of revisiting or re-trying the contested events.[22] At times, civil trials may offer a more satisfactory treatment and resolution of matters incompletely or badly handled in criminal trials; in the United States, the Bernard Goetz and O.J. Simpson supply examples of this renegotiation of history in a civil proceeding. Indeed, when we speak of the didactic trial, the *individual* trial, as a discrete legal event, is perhaps the wrong frame of reference. Instead, attention must be paid to ways in which specific trials revisit and revise their juridical precursors, and in so doing, participate in, and contribute to, an evolving juridical understanding of traumatic history. In this regard, we can understand the Eichmann trial as a revision of Nuremberg. By placing the Holocaust at the legal fore of the trial, and by satisfying the testimonial need of survivor-witnesses, the Eichmann trial offered a far more comprehensive and, from the perspective of the survivors, more satisfying treatment of the traumatic history presented in incomplete fashion at Nuremberg. The French experience is also instructive, inasmuch as the very definition of crimes against humanity – and the role that the Vichy state played in the perpetration of these crimes – importantly changed from the Barbie trial to the Touvier trial to the Papon trial.[23] Trials before International Criminal Tribunal for the former Yugoslavia, such as the *Foca* case, have similarly led to a redefinition of the meaning of crimes against humanity, expanding them to now include the crime of rape. And with the expansion of the legal category, comes a broadening of the historical narrative that can be told through the law.

A fourth set of criticisms directed at the didactic trial focuses on what we may describe as the essential subject matter of these trials. Here it is claimed that criminal trials, by necessity, occupy themselves with the specific actions of a discreet defendant or group of defendants. In so doing, trials necessarily exaggerate the roles of individuals in events of greater historical sweep and compass. By focusing on the actions of individuals, the law overlooks and mischaracterizes the larger forces – political, ideological, military, bureaucracy – that inform the dark logic of genocide. Didactic trials thus allegedly create an odd disconnect between the magnitude of the crimes adjudicated and the solitary individual in the dock – a disconnect – that can only be overcome by demonizing the defendant. This,

---

[20] This, of course, is not to declaim the superiority of trials over truth commissions as tools for "calling to account"; indeed, it would be foolish to do so. In certain cases, trials may be more appropriate; in other cases, not. Context is all. Nor should we see trials and truth commissions as mutually exclusive alternatives; the two may work in tandem, with one supplementing the work of the other.

[21] Perhaps the best example of this in the context of Holocaust trials was the Israeli Supreme Court's decision to throw out Ivan Demjanjuk's 1987 conviction. Demjanjuk had been extradited to Israel from the United States, tried by a Jerusalem court, and was sentenced to death for engaging in sadistic practices while serving as a guard at Treblinka; the Supreme Court vacated the conviction once evidence emerged that Demjanjuk had served not at Treblinka, but at Sobibor, a less well known, though equally murderous death camp. At the time, observers lamented the Supreme Court's decision as an insult to the sacral memory of survivors (who had apparently misidentified Demjanjuk) and as giving succor to Holocaust deniers. See Yoram Sheftel, *Show Trial: The Conspiracy to Convict John Demjanjuk as 'Ivan the Terrible'* trans. Haim Watzman (London, 1994), 342.

[22] See Shoshana Felman, "Forms of Judicial Blindness: Traumatic Narratives and Legal Repetitions", in: Austin Sarat and Thomas Kearns eds., *History, Memory and the Law* (Ann Arbor, 1999).

[23] See Leila Nadya Sadat, "The Legal Legacy of Maurice Papon," in: Golsan, *The Papon Affair*.

indeed, is a crucial aspect of Arendt's critique of the Eichmann trial. At worst, then, genocide trials threaten to transform the defendant into something of a scapegoat, creating a false sense of legal closure and historical reckoning, as other perpetrators go unpunished and history remains unexamined, undigested. This is also the gist of Geoffrey Robertson's criticism of the trial of *Dusko Tadic* by the ICTY. While acknowledging that Tadic was "a licensed thug, a freelance torturer," Robertson insists that the defendant, as a low-level perpetrator, "takes on a symbolic capacity, a scapegoat almost, for the community of which he was part. His punishment is less an example of individual responsibility than collective guilt."[24]

This criticism is hardly trivial, and here I'll confine myself to two responses. First, it is important to distinguish between the notion of collective guilt which unfairly blames an entire nation or a people for the acts of specific groups, and the notion of collective guilt that rightly recognizes the corporate nature of mass atrocities – that such acts, to be successful, require extensive technical assistance, bureaucratic organization, and logistical support. Indeed, as I have suggested, some have faulted the legal process precisely because they believe it incapable of addressing the corporate dimension of genocide. And yet even this criticism is overstated. Nuremberg, for example, was not simply a trial of twenty-two individuals. Also on trial were a number of Nazi organizations, including the entire Gestapo. Indeed, Robert Jackson, the lead prosecutor for the Allies, melodramatically insisted, "It would be a greater catastrophe to acquit these organizations than it would be to acquit the entire twenty-two individual defendants in the box."[25]

Second, I think we should be very careful about describing an architect or even a low-level perpetrator of genocide as a scapegoat. A scapegoat is an innocent creature saddled with undeserved guilt. Wrongdoing has been *displaced* upon the scapegoat. An architect or accomplice or perpetrator is not, however, an innocent creature, and does not become a scapegoat when asked to answer in law for crimes orchestrated by more prominent individuals or facilitated by groups or collectives. Here wrongdoing has not been displaced but *condensed* in the figure of the perpetrator.[26] It seems odd, then, to criticize perpetrator trials as performing a "symbolic function". In a way, all criminal trials can be said to play this symbolic function, inasmuch as only a small percentage of those who violate norms of social order ever find themselves in the dock at a criminal trial. It is well accepted that trials of organized crime figures will invariably focus on the conduct of a few. Obviously, the goal is to go after the leaders of a criminal organization. At times, however, circumstances may conspire to force prosecutors to settle for underlings. The compromises may be unfortunate, but they are not unjust. In either case – the trial of the underling or the architect – the trial remains a symbolic act. But symbolic gestures are not to be shunned because they are selective. On the contrary – that is their justification and their potency.

Yet even if one were to acknowledge the limitations of the didactic trial, one must ask what follows. Here I would respond, very little. For it is one thing to agree that the most nuance renderings of the past issue from the pen of the professional historian, another to conclude, therefore, that didactic trials have no valuable role to play as a tool of instruction in the wake of episodes of mass atrocity. So I will gladly concede that such trials are not well equipped to render history in its complexity; nor are they structured self-consciously to acknowledge the limitations of their representation of the past. In this respect, these trials are a bit like television dramas – though, again, we should recall the limits of this analogy. Television dramas, even those occasional mini-series that seek to do justice to a topic of history, tend to be controlled by the logic of entertainment. By contrast, the peculiar mix of sobriety and spectacle, as I have argued, will always characterize didactic trials. That said, the analogy to TV, however imperfectly drawn, supplies for many commentators a potent justification for eschewing law to teach history – the

---

[24] Geoffrey Robertson, *Crimes Against Humanity: The Struggle for Global Justice* (London: Penguin Books, 2000), 309, 310.
[25] Quoted in Douglas, *The Memory of Judgment,* 88.
[26] And it should be noted that this process of condensation – using the crimes of the perpetrator to tell a story of greater historical sweep – cuts both ways; as the Milosevic trial has made abundantly clear, once history is brought into the courtroom, it does not simply serve at the behest of the prosecution.

last thing we want, is the kind of trivial caricature of the past supplied by network television. Yet here I am reminded of the debates that surrounded the broadcast of the NBC miniseries *Holocaust: the Story of the Family Weiss* on German television some twenty-five years ago. Before the series was aired, numerous historians bemoaned the "hollywoodification" of the Holocaust, the dreadful trivialization of traumatic history into digestible bits of television drama.[27] Amid the protests and hand-wringing the series was broadcast, and to the shock of the pundits, it occasioned a critical moment of national collective reckoning, stimulating a new generation of Germans to its own *Vergangenheitsbewältigung* – a wrestling with the meaning of their collective past.

Almost two decades earlier, the Eichmann trial served a similar purpose in Israel. By turning the history of the Nazi campaign of extermination into a legal drama broadcast live on Israeli radio and televised around the world, the trial permitted survivors to transform acts of tragic witnessing enveloped in silence and shame into potent juridical acts. Indeed, the Eichmann trial served in crucial respects to *create* the Holocaust.[28] By this I mean the trial importantly served to transform cultural understandings of Nazi genocide. No longer simply a horrific episode of mass killing, the Holocaust emerged from the Eichmann trial as an emblematic act of the twentieth century – an act no longer continuous with the history that proceeded it, but radically disruptive of it.

But if, as I have tried to suggest, the interests of justice conventionally conceived and didactic uses of a trial are not inherently antagonistic, this is not to deny the risks that attend the staging of the high-profile perpetrator trial. The legal theorist Otto Kirchheimer located at the heart of every just criminal trial an element of "irreducible risk" – the possibility that the trial conclude in an acquittal. Absent this aspect of risk, the trial threatens to degenerate into a sham, a legal fraud.[29] Obviously prosecutors will try to master this risk, but they may not engage in practices that would predetermine the outcome. Keeping in mind Kirchheimer's insight, I believe it is important to note that as we move from the ordinary criminal trial to the didactic perpetrator trial, the risks multiple. In the case of the perpetrator trial, conventional prosecutorial success – winning a conviction – does not necessarily translate into the didactic success of the proceeding. Here I should add that prosecutorial success does not necessarily require conviction of all defendants on all charges. Nuremberg concluded in the acquittal of three of the twenty-one defendants present, and though the acquittals were controversial at the time, one can say with hindsight that they importantly served to legitimate the IMT – by demonstrating the tribunal's independence and neutrality. Still, a perpetrator trial that unravels entirely – for example, the Israeli prosecution of Ivan "the Terrible" Demjanjuk that originally issued in a conviction that was later tossed out on appeal – will invariably be considered a didactic disaster. A prosecutorial failure cannot help be but seen as a didactic failure as well – unless the didactic goal is solely to make visible the sober logic of procedural justice, which, I have tried to suggest, is usually but one goal among others.

But if prosecutorial success is generally speaking a necessary condition for didactic success, it is not sufficient. A perpetrator trial can succeed in our first sense – end in a conviction – yet fail in the second – as a didactic exercise. This will most often happen, I believe, in cases in which the *defense* puts history on trial. So far I have considered the didactic trial as an affair of the prosecution; the didactic trial of the *defense* is, however, a far more problematic and destabilizing affair. A didactic trial staged by the prosecution must remain ever mindful of the basic need to secure a conviction while respecting the conventional requirements of due process. The didactic trial of the defense is burdened with no such reciprocal obligation. In these cases, we often encounter a defendant less interested in acquittal than in martyrdom, intent upon hijacking history toward this end. In such cases, the defense attorney – or the defendant mounting a *pro se* defense – acts less like a conventional advocate, focusing on the conduct of the accused, than as a radical historical revisionist. Here we think of Jacques Verges and his "trial of

---

[27] For a discussion of the reception of the mini-series, particularly in the United States, see Jeffrey Shandler, *While America Watches: Televising the Holocaust* (New York, 1999), 159-178.

[28] See Douglas, *The Memory of Judgment*.

[29] Otto Kirchheimer, *Political Justice: The Use of Legal Procedure for Political Ends* (Princeton: Princeton University Press, 1961).

rupture", threatened though only incompletely delivered upon in his defense of Klaus Barbie,[30] and of Slobodan Milosevic, who, alas, has been quite effective in taking history hostage in The Hague. In such cases (and one worries that the future trial of Saddam Hussein might supply another example), the perpetrator trial turns into a revisionist, or even negationist, spectacle, as the disputed terms of history take the legal fore of the proceeding. Courts can, of course, muzzle disruptive defendants, but it is hardly surprising that judges have on the whole proved reluctant to do so in high-profile perpetrator trials. Inasmuch as didactic trials are, as I have argued, anomalous proceedings, we should hardly be surprised to find judges struggling to demonstrate legitimacy by bending over backwards to accommodate even the most tendentious displays by the defense – a phenomenon vividly on display in the Milosevic trial.

The risk of subversion by the defense thus remains a substantial risk of didactic trials. The Eichmann trial remains instructive in this regard, if only as a counter-example. Much as been written about the character of Adolf Eichmann; for some – most notably Raul Hilberg – Eichmann was a zealous and brilliant technocrat of death; for others, such as Arendt, he was a completely replaceable cog, a dreary exemplar of the banality of evil. But whatever our take on the issue, it is clear that Eichmann contrived to make his trial a success. Through his submissive behavior and obedience, Eichmann curiously helped to legitimate the court that sentenced him to death. Gabriel Bach, an assistant prosecutor at the Eichmann trial and later a Justice on the Israeli Supreme Court, recalls as his sharpest and proudest memory of the trial the moment that Eichmann rose to his feet and stood as the judges entered the court for the first time.[31] On one hand, Bach's sense of pride can be easily understood – here we have the once-powerful SS officer – a key player in the effort to destroy the Jewish people – humbly submitting to the authority of a Jewish court. And yet the defendant's gesture must be seen as more than an act of submission to superior power; it is also an act that acknowledges the authority of the force arraigned against him – an acknowledgement that Milosevic has tenaciously refused to tender in The Hague. But memorable as Eichmann's gesture may have been, it was also entirely consistent with his character: the very craven obedience to authority that arguable made him a morally ungrounded perpetrator of genocide also made him into a model defendant.

But if the Israeli court had the good fortune of having an obedient defendant – and by that I do not mean cooperative: Eichmann's answers routinely mixed *bona-fide* candor with infuriating obfuscation – it other regards, the trial created its own success. Most crucially, the prosecution and the judges serendipitously struck a balance between the conventional legal interests of justice and the didactic purposes of the trial. As I have mentioned, the Eichmann prosecution sought not simply to win a conviction, but to use the trial as a tool of instruction and commemoration. In its written judgment, however, the court largely ignored the didactic ambitions of the prosecution and focused narrowly on the materiality of the evidence as it applied to the charges brought against the accused. This is as it should be. This dialectic, in which the prosecution presented its case in broadly didactic terms while the court hewed to its juridical function conventionally conceived, permitted the trial to succeed as both an exercise in collective pedagogy and as a instrument of legal justice. Here the balance between spectacle and sobriety was largely, if fortuitously, maintained.

By way of conclusion, I think it is also important for us to bear in mind that the success of the didactic trial can only be measured over broad space and time. Such trials play before multiple audiences: the victims clamoring for justice; the perpetrators, wrapped in their own misplaced sense of aggrievedness and victimization; a legal community both on the ground and abroad; and a larger international community watching with periodic spasms of interest amid long stretches indifference. The multiple and far-flung audiences of the didactic trial raise important concerns about what might be described as the "spatiality" of justice, a matter which has gained increasing salience as legal scholars and actors weigh international tribunals against domestic courts as the most efficacious tools for dealing

---

[30] See Alain Finkielkraut, *Remembering in Vain: The Klaus Barbie Trial and Crimes Against Humanity* Roxanne Lapidus, trans. (New York: Columbia University Press, 1992).

[31] Gabriel Bach, in conversation with the author.

with mass atrocity. Here I will confine myself to two observations. Many of the most famous photographs associated with the Eichmann trial, at least at the time of its staging, were not the images of the man in the glass booth. Rather, they were shots of the spectators at the trial reacting to the testimonial drama in the courtroom: expressions of grief, disbelief, anger, horror. If at the Eichmann trial the glass booth made the defendant into a specimen of display and scrutiny, the spectators were organically part of the proceeding. Their gasps, snickers, whispers, and occasional violent outbursts were part of the trial and constituted a crucial point of primary reception for the journalists following the case. Contrast this to the organization of space and spectatorship at the Milosevic trial in The Hague. There it is the court itself that sits in the glass booth, sealed from the gallery of spectators by sheets of glass thick enough to repel rocket propelled grenades. The glass is also soundproof; the only sounds that the spectator can hear are those broadcast over the headsets made available to each observer; the court is likewise sealed from any sounds from the spectators. As a consequence, there is no interaction between the court and the spectators – usually no more than a handful, though on occasion, filling the gallery. For the observer, the feeling is akin to watching an elaborate psychology experiment through one-way glass: the spectator cannot suppress the feeling that he or she is entirely invisible to the Tribunal. The spectator gallery is supplied with TV-monitors that track the proceeding; one finds oneself watching the monitors instead of the courtroom – as powerful a trope as any for the formal removal of the court from the region in which the crimes took place. This element of spatial displacement must, I believe, undercut the didactic value of the trial, particularly in terms of its contemporaneous reception. Still, we must remember that perpetrator trials play before multiple audiences, each of which will perceive the trial differently and will measure its success by different standards. Perhaps more to the point, these perceptions will also transform over the course of years, as the dynamics of space yield to the imponderables of time.

In part this is a consequence of the fact that it is very difficult to predict what aspects of a trial will live on in collective memory. In the United States, the O.J. Simpson murder trial is remembered in an ungrammatical ditty, "If the glove don't fit, you must acquit." The Nuremberg trial remains remembered in the American popular imagination through the vehicle of the famous Hollywood movie, *Judgment at Nuremberg,* which, in fact, had nothing to do with the trial before the International Military Tribunal. In Israel, the Eichmann trial is powerfully associated with the collapse on the stand of Yehiel Dinur, aka Katzetnik, a sequence captured on film that is ritually rebroadcast on Israeli television on Yom Hashoah, the national day of Holocaust remembrance. These moments of collective memory can all be described as juridically unstable, in that they evade the sober ordering strategies deployed by courts at the time of trial. They remind us that regardless of the power of courts to control difficult proceedings and to submit refractory histories to legal judgment, they are unable to control the way in which the trial will itself become a cultural artifact and an article of collective memory.

But if the workings of time refuse to submit to juridical control, that does not mean that such instabilities are necessarily deleterious. At the time of its staging, the Nuremberg trial aroused utter indifference in the vast majority of Germans. In the fifties, Germans viewed the trial with contempt, as an exercise in victor's justice.[32] (In particular, Germans vilified Nuremberg for treating "aggressive war" as an international crime.) Now, however, the trial is generally viewed in Germany with respect – both as an event that prodded Germans to a collective reckoning with their troubled past, and as a vital contribution to the developing body of international law. And today it is German jurists who have taken the lead in codifying "aggressive war" as a crime to be judged before the fledgling International Criminal Court,[33] the court that the US is shamefully boycotting. And so success must be measured over broad space and time. Just as the didactic trial must struggle to do justice to history, history also takes time to do justice to the trial.

---

[32] For an excellent study of the politics of collective memory of the Nuremberg trial in Germany see, Norbert Frei, *Vergangenheitspolitik: die Anfänge der Bundesrepublik und die NS-Vergangenheit* (Munich: Beck, 1996).
[33] I'm grateful to David Scheffer for pointing this out.

Lawrence Douglas

Geschichte und Erinnerung im Gerichtssaal: Reflektionen über Kriegsverbrecherprozesse

Dass Verbrechen gegen die Menschlichkeit rechtlich als Straftaten anerkannt und die Täter dafür gerichtlich zur Verantwortung gezogen werden sollen, kann kaum bestritten werden. Über die Durchsetzung im Einzelnen kann man hingegen unterschiedlicher Auffassung sein. Ein Strafverfahren wird allerdings als Erfordernis der Gerechtigkeit angesehen, wodurch die Balance zwischen nationaler und internationaler Macht aufrechterhalten wird, Straflosigkeit der Verbrecher zugleich als Übel an sich. Insbesondere kann dadurch, dass den Opfern ein Forum geboten wird, ihr Leid zu artikulieren, und dieses im Verfahren öffentlich anerkannt wird, die Gefahr von Racheakten und neuerlichen Grausamkeiten im Zaun gehalten und Versöhnung möglich werden. Eng damit verbunden wiederum ist die Vorstellung von Strafverfahren als didaktisches Lehrstück, als normative Demonstration der Wirksamkeit und Legitimität rechtsstaatlicher Verfahren. In diesem Zusammenhang wurden auch die Nürnberger Prozesse als das „größte historische Seminar" bezeichnet, das jemals stattgefunden hat.

Die eigentliche, nicht aber, wie von Hannah Arendt behauptet, einzige Aufgabe eines Strafverfahrens ist es, die Schuld des Angeklagten zu klären. Die Frage ist nicht, ob ein Prozess gegen hochrangige Verbrecher Auswirkungen auf die Öffentlichkeit hat; solche bestehen zwangsläufig. Fraglich ist hingegen der verantwortliche Umgang mit dieser Wirkung. Dabei gilt es die durch formalisierte Beweisaufnahme und prozessuale Fairness beschränkte Möglichkeit der Einbeziehung des traumatisierten Umfelds im Strafverfahren zu akzeptieren. Trotz der unterschiedlichen epistemologischen und beweisrechtlichen Konventionen haben Strafverfahren und Geschichtsforschung doch ein gemeinsames Ziel: die Wahrheit. Sowohl die Nürnberger Prozesse wie auch der Eichmann-Prozess haben zur geschichtlichen Wahrheitsfindung ihren Beitrag geleistet. ohne die dort gewonnenen Erkenntnisse hätten etliche geschichtswissenschaftliche Abhandlungen nicht verfasst werden können. Zu berücksichtigen ist außerdem, dass die Terminologie der Strafnorm und des Strafprozesses nicht der Umgangssprache entspricht. Verwirrungen um die Verneinung des Genozid-Vorwurfs in der Dafur-Region im Sudan durch den Bericht der UN-Untersuchungskommission finden darin ihren Grund. Schließlich besteht die Gefahr, dass die Suche nach der strafrechtlichen individuellen Verantwortlichkeit im Strafverfahren den Blick auf die Gesamtumstände und -zusammenhänge, politische, militärische, ideologische oder bürokratische, verstellt, ebenso wie umgekehrt der Angeklagte als Sündenbock oder Märtyrer politisch missbraucht werden kann.

Der Effekt von öffentlichen Strafverfahren gegen Menschenrechtsverbrecher muss über einen langen Zeitraum betrachtet werden. Das kollektive Erleben von Geschichte wird nicht unbedingt durch das nüchterne Strafverfahren geprägt und ist außerdem wandelbar. Dafür sind oft Filme oder Fernsehberichterstattungen verantwortlich. Das zeigt sich z.B. aber auch im Positiven: Die ablehnende Haltung Deutschlands gegen das „Verbrechen des Angriffskriegs" im Nürnberger Prozess hat sich zwischenzeitlich in eine Führungsrolle bei der Kodifizierung des „Verbrechens der Aggression" im Statut des ICC gewandelt. In gleichem Maße wie der didaktische Strafprozess darum bemüht sein muss, der Geschichte gerecht zu werden, braucht es Zeit, bis die Geschichte dem Strafprozess gerecht wird.

Whitney R. Harris

Tyranny on Trial – Trial of Major German War Criminals at Nuremberg, Germany, 1945-1946

Ten years ago I was standing at a podium in this very courtroom at the invitation of the Mayor of Nuremberg in remembrance of the trial of the major German war criminals at Nuremberg at the end of World War II. The trial before the International Military Tribunal commenced on November 20, 1945 and concluded on October 1, 1946. There were other war crimes trials following World War II, including the Tokyo trial in Tokyo and numerous trials conducted before national courts, including the twelve trials by American Military Tribunals at Nuremberg. There was, however, only one trial conducted against the twenty-two German war defendants by the International Military Tribunal at Nuremberg. I was the only American representative and the only former prosecutor present, and was invited to deliver the opening address.

It was a moment of intense nostalgia for me then, as it is this evening, to be speaking in the very courtroom where I spent a year of my life prosecuting the major Nazi war criminals. And it was particularly emotional then, as it is today, to realize that after the passage of so many years the German people, and in particular, the citizens of Nuremberg, itself, have come to accept the importance of the hard work which we did at Nuremberg in the advancement of international law in the Twentieth Century.

As I glance about this familiar room I note the three bronze plaques, which still adorn the lintel above the entrance to this courtroom. The centre plaque represents human frailty in the offering by Eve of the apple to Adam. On one side are the Roman fasces for authority; and on the other side a kneeling figure holding a sword, representing Justice. In this courtroom, sixty years ago, Justice vanquished Authority.

The genesis of the Nuremberg trial was the Moscow Conference of October, 1943 at the conclusion of which a statement was issued by President Roosevelt, Prime Minister Churchill, and Premier Stalin declaring the determination of the three powers to hold individuals responsible for crimes committed by them in the course of World War II. The statement warned that officers and men and members of the Nazi Party, who were responsible for or took a consenting post in atrocities, massacres or executions would be punished by joint decision of the governments or the Allies. The statement concluded: "Most assuredly the three Allied Powers will pursue them to the uttermost ends of the earth and will deliver them to their accusers in order that justice may be done."

On May 8, 1945 President Harry Truman appointed Supreme Court Justice Robert H. Jackson the United States Chief of Counsel charged with obtaining the agreement of the Allies to a trial of the major Axis war criminals before an international military tribunal. Jackson succeeding in persuading the British to agree to the proposed trial and on June 26, 1945 representatives of the United States, Great-Britain, France and the Soviet Union met in London for the purpose of drafting an agreement for the trial of the Axis war leaders. I had served as a line officer in the Navy throughout the war. Toward the end of the war the Navy assigned me to active duty with the Office of Strategic Services. OSS sent me to London in charge of the investigation of Axis war crimes. I was in London on this mission when representatives of the Allied Powers convened to negotiate the London Agreement of August 8, 1945 for the trial of the major Axis war leaders.

From time to time I was able to provide the American negotiators with incriminating Nazi documents. I was invited to join the prosecuting staff, and with the consent of OSS moved with the first contingent to Nuremberg in August.

The principal repressive agency of the Nazi regime was the Reich Main Security Office, or RSHA. Both intelligence and special police agencies were combined in this office. Since I had acquired some knowledge of the Nazi intelligence system while serving in OSS, I was assigned the case against the Gestapo and SD, two organizations within the Reich Main Security Office, and against the chief of that office, the defendant Ernst Kaltenbrunner, who had succeeded Reinhard Heydrich in that position on January 30, 1943 after Heydrich's assassination in Czechoslovakia. I was provided an office down the hall from here, a second-hand typewriter, and a German secretary, and told to assemble evidence and write briefs against these defendants.

The major crime against humanity charged to the Nuremberg defendants was the extermination of Jews, Gypsies, Polish and Soviet intelligentsia and other unwanted minority groups. This crime was primarily the responsibility of the Gestapo and SD within the government and the SS within the Party. Thus, this part of the case fell primarily into my hands.

Our basic evidence against the Nazi defendants was documentary. I had collected documents in Great Britain while serving in OSS. Colonel Storey, Justice Jackson's first executive trial counsel, had assembled a much greater collection in Paris. All these incriminating documents were assembled in the Palace of Justice, classified, translated, and made available to both prosecution and defense counsel. In preparing the case against the Gestapo and SD, and Kaltenbrunner, I searched the Document Room seeking evidence of Nazi crimes against humanity.

One document which I found was a letter written by SS Untersturmführer Becker, the operator of a gas van in the Eastern territories, to Walter Rauff, the head of the motor vehicles department of the Gestapo, in which he complained of the malfunctioning of a gas van he was operating which caused victims to die in suffocating agony rather than in gentle sleep as intended.

Shortly before the trial began, I learned that the British had under interrogation in London, Otto Ohlendorf, the head of Amt III of the RSHA, which dealt with matters of intelligence within Germany. I asked that the British send Ohlendorf to Nuremberg so that I might interrogate him on the organization of the RSHA of which my defendant, Kaltenbrunner, was the chief. The British did so, and I began my interrogation of Ohlendorf by asking him about his activities during the war. He said that, except for 1941, he had served as chief of Amt III of the RSHA. Naturally, I asked what he had done during that year. When he replied that during 1941 he had been in command of Einsatzgruppe D, I immediately recalled the Becker letter, which had been written from an Einsatzkommado, and was inspired to ask: "Well, Ohlendorf, how many men, women and children did your group kill during that year?" And he replied: "90,000!" That broke the case on the extermination program of the Einsatzgruppen in the Eastern territories, and we were able to establish through the testimony of Ohlendorf, and others, that approximately 2,000,000 persons, mainly Jews, were murdered by these units of the RSHA. It was the initial proof of the Holocaust. My esteemed colleague, Ben Ferencz, who is with us at this conference, was the chief prosecutor in the subsequent trial before an American Military Tribunal in which Ohlendorf and thirteen other defendants received the death sentence and seven others were imprisoned for this horrendous crime.

An especially dramatic moment of the trial was the cross-examination of Hermann Göring by Justice Jackson. Göring had assumed the role of leader of the defendants. He occupied the first seat in the prisoners dock. He was irritated by the apparent disinterest in the proceedings of Rudolf Hess, who sat next to him. But at every opportunity be sought to stimulate the other defendants to challenge the prosecution in every possible way. It was, therefore, of great interest to the press when Göring was brought under cross-examination by Justice Jackson. I was Jackson's assistant in this dramatic moment of the case and sat beside him at the prosecutor's podium. Among the issues raised was Göring's role in the terrible pogrom of November 9/10, 1938 which has come to be known as Kristallnacht, the Night of Broken Glass.

This was the Nazi reaction to the murder of a secretary in the German Embassy in Paris by a German Jew named Grynspan. During the night Jewish stores were destroyed in Germany. Thousands of Jews were taken into custody and sent to concentration camps. Many were killed.

Göring met with Hitler and Goebbels to consider further repressive measures. Göring proposed imposing a fine of one billion Reichmarks on the Jews whose property had been destroyed so that all insurance benefits to which they would be entitled would, instead, be paid to the State. At a meeting the Reich Air Minister Göring declared that Jews should be forced out of the economy. Their property should be seized and only interest paid upon its under-valuation. "We must agree on a clear action", he said, "that will be profitable to the State". And he closed the meeting with these prophetic words: "I'd like to say again that I would not like to be a Jew in Germany ... . If in the near future, the German Reich should come into conflict with foreign powers, it goes without saying that we in Germany should first of all let it come to a showdown with the Jews ... ." Göring admitted making those statements. And he did not deny that in a letter dated July 31, 1941, shortly after the invasion of the Soviet Union, he had charged Reinhard Heydrich with the complete solution of the Jewish question in the German sphere of influence in Europe, some six months before Heydrich disclosed to high-ranking civil servants, meeting in a villa at Wannsee, Berlin, that the final solution of the Jewish question in Europe was to be, in fact, the annihilation of the Jewish race.

By the time we had rested our case we had not found the greatest killer of the regime, Rudolph Höss, the Commandant of Auschwitz Concentration Camp. It was, therefore, a dramatic moment when I was informed that Höss had been captured by the British near Flensburg. Although I had no idea how we could get his testimony into the record, I asked that he be sent to Nuremberg and interrogated him over a period of three days, reducing his testimony to an affidavit in which he confessed to the killing of two and a half million victims in Auschwitz and provided the details of this incredible human extermination. But how, having rested our case, were we to gel this affidavit into the record?

After I had finished with Höss I turned him over to Kaltenbrunner's attorney, Dr. Kurt Kauffman. Kauffman's defense of Kaltenbrunner had been that when be had been named by Himmler to head the Reich Main Security Office Kaltenbrunner had been instructed to confine himself to matters of intelligence and to leave the administration of concentration camps to Gestapo chief Heinrich Müller. When Kauffman learned that Höss would testify that Kaltenbrunner had never visited Auschwitz, the most terrible extermination facility of the Nazi regime, he decided to buttress this defense by calling Höss as a witness for the defense. As a consequence we were able to put into the record the complete story of Auschwitz, and the mass killings of Jews, Soviet POWs and other victims in the camp, through the testimony of its Commandant.

In his closing speech to the Tribunal, Justice Jackson summarized the evidence supporting the guilt of the defendants, concluding with the following peroration:

"It is against such a background that these defendants now ask this Tribunal to say that they are not guilty of planning, executing or conspiring to commit this long list of crimes and wrongs. They stand before the record of this Trial as bloodstained Gloucester stood by the body of his slain king. He begged of the widow, as they beg of you: 'Say I slew them not.' And the Queen replied, 'Then say they were not slain. But dead they are...' If you were to say of these men that they are not guilty, it would be as true to say that there has been no war, there are no slain there has been no crime."

On the first day of October, 1946, the eight judges constituting the First Nuremberg Tribunal took their seats at the bench facing the prisoners' dock, which was empty. Before it, the defense counsel occupied their chairs. To the left were the prosecution tables, occupied by the four Allied prosecutors and the principal members of their staffs. I sat at the American table. Behind us the visitor's gallery was packed with members of the press and visitors. The defendants were to be brought into the courtroom, one at a time, to hear the sentences pronounced against them.

At ten minutes before three, the panelled door in the back of the prisoners' dock slid silently open. The defendant Herrmann Göring stepped out of the elevator which had brought him from the ground floor where the defendants waited. Göring put on a set of headphones which had been handed to him by one of the white-helmeted American guards. The president of the Tribunal began to speak. Göring signalled that he was unable to hear through the headphones, and there was an awkward delay while the technicians sought to correct the difficulty. A new set of headphones was produced, and once again Göring quietly awaited the words which were to decide his fate.

"Defendant Hermann Wilhelm Göring, on the counts of the indictment on which you have been convicted, the International Military Tribunal sentences you to death by hanging."

The number two Nazi turned on his heel and passed through the panelled door into the waiting elevator. The door closed, and there was a hum of whispered voices in the courtroom as those present awaited the arrival of the next defendant, Hess. Rudolf Hess, who had flown his Messerschmitt to England in a futile effort to persuade the British to abandon the fight with Germany, was sentenced to imprisonment for life. The other defendants appeared in turn and received their sentences. Twelve, including Martin Bormann who had been tried *in absentia* and the defendant, Ernst Kaltenbrunner, received death sentences; three were acquitted; and the remaining seven received varying terms of imprisonment. The Tribunal declared as criminal organizations the Leadership Corps of the Party, the Gestapo, the SD, and the SS.

Appeals were taken by all of the defendants to the Allied Control Council, except Kaltenbrunner. The appeals were uniformly denied at a meeting of the Council on October 10. I had been designated by Justice Jackson as his personal representative at the executions and was present in the Palace of Justice on the fateful night of October 15-16, 1946. Shortly before midnight the electrifying word was released that Göring had cheated the hangman by taking poison while lying, ostensibly asleep, upon the bed in his cell. Death thus came to Göring by his own hand, as it had come to Hitler, Himmler and Goebbels, before him, even as the prison officer was walking to the cell block to give formal notice of the executions to take place that night.

At eleven minutes past one o'clock in the morning of October 16, the white-faced former foreign minister, Joachim von Ribbentrop, stepped through the door into the execution chamber and faced the gallows on which he and the others condemned to die by the tribunal were to be hanged. His hands were unmanacled and bound behind him with a leather thong. Ribbentrop walked to the foot of the thirteen steps leading to the gallows platform. He was asked to state his name, and answered "Joachim von Ribbentrop". Flanked by two guards and followed by the chaplain, he slowly mounted the stairs. On the platform he saw the hangman with the noose of thirteen coils and the hangman's assistant with the black hood. He stood on the trap, and his feet were bound with a webbed army belt. Asked to state any last words, he said: "God protect Germany, God have mercy on my soul. My last wish is that German unity be maintained, that understanding between East and West be realized, and there be peace for the world." The trap was sprung and Ribbentrop died at 1:29. In the same way, each of the remaining defendants approached the scaffold and met the fate of common criminals. All, except the wordy Nazi philosopher, Rosenberg, uttered final statement. After the executions the body of each man was placed upon a simple wooden coffin. A tag with the name of the deceased was pinned to coat, shirt or sweater. With the hangman's noose still about the neck, each hanged man was photographed. The body of Hermann Göring was brought in and placed upon its box, to be photographed with the others.

In the early morning hours two trucks, carrying the eleven caskets, left the prison compound at the Palace of Justice bound for a Munich crematory. There, during all of that day, the bodies were burned, one after the other. It was reported that in the evening the eleven urns containing the ashes were taken away to be emptied into the River Isar. The dust of the dead was carried along in the currents of the stream to the Danube – and thence to the sea.

The defendants who had received sentences of imprisonment were transferred to Potsdam prison, which had been designed for some 600 prisoners, but was now reserved for the seven from Nuremberg. As the years passed, the defendants completed their terms and were released. The last prisoner was Rudolf Hess, who had been sentenced for life. On August 17, 1987 forty-one years after the final judgment of the Tribunal, Hess managed somehow to commit suicide. With his death the Hitler tyranny ended.

The tyrant and his chief cohorts were gone. They had sought to achieve greatness in history. But they inscribed their names in sand, and clean waters fell upon the beach and washed them out. They had intended to establish a new order for Europe. But they built upon pillars of hate, and what they stood for could not stand.

The legacy of the trial of the major German war criminals before the International Military Tribunal at Nuremberg is a law-ordered world in which nations live at peace. It is not the fault of the Tribunal or its judgment that this legacy has not been fully accepted in the second half of the Twentieth Century. If Nuremberg had not occurred, and the anger of the Allies had been assuaged by execution of alleged war criminals without trial, world society would not have advanced an iota toward peace under law.

By a resolution of December 10, 1946 the General Assembly of the United Nations affirmed the principles of the Charter and Judgment of the International Military Tribunal and declared that any person who commits an act which constitutes a crime under international law is responsible and subject to punishment, and that the planning and waging of aggressive war constitutes such a crime. The precedent of Nuremberg is now a part of the law of nations, binding upon all governments and the leaders of all states.

Moreover its principles have been re-formulated in the Rome Treaty for a permanent International Criminal Court. At a special ratification ceremony held on April 11, 2002 at the United Nations headquarters in New York, ten countries simultaneously deposited instruments of ratification. Hans Corell, the Under Secretary General for Legal Affairs, declared: "In accordance with Article 26, the Rome Statute of the International Criminal Court will enter into force on the first day of July, 2002. A page in the history of mankind is being turned." The Court is now dealing with its first case – the grave crimes against humanity committed in the course of the conflict in the Sudan.

Although of the great powers only the United States, China and Russia remain non-signatories, Germany, the nation whose despotic leadership brought on the Second World War, was the twenty-third nation to ratify by a resolution adopted on October 27, 2000. I was present in the Reichstag on that historic day, at the invitation of Hans-Peter Kaul, German delegate to the Rome Conference, judge of the International Criminal Court and a delegate to this conference. I was assigned a front seat in the gallery and was introduced from the floor. All the top leaders of the government were present, including Chancellor Gerhard Schröder, Secretary of State Fischer, Minister of the Interior Schily, Minister of Justice Däubler-Gmelin and Vice-Secretary of State Vollmer. After extensive discussion the Rome Treaty was ratified by the Reichstag without a single dissenting vote. No more significant approval of the principles of the Nuremberg Trial, and, indeed, of the principles of law and justice essential to peace on planet Earth, could ever have been made. After the vote Hans-Peter and I retired to a near by restaurant to toast this great victory of law over tyranny with fine German wine.

I concluded *Tyranny On Trial,* my book on the great trial at Nuremberg, with these words:

"Nuremburg stands firmly against the resignation of man to the inhumanity of man. Because of Nuremberg – and the effort which it represents of man's attempt to elevate justice and law over inhumanity and war – there is hope for a better tomorrow. We may enter the atomic age determined that tyranny shall not extend its sway, nor war become its game – placing our faith in the cause of justice, in the freedom of man, and in the mercy of God."

Whitney R. Harris

Tyrannen vor Gericht – Das Strafverfahren gegen die NS-Hauptkriegsverbrecher in Nürnberg, 1945-1946

Whitney Harris berichtet als Zeitzeuge von dem Verfahren gegen die NS-Hauptkriegsverbrecher. Gegen Ende des Krieges war er als Marinesoldat dem Office of Strategic Services (OSS), dem US-Geheimdienst zugewiesen. Während im Sommer 1945 in London die Alliierten über das Statut des zu schaffenden Militärtribunals (IMT) debattierten, konnte Harris immer wieder Beweismaterial über NS-Kriegsverbrechen herbeischaffen, was ihm schließlich die Aufforderung einbrachte, mit dem US-Anklageteam nach Nürnberg zu gehen. Wegen seiner geheimdienstlichen Erfahrungen wurde ihm schließlich die Anklage von Ernst Kaltenbrunner, dem Leiter des Reichssicherheitshauptamtes (RSHA), sowie von SD und Gestapo anvertraut. Im Rahmen der Vorbereitung dieser Anklage war es Whitney Harris möglich, Otto Ohlendorf in seiner Eigenschaft als Mitarbeiter des RSHA zu vernehmen. Bei diesem Verhör kamen die Grausamkeiten der SS-Einsatzgruppen in Osteuropa ans Tageslicht, für die Ohlendorf später in einem der sog. Nürnberger Nachfolgeprozesse mit dem Tod bestraft wurde.

Whitney Harris war außerdem Stellvertreter des Chefanklägers Robert Jackson, als dieser den wichtigsten und ranghöchsten Angeklagten Göring im Prozess verhörte. Dieser musste nicht nur seine Verwicklung in die Umstände der Reichspogromnacht am 9./10. November 1938, sondern auch seine unmittelbare Anordnung, „die Judenfrage der Endlösung" zuzuführen, gestehen.

Harris berichtet von dem dramatischen Moment, als die Ankläger die Möglichkeit hatten, den Kommandanten des KZ Auschwitz, Rudolf Höss, ins Kreuzverhör zu nehmen, und so zum ersten Mal der Holocaust gerichtlich dokumentiert werden konnte.

Bei der Urteilsverkündung kam es zu einem peinlichen Zwischenfall, als Görings Kopfhörer zunächst nicht funktionierte und sich die Bekanntgabe des Todesurteils dadurch verzögerte. Göring gelang es allerdings, sich dem Strang durch Selbstmord zu entziehen. Harris wohnte als Vertreter Jacksons den Hinrichtungen der anderen zum Tode verurteilten Nazi-Verbrecher bei, die in der Nacht vom 15.-16. Oktober 1946 stattfanden, und wurde so Zeuge des Endes der Nazi-Tyrannei.

Die Prinzipien von Nürnberg wurden von den Vereinten Nationen weitergetragen und schließlich im Statut des Internationalen Strafgerichtshofs (IStGH) niedergelegt. Deutschland ist Mitglied beim IStGH. Whitney Harris war auf Einladung der Bundesregierung im Reichstag anwesend als das IStGH-Statut vom Deutschen Bundestag einstimmig ratifiziert wurde. Ein stärkeres Zeichen für die Wirksamkeit der Nürnberger Prinzipien kann es nicht geben.

**III. Civilized People – Heinous Crimes, Philosophical-Historical Perspectives/
Zivilisierte Menschen – grauenhafte Verbrechen, historisch-philosophische
Perspektiven**

Herbert R. Reginbogin

Confronting "Crimes Against Humanity", from Leipzig to the Nuremberg Trials

In 1945, an International Military Tribunal began indicting Nazi war criminals. Information about Nazi atrocities had been available throughout World War II. However, the occurrence of such abominable acts had all too often been discounted or flatly dismissed as no more than wartime propaganda that was too exaggerated to be believed. When in 1943 Jan Karski, a leader of the exiled Polish government in London, who had twice risked his life entering into the Warsaw ghetto came to the United States, he met at the Polish Embassy in Washington D.C. a Justice Felix Frankfurter of the U.S. Supreme Court. Justice Frankfurter was a prominent Jew and personal confidante of the President of the United States Franklin D. Roosevelt. Karski recounted during his meeting with Frankfurter what he had seen in Warsaw, to which Justice Frankfurter replied, "Mr. Karski, a man like me talking to a man like you, I want to be totally frank – I am unable to believe you." Also present was the U.S. Ambassador to the exiled Polish government, who cautioned his learned colleague: "Felix, you don't mean it. You cannot say such a thing. You cannot call him a liar." "I did not say he is lying," responded Justice Frankfurter. "I am just unable to believe what he told me."[1] Eventually Jan Karski would meet Franklin D. Roosevelt on July 28, 1943. Yet it would not be until once the Allied forces entered the extermination camps some 1½ years later, the all too tragically unreal became the all too horribly real.

After the trials began in Nuremberg on November 20, 1945, few people were of the belief that sufficient evidence existed to charge surviving Nazi leaders with crimes involving the commission of conspiracy, crimes against the peace, war crimes, and 'crimes against humanity' (involving persecution, mass deportation, and extermination on political, racial, or religious grounds). In opening the first trials in history for crimes against the peace, Allied leaders took on the grave responsibility of holding other former leaders and military officials responsible as individuals for crimes against humanity. "The wrongs which we seek to condemn and punish," declared Justice Robert Jackson in his opening statement, "have been so calculated, so malignant, and so devastating, that civilization cannot tolerate their being ignored, because it cannot survive their being repeated."[2] History, he argued, had never recorded a crime perpetrated against so many victims "or one ever carried out with such calculated cruelty"[3] against the 'inalienable rights' of all human beings." "Our proof," he predicted without exaggeration, "will be disgusting."[4]

And indeed, it was. Massive amounts of meticulously-kept records revealed the names and numbers of exterminated men, women and children. The annihilation of tens of thousands of civilians was not singular in comparison to similar horrific crimes. However, it *is* singular insofar as Nazism succeeded

---

[1] http://www.remember.org/educate/hrintrvu.html, interview with Jan Karski, 9. February 1995. See Arthur D. Morse, While Six Million Died: A Chronicle of American Apathy (New York, 1998). A shocking detailed account of President Franklin D. Roosevelt's acquiescence, and that of his top staff, in the genocide of Jews and other victims. Rudolf Vrba, "Die missachtete Warnung. Betrachtungen über den Auschwitz-Bericht 1944," in: Dietrich Bracher et. al (eds.), Vierteljahrshefte für Zeitgeschichte. Heft 1 (München, 1996), 1-24; Yehuda Bauer, 'Anmerkungen zum ‚Auschwitz Bericht' von Rudolf Vrba," in: Dietrich Bracher et. al (eds.), Vierteljahrshefte für Zeitgeschichte. Heft 2 (München, 1997), 297-307; Ruth Linn, Escaping Auschwitz. A Culture of Forgetting (Ithaca, 2004). This is about Alfred Weczler and Rudolf Vrba, two Slovakian Jews who had escaped from Auschwitz on April 7, 1944, and found refuge in Bratislava. Rabbi of the community, Rabbi Weissmandel, wrote a report based on their eyewitness account of Auschwitz known as the Vrba-Wetzler report, which was the first document about the Auschwitz death-camp to reach the free world and to be accepted as credible. Its authenticity broke the barrier of skepticism and apathy that had existed up to that point. However, though their critical and alarming assessment was in the hands of Hungarian Jewish leaders by April 28 or early May 1944, it is doubtful that the information it contained reached more than just a small part of the prospective victims – during May and June 1944, about 437,000 Hungarian Jews boarded, in good faith, the "resettlement" trains that were to carry them off to Auschwitz, where most of them were gassed on arrival.

[2] http://www.yale.edu/lawweb/avalon/imt/imt.htm – The Avalon Project at Yale Law – Nuremberg Trial Proceedings, Vol. 2, Wednesday 21 November 1945 – Morning Session, Section 98.

[3] Ibid., Section 118.

[4] Ibid., Section 129.

in the industrial-scale killing of Jews and other unacceptable groups of people. We observe that the ideology of hate, the teaching of contempt, and the demonizing of the "other" continue to kindle the fires of crimes against humanity. Witnessing genocide in Europe, Africa and Asia in the last few years, we recognize that previous lessons – even those exposing the evils of state-orchestrated incitements to ethnic cleansing and genocide – have not been learned. We are witnesses even today to a growing trafficking in hate; Bosnia, Kosovo, Rwanda and Sudan are but a few of many examples.

So why did the Holocaust occur? Why is genocide perpetrated even today? How shall we confront crimes against humanity? Who are the people behind such crimes? Why is there so much indifference still today in regard to ideology of hate against Jews? During a gala event in Paris in January 2004 young French Muslims sitting in the first rows interrupted the performance by a French singer with shouts of "dirty Jew", "death to the Jews", and "we'll kill you" while all attending the event including public figures remained silent with no one condemning the blatant anti-Semitism.[5] In Ingo Müller's book on "Hitler's Justice",[6] we read of the complicity and criminality of judges and lawyers. Robert Jan van Pelt's highly acclaimed books[7] expose Auschwitz as a site at which architects and engineers were closely involved in the day-to-day minutia of designing death camps. Many purport to answer these questions; scholars such as Daniel Goldhagen[8] and Christopher Browning[9] have asserted that Nazism almost succeeded in achieving its 'final solution'. The answer for ordinary Germans supporting the killing of Jews was associated supposedly with Nazi bureaucracy as Robert Lifton and Erik Markusen cite Raul Hilberg in their book pointing out "careerism could be exploited to harness ordinary people in the service of mass murder," while technical achievements within careerism fed competition to design and develop the most effective killing agent and gas chamber "to achieve the highest totals of mass murder."[10] The social dynamics of supporting anti-Semitism and the Nuremberg Race Laws demonstrated the complicity of the German elites – physicians, church leaders, judges, lawyers, engineers, architects, educators, and the like – who ultimately helped buttress the Nazi regime and their killings fields. However, this obsession to achieve the "Final Solution" according to Goldhagen and Browning is rooted much deeper in an internalized legacy of religious and racial discrimination.[11] This ingrained culture of racism and anti-Semitism is expressed by Johann Gottfried Fichte, a moral and metaphysical philosopher at the turn of the 19th century.

Although Fichte was perceived as an agitator by most Germans and had few admirers at first, his writings would make him later into a national hero. He wrote about the inner spirit of the individual to create its own moral universe, which was much admired by such American transcendental philosophers like Ralph Emerson. However, following the occupation of Prussia and other German states by the French Napoleon Forces in the early 1800s, Fichte became intensively and self consciously German. He saw the idea of the Volksgeist (the peoples' spirit): no longer only in terms of the individual spirit creating its own moral universe, but the spirit of a people creating a kind of moral universe as well, manifested in its customs, language, arts, institutions and ideas. Fichte had declared that there was an ineradicable German spirit, a primordial and immutable national character, more noble than that of

---

[5] Proche-Orient.info, Feb. 2, 2004; See Olivier Guitta, "The Chirac Doctrine", in: *Middle East Quarterly* Fall 2005 http://www.meforum.org/article/772.

[6] Ingo Müller, Hitler's Justice: The Courts of the Third Reich (Cambridge, 1991).

[7] Robert Jan van Pelt and Carroll William Westfall, Architectural Principles in the Age of Historicism (New Haven/London, 1991); Deborah Dwork and Robert Jan van Pelt, Auschwitz: 1270 to the Present (New York/London, 1996).

[8] Daniel Jonah Goldhagen, Hitler's Willing Executioners (London, 1996).

[9] Christopher Browning, Die Entfesselung der 'Endlösung'. Nationalsozialistische Judenpolitik 1939-1942 (München, 2003).

[10] Robert Jay Lifton and Erik Markusen, The Genocidal Mentality. Nazi Holocaust and Nuclear Threat (New York, 1988), 166.

[11] Daniel Jonah Goldhagen, A Moral Reckoning. The Role of the Catholic Church in the Holocaust and Its Unfulfilled Duty of Repair (New York, 2002).

other peoples, to be kept pure from Jews, foreigners etc. at all costs from all outside influence.[12] The movement of thought perpetuated by Fichte centered round a dream of a great united and awakened Germany of the future, a sentiment, which influenced, indirectly, a rising up against the ruling dynasties of the Fatherland in whole of Europe in the 19th century.

Indeed racism and anti-Semitism were anchored in the theory and practice of German nationalism but also in the Nuremberg Race Laws, which contributed in turning 'ordinary loyal and law abiding Germans', into 'Hitler's willing executioners'. If this be true of Germans, is it not true of others? Irwin Cotler raised this identical question almost five years ago at the Stockholm International Forum on the Holocaust in 2000.[13] Not only had ordinary Germans become executioners in the Baltics and Balkans but also helpers' helpers in Holland, Norway, and Vichy France in deporting their own Jewish population to Auschwitz and other death camps. Culture did not exclude people from torturing and committing mass murder and it proved ironically that a person can both appreciate love poems and kill children.

So while forms of nationalism emerged as an ideological doctrine at the end of the 18th century presupposing that humanity was divided into nations characterized as individuals with their own culture and history where freedom and personal wealth could be achieved by identifying with a nation, anti-Semitism still flourished. The rhetoric of nationalism relied upon the idea that peace and security is a result of the freedom and security of every nation as member of the family of nations. As the great family of nations proclaimed constitutional principles of religious tolerance based on expanded civil liberties at the Congress of Vienna during 1814 and 1815 much optimism was shed recalling the Age of Enlightenment. While the beginnings of an international right of religious freedom began to be acknowledged as it became evident that religious intolerance had the greatest potential of jeopardizing international security and peace, different forms of anti-Semitism continued to be displayed. European nations like Belgium[14] and Switzerland[15] pledged themselves to maintain religious equality and assure equal protection and favor to every sect to guarantee without any distinction of religion the same political and civil rights, which are enjoyed by other inhabitants. Germany committed that "an amelioration in the civil state of those who profess the Jewish religion in Germany,' paying 'particular attention to the measures by which the enjoyment of civil rights shall be secured and guaranteed to them"[16] These provisions occurred as an integral part of multilateral treaties, established the principle and practice of international guarantees to protect such rights and entailed the implication that any failure by the responsible government to abide by these conditions due to religious or ethnic persecution could result in international enforcement.

Treaties like those of 1856 in Paris and 1878 in Berlin addressing the rights and security of persons living under the rule of a foreign sovereign in time of peace; or the innovative multilateral treaty Geneva Convention for the Amelioration of the Condition of the Wounded in Armies in the Field of 1864, the first designed to protect the individual in time of war; or the 1899 and 1907 Hague Peace Conferences about humanitarian law in armed conflicts were all global efforts to establish laws of humanity.[17] At the core of this 19th century system of international justice were undercurrents of prevailing contrary guidelines arising from nationalism, imperial conquests, racism, anti-Semitism, laissez-faire etc. While at the time war was very much seen as a totally normal tool of international policy (Clausewitz), international law was paradoxically supposed to reduce and deter international violence. As the Great Powers demonstrated their willingness to intervene on behalf of the persecuted to

---

[12] H.C. Engelbrecht,, Johann Gottlieb Fichte: "A Study of His Political Writings with Special Reference to His Nationalism", in: Columbia University Studies in the Social Sciences Nr. 383 (New York, 1968).
[13] http://www.holocaustforum.gov.se/conference/official_documents/abstracts/cotler.htm.
[14] Edward Hertslet, The Map of Europe by Treaty, Vol. I (London, 1875), 38.
[15] Ibid., 255.
[16] Ibid., 205.
[17] "Convention with Respect to the Laws and Customs of War on Land," (Hague II) July 29, 1899; http://www.yale.edu/lawweb/avalon/lawofwar/hague02.htm. "Convention with Respect to the Laws and Customs of War on Land," (Hague IV) October 18, 1907; http://www.yale.edu/lawweb/avalon/lawofwar/hague04.htm.

protect their rights in the Ottoman Empire, the very same nations prosecuted and discriminated against indigenous peoples within their own territorial possessions. It became evident that the principles of humanity and human rights had become a pretext to serve national interests.[18] In President Woodrow Wilson's view the crisis of the First World War was due to the 19th century diplomacy in achieving peace and security by holding dear to a 'balance of power policy'. This should be replaced by a "community of power" by doing away with the nationalistic cabinet-room intrigues drawing on a spirit of international cooperation.[19] Yet nationalism imbued by racism and anti-Semitism would continue.

Great hope and dramatic expectations unfolded as the Allied representatives arrived in Paris at the conclusion of World War I what became known as the 'war to end all wars'. There were crucial differences among the leaders about the function and objectives of international law in international relations and the objectives of peace. However, they had a one thing in common. They wanted that the silenced guns of World War I would pay tribute to the millions who had fallen by drafting a treaty that would make sure that they had not died in vain. The negotiations in Paris provided an opportunity to discuss different proposals that would change the political map of Europe and attempt to make the world a safer place for democracy.

The Paris Peace Conference was about punitive justice against Germany and a new world order. The Germans hoped for a just postwar settlement based on Wilson's Fourteen Points at the Paris Peace Conference, which officially convened on January 18, 1919, would succeed against the ancient policy of punitive justice and demand for massive reparations.

At the first meeting the punishment of war criminals was the first item on the agenda at the Paris Peace Conference.[20] Although there were other nations that had clearly committed war crimes, Germany was practically the only nation on trial. The Austrian-Hungarian Empire whose Emperor Franz-Josef had died during the war and was succeeded by the ex-Emperor Karl at the time of the Paris Peace Conference, could not be held accountable by the Allies. The war crimes committed by Austrian-Hungarian armies in fighting the Russians were ignored because the Bolshevik government in Russia (the Soviet Union) was absent from the Peace Conference and the widely-shared apprehension that the new successor states arrest soldiers of the Austrian-Hungarian forces that had been composed of many populations, which lived in territory taken over by new successor states be required to turn over newly acquired citizens to the Allies as war criminals would be deemed infeasible and pose domestic and international instability.[21] The peacemakers did not have a major invested interest in exploring evidence and handling of what is referred to as the Turkish genocide of the Armenians since according to The Hague conventions Turkish treatment against their own Armenian citizens was an internal matter and not subject to the jurisdiction of another government.[22] Not until 1948, would genocide be clearly defined by treaty as an international crime, and in 1919 adherence to time-honored-notions of sovereignty placed limitations upon the scope of the traditional laws and customs of war. It was this reasoning that laid the foundation for Hitler's deputy German Göring to declare at the Nuremberg Trial: "But that was our right! We were a sovereign State and that was strictly our business."[23] Although the British among the Allies were very interested in bringing criminal charges against Turks outside of Germany because of neglect and brutality towards British prisoners of war that led to the deaths of half of the 13,000 soldiers captured at Kut-el-Amara, political circumstances prevented Britain from

---

[18] Michael Walzer, Just and Unjust Wars (New York, 1992), 101-104.

[19] Committee on Public Information of the United States (ed.), Die Reden Woodrow Wilson's (Bern, 1919), 9.

[20] Foreign Relations of the United States, (FRUS), Paris Peace Conference, 1919 Council of Ten meeting, 17 January 1919 at 3:00 p.m., 606-607; Preliminary Peace Conference, Protocol No. 1, Session of 18 January 1919, 169.

[21] James F. Willis, Prologue to Nuremberg. The Politics and Diplomacy of Punishing War Criminals of the First World War (Westport, 1982), 150.

[22] Conference titled "Ottoman Armenians During the Decline of the Empire: Issues of Scientific Responsibility and Democracy" was held at the Bigli University, Turkey, end of September 2005, contributing to the discussion of the Armenian issue of "genocide" in Turkish society.

[23] G. M. Gilbert, Nuremberg Diary (New York, 1961), 39.

bringing these criminals to justice.[24] As the Council of Four permitted Turkey's arch enemy Greece to send soldiers to occupy Smyrna (Izmir) to support the Sultan's attempt to fulfill demands made by the Allies to try war criminals while the country was in the midst of a civil war, the move was interpreted to be that the Allies were possibly thinking of annexing a part of Turkey by their old enemy. When Greek forces landed at Smyrna on May 15, 1919 hostilities emerged with the Greeks committing flagrant atrocities in their occupation, which for the most part went unpunished, thus making the Allies appear hypocritical and raising objections "in holding Turkey to a double standard of conduct."[25] Thus, Germany remained the only nation on trial.

These failures to extend the policy of punitive justice elsewhere only intensified the perception that Germany was a scapegoat and a proving ground of Wilson's new vision of international justice. Feelings of outrage over Germany were beyond dispute. The French President Raymond Poincaré expressed the sentiments of many Allied leaders and their peoples in a speech held a few weeks after the outbreak of World War I. He accused the Germans of being guilty of a "brutal and premeditated aggression which is an insolent defiance of the law of nations."[26] "In August-October 1914, some 6,500 Belgian and French civilians were massacred by German soldiers, over twenty thousand buildings were deliberately destroyed by arson and artillery fire, civilians were widely used as 'human shields' by German troops advancing into battle, and tens of thousands of inhabitants of the invasion zone were deported to Germany where they were interned. In the most notorious incidents, the historic university library of Louvain was destroyed while much of Dinant was razed...."[27] These were some of the German war crimes along with using poisonous gas, deporting French and Belgium civilians to labor force camps[28] and launching zeppelins over London[29], which also caused the British as early as 1915 to make war crimes trials part of its stated war aims.[30] The Paris Peace Conference created a Commission on the Responsibility of the Authors of the War and on Enforcement of Penalties to study "German atrocities". The Report of that Commission called for necessary action "to try all persons, including heads of state, accused of ordering or failing to prevent, violations of the laws and customs of war and laws of humanity."[31] In the case of the Kaiser of Germany, a special tribunal was supposed to try him, which the Americans rejected by proclaiming a sovereign's immunity from a foreign state's jurisdiction, for to do otherwise was to deny "the very conception of sovereignty."[32] Efforts to establish an international "high tribunal" were quickly rejected by the Americans because there was, "no precedent, precept, practice, or procedure."[33] But the drafted Treaty of Versailles contained provisions that was drafted to contain provisions for the trial by the Allies of Germans who were alleged to have committed violations of the law of war during the course of the then recently concluded World War I. According to Article 228:

The German Government recognizes the right of the Allied and Associated Powers to bring before military tribunals persons accused of having committed acts in violation of the laws and customs of law....The German Government shall hand over to the Allied and Associated Powers...all persons accused of having committed an act in violation of the laws and customs of war....[34]

According to Article 229:

---

[24] Op.cit., 154.
[25] Ibid., 155.
[26] Ibid., 8.
[27] John Horne and Alan Kramer, German Atrocities, 1914, A History of Denial (New Haven/London, 2001).
[28] Gary Jonathan Bass, Stay the Hand of Vengeance. The Politics of War Crimes Tribunals (Princeton/Oxford, 2000), 94.
[29] Ibid., 79.
[30] Ibid., 60.
[31] James F. Willis, Prologue to Nuremberg. The Politics and Diplomacy of Punishing War Criminals of the First World War (Westport, 1982), 75.
[32] Ibid., 76.
[33] Ibid.
[34] Carnegie Endowment for International Peace, The Treaties of Peace, 1919-1923. Vol. I (New York, 1924).

Persons guilty of criminal acts against nationals of one of the Allied and Associated Powers will be brought before the military tribunals of that Power.[35]

Furthermore, Article 330 called for:
The German Government undertakes to furnish all documents and information of every kind, the production of which may be considered necessary to ensure the full knowledge of the incriminating acts, the discovery of offenders and the just appreciation of responsibility.[36]

These demands caused political outcry on the part of the Germans, which resented the Allied related to war crime demands. The German Army warned it would not turn over Kaiser Wilhelm II. The compromise solution was that Germans were to try their own nationals. There was a good deal of wrangling among the Allies about the number and composition of suspects to be tried; the first combined list included some 3,000 names, reflecting a "kind of rough mathematical ratio of wartime suffering" by each country involved.[37] Such an amount was quickly dismissed as unwieldy and unwise, given its likely reception in Germany. By the end of 1919 the Allies handed German delegates dossiers on 890 suspected "war criminals" with instructions to press for prosecution; the listed included such notables as Generals Ludendorff, von Gallwitz, von Bülow, Field Marshall Hindenburg, Reich's Chancellor Bethmann-Hollweg and Admiral von Tirpitz.[38] After stiff German protest and delicate diplomatic negotiations, the Allied submitted a sample "abridged list" of 45 Germans to be arraigned before the German Supreme Court in Leipzig in 1921. Of the 45 submitted cases, merely 12 were tried by the German court, and of these only six were convicted. Of the almost 900 arrangements in Leipzig during the interwar years, almost all of the accused were acquitted. Several of the dozen or so found guilty were allowed to escape with the help of prison guards, who "were publicly congratulated for assisting"[39]

In a recent study by Gerd Hankel *Die Leipziger Prozesse. Deutsche Kriegsverbrechen und ihre strafrechtliche Verfolgung nach dem Ersten Weltkrieg,* there were in fact some 1,700 different forms of trials held in Leipzig between 1921 and 1927 dealing with murder, torture, mistreatment of Prisoner's of War (POWs), forced labor, submarine and air warfare.[40] The prosecution at the Leipziger Trials was undermined by the constant poorly defined concepts like "war crimes" and enforceable international norms. The trials provided a venue for the legitimization of concepts that justified atrocious acts in war by referring to such terminology as "Kriegsnotwendigkeit" (necessity of war), "Kriegsbrauch" (custom of war), und "Handeln auf Befehl" (responding to orders by superiors). These words illustrated concepts that allowed judges to accept that the accused could not have been acting criminally as long as their atrocities were not the intended goal of their actions but the consequence of pursuing a legitimate military goal, which diluted the whole concept of war crimes in the course of the trials as to become meaningless.[41]

One case in particular provides insight into the types of cases actually tried and decided by the German Court not only in terms of its findings but also the continuity it reveals in terms of arguments raised to justify brutal atrocities in World War I and later in World War II. The case against General Karl Stenger, who was tried on the charge of having ordered his men to give no quarter and to shoot all prisoners of war, is exemplary. Despite substantial evidence that such an order had been given and had

---

[35] Ibid.
[36] Ibid.
[37] Gary Jonathan Bass, Stay the Hand of Vengeance. The Politics of War Crimes Tribunals (Princeton/Oxford, 2000), 78.
[38] Gerd Hankel, Die Leipziger Prozesse. Deutsche Kriegsverbrechen und ihre strafrechtliche Verfolgung nach dem Ersten Weltkrieg (Hamburg, 2003), 40-41. Sometimes in the literature reference is made to 901 arrangements in Leipzig. This is due to duplication of the names of the accused.
[39] Geoffrey Robertson, Crimes Against Humanity. The Struggle for Global Justice. (London, 1999), 197.
[40] Op. cit., 103.
[41] Ibid., 256.

been compiled (evidence which included the testimony of fellow accused, the staff Major to whom the order was given; and, that of another office who testified to seeing prisoners of war shot in Stenger's presence; and, that several German enlisted men who testified to having shot prisoners of war in the General's presence), he was acquitted by the Court, apparently on the premise that no Prussian general officer would have issued such an order. His co-accused was found guilty of 'killing through negligence'. There can be no logical explanation for Stenger's acquittal of the charge with respect to the shooting of prisoners of war in view of testimony of the two German officers and the enlisted men. At the very least, he should have been found guilty of having permitted his men to commit a flagrant war crime in his presence and of having taken no action either to terminate it or punish the actual perpetrators.[42] Needless to say, the Allies were outraged. So incensed were the French and Belgians that they tried and convicted hundreds of accused Germans in absentia in their own national courts, and even attempted to use the war crimes issue to force compliance on reparations.

Conclusion

There are similarities between the arguments put forth at both the Nuremberg and Leipzig trials. The permissive attitude toward violence argued at the Leipzig trials was an ideological platform for the Nazi regime. Although there are major differences between Nuremberg and Leipzig, the legal-theoretical grounds of legitimization as set forth in the rulings made by the judges at the Leipzig trials against the accused in regard to war crimes exemplify the legal reasoning that continued to be used to defend atrocious German conduct in both World War I and II.

The Versailles Treaty was extremely severe because the Allies held Germany to "be responsible for the war and for the 'savage and inhumane manner in which it was conducted,' had committed 'the greatest crime against humanity and the freedom of peoples that any nation, calling itself civilized, has ever consciously committed'. Seven million dead lie buried in Europe, more than twenty million bear wounds and sufferings 'because Germany saw fit to gratify her lust for tyranny by resort to war'."[43]

It was less than ten years after the Treaty of Versailles that an extraordinary amount of political and academic energy on the part of German politicians, historians, and publicists had been devoted during the interwar years to refute the war guilt clause in order to rehabilitate Germany similar to what occurred after Nuremberg and the early release of Nazi war criminals. They reveal yet another facet of the Weimar and Federal Republic of Germany judiciary's permissive attitude toward violence imbued with nationalism causing a nation to lack the willingness to seriously prosecute 'their own' for crimes committed in violation of international laws.

In these last two centuries, nationalism has harnessed peoples' imagination to achieve unbelievable results transforming the love for their country into blind loyalty. Xenophobia and total isolation from the outside world were the by-products of such fear. In the name of ones country, men and women have lost their lives because of so-called potential dangers from outside by endangering the existence of other nations. The Leipzig and Nuremberg Trial are crossroads in a testimonial struggle between justice and political expediency. It is more than just about seeking justice for human frailty. It is about a paradox in which nationalism is an idea that emphasizes the bonding of citizens into what is called 'a nation' while citizenship touches upon the rights and duties of individuals providing for a greater range of humanitarianism. The rhetoric of nationalism relies upon the idea that the peace and security of the world is the result of the freedom and security of every nation as a member of the world's great family of nations. Can the limitations of humanity be only overcome by nations or will the citizenship of individuals bring to life what nations fear so much is criticism by their bonding population. What will the crossroad of Leipzig and Nuremberg in the 21st Century be?

---

[42] http://atlas.usafa.af.mil/dfl/documents/commresp.doc. Howard S. Levie, Command Responsibility. See, Gerd Hankel, Die Leipziger Prozesse. Deutsche Kriegsverbrechen und ihre strafrechtliche Verfolgung nach dem Ersten Weltkrieg (Hamburg, 2003), 123-142.
[43] H.W.V. Temperley (ed.), A History of the Peace Conference of Paris, Vol. II (London, 1920), 11.

Herbert R. Reginbogin

„Verbrechen gegen die Menschlichkeit" – von Leipzig nach Nürnberg

Als Reaktion auf die ungeheuerliche Aggressivität der Kriegsführung, den Einsatz von „menschlichen Schutzschildern", Massakern an Kriegsgefangenen, Giftgasangriffen und ähnlichen Verletzungen von Kriegsrecht wurde Deutschland nach Ende des 1. Weltkrieges durch den Versailler Vertrag strafrechtlich zur Verfolgung von Kriegsverbrechern in den eigenen Reihen verpflichtet. Der deutsche Kaiser, Wilhelm II., sollte vor einem internationalen Kriegsgericht wegen des Angriffskriegs verfolgt werden, was aber wegen internationalen Widerstands nicht zustande kam.

Humanitäres Recht hatte zu diesem Zeitpunkt bereits eine längere Geschichte, wurde aber nie wirklich durchgesetzt. Schon ein Jahrhundert früher, nach Ende der Napoleonischen Kriege, wurde auf dem „Wiener Kongress" von 1814/15 das aufklärerische Recht der Religionsfreiheit als Minderheitenrecht anerkannt. Der Respekt für die Freiheit der Person, der auch und gerade gegenüber dem Machthaber Gültigkeit hat, sollte in gemeinsamen Anstrengungen im Pariser Vertrag von 1856, dem Berliner Vertrag von 1878 und in den großen Friedenskonferenzen von 1899 und 1907 in Den Haag zu einem humanitären Recht weiterentwickelt werden. Gerade der europäische Antisemitismus, der nicht zuletzt im deutschen Idealismus seine philosophische Rechtfertigung fand, zeugt von dem politischen Unwillen, die Staatssouveränität zugunsten von Menschenrechten und Minderheitenschutz zurückstehen zu lassen. Die Pariser Konferenz von 1918/19 lastete Deutschland die gesamte Bürde der Kriegsschuld und Verantwortung für die humanitäre Misere an und ließ den Völkermord anderer Länder ungesühnt.

Nicht zuletzt aus dem Gefühl heraus, für die Rolle des Sündenbocks herhalten zu müssen, bemühte Deutschland sich in den Leipziger Prozessen nicht wirklich um eine strafrechtliche Verfolgung der eigenen Kriegsherren, die schließlich teilweise als Helden gefeiert wurden. Am Ende wurden zwölf Verfahren durchgeführt und sechs Angeklagte verurteilt, denen allerdings teilweise von den Gefängniswärtern zur Flucht verholfen wurde. Die Geschichte der Leipziger Prozesse ist zugleich ein Beispiel des Paradoxons Nationalismus. Darin zeigt sich eine Überbetonung der Zugehörigkeit von Bürgern zu einer sog. Nation, während der Status des Bürgers mit individuellen Rechten und Pflichten das größere Spektrum der Humanität in den Mittelpunkt rückt. Die durch Nationalismus geschürte Xenophobie war schließlich ein Grund dafür, dass die „Endlösung" in Deutschland so viele „willige Vollstrecker" fand. Vielleicht ist der Konflikt zwischen dem Staat und dem Individuum der Punkt, wo sich Leipzig und Nürnberg treffen.

Klaus Kastner

Rückblick: NSDAP, Reichsparteitage, Rassengesetze

In Nürnberg, einer Stadt, die an der Wende des Mittelalters zur Neuzeit gelegentlich auch als „caput Germaniae" bezeichnet wurde, sind seit mehr als neun Jahrhunderten Kunst und Kultur, Handel und Gewerbe und seit der Mitte des 19. Jahrhunderts auch die Industrie „zu Hause". In der ersten Hälfte des 20. Jahrhunderts war eben dieses Nürnberg für zwei Jahrzehnte – freilich neben anderen deutschen Städten, wie Berlin, München oder Weimar – auch einer der Schauplätze des Nationalsozialismus und damit ein Ort totalitärer Herrschaft.

Drei Begriffe machen für manche den Namen der Stadt Nürnberg geradezu zum Synonym für den Nationalsozialismus, nämlich: die NSDAP, die Reichsparteitage und die Rassengesetze. Ein vierter topos folgt schließlich in den Jahren nach 1945, nämlich die Nürnberger Prozesse.

Die NSDAP

Es stellt sich als erstes die Frage, wie es dazu kommen konnte, dass eine Stadt, in der beispielsweise bei den Reichstagswahlen vor dem Ersten Weltkrieg die Sozialdemokratische Partei die meisten Stimmen erhielt und in der während der Weimarer Republik die Sozialdemokraten und Kommunisten fast die Hälfte aller Stimmen auf sich vereinigen konnten, sich zu einem Ort entwickelte, der von den Nationalsozialisten gewissermaßen zum Forum für viele ihrer Aktivitäten auserkoren wurde.

Die Wurzel liegt zum einen – wie in vielen Teilen Deutschlands nach 1920 – in dem verlorenen Ersten Weltkrieg, in der darin begründeten wirtschaftlichen Misere und in der Tatsache, dass man sich mit dem Ergebnis des sogenannten Versailler Friedensvertrages nicht abfinden wollte. Bereits 1923 begannen die Nationalsozialisten zusammen mit anderen deutsch-nationalen Gruppierungen, sich in Nürnberg darzustellen. Man beging hier den „Deutschen Tag". Hitler und seine NSDAP waren damals noch nicht dominierend. Doch der erste Mann der Nürnberger NSDAP, Julius Streicher, ein seit 1909 in Nürnberg lebender Volksschullehrer, der 1922 eine Ortsgruppe der NSDAP in Nürnberg gegründet hatte, war ein Einpeitscher, der sich Hitlers absolutem Führungsanspruch unterworfen hatte. Streicher vertrat in Nürnberg das nationalsozialistische Gedankengut nicht nur persönlich, sondern brachte es demagogisch auch unter die Bevölkerung. Er gab seit 1923 in Nürnberg den „Stürmer" heraus. Diese ursprünglich als allgemein politisches Lokalblatt konzipierte Wochenzeitung – sie gehörte Streicher persönlich, war also keine offizielle Parteizeitung – entwickelte sich im Laufe der Jahre zu einem über ganz Deutschland verbreiteten antisemitischen Hetzblatt mit einer Wochenauflage von meist 500.000. Das Zitat „Die Juden sind unser Unglück" (es stammte von dem Historiker Heinrich v. Treitschke) prangte auf der Titelseite einer jeden Ausgabe des „Stürmer". 22 Jahre lang verbreitete dieses Periodikum übelste Diffamierungsparolen gegen den Weltfeind „Alljuda". Karikaturen, erfundene Geschichten, beispielsweise über Ritualmorde und Hostienschändungen durch Juden, und Berichte über die „Verschwörung des internationalen Finanzjudentums" schürten den Hass gegen alles Jüdische.

Nicht zuletzt dieses planmäßige Hetzen gegen alles Jüdische und das damit verbundene Verhetzen weiter Volksschichten, nicht nur in Nürnberg, sondern auf dem Weg über die Wochenzeitung „Der Stürmer" im gesamten Deutschen Reich, war dann – ich greife jetzt 20 Jahre weiter – der maßgebliche Grund dafür, dass das Internationale Militärtribunal in Nürnberg im Oktober 1946 Julius Streicher wegen Verbrechen gegen die Menschlichkeit (Straftatbestand vier im Sinne der Anklage) zum Tod durch den Strang verurteilte.

Streicher gründete in Nürnberg am 20.10.1922 die erste Ortsgruppe der NSDAP außerhalb von München. Als treuer Vasall Hitlers „trommelte" er wie kein zweiter für die nationalsozialistische „Bewegung", so dass die NSDAP in Nürnberg im Jahre 1927 schon 2000 eingeschriebene Parteimitglieder hatte. Bei der bayerischen Landtagswahl am 24. April 1932 wurde die NSDAP in Nürnberg mit 37,6 % der Stimmen erstmals die stärkste politische Kraft. Doch eine demokratisch legitimierte, absolute Mehrheit errang die NSDAP in Nürnberg nie. Bei der Reichstagswahl am 5. März 1933, der letzten freien Wahl, bekam die NSDAP in Nürnberg nur 41,7 % der Stimmen, während es im

Reichsdurchschnitt immerhin 43,9 % waren. Also: Nürnberg war keineswegs eine Stadt, in welcher der Nationalsozialismus vor 1933 politisch dominierend war.

Als aber der Nationalsozialismus in Berlin die Regierungsgewalt errungen hatte, ging es auch in Nürnberg mit den demokratischen Rechten rasch dahin. Nach den „Gleichschaltungsgesetzen" verhafteten die Nationalsozialisten sofort den Nürnberger Oberbürgermeister Luppe und Bürgermeister Treu. Der zugleich entfachte „braune Terror" hatte es auf alle Repräsentanten der Demokratie abgesehen. Schon kurz nach der NS-Machtübernahme wurden in Nürnberg etwa 250 Kommunisten verhaftet und ins rasch eingerichtete KZ Dachau verschleppt. Führende Sozialdemokraten erlitten das gleiche Schicksal. Die ersten Opfer in Dachau waren also deutsche Demokraten. Ab dem 30. August 1933 saßen nur noch Nationalsozialisten im Nürnberger Stadtrat.

Auch wenn, wie gesagt, die NSDAP in Nürnberg in den Jahren vor 1933 keineswegs politisch dominierend war, so konnte sie nach der so genannten Machtergreifung auch in Nürnberg im Wesentlichen alles bestimmen. Daher kommt es, dass zwei Elemente des NS-Regimes – fortwirkend bis jetzt – mit dem Namen der Stadt eng verbunden sind, nämlich die Reichsparteitage der NSDAP und die sogenannten Nürnberger Gesetze.

Die Reichsparteitage

Die Entscheidung für Nürnberg als Austragungsort der ab 1933 alljährlich stattfindenden Reichsparteitage fiel im Juli 1933. Auch Stuttgart hatte sich darum beworben. Hitler favorisierte jedoch Nürnberg. Dahinter stand – neben dem Umstand, dass zur Durchführung einer solchen Massenveranstaltung die Infrastruktur einer Großstadt notwendig war – die Idee, an die Reichstage des Heiligen Römischen Reiches Deutscher Nation anzuknüpfen. In der sogenannten Goldenen Bulle des Jahres 1356 hatte Kaiser Karl IV. verfügt, dass jeder neu gewählte deutsche Kaiser, der in Frankfurt gewählt und in Aachen gekrönt werden sollte, in Nürnberg den ersten Reichstag abzuhalten habe. An diese alte Reichstradition, die allerdings im 16. Jahrhundert abbrach, und an das Renommee Nürnbergs, die „deutscheste der deutschen Städte" zu sein, wollte Hitler anknüpfen. Vor dem historischen Hintergrund der Stadt wähnten sich die Nationalsozialisten als die Vollender der deutschen Geschichte.

Mit dem im Juli 1933 gegebenen Einverständnis des Nürnberger Oberbürgermeisters und kraft der Bestimmung durch Hitler, wonach Nürnberg der ständige Ort der Reichsparteitage ist, stand die Stadt im Dienst des NS-Regimes. Dessen Werbestrategen zogen eine direkte Linie von den Reichstagen des Mittelalters zu den jetzt – alljährlich im September stattfindenden – einwöchigen Staats- und Parteifeiern. Die NSDAP schuf sich mit dem Reichsparteitagsgelände eine riesige Versammlungsstätte. Rund eine Million Menschen nahmen jeweils als Aktive oder als bloße Zuschauer an diesem Spektakel, einer Mischung aus Machtdemonstration und Faszination, teil. Im Vordergrund der Veranstaltungen stand jeweils die Einschwörung der Massen auf den „Führer" Adolf Hitler und die Inszenierung der propagierten „Volksgemeinschaft".

Ein Architekt für das „Gigantenforum" als „Weihestätte der Bewegung" mit Aufmarschflächen, Versammlungs- und Lagerstätten fand sich in der Person des jungen Architekten Albert Speer, dem Adolf Hitler im Herbst 1934 den Auftrag erteilte, einen Gesamtplan für das Reichsparteitagsgelände zu entwerfen, das eine Größe von nicht weniger als 11 qkm umfasste.

Fertig gestellt wurden lediglich die Luitpoldarena, die 150.000 Teilnehmern aus dem Kreis der SS und der SA und zudem 50.000 Zuschauern Platz bot. Als weitere Anlage wurde das Zeppelinfeld vollendet. Es war eine fast quadratische Anlage mit Tribünen für rund 70.000 Zuschauer. Dieses Feld – sein Name erinnert an die erste Landung des Luftschiffes „Zeppelin" im Jahre 1909 – erlebte die Aufmärsche der politischen Leiter der NSDAP, des Reichsarbeitsdienstes, den „Tag der Gemeinschaft" und Vorführungen der Wehrmacht.

Weitere Bauvorhaben blieben unvollendet: die Kongresshalle für 50.000 Teilnehmer, das Deutsche Stadion für 400.000 Besucher und das Märzfeld für Vorführungen der Wehrmacht, das bis zu 500.000 Besucher fassen sollte.

Der Architekt des Ganzen, Albert Speer, stand auch als Angeklagter vor dem Internationalen Militärtribunal in Nürnberg, freilich nicht in seiner Eigenschaft als Architekt des Führers, sondern als

Rüstungsminister des Reiches (seit Februar 1942). Als solcher wurde er unter dem Aspekt des Völkerstrafrechts unter anderem zur Verantwortung gezogen wegen des Einsatzes von Zwangsarbeitern in der Rüstungsindustrie.

Die sogenannten Nürnberger Gesetze

Der Reichsparteitag des Jahres 1935 wurde zum Ort für die Verkündung von zwei Reichsgesetzen, die für alle deutschen Bürger jüdischer Abstammung in der Folgezeit katastrophale Folgen hatten. Diese Gesetze, das „Gesetz über das Reichsbürgerrecht" und das „Gesetz zum Schutze des deutschen Blutes und der deutschen Ehre", waren zwar in den Berliner Ministerien erarbeitet, in Nürnberg jedoch abschließend beraten und verkündet worden. Deshalb werden sie umgangssprachlich heutzutage als Nürnberger Gesetze bezeichnet. Dieser Begriff ist nach wie vor ein Makel auf dem Namen der Stadt, obwohl die Kommune eigentlich eher beiläufig zum historisch-geographischen Ursprung dieser menschenverachtenden Normen wurde. Was war geschehen?

Ursprünglich hatte man keineswegs geplant, dieses Massenspektakel zum Fanal für die Degradierung jüdischer Mitbürger zu machen. Zwar war schon im Parteiprogramm der NSDAP (1920) die Forderung enthalten gewesen, dass nur ein Mensch „deutschen Blutes" auch deutscher Staatsbürger sein könne und jeder andere als Gast „unter Fremdengesetzgebung" stehen müsse. Diese radikalen Forderungen der NSDAP bekamen aber erst nach der sogenannten Machtergreifung am 30. Januar 1933 „Oberwasser". In der Folgezeit war man jedoch innerhalb der federführenden Ministerien – Innen- und Justizministerium – uneins, *wie* man diese Forderungen gesetzlich normieren solle. Diesem Tauziehen machte Hitler persönlich während des Reichsparteitages 1935 ein Ende. Es war geplant gewesen, am Abend des 15. September, des Abschlusstages, den formal noch bestehenden Reichstag, also das Parlament, einzuberufen und das vom Reichsinnenministerium vorbereitete Reichsflaggengesetz zu verabschieden, das die Hakenkreuzflagge zur Nationalflagge bestimmen sollte. Doch dies genügte Hitler für die als Höhepunkt des Reichsparteitages gedachte Reichstagssitzung nicht. Er gab daher am 13. September – also während des Parteitages, nur zwei Tage vor der geplanten Sitzung – dem Reichsinnenminister Frick den Auftrag, „zur Auffüllung des Programmes" ein Rassengesetz zu entwerfen, das der Reichstag neben dem Reichsflaggengesetz verabschieden sollte. Die Forderung nach einem Rassengesetz seitens der NSDAP war nicht neu – und Entwürfe gab es in den Schubladen der Berliner Ministerien schon etliche. Nun sollte binnen 24 Stunden alles perfekt sein. Die Staatssekretäre Pfundtner und Stuckart aus dem Reichsinnenministerium hatten die Vorlage für das Rassengesetz zu entwerfen. (Ein zeitlicher Vorgriff auf das spätere Schicksal der beiden: Pfundtner beging am 25. April 1945 in Berlin Selbstmord; Stuckart, der auch am 20. Januar 1942 an der Wannseekonferenz über die „Endlösung der Judenfrage" teilgenommen hatte, wurde durch ein US-Militärtribunal in Nürnberg am 11. April 1949 zu vier Jahren Haft verurteilt). Noch in der Nacht vom 13. zum 14. September wurde ein Mitarbeiter des Reichsinnenministeriums – Dr. Löser – von Berlin nach Nürnberg beordert. Die Genannten entwarfen dann anhand der vorhandenen Textvarianten die beiden Gesetze. Die erste Vorlage wurde von Hitler sofort abgelehnt und die Ausarbeitung von vier Entwürfen mit unterschiedlicher Schärfe befohlen. Es ging dabei nicht nur um die Staatsbürgerschaft, sondern auch um Berufs- und Gewerbebeschränkungen, um das Verbot der Heirat zwischen Ariern und Nichtariern, um Strafbestimmungen und anderes mehr. Die Ministerialbürokratie wollte den „mildesten" Entwurf, der zudem nur „Volljuden" betreffen sollte, bei Hitler „durchbringen". Denn man befürchtete bei der Ausweitung des in Betracht kommenden Personenkreises Schwierigkeiten in der praktischen Umsetzung einer solchen Regelung. Letztlich entschied sich Hitler einerseits für die mildeste Form der Entwürfe. Er strich aber andererseits eigenhändig im Entwurf die Bestimmung, dass das Gesetz nur für „Volljuden" gelten solle. Um dessen Außenwirkung – wohl auch mit dem Blick auf das Ausland – etwas abzuschwächen, ordnete Hitler jedoch an, dass die Nachrichtenagentur DNB („Deutsches Nachrichten-Büro") melden solle, diese Regelungen würden nur für „Volljuden" gelten.

Zwei Tage später, am Sonntag, dem 15. September, trat um 21 Uhr im Jugendstilbau des „Kulturvereins" der Reichstag unter dem Vorsitz des Präsidenten Göring zusammen. Neben dem Reichsflaggengesetz wurden sodann das sogenannte Reichsbürgergesetz und das Blutschutzgesetz beschlossen. Damit waren jüdische Bürger im NS-Regime erstmals r e c h t l i c h und s o z i a l zu Menschen zweiter Klasse geworden.

Wie scheinheilig man damals diesen Schritt zur Verfolgung deutscher Juden der deutschen Öffentlichkeit präsentierte, zeigt ein Bericht der für damalige Verhältnisse durchaus noch als „freie" Presse zu wertenden „Bayerischen Volkszeitung" vom 17. September 1935. Darin heißt es: „Bei einem Abschiedsabend im ‚Deutschen Hof' erklärte der Führer, dass den Juden in Deutschland nach diesen Gesetzen Möglichkeiten ihres völkischen Eigenlebens auf allen Gebieten eröffnet würden, wie sie bisher in keinem anderen Land zu verzeichnen wären. Im Hinblick darauf erneuerte der Führer den Befehl für die Partei, jede Einzelaktion gegen Juden wie bisher zu unterlassen". – In einem weiteren Bericht über diese gesetzliche Neuregelung steht zu lesen: „Indem Deutschland der jüdischen Minderheit Gelegenheit gibt, sich selbst zu leben und diesem Eigenleben (d.h. durch eigene Schulen, Theater, Sportverbände u.a.m.; d.Verf.) der jüdischen Minderheit den staatlichen Schutz gewährt, fördert es die Volkwerdung des Judentums und trägt dazu bei, das Verhältnis zwischen den beiden Nationen wieder erträglicher zu gestalten". Mit diesem Hinweis sollte ein Bezug hergestellt werden zu dem kurze Zeit vorher in Zürich abgehaltenen Zionistenkongress, der festgestellt hatte, dass das Judentum nicht nur eine Religion, sondern dass die Juden ein eigenes Volk seien.

Die Weltöffentlichkeit reagierte auf die Entrechtung jüdischer Bürger nicht sonderlich. Zwar gab es Aufrufe internationaler Sportverbände, deutscher Emigranten und anderer, die für das Jahr 1936 nach Deutschland vergebenen XI. Olympischen Spiele (Garmisch und Berlin) zu boykottieren. Das Internationale Olympische Komitee blieb aber bei seiner im Jahre 1931 getroffenen Entscheidung, obwohl sich die NSDAP unverblümt dagegen ausgesprochen hatte, Wettkämpfe gemeinsam mit „Negern und Juden" durchzuführen. Wie wenig Resonanz die „Nürnberger Gesetze" im politischen Leben der Völker fanden, erhellt geradezu beispielhaft die Tatsache, dass bei dem Reichsparteitag des Folgejahres – 1936 – mehr ausländische Diplomaten als früher in Nürnberg zu sehen waren. Und im Jahre 1937 nahmen erstmals auch die Botschafter Frankreichs und Großbritanniens, Francois-Poncet und Henderson, an der Selbstdarstellung des Nationalsozialismus in Nürnberg teil; die USA vertrat der Geschäftsträger ihrer diplomatischen Vertretung. Für hochrangige ausländische Besucher eröffnete der „Zweckverband Reichsparteitage" im Jahre 1936 sogar ein eigenes „Diplomatenhotel" unmittelbar neben dem renommierten Grand Hotel gegenüber dem Nürnberger Hauptbahnhof.

Nimmt man alles in allem, so war die Stadt Nürnberg ein Ort, an dem sich das nationalsozialistische System der Weltöffentlichkeit darstellte. Eine Legende ist es allerdings, dass eben deshalb die Alliierten im Jahre 1945 Nürnberg zum Sitz des Internationalen Militärtribunals gewählt hätten. Bei allen Vorgesprächen plädierten die Sowjets stets für Berlin, die ehemalige Reichshauptstadt, die sie erobert und besetzt hatten, auch wenn seit Juni 1945 den Westalliierten drei Sektoren der Stadt als Besatzungsgebiet zugeteilt waren. Die USA wollten den Prozess von Anfang an in ihrer Besatzungszone abhalten, denn sie organisierten und finanzierten alles. Auf der Suche nach einem geeigneten Gerichtsort ließ sich der *spiritus rector* des IMT, Robert H. Jackson, von dem stellvertretenden US-Militärgouverneur, General Lucius D. Clay, beraten. Jackson wusste, dass er ein weitläufiges Gebäude brauchte, da die Personalplanungen Raum für mehr als 1000 Mitarbeiter vorsahen. Auch sollte in nächster Nähe ein Gefängnis vorhanden sein, das nicht nur die Kriegsverbrecher selbst, sondern auch Tausende von Zeugen, die überwiegend aus Kriegsgefangenen- oder Internierungslagern für längere Zeit nach Nürnberg gebracht werden mussten, aufzunehmen hatte. Clay stützte sich bei seinem Vorschlag an Jackson auf ein Gutachten des US-Army Generalanwalts Murray Barnays, der in Nürnberg den verhältnismäßig wenig kriegsbeschädigten Justizpalast und das nebenan gelegene Gefängnis besichtigt hatte. Nirgendwo anders in Deutschland fand sich eine solch ideale räumliche Konstellation. So einigte man sich schließlich mit den Sowjets in Artikel 22 des Statuts für den Internationalen Militärgerichtshof vom 8. August 1945 kompromissweise darauf, dass der ständige Sitz des IMT in Berlin ist, dass aber der erste Prozess, welcher wegen des Kalten Krieges der einzige blieb, in Nürnberg stattfindet.

Nürnberg trug viele Jahre schwer an der Bürde, dass der Name der Stadt weltweit mit dem Nationalsozialismus geradezu identifiziert wurde. Sieht man indes näher hin, kann man unschwer feststellen, dass Nürnberg nur e i n e Station von etlichen auf dem mörderischen Weg eines Regimes war, das sich anschickte, Europa bis zum Ural unter seine Gewaltherrschaft zu zwingen.

Literatur:
Benz, Wolfgang, Hermann Graml und Hermann Weiß (Hrsg.), Enzyklopädie des Nationalsozialismus (München 2001).
Burleigh, Michael, Die Zeit des Nationalsozialismus – Eine Gesamtdarstellung (Frankfurt 2000).
Fritzsch, Robert, Nürnberg unterm Hakenkreuz – Im Dritten Reich 1933 – 1939 (Düsseldorf 1983).
Gruchmann, Lothar, „Blutschutzgesetz" und Justiz. Zu Entstehung und Auswirkung des Nürnberger Gesetzes vom 15. September 1935, in: VjZ 1983, 418.
Hambrecht, Rainer, Der Aufstieg der NSDAP in Mittel- und Oberfranken 1925 – 1933 (Nürnberg 1976).
Kulka, Otto Dov, Die Nürnberger Rassengesetze und die deutsche Bevölkerung im Licht geheimer NS-Lage- und Stimmungsberichte, in: VjZ 1984, 582.
Nadler, Fritz, Eine Stadt im Schatten Streichers (Nürnberg 1963).
Ogan, Bernd und Wolfgang W. Weiß (Hrsg.), Faszination und Gewalt. Zur politischen Ästhetik des Nationalsozialismus (Nürnberg 1992).
Pohl, Dieter, Verfolgung und Massenmord in der NS-Zeit 1933 – 1945 (Darmstadt 2003).
Zelnhefer, Siegfried, Die Reichsparteitage der NSDAP in Nürnberg (Nürnberg 2002).

Klaus Kastner

In Retrospect: Nazi Party, the Rallies, the Racial Laws

Decades after the National Socialist Germany had ceased to exist, Nuremberg continued to be remembered as a city, which had fulfilled a prominent role under the NS-regime. Although National Socialism in Nuremberg was not more predominant than elsewhere in Germany, the Nazi regime had skilfully misused Nuremberg's historical backdrop by turning it into a place that the Nazis used to mystically expose themselves as something empowered and revitalized.

The National Socialist Party (NSDAP) was founded 1920 not in Nuremberg, but Munich. However, Julius Streicher, an elementary school teacher and exceptionally repulsive anti-Semite, founded in 1922 a regional NSDAP group in Nuremberg. He "drummed up" enormous support for the Nazi movement. For over twenty years from 1923, he published in Nuremberg a series of nauseating anti-Semitic articles in "Der Stürmer" ("Storm Trooper"). The newspaper had a peak circulation close to 500,000 per issue. It thrilled its anti-Semitic readers with hair-raising stories about Jewish misconduct or crimes such as ritual child murder, rape, sinister political plots and so on. These anti-Semitic portrayals and demagogic campaigns would constitute an important step in mobilizing Germans to exterminate a whole group of people because they were Jews. Streicher was found guilty by the IMT and sentenced to death by hanging.

In summer of 1933, Hitler chose Nuremberg to be the permanent site for the NSDAP Annual Party Rally. He preferred this large town equipped with a more than adequate infrastructure to accommodate millions of spectators because he believed Nuremberg was the "most German of all German cities" by taking into consideration the predominant position Nuremberg had within the Holy Roman Empire of the German Nation and using it for his propaganda.

The early political claims of the NSDAP were transformed into law with the passage of the so-called Nürnberger Rassengesetze (Nuremberg Racial Laws). "Aryan" descent should become the prerequisite for citizenship in the German Reich. Hitler personally ordered at short notice that the laws should be proclaimed during the 1935 Party Rally in Nuremberg. Within two days, drafts of the "Citizens' Rights Act" and the "Protection of German Blood and German Honour Act" were prepared and subsequently passed by a special session of the Reichstag (parliament) in Nuremberg on September 15, 1935. Regardless of the legal discrimination against Jews, the XI Olympic Games were anyways held in Berlin the following year. At subsequent party rallies the number of diplomats and guests from abroad attending the procession were even higher than the years previously!

It was a heavy burden for Nuremberg that worldwide the name of the city was seen as a synonym for National Socialism. Nuremberg was only one of many stations along the murderous path of a totalitarian regime preparing to tyrannically and coercively control Europe to the Ural.

John Q. Barrett

"One Good Man": The Jacksonian Shape of Nuremberg*

Robert H. Jackson (1892-1954) was a Justice of the Supreme Court of the United States when President Truman asked him in April 1945 to take on, and Jackson accepted responsibility to be the chief United States prosecutor of Nazi war criminals. The International Military Tribunal proceedings that commenced seven months later in Nuremberg, Germany – the first and, in public memory, *the* Nuremberg trial – are, like Jackson himself, well-known, especially to this audience of participants, witnesses and experts.

The Nuremberg story of Justice Jackson – he who was first among Allied equals at Nuremberg; he who was its architect – is not, however, merely a story of one man in the place where he spent a year trying criminal cases of enormous, and permanent, significance. Much of Jackson's "Nuremberg" actually occurred elsewhere, in Jackson's fifty-three years of living before Lord Geoffrey Lawrence gaveled the IMT trial proceedings to order on Tuesday, November 20, 1945.

I. Jackson's Preparation for Nuremberg

The key component of Robert Jackson's preparation for his role at Nuremberg was his deep reverence toward, and his expertise in, law itself. As a very young man, Jackson came to the law in 1910 primarily through training as an apprentice. A lawyer by 1913, when he was only twenty-one years old, he then worked for 20 years in his native New York State in private practice. Jackson's legal experiences during those decades were full and diverse, including civil and criminal trial and appellate litigation, client counseling, sophisticated business matters, government regulation, municipal lawyering, regional and national professional organizing, political party service, and involvements in state government. In all of this, Jackson interacted with many, but he ran primarily his own shop, doing most of his investigating, writing, negotiating and advocacy. In a quick span of years, Jackson rose to prominence across his state and even nationally, becoming a member of the American Law Institute and a leader in the American Bar Association.

Attorney Robert H. Jackson of western New York State was not merely an American domestic figure, however. Jackson's early years and prosperity soon brought international travel that greatly expanded his range of contacts, and experiences. In 1924, he was part of an American Bar Association trip to England. During this trip, Jackson began an acquaintance with former Supreme Court Justice, near president, Secretary of State and future Chief Justice Charles Evans Hughes. This trip also took Jackson for the first time to Middle Temple in London, in which one of his ancestors, who later immigrated to the United States, had been born. This trip to England also gave Jackson an initial exposure to Lord Chancellor Richard Haldane, who in many ways became a Jackson role model and influence in later years.

As Jackson developed this deep intellectual, personal, practical and expansive engagement with law, he also pursued a formative political path. He had an acquaintance with Franklin D. Roosevelt beginning in Albany in 1911, when Jackson was a law student and Roosevelt was a freshman state senator. Over the next two decades, that acquaintance developed as Roosevelt rose in the Wilson administration, to the New York governor's mansion and ultimately to the White House, becoming a series of deepening political, policy and law involvements and a friendship.[1] After being deeply involved in FDR's 1932 presidential campaign, Jackson paused a year before committing to join the New Deal in Washington. Ultimately, in early 1934, he was appointed by President Roosevelt,

---

* I am very grateful to Dean Lawrence Raful, his Touro College Jacob D. Fuchsberg Law Center colleagues and the other conference sponsors for organizing this special event, to Professors Michael J. Bazyler, Herbert R. Reginbogin and Christoph J.M. Safferling for their vision and expertise, and to law students Eleni Zanias and Jessica Duffy for research assistance.

[1] *See generally* ROBERT H. JACKSON, THAT MAN: AN INSIDER'S PORTRAIT OF FRANKLIN D. ROOSEVELT (John Q. Barrett, ed., 2003).

confirmed by the Senate and joined the Treasury Department's Bureau of Revenue as assistant general counsel.

In federal government work, Jackson quickly rose to his own great successes. In spring 1935, he was the U.S. government's lead prosecutor in an American, domestic, civil law version of a "trial of the century": the tax evasion case against Andrew W. Mellon, the former Secretary of the Treasury and Ambassador to the Court of St. James's in London under Presidents Harding, Coolidge and Hoover. Although Mellon was defended aggressively by his attorney, the American Bar leader Frank Hogan, Jackson's cross-examination of the defendant and the sizeable judgment he won, garnered him nationwide press and name recognition.

Later in 1935, Jackson led the U.S. government's investigation regarding the finances and affairs of the recently-deceased "Match King" Ivar Kreuger. His International Match Company had collapsed spectacularly (it was the Enron of its day), leaving financial mysteries, creditors and business wreckage in the United States and abroad. Roosevelt sent Jackson to Europe that fall to investigate Kreuger's and the corporation's actual financial circumstances. This investigation took Jackson to Sweden, France ... and into Germany. Jackson's first visit to Germany occurred, in other words, in Hitler's third year in power. Jackson met there with the United States ambassador and many senior officials and got to observe National Socialism in its early governmental form.

From Treasury, Jackson moved on to the Department of Justice. Over the next few years, Roosevelt appointed him first as an Assistant Attorney General heading the Tax Division, then Assistant Attorney General heading the Antitrust Division, then Solicitor General of the United States, then finally Attorney General. In each of these positions, Jackson had enormous responsibilities and was the Roosevelt Administration representative on the pressing issues, and in the leading legal and political battles, of the day. Jackson came to be known even more widely as a great talent and a personal favorite of President Roosevelt. Jackson was, by late 1937, one whom Roosevelt contemplated succeeding him in the White House when he retired to Hyde Park, New York in 1941 after two terms.

Events in Roosevelt's career, of course, took different turns, as did Jackson's own career. In 1941, Roosevelt appointed Jackson to the Supreme Court as an Associate Justice. During the next four Terms, Jackson wrote landmark opinions in civil liberties and other notable cases. Through his beautifully written opinions, Jackson demonstrated legal expertise and range and a level of personal independence that distinguished him from some of his colleagues on the Court. It became generally known that Roosevelt's intention was to appoint Jackson to serve as chief justice of the United States whenever Chief Justice Harlan Fiske Stone decided to step down. Thus Jackson was visibly, by spring 1945, in legal circles and beyond, in the United States and internationally, much more than "just" a Supreme Court justice. When new President Truman officially appointed Jackson on May 2, 1945, to prosecute Nazi war criminals, Jackson's stature and qualities themselves demonstrated the seriousness of the president's commitment to a path of law.

II. The Intellectual Seeds of Jackson's Nuremberg

What Jackson did at Nuremberg has many intellectual origins, but three are particularly noteworthy:

First, Jackson's personal background was philosophically anti-war. During World War I, when Jackson was merely a young attorney based in western New York State, he was involved in regional politics and spoke regularly on many public issues. He advocated President Wilson's reelection in 1916 because "he kept us out of war." Jackson was deeply skeptical and critical in the first months of 1917, when the president's perspective on the European war changed. Unlike many of his contemporaries, Jackson did not enlist after war was declared in April 1917. He spoke loyally in support but kept his distance from actual war efforts. Two decades later, Jackson was deeply involved in President Roosevelt's reelection campaign. In August 1936, when FDR delivered his famous "I Hate War" speech at Chautauqua Institution in Jackson's adult home region of Chautauqua County, New York, Jackson was present at the president's side, mouthing along with him that famous punch line – which was, in its particular, a Roosevelt commitment to non-involvement in the new civil war in Spain.

Second, as a Roosevelt administration executive branch official in the late 1930s until summer 1941, Jackson was deeply involved in numerous projects that were important responses to, and legal condemnations of, Germany's aggressive war making. In summer 1940, Jackson as attorney general provided to President Roosevelt the ultimate legal justification that undergirded and justified his deal with Prime Minister Churchill that provided 50 over-aged United States destroyers in exchange for naval base leases on various Atlantic territories. From this Destroyer Deal came the larger Lend-Lease arrangements, again built on policy and legal work by Jackson, with Great Britain and with the U.S.S.R. In 1941, Jackson wrote and prepared to deliver in Havana, Cuba, a speech to the Inter-American Bar Association that attacked Germany's aggressive and illegal war making.[2] This speech, which Jackson finalized after discussing it privately with President Roosevelt on his yacht off the coast of Florida, in fact was not delivered by Jackson – rough waters and bad weather made it impossible for the seaplane that would have taken Jackson to Cuba to land near the yacht, but the speech made it there without Jackson and was delivered in his name by a prominent U.S. diplomat. This widely-reported speech formed an intellectual framework for Roosevelt Administration policy through the rest of that year and then, as war came to the United States, during later planning for prosecuting the perpetrators of such aggression.

Third, Jackson's work and career involved regular and committed engagement with issues that we today would call human rights questions. In the Department of Justice, he was deeply involved in civil liberties policy determinations. On the Supreme Court, he penned the *West Virginia State Board of Education v. Barnette* opinion that invalidated compelled flag salutes in public schools, protecting Jehovah's Witness schoolchildren in their freedom of belief and conscience.[3] Jackson also stood away from the majority of the Court, for human rights in clashes with executive power, military imperatives and his own president and friend. The most notable of these moments is Jackson's dissenting opinion in *Korematsu v. United States*, where he branded as unconstitutional the military orders of 1942 that had excluded Japanese Americans, including tens of thousands of U.S.-born citizens, from the west coast regions where they lived and worked.[4]

III. Jackson's Nuremberg Assignment: The Law/Trial Path

When Japan attacked the United States on Sunday, December 7, 1941, Jackson had been a justice of the Supreme Court and thus out of the executive branch for only six months. He felt immediately that the legal work of the Court had become much less important than the military work of the nation and its allies. Jackson's feelings of discontent crystallized in the very first week after Pearl Harbor when he and the other justices heard oral arguments in the now long-forgotten *Winchester Country Club* and *Merion Cricket Club* cases.[5] The weighty issue they raised was whether country club members' annual payments constituted "dues and membership fees" and were therefore subject to federal taxation. Jackson railed in the justices' private conference about the stupidity of giving a moment's thought, at that juncture, to such a pedestrian issue – which led Chief Justice Stone to assign responsibility for writing those Court opinions to Jackson. In this context, Jackson volunteered to President Roosevelt, early and often, that he would leave the Court and return to the executive branch in any capacity where he could be useful.

Roosevelt appreciated Jackson's offer and conversed with him occasionally and informally about various war-related matters, but the president recognized, and he told Jackson, that Court-work had permanent importance. FDR also told Jackson to stay put because of the president's intention eventually to elevate Jackson to chief justice. Thus, Jackson stayed put on the Court, although his reading and thinking did gravitate toward international topics and matters as time permitted. In part, this may have

---

[2] *See* Robert H. Jackson, *International Order*, 35 AM. J. INT'L L. 348 (1941) & 27 A.B.A. J. 275 (1941).
[3] 319 U.S. 624.
[4] *See* 323 U.S. 214, 242-48 (1944) (Jackson, J., dissenting); *see generally* John Q. Barrett, *A Commander's Power, A Civilian's Reason: Justice Jackson's* Korematsu *Dissent*, 68 L. & CONTEMP. PROBS. 57 (2005).
[5] *White v. Winchester Country Club*, 315 U.S. 32 (1942); *Merion Cricket Club v. United States*, 315 U.S. 42 (1942).

reflected Jackson's understanding of Roosevelt's vague references to tasks he would want Jackson to perform after the war was won.[6] Without in any way meaning to compare Andrew Mellon or other large domestic legal challenges to the criminality of Hitler and the waging of aggressive world war, Roosevelt and his other close advisers knew and valued Jackson as an excellent lawyer of great stature – he would be their counsel of choice for any challenging legal project. Thus even very early on, Roosevelt contemplated Jackson performing a task on the order of what ultimately became his Nuremberg assignment.

During the War, President Roosevelt made general, public commitments that the German perpetrators of this criminal calamity would, following their military defeat, be tried and punished through legal processes rather than summarily executed. This decision emerged from a battle within the Roosevelt administration, pitting principally Secretary of War Henry L. Stimson advocating legal prosecution against Secretary of the Treasury, Henry Morgenthau Jr., advocating summary punishment. FDR first committed generally to prosecution but then endorsed Morgenthau's proposal for extreme and extralegal measures, only to be persuaded by Stimson to rescind that decision and return to the law path. In February 1945, Roosevelt, Stalin and Churchill at Yalta reiterated their general commitment to war crime prosecution. They discussed the topic in no detail, however, referring it instead to foreign ministers for further negotiation and implementation. That work, including detailed negotiations that Roosevelt's White House counsel Samuel I. Rosenman was having with counterparts in London, was ongoing when Roosevelt died on April 12, 1945.

Although Jackson in that early April was barely aware of these diplomatic processes, he was by that time organizing and advancing his own thinking about post-war prosecutions of war criminals. On April 13, 1945, literally the night after Roosevelt's sudden death in Warm Springs, Georgia, Jackson delivered the principal speech at the annual meeting of the American Society of International Law.[7] Jackson addressed the topic of war criminals and starkly delineated the choice between executive disposition and trial. Jackson declared that he would not presume to say which option should be chosen – that was, in his view, an executive decision that a new president now would have to make. When Jackson mentioned President Roosevelt, he departed from his prepared text and noted tearfully that events now would be proceeding on a course that he had not anticipated even a day earlier, meaning a new president. But as to the trial option, Jackson declared that a decision to pursue trials should mean committing the United States to conducting real trials, by which he meant American due process standards of public proceedings, specified charges, defense counsel, discovery of evidence, a burden of proof beyond a reasonable doubt on prosecutors, and an independent judicial decision-maker.

In the days following Jackson's ASIL speech, Judge Rosenman returned to Washington, first for the Roosevelt funeral and then to brief President Truman on pending matters. One topic of their discussion was Rosenman's negotiations with the British regarding the fate of captured German leaders following their imminent defeat. Based on discussions with Rosenman, Truman quickly decided to pursue the law path – the Stimson, rather than the Morgenthau, path – just as Roosevelt had. This meant that the project would require more than armed force. Through Rosenman, Stimson and his deputy John J. McCloy, the recommendation reached Truman that Justice Jackson, among other possibilities, was a person of the stature and ability to do this job for the United States. Truman, who knew Jackson quite well and held him in very high regard, agreed to give this project this leader. He dispatched Rosenman to the Supreme Court, where he opened discussions and on the president's behalf ultimately offered the job to Jackson. In direct discussions over a matter of a few days, Jackson and Truman reached a detailed understanding on their shared vision of real prosecution in real trials of Nazi war criminals. On May 2, 1945, Truman announced publicly Jackson's appointment to serve as United States Chief of Counsel.

---

[6] *See* ROBERT H. JACKSON, *supra* note 1, at 107: "He [FDR] said that it was quite possible … that when the peace came and the time for settlement arrived, there would be important things that I was particularly qualified to do. What it was he did not say, and of course I did not ask. The matter dropped at that."

[7] *See* Robert H. Jackson, *The Rule of Law Among Nations*, 39 AM. SOC'Y INT'L L. PROC. 10 (1945), 31 A.B.A. J. 290 (1945), 19 TEMP. L.Q. 135 (1946) & 39 AM. J. INT'L L. 533 (1945) (excerpt).

IV. Jackson's Getting to Nuremberg

When Jackson publicly accepted President Truman's appointment, he believed that he was accepting a summer job that he could complete before the next Supreme Court Term would begin on the first Monday in October. The job, as Jackson understood it at the start, involved preparation and prosecution of the principal war criminals. He would, in other words, take ready-to-go cases based on overwhelming evidence, master them quickly and try them swiftly to verdicts. Given the assurances of the War Department and the obvious criminality of the Nazi defendants, Jackson believed that such trials were plausible, and that they were destined to be successful.

What Jackson learned in his first weeks on the job, performed while also juggling his end-of-term work on the Supreme Court, was that he had been sold a bill of goods. There were no cases ready to be tried. In fact, there was very little evidence that had been collected. Most shocking for the objective of international prosecution was the absence of any diplomatic agreement among the Allies of how to proceed – Jackson quickly learned that significant diplomatic work needed to be done before any prosecution could take place. He therefore arranged formally to be assigned the task of negotiating the diplomatic agreement. Within weeks, all negotiations, including those that had occurred at the United Nations conference in San Francisco, were consolidated as Jackson's responsibility. On June 18, 1945, he embarked for Europe to negotiate with his British, Soviet and French counterparts.

What Jackson accomplished first, and personally, in this enormous, unexpected task was the public definition of an intellectual framework for prosecuting Nazi war criminals. Jackson's vision is embodied in the June 6, 1945-report that he delivered to President Truman following an initial organizational trip to the European continent.[8] As Jackson's report makes clear, an overriding concern of the prosecution project was to prevent resurgent Nazism in Germany. The legal framework for addressing this concern was a charge that the Nazi planning and perpetration of aggressive war and related crimes was itself criminal – in other words, it was conspiracy in the nature of that crime in United States law. Jackson also articulated a theory of bringing charges against specified organizations that had been key components of the Nazi governmental system. Jackson asserted that these organizations were central entities in the conspiracy, and that obtaining guilty verdicts against organizations in an initial trial would permit more efficient later prosecutions of their most culpable members. The Jackson model, in other words, envisioned the trial of an organization such as the Gestapo and, once its criminal guilt was adjudged, prosecutions of individual Gestapo members limited to their roles in that now-established criminal organization. Jackson's vision at this very early moment also included a preferred mode of trial evidence: the Nazi individuals and organizations would be prosecuted based not on the fallible and suspect testimony of cooperating individuals, but rather on authenticated, enormously detailed captured Nazi documents – in other words, on proof from the defendants' own offices and fountain pens.

Following his report to Truman and the completion of the Supreme Court's term, Jackson decamped to London to do the actual negotiating with his Allied counterparts. He went there with the full authority of the United States, which President Truman had communicated anew in June when he received and embraced Jackson's initial report. Over the ensuing seven weeks, Jackson accomplished for the United States and its Allies a diplomatic feat that is, in the recollections of "Nuremberg" as a trial in Germany, appreciated far too little. Meeting over many, many hours in Church House at Westminster Abbey, Jackson and the Allies negotiated the details and agreed on the legal framework that became the IMT trial at Nuremberg.[9] Their starting-point was four significantly differing legal systems and at least two divergent views – the American-British view versus the Soviet perspective – of what a war criminal trial actually would be. In the western view (and on this the British quite quickly deferred to the American lead), the trial would be of the type that Jackson had described three months earlier to the

---

[8] Report to the President by Mr. Justice Jackson, June 6, 1945, *reprinted in* U.S. DEPARTMENT OF STATE, INTERNATIONAL CONFERENCE ON MILITARY TRIALS, LONDON, 1945, at 42-54 (Publication 3080, released Feb. 1949).

[9] The full London Conference proceedings and other related documents were published as U.S. DEPARTMENT OF STATE, INTERNATIONAL CONFERENCE ON MILITARY TRIALS, LONDON, 1945 (Publication 3080, released Feb. 1949).

American Society of International Law: it would be a real trial, not a show-trial, with prosecutors carrying a significant burden of proof at trial against defendants, who had adequate and independent defense resources, in a proceeding before an independent adjudicator, all of which meant that acquittal was a real prospect for each defendant. In the Soviet view, by contrast, these trials were to be conducted against persons whom the Allies had already declared to be guilty, which meant a view of the trial function as revealing crimes as a step preliminary to imposing foreordained punishments.

Jackson's authority to insist on the international framework he envisioned or, failing to persuade allies of his course, to abort the international effort and instead to go it alone in U.S.-only prosecutions, was reconfirmed near the end of the London negotiations. In late July 1945, Jackson flew to Berlin and traveled to Potsdam, where President Truman was meeting with his counterparts Stalin and Churchill (and then, after the British election and the Conservative Party's defeat, with new Prime Minister Clement Attlee). Each of the new "Big Three" was accompanied in Potsdam and assisted by his foreign minister and a large supporting contingent. Jackson met with the new U.S. Secretary of State, James F. Byrnes, who had been Jackson's Supreme Court colleague during his first year on the Court and was a peer and a friend. Byrnes at Potsdam reconfirmed Jackson's full authority to conclude the London negotiations for the United States in any fashion he saw fit.

Back in London and within days, Jackson used this authority – his ultimate ability to walk away from the international effort – to win Soviet agreement to Jackson's trial model. On August 8, 1945, Jackson and his Allied counterparts signed the London Agreement and Charter.[10] It defined the crimes that would be prosecuted by the Allies and created the International Military Tribunal that would adjudicate cases against Nazi defendants. (Within days, of course, Japan surrendered following the U.S. atomic bombings of Hiroshima and Nagasaki, and this unexpectedly early Allied victory in the Pacific and full conclusion of World War II explains why the London Agreement did not, even in its time, attract the global notice it deserved.)

V. Jackson at Nuremberg

On November 21, 1945, Justice Jackson went to the podium in courtroom 600 at the Palace of Justice in Nuremberg and delivered his opening statement on behalf of the United States. Jackson was the first of the four prosecutors to speak, and his presentation took more than half the day. In eloquent terms, demonstrating his writing prowess and the drafting and redrafting that produced it, he canvassed in one speech the full span of Nazi criminality. He reviewed in detail the evidence against the individuals who sat in the dock and located them within the system of culpability and accountability that ran upwards to the would-be defendants who were not present, including Hitler, Himmler and Goebbels. Jackson also located the individual crimes within the overall conspiracy to engage in aggressive war, the supreme crime, explaining a theory of that crime as the taproot that made the further war crimes and crimes against humanity possible. For Jackson and the Allies generally, this framework of conspiracy to breach the peace as the principal crime connected the individual defendants to the culpable Nazi organizations, and it addressed this culpability in a public venue that would, it was hoped, help to thwart any resurgent Nazism among the German people.

After the American conspiracy case was completed in late 1945, Jackson turned personally to the completion of two additional tasks during the many remaining months of trial. He first presented the detailed argument defending the criminal charges against the Nazi organizations, ultimately persuading the Tribunal to proceed with their trial and, in the end, to return guilty verdicts against some of the organizations.

Jackson also participated actively during the 1946 trial months in cross-examining selected defendants and principal defense witnesses. Most famous, and controversial, was his cross-examination of Hermann Göring, the *de facto* lead defendant. The general public impression of this examination is

---

[10] *See id.* at 420-28.

that Jackson was less than successful, and indeed that Göring got the better of Jackson in their verbal exchanges.

Although the trial record, films and audiotapes demonstrate that this impression is accurate to a point, the belief that Göring bested Jackson reflects, I believe, an over-emphasis on a few reporters' partial, if harshly judgmental, accounts, their unrealistic expectations for the examination, their disproportionate focus on Jackson's rough patches and, at the bottom line, their overlooking the decisive admissions that Göring made. In other words, while there is no question that Jackson's cross-examination of Göring got off to a bumpy start, that some questions were compound or just loose, that Jackson wasted time arguing to the Tribunal objections that to us seem trivial, and that Jackson in spots got flustered, negative reportage and impressions fail to notice what the examination achieved: Göring's many admissions and his authentications of damning documentary evidence. As the United States judges Francis Biddle – Jackson's longtime friend and colleague and then, at Nuremberg, his judicial antagonist to a degree – and John Parker put it privately to Jackson shortly after he completed this cross-examination, the prosecution was getting on better than they had thought possible.

Negative reporter accounts of Jackson's cross-examination of Göring seem to reflect particularly unrealistic, but experience-based, expectations that Jackson would knock this witness out of the ring. Before Göring took the stand, his lawyer Dr. Otto Stahmer had opened his defense case by calling two principal defense witnesses, German Air Force General Karl Bodenschatz and General Field Marshal Erhard Milch, to testify. In each instance, Jackson handled the cross-examination and was extremely effective. Indeed, Jackson's cross-examination elicited from Bodenschatz and Milch such strong evidence against Göring that Dr. Stahmer, almost in a panic, decided to dispense with further witnesses and instead to rush Göring himself onto the stand unexpectedly. Reporters, witnessing all of that, probably expected more of the same from Jackson, overlooking Göring's brilliance, his restored health since jailers had weaned him from drugs and his attitude of fatalistic confidence without remorse. They also did not anticipate the Tribunal's decision, surely a fair one, to let a defendant explain, even quite discursively, his answers to a prosecutor's questions.

In the later months of trial, Jackson personally handled cross-examinations of other defendants and witnesses. Two of these – Hjalmar Schacht, former head of the Reichsbank, and Albert Speer, former Hitler confidant, architect and armaments minister – were notably challenging. Although each examination is a complex and mixed story, Jackson believed that he succeeded each time in establishing the defendant's guilt beyond a reasonable doubt. The Tribunal agreed as to Speer, but Schacht was acquitted.

Jackson's final trial contribution at Nuremberg trial was his July 26, 1946, closing address. In this speech, again written, edited, rehearsed and perfected by Jackson himself, he canvassed the overwhelming evidence that he and his Allied counterparts had presented. Interestingly, although he argued vehemently for verdicts of guilty, Jackson advocated no particular punishment for any of the defendants. Some combination of his own disdain for execution and respect for judicial independence seems to have reinforced Jackson's determination to be only, in this moment, a prosecutor, summarizing the evidence presented and arguing for the verdicts he believed it justified legally.

VI. Jackson's Nuremberg Successes

In the complex story of Nuremberg, Jackson's achievements are at least four-fold:

First, Jackson's accomplishment was the legal task completed. He demonstrated, even to skeptical audiences at home and abroad, that this trial had indeed lived up to high standards of fairness and due process. One example of this developing reaction was the move that Judge Charles Wyzanski, one of Jackson's friends and former colleagues and one of his most thoughtful early critics, made during the course of the Nuremberg trial year. Judge Wyzanski, with whom Jackson had argued and won the Social Security cases in the Supreme Court in the late 1930s[11] and who in 1941 had been appointed a

---

[11] See *Steward Machine Co. v. Davis*, 301 U.S. 548 (1937); *Helvering v. Davis*, 301 U.S. 619 (1937).

Federal District Judge in Boston, spoke privately and then wrote publicly, near the start of the Nuremberg trial, about his deep misgivings about its legality.[12] Months later, after evaluating the record of what actually had transpired in the Palace of Justice, Wyzanski, with private grace and public courage, reassessed and to a large degree recanted his earlier criticism by publishing these words in late 1946:

"…[T]he outstanding accomplishment of the trial, which could never have been achieved by any more summary executive action, is that it has crystallized the concept that there already is inherent in the international community a machinery both of the expression of international criminal law and for its enforcement. …

No doubt such an *ad hoc* method is not so satisfactory as a covenant made by all the powers in advance of wrongful conduct…. But until the world is prepared to follow the more satisfactory method, it has every reason to be profoundly grateful to Mr. Justice Jackson and his associates, who, in the face of enormous practical difficulties and widespread theoretical criticisms, persisted until they demonstrated the justice of the *ad hoc* method adopted at Nuremberg."[13]

Jackson himself summarized the legal task well completed, including its procedures, evidence, judgments and relative speed, in his October 7, 1946, final report to President Truman.[14]

The second success Jackson had at Nuremberg is the building of the historical record that is embodied in the forty-two volume Nuremberg trial transcript and millions of pages of supporting documents. As Jackson had envisioned from the beginning, this documentary record, largely captured from the Nazis and authenticated by them during interrogations and at trial, demonstrates without ambiguity the scope, complexity, and personal perpetration of myriad crimes. It took subsequent decades for people to understand from this record the enormity of the crimes perpetrated by the Nazis, including the magnitude and details of the Holocaust. This comprehension might not have been possible, and "Holocaust denial" might be more than a crackpot venture today, had Jackson not led the Allies on the path of gathering and using documentary evidence to prove the guilt of the individual and organizational defendants.

Another Jackson success at Nuremberg is what he recognized even then as its durability as a challenge. In the remaining eight years of his life, Jackson wrote, spoke and thought constantly about Nuremberg while also handling his sizeable work as a Supreme Court Justice. He regarded his time at Nuremberg as the most important work of his life, and he viewed it as work that was undone in the sense of having a meaning that would continue to be worked out over the course of many years. In Jackson's phrase, the meaning of Nuremberg would start to become clear in the "century run," and it would turn on the uses and building and commitment that future generations brought to what he started.

A final Jackson success was the one that connects him personally to the bottom line of the project: He got the world, quite literally, to Nuremberg, and to all that that achievement has come to mean in six decades since his day. Another leading lawyer might have been able to do something similar, laudable and lasting, of course. But that doing of Nuremberg would have required, in that hypothetical alternative to Jackson, the uncommon qualities that made him, by 1945, such a special fit for this enormous, personal task.

And yet that may overstate the need. President Truman instead may have had it exactly right when he offered a much simpler description in late summer 1945 of what Jackson was, in his performance of this task, which made him the right man to pursue all the challenges that became the achievements of Nuremberg. On Wednesday, September 5, 1945, Justice Jackson met with the president in the White House. The London Agreement had been reached and the project of prosecuting leading Nazi war

---

[12] *See* Charles E. Wyzanski, Jr., *Nuremberg – A Fair Trial?*, ATLANTIC MONTHLY, Apr. 1946, *reprinted in* CHARLES E. WYZANSKI, JR., WHEREAS – A JUDGE'S PREMISES 164 (1965). Judge Wyzanski's article originated in his December 15, 1945, lecture to the American Academy of Arts and Sciences.

[13] Charles E. Wyzanski, Jr., *Nuremberg in Retrospect*, ATLANTIC MONTHLY, Dec. 1946, *reprinted in* CHARLES E. WYZANSKI, JR., WHEREAS – A JUDGE'S PREMISES 180 (1965).

[14] Report to the President by Mr. Justice Jackson, Oct. 7, 1946, *reprinted in* U.S. DEPARTMENT OF STATE, INTERNATIONAL CONFERENCE ON MILITARY TRIALS, LONDON, 1945, *supra* note 9, at 432-40.

criminals was then in transition to Germany, where individuals and organizations would be indicted and then the international trial would commence. Jackson, in this meeting, described for the president the kinds and quality of evidence that the Allies had gathered for use at trial, including some that Jackson personally had just obtained from the Vatican following his personal meeting with Pope Pius XII. President Truman told Jackson of his inclination to appoint Francis Biddle, recently fired as Attorney General of the United States and before that the Solicitor General, who had served under Attorney General Jackson, as the chief American judge at Nuremberg. Truman gave Jackson an opportunity to object, and thus to veto, the Biddle appointment, but Jackson did not.

And then, after the meeting was done, President Truman jotted a few words on his daily appointment page alongside the entry noting this scheduled meeting. Jackson had, Truman wrote, already "[m]ade a great contribution to International Law." And then the President summarized what Jackson was – which is all that the world will ever need to accomplish something like Nuremberg – by writing three more words: "One good man."[15]

---

[15] President Truman's handwritten note on his Appointment Sheet, Sept. 5, 1945, in PSF Box 82, Harry S. Truman Library, Independence, MO, *quoted in* OFF THE RECORD: THE PRIVATE PAPERS OF HARRY S. TRUMAN 64 (Robert H. Ferrell, ed., 1980).

John Q. Barrett

„Ein guter Mann": Jacksons Einfluss auf Nürnberg

Robert H. Jackson (1892-1954) war Richter am Obersten Gerichtshof der Vereinigten Staaten von Amerika (US Supreme Court), als ihm der damalige Präsident Truman im April 1945 die Verantwortung für die Strafverfolgung der Nazi-Kriegsverbrecher übertrug. Diese für ihn selber wichtigste Aufgabe seines Lebens, die ihn wie keine andere prägte, lässt sich aber nur im Kontext seiner Lebensgeschichte betrachten.

Jackson startete seine juristische Karriere im Alter von 21 Jahren und war 20 Jahre lang in seinem Heimatstaat New York meist als selbständiger Anwalt tätig. Seine Bekanntschaft mit dem späteren US-Präsidenten Roosevelt führte ihn auf verschiedene Positionen in der US-Bundesverwaltung. Bereits 1941 wurde er schließlich zum Richter am Supreme Court gewählt und gewann rasch nicht nur an Profil bei Gericht, sondern auch an Renommee in der amerikanischen und internationalen Öffentlichkeit. Unter den vielen Gründen, ihn für die wichtige und neue Aufgabe auszuwählen, stechen drei besonders heraus: Zum einen war Jackson bekanntermaßen Kriegsgegner; zum anderen war er mit verantwortlich für verschiedene diplomatische Verurteilungen des deutschen Aggressionskriegs seitens der Roosevelt-Administration; schließlich zeugt seine Rechtsprechung am Supreme Court für ausgesprochene Sensibilität im Hinblick auf Menschenrechte.

Von besonderer Bedeutung auf Jacksons Weg nach Nürnberg war seine Rede am 13. April 1945 (am Abend nach Roosevelts überraschendem Ableben) in Warm Springs, Georgia, bei der Jahresversammlung der American Society of International Law. In dieser Rede setzte er sich vehement dafür ein, dass, wenn politisch eine Strafverfolgung der deutschen Kriegsverbrecher gewünscht sei, die Einhaltung der rechtstaatlichen Verfahrensregeln Pflicht sei, und dass ein fairer Prozess und nicht ein Schauprozess stattfinden müsse. – Kurz nach dieser Rede, am 2. Mai 1945, wurde er offiziell mit der Vorbereitung der Strafprozesse betraut.

Die unmittelbare Vorbereitung des Statuts des Tribunals war ein langwieriger politischer Prozess, in welchem Jackson gemeinsam mit seinen englischen Kollegen vor allem die sowjetische Seite vom Erfordernis der Fairness überzeugen musste. Am 21. November 1945 stand es dann auch Jackson zu, die Anklage mit seinem Plädoyer zu eröffnen. Auch wenn ihm ein möglichst objektiver Prozess, der sich vor allem auf Urkundsbeweis stützt, vorschwebte, übernahm er das Kreuzverhör von Göring, Schacht und Speer selbst. Dabei ist die kritische Rezeption der Einvernahme Görings in den Medien nicht unbedingt gerechtfertigt, mag aber zum Teil auch an überzogenen Erwartungen gelegen haben.

Jacksons Errungenschaften lassen sich in folgenden Punkten zusammenfassen: Zum einen hat Jackson gezeigt, dass ein fairer Prozess möglich ist; zum anderen hat er eine Dokumentensammlung geschaffen, die es ermöglicht, den Holocaust und andere Nazi-Verbrechen nachzuvollziehen; schließlich hat er den Grundstein gelegt für eine internationale Strafrechtordnung, die sein eigenes Leben weit überdauerte. Dafür verantwortlich sind auch Jacksons Charakterstärke und Engagement. Als Präsident Truman am 5. September 1945, nach Verabschiedung des Statuts des IMT, Jackson im Weißen Haus traf, schrieb er nach dem Treffen drei Worte in seinen Kalender, die besonders treffend Jacksons Persönlichkeit beschreiben: „One good man" – „Ein guter Mann".

Rodger D. Citron

The Nuremberg Trials and American Jurisprudence: The Decline of Legal Realism and the Revival of Natural Law[*]

I will discuss the influence of the Nuremberg trials on legal philosophy in the United States, focusing on the decline of legal realism as an autonomous jurisprudential movement and the revival of natural law philosophy. Legal realism emerged in the late 1920s as a jurisprudential movement that criticized the formalist approach to law, expressed skepticism about the influence of the rules of law, and sought to demystify how courts operated and judges made decisions. The legal realists generally urged the incorporation of social science into efforts to understand how courts operated and to improve their operations.

The legal realists were viewed as intellectual provocateurs. By the early 1930s, legal realism had become a prominent jurisprudential movement – not dominant, yet extensively discussed. Critics complained that the legal-realists divorced morality from law, worshipped at the altar of power, and were engaged in a fruitless quest to impose the precision of scientific methods on the understanding of law and the legal system. As the decade progressed, the emergence of fascism abroad gave these criticisms additional urgency. In the aftermath of World War II, the horrors of Nazi Germany and the emerging totalitarian threat of the Soviet Union contributed to the decline of legal realism as an independent jurisprudential movement. Quite simply, the United States could not embrace a legal philosophy in which morality was detached from the legal system. This concern for morality in the legal system contributed to the revival of natural law philosophy.[1]

I must acknowledge that this brief summary oversimplifies the relevant developments. My topic is enormously broad and spans nearly three decades. Therefore, at the outset, I have taken the following steps to make the topic more manageable. First, my discussion focuses on two authors: Jerome Frank and Lon Fuller. Each man is, deservedly, a towering figure in American jurisprudence. Jerome Frank practiced corporate law in Chicago and New York City, held a number of high-level positions in the federal government during the New Deal (including Chairman of the Securities and Exchange Commission), and was appointed to the Second Circuit Court of Appeals in 1941. He wrote a number of books, including Law and the Modern Mind – a provocative and popular legal realist tract – and taught at Yale Law School. Frank was, to be sure, a committed legal realist.

After World War II, Frank made clear in his writings that he saw a place for morality in the law, and that he cared deeply about the fate of democracy in a world threatened by totalitarianism. Frank's efforts to acknowledge the role of morality in the law, to pronounce, repeatedly, his concern for democracy, and to broaden his focus from describing the insights available to judges through psychoanalysis to proposing reforms for the judicial fact-finding process reflect broader shifts in American jurisprudence. That shift occurred, in part, because of events like the Nuremberg trials.

Lon Fuller, a lifelong law professor who spent more than 30 years at Harvard Law School, was one of the most thoughtful proponents of natural law theory. Initially Fuller appreciated the anti-formalist insights offered by the legal realists, though he insisted on a more purposive and value-laden understanding of the law and the legal system through which it developed. As the 1930s progressed,

---

[*] Mr. Citron wishes to thank Dean Lawrence Raful, Andrea Cohen, Dan Derby, Beth Mobley, and April Schwartz for their time and assistance, Robert S. Summers for providing a prompt response to a request for more information about Lon Fuller, and Albert Messina for valuable research assistance. Needless to say, they are not responsible for any errors.

[1] Natural law philosophy, broadly speaking, insists that positive law – statutes, court decisions interpreting statutes – should be evaluated according to a higher moral law. To put it another way, natural law also, generally, insists upon the existence of foundational principles of morality that exist apart from the legal rights and duties established by positive law. Natural law philosophy may be defined in relation to the legal philosophy of positivism. See, e.g., Philip Soper, "Some Natural Confusions about Natural Law," 90 Mich. L. Rev. 2393, 2395 (1992) ("the legal positivist claims that no necessary connection exists between law and morality; the natural law legal theorist denies that a sharp separation of these concepts is possible").

Fuller joined the chorus of natural law scholars criticizing legal realism. In 1940, Fuller's book, "The Law in Quest of Itself," sharply and specifically condemned the legal philosophies of positivism (and its related successor, legal realism) for contributing to the emergence of fascist governments in Germany and Spain.

Fuller continued to develop his theory of natural law after World War II. Fuller's 1958 debate with the English philosopher H.L.A. Hart over positivism in the Harvard Law Review is perhaps the most famous jurisprudential exchange of the 20th century.[2] As I will discuss, the specter of Nazi Germany informed – even, to some extent, framed – the exchange. Central to the debate was a disagreement over judicial treatment of laws enacted and enforced while the Nazi government was in power. Although neither Fuller nor Hart specifically discussed the Nuremberg trials, the debate over retroactive invalidation of Nazi laws paralleled the retroactivity issue raised by the war crimes prosecutions.

Second, I want to be clear on the way in which the trials should be understood in my discussion of the relevance of the Nuremberg trials to the development of American jurisprudence. First, the trials loomed large in world politics during and after World War II, and inspired an extensive debate over their legitimacy.[3] The trials were a significant event for legal philosophers. Second, the Nuremberg trials received extensive press coverage, and widely publicized the nature and extent of the Nazi atrocities during World War II. The trials therefore both reflected and contributed to serious post-war concerns about totalitarianism. The debate inspired by the Nuremberg trials therefore is one measure of a broader shift in American legal thought – a change in which legal realism continued to decline as an autonomous jurisprudential movement, and natural law philosophy returned to prominence.

I. Situating American Legal Realism: Context and Definitions

Legal realism in the United States emerged early in the twentieth century as a response to the dominance of formalism in legal thought and practice. Harvard Law School Dean Christopher Columbus Langdell, who devised a new approach to legal education in the 1870s, is perhaps the archetypal legal formalist of this era.[4] Langdell maintained that law is an inductive science, and "that all the available materials of the science are contained in printed books" of judicial opinions.[5] For Langdell, as Bruce Ackerman has explained, "the task of the legal scholar, like that of the natural scientist, was to transform the disordered data found in judicial opinions and render them intelligible by demonstrating the way in which each term could be explained in terms of the fundamental legal principles implicit in the common law."[6]

Oliver Wendell Holmes, Jr., was an early critic of legal formalism. Although Holmes respected Langdell's contribution to legal education, he disagreed with Langdell on the idea that logic was vital to

---

[2] See H.L.A Hart, "Positivism and the Separation of Law and Morals," 71 Harv. L. Rev. 593 (1958); Lon Fuller, "Positivism and Fidelity to Law – A Reply to Professor Hart," 71 Harv. L. Rev. 630 (1958). This debate has been described as "the most interesting and illuminating exchange of views on basic issues of legal theory to appear in English in" the 20th century. See Robert S. Summers, LON L. FULLER, 10 (1984). Many commentators have acknowledged both the quality as well as the significance of the exchange. See, e.g., Carl Landauer, "Deliberating Speed: Totalitarian Anxieties and Postwar Legal Thought," 12 Yale J. Law & Humanities 171, 217 (2000) (referring to Fuller's "famous 1958 exchange with H.L.A. Hart in the Harvard Law Review").

[3] See, e.g., Richard Primus, Note, "A Brooding Omnipresence: Totalitarianism in Postwar Constitutional Thought," 106 Yale L.J. 423, 430 n.50 (1996) (collecting articles); see also, e.g., Hans Kelsen, "The Rule Against Ex Post Facto Laws and the Prosecution of the Axis War Criminals," Judge Advocate J., Fall-Winter 1945, at 8; Bernard D. Meltzer, Comment, "A Note on Some Aspects of the Nuremberg Debate," 14 U. Chi. L. Rev. 455 (1947).

[4] See Thomas Grey, "Langdell's Orthodoxy," 45 U. Pitt. L. Rev. 1, 11-12 (1983) (Langdell's "orthodoxy" was "doubly formal" because, first, "the specific rules were framed in such terms that decisions followed from them uncontroversial when they were applied to readily ascertainable facts," and, second, "one could derive the rules themselves analytically from the principles.").

[5] Christopher Columbus Langdell, Record of the Commemoration, November Fifth to Eighth, 1886, on the Two Hundred and Fiftieth Anniversary of the Founding of Harvard College, at 98 (1887), quoted in Bruce Ackerman, "Law and the Modern Mind," 103 Daedalus 119, 126 n.3 (1974).

[6] Ackerman, "Law and the Modern Mind," 103 Daedalus at 119-20.

the development of legal thought.[7] In his 1881 book The Common Law, Holmes essentially "argued that practical expedients, necessitated by the needs and conflicts of human society, were more central to the development of law than were any logical propositions."[8] Furthermore, Holmes maintained a skeptical attitude towards the law, defining it as nothing more than "the incidence of the public force through the instrumentality of the courts."[9] By early in the twentieth century, Holmes' criticism of Langdell and legal formalism began to attract followers, planting the seeds that would develop into the legal realism movement.[10]

Holmes' legal philosophy loomed large in the work of Jerome Frank and other legal realists, who shared Holmes' skepticism of Langdell's formalism. They focused their efforts on investigating and explaining how judicial decisions really were made, and "attempted to move beyond the talk of rules and principles heard in the courtroom and the academy and to expose them as myths obscuring most of the principal factors at work in the decision-making process."[11] The idea of science figured prominently in the efforts of the realists, but it was not the self-contained, inductive logic of Langdell. Instead, the realists were dogged empiricists who consulted the social sciences – Frank, for example, turned to psychiatry – to locate the extra-legal factors that, they argued, determined the outcome of judicial decisions.

II. Jerome Frank, Law and the Modern Mind, and Legal Realism

To simplify matters, I have decided to explain legal realism through the writings of Jerome Frank. Frank offered a comprehensive critique of formalist legal thought. His views made him an extreme – and extremely clear-spoken – legal realist. In addition, Frank's views were well known outside the legal academy. His first book, Law and the Modern Mind, sold well when it initially was published in 1930, and went through a number of printings. As a result of his extremism, clarity and prominence, Frank inspired a substantial response from both fellow realists and ardent critics of legal realism.

In Law and the Modern Mind, Frank described "the basic legal myth" – the myth of certainty – and explained its causes. He did not, however, prescribe a solution for it. Frank proclaimed that "[t]he law always has been, is now, and will ever continue to be, largely vague and variable."[12] And yet, according to Frank, the necessity of uncertainty in the law – even the existence of it – is denied. Why? To answer this question, Frank turned to psychiatry – in particular, the child psychiatry of Jean Piaget.[13] Frank attributed the need for, and belief in, certainty in the law to a child-like need for certainty.[14]

---

[7] See Neil Duxbury, PATTERNS OF AMERICAN JURISPRUDENCE, 37 (1995).
[8] Edward Purcell, THE CRISIS OF DEMOCRATIC THEORY, 75 (1973) (discussing Oliver Wendell Holmes, Jr., THE COMMON LAW (1881)).
[9] Oliver Wendell Holmes, "The Path of the Law," 10 Harv. L. Rev. 457, 457 (1897).
[10] See Ackerman, "Law and the Modern Mind," 103 Daedalus 121 (identifying first generation, including Holmes and James Bradley Thayer, as critics denying "the assumption of the scientific school that the Common Law had a fundamental structure discernible by the architectonic intelligence"; second generation "affected by Progressive politics and Deweyite pragmatism," including Louis Brandeis, Felix Frankfurter, and Roscoe Pound; and third generation of legal realists, including Frank).
[11] Ackerman, "Law and the Modern Mind," 103 Daedalus 121.
[12] LAW AND THE MODERN MIND, 6.
[13] Jean Piaget was a Swiss psychologist who worked with Alfred Binet in testing the intelligence of children, and wrote a number of books on childhood development. Frank acknowledged that, in Law and the Modern Mind, he "relied chiefly upon Piaget, an eclectic psychologist, who has done an immense amount of first-hand work with children." LAW AND THE MODERN MIND, 326 n.1 (notes to Part One, Chapter II); see also id. at 69 n.* (citing three articles by Piaget).
[14] LAW AND THE MODERN MIND, 13-16. To be fair, Frank asserted that he was providing only a "partial explanation" of the phenomenon he described, and included an appendix offering 14 other "suggested or possible explanations of the basic legal myth." LAW AND THE MODERN MIND, at xiii, 13, and 263 (Appendix I). On the other hand, Frank's writing style was both provocative and repetitive, so it was easy for the reader to form the impression that the "partial explanation" is dominant, if not exclusive. See Robert Glennon, THE ICONOCLAST AS REFORMER: JEROME FRANK'S IMPACT ON AMERICAN LAW, 48 (1985).

Frank's account of child development was relevant to the myth of legal certainty because, ultimately, according to Frank, the law "inevitably becomes a partial substitute for the Father-as-Infallible-Judge."[15] Caught between the uncertainty attendant to the practice of law – with its "changing realities," which require "recognition of novel circumstances, tentativeness, and adaptation" – and the desire to "achieve certainty, rigidity, security, uniformity" (the result of "unconscious longing for the re-creation of a child's world stimulated in all men ... by the very nature of law"), the lawyer essentially becomes a "professional rationalizer."[16] Frank, needless to say, objected to this state of affairs. In response, he urged the legal profession, essentially, to grow up and embrace uncertainty, rather than attempt to avoid it or conceal it.[17]

Frank also focused his analysis on the understanding of rules and judicial decisions in the legal system. Frank chose Joseph Henry Beale, an accomplished Harvard Law School professor (and former student of Dean Langdell), to personify the conventional formalist view of what constitutes law.[18] According to Frank, Beale defined law as "(1) Statutes, (2) rules, and (3) 'the general body of principles accepted as the fundamental principles of jurisprudence.'" Moreover, for Beale, "[t]his third element is 'the one most important feature of law: that is ... a body of scientific principle.... Law, therefore, is made in part by the legislature, in part it rests upon precedent; and in great part it consists in a homogeneous, scientific, and all-embracing body of principle" which is "'truly law' even 'though no court has lent its sanction to many [of its] principles.'"[19]

Frank railed against this view. The law according to Beale bore no resemblance to the law experienced by practicing lawyers. "Particular judgments of particular controversies are only vaguely predictable," observed Frank. "Decisions in the courts of any given state vary."[20] Borrowing from Holmes, Frank offered his own definition of the law "from the point of view of the average man," which he described as "a decision of a court with respect to [any particular set of] facts as far as that decision affects that particular person."[21] So far, Frank's critique was familiar, even, in its own way, conventional. Holmes, after all, already had observed that "[a] legal duty so called is nothing but a prediction that if a man does or omits certain things he will be made to suffer in this or that way by judgment of the court."[22]

Frank extended this criticism, however, drawing upon the lessons he had learned from the emerging discipline of psychiatry. Focusing on the judge, Frank challenged the conventional view that "the judge begins with some rule or principle of law as his premise, applies this premise to the facts, and thus arrives at his decision."[23] Nonsense, insisted Frank; instead, he argued that, "[j]udicial judgments, like other judgments, doubtless, in most cases, are worked out backward from conclusions tentatively formulated."[24] Frank elaborated upon his challenge to the conventional view of judicial decision-making. He quoted favorably the description of Judge Joseph C. Hutcheson, Jr., that judging consisted of arriving at a "hunch," and then providing the "ratiocination" for the decision in the written opinion.[25] Frank recognized the consequences of his argument: "Whatever produces the judge's hunches makes

---

[15] LAW AND THE MODERN MIND, 18; see also id. 20 ("Hence the basic legal myth that law is, or can be made, unwavering, fixed and settled.").

[16] LAW AND THE MODERN MIND, 30-31.

[17] LAW AND THE MODERN MIND, 17-18 (discussing the career of William James, who made "a sudden shift from panic fear of insecurity to a deep enthusiastic bliss in the absence of security" which "marked for James the advent of emotional adulthood.").

[18] LAW AND THE MODERN MIND, 48 (describing Beale as "one of America's influential legal writers from whom, at Harvard Law School, many of the leading lawyers of this country have received valued instruction. Beale's opinion, which is representative of the conventional doctrine, commands attention.").

[19] LAW AND THE MODERN MIND, 51-52.
[20] LAW AND THE MODERN MIND, 53.
[21] LAW AND THE MODERN MIND, 46.
[22] Holmes, "The Path of the Law," 10 Harv. L. Rev. 458.
[23] LAW AND THE MODERN MIND, 101.
[24] LAW AND THE MODERN MIND, 101.
[25] LAW AND THE MODERN MIND, 103-04.

the law."²⁶ Although he acknowledged that the "rules and principles of law" were part of the stimuli that produced the judge's hunches, Frank nevertheless insisted that there were many "complicated" and "hidden" factors that influenced the individual judge.²⁷

Frank did not confine his critique to the vagaries of the judge's personality. In addition to the fact that judges made decisions based upon hunches, Frank argued, the judicial fact-finding process was full of opportunity for error. Even honest witnesses made mistakes when they testified, and the risk for error increased due to the possibility that the judge or jury did not correctly understand the testimony or became distracted while listening to the witness.²⁸

One should not exaggerate the novelty of Frank's insights – even Frank acknowledged that much of his book merely debunked myths for the general audience told by lawyers and judges about the legal system. In part, it was the vehemence of his assault on the legal system that made his claims bold and provocative, especially for the era in which they were written. Frank effectively held up a mirror to the legal system, and reflected back was something akin to the abyss. It is difficult to conceive of a more direct assault on the inductive logic of formalism. The operating legal principles, said to be discoverable in the law books and reported cases in the library, did not resolve cases, and did not provide definitive guidance on the outcome of a legal dispute. Frank did not shy away from the implications of his argument: if the administration of justice was idiosyncratic, it could not be said that litigants received equal treatment in the legal system.²⁹

Frank did not provide a programmatic solution to improve the judicial system he described in Law and the Modern Mind. He agreed with reformers that psychology could provide further insights into how individual judges decided cases, but acknowledged that such efforts depended upon the willingness of the "judges to engage in searching self-analysis."³⁰ However, he did not expect most judges to be willing to engage in such self-analysis.³¹ Still, the best lawyers and judges can do, according to Frank, is grow up. This meant embracing change, accepting uncertainty, and liberating civilization from "father-governance."³²

Law and the Modern Mind received a broad but divided reception. Although critics agreed that Frank's book was "provocative,"³³ not every reviewer employed that description with favor. A number of prominent professors and writers praised Law and the Modern Mind.³⁴ More revealing than the

---

[26] LAW AND THE MODERN MIND, 104. See also id. 133 (" ... the personality of the judge is the pivotal factor.").

[27] LAW AND THE MODERN MIND, 105.

[28] LAW AND THE MODERN MIND, 106-111. See, e.g., id. at 111 ("If [the judge's] final decision is based upon a hunch and that hunch is a function of the 'facts,' then of course what [the judge], as a fallible witness of what went on in his courtroom, he believes to be the 'facts,' will often be of controlling importance. So that the judge's innumerable *unique* traits, dispositions and habits often get in their work in shaping his decisions not only in the determination of what he thinks fair or just with reference to a given set of facts, but in the very processes by which he becomes convinced what those facts are.") (emphasis added).

[29] LAW AND THE MODERN MIND, 111-12.

[30] LAW AND THE MODERN MIND, 113-14.

[31] LAW AND THE MODERN MIND, 116-17.

[32] LAW AND THE MODERN MIND, 243-52.

[33] See Felix S. Cohen, "Among Recent Books," XVII ABA Journal, 111 (Feb. 1931) (located in Jerome Frank Papers, Box 128 Folder 3) (describing Law and the Modern Mind as "the most provocative stimulus to thinking on fundamental legal problems in the Anglo-American literature of jurisprudence since Dean Pound's Spirit of the Common Law."). See also Charles E. Clark, "Jerome E. Frank," 66 Yale L.J. 817, 817 (1957) (Law and the Modern Mind "fell like a bomb on the legal world.").

[34] See "Law and the Modern Mind: A Symposium," 31 Colum. L. Rev. 82 (1931); Karl Llewellyn, "Legal Illusion," 31 Colum. L. Rev. 82 ("This book excites ... . It is well nigh unique in attempting exploration of emotional drives and genetic psychology for their contribution to understanding of the ways of law."); Walter Wheeler Cook, "Legal Logic," 31 Colum. L. Rev. 108-15 (defending Law and the Modern Mind against attack by Mortimer Adler). See also Thurman Arnold, "Law and Men," Saturday Review of Literature (March 7, 1931) (located in Jerome Frank Papers, Box 128 Folder 3). Earlier in 1931, Arnold wrote a letter to Frank in which he observed that Mortimer Adler – in his review in the Columbia Law Review – "appears to throw big words at you like a comedian throws custard pies." Thurman Arnold to Jerome Frank, January 15, 1931, Jerome Frank Papers, Box 4 Folder 108. Arnold returned to this image in his article for the Saturday

positive reviews, however, were the critical ones. Initially Law and the Modern Mind was challenged for its method, or its science. These reviews questioned, for example, whether Frank had accurately described the operation of the legal system, whether he had properly weighed the value of certainty in a legal system, and whether he reasonably relied upon psychiatry as the explanatory extra-legal discipline.

For example, Mortimer Adler, a University of Chicago philosopher who embraced foundational principles,[35] sounded a sharp note in his assessment of Law and the Modern Mind in the Columbia Law Review in 1931. Frank's book offended Adler from start to finish. According to Adler, *Law and the Modern Mind* was a lawyer's brief rather than a philosopher's discussion; it demonstrated flaws in logic and argument; and the book erred even in its understanding of psychiatry.[36] Adler dismissed Frank as "an extreme nominalist" for whom "nothing exists except particulars, and words are merely their names."[37] Adler's assault, though sweeping, centered on the shortcomings of Law and the Modern Mind as a work of philosophy. Frank's book did not, in 1931, pose a threat outside the academy.

What is worth noting about the reception of Law and the Modern Mind immediately after its publication is that the debate over the book revolved around the soundness of its science. This inquiry did not focus on the political implications associated with an arbitrary judicial system. As the decade progressed, this would change, and Frank and the legal realists came under fire for the political values associated with their jurisprudence. On the eve of and during World War II, those critics could be sharp: legal realism, they charged, permitted – indeed, was synonymous with – fascism.

Indeed, by the end of the 1930s, virtually no academic discussion could occur without reference to the political developments in Europe and elsewhere. An increasingly popular attack on legal realism was that it permitted fascism. This development is reflected, in part, in the Julius Rosenthal Lectures Fuller gave at Northwestern University in 1940. In his second speech, Fuller addressed legal realism. He viewed legal realism as a modern form of positivism – one that sought "to anchor itself in some datum of nature, which considers that the law's quest of itself can end successfully only if it terminates in some tangible external reality."[38] In their studies of judicial behavior, according to Fuller, the legal realists modified positivism, focusing on what judges do, rather than on what they say.[39] Indeed, Fuller argued, the legal realists insisted upon a "sharp line between the rules that judges act on and those they talk about" – a "field" of "pure judicial behavior" that corresponded to Austin's sovereign.[40]

In his final lecture, Fuller connected his critique of positivism to current political developments. "We live in a period when major readjustments in our economic and social order have become necessary," he wrote. "It would seem that the present is a time when our social structure requires to be held together by a cement firmer than that supplied by the abstract principle for law as such. If Renan was right in assuming that men have the capacity for developing the illusions necessary for their survival, we ought to be seeing a revival of natural law."[41] This prediction turned out to be correct. Under the philosophy of positivism, Fuller continued, "[s]ince power rests ultimately on the acquiescence of the governed, the most logical principle of government is that of majority rule, since this offers the broadest base for the order set up." Fuller was dismayed by this view of democracy: it did not provide for justice, and did not come "closer to the inner essence of things than the will of any

---

Review of Literature; Max Radin, "Giving Away the Legal Show," New York Herald Tribune (Dec. 21, 1930) (located in Jerome Frank Papers, Box 128 Folder 3).

[35] Purcell, THE CRISIS OF DEMOCRATIC THEORY, 3 (noting that Adler believed "that human reason could discover certain immutable metaphysical principles that explained the true nature of reality").

[36] Adler, "Legal Certainty," 31 Colum. L. Rev. 91-108.

[37] Adler, "Legal Certainty," 31 Colum. L. Rev. 98.

[38] Fuller, THE LAW IN QUEST OF ITSELF, 47; see also id. 55 ("the psychology involved in the realist view is largely indigenous to the soil of legal positivism."). Fuller cited Frank's Law and the Modern Mind as one the "most important expositions of the realist conception of law." Id. 52 n.11

[39] Fuller, THE LAW IN QUEST OF ITSELF, 52.

[40] Fuller, THE LAW IN QUEST OF ITSELF, 59.

[41] Fuller, THE LAW IN QUEST OF ITSELF, 115, 116.

particular individual."[42] Moreover, he argued that this "purely negative ... conception of democracy" – based upon only the exercise of power by the majority – has "played an important part ... in bringing Germany and Spain to the disasters which engulfed those countries."[43]

As world events brought the United States closer to and then into World War II, critics of legal realism compared the realists to the emerging fascist governments in Europe, in particular the Nazi regime in Germany. By divorcing law from morality, insisting upon retaining an air of scientific detachment, and denying the significance of legal rules, the realists appeared to embrace the notion that power - and only power – was relevant to and necessary for governance. Compared to claims made by other natural law scholars in the early 1940s, Fuller's critique seemed positively mild. In 1942, for example, Father Francis E. Lucey of Georgetown wrote: "Realism is being tried today in Germany and Russia," he argued. "The Jurisprudence of these countries is that 'Is' Instrumentalism or Pragmatism of the Realist. What works is good. They exclude principles and morals and God from the picture of law, national and international."[44] Lucey continued: "For Holmes and the realist [man] is a sort of superior animal. ... If man is only an animal, Realism is correct, Holmes was correct, Hitler is correct."[45]

III. World War II, the Nuremberg Trials, the Decline of Legal Realism, and the Revival of Natural Law Theory

After World War II, attention turned to development of a new political order. Immediately after the war, some in the United States desired – and even were optimistic about the prospect of – a new world order governed by international law. The idea of human rights, for example, reflected this sentiment.[46] A working definition of human rights, from the perspective of the United States in 1945, was the idea that individuals in a foreign state "have universal, objective human rights ... regardless of the content of [that foreign state's] positive law."[47] This idea of human rights reflected natural law principles.

However, the vindication of human rights potentially conflicted with another fundamental legal principle, the due process protection against retroactive laws. Although there was (and is) not an absolute protection against retroactive lawmaking, the principle of due process protects individuals against liability – and even more strongly, against criminal punishment – for conduct that was not illegal or prohibited when it occurred. This concern about retroactive lawmaking reflected positivist principles. In the post-war period, the protection against retroactive lawmaking was subordinated to the human rights principle that some rights exist independent of the state's laws, and that some conduct is wrong – and may be judged as such – even if that conduct is not prohibited by law.[48]

---

[42] Fuller, THE LAW IN QUEST OF ITSELF, 121.

[43] Fuller, THE LAW IN QUEST OF ITSELF, 121, 122. With respect to Germany, Fuller elaborated: "It was only this conception [of democracy] which could mislead men into believing that power relations inside a society could be radically displaced by the mere will of a numerical majority or that a social or economic revolution could be accomplished through a democratic control un-sustained by any common faith or program. It was this conception which lulled men into the dangerous dream that a kind of political euthanasia of vested interests would be possible. In the rude awakening which followed this dream there was demonstrated, at least in Germany, not only the futility of the dream itself, but the inability of repressive violence to fill the void left by a defaulting principle of majority rule, for the purported counter-revolution of Nazism has in many cases only increased the tempo and violence of the disintegrative forces from which it claimed to be rescuing Germany." Id. 122.

[44] Francis E. Lucey, "Natural Law and American Legal Realism: Their Respective Contributions to a Theory of Law in a Democratic Society," 30 Geo. L.J. 493, 523 (1942). Purcell describes the attack by Catholic natural law scholars on legal realism in THE CRISIS OF DEMOCRATIC THEORY, 164-172.

[45] Lucey, "Natural Law and American Legal Realism," 30 Geo. L.J. 531. See also Purcell, THE CRISIS OF DEMOCRATIC THEORY, 157-58 (quoting Robert Hutchins, former Yale Law School Dean, as saying, "There is little to choose between the doctrine I learned in American law school and that which Hitler proclaims.").

[46] Primus, "A Brooding Omnipresence," 106 Yale L.J. 429-30.

[47] Primus, "A Brooding Omnipresence," 106 Yale L.J. 430.

[48] See Primus, "A Brooding Omnipresence," 106 Yale L.J. 431 (noting that although the "International Military Tribunal tried to limit the trial[s] to issues of positive law codified in treaties and international conventions of war, ... the propriety of Nuremberg rested on the distinctly nonpositivist principle that some things were simply wrong, whether codified or not, and that justice sometimes calls upon courts to act when they lack formal legal authorization").

The clash between the natural law notion of human rights and the positivist concern about retroactive lawmaking is reflected in the writings of both Frank and Fuller after World War II. Fuller discussed it in a debate about the validity of Nazi laws after the war, while Frank addressed this conflict in the context of the Nuremberg trials. In an article published in Collier's in 1945, Frank defended the necessity of the trials for the sake of world peace. In this discussion, he specifically noted "the moral effect of the trials," and enlisted this value in the cause of establishing a new world order.[49]

The Nuremberg trials were an extraordinary event, and important to United States post-war foreign policy. It therefore is not entirely surprising that Frank would set aside his skepticism of judges and the judicial process in endorsing the efforts of Justice Jackson and the goals of the war crimes trials. Nevertheless, it is worth noting, that his discussion of the Nuremberg trials did not even resonate with, much less mention, his usual criticisms of the trial process – the childish quest for certainty, the limits inherent in the judicial fact-finding process, the intuitive quality of judging. This silence is even more notable given the novelty of the tribunal, as well as its task – to pass legal judgment on the conduct of individuals pertaining to international affairs and war.

The Collier's article is important also because it is one of the earliest indications of Frank's acknowledgment – if not embrace – of natural law principles.[50] In his post-war books, Frank responded to criticism that his emphasis on "fact skepticism" indicated a lack of commitment to values – by acknowledging basic natural law values, and by emphasizing that his work aimed to improve fairness in the judicial system (and was intended to promote democratic government). To be sure, Frank did not abandon his earlier views and become a disciple of natural law. He continued to address the limits of the trial process, and to insist that psychiatry remained crucial to understanding the individual decisions made by trial judges. Natural law was not, and could not be, "practically meaningful" because "Natural law aims at justice, and at moderate certainty ... in the more or less abstract, generalized human formulations of what men may or may not lawfully do," and "judicial justice must be justice ... in the concrete – in the courts' decisions of the numerous particular individual cases."[51]

Frank was more vehement about his concern for democracy in the post-war era. Even before the Cold War dashed hopes for a world order regulated by a regime of international law, there was anxiety in the United States about the fate of democracy in the post-war period. Some of this anxiety stemmed from the example of Nazi Germany, which revealed the nightmare possible through tyranny of the majority. Frank's post-war writings consistently noted and addressed this concern for democracy. In the sixth printing of Law and the Modern Mind, published in 1949, Frank emphasized that his efforts to demystify the trial court process were motivated by an effort to ensure fair trials, which were vital to democracy.[52] It may be argued that Frank's concern for democracy, acknowledgment of natural law, and proposals for reforming the judicial system resulted from his own efforts to "grow up" since he wrote Law and the Modern Mind in 1930. Yet it is also the case that these developments in Frank's jurisprudence reflected the revival of natural law in the United States – a shift that itself resulted from and reflected concerns about totalitarian governments, in particular Nazi Germany.

---

[49] Jerome Frank, "War Crimes: Punishment for Today – Precedent for Tomorrow," Collier's (Oct. 13, 1945), 11, 73 ("the principal purpose of the trials is not the regeneration or re-education of Germany. Far more important is the moral effect on other peoples. ... . With the dropping of the first atomic bomb on August 6, 1945, lasting world peace became the immediate concern of everybody on this planet, including the hard-headed practical realists. For the maintenance of such peace a vigorous, organized world order is imperative. The Nuremberg trial signalizes the emergence of such a world order. ... . To the prisoners' dock are called men once mighty – among others, a Reich Minister Goering, a Foreign Minister Von Ribbentrop, a Labor Minister Ley, a Field Marshall Keitel. Their very presence dramatically affirms that a robust world morality is alive at this moment, that a world conscience is on its way to becoming an accepted world custom.").

[50] Duxbury, "Jerome Frank and the Legacy of Legal Realism," 18 J. of Law and Society 194 & n.130 (In "the 1940s Frank 'found' natural law"). The Collier's article is the earliest writing by Frank cited in Duxbury's discussion of Frank and natural law.

[51] Frank, LAW AND THE MODERN MIND xviii (6th ed. 1949). Frank elaborated on these points in his other book published in 1949, Courts on Trial. See Jerome Frank, COURTS ON TRIAL: MYTH AND REALITY IN AMERICAN JUSTICE 346-74 (1949).

[52] Frank, LAW AND THE MODERN MIND, xix.

The issue of retroactivity, briefly taken up by Frank in his Collier's article, is at the heart of the debate between Professors Hart and Fuller. The specific question addressed in the exchange is the validity of laws that had been enacted by the Nazi government, and had been invoked to perpetrate wrongful acts. In German legal proceedings after World War II, could litigants defend their actions on the grounds that they were authorized by Nazi laws? This question paralleled the retroactivity debate over the Nuremberg prosecution: in the post-war German cases, the courts relied upon natural law principles to invalidate Nazi laws, and thereby denied litigants the protection claimed by positive Nazi law. In the Nuremberg trials, the prosecution effectively relied upon natural law principles to retroactively criminalize conduct that previously had not been illegal under international law. The specter of Nazi Germany framed the debate: Hart vigorously denied the connection between positivism and Nazism.[53] Fuller – citing the history of positivism in German jurisprudence – argued to the contrary.[54]

In presenting his case for positivism, Hart argued for the separation of law and morals through an account of the utilitarian philosophy of Bentham and Austin. He connected positivism with their political reforms. Bentham and Austin "were not," Hart wrote, "dry analysts fiddling with verbal distinctions while cities burned, but were the vanguard of a movement which laboured with passionate intensity and much success to bring about a better society and better laws."[55] When Hart turned to criticism of positivism based upon the example of Nazi Germany, he sought to downplay the argument by describing it as "less an intellectual argument ... than a passionate appeal supported not by detailed reasoning but by reminders of a terrible experience."[56] Nevertheless, Hart seemed defensive as he began his presentation.[57]

Hart then addressed the retroactivity issue. After World War II, the German courts had to decide cases in which "local war criminals, spies, and informers under the Nazi regime were punished."[58] The cases presented a dilemma: the persons punished after the war had been prosecuted for actions authorized by laws enacted during the Nazi regime; now, however, those laws did not provide a defense because they were immoral, and therefore were not valid. For example, as Hart summarized:

"In 1944 a woman, wishing to be rid of her husband, denounced him to the authorities for insulting remarks he had made about Hitler while home on leave from the German army. The wife was under no legal duty to report his acts, though what he had said was apparently in violation of statutes making it illegal to make statements detrimental to the government of the Third Reich or to impair by any means the military defense of the German people. The husband was arrested ... and was sent to the front. In 1949 the wife was prosecuted [pursuant to an 1871 law that had been in force since its enactment] in a West German court for an offense which we would describe as illegally depriving a person of his freedom. ... The wife pleaded that her husband's imprisonment was pursuant to the Nazi statutes and hence that she had committed no crime."[59]

Ultimately the wife was found guilty of depriving her husband of his freedom. The German appellate court invalidated the Nazi law cited by the wife as "contrary to the sound conscience and sense of justice of all decent human beings."[60]

Although, as Hart noted, "[m]any of us might applaud the objective" of the court's decision, Hart was disturbed by the result because the court had found that a validly enacted law did not, in fact, have

---

[53] Hart, "Positivism and the Separation of Law and Morals," 71 Harv. L. Rev. 617-18. The literature on this debate is extensive, and continues today. See Primus, "A Brooding Omnipresence," 106 Yale L.J. 432 & n. 61.
[54] Fuller, "Positivism and Fidelity to Law," 71 Harv. L. Rev. 657-661.
[55] Hart, "Positivism and the Separation of Law and Morals," 71 Harv. L. Rev. 596.
[56] Hart, "Positivism and the Separation of Law and Morals," 71 Harv. L. Rev. 615.
[57] Hart, "Positivism and the Separation of Law and Morals," 71 Harv. L. Rev. 616. Hart acknowledged that among the post-war critics of positivism were "German thinkers who lived through the Nazi regime and reflected upon its evil manifestations in the legal system," citing Gustav Radbruch, who had "shared the 'postivist' doctrine until the Nazi tyranny" but essentially recanted those views after the war. Id.
[58] Hart, "Positivism and the Separation of Law and Morals," 71 Harv. L. Rev. 618.
[59] Hart, "Positivism and the Separation of Law and Morals," 71 Harv. L. Rev. 618-19.
[60] Hart, "Positivism and the Separation of Law and Morals," 71 Harv. L. Rev. 619.

the force of law. The better solution, Hart argued, would have been for the legislature to pass "a frankly retrospective law" that at least would have acknowledged that "in punishing the woman a choice had to be made between two evils, that of leaving her unpunished and that of sacrificing a very precious principle of morality endorsed by most legal systems."[61] Positivism demanded candor, and Hart believed it was necessary to expressly resolve the moral dilemma between delivering justice in the woman's case and observing the duty to obey the law by passing a new law to supersede the prior Nazi laws.

Fuller did not believe that the case presented such a dilemma. In a more detailed response, he analyzed the Nazi statutes relied upon by the wife, and argued that they did not provide a valid defense because they did not have the quality of law. Fuller argued that one of the statutes, enacted in 1934, had been applied in an overbroad manner, while the other statute, enacted in 1938, was a "legislative monstrosity" that permitted "uncontrolled administrative discretion."[62] Whether a court or an individual was required to follow such laws (simply because of their status as laws) or to instead "do what we think is right and decent" did not create a dilemma for Fuller. "I do not think it is unfair to the positivistic philosophy to say that it never gives any coherent meaning to the moral obligation of fidelity to law," Fuller concluded.[63] Although Fuller also endorsed the enactment of a new statute to invalidate the earlier laws, he justified that choice on entirely different grounds: the adoption of a new law would "symboliz[e] a sharp break with the past," and help usher in a new, lawful regime.[64] Although Fuller did not discuss the Nuremberg trials, his remarks endorsed the natural law justifications for the Nuremberg trials.

IV. Nuremberg, Legal Realism, and Brown v. Board of Education

So far, I have discussed the influence of the Nuremberg trials and the example of Nazi Germany only in the American legal academy, in the decline of legal realism and the revival of natural law after World War II. Nuremberg and Nazi Germany also influenced the development of constitutional law during the post-war period as well. With respect to Nuremberg and the example of Nazi Germany, the case law runs the same way as the academic discussion – in the direction of natural law foundationalism.

Perhaps the most compelling illustration of the influence of Nazi Germany on the Supreme Court is – as Richard Primus and others have suggested – Brown v. Board of Education, in which the Court held that separate-but-equal public schools for African-American children violated the Constitution's equal protection clause.[65] The Nuremberg trials contributed to the growing sentiment against segregation which enabled the Court's decision in Brown.[66]

Brown represents the culmination of the developments discussed thus far in at least three ways. First, a foundational principle in the post-war world was racial nondiscrimination.[67] Brown enshrined that principle in the law of the United States, in a morality-based decision.[68] Second, Brown launched an era of greater judicial activism. This development was necessary to guarantee the protection of

---

[61] Hart, "Positivism and the Separation of Law and Morals," 71 Harv. L. Rev. 619.
[62] Fuller, "Positivism and Fidelity to Law," 71 Harv. L. Rev. 652-54.
[63] Fuller, "Positivism and Fidelity to Law," 71 Harv. L. Rev. 656.
[64] Fuller, "Positivism and Fidelity to Law," 71 Harv. L. Rev. 661.
[65] Brown v. Board of Education, 347 U.S. 483 (1954). See Primus, "A Brooding Omnipresence," 106 Yale L.J. 437, 447-49. See also Constance Baker Motley, "The Historical Setting of Brown and its Impact on the Supreme Court's Decision," 61 Fordham L. Rev. 9, 12 (1992) (explaining that racial segregation during World War II embarrassed the United States, and helped bring about Supreme Court's decision in Brown).
[66] See William E. Nelson, "Brown v. Board of Education and Legal Realism," 48 St. Louis U. L.J. 795, 812 (2004) ("The Nuremberg trials, as well as massive press coverage of Nazi atrocities, served to inform the wider American public of the horrors of the Third Reich's Final Solution. All of this would help make the kind of easy yet deep racial prejudice common earlier in the century far less respectable after the Second World War.").
[67] Primus, "A Brooding Omnipresence," 106 Yale L.J. 447-48.
[68] See Richard Fallon, "Legitimacy and the Constitution," 118 Harv. L. Rev. 1787, 1836 (2005) (arguing that Chief Justice Warren's "reasoning" in Brown "can easily be understood as advancing a substantially moral justification.").

foundational principles, and reflected the post-war rejection of the legal realist's demystified depiction of the judge. Third, Brown demonstrated that although legal realism no longer remained viable as an autonomous legal philosophy, it continued to influence American case law and jurisprudence.[69] This influence is shown in Brown in the Court's reliance upon extra-legal materials to support its decision – specifically, the social science studies involving dolls cited by the Court, which demonstrated that racial segregation "generates a feeling of inferiority."[70]

---

[69] See Robert J. Cottrol, "Justice Advanced: Some Comments on William Nelson's Brown v. Board of Education and Legal Realism," 48 St. Louis U. L.J. 839, 850 (2004) (concluding "that Brown made a difference precisely because the advocates urging desegregation and the Court that accepted their arguments tapped into the changed mood and needs of the nation. In doing so they proved that they had learned the realist lesson well.").

[70] Brown, 347 U.S. 494 & n.11 ("Whatever may have been the extent of psychological knowledge at the time of Plessy v. Ferguson, this finding is amply supported by modern authority," citing psychology studies).

Rodger Citron

**Die Nürnberger Prozesse und die amerikanische Rechtswissenschaft:
Der Niedergang des Rechtsrealismus und die Wiedererstehung des Naturrechts**

Dieser Beitrag beschäftigt sich mit dem Einfluss der Nürnberger Prozesse und darüber hinaus des Nazi-Faschismus insgesamt auf die amerikanische Rechtswissenschaft. Das Hauptaugenmerk wird dabei auf den Rechtsrelativismus und das Wieder-Erstarken von Naturrechtstheorien in der Zeit vor und nach dem Zweiten Weltkrieg gelegt. Beide Strömungen gründen teilweise auf Angst vor dem Faschismus und der Sorge um Demokratie – diese Anliegen wurden durch das NS-Regime ausgelöst und riefen eine ausgeprägte Berichterstattung und Auseinandersetzung mit den Nürnberger Prozessen hervor, die sich zugleich in diesen widerspiegeln. Die Darstellung weist dies exemplarisch an den vor und nach dem Krieg verfassten Schriften von Jerome Frank und Lon Fuller nach. Weiter zeigt dieser Beitrag, dass jenseits der Rechtswissenschaft der Einfluss der Nürnberger Prozesse sich am offensichtlichsten in der Entscheidung des Supreme Court im Fall Brown v. Board of Education, 347 U.S. 483 (1954), erkennen lässt. In dieser Entscheidung wurde Segregation in öffentlichen Schulen für rechtswidrig erklärt. Nach dem Zweiten Weltkrieg und den Urteilen von Nürnberg konnte in den USA unmöglich an einer staatlich unterstützen Segregation festgehalten werden.

IV. The Later Nuremberg Trials/Die Nürnberger Folgeprozesse

Benjamin Ferencz

The Einsatzgruppen Trial

Danke schön für diese schöne kurze Einleitung. (Thank you for this brief introduction) I am sorry, but I have got to speak English now. You'll pardon me for not getting behind the podium, but then you would only hear my voice. If I sat here it would be the same, so I have agreed with the photographers to stand right here. If I should fall off the platform would somebody pick me up? Well, as you see, I have no prepared text, but after talking to some members of the audience I think what I'll try to do in the course of perhaps twenty minutes, half an hour or so, [is to] explain what have been my personal experiences on the subjects, which we have been [discussing].

You have been very fortunate to have a large group of scholars giving you very interesting and exciting reports. Between my friend Whitney Harris' very moving address yesterday giving you the feeling of a prosecutor at the International Military Trial and Professor Barrett's report this morning about the inspiration which justice Jackson gave to all of us, I won't have to go into the International Military Tribunal, but I will take it from there ... and speak about my actual experiences, which falls into four different categories:

First, I had to stop the killing, which is my war-time experience and happened during the war. The next thing is the prosecution of criminals. [Thirdly,] what happened after the International Military Tribunal trial isn't very well known and will be touched upon by Professor Harmon dealing with the Medical Case, in the afternoon, while I will talk to you about the "Einsatzgruppen". And then came the most important problem of all – how do you prevent it from happening again? That's the most difficult and the most important. First of all, no one can translate "Einsatzgruppen". So for the benefit of the German audience "Einsatzgruppen" has been interpreted to mean killing squads. I will explain: how did I get that job? Because people always ask me that question, I will also explain where we did get the evidence. What did the evidence show? How did we pick the defendants? What arguments did we make as prosecutors? What arguments did they make as defence counsel? What was the decision of the judges? And what does it add up to? This will be the major focus of what I'll have to say because that's what it says in the programme I'm supposed to do. I try to be a good fellow. But there is more to it than that. We have to deal with what happened to the victims. It is always more dramatic to talk about the criminals, but what about the victims? I stayed on in Nuremberg to deal with that problem.

So I will touch on all of these, I hope within half an hour, and then I will open the floor to questions. You may ask me whatever you want, on any subject, and I promise to give you an answer. I don't promise that it'll be correct, but it'll be an answer. So let me begin where I came in. I came into Germany via Normandy Beach. Sainte Mère Eglise. Someone had tipped off the Germans that I was coming, so they ran in the opposite direction. Fortunately, I had a fellow along by the name of General Patton, and about 10,000 tanks. I crossed the Rhine at Remagen on a pontoon, I went through the Siegfried line and the Maginot line, and was assisting in the liberation of the 101st Air-Borne Division surrounded in Bastogne by the last gasp of the German army. At that time I had the exalted rank of a sergeant of the infantry. They had recognised my talent in the army right away. Well, then an interesting thing happened. One day I was told to report to General Patton's headquarters. There I met a colonel, and he said: "I have been instructed to set up a war crimes branch. And your name has been forwarded to me from Washington. What's a war crime?" And that's the truth. The Army had no idea of what a war crime was. And I have no time to go into the detail now, but I became the first investigator in the United States Army to investigate war crimes. At that time initially it meant dealing with the cases where Allied fliers had come down in some German towns and they were almost invariably murdered by the people on the ground. They came out, they beat them to death, sometimes they turned them over to the SS who shot them and threw the bodies in a river. My job was to go [and] find the bodies, dig them up, sometimes with my hands, because you can't use a pick, then you don't know a bullet wound [from] a bayonet wound, and then write up a report [about] what happened, who ... [did it], and I would interrogate as many witnesses as I could from the town.

The standard routine was for me to find the "*Bürgermeister*" (mayor of the town) or the Chief of Police, and tell them to arrest everybody who was within a hundred yards of the event. He would bring them in; I would line them up against a wall, and tell them I want them to sit down and write an exact statement of what they saw and what they did and anybody who lies would be shot. This is no place for confessing war crimes, but that was standard routine. The German *Bekanntmachung* when they ordered people to appear somewhere always had on the bottom [of the notice] the threat of *Todesstrafe,* (death penalty). I thought there was nothing wrong with my having a little reciprocity. After reading about twenty statements, of course, I knew what happened exactly. I would then go out and try to catch the criminal, who had usually fled. Then I'd write up a report: This is what happened, these are the witnesses, and these are the bodies that I dug up at this and this place. Photographers would come in, photograph the bodies, I would make a report, and I was ready for trial. Murder would be the charge for killing prisoners of war. Then some even more interesting things happened: we began to run into concentration camps. I remember very well the first camp was Ordruff. It was an outer camp of Buchenwald. And I won't go into the details of the concentration camps because they are too well-known. But just of my personal experiences, and how I approached the problems. Buchenwald, for example, was next in line. The Russians were coming in from the other side. I met them at the Elbe. From Buchenwald, I went on to other camps, Ebensee, Mauthausen, and eventually everything in between down to Linz, Austria.

My goal was to obtain the evidence of the crimes that were committed there. The procedure was that I would go directly to the *Schreibstube* (the office), and seize all the records, for example the *Totenbücher,* (the death registries), in Buchenwald. They were big black ledgers, which showed exactly which transports arrived at which dates, how many people, very often their names, which people – I don't like to say "died", because they didn't die, they were murdered – which people were murdered through beatings or starvation, and the list of the dead people. Frequently with the help of some of the inmates – and I don't have time to go into the stories of some of the heroic inmates – I got the names, some of the names, sometimes photographs of all the SS officers who ran the camp. The objective was to get in and get out as fast as humanly possible, because that was no place to be: dysentery, lice, malaria. I don't know what other diseases they had there, typhus, the bodies were lying all over the ground, bones wrapped in skin, and rags, and occasionally they would move when you thought they were dead. Cords of bodies stacked in front of the crematoria. This was the scene. I have flashbacks from time to time, so I don't like to pause on this. And this was the basis for reports for war crimes trials. Very few people have heard of the war crimes trials that existed immediately after the war. The war was still on. I was in, I think, Ebensee, on May 1st, when they were having a big celebration of the liberation where incidentally the French marched, the Russians marched, and the Germans marched, but the Jews marched separately. They were not accepted by the other inmates to march with them. That made a big impression on me, too. That phase of my work ended, when we prepared these reports of the concentration camps as well. I had nailed up the first sign saying "US Third Army War Crimes Trials" in Dachau.

You [referring to the audience] are going to be in Dachau, I think there is a trip planned for perhaps this afternoon. I am not going, I have been there. You can ask about it. Also, Joshua Greene is here who wrote a book [titled] "Justice at Dachau", which describes the work of one of the American prosecutors, Colonel Denson, who came in just as I was leaving, and how the US Army conducted those trials. There were about a thousand people tried at Dachau, the trials lasted a couple of minutes, the people were lined up, thirty, forty in a room, usually an old barrack, with a number on them – like this but bigger – , they were called upon to admit or deny being an accomplice to mass murder and other war crimes. They invariably said they were innocent, they were acting under orders or whatever, some alibi, they were usually all convicted, they were usually all sentenced to death, and many of them were executed. Not all of them, but many of them. Those were the Dachau trials. I really didn't think much of the Dachau trials. I was then a sergeant of Infantry. I didn't think much of the Army. I didn't think much of my officers frankly, either. And I was very happy when the war was over. That was the reason I joined the Army to help them win. We won. I went home. I never wanted to come back to Germany again. Then a strange thing happened. I got a telegram from the Pentagon, saying "Dear Sir" – in three years they had never called me Sir – would I please come to Washington, Sir, at their expense, Sir, they want to talk to me. And so I went and they said: "Look, we want you to go back to Germany. We'll make you a full Colonel. From Sergeant." I said: "I should go back in the Army?" I said: "First you have to declare war on Germany again. And you have to be losing." So they said: "Well, look, we need you. We need you. We'll give you a civilian rank. You don't have to be in the army. We'll make you a Colonel with all the rights and privileges, and you'll be a civilian." I said: "How long do you have in mind?" And they said: "You name it." I said: "Now you're talking my language. I'll let you know right away." I then called up what we used to call my fiancée, my girl-friend. Today they have other words. And she'd been waiting patiently while I went off to Law School and then went off to the Army to win the war. And I said: "How would you like to go to Europe for a brief honeymoon?" She said: "This is so sudden. Yes." And so I accepted the job. I swear to you it was my serious intention to do absolutely nothing. But get even with all those Lieutenant-Colonels who had been sticking it to me for three years.

However, another strange thing happened. I was intercepted by then a Colonel by the name of Telford Taylor. And he said: "I want you to go with me, not back to Dachau. You go with me." I said: "What for?" He said: "Well, I have been assigned by the President to take over the trials which Justice Jackson was just finishing. And we are going to conduct about a dozen trials, and I think you are the right guy. You have the experience. You were a war crimes investigator, you've seen what happened, you wrote the reports, and you prepared the materials for trials." He said: "I'd like you to go with me." I had checked up on him. Just as he had checked up on me, and he had discovered that I was occasionally insubordinate. I told him that was not true, I was usually insubordinate. So I went back with the best of intentions to have nothing but a brief honeymoon. Well, the first assignment he gave, he said: "Look, we have twelve planned trials, and we don't have the evidence." Now, as all the lawyers here will know, if you have the defendant and you have no evidence, you have nothing. And if you have the evidence and you don't have the defendant, you've got almost nothing. So you had to put the two together. And, of course, most of the crew that Taylor was putting together were young fellows with no experience whatsoever in this field. Where should they get that experience? So he said: "You go to Berlin, set up an operation there, and find the evidence." Okay, so I became chief of the Berlin branch with about 50 people. We had offices in Harnack House, for the Berliners, which was then all bombed out. And I said: "This won't do." And I called the first Lieutenant-Colonel, and I said: "I want better quarters than this." So they moved us over next door to General Clay who lived in Clay-Allee, which used to be called Adolf-Hitler-Straße, I think. And there we began.

How do you begin to find the evidence of massive crimes? The theory was that the handful of defendants in the International Military Trial which was also partly at random, you put Streicher in the same shoes as Ribbentrop, and Göring and so on and Speer, for that matter. We wanted to get a broader picture. How was it possible that a civilised country like Germany can engage in this kind of criminality? They must have the help of the entire structure of social society. They must have help from the industrialists who built the concentration camps or the bankers who financed it, from the ministries of the Foreign Office, who were planning these aggressions, from the Justice Department, from the medical department, the doctors, who were performing medical experiments, and that was the function of what is here called "the later trials". At that time it was called "the subsequent proceedings". And I had to go find the evidence. Well, Germans, however, are gifted people. They keep records. That was very handy. The Berlin Document Center, for those of you who live in Berlin, take a walk through the park at Dahlem, and ask anybody on the road "Where is the Document Centre?" They won't know, unless they are very old. There's a little villa, from the air it looks like any other little villa in the park. Underneath that villa, there are subterranean chambers much bigger than this room, many of them. And there are stored all the Nazi Party files. Everybody who applied for a position, for membership in the Party, has a folder, an "Akte", and we captured that. Very nice, thank you very much! Anybody who got a promotion in the SS or who wrote a letter, it's in his file. In addition to that we had the archives in the buildings which were not destroyed. Most of [the buildings had been] destroyed. At Gestapo, we found some things in the basement, we found some records of the "Einsatzgruppen" in the basement, but only a few. As Whitney Harris pointed out, we had already Ohlendorf. He was already "in the can", as we called it, in Nuremberg, and he had admitted his unit had killed 90,000 Jews. So we were looking for the rest of those reports.

One day, one of our researchers – we had about 50 of them working and you may want to know how they worked. They had to go through the files. If they found an interesting document, they prepared a one page sheet. These were people who knew German, mostly German American refugees, who came back to Germany to help with this process. They would find something of interest, they would summarise it, on what we call an S.E.A., Staff Evidence Analysis. Put the name of the document, where it was found, by whom, what it dealt with, a brief summary of what was in it. That was then shipped down from Berlin to Nuremberg where the lawyers who were preparing the industrialists' case against IG Farben, Krupp, Siemens etc. or the Justice Case received that. If their wanted additional information on that subject they would communicate with me in Berlin. I would pass it down to the analyst, make the more complete report or copy the whole document. And we sent the whole document down to Nuremberg. Wannsee Protocol was one of them. One of the problems there was: which lawyer grabs it? Some of you in Germany will remember the name of Robert Kempner who was very popular here, and he loved to collect documents. And he had the Wannsee-Konferenz document in his file. And he put it in his drawer and he locked it up! There was only one trouble: one of the persons named there – which was the conference, you'll recall, where they decided on the final solution of the Jewish question – and the final solution was that Eichmann lines them all up, ships them to the East and then they murder them all. There was another name of another defendant who was being worked on by one of our prosecutors, by the name of Charles Lochalid [?]. I don't think I have ever told this story anywhere. One day, Charlie came rushing in. "I am going to kill Kempner!" I said: "Why are you going to kill Kempner?" He said: "He's got one of the documents which I need for my trial, and he's hiding it!" – "How do you know?" The researcher, who found it, blew the whistle and called the other lawyer who felt he needed it for his case; he also had a lead defendant.

So anyway, to make that story short, I said: "You can't kill Kempner." I went to Taylor who was my boss, later my law-partner, and I said: "Bob [ought to be Charlie?] wants to kill Kempner." Taylor said: "Why?" I said: "Well, he's hiding one of his documents." "Oh", he said, "do you think we should kill him?" I said: "No, no, we can't kill him. We need him; he is the only one who knows about the Ministries' Case." He'd been in a ministry before. I mention this en passant as the type of real problems that we had. We straightened it out. I talked to Kempner, I said: "Bob, come on, give me the document. Never mind this business." And so it went.

Now one day, I started to say, one of the researchers came in and said: "Look what I found." In the Foreign Office, the Foreign Ministry near the old Tempelhof Airport in Berlin, he'd found a complete set of what was called, for the German translators, *Ereignismeldung aus der UdSSR*, English translation "operational reports from the Soviet Union". And in those reports, the *Einsatzgruppen* described very precisely which unit had entered which town and bragged about how many people they had killed. And a typical report would say:

"We entered such and such town, in the first 24 hours, we succeeded in eliminating – they never said kill, they were too refined for that – eliminating 4327 Jews. (I am fabricating the figures now.) Or plus 862 gypsies. And 46 others"

I took those reports, I took a little hand adding machine and I began to add up how many people had been murdered by these units. Where we had the name of the unit, the name of the commander, the place and the time and the number, when it said the town was "cleansed" of Jews, I put [down] number one. I didn't know how many they were, could have been a thousand and I added it [up]. When I reached over a million I stopped. I said, that's enough for me. I grabbed copies of some of the files. I flew down to Nuremberg. And I said to then General Taylor: "Sir, we have to put on another trial." He said: "What for?" I said: "Look at this. I got proof here of over a million murders – Cold-blooded, calculated murders – and I can prove it." He said: "We don't have budget for any new cases. We have submitted our budgets. We don't have staff, we don't have people. We're not putting on any new trial now." IMT was already finished; he was beginning with the Medical Case which was going to be the first case. And I said: "You can't do this! This is mass murder. This is Holocaust on grand scale. Genocide." I knew Rafael Lemkin in Nuremberg, who had taught me the word genocide. So Taylor said: "Can you do it in addition to your other work?" And I said: "Sure." And he said: "You got it." So there it came about that I became the Chief Prosecutor in what was certainly the biggest murder trial in human history. I came back to Nuremberg. I selected the defendants.

How do you select the defendants? Well, our intelligence services had indexed people according to their position. We sent notices around to the CIC, the intelligence service. "Please, anybody who is listed membership in an Einsatzgruppe or Einsatzkommando, send us the names, send us the ranks, and send us the position." We got the lists, and I said okay. I went down the list and I selected them by rank and by education. I had six SS generals, the rest of them were all high-ranking officers, I have forgotten the number of colonels and majors, and the interesting thing, too, for me was, I picked them because they had a doctor title. I love that. Germans are so proud to be doctors. And one of them I was particularly happy to have, Dr. Dr. Rasch. R A S C H. Double doctor! I was an American, and we're not used to that. I thought somebody was stuttering. But they explained to me: "No, he is a very learned fellow." Okay, he murdered, according to his report, 33,771 Jews in two days, 29/30 September 1941, which happened to be the Jewish High Holidays. Imagine, a number like that! More than ten Trade Centers, more than all the other horrors that we've heard about. One unit. Dr. Dr. Rasch. A double doctor. One day, his defence counsel, before the trial started, came to see me. He said: "You got to drop the charges against Rasch." I said: "What for?" He said: "He's sick." – "What's he suffering from?" – "Parkinson's disease." – "What's Parkinson's disease?" – "He shakes." I said: "If I had killed that many people, I'd shake too." I said: "Is he breathing?" He said: "Yes, he is breathing." I said, "if he is breathing, I am going to indict him." And I have photographs of Dr. Dr. Rasch being carried in on a stretcher to the court room, to answer whether he understood the charges or whether he was able to reply, and he was. But then, there was an intervening event. He was judged by higher authority. He died before we could open the trial. So we dropped him. He was dead.

Now how do we pick the number of defendants? It's also of interest. I ended up with 22 defendants. I started with 24. And the reason we had only 22 instead of 3,000, which were the units who for every day for two years their main job was to go out and commit mass murder. How did we pick 22? I told you I picked them by rank. Why only 22? That's the only number of seats we had in the dock. We were sold out! Ridiculous? Sure, it's ridiculous. But that's the reality. That's what it was. We never intended to try all those who were guilty of mass crimes. We only intended, at best, to have a meagre sampling of the different categories of people who made all of this possible. And that's what we tried to do. What were the charges? The charges were very easy there. We charged them: crimes against humanity, genocide, and genocide was mentioned in my opening paragraph, in which I laid it out from courtroom 6[00] where we were yesterday, from the middle of the room, the judges standing on this side, the defence counsel on the other side. I accused them of committing these horrible crimes and made it clear that vengeance was not our role, that we are seeking merely a rule of international law, which will protect humanity against this type of crime. These people were murdered because they didn't share the race or the religion or the ideology of their executioners. And I thought then and I think now that it's a terrible reason to kill people, and we cannot tolerate a world in which we condone that kind of behaviour and grant immunity to those leaders who are responsible for it. So that was the gist of our approach.

Now what were the defendants' positions? What did they say? My time is limited and I will just focus on the one defendant who has already been mentioned by Whitney Harris, Otto Ohlendorf, who was the lead defendant. Incidentally, I never spoke to any of the defendants before they came into the courtroom. I never wanted to. I had interrogators who went down and interrogated them, I had affidavits, I knew their alibis, I knew their excuses, but I never personally confronted any of them. I didn't want to be tainted with any feeling of sympathy towards a human being who was responsible for those terrible crimes. I wanted to judge them by their deeds. So I did not plan to call any witnesses, and I did not. The DP camps were full of survivors any one of whom would have come in gladly to testify that everyone of those defendants murdered his mother. No problem getting witnesses. But I was afraid that would happen to me what happened in Israel, when Ivan the Terrible was not the Ivan so Terrible, but Ivan not so terrible, from another camp. I said: "I don't need them. I will hang them with their own documents." When they were presented, Ohlendorf who was a father of five children, intelligent, handsome man, he said: "Well, I can't say for sure whether we killed 90,000, you know, sometimes the troops were bragging." Talk about willing executioners. These were eager executioners; they were trying to show they killed more. I said: "But would you say there was … eighty thousand? …seventy thousand?" – "Yeah, could be." – "Could it be more?" "Yeah, that's also possible, but", and he made the point, he never allowed his men to do what some other units did. They threw the babies up in the air; they used them for target practice. They smashed their heads against a tree. He said: "I never let them do that. I told them: If a mother is there with an infant child, you allow the mother to hold the child to her breast. Otherwise she starts screaming and she has a scene, and you aim for the child, and you shoot through both of them. You save ammunition. You quiet down your mother. That's a more humane way to do it." Ohlendorf was a gentleman. He also explained about the gas vans. You know they sometimes had to move the people out of town. Didn't want to do it in the middle of a city. Well, the old people couldn't run fast enough. And the young kids, they couldn't run at all. So somebody got the good idea: we put them in a gas van. The gas van looked like a regular house trailer. They even disguised some of them by putting windows on the sides so it looked like a *Wohnwagen,* a house trailer to go on vacation with. They'd jam it full with thirty or forty people. It was so arranged that when the motor was started, carbon monoxide gas would flood into the van. And the theory was that within fifteen minutes or so they are already dead when you get to the burial side which the other inmates were busy digging, and you'd dump them into the site. Well, it didn't quite work that way. Sometimes they didn't die. Sometimes, the brakes would fail on the van. Instead of just dying quietly – which the advertisers was for the manufacturer who manufactured these nice vans, and we have his name – they would start clawing at each other trying to get out as soon as the gas came in. So when you opened it, it was full of excrement and vomit and blood and a mess, and these kids had to be separated from their parents and the old parents and the grandparents, and they had to do it by hand. And he said: "This was very tough on my men." He said: "I didn't like gas vans at all." Sensitive fellow. Well, I don't want to get too gory here. Ohlendorf was sentenced to death.

All of my defendants were convicted. Thirteen of them were sentenced to death. And Ohlendorf explained why he did this. It was very important. I said: "How do you explain this, a man of your intelligence, background, education, a family man? How do you explain it?" He said: "It's easy, it's self-defence." – "Self-defence? Germany attacked France, Holland, Belgium, Poland, and Russia, all of a dozen countries. Nobody has attacked Germany, and you say it's self-defence?" – "Oh yes, of course it's self-defence. Because we knew that the Bolsheviks were planning to attack us. So we were going to have to, in self-defence, move against them first." – "Well, why did you kill the Jews?" – "Well, we knew the Jews were sympathetic to the Bolsheviks. So you got to eliminate them, too. And the gypsies, well the gypsies, they played both sides of the street, so we can't have them hanging around loose." – "But why then did you kill the children, the little children?" – "Well", he said, "they would grow up knowing that we had killed their parents, they would be enemies of Germany. And so we had to kill them, too. Because we were interested in the long-range plans." – "And how do you justify this?" – "Well, Hitler had all the information. I was not in a position to judge that. I had to assume that he was more informed and he knew better what was in the interest of our country. And I accepted that. And that's what I did." And he brought in, as all the Germans did, *Gutachten,* expert opinions, we called them affidavits by the dozen, by the bushel, one was from a Professor Reinhart Maurach of Munich, a five hundred page *Gutachten* explaining that in order to commit a crime you must have a criminal intent. And if what you do, you believe, is in the interest of the government, and is self-defensive, then, of course, there is no criminal intent, and it is not a crime. And you cannot convict him. Professor Maurach, a very distinguished professor at the University of Munich, continued to preach and teach that doctrine for many years. So what it boiled down to, and that was the language that Maurach used, I hesitated to use it out of pity for our translators, but I will translate it – *putativer Notstand* in German literally means "presumed emergency" – as justification for the action. The modern terminology is "anticipatory self-defence". Anybody heard that recently? Well, the tribunal consisting of three American judges led by Judge Michael Musmanno of Pennsylvania, a very competent man, found them all guilty. And then came the day of sentencing. "For the crimes of which you have been committed this Tribunal sentences you to death by hanging." They'd stand to attention, take off the earphones, and step back into that side door which many of you may have noticed in Room 600. The panel would open; they'd step into the Black Maria, the lift that went all around. They were dropped down; the door would close, as if they had dropped into Hell one after the other. Very, very dramatic.

Somebody asked me how did I feel about that, did I have jubilation? I had never asked for the death penalty. Not that I am opposed to it under certain circumstances. But I felt that there is no penalty, no penalty which could balance out the enormity of the crimes committed by these men. And so I left it to the judge to fix the sentences. And he did. And I had a score card, and he was rougher than I would have been. Had I imposed the sentences, they would have been more lenient. And there was no jubilation in my heart at all. It was the practice at Nuremberg in those days, Whitney will probably remember it, when a trial ended, the prosecutors, the chief prosecutor for that trial, served as host at a party at his house to celebrate the ending of a difficult trial. I couldn't go to my own party. I went to bed. Well, that gives you some idea of how it is that educated, intelligent men of families of their own, can go out and murder in cold blood hundreds of thousands of little children and seek to justify it on the spurious argument that our system is so corrupt that if you can use anticipatory self-defence as an argument you feel that gives you permission to engage in that type of monstrosity and atrocity. So much for the trial. The trial was over. I decided to stay on in Germany. I was approached by leading Jewish organisations that had an idea. The idea was to recover the property which had been taken from the Jews ... the heirless Jewish property. They didn't have any money, of course, but they thought I was the right man to do the job. Military government had passed a law calling for the restitution of property. And also a provision in case property was unclaimed, it was presumed heirless, it would go to a successor organisation instead of to the State, to be used for the benefit of survivors. I was named the Director General of that organisation. I gave myself that title, because I was the only employee at the time. And we began to work.

My time is running out on me, I'll be very brief. But I promised Dr. Kress, who is here in the audience somewhere. You're holding up your hand somewhere, where are you? Are you hidden away? Dr. Kress, are you here? Ah, wherever he is, he's over there, hiding over there. I promised, because he's an old-timer he and Ambassador Kaul now, Judge Kaul, and Zimmermann, they have been a powerful German force in the negotiating of the International Criminal Court. I promised to say something, which I said he probably doesn't know about the law, and that's hard to come by. What I am going to tell him is the main problems on the restitution programme. We had a Court of Restitution Appeals, Allied lawyers originally, later mixed, who decided difficult legal issues. The first legal issue was the repayment of the purchase price. The principle of law was one I had learnt in Law School: If a contract is entered into under duress, when the duress is gone, you can void the contract. You have an option: you give back what you got, you get back what you had to give up, and you give back what you got. For example, if Hans Kohn had to sell his house, because Hitler said under the Nuremberg Laws, which were explained to you this morning, that no Jew can own property, he sold it to his neighbour for a hundred thousand marks. It was Reichsmarks. By the time the war was over, the Reichsmark was worthless. The German law provided one Deutschmark equals ten Reichsmarks. So if he got a hundred thousand Reichsmarks when he was forced to give up his property, in order to get it back he would have to give back a hundred thousand marks of some kind. If he had to give back a hundred thousand Deutschmarks, nobody would have claimed restitution under those circumstances. Nobody. It would have made no sense whatsoever; because first of all the house wasn't worth it, secondly we were afraid the Russians might come in the next day. We were always on the alert during those early years against the possibility of an invasion, as the Russians were sweeping to the West. And the needs were immediate. Advisory opinion number one issued by the Court of Restitution Appeals, and I wrote the brief and made the argument in the courthouse at Nuremberg, room number 600, was that ten to one applies. It applied to other cases. So it was possible to have that programme.

The second important decision in the Court of Restitution Appeals, and then I will fulfil my obligation to Dr. Kress, was a case I argued against the Jewish community of Augsburg. There was communal property – Jewish communal property – the Jews had their own schools, their own synagogues, their own hospitals and institutions of various kinds. It was a congregation, like other Christian, non-Jewish congregations, part of the German state mechanism. Americans don't understand that here. That's the way it worked in Germany. And what happened? The Jews were all driven out, new immigrants came in, they occupied the town, they started to build, and they took over the Jewish cemeteries. I am a great expert on hundreds of Jewish cemeteries. And they claimed all the assets. I said "I am sorry." I appeared before the court, and I said: "You know, I stood on this spot and prosecuted the Einsatzgruppen", I never thought I would see the day when I'd stay here and argue a case against the newly created Jewish community, the *Gemeinde*, which was the defendant in that case. I said: "But my duty under the law is to bring back the assets for the benefit of all the persecuted, and to distribute it where it's most needed. And therefore I cannot agree that it should go to one small group." And I won that case. If I had lost that case, there would have been no restitution programme. Anyway, let me move on, because I am already trespassing on the time of Louise Harmon, I apologize for that. The restitution programme consisted of other parts as well, not only the restitution of property, but the compensation laws, which have been forgotten. In 1951, as a result of an initiative announced by Chancellor Adenauer, a devout Catholic, Germany agreed to make amends, insofar as they could. Tremendous battles about how much should be paid for what. Impossible problems! How much do you pay for a human life? Six million people presumably were killed. How much do you ask for each one? Is grandma worth more than grandpa? Is he worth more than she? These were the problems. We decided, we ask for nothing for a human life, because we put no value on it. How much do you ask for fear? Every day they were afraid. They woke up; they didn't know if they'd be dead the next day. They lived with constant fear in all the concentration camps and everywhere. We put no price on fear. We charged for things which were normally measurable. *Haftentschädigung,* false imprisonment, for time spent in Auschwitz, five marks a day, which was the equivalent then of one Dollar. And the Finance Minister said: "Ach, we're going to go bankrupt." Fritz Schäffer was his name: "This programme will cost us a lot of money. Compensation for all the injuries that we imposed, disability, loss of economic rights, loss of positions, loss of jobs." And we said: "He is an old Nazi, he is against restitution, he is exaggerating the claims." In the end it cost them ten times more than any of us had ever dreamed of. The injuries were so great. I've tried and negotiated with the German companies, after Nuremberg, when they were released from prison. And I said: "Look, you have worked these people to death. Don't you think you owe them something?" And they said: "We? We never worked anybody to death. We had nothing to do with it." – "But I show you the proof that you have." – "Oh, well, of course, we had to, we were under orders. We had to be loyal patriots." – "But did you have to treat them like dying dogs?" – "Oh well, everybody was suffering. We treated them well." And these were the arguments they made, and invariably, all of them, IG Farben, Krupp, Siemens, AEG, Telefunken, every company I approached, made the same arguments. And when Albert Speer came out of Spandau prison, which is no picnic, I have been in Spandau, after twenty years, I met him secretly in Frankfurt Airport, and I said: "Herr Speer, I have read all of your reports. You make it very clear that they cannot use labourers without a request to the SS. That they must have the best of connections, they must be able to show that they need it for their war production. Why do all of these people tell me they didn't employ them, they didn't request them, they treated them well, etc.?" And he said: "They're lying." I was afraid he was going to say: "Ey, Mr. Prosecutor, get lost. I served my time. Your case is over." He said: "No, they're lying." I said: "Can I quote you?" He said: "Yes, you may." And I quoted him in a book called "Less Than Slaves" which was published by Harvard University Press. It appeared in Germany under the title of *Lohn des Grauens*. It appeared as a documentary film by Lea Rosh, from Zweites Deutsche Fernsehen [ZDF] I think it was: *Vernichtung durch Arbeit.* The record was clear. I don't sell books. My rights have been given away to the Holocaust Museum in Washington for everything that I have ever written. It was a courageous act on the part of Mr. Speer, after twenty years to come back. The arguments about his sincerity? I don't believe. He could have told me to get lost.

Anyway, let me move on. So much for restitution. The most difficult problem of all, of course, is to prevent it from happening again. And that's what I have been doing. How do you do that? Well, nobody pays me. Nobody hired me, so nobody can fire me. I have a big advantage. I go to the UN, I go to the meetings, I prepare memoranda, I prepare arguments, to create an International Criminal Court. I want to pay tribute to Germany on this occasion, too, because the German delegation led by Ambassador Kaul then, has been a strong advocate of the Court, and in their subsequent legislation with

Zimmermann and with Kress, trying to pass laws to implement that, they have been ahead of the rest of the world. Because they know better than everybody else what war means. Aggression is the supreme international crime, according to the IMT judgement. And we just barely got it into the Roman Statute with the proviso, however, that the court can't act on it until there is agreement reached on a re-definition which is not necessary, and its relationship to the Security Council, which they'll never get. And that's been postponed. It's too technical to go into here. I've written lots of articles, and I encourage you who are seriously interested to read my website which is benferencz.org for more information. So let me wrap it all up. What does it all add up to? Well, it's a complicated world, and it's very difficult. People say "How are you?" and I say "I am always fine." – "How can you be always fine?" – "I am aware of the alternatives." I have seen man's degradation. I have experienced it. I have lived through it. And I have a strong conviction that we can make it a better world. I refuse to believe that a society which is capable of giving me a box which I can push a button and see when there was a train accident in Paris a week ago or a minute ago and in China; and which can repair satellite a million miles out into outer space; and which can give me a telephone that I carry in my pocket and call any place in the world; that they are incapable of divining a system where human beings can live in peace. I don't believe that. The will is lacking because they don't believe it can be done. There are those who believe not in the rule of law, which Whitney Harris also spoke about, who believe only in the rule of power. And that was mentioned also in connection with the Jackson speech. Reason versus power or I put it another way, some thought that law is better than war. If you believe that law is better than war, then what you have to do is work for law and work against war. You have to stop glorifying war. You have to stop treating it as a holy grail, a holy mission, where young people are encouraged to give their lives and take lives of innocent people in pursuit of their own particular goals whatever they [happen] to be. Is it possible to change the way people think? Sure, it is possible. I've seen it in my life time. In my lifetime we have eliminated colonialism, in my lifetime we have seen the beginning of the emancipation of the black man and of women in the United States. We have seen such radical changes in the way people think that I think it's folly to assume that we can't do it. And let me say what really drives me: I believe that we owe it to the memory of all those who died in wars, all of them in all countries, never to stop trying to make it a more humane and peaceful world. I think it can be done. Never lose hope that it can be done. And keep trying. Thank you very much.

I will take a couple of questions. I am sorry, I have already trespassed on Louise's time and generosity. So let's get a few questions. Whoever you are, wherever you are, if you have some questions, just take the microphone. My ears are now over 170 years old, combined, so speak up, and I'll try to answer it.

Question: Sir, after the end of your short presentation, it is very difficult to come back to the beginning. But I still would like to do that. You were then talking about show down pilots who were killed in some German cities. We know about those cases. But do you agree that – I may add that I was in the anti-aircraft artillery for nineteen months myself, and I know what happened with shot down planes. We had to report to the Division, and immediately some officers went to the shot down planes and captured the pilots to prevent the killings you mentioned in the beginning. It happened immediately. So would you agree on this, because otherwise in my opinion it would not have been possible that thousands of pilots were prisoners of war?

Answer: I get your point. You're quite right. Of course, there were cases where the pilots were rescued. We did have rescued pilots. And I didn't go out and investigate the cases of rescued pilots. I only went out to investigate the cases where the pilots were murdered on the ground. And I can assure you from having dug up such bodies with my hands that those cases existed and they were crimes committed by the local ordinary house people, very often the housewives, who came out and beat them on the head with shoes if they did not have a shovel. And then the firemen would come out and use a crowbar, and split their head open. But, of course, some of them were rescued. If a flier came down somewhere near a farmhouse, and he was lucky, he met a decent person who was unaware of any orders from Berlin, he was saved, and I am grateful to all those who behaved in a humane manner, and I didn't mean to imply that it happened to everyone. At Nuremberg, we were very particular. We wanted to hold accountable only those who could be proved guilty beyond a reasonable doubt. This was pointed out by

Professor Barrett in his talk about Jackson. There were some Americans who said: "No, we'll turn all of Germany into a meadowland. Morgenthau was one such. That was not the policy of the US government; the policy was to hold accountable only those who are proved guilty after a fair trial. And that's what they had. We never condemned all of the German people. If we had, we would not have needed the trials. We had the capacity to kill them all, if we wanted to. We didn't want to. We stopped. And that was the end of the war. And I am grateful to those who then may have helped Americans, and I am certainly grateful to those who today realise how dangerous wars can be and how awful they can be and are working now so carefully to create an International Criminal Court as an important step in the direction of a more rational world of the law.

Question: I have another question.

Answer: Is there somebody else with another question to give somebody else a chance? There's nobody else? Here's a gentleman right here, he has a question.

Question: My question refers to your "putativer Notstand" or anticipatory self-defence. Would you say, that those terms describe the rationale for the invasion of Iraq by the American government?

Answer: The question relates to the American invasion of Iraq. In my judgement which is not shared by all lawyers, I want to draw your attention to that, it certainly is not shared by the government's lawyers, the United Nations' system that what set up after 40 million people were killed in World War II, provided that you are not allowed to use armed force, except under very restricted circumstances, if you are attacked, armed attack against you, or if you are directed by the Security Council to do so. The last resolution of the Security Council before the invasion of Iraq which had already been planned was "Come back to us with a report of the arms inspectors, and then we will decide what to do." They did not authorise any invasion of Iraq by the use of armed force. Ten years before, they had resolutions which authorised all nations to use whatever means necessary to kick Iraq out of Kuwait and stop there. And Bush's father stopped, I think from a political point of view unfortunately, without going into Baghdad to arrest a criminal. So the action by the United States in my judgement, and I repeat it is a judgement which is shared by many lawyers, but not by everyone, was an act of aggression, the supreme international crime, for which the leaders, I emphasise the point, because Judge Kaul was very strong in all the negotiations on making it a point that this is a leadership crime only, with no threat to an enlisted man, a sergeant or a corporal, it's a threat to those who planned and perpetrated this act in violation of the UN Charter, which binds all nations, including the United States. I regret it very much, I am ashamed of it very much, I do whatever I can to change it, and I will continue to do whatever I can to change it. Sometimes I succeed, sometimes I don't. That's the world in which we live.

Any more questions? If not, I am very happy, with apologies to Louise …

Question: I have one here. Given your indication earlier that you had to be selective in your prosecution of the members of the Einsatzgruppen, can you tell us whether the individual leaders of Einsatzgruppen A, B, C and D were prosecuted? Two, was von dem Bach-Zelewski among those prosecuted? And three: did the Soviets conduct their own prosecutions?

Answer: The answer to your first question which was did we try the leaders of the other Einsatzgruppen and Kommandos. The answer was no. We were in a hurry, we had limited budget, we had to get going with the trial then and there, we had no time to go searching the world and send out arrest warrants to countries to cooperate. There was no co-operation, as there is no developing, thanks to Germany, I hope as well, with the International Criminal Court. We did not try Bach-Zelewski in the Einsatzgruppen Case, he was put on trial later on in another trial, but not in the Einsatzgruppen Case, and the result was: we turned the files over, I was responsible for that later, I was executive counsel, turning the files over in Bavaria, to the Ministry of Justice, I remember Camille Sachs who was liberated in a concentration camp, and SPD man who was minister of justice, his son, also named Sachs, Hans Sachs, for Nuremberg, who received the files, and later they set up the *Zentralstelle* in Ludwigsburg to try other members, and there were some trials, but so many years after the war, it was very difficult to find witnesses, it was very difficult to find witnesses who were willing to co-operate, and so most of them got away with murder. That's another reality of the life in which we live. So, if you'll allow me now, I turn over to Louise, again with my apologies, thank you very much.

Benjamin Ferencz

Der Einsatzgruppen-Prozess

Hier erzählt Ben Ferencz, der als Chefankläger im Verfahren gegen Hitlers mobile Tötungstrupps, genannt Einsatzgruppen, amtierte, eine eindrucksvolle Geschichte. Eines Tages während des Krieges wurde er aufgefordert, sich in General Pattons Hauptquartier zu melden. Dort erhielt er den Auftrag, eine Abteilung für die Untersuchung von Kriegsverbrechen aufzubauen, deren Aufgabe es sein sollte, Kriegsverbrechen an alliierten Flugzeugbesatzungen, die in einigen deutschen Städten heruntergekommen und von der Bevölkerung oder der SS erschossen worden waren, zu untersuchen.

Als Konzentrationslager entdeckt wurden, verschob sich der Schwerpunkt der Ermittlungen auf dieses Gebiet. Das erste Lager, das er besuchte, war das Lager Ordruff, ein Außenlager von Buchenwald. Seine Aufgabe war nun, Beweise für die dort stattgefundenen Verbrechen zu finden. Es gelang ihm, in Buchenwald entsprechende Aufzeichnungen zu beschlagnahmen, beispielsweise die Totenbücher, dicke schwarze Bücher, in denen exakt vermerkt war, welche Transporte an welchen Tagen mit wie vielen Menschen, die oft auch namentlich aufgeführt waren, ankamen. Außerdem war erfasst, wie viele Menschen zu Tode geprügelt wurden oder verhungerten. Eine Totenliste mit den Todesursachen.

Nach seiner Rückkehr in die USA traf Ferencz durch Zufall einen Oberst namens Telford Taylor, der vom Präsidenten beauftragt worden war, die Nachfolgeverfahren des Hauptkriegsverbrecherprozesses, den Richter Jackson gerade im Begriff war zu beenden, zu übernehmen. Taylor bat nun Ben Ferencz, nach Deutschland zurückzukehren und ihn bei der Auffindung von Beweisen für die vorgesehenen zwölf Folgeprozesse zu unterstützen. Dieser tat, worum er gebeten worden war, kehrte nach Deutschland zurück und fand in der Folge die Aufzeichnungen über die „Einsatzgruppen". Diese informierten präzise darüber, welche Einheit welche Stadt aufgesucht hatte. In prahlerischer Art war vermerkt, wie viele Menschen man dort jeweils eliminiert hatte. Von den 3.000 Mitgliedern der Einsatzgruppen, die im Zeitraum von zwei Jahren Tag für Tag Massenmorde begangen hatten, wurden gerade einmal 24 angeklagt.

Unter den Angeklagten stellten die SS-Generäle die ranghöchsten Offiziere dar. Ihr Anführer war General Otto Ohlendorf, Vater von fünf Kindern, intelligent und gut aussehend. Voller Stolz betonte er, dass er den Männern seiner Vernichtungseinheit niemals erlaubt habe, so zu handeln wie dies bei anderen Einsatzgruppen üblich war, die Kleinkinder in die Luft warfen, um sie als Zielscheiben zu benutzen oder ihre Köpfe gegen Baumstämme geschmettert hatten. Er habe seinen Leuten dies niemals gestattet. Er habe ihnen gesagt, dass es einer Mutter mit einem kleinen Kind erlaubt werden müsse, ihr Kind an ihre Brust zu halten; andernfalls würde sie zu schreien beginnen und es gäbe eine unangenehme Szene. Dann sollte man das Kind ins Visier nehmen und mit einem Schuss beide, Mutter und Kind, erschießen. Damit könne Munition gespart werden, und außerdem sei dies eine humanere Art zu töten. Alle Angeklagten wurden verurteilt, dreizehn von ihnen erhielten die Todesstrafe.

Louise Harmon

The Doctors' Trial at Nuremberg

I've been thinking about the Doctors' Trial at Nuremberg for the past year. It wasn't a subject I sought out; it found me. I thought I was researching something else altogether, and then one day I got stuck in Telford Taylor's Opening Statement for the Prosecution in the Doctors' Trial, spoken on December 9, 1946 in the Palace of Justice in Nuremberg. I got stuck in that Opening Statement and I couldn't get out. I'm still there.

I should say at the outset that I usually hate to speak at conferences. I know most academics enjoy it, but I don't. I'd much rather stay home and read and write and burrow into my cozy little hole on Long Island. Still, I've crawled out of that hole to be here today because I thought it would be good for me to teach someone else about the Doctors' Trial. To talk it out loud – to worry about it publicly – to see if this process might help me make sense of the Doctors' Trial. And truth to tell, it wasn't the Doctors' Trial I was trying to make sense of, but the conduct described in Taylor's Opening Statement that formed the basis of the charge. How could doctors, healers, upholders of the Hippocratic Oath of *do no harm* have performed those medical experiments on unwilling, suffering human beings?

The holocaust itself is a horrible package to unwrap. These human subjects were, after all, prisoners. They had been rounded up, forced out of their homes, and out of their families, transported on cattle cars to work camps, and put to slave labor. Had they not been found fit for work, they would have been killed. So this is the context in which this human experimentation took place. Once you've unwrapped the horrible package of the holocaust, and find yourself inside that box, you'll discover another horrible package inside, smaller, more discrete, needing to be unwrapped as well. Inside that package is what happened to some of those prisoners when they were drafted as human research subjects in experiments by Nazi doctors; a box within a box – a horror within a horror – evil squared – that's what I was trying to make sense of.

So I thought maybe speaking at a conference would help. How hard could it be? I asked myself. I'll take twenty minutes to describe what happened, and then leave ten minutes to ponder deep questions. It'll be just like teaching. Inform them a little, disturb them a lot. And just like teaching, I was hoping for revelation. It's been my experience that when you sing for your supper, you end up learning something about the song.

So let me inform you a little first. The Doctors' Trial was the first trial in Nuremberg after the War Crimes Trial of the most infamous Nazi war criminals. It was prosecuted solely by the United States. It was called the Doctors' Trial for the obvious reason that 20 of its 23 defendants were Nazi doctors; the other three were public health officials. The defendants were tried for a broad assortment of crimes, war crimes and crimes against humanity, including genocide and murder. They were also accused of carrying out forced sterilizations, and of taking part in the selection process on the arrival platforms of the concentration camps. Doctors were complicit in a wide array of Nazi crimes, but most of the evidence of the Doctors' Trial focused on the horrific medical experiments conducted on inmates of the Nazi concentration camps.[1]

Students of the holocaust are all familiar with the Doctors' Trial, but I'm surprised by how many people, even in academic circles, have never heard of it. The only people in the academy who I can absolutely count on to know something about the Doctors' Trial at Nuremberg are those who are engaged in medical ethics. The Doctors' Trial looms large in the field of medical ethics, particularly in the area of human experimentation. At the end of the Tribunal's written judgment in the Doctors' Trial, the judges wrote a ten-point code about how doctors should behave when using other human beings in their research. This code came to be known as the Nuremberg Code. It was the first international

---

[1] Arthur L. Caplan, *The Doctors' Trial and Analogies to the Holocaust in Contemporary Bioethical Debates*, in THE NAZI DOCTORS AND THE NUREMBERG CODE 258, 259 (George J. Annas and Michael A. Grodin, eds., 1992) [hereinafter THE NAZI DOCTORS].

standard for the protection of human research subjects. Virtually all contemporary debate on human experimentation is grounded in the Doctors' Trial at Nuremberg, and in the Nuremberg Code.[2]

The principles of the Nuremberg Code are elegant and simple, and derive from what purports to be a universal, natural law. Its central tenet is that the research subject must give his informed consent. He must be told of any and all risks of participating in the experiment, and then he must voluntarily agree to participate. The experiment must be based on the results of animal experimentation. Moreover, the experiment must yield results for the good of society, and must not be procurable by other methods of study. It must not be random and unnecessary in nature, and must be conducted only by scientifically qualified persons.[3] In the last sixty years, a second, even a third, generation of international codes have been spawned,[4] but the Nuremberg Code still remains the grand-daddy of all international standards for the protection of human research subjects.

---

[2] Michael A. Grodin, *Historical Origins of the Nuremberg Code, in* THE NAZI DOCTORS, *supra* note 1, at 121, 122.

[3] The Nuremberg Code, *in* THE NAZI DOCTORS, *supra* note 1, at 2.

[4] While the Nuremberg Code was the first effort to set an international standard for human experimentation, because the Code was created during the Nuremberg trials, it created the impression that it was merely a response to the horrific experiments of Nazi Germany. Dawn Joyce Miller, *Research and Accountability: The Need for Uniform Regulation of International Pharmaceutical Drug Testing,* 13 PACE INT'L L.REV. 197, 202-203 (2001). Furthermore, the experiments were all performed on healthy people who were prisoners of the state; the Code failed to distinguish between clinical research on healthy subjects and therapeutic clinical research that might offer a benefit for the presumably ill subjects. Sharon Perley, Sev S. Fluss, Zbigniew Bankoski, Francoise Simon, *The Nuremberg Code: An International Overview, in* NUREMBERG, THE NAZI DOCTORS, *supra* note 1, at 149, 156. Some of the principles of the Code were criticized as well. *See id.* at 154-156. In an effort to create a more comprehensive international code on human experimentation, the Helsinki Declaration was adopted by the World Medical Association (WMA). What is often referred to as "Helsinki I" was adopted by the World Medical Association in 1964, followed by three other congresses, "Helsinki II" adopted in Tokyo in 1975, "Helsinki III" adopted in Venice in 1983, and Helsinki IV, adopted in Hong Kong in 1989. DECLARATION OF HELSINKI RECOMMENDATIONS GUIDING DOCTORS IN CLINICAL RESEARCH, *in* THE NAZI DOCTORS, *supra* note 1, at 331[hereinafter DECLARATION OF HELSINKI] The Helsinki Declaration embodied all of the provisions of the Nuremberg Code, but distinguished between therapeutic clinical research and "pure" clinical research which anticipated little value or benefit to the subject. M. Cherriff Bassiouni, Thomas G. Baffes, John T. Evrard, *An Appraisal of Human Experimentation in International Law and Practice: The Need for International Regulation of Human Experimentation,* Vol. 72, No. 4, THE JOURNAL OF CRIMINAL LAW AND CRIMINOLOGY 1597, 1610 (1981). Different guidelines were formulated for "Clinical Research Combined with Professional Care" and "Nontherapeutic Clinical Research." *Id.* The Helsinki Declaration also required an independent ethical committee to provide researchers with comments and guidance on their research protocol. "The design and performance of each experimental procedure involving human subjects should be clearly formulated in an experimental protocol which should be transmitted for consideration, comment and guidance to a specially appointed committee independent of the investigator and the sponsor..." DECLARATION OF HELSINKI, *supra* at 340. This committee had the responsibility for verifying that the researchers were qualified to conduct the experiment, that the experiments were properly designed, that test subjects had been equitably chosen, that privacy of the subjects would be respected, and that the potential humanitarian benefits arising from the experiment would justify the risk to the individual subjects. *Id.* at 340-341. Both the requirement that the research be guided by an independent committee, and the principle that "reports of experiments not in accordance with the principles laid down in this Declaration should not be accepted for publication," sought to shift the burden of determining whether research complied with ethical standards from the individual researcher's conscience to the professional community of researchers. *Id.* at 341. A system of checks and balances that did not exist in the Nuremberg Code was thus created by the Declaration of Helsinki; it sought to establish mechanisms to monitor and enforce ethical standards in human experimentation.

In addition to the Nuremberg Code and the Helsinki Declaration, in 1991 the Counsel for International Organizations of Medical Sciences (CIOMS), in collaboration with the World Health Organization, published the International Ethical Guidelines for Biomedical Research Involving Human Subjects (the Guidelines). The Guidelines represent the most recent effort by the international community to establish ethical principles for research involving human subjects. The Guidelines were first distributed for comment by the CIOMS in 1982 to ministries of health, medical research councils, medical faculties, non-governmental organizations, research-based pharmaceutical companies, developing countries, and medical journals. The final product includes fifteen guidelines, providing for: 1) individual informed consent; 2) essential information for prospective research subjects; 3) obligations of investigators regarding informed consent; 4) inducement to participate; 5) research involving children; 6) research involving persons with mental or behavioral disorders; 7) research involving prisoners; 8) research involving subjects in underdeveloped communities; 9) informed consent in epidemiological studies; 10) equitable distribution of burdens and benefits; 11) selection of pregnant or nursing (breast-feeding) women as research subjects; 12) safeguarding confidentiality; 13) right of subjects to compensation; 14)

It is somewhat ironic to me that the Nuremberg Code with its high ideals and implicit respect for persons was the product of systematic, on-going torture and abuse. The Nazi experimentation represents the paradigmatic worst case scenario for human research subjects. It was a nightmare that generated the Nuremberg Code. But that pattern often repeats itself in history: Nightmares generate norms. When moral boundaries are transgressed, we put the offenders on trial and punish them to manifest our disapproval. Most recently we have seen it in our prosecution of the American soldiers who engaged in that shocking, degrading treatment of Iraqi prisoners in Abu Graib. As part of that process, there is often a ritualistic articulation of ideal behavior – a mantra to ward off further evil. When the horrible thing was done by ourselves, we may engage in that ritual out of guilt. Perhaps we harbor the belief that if we had only written it down – how we are supposed to treat one another – the horrible thing would not have happened. In other instances, where we stand in judgment of others – as was the case in Nuremberg – the ritual has other dimensions. Not only does a document like the Nuremberg Code silently condemn, but it creates a vast symbolic distance between the authors of the norms and those people who transgressed them.

But let's return to the Doctors' Trial itself. Officially designated as *United States v. Karl Brandt*, it was a long trial, lasting for eight months. It started in late 1946 and ended in August 1947. For people who love to count things, there are a lot of things about the Doctors' Trial to count. For example, the Tribunal convened 139 times. There were a total of 85 witnesses, and over 11,000 pages of transcript. Seven of the defendants were sentenced to death by hanging; five were sentenced to life imprisonment; four were given lesser prison terms; and seven were acquitted and freed.[5] Lots of numbers to count, except for victims. Telford Taylor refers to them as the nameless dead,[6] but if you are in the counting game and you're counting victims, there are comparatively fewer nameless dead to count. One scholar speculates that there were probably no more than a few thousand prisoners used as human research subjects in the Nazi experiments, but no one knows for sure.[7]

But we do know that the total number of individuals actually harmed by the defendants in the Doctors' Trial was far smaller than the number of those who were killed as part of the final solution, or who died of disease or malnutrition in the concentration camps. Why would these medical experiments that only affected a few thousand prisoners form the heart of the prosecution's charge against the Nazi doctors? Surely the Nazi doctors were complicit in the mass murder of millions – so why go after them for the torture of a few thousand?

The most obvious explanation for this was evidentiary. The prosecution had to prove up its case against individual defendants, and it was much more difficult to assign individual responsibility for the murder of millions. The scale of those massive killings in the gas chambers required a complex bureaucracy with multiple players and tiers of authority. Individual responsibility became buried and impossible to dig out. And while the planning phases of the killing operations were all written down in incredible detail with illustrations, once the operations were put into place, the oral tradition took over.

---

constitution and responsibilities of ethical review committees; and 15) obligations of sponsoring and host countries. INTERNATIONAL ETHICAL GUIDELINES FOR BIOMEDICAL RESEARCH INVOLVING HUMAN SUBJECTS (Council for International Organizations of Medical Sciences 1983) [hereinafter CIOMS Guidelines]. One of the goals of the CIOMS Guidelines was to provide strategies on how to implement the more abstract principles of the Helsinki Declaration. Unlike the Helsinki Declaration, the Guidelines require the approval of every research protocol involving humans by an independent ethical review committee. (Ethics and Research on Human Subjects) By mandating the review of all protocols using human subjects, the drafters of the CIOMS Guidelines believed that the principle of informed consent was insufficient to ensure the protection of human test subjects. The CIOMS Guidelines also represent the first international effort to tackle the issues arising out of clinical research conducted on an international scale; there are provisions that specifically apply to research in developing countries. Guideline 8 requests that research subjects from developing communities not be used in research that could be carried out reasonably well with subjects from developed countries. CIOMS Guideline 8.

[5] *Introduction* to THE NAZI DOCTORS, *supra* note 1, at 4. There were also over 1400 documents introduced.

[6] *Opening Statement of the Prosecution, December 9, 1946, reprinted in* THE NAZI DOCTORS, *supra* note 1, at 67.

[7] Arthur L. Caplan, *The Doctors' Trial and Analogies to the Holocaust in Contemporary Bioethical Debates,* THE NAZI DOCTORS, *supra* note 1, 258, 265.

Orders for the killings were sounded in the air, not written down. But the Nazi medical experiments purported to be science, and science ensured a well-documented record. It was relatively easy to prove up these cases against individual Nazi doctors. That ease of proof at least in part explains the prosecution's charging strategy.

I want to show you some photographs now. The first seven, I borrowed from an excellent book that I have relied upon a lot, edited by George Annas and Michael Grodin, *The Nazi Doctors and the Nuremberg Code*, published by Oxford University Press.[8] I am using those photographs with their permission. The last few are from the Photographic Evidence of the Prosecution.[9] I should warn you that a number of them are disturbing. I don't mean to be disrespectful of the victims by showing these pictures to you. I just think it is important to keep in mind just exactly what went on, and these pictures tell the story better than any words could.

PHOTOGRAPHS[10]:

[1] Here is a photograph of the Judges of the United States Military Tribunal No. One. Each of these judges was appointed by President Truman. Left to right: Harold L. Sebring, justice of the Supreme Court of Florida; Walter B. Beals, the presiding judge and justice of the Supreme Court of the state of Washington; Johnson T. Crawford, former justice of the Oklahoma District Court in Ada, Oklahoma; and Victor C. Swearingen, alternative member and former assistant attorney general of Michigan.

[2] This is a photograph of the Chief of Counsel for War Crimes, Brigadier Telford Taylor.

[3] Here is a photo of the general view of the courtroom on the opening day of the trial. Taylor is at the podium, delivering the Opening Statement.

[4] Here is a picture of the defendant physicians in the "Dock."

[5] This photograph is of the named defendant, Karl Brandt. He is age 43 here, and was the personal physician to Hitler, and the Reich Commissioner for Health and Sanitation. When Brandt was sentenced to death by hanging, he tried to avoid it by offering his living body for medical experiments, but he was turned down by the American authorities. At the gallows, Brandt declared, "It is no shame to stand on this scaffold. I served my fatherland as others before me."[11] He refused to end his speech, and finally the black hood was dropped over his head in mid-sentence.[12]

[6] This is a photograph of Dr. Leo Alexander, a Boston neurologist and psychiatrist, who was a consultant to the trial, and along with Dr. Andrew Ivy, drafted the Nuremberg Code. Here Dr. Alexander is examining a Polish girl who was permanently crippled from being a subject in an experiment.

[7] This is a freezing experiment at Dachau. The human subject is a political prisoner. He is being immersed in ice water. The freezing experiments were instigated by the German Air Force that wanted to know how to warm up aviators who were forced to parachute into the cold North Sea. In these experiments, human subjects were put in tanks of ice water for up to 3 hours, and then rewarmed by various means, including surrounding them by naked women. In other experiments, subjects were kept naked outdoors in freezing weather.[13] Many died.

---

[8] THE NAZI DOCTORS, *supra* note 1, at 113-119.

[9] Photographic Evidence of the Prosecution. Trials of War Criminals Before the Nuremberg Military Tribunals Under Control Council Law No. 10, Vol. I, 898-908 [hereinafter Trials of War Criminals, Vol. I].

[10] http://www.tourolaw.edu/Nuremberg.

[11] Alexander Mitscherlich and Fred Mielke, *Epilogue: Seven Were Hanged*, in THE NAZI DOCTORS, *supra* note 1, at 106.

[12] In the transcript at the end of the trial, each of the defendants was given a chance to address the Tribunal, and Karl Brandt's final statement before the Tribunal was very revealing. About the euthanasia programs, he characterized the conduct not as a crime against humanity, but as "pity for the incurable". *Final Statement of Defendant Karl Brandt, in* Trials of War Criminals: Nuremberg Military Tribunals, Vol. 2, at 139. Here is quote from Brandt's final statement, "…when I said 'yes' to euthanasia I did so with the deepest conviction, just as it is my conviction today, that it was right. Death can mean deliverance. Death is life – just as much as birth. It was never meant to be a murder." *Id.* at 140.

[13] *Opening Statement of the Prosecution, December 9, 1946, reprinted in* THE NAZI DOCTORS, *supra* note 1, at 74.

[8] These are photographs of an inmate from Dachau who is undergoing the terrific pain of low pressure in the high altitude experiments, also instigated by the German Air Force. They would lock the research subject in a low-pressure chamber and simulate pressures at high altitude, up to 68,000 feet. Then they would plunge him into a rapid descent without oxygen and witness and record his painful death.[14]

[9] Here are some pictures of phosphorus burns that were inflicted on inmates of Buchenwald. They would burn the human subjects, and then rub the burns with various preparations, to see which ones might heal, and which would cause infection, necrosis, and finally death.[15]

[10] This is a photograph of a young woman who underwent bone experiments. In these experiments, human subjects would have their legs broken, and then bone transplants performed. Transplantations of entire limbs from one person to another were performed. Usually the amputee would then be killed.[16]

[11] Here are corpses that were part of the transplantation experiments assembled in tanks containing formaldehyde for their preservation. To me, these have an otherworldly look to them, particularly the one there with just the amputated legs.

[12] Here is what the tanks looked like that preserved the corpses.

[13] Here is a corpse that has been carved up in preparation for dissection.

I've asked myself many times: with what degree of detail should I describe the horrific Nazi medical experiments at the conference? It's true, I just showed you some disturbing pictures, but I assure you, if you read the transcript of the Doctors' Trial, you would appreciate there were many worse tortures that I've left out that were not, and could not be, captured in photographic evidence. And I discovered something: I simply could not bring myself to say some of the things that happened to those people out loud. That was one of the surprises I did not anticipate in singing this song: that I would be unable to be a reporter of the truth.

I am reluctant to admit this, but there is something compelling about reading what happened in the research bays of the camps. The victims of the human experimentation *were* able to tell the truth, and many times I found I couldn't put the transcript down. I couldn't breathe as I read their testimony, spoken over sixty years ago by people who are long dead. But you can feel their suffering coming from the printed page. I don't think I will never read those transcripts again, but I do remember being there, inside that horrible little box of Nazi experimentation, in the pursuit of damnable knowledge about what might happen if you force the human body to exceed its limitations.

Perhaps too, this helps explain why the prosecution chose the medical experiments as the basis of their charge. They knew those survivors' stories were compelling. And so imaginable. Many of the deaths in the concentration camps took place in unimaginable circumstances, like lining up to take a shower that turns out to be a poisonous gas – who has ever been in such a situation? But it's not so hard to imagine how it might feel to be a human research subject. The setting would be familiar to all of us in this room: a medical facility of some kind, perhaps a laboratory in the doctor's office. I don't know about the rest of you, but I always feel so vulnerable when I go to the doctor, sitting there, waiting all alone in an examining room, half naked, dressed only in a white paper gown. Not only do I feel stripped of my clothes, I feel stripped of my identity and my dignity, and if there's something wrong with me physically, I feel anxious and mortal. I feel trapped inside this imperfect, confining, aging physical entity that weighs too much and hurts so much in the morning. All things considered, I'd rather be somewhere else.

The truth is: at times, the human body is a prison, and living inside of one is hard – that is the most basic fact of our universal human condition, and the basis of much of our suffering. So the stories described in the Doctors' Trial are ones that we can imagine. We can feel how trapped those human

---

[14] *Counts Two and Three of the Charge at the Doctors Trial, Judgment and Aftermath, in* THE NAZI DOCTORS, *supra* note 1, at 94-97.
[15] Trials of War Criminals, Vol. I, *supra* note 9, at 653-669.
[16] *Id.* at 391-418.

research subjects must have felt in their multiple prisons – the prison of the concentration camp, and then that other prison we all know too well – the prison of the human body. Except in the concentration camps, the doctor wasn't there to help you feel better, to transform your prison into a room with a door, or a place you could live in and with. He was there to use you, to cause you suffering, and to do you harm.

And so I have to confess to finding the stories of the Nazi experimentation compelling, and I own up to some morbid fascination about them. Perhaps some of you know what I'm talking about. I wonder – fear really – whether some emotions in the same genre – compulsion and morbid fascination – may have motivated the Nazi doctors themselves to perform those experiments. I shudder at the thought that I might understand them.

I suspect that Telford Taylor had the same conversation with himself about how much detail to go into about the experiments. He took the high road. His description of the experiments in the Opening Statement was purely factual, and devoid of any details of suffering. His list included, besides the experiments I just described, infecting prisoners with malaria and typhus, inflicting wounds that were then infected with mustard gas or pus to induce blood poisoning, forcing inmates to drink salt water, sterilization experiments, castrations, experiments on effective methods of poisoning in practice for the final solution, burning inmates with incendiary bombs, and killing Jewish inmates in order to help build a skeleton collection.[17]

How could we be talking about doctors? Doctors are healers. Doctors help people, prevent and cure disease, alleviate human suffering. We know that the Nazi doctors swore to the Hippocratic Oath. How could they have sworn to do no harm to their patients and then engage in gruesome scientific experiments on human subjects that not only did not benefit them, but harmed them, and caused them to suffer, and often to die?

I suppose the cheap answer might be: The Hippocratic Oath applies only in a therapeutic context, and this is scientific research. In a therapeutic doctor/patient relationship, the doctor's duty is clear. But these human subjects were not their patients, but their prisoners. And even if they were research subjects, who knew what the ethics were of using them in scientific experiments? That was how the defense argument went. But they *did* know. There *were* German codes predating the Second World War that set out the ethically permissible boundaries of research on human beings. A 1900 document called the Prussian Directive required the fully informed consent of the human subject in research; he had to be told of all "the adverse consequences that may result from the intervention."[18] Then again, in 1931, the Reich Minister of the Interior promulgated a set of guidelines for medical experimentation. The Reich Circular demanded that the researcher obtain the informed consent of the human subject, that he document any deviations from protocol, and that he justify the study of especially vulnerable populations.[19] Some have argued that the principles in the 1931 Reich Circular were "even more inclusive and formalistic than the Nuremberg Code in that they demand complete responsibility of the medical profession for carrying out human experimentation."[20]

So it is just historically inaccurate to say that there were no norms of proper research conduct before the Second World War. When Dr. Ivy cited the 1931 Reich Circular in his testimony to show that the Nazi doctors were surely familiar with the ethics of human experimentation, defense counsel responded

---

[17] Not listed, of course, since he was not a defendant, having slid away into the night, were the experiments on twins performed by Dr. Joseph Mengele. Infecting one twin with a germ, and using the other as a control, attempting to create Siamese twins on Gypsy twin girls by connecting blood vessels and organs, trying to connect the urinary tract of a seven year-old-girl to her own colon. Eva Mozes-Kor, *The Mengele Twins and Human Experimentation: A Personal Account*, in THE NAZI DOCTORS, *supra* note 1, at 53, 57.

[18] Michael A. Grodin, *Historical Origins of the Nuremberg Code*, in THE NAZI DOCTORS, *supra* note1, at 121, 127. The Prussian Directive was probably the first document ever to recognize the need to protect vulnerable populations from being used as subjects in experimentation. It banned nontherapeutic research on children and incompetents. *Id.*

[19] *Id.* at 131-132.

[20] *Id.* at 129.

that it was only a guideline, and did not have the force of law.[21] Frankly I don't care if the 1931 Reich Circular had the force of law. As far as I'm concerned, ethics need not have the force of law to be binding, but then again, I'm not much of a legal positivist. The Nazis were. I don't care what you call them, law, directives, guidelines, ethical principles – those documents described in detail how a doctor was supposed to treat a human research subject. I suspect that each of those Nazi doctors knew about those moral principles, and if they didn't, they should have as members of the medical profession.

But even if they had known about the ethics of human experimentation, it wouldn't have mattered. The racist theories about Aryan supremacy – theories embraced by most doctors in Germany in the 1930s – managed to move the subjects of those experiments out of the category of humanity. Hence there was little ethical *Angst* about how to treat them. The packages of the holocaust, and the little box within the box we are looking at right now – both of these packages were wrapped in a set of prevailing ideas known as "social Darwinism."[22] Fearing degeneration of the human race and of the Nordic German race in particular, the social Darwinists established a kind of Rassenhygiene, or racial hygiene.[23] By the mid-1920s, Rassenhygiene merged with the ideologies of National Socialism,[24] and the creation and maintenance of racial purity became a vital component of Nazi ideology.[25]

Given the importance of biology in the Nazi ideology, many doctors were attracted to the Nazi movement.[26] By 1942, more than half the doctors in the country were members of the Nazi party, and doctors were represented in the SS seven times more than the average for the employed male population. Most of the twenty or more institutes for racial hygiene were established at German universities before Hitler rose to power, and by 1932 Rassenhygiene was a fixture in the German medical community.[27] The practical results of the Nazi ideology of Rassenhygiene were three state programs: the Nuremberg Laws,[28] the Sterilization Law,[29] and the euthanasia program.[30] German

---

[21] *Id.*

[22] Robert N. Proctor, *Nazi Doctors, Racial Medicine, and Human Experimentation, in* THE NAZI DOCTORS, *supra* note 1, at 17 [hereinafter PROCTOR]. Many more Nazi doctors were involved in human experimentation beyond those 23 Nuremberg defendants; they were just the "tip of the iceberg." Christian Ross, *Nazi Doctors, German Medicine, and Historical Truth, in* THE NAZI DOCTORS, *supra* note 1, at 32, 34. Many who conducted experiments held prestigious academic positions. *Id.* at 24-28.

[23] PROCTOR, *supra* note 22, at 18. The founders of Rassenhygiene were Alfred Ploetz and Wilhelm Schallmayer. *Id. Rassenhygiene* was viewed as a complement to personal and social hygiene; it was characterized as a form of preventive medicine for the "German germ plasm," by "combating the disproportionate breeding of 'inferiors,' the celibacy of the upper classes, and the threat posed by feminists to the reproductive performance of the family." *Id.*

[24] Initially the eugenicists were worried more about "the indiscriminate use of birth control (by the "fit") and the provision of inexpensive medical care (to the "unfit") *Id.*

[25] *Id.* at 18-19.

[26] *Id.* In 1929, a number of physicians formed the National Socialist Physicians' League. Its purpose was to coordinate Nazi medical policy and to "purify the German medical community of 'Jewish Bolshevism.'" *Id.* Nearly 6 % of the medical profession had joined by 1933 before Hitler had risen to power. By 1942, more than 38,000 doctors were members of the Nazi Party, about half of the doctors in the country. In 1937, "doctors were represented in the SS seven times more than the average for the employed male population; doctors assumed leading positions in German government and universities." *Id.*

[27] *Id.* at 19-20.

[28] *Id* The Nuremberg laws excluded Jews from citizenship, prevented marriage or sexual relations between Jews and non-Jews, requiring the medical exams to ensure racial purity. *Id.*

[29] *Id.* at 20-21. The law was entitled the Law for the Prevention of Genetically Diseased Offspring. Physicians, dentists, nurses, midwives, and directors of mental institutions were required to register anyone suffering from the infirmities listed by the law, such as feeblemindedness, schizophrenia, manic depression, epilepsy, Huntington's chorea, genetic blindness, deafness, and alcoholism. Children under age 14 could not be forcibly sterilized, but a petition for sterilization could be issued for anyone over age 10. *Id.* at note 8, 30. Local health offices were empowered to inspect municipal and private institutions to ensure anyone falling within the categories established by the law was brought before the courts. Genetic Health Courts were established throughout Germany, and doctors were required to register every case of genetic illness; failure to register such an illness resulted in a fine. In 1935, The Genetic Health Courts were granted powers to "disbar any attorney who persisted too vigorously in arguing that their clients should not be sterilized." *Id.* There were also Appellate Genetic Health Courts. These courts were usually attached to local civil courts, and were presided over by two doctors and a lawyer; one of them had to be an expert on genetic pathology. *Id.* at 21. Physicians were also required to undergo training in genetic pathology at racial institutes created throughout the county. *Id.*

doctors were intimately involved in all three of them. Somewhere between 350,000 and 400,000 people were sterilized by German doctors.[30] Between 1939 and 1941, German doctors killed 70,000 patients from mental hospitals, in what turned out to be a "rehearsal for the subsequent destruction of Jews, homosexuals, Communists, Gypsies, Slavs and prisoners of war."[31] It was a logical extension of their medical power to use concentration camp prisoners as human subjects in experiments. It should have come as no surprise.

Rassenhygiene made all of these medical practices morally defensible to the doctors who engaged in them. That was what made the idea so potent. It urged the doctors to relieve the groaning lifeboat of useless eaters and the racially impure in order to save the human race. Rassenhygiene looked like a superseding moral principle to trump the Kantian notion of respect for persons. Elie Wiesel wrote about a dissertation he once read in which a psychiatrist argued that the sense of morality of the Nazi killers was not impaired. They knew how to differentiate between good and evil. Their sense of reality was impaired. Human beings were not human beings in their eyes. They were abstractions.[33] I quarrel with that psychiatrist's characterization. The impairment was one of morality, not of reality. To move another human being out of the moral community, to treat him as an abstraction, as nonhuman, as a means to another's end – that maneuver is a violation of morality. But Rassenhygiene created the illusion that the so-called science the doctors were engaged in promoted the public good. It was a moral sleight of hand, and enabled them to sleep at night – at least some of them, probably most of them. But it is important to have clarity about this: Believing in that illusion was a wrong thing to do. It may have skewered what the Nazi doctors believed to be reality, but at its heart, the impairment was moral, not ontological.

The transcripts of the Doctors' Trial reveal that some doctors in the concentration camps could not sleep at night. One defendant, for example, Dr. Romberg, testified about his efforts to protest what was going on. Dr. Romberg was an assistant to Dr. Rascher, a minor satellite of Himmler's. Himmler had given his consent to the high altitude experiments using concentration camp inmates who were condemned to death. The inmates in Dachau were supposedly going to receive some form of clemency if they survived the experiments, so in Dr. Romberg's mind he considered these human subjects as 'volunteers.' But there was an incident in the laboratory one day that upset Dr. Romberg very much. He was assisting Dr. Rascher in conducting an experiment with the altitude machine on one of the human subjects. The electrocardiograph indicated that the prisoner's medical condition was "getting dangerous." Dr. Romberg said to his superior, Dr. Rascher, "You had better stop now." I will read from the transcript:

"Question: And what did Rascher do?

Answer: Nothing. He kept that altitude and later death suddenly occurred.

---

[30] *Id.* at 23. In 1939, Hitler ordered that certain doctors be commissioned to declare individuals "incurably sick by medical examination," and to grant them *Gnadentod*, or "mercy death." Between 1939 and 1941, German doctors killed over 70,000 hospitalized mental patients, and the operation turned out to be a "rehearsal for the subsequent destruction of Jews, homosexuals, Communists, Gypsies, Slavs, and prisoners of war." *Id.* As with the Sterilization Law, German doctors planned and implemented the Nazi euthanasia programs. Upon the occasion of killing patients in the Brandenburg Hospital in 1940, the head of the operation, Victor Brack, emphasized that the gassings "should be carried out only by physicians," citing the motto: "The needle belongs in the hand of the doctor." *Id.* at 24-25. The medicalized euthanasia operation and the "final solution" to the "Jewish question" was linked in both theory and practice. *Id.* at 25. The belief that some lives were not worth living and could therefore be eliminated on a mass scale in Germany's mental hospitals was merely expanded to justify the gassing of the Jews in work camps. The medical profession had already developed a successful technical apparatus to destroy the mentally ill; that apparatus was merely dismantled and shipped east to Majdanek, Auschwitz, and Treblinka. *Id.*

[31] *Id.* at 21.

[32] *Id.* at 24.

[33] *Introduction* to THE NAZI DOCTORS, *supra* note 1, at ix.

Question: When you observed the electrocardiogram was it quite clear to you that the person would die in the next second?

Answer: No, of course not. First of all I had never seen a death from high altitude. That was the first one I ever saw….the electrocardiogram change was, shall we say, doubtful. I myself would have stopped the experiment at this stage but he didn't. I only spoke up because I would have stopped the experiment at that moment.

Question: Did you speak to Rascher about this after the experiment?

Answer: It was not possible for me to object in view of Rascher's position, but I told him that such things should not happen."[34]

Dr. Romberg ended up going back to Berlin and reporting the death to another superior. This was in violation of an agreement that he had signed under Himmler's orders promising that everything that happened at the concentration camp would remain a secret. Dr. Romberg's superior convinced him not to report the death of the research subject in the altitude chamber. What good would it do? Dr. Rascher reported to Himmler, and Himmler was not going to give up the experiments. Not only that, Himmler would have started proceedings for treason or for sabotage of an essential war experiment against Dr. Romberg. Dr. Romberg ended up going back to Dachau, and continued to argue with Dr. Rascher when later deaths occurred in the altitude machine, but to no avail.[35]

When asked at the trial whether there was any possibility in Germany for a doctor in his position to resist, Dr. Romberg answered there were three types of resistance: to emigrate if you were able; open resistance which meant the complaining doctor would himself end up in a concentration camp or subject to a death penalty; or passive resistance, to apparently yield to orders, but to misplace and delay them. He referred to this third method of passive resistance as "internal emigration," and this was the mode Dr. Romberg chose for himself.[36] He felt he could not do otherwise, "in view of Rascher's position."

That phrase is so chilling to me, and yet I have some empathy for Dr. Romberg. I don't know what his circumstances were. He may have had children of his own to protect. I don't know, but I'm loath to judge him too harshly. It must be so difficult to keep your moral compass when you're in an inherently immoral context. That Dr. Romberg was acquitted, although somewhat reluctantly by the Tribunal, speaks well for the judicial process, and for the monumental effort of the prosecutors, defense attorneys and judges in the Doctors' Trial at Nuremberg to fine-tune degrees of culpability. Those eight months of testimony and documentary evidence and briefing and arguing by counsel made it possible for them to discriminate between the Dr. Raschers and the Dr. Rombergs. There is great virtue in that.

And so my time is about up. I have sung my song, and I did learn something. Two problems arose as I tried to write this; the first revealed something to me about the Doctors' Trial, and the second revealed something to me about myself. The first problem had to do with sequencing. I thought I would cover the experiments, the Doctors' Trial, and then explain the importance of the Nuremberg Code. That would have been neat and tidy, but it didn't work. The experiments and the trial clung together in a horrific unit of thought, but a chasm existed between that unit of thought and the Nuremberg Code. Between the horror within a horror, and the articulation of the elegant doctrine of informed consent – I felt like I was trying to paste the two sides of the Grand Canyon together with one tube of Crazy Glue.

There is little recognition in the Nuremberg Code of the horrific bigger box of the holocaust that the Nazi human experimentation took place in. Indeed, I find myself staring at the Nuremberg Code in some amazement, saying over and over to myself: What does this Code of ideal principles about

---

[34] *Extracts from the Testimony of Defendant Romberg, in* Trials of War Criminals, Vol. 1, *supra* note 9, at 192-193.
[35] *Id.* at 194-195.
[36] *Id.* at 198. Ironically, this term was also used by prisoners in concentration camps.

informed consent in medical research really have to do with the horrible things that happened to those people in the concentration camps? Is the doctrine of informed consent the most forceful moral principle that the Tribunal could come up with? Surely it represents noble ideals. I am heartily in favor of it being put into operation when researchers are testing new drugs or new medical procedures. But do we really think the norms of the Nuremberg Code reflect the nightmare that generated those norms? What possible good would it have done those prisoners? Voluntary, informed consent of the human subject would have been utterly irrelevant in the horrific bigger box of the holocaust. The Nuremberg Code is like looking at a roaring, rushing, flooding red river of blood, and offering a box of Q tips to stem its waters. I wonder if perhaps the Tribunal was morally shell-shocked, and could think of nothing else to say. It would be both understandable and forgivable.

The second problem I had in writing this I've already revealed to you. In thinking about how much detail to offer about the human suffering involved in the Nazi experiments, I had to own up to my own morbid fascination. I won't belabor the point, but it has profound implications for me. It implies in a very disturbing way that the duality between good and evil may itself be an illusion. It is far too easy to label those doctors at Nuremberg as Nazi monsters, to characterize what happened in those experiments as evil squared, to identify only with the humanity of their victims. It is far more difficult to look into your own heart, and to come, shuddering, to a threshold of understanding, of daring to contemplate the humanity of the defendants.

That contemplation is painful. I see a mirror there, and in that mirror I see not only morbid fascination with the human experiments, but I see racism. I see racism, in myself, and everywhere I look in the United States, perhaps here in Germany too. True, it is not the overt, foul racism of social Darwinism. But there are other subtler versions of racism still out and among us today. Julius Streicher's virulent anti-Semitism did not operate in a vacuum. It needed a receptive audience for his ideas to hold sway.

So I may not like the reflection in the mirror when I contemplate my own potential for complicity. Our potential for complicity. I don't think it is a good idea to look away either. Only by looking into that mirror of self, by recognizing the universality of our humanity, that we all possess both goodness and evil in our own hearts, each and every one of us – only then are we going to be able to generate norms that might really reflect the nightmares we are capable on imposing on each other.

Louise Harmon

Der Mediziner-Prozess in Nürnberg

Direkt nach dem Abschluss der Kriegsverbrecherprozesse begann in Nürnberg der so genannte Mediziner-Prozess. Von den Vereinigten Staaten als alleiniger Nation wurden 23 Nazi-Ärzte und Administratoren für eine ganze Reihe von Verbrechenstatbeständen angeklagt, einschließlich Kriegsverbrechen, Verbrechen gegen die Menschlichkeit, Genozid und Mord.

Diese angeklagten Ärzte hatten in weitem Umfang bei medizinischen Experimenten, u.a. Zwangssterilisationen und Selektionsprozessen in den Konzentrationslagern, mitgewirkt. Der Hauptanteil des bei dem Ärzte-Prozess vorgelegten Beweismaterials stammte aus den entsetzlichen medizinischen Experimenten, die an Insassen von Konzentrationslagern durchgeführt worden waren. Nach dem Gerichtsurteil, das sieben der Angeklagte zum Tode und neun andere zu Gefängnisstrafen verurteilte, formulierte das Gericht den „Nürnberger Code", durch den zum ersten Mal internationale Standards zum Schutz von menschlichen Versuchsobjekten in der medizinischen Forschung aufgestellt wurden.

Der Beitrag von Louise Harmon beschreibt die Experimente, die Prozesse, den „Nürnberger Code" und seine Bedeutung im Bereich der medizinischen Ethik und untersucht, wie Ärzte, die den Hippokratischen Eid geschworen hatten, derart grauenhafte medizinische Experimente durchführen konnten. Die Nazi-Ideologie der Rassenhygiene und eines nationalsozialistisch gefärbten Darwinismus motivierten viele der in der medizinischen Forschung engagierten Angeklagten und vermittelte ihnen die Illusion einer moralischen Rechtfertigung für eine ethisch nicht zu rechtfertigende Haltung.

Am Ende ihres Beitrages stellt die Autorin die Frage, ob die Doktrin der im „Nürnberger Code" artikulierten „informierten Zustimmung" den menschlichen Versuchsobjekten, die aus der an sich schon schrecklichen Umgebung eines Konzentrationslagers selektiert wurden, in irgendeiner Form von Nutzen gewesen wäre.

Harry Reicher

The Jurists' Trial and Lessons for the Rule of Law

Introduction

In its Opinion and Judgment in "The Justice Case", in which leading figures in the Nazi legal establishment were brought to trial, the Tribunal summed up very powerfully: "The dagger of the assassin was concealed beneath the robe of the jurist."[1] The lesson delivered in these words is a somber one: Lawyers can commit hideous crimes, even mass murder, while going about their "normal" functions. Adopting that notion as its central theme, this paper addresses three issues of particular interest:

1. The most important crime with which the Defendants in The Justice Case were charged with crimes against humanity.[2] Yet it seems deeply incongruous when applied to members of the legal profession apparently practising their craft. Crimes against humanity are usually associated with massive atrocities: with concentration camps and death camps; with gas ovens and crematoria; with the *Einsatzgruppen*, being mobile killing squads that roamed the Soviet Union, shooting Jews into mass graves which they themselves had been forced to dig; with slave labor; and so on. In the modern era, we associate the term with ethnic cleansing in the former Yugoslavia, with wholesale macheting of people to death in Rwanda and the use of chemical weapons on the Kurds by the Iraqi regime. We do not naturally associate crimes against humanity with practise of the legal profession. When we think of lawyers, we think, first and foremost, of judges, wearing judicial robes, sitting in detached objectivity, listening carefully and impartially to the evidence and deciding cases fairly and strictly in accordance with the evidence and a reasonable interpretation of the applicable law. In criminal cases, we think of them bending over backwards to be fair to the defendant, insuring that no-one is convicted unless the case against them is proven beyond a reason doubt. In short, judges embody all we associate with the term "justice". In western systems of justice, we often view the role of prosecutors as not that of people intent on obtaining convictions at any cost; rather, we think of them as being officers of the court, whose duty is to inform the court fully, and advise the defense fairly and fully what the case against it is, and furnishing it with potentially exculpatory information. Finally, we think of civil servants, in positions in ministries of justice, as being faithful administrators of the law, under a legal duty to act fairly and properly vis-à-vis the general population affected by the law. All of which leads directly into the central question: How can these three categories of lawyers commit crimes against humanity, while pursuing their professional calling? (These lawyers are to be contrasted with other leading figures in the Nazi regime, who while qualified as lawyers, were responsible for the commission of atrocities, albeit not by practising law *per se*, eg Ernst Kaltenbrunner, Hans Frank and Wilhelm Frick.)

2. What was the fate of the Defendants in The Justice Case, given that so many of them were found guilty of crimes against humanity, and that, as a result, they may be said to represent the worst face of the legal profession under the Nazi regime?

3. Finally, what lessons may be derived from the Nazi judicial system, as represented in The Justice Case?

The Defendants

On trial in The Justice Case were 16 defendants, of whom six were judges in the Nazi era, four were prosecutors and nine were civil servants. (Some occupied more than one category of position, which accounts for the discrepancy in the numbers.)[3]

---

[1] Opinion and Judgment of Military Tribunal III, in Case 3, The United States of America v Altstoetter and Ors, "*The Justice Case*", *Trial of War Criminals Before the Nuremberg Military Tribunals Under Control Council Law No 10*, Vol. III (United States Government Printing Office, Washington, 1951) (henceforth, "The Justice Case"), 985.
[2] The Justice Case, 23-25.
[3] *Id*, 15-17.

Crimes with which the Defendants were Charged

The principal crime, as mentioned above, was crimes against humanity, being the commission of atrocities such as murder, extermination, enslavement, deportation, illegal imprisonment, torture, rape and persecution on political, racial and religious grounds.[4] The net was cast wide, in the sense that the Defendants could be found guilty not only if they were principals in the commission of the above acts, but also if they were accessories to them or ordered, abetted, took a consenting part in, or were connected with plans and enterprises relating to the listed acts.[5] In sum, the defendants were charged with the destruction of the German legal system, and with using the shell for wide-scale atrocities – judicial murder.[6] The other charges, which are not centrally relevant here, were war crimes, conspiracy to commit both crimes against humanity and war crimes and membership in criminal organizations.[7]

Lawyers Committing Crimes Against Humanity: Three Case Studies

Three of the Defendants may be singled out for consideration, in order to illustrate the role of lawyers.

Franz Schlegelberger[8]

As a bureaucrat in the Justice Ministry, he played a central role in the tragic case of Markus Luftglass, an elderly Jew who was convicted on a charge of stealing a large quantity of eggs, and sentenced to two-and-a-half years' imprisonment. A brief report of the case appeared in a Berlin daily newspaper, and it was brought to the attention of Hitler himself, who expressed the view that the sentence was manifestly inadequate, and that the death penalty was appropriate. Correspondence involving Schlegelberger passed between various departments, with the result that Luftglass was ultimately handed over to the Gestapo for execution.[9] The correspondence is chilling in three respects.

1. The callous fate of a human being in his 70s, which is its subject-matter.

2. The deep personal reach it reveals of Hitler into the daily workings of the legal system, being emblematic of the very antithesis of US-style separation of powers, represented by the "Führer-principle".

3. The bland, almost matter-of-fact bureaucratese in which the correspondence is couched, completely belying the seriousness of the subject-matter.

The case of Marcus Luftglass was by no means an exception, and Schlegelberger was involved many times.[10] Indeed, the Tribunal focused on the fact that Schlegelberger disregarded legal judicial process in his efforts to fulfill the will of Hitler, contributing to the destruction of judicial independence;[11] specifically, that he concocted many "legal justifications" for SS shootings of defendants whose court sentences were deemed disapproved of, as insufficient, by Hitler.[12] If it happens once, as in the case of Marcus Luftglass, it is murder; if it happens twice, that is two counts of murder. And if it happens enough times, it is a crime against humanity.

Curt Rothenberger[13]

As a judge, who coveted the position of State Secretary of the Reich Ministry of Justice, Rothenberger wrote an infamous Memorandum,[14] in which he sought to curry favor with Hitler, and to

---

[4] *Id*, 23 (para 20), 32.
[5] *Id*.
[6] *Id*, 32-33.
[7] *Id*, 17-23, 25-26.
[8] *Id*, 16 (biographical notes), 126-130 (opening statement on his behalf).
[9] *Id*, 429-431, 1085.
[10] *Id*, 417 *et subs*.
[11] *Id*, 1083.
[12] *Id*, 1085.
[13] *Id*, 16 (biographical notes), 142-149 (opening statement on his behalf).
[14] *Id*, 469-483.

which he attributed his eventual appointment as State Secretary. In the Memorandum he said, among other things: "Law must *serve* the political leadership";[15] "[T]he Führer is... the *supreme judge*. Theoretically, the authority to pass judgment is therefore only his";[16] *"[A] judge who is in direct relation of fealty to the Fuehrer must judge 'like the Führer'."*[17] The message was absolutely clear and unequivocal: There was no such thing as judicial independence; the role of judges was, quite simply, to execute the political will, as embodied in, and expressed by, the Führer himself.

Quite extraordinarily, when under cross-examination in The Justice Case, in a passage that reads like an excerpt from Alice in Wonderland, Rothenberger steadfastly maintained (presumably with a straight face) that his Memorandum had been an argument for judicial independence![18] In relation to Rothenberger, the Tribunal focused, among other things, on actions which had "materially contributed toward the prostitution of the Ministry of Justice and the courts and their subordination to the arbitrary will of Hitler..."[19]

Oswald Rothaug[20]

There are many ways of illustrating what Kurt Rothenberger meant when he declared that judges "must judge like the Fuehrer", at the levels of both form as well as substance. At the formal level, one may, for instance, point to scenes, captured for posterity in archival film footage, in which judges are seen entering the courtroom and giving the "Heil Hitler!" salute before taking their places on the bench, thereby affirming their primary loyalty to Hitler himself, as opposed to the constitution. This was not, they thereby declared, a government under law, but very much a case of law being subordinated to government. Indeed, their oath of office, declaring loyalty first and foremost to the Fuehrer, affirmed as much. Or, one may recall archival footage showing the President of the People's Court, Roland Freisler, in action, in the trial of the plotters who attempted to assassinate Hitler on July 20, 1944. Freisler, who had the dubious distinction of sentencing some 5,000 people to death, and was characterized by William Shirer, in his classic work *The Rise and Fall of the Third Reich: A History of Nazi Germany*, as a "vile, vituperative maniac",[21] is seen and heard yelling and screaming, and generally carrying on in decidedly unjudicative fashion.

And at the substantive level, Oswald Rothaug gave expression to Rothenberger's dictum in the infamous Katzenberger case,[22] which was immortalized in Stanley Kramer's film *Judgment at Nuremberg*. In that case, Rothaug resorted to blatant distortions and machinations in order to guarantee that the hapless Leo Katzenberger, who was charged with "racial pollution",[23] arising out of an alleged relationship with an Aryan woman, was sent to his death[24] on the basis of no credible evidence. Consistent with the goal of "judging like the Führer", Rothaug had two clear objects in presiding over the Katzenberger case: Most importantly, the Jew had to lose and, further, he had to lose big, meaning, in the case of Leo Katzenberger, that he had to be sentenced to death. The problem for Rothaug, however, was that each of these goals faced what, in normal circumstances, would have been insurmountable obstacles.

Finding the defendant guilty was confronted by the problem of there being no credible evidence against him; such evidence as there was consisted only of rumor, hearsay and flimsy circumstantial material. The only credible witness in the case was Irene Seiler, the woman with whom the alleged

---

[15] *Id*, 471 (emphasis in original).
[16] *Id*, 474 (emphasis in original).
[17] *Id*, (emphasis in original).
[18] *Id*, 499-502.
[19] *Id*, 1118.
[20] *Id*, 16 (biographical notes), 154-158 (opening statement on his behalf).
[21] (New York, 1960), 1070 (henceforth "Shirer"). Shirer also describes Freisler as "perhaps the most sinister and bloodthirsty Nazi in the Third Reich after Heydrich..." (at 1023).
[22] The Justice Case, 650-664.
[23] *Id*, 653.
[24] *Id*, 654, 663.

improper relationship had taken place.[25] The difficulty was that Seiler's evidence exonerated Katzenberger; her position was, quite unequivocally, that the "crime" had not been committed.[26] Rothaug, however, got around this inconvenience by having Seiler charged with perjury,[27] arising out of her statement on interrogation, and conducting the perjury trial concurrently with the trial of Katzenberger himself. He then found Seiler guilty of perjury[28] and, having done so, could therefore brush aside her evidence, and convict Katzenberger; in fact, if Seiler had perjured herself in denying crime, it followed that the crime had in fact taken place.

That still left the object of ensuring that the death sentence was passed. Here, too, there was a difficulty in Rothaug's path. The crime of "racial pollution" arose under the *Law for the Protection of German Blood and Honor*[29], one of the infamous so called Nuremberg laws, enacted on September 15, 1935. But the penalty for that crime was set at a maximum of a prison term or hard labor.[30] In fact, nowhere in the law was there provision for the death penalty. In this light, a curious aspect of the judgment in the Katzenberger case suddenly takes on a different mien. Although the charge against Katzenberger was "racial pollution", the judgment gradually elides into another crime, namely that of being a "public enemy",[31] and in fact when Katzenberger was ultimately sentenced, it was for that crime, in addition to the crime with which he was charged.[32] The difference, and therefore the importance of superimposing the additional crime even though the case had begun on a very different basis, lay in the fact that the penalty for being a public enemy was death.[33] So far as Rothaug was concerned, the Tribunal in The Justice Case focused, among other things, on the fact that he "made his court an instrumentality of terror…He was and is a sadistic and evil man…"[34]

Sentencing of the Three Defendants and Their Respective Fates after the Trial[35]

There were 16 Defendants in The Justice Case. Of these: ten were convicted on one or more counts,[36] four were found not guilty,[37] one suffered from ill health, and could not attend most of the trial, as a result of which a mistrial was declared,[38] one committed suicide in prison, after being indicted and before the trial opened.[39]

Franz Schlegelberger was sentenced to life imprisonment[40] but was released in 1950.[41] After his release from prison, he received a monthly pension of 2,894 Marks (compared with the earnings of an average skilled worker of about 400 Marks).[42] In addition, he received 160,000 Marks, by way of back pension, which included payment for the time he had spent in prison.[43]

---

[25] *Id*, 653-654.
[26] *Id*, 656.
[27] *Id*, 653, 654, 657.
[28] *Id*, 663.
[29] Section 2 provided: "Relations outside marriage between Jews and nationals of German or kindred blood are forbidden."
[30] Section 5(2).
[31] The Justice Case, 661-662.
[32] *Id*, 662-663.
[33] *Id*, 663.
[34] *Id*, 1156.
[35] *Id*, 1199-1201.
[36] *Id*, 1200-1201.
[37] Muller, *Hitler's Justice: The Courts of the Third Reich* (Harvard University Press, Cambridge, MA, 1991 – henceforth "Muller"), 272.
[38] The Justice case, 3.
[39] *Id*, 3, 27.
[40] *Id*, 1200.
[41] Muller, 210, 273.
[42] *Id*, 208.
[43] *Id*.

Curt Rothenberger was sentenced to seven years' imprisonment[44] and was released in 1951.[45] After his release, was awarded a pension of 2,073 Marks per month, plus a back pension.[46]

Oswald Rothaug was sentenced to life imprisonment,[47] and was the last of the convicted defendants released, in 1956,[48] all the others having been released by 1951.[49]

Rothaug's co-judges in the Katzenberger case were charged in Germany, but were held to be unfit to stand trial in 1976. This was despite the fact that one of the two was actively conducting a law practice at the time. The Nuremberg County Court held that that was not a bar to holding that he was unfit to stand trial, because he suffered from "intellectual and emotional disturbances".[50]

Roland Freisler was killed by a direct hit by a United States bomb on the courthouse where he was presiding over the People's Court, on February 3, 1945.[51]

The leniency with which the Defendants in The Justice Case were treated was symptomatic of the continuity which by and large characterized the legal system of the Federal Republic of Germany in the post-War years, one aspect of which was the re-employment of Nazi-era officials as judges, prosecutors and civil servants.[52]

Duration of the Justice Case

The trial opened on March 5, 1947,[53] and concluded on October 18, 1947,[54] with sentences being handed down on December 3 and 4, 1947.[55] From beginning to end, therefore, it lasted exactly nine months, and makes an interesting contrast with the current trial of Slobodan Milosevic, which is now mid-way through its fourth year.

The Judges

It is interesting to reflect on the positions, which the judges in The Justice Case held in the United States, before presiding at Nuremberg. One was a former Chief Justice of the Supreme Court of Ohio, another was a Justice of the Supreme Court of Oregon, the third was an Associate Justice of the Court of Civil Appeals for the Third District of Texas, and the fourth was a former Assistant Attorney-General of Ohio and a District Judge of the First Division of the Territory of Alaska.[56]

On the one hand, this was a reflection of the fact that, by the time The Justice Case was held, interest in bringing Nazi-era perpetrators to justice had waned in the United States; in fact, continuing prosecution of Nazi-era crimes had become so unfashionable that, in certain judicial circles, accepting a position on one of the tribunals was considered an obstacle to advancement in the US.[57] At the same time, though, it illustrates one of the profound lessons about judicial character and temperament, as brilliantly portrayed in the counter pointing of two central characters in *Judgment at Nuremberg*. Ernst

---

[44] The Justice Case, 1200.
[45] Muller, 273.
[46] *Id*, 208.
[47] The Justice Case, 1201.
[48] Muller, 273.
[49] *Id*.
[50] *Id*, 250.
[51] Shirer, 269, 1071.
[52] See, generally, Muller, Section III, "The Aftermath", chaps 23- 30, 199 *et subs*.
[53] The Justice Case, 31 (opening statements).
[54] *Id*, 941 (final statements of the defendants).
[55] *Id*, 1199, 1201.
[56] *Id*, 13.
[57] Mann, *Judgment at Nuremberg* (Samuel French, New York, 2001), 6.

Janning (portrayed in an Academy Award-winning performance of Maximillian Schell) was endowed with an exceptionally brilliant mind, and had stellar careers in academe and the judiciary, but a fundamental element was missing at the core of his judicial persona; indeed, of his very being. As a result, he was capable of committing terrible atrocities, thereby debasing the very notion of law. By contrast, Judge Haywood (portrayed by Spencer Tracy), who presided over the trial, was no intellectual heavyweight. But, at his core, he was a decent human being, endowed with genuine common sense, and, very importantly, with a highly-tuned moral compass that allowed him instinctively to differentiate between right and wrong. The two personalities together represent the moral equivalent of the hare and the tortoise.

Other Lessons Emerging from The Justice Case

Among the sobering lessons that emerge clearly from The Justice Case are the following: First and foremost, perhaps, the critical importance of a system of constitutional separation of powers, with its concomitant checks and balances. The underlying message is that the ultimate guarantee of individual freedoms is a diffusion of power, as opposed to the aggregation of power in few sets of hands, and ultimately in one set of hands, namely that of the Führer, which resulted in Hitler being not only chief legislator and chief executive, but also Chief Justice. Within that, the importance of an independent judiciary, which is empowered to judge governmental action by reference to constitutional standards and, if the occasion arises, is prepared to tell the government that it has gone too far At its heart, all this means that government must be under law, and not the reverse.

Law, in its judicial aspect (and the same applies to its legislative aspect) is inherently neutral. If it is administered by righteous people, it can accomplish the greatest good in a society. But if it falls into evil hands, it can become the instrument of the greatest brutalities, inflicting untold amounts of suffering, misery and loss of life.

The case also underscores the fragility of democracy itself, when it is borne in mind that Hitler came to power lawfully, under the Weimar Constitution, which was never repealed, yet managed to turn the court system into a grotesque caricature of a judiciary which, in parrot-like fashion, spewed out the Government's hatred and poison, directed at the targets of its racial ideology.

The case also illustrates an important principle, which is emblematic of a theme which links all the twelve subsidiary trials conducted by the United States, after the conclusion of the trial of the major war criminals. The notion of "crimes against humanity" is normally associated with politicians, and military personnel; in other words, those who make the policy decisions, and those who actually carry out the atrocities, namely the killings, the torture, the enslavement, and so on. In the case of Nazi Germany, as Professor Raul Hilberg has pointed out, all corners of German society were involved in some way or other.[58] In prosecuting the twelve subsidiary trials, the defendants were categorized by "profession" – the doctors, the lawyers, the industrialists, and so on.[59] The message for future generations was clear: If all corners of society are complicit, then all corners of society are potentially liable to give account for their actions and, if found guilty, to face the consequences. The Nazi regime went to extraordinary lengths to "legalize" the Holocaust, in the process harnessing the German legislative system as well as the judiciary and the legal bureaucracy to accomplish its ends. Legalization of the Holocaust could not have taken place without the active participation of lawyers, and The Justice Case therefore teaches the lesson that, in the context of major human rights violations, lawyers, like anyone else, are ultimately liable to face the consequences of their actions.

---

[58] Hilberg, *Perpetrators, Victims, Bystanders: The Jewish Catastrophe 1933-1945* (Harper Collins, 1992), 65.
[59] The Justice Case, IX.

Harry Reicher

Der Juristenprozess und die Lehren für den Rechtsstaat

Im so genannten Juristenprozess standen die Verantwortung der Juristen für die Umsetzung des NS-Unrechts und die legale Fassade, die sie dem totalitären Regime gaben, im Mittelpunkt. Das Urteil des Juristenprozesses sendet eine ernüchternde Botschaft: In Ausübung ihrer „normalen" beruflichen Funktionen können Juristen abscheuliche Verbrechen und sogar Massenmorde begehen. Zwar scheinen Verbrechen gegen die Menschlichkeit sich mit dem beruflichen Umfeld von Richtern, Staatsanwälten und Beamten nicht vereinbaren zu lassen, die Karrieren von drei im Juristenprozess angeklagten Juristen veranschaulichen jedoch das Gegenteil. In erschreckender Weise wird deutlich, wie das deutsche Rechtssystem von denen, die es professionell anwenden, entwertet und zerstört wurde, um es dann in ein brutales und mitleidloses Instrument der zentralen nationalsozialistischen Rassenideologie umzuwandeln.

Für Franz Schlegelberger gab Hitlers Unzufriedenheit über die inadäquate Verurteilungspraxis der Gerichte einen ausreichenden Anlass, Todesurteile zu fällen; Kurt Rothenberger trug zur Zerschlagung der juristischen Unabhängigkeit bei, indem er die Richter aufforderte, „wie der Führer" zu urteilen und Oswald Rothaug (sowie auch Roland Freisler und viele andere) zeigten in einer eiskalten Weise, was dies in der Praxis bedeutete.

In Anbetracht des von den Angeklagten verursachten Leidens und der von ihnen zu verantwortenden Todesurteile fielen ihre Strafen beunruhigend milde aus. Trotzdem hat der Fall weitreichende Bedeutung; insbesondere wird einmal mehr die Bedeutung einer unabhängigen Justiz in einem System der Gewaltenteilung deutlich.

Roland Bank

The Role of German Industry: From Individual Criminal Responsibility of Some to a Broadly Shared Responsibility for Compensatory Payments

Hitler's wars would not have been possible without a cooperating industry and the massive abuse of forced labourers.[1] Several million people were coerced to work under the cruelest conditions – according to estimates by Marc Spoerer ten million people (not counting prisoners of war) were forced to work on the territory of the German Reich alone during World War II.[2] The exploitation of forced labour was among the deeds for which the major war criminals were sentenced by the Nuremberg International Military Tribunal. Moreover, some industry leaders were put on trial later on in the so called "subsequent Nuremberg trials" before the US Military Court in Nuremberg and were held criminally responsible for what they had done to millions of forced labourers during World War II.

The Flick Trial was the first of three trials of leading industrialists of Nazi Germany for their conduct during the Nazi regime. The defendants in this case were Friedrich Flick and five other high-ranking directors of the Flick concern. The charges centred on slave labour and plundering, but Flick and the most senior director were also charged for their membership in the "Circle of Friends of Himmler", the purpose of which was the financial support of the Nazis. Its members "donated" annually about one million Reichsmark on a "Special Account S" in favour of Himmler.

The Flick Trial was followed by the IG Farben Trial. The defendants in this case were all directors of IG Farben, a large German conglomerate of chemical firms. In World War II, IG Farben developed chemical processes for synthesizing gasoline and rubber from coal, and contributed significantly to Germany's effort to wage a war despite the absence of large natural oil reserves. Charges were put forward namely for waging a war of aggression., slave labour and pillaging.

In the Krupp Trial, twelve former directors of the Krupp Group were accused of having enabled the armament of the German military forces and thus having actively participated in the Nazis' preparations for an aggressive war, and for having used slave labourers in their companies. According to conservative estimates, the Krupp enterprises used nearly 100,000 persons in the forced labour programme among them about 23,000 prisoners of war.

As a result of these trials, a number of high ranking industrialists were found guilty and sentenced to an imprisonment ranging between 2½ to 12 years.

This is the criminal aspect as to the responsibility borne by representatives of the German State and industry. However, vis-à-vis the victims, responsibility does not end with bringing to trial some of those individuals who are the most responsible for what had been done. The other aspect of responsibility is to provide some form of reparation to those who have suffered such cruel abuse. I have been invited by the organisers of the Conference to focus my presentation on this side of the coin. Germany's industry serves as a good example for the joint responsibility between state and private enterprises in abusing millions of people through forced labour. The joint responsibility is particularly illustrated by the fact that, finally in the year 2000, the German government and companies together funded a Foundation with the task, among others, to make financial restitution to surviving victims of forced labour.

---

[1] Most recently, the German historian Götz Aly claimed that the exploitation of forced labour was also central for maintaining support among the German population for Hitler's politics by providing a number of material privileges to the overall German population, see Götz Aly, Hitlers Volksstaat, 181et subs. (2005).

[2] See Mark Spoerer, Zwangsarbeit im Dritten Reich und Entschädigung: ein Überblick, in: Zwangsarbeit in der Kirche (K. Barwig/D.R. Bauer/K. J. Hummel, eds., 2001); quoted from the internet www.adademie-rs/publikationen/hp56_spoerer.htm (visited 30 June 2005). According to Spoerer, this estimate includes 1,000,000 people, who came voluntarily to Germany to work; taking heed to the pressure exerted by Germany as the occupying power on the local population the term "voluntariness" frequently does not stand closer analysis.

What did Germany and German Companies Do to Live Up to Their Responsibility to Provide for Compensation?

Germany has a long history of financial efforts to provide some form of compensation. In 1951, Adenauer said in his landmark speech on German responsibility to the Bundestag: "The Federal Government, and with it the vast majority of the German people are conscious of the immeasurable suffering that was brought to bear upon the Jews in Germany and in the occupied territories during the period of National Socialism (...). But unspeakable crimes were perpetrated in the name of the German people which impose upon them the obligation to make moral and material amends, both as regards the individual damage which Jews have suffered and as regards Jewish property for which there are no longer individual claimants."[3]

This promise was fulfilled when in 1952 the Federal Republic of Germany, the State of Israel and the Conference on Jewish Material Claims against Germany signed the Luxembourg Agreements. These Agreements formed the basis for the German Federal compensation and restitution programmes for Holocaust survivors. Germany acknowledged in these Agreements its debts to both individuals and to the Jewish world by agreeing to pay three Billion Deutsch Marks in annual instalments to Israel in the form of goods and services. Moreover, Germany committed to enact legislation requiring compensation to be directly paid to individual claimants for damages including the loss of life, liberty health, property, or professional opportunity. Finally, Germany agreed to pay 450 Million Deutsch Marks to the Jewish Claims Conference for the relief, rehabilitation and resettlement of Jewish victims.

Partly in implementation of these agreements, the Federal Law on Compensation was adopted in 1953 and later on reformed in 1956. This law established a detailed legal framework for compensating victims of Nazi persecution. Not only the conditions for a claim were set out in detail but also – and even more complicatedly – details on the amount to be awarded. The damage suffered as a result of persecution was evaluated in each and every individual case – ranging from generalised sums per day in a concentration camp over the definition of health damage by certain percentages of full capacity to a calculation of financial implications of lost professional opportunities.

At the same time, Germany was largely protected under international law from reparations claims by virtue of the 1953 London Debt Agreement which postponed remaining reparations claims to be settled by a final peace treaty. According to the German government's understanding, such a final peace treaty is to be seen in the 2+4 Treaty. This treaty does not address any reparation claims and consequently the reparation question is perceived as settled by the German government.[4]

A number of so called "Globalabkommen" – treaties concluded with some of the victims' States – provided for a global sum to be paid to the respective government of the formerly occupied State. This sum was then to be paid out to the individual victims by the respective government. A first round of treaties was prompted by the exclusion of forced labourers from Western States from compensation under the Federal Law on Compensation[5]: since these persons were not persecuted for political or racial reasons according to the understanding in post-war Western Germany, they were not eligible under this compensation scheme. In a last round of such global payments after the conclusion of the 2+4 Treaty, 1.5 billion German Marks (3/4 billion Euro) were transferred to the governments of Poland, Ukraine, Russia and Belarus with a view to providing for some relief to victims of Nazi terror.

Some German companies established their own compensation schemes over the years providing for payments to "their" forced labourers during the war. In the years 1950 and 1960, IG Farben, Krupp,

---

[3] This English translation is provided in The Conference on Jewish Material Claims against Germany, 1951-2001 – 50 Years of Service to Holocaust Survivors, 2001, p. 6.

[4] The question of statute of limitations applying to eventual claims under German law cannot be discussed here in detail. There is, however, a strong argument that legal claims under German law – if existing at all – expired only a certain time after the 2+4 Treaty, i.e. that statute of limitations only started running with the entry into force of the 2+4 Treaty or their expiry was suspended during the time between the entering into force of the London Debt Agreement and the 2+4 Treaty.

[5] Op. cit.

AEG and Telefunken, Siemens and Rheinmetall started payment programmes with sums of up to 30 Million DM. Only the IG Farben programme also addressed non-Jewish concentration camp inmates. More companies joined in during the 1980ies and particularly the 1990ies and some increased the funding of their payment schemes. However, others never established any compensation scheme. The overall sum paid by German companies – as far as payments have been made public – amounts to 280 million DM calculated on the basis of prices in the year 2000.[6]

Finally, – and more than 55 years after the end of World War II – Germany established a foundation with the name "Remembrance, Responsibility and Future" with a view to making payments for a number of National Socialist injustices, in particular, forced labour. The Foundation was jointly funded by German companies and the German State providing for an overall sum of 10 billion DM.[7]

Why was the Foundation Established and Why so Late?

Among a greater scope of relevant factors, the new readiness for further efforts to grant some compensation to former victims of Nazi-injustice, in particular, forced labourers, has been encouraged decisively by four aspects: Firstly, the gap in compensation efforts regarding forced labour; secondly, the fall of the iron curtain in 1989; thirdly, a wave of class-action law suits against German companies in the late 1990ies; and finally, the political will of the new German government which came into power in autumn 1998.

The compensation gap: Amazingly, the historical situation of forced labour had never been a criterion for compensatory payments before the establishment of the Foundation. In particular, compensation under the Federal Law on Compensation was restricted to cases of persecution because of political, racial, religious or conscience related reasons.[8] In particular, this did not include forced labourers from Slavic countries since they were not persecuted for racial reasons but for reasons of their nationality according to the Western German understanding.[9] As a consequence, a great number of former forced labourers had received no or only little compensatory payments from the German State(s).

Moreover, neither the laws providing victims with legal claims nor any of the hardship payments had foreseen any compensation specifically addressing forced labour. And, whereas certain companies have paid out some compensation to "their" former forced labourers, individual amounts varied considerably and sometimes payments were initiated only quite recently. The situation of forced labourers therefore had constituted a gap in Germany's record of compensatory efforts for atrocities committed during the period of the Nazi regime.

The fall of the iron curtain: Throughout the Cold War, the Federal Republic of Germany had excluded States of the Communist block and victims living in those states from compensatory payments. Only after the political turnover in Central and Eastern Europe in 1989 and the ensuing disruption of the Soviet Union, the motivation to withhold payments to victims living in the communist world in order not to subsidise the political "enemy" had ceased to exist. To put it in a simplified way, until then, compensation had been channelled predominantly to those victims residing in the Federal Republic of Germany or somewhere abroad in the Western world including Israel.[10] The application deadline under the Federal Law on Compensation had expired already at the end of 1969. In addition,

---

[6] Ibid.

[7] The statute of the Foundation together with other basic texts and documents can be found in both German and English at www.stiftung-evz.de.

[8] Section 1 of the Bundesentschädigungsgesetz (Federal Law on Compensation) as of 29 June 1956, BGBl: (Federal Law Gazette) I 562 (1956).

[9] These victims could obtain some compensation under narrow preconditions, if they had suffered a lasting bodily injury, Art. VI No.1 para. 1 Final Law on the Federal Law on Compensation of September 14, 1965, BGBl. I 1315 (1965).

[10] See in particular the territoriality principle in Section 4 para. 1 and the diplomatic clause in Section 238a of the Federal Law on Compensation, (Bundesentschädigungsgesetz) as ammended by the Final Law on the Federal Law on Compensation (BEG-Schlussgesetz) as of 14 September 1965, BGBl. I 1315 (1965).

due to the political situation before 1989 there had been no agreements with Eastern European States providing for lump sum payments in order to address the historical responsibilities.

After the end of the East-West confrontation, political bodies in Germany were no longer principally opposed to providing some late justice to those victims who were living in Central and Eastern Europe. Already in connection with the 1990 Treaty on Unification of Germany an additional agreement had provided for hardship payments to Jewish Nazi-victims in the East who so far had obtained no or only little compensation (so called Article-2-Fund).[11] As a consequence of the political changes, Germany also provided lump sum payments to Poland, Russia, Ukraine and Belarus already in the years 1990 as it had done before to Western European countries. However, the overall volume of 1.5 billion German Marks did not allow individual amounts paid out to victims to reach a substantial level – broken down to individual payments that meant that in Ukraine, for instance, a victim of a concentration camp received some 900 Deutsch Marks (450 Euro).[12] And, the definition of victims eligible for receiving the monies was largely left to the discretion of the receiving country; in practice, the former forced labourers in those countries were usually the beneficiaries of most of the monies distributed under these programmes even though an explicit reference to forced labour was avoided. Finally, the idea to leave the responsibility for the just and prompt distribution of the monies to the Central and Eastern European States and their reconciliation foundations was cast into doubt when some parts of the monies disappeared due to improper financial practices or bankruptcies of national banks. Consequently, a significant discontent with the measures adopted remained and the compensation gap with a view to forced labour was not really closed.

This may have been one of the factors which inspired the wave of class actions in US courts against German companies which started in 1998. What is relevant here is that the increasing use of class action litigation against companies and the relaxed requirements for establishing a forum of territorial jurisdiction in the US have made this kind of court procedures a political factor of potentially high relevance for the economic performance of a company in the US. Irrespective of their prospect for success, pending class action cases have made it attractive for German companies to look for solutions which may save them from a court's judgment with unpredictable results after years of extremely costly proceedings and negative publicity. This explains the increased readiness of companies to contribute to a foundation solution but also prompts the justified interest on the part of those companies to get a certain protection against future proceedings in return for their financial engagement.

It is difficult to judge how far judicial proceedings in Germany brought forth by former forced labourers both against the authorities and German companies have contributed to the foundation solution. No final judgment is known in which a company has been obliged to pay compensation to a former forced labourer.[13] However, it cannot be disputed that the legal situation was far less than clear both with regard to eventual claims against German companies and against the authorities.[14] What became evident during the years 1990 was that protracted legal proceedings with unpredictable results could not suffice to meet the moral and political responsibilities having in mind the advanced age of the victims which turned any effort to provide some satisfaction into a race against time.

It was a combination of these moral, legal and economical factors that forms the background to the creation of the Foundation Initiative of German Companies ("Stiftungsinitiative der deutschen Wirtschaft"), a loose association[15] of those leading German companies which had been involved in

---

[11] Article 2 Additional Agreement to the Treaty on Unification of September 18, 1990, BGBl. II 1239 (1990).

[12] Cf. Igor Luchnikov, Ansprüche aus Zwangsarbeit seitens der Geschädigten – Ukraine, in: Entschädigung für NS-Zwangsarbeit 179, 181 (Klaus Barwig, Günter Saathoff, Nicole Weyde, eds.,1998).

[13] Cf. Explanatory Report of the Draft Federal Law on the Establishment of a Foundation, Section 16, BT-Drs. 14/3206, 17.

[14] See B. Heß, Völker- und zivilrechtliche Beurteilung der Entschädigung für Zwangsarbeit vor dem Hintergrund neuerer Entscheidungen deutscher Gerichte, in: Entschädigung für NS-Zwangsarbeit: Rechtliche, historische und politische Aspekte, 65 et subs. (K. Barwig et al., eds., 1998).

[15] The legal nature of the Foundation Initiative still remains somewhat obscure (association under German civil law, so called "BGB-Gesellschaft", or a corporation *sui generis*).

forced labour. Regardless of the motives, it is evident that the principal interest of German companies was to avert legal proceedings by creating a foundation which would make payments to victims. The momentum of events matched well with the idea of a foundation that had been already promulgated by the German Green Party several years beforehand, which became an instrumental part of the German political party system after the 1998 elections at which time the new Social Democrat/Green government made it a mutual project of their coalition agreement.[16] Subsequently, the German Chancellor appointed a special envoy with the task to negotiate with the US and all other relevant governments as well as victims' lawyers and victims' organisations an overall solution. In several rounds of negotiations the overall amount of money to be inserted into a foundation and the basic features of a law creating the respective foundation as well as a plan of allocation were agreed on. The most important parts of the basic features are comprised in an annex to the government agreement between the US government and the German government of 17 July 2000[17] and confirmed by other governments of victim states, an organisation representing the worldwide Jewish community, the victims' lawyers and the Foundation Initiative of German Companies in the Joint Statement on the occasion of the final plenary meeting concluding international talks on the preparation of the Foundation "Remembrance, Responsibility and the Future" of 17 July 2000.[18]

Main Elements of the Foundation Solution

The solution to the pending problems by establishing a Foundation is characterised by three elements: It is based on a mass claims approach which favours expediency over a detailed individual justice. It is intended as a gesture of reconciliation towards those victims who were still alive when the Foundation idea was agreed on. And, as a second aim, it seeks to provide legal closure for the German State and German companies in order to protect them against further lawsuits.

Mass claims approach: The Foundation Law provides for only three main categories involving forced labour. One category includes detention in a concentration camp, a ghetto or a similar institution; the second category addresses former forced labourers who were deported from their home country, kept in detention, detention-like or comparable harsh living conditions and forced to work except in agriculture; and a third category provides for payments for "other National Socialist injustice" which may include forced labour in agriculture or without detention or deportation.[19] The law defines certain sums as maximum amounts for each of these categories; despite the possibility to do so to a certain extent, in practice hardly any differentiation was made regarding groups of individual fates within the categories. Consequently, the individual fate is only analysed with a view to falling under one of the categories which then prompts a payment of a specific sum irrespective of the exact circumstances of the individual suffering. Relaxed standards of proof are applied: a claim can be made credible by any means including credible individual anecdotal statements if no documentation can be found. Review of decisions is limited to recourse to an independent appeals body. Consequently, the concept is putting more emphasis on expedient payments to eligible applicants than on examining the particularities of each application in detail. This approach was justified for two reasons: firstly, to process and decide on more than two million applications would have taken a very long time had the cases been evaluated in a detailed manner. In situations of mass claims, a generalising approach may therefore be preferable anyway. And secondly, in this specific situation, the entire programme was a race against time since victims were very old already and the purpose of the programme was to make a gesture towards them rather than to their heirs.

---

[16] Aufbruch und Erneuerung – Deutschlands Weg ins 21. Jahrhundert, Koalitionsvereinbarung zwischen der Sozialdemokratischen Partei Deutschlands und BÜNDNIS 90/DIE GRÜNEN, Bonn, 20. Oktober 1998, IX. 3.

[17] Agreement between the Government of the Federal Republic of Germany and the Government of the United States of America on the Foundation "Remembrance, Responsibility and the Future", Annex A, BGBl. II 1373 et seq. (2000).

[18] BGBl. II 1383 et seq. (2000).

[19] Section 11 para. 1 sentence 1 No. 1, 2 and sentence 2 Law on the Establishment of a Foundation "Remembrance, Responsibility and Future", subsequently: German Foundation Law. of 2 August 2000, BGBl. I 1263 (2000).

Payment as a "gesture": The Foundation Law openly recognises that it is impossible to make good by way of financial compensation for any of the harm caused.[20] This is first of all due, of course, to the immensity of the suffering involved in the cruel treatment at the hands of Germans and its allies during the Nazi era. Deportation to a foreign country, long periods of forced labour under constantly degrading and life-threatening conditions or let alone exploitation by labour while awaiting extinction in a programme of racial persecution may never be fully compensated. But it is also due to the fact that any attempt to compensate for the suffering comes too late for those who were killed already during the war or who have died in the meantime before the Foundation was established. On the other hand, the founders wished to acknowledge the injustice and the suffering caused by the German State and by German companies and to accept their responsibility by granting a modest sum to those victims still alive. Therefore, the concept is aimed at making a gesture in the spirit of reconciliation.

At the same time, the concept of legal closure is pursued with the establishment of the Foundation. It is clear that this was part of the motivation underpinning the idea of a Foundation. A number of measures have been adopted in this respect. The US government has taken on an obligation to intervene in eventual future legal action in US courts against Germany, Austria or the respective companies. To this end the US government is obliged to issue a so called "Statement of Interest" making the point that it is in the foreign policy interest of the United States that cases concerning Nazi injustice are dismissed by US courts in favour of the solutions agreed on in the Austrian and German Foundation solutions.[21] Additionally, the beginning of payments was made dependant on the dismissal of claims pending in US courts.[22] Moreover, the requirement to sign a waiver has been made a condition for payments in the German and all Austrian programmes.[23] Finally, the current programmes have partly been designated as the sole and exclusive forum for any claims relating to that period apart from already existing provisions.[24]

What are the Effects of the Work of the Foundation?

Of course, the primary effect of the work of the Foundation so far is that some 1.6 million victims of Nazi injustice have received at least a first instalment of the payment foreseen. Most of the recipients have also received the second instalment of their payment. Beyond this immediate effect of the payment programme, both the work of the Foundation as well as the discussions around its establishment also has a number of additional positive effects.

First and foremost, the gesture of reconciliation seems to have been accepted in many cases. Although there is no empirical evaluation of the reaction to the reception of payments, at least in contacts with victims' organisations the German efforts were appreciated on their part. Of course, reactions to the programme were rather negative where applicants felt excluded for unjustified reasons. In particular, this remark pertains to former prisoners of war who were excluded from the programme as a result of the international negotiations in the Foundation Act.

Additionally, the payment programme has given back their personal history to victims of forced labour in the former states of the Soviet Union. Upon return, many of the forced labourers from the Soviet Union upon return were screened for the GULAG for "having collaborated with the enemy" according to Stalin's ideology. Also after Stalin's death, their double suffering was suppressed for decades. It seems that it was very important especially for these victims that the injustice committed

---

[20] German Foundation Law, Preamble.
[21] Agreement between the Government of the Federal Republic of Germany and the Government of the United States of America on the Foundation "Remembrance, Responsibility and Future" of 17 July 2000, Article 2.
[22] Joint Statement on Occasion of the Final Plenary Meeting Concluding International Talks on the Preparation of the Foundation "Remembrance, Responsibility and Future", Section 4 d.
[23] Agreement between the Government of the Federal Republic of Germany and the Government of the United States of America on the Foundation "Remembrance, Responsibility and Future" of 17 July 2000, Annex A, Section 14.
[24] Joint Statement on Occasion of the Final Plenary Meeting Concluding International Talks on the Preparation of the Foundation "Remembrance, Responsibility and Future", Preamble; Section 16 (1) Foundation Law.

against them was recognised as such by the successors of the former perpetrators and that their personal story was finally listened to.

The discussion around its establishment as well as the work of the Foundation also gave a boost to consciousness in German society of the historical situation of forced labour. This was of particular importance since consciousness of the treatment accorded to forced labourers from Central and Eastern Europe had been much less developed than that of the Holocaust. Throughout the last five or six years, the media have frequently reported on this aspect of German history. In addition to the Federal payment programme carried out by the Foundation a number of German cities established own payment programmes. Moreover, a lot of communities invited former forced labourers to visit their home towns in order to tell the young generation about their suffering.

As outlined above, one of the aims of establishing a Foundation was to bring legal closure for those violations covered by the Foundation solution. The forum at which this attempt to bring closure was aimed at was that of US courts. Even though in the beginning there had been serious problems with achieving closure it seems to have worked in the longer run.

The attempt to bring closure had led to a delay in the beginning of payments in early 2001. A nexus had been established between the dismissal of certain legal actions pending before US courts and the beginning of payments to former victims. The dismissal did not go as smoothly as expected. This was partly due to the fact that German industry did not collect the monies quickly enough and partly due to the refusal of a US judge to dismiss the claims pending before the court of the Southern District of New York. The latter situation also proved that it was possibly the failure to establish a binding legal obligation to dismiss the cases concerned was not the best solution. However, over the years, it seems that US courts have accepted the Foundation solution, and subsequent legal actions in this field were usually dismissed. In the German forum, legal closure has worked comprehensively. Any subsequent legal actions were dismissed on the basis of the explicit provision in the Foundation Law.

Concluding Remarks

I have said at the outset of my presentation that there is a joint responsibility of the German State and German companies. Did they live up to their responsibilities? Focussing on the Foundation, I see it as a positive signal that not only governments have accepted the Foundation solution and the way it was put into practice but also numerous victims' organisations which have also been involved in the process of implementing the programme. On the other hand – despite the fact that Germany has undertaken great efforts in field of individual compensation since the 1950ies – it cannot be overlooked that the compensation gap concerning forced labour remained at least partly open until more than 55 years after the atrocities were committed. Consequently, the German legislator openly admits in the Preamble of the Foundation Law that the Foundation comes too late for all those having deceased in the meantime. Moreover, the far reaching exclusion of former prisoners of war from any direct compensation irrespective of whether they were treated in accordance with international humanitarian law[25] led to major disappointment in particular among those former prisoners who were denied even most existential conditions, i.e. prisoners from the Soviet Red Army and from Italy after Italy had quit the Axis with the German Reich and concluded a separate cease-fire with the Allied Forces before subsequently joining them in their fight against the Reich.

Talking about closure, it is important to emphasise that this means legal closure, not moral closure. To the contrary, the Foundation also constitutes an attempt to avoid moral closure. This is not only due to the effects of the awareness for the situations addressed under the Foundation's payment scheme. It is also reflected in the second pillar of the Foundation which is the so called Fund "Remembrance and Future". This permanent Fund has the task to support projects fostering, in particular, the understanding

---

[25] There was one important exception to the rule excluding prisoners of war from the compensation scheme: those prisoners of war who were transferred to concentration camps – usually run by the SS – received an award for their suffering in a concentration camp irrespective of their legal status as prisoners of war. The reason for this exception was that these persons were completely stripped of their status and merged into the persecution system.

of peoples as well as the remembrance of the threats which emanated from totalitarian systems. Among other things the Fund has been supporting projects for maintaining the historical consciousness for the atrocities committed during the era of the Third Reich among young people. An attempt to bring moral closure would also run contrary to the broad concept of reparation which should include measures of moral recognition of the injustice committed. In this sense, moral reparation could not work if financial compensation were combined with the expectation never to hear anything again about the guilt incurred by the nation bearing responsibility for atrocities. It is important to state that the idea of moral closure would run contrary to the aim and purpose of the Foundation.

Let me close with a remark on the relationship between what I see as constituents of international justice: criminal prosecution of those responsible for atrocities and compensation for the victims. It is important to hold perpetrators criminally responsible. The Nuremberg Tribunal constituted a major step towards a system of international justice which was later followed by other steps to the same end. The question of reparation has added the perspective of the victims to the concept of international justice. The example of the German history of individual compensatory payments for atrocities committed under the Nazi regime is an example for the growing respect for the perspective of the victims. Other examples are the United Nations Compensation Commission, established with a view to compensatory payments to victims of Iraq's illegal invasion of Kuwait, or the Eritrea-Ethiopia Claims Commission, established with the purpose to provide for reparation for damages incurred in the war between the two states. The increasing perception that international justice does not only encompass the prosecution of the guilty with the means of international criminal law but also reparation to victims now is corroborated by the provisions of the ICC Statute on victims' participation and compensation. It remains to be hoped that the tendency to strengthen the victims' role in the process of international justice will continue.

Roland Bank

Die Rolle der deutschen Industrie: Von individueller strafrechtlicher Verantwortung zur gemeinsamen Verantwortung für Entschädigungszahlung

Ohne eine kooperierende deutsche Industrie wären die Kriege Hitlers nicht möglich gewesen. Die Kriegswirtschaft konnte nur durch den massiven Einsatz von Millionen von Zwangsarbeitern gewährleistet werden. Für diese Menschenausbeutung wurden die Hauptkriegsverbrecher vor dem IMT in Nürnberg zu Rechenschaft gezogen. In den sogenannten Nürnberger Nachfolgeprozessen wurde darüber hinaus in drei separaten Verfahren, gegen Flick, IG Farben und Krupp, gezielt Industriellen an erster Stelle wegen des brutalen Einsatzes von Zwangsarbeitern und Kriegsgefangenen der Prozess gemacht. Viele der Angeklagten wurden zu Haftstrafen zwischen 2½ und 12 Jahren verurteilt. Neben dieser individuellen strafrechtlichen Verantwortlichkeit besteht eine Verantwortung der beteiligten Unternehmen, der deutschen Industrie insgesamt und der deutschen Gesellschaft. In den Nachkriegsjahren wurde über das Bundesentschädigungsgesetz in erheblichem Umfang Wiedergutmachung finanzieller Art an Opfer nationalsozialistischer Verbrechen geleistet, wovon jedoch Zwangsarbeiter ausgeschlossen blieben. Auch nach dem Erhalt vollständiger Souveränität Deutschlands durch den 2+4 Vertrag im Jahr 1990 wurden Entschädigungsforderungen von Zwangsarbeitern nicht anerkannt. Unter massivem Druck vor allem durch Massenklagen, sogenannte class actions, gegen deutsche Firmen in den USA wurde nach bilateralen Verhandlungen zwischen den Regierungen Deutschlands und der USA unter Einbeziehung der deutschen Industrie und der Opferanwälte im Jahr 2001 die Stiftung „Erinnerung, Verantwortung und Zukunft" mit einem Gesamtvolumen von fünf Milliarden Euro ins Leben gerufen, um ehemalige Zwangsarbeiter zu entschädigen und pädagogische Projekte zu finanzieren.

Lisa Yavnai

Military Justice: War Crimes Trials in the American Zone of Occupation in Germany, 1945-1947

Scholars of war crimes trials have often focused on the question of whether the trials were fair and just. More recently, the research has shifted to whether war crimes trials are an effective tool for educating civilians about the crimes of a previous regime. Mark J. Osiel in his book *Mass Atrocity* argues that war crimes trials should be designed as monumental spectacles to maximize their educational impact, affording the affected society a forum for exploring its past and reshaping its collective memory.[1] Lawrence Douglas in *The Memory of Judgment* supports this argument by suggesting that war crimes trials may be an imperative "born of the scars left on an outraged collective consciousness," and that such trials can contribute to the historical understanding of a traumatic past.[2] But Martha Minow in *Between Vengeance and Forgiveness* warns that varying prosecution strategies and the self-serving interests of the defendants may distort the historical record presented at trial.[3] Because of such inherent dangers, Michael Marrus argues that the historical narrative presented at trials should be viewed critically.[4] Hannah Arendt goes further in *Eichmann in Jerusalem* to suggest that creating a historical record in war crimes trials could only distract from the law's main purpose: to "render justice, and nothing else."[5]

This tension between the law and history, as it manifested in the U.S. Army war crimes trials in Germany, is the focus of this paper. Between 1945 and 1947 the U.S. Army prosecuted 1,676 lesser war criminals, defined as perpetrators "other than those who held high political, civil, or military positions," in 462 trials conducted in the American zone of occupation in Germany.[6] The accused included concentration camp personnel, Nazi military and state officials, as well as ordinary German civilians accused of violations of the laws of war. The Dachau trials – as they later became known for the location where most of them took place – were meant to serve both punitive and educational purposes. By punishing the perpetrators the army hoped to establish individual responsibility for violations of the laws of war. At the same time, by presenting evidence of Nazi criminality in open court, the army also sought to educate the Germans about the crimes of their past regime. Through an overview of the Dachau trials, this paper will demonstrate how the law shaped the historical record prosecutors could present and how it influenced the army's ability to achieve the didactic goals it set for the trials.[7]

In the aftermath of the Second World War, the United States prosecuted war criminals in Germany under three separate jurisdictions: the International Military Tribunal at Nuremberg (IMT), the successor Nuremberg Trials, and the U.S. Army trials at Dachau. First, the IMT, which convened under the London Charter by the United States, Great Britain, the Soviet Union, and France, indicted 24 of the highest ranking military and political leaders of the Third Reich captured by the allies. The indictment included three categories of crimes: crimes against peace – defined as "planning, preparation, initiation, or waging of a war of aggression"; war crimes – defined as "violations of the laws and customs of war;" and crimes against humanity – defined as "murder, extermination, enslavement, deportation, and other inhumane acts committed against any civilian population… or persecutions on political, racial or

---

[1] Mark J. Osiel, *Mass Atrocity, Collective Memory and the Law* 1-3 (NJ, 1997).
[2] Lawrence Douglas, *The Memory of Judgment: Making Law and History in the Trials of the Holocaust* 259-261 (New Haven, 2001).
[3] Martha Minow, *Between Vengeance and Forgiveness: Facing History after Genocide and Mass Violence* 47 (Boston, 1998).
[4] Michael Marrus, 'History and Holocaust in the Courtroom,' in Ronald Smelser, ed., *Lessons and Legacies V: The Holocaust and Justice* 215-239 (Illinois, 2002).
[5] Hannah Arendt, *Eichmann in Jerusalem: A Report on the Banality of Evil* 233 (New York, 1963).
[6] Combined Chiefs of Staff Order 19 June 1945.
[7] This data for this paper is based on Lisa Yavnai, *Military Justice: The U.S. Army War Crimes Trials in Germany, 1945-1947* (unpublished dissertation).

religious grounds...whether or not in violation of the domestic law of the country where perpetrated."[8] During the IMT proceedings, which began on 20 November 1945 and lasted for ten months, the court examined mostly documentary evidence about the crimes of the Nazi regime. Of the 22 defendants sentenced, twelve received death sentences, three received life imprisonment, four received lesser prison terms, and three acquitted.[9]

The second group of cases, closely linked to the IMT, was the successor Nuremberg trials. Established by the American Military Governor in Germany in accordance with Control Council Law No. 10, the twelve trials indicted 185 leaders of the Third Reich ministries, military, industrial concerns, SS, and legal and medical professions.[10] The accused were charged with war crimes, crimes against peace, crimes against humanity, and membership in groups or organizations declared criminal by the IMT.[11] The trials took place after the IMT proceedings concluded, beginning in December 1946 and ending in April 1949. Of the 177 defendants sentenced, the courts sentenced 24 to death, 20 to life imprisonment, 98 to lesser prison terms, and 35 acquitted.[12]

The third group of cases, constituting the largest and longest American effort to bring war criminals to justice, included the U.S. army trials of lesser war criminals. The fate of the lesser war criminals, in contrast to the major war criminals, was determined as early as 30 October 1943, when the United States, Great Britain, and Soviet Union signed the Moscow Declaration. The Declaration stated that perpetrators who committed crimes in known geographical locations would be brought back to the scene of their crimes after the war to be prosecuted by the countries in which their crimes took place, "according to the laws of those liberated countries."[13] The U.S. Army, as occupier of Germany, had authority to prosecute war crimes within its zone of occupation, whether committed in concentration camps liberated by U.S forces, or committed against American nationals.[14]

The U.S. Army became involved in the war crimes issue soon after the D-day invasion. On 25 September 1944, the army's Judge Advocate General established the National War Crimes Office in Washington, DC, to collect evidence on Nazi criminality in anticipation of possible war crimes trials in the future.[15] Initially, army commanders in the field only collected evidence on Nazi perpetrated crimes against American servicemen.[16] But with the liberation of Nazi concentration camps by American forces, the army created nineteen professional war crimes investigation teams that were able to expand the scope of the investigations to include mass atrocities against allied nationals.[17]

The American war crimes investigation teams attempted to gather evidence under extreme conditions and with little manpower. Often, investigators were unprepared for what they found and had to rely on their own creativity in order to accomplish their incredible task. Benjamin Ferencz, a war crimes investigator before he became a prosecutor at Nuremberg, wrote of his experience investigating crimes committed inside Flossenbürg concentration camp:

---

[8] Charter of the International Military Tribunal, August 8, 1945, reprinted in Robert H. Jackson, *Report of Robert H. Jackson , United States Representative to the International Conference on Military Trials*, 420-429 (London, 1945).

[9] *Trial of the Major War Criminals before the International Military Tribunal Nuremberg, 14 November 1945 - 1 October 1946,* 365 (Nuremberg, 1947).

[10] Telford Taylor, *Final Report to the Secretary of the Army on the Nuremberg War Crimes Trials Under Control Council Law No. 10* 73-85 (Washington DC, 1949).

[11] Ibid. 64-65.

[12] Subsequent to the indictment four accused committed suicide, and four others were severed from the proceedings because of illness. Ibid., 91.

[13] Moscow Declaration signed 30 October 1945 by Roosevelt, Churchill and Stalin.

[14] Report to the President by Mr. Justice Jackson, 6 June 1945. Reprinted in Jackson, *Report by Robert H. Jackson*, 42-54.

[15] From Henry L. Stimson to the Judge Advocate General, "Punishment of War Criminals" letter, 25 September 1944. NARA, RG 153, General Records, Box 1; "A History of The War Crimes Office," Secret Report, 4. NARA, RG 153, JAG Law Library, Box 57.

[16] Ibid., 11.

[17] From R. B. Lovett, Brigadier General, to Commanding Generals, "Establishment of War Crimes Branches," memo, 24 February, 1945. NARA, RG 153, JAG Law Library, Box 57.

"I took over two large offices [in the camp] for our headquarters... Some of the inmates had hidden the books with the names and statistics of the prisoners, and those were now brought out and I put a crew to work tabulating the data. I had two long-time French inmates, as well as one Polish journalist start writing a complete history of the camp. To another I assigned the job of compiling the names of all known SS men who were ever in the camp. A Dr. was gathering statements from persons in the hospital, and I went to work furiously gathering statements from others whom I started calling to the office."[18]

American war crimes investigators who entered Mauthausen, Dachau, Buchenwald, and Nordhausen concentration camps had similar experiences.[19] Yet despite these difficulties investigators gathered over 12.5 tons of documentary evidence,[20] and opened 3,887 war crimes cases,[21] which formed the basis for the army's trials of lesser war criminals.

The army relied on established international law to prosecute its war crimes cases at Dachau. The indictments focused exclusively on violations of the laws and usages of war in accordance with the Army's own rules and regulations. The exclusive focus on war crimes was in contrast, however, with the broader charges of crimes against peace and crimes against humanity used in the IMT and subsequent Nuremberg proceedings. The army's use of a narrow legal framework made it less susceptible to accusations of retroactivity of the law, but at the same time presented unique challenges for prosecuting crimes of an unprecedented scale and nature.

Between June 1945 and December 1947, the army prosecuted two types of cases at Dachau: cases dealing with crimes against American nationals and cases of mass atrocities. The first group involved 253 trials against 646 defendants who mistreated American aviators or ground troops in violation of the laws of war. The aviators were shot down from their planes over the German countryside. Upon their surrender as POWs on the ground, the flyers suffered mistreatment by the local population. Later, they were either lynched by mobs of civilians or executed by local police or party officials. The surrendered American ground troops, on the other hand, were either shot by German soldiers on the battlefield, or mistreated in Nazi POW camps. The prosecution presented evidence in court to show that the deaths of the American servicemen were the result of an official policy developed by Himmler and Bormann to encourage the killing of captured allied soldiers in violation of the laws of war. Introducing this evidence assisted the army in educating the German public about the criminal policies of the Nazi government. It also illustrated to the Germans that the execution of these policies was carried out not only by government officials but also by ordinary civilians.[22]

The 646 accused, including fifteen women, were mostly German or Austrian nationals but also included six Hungarians, two Czechs, two Romanians, and one Dutch citizen. They were civilians, Nazi police and party officials, as well as German military personnel, and ranged in ages between 18 and 72 years old.[23] Many did not belong to the Nazi Party. Some defendants maintained that their actions were the consequence of the relentless Nazi propaganda, which encouraged them to kill downed flyers. Others attributed their acts to the trauma they suffered either on the battlefield or after losing family members or property to allied bombings. Yet others claimed that they only followed orders and that disobeying their superiors would have resulted in their own deaths. In most cases the court did not

---

[18] Ferencz to Trudy, 29 April 1945. Benjamin Ferencz Papers, RG 12.001.03*01, United States Holocaust Memorial Museum, Washington, DC.

[19] From Major Eugene S. Cohen, JA Section, Third U.S. Army, Investigator-Examiner, to Commanding General, Twelfth Army Group, Re: Report of Investigation of Alleged War Crimes, 17 June 1945. NARA, RG 338, Cases Tried, Box 345.

[20] Memorandum for The Secretary of the Army, "Survey of the Trials of War Criminals Held at Dachau, Germany," from Gordon Simpson, Colonel, JAGD, Edward L. Van Roden, Colonel, JAGD, and Charles W. Lawrence, JR., Lieutenant Colonel, 14 September 1948. NARA, RG 338, Cases Tried, Box 14.

[21] "Report of the Deputy Judge Advocate for War Crimes", 160. NARA RG 338, General Administration, Box 13.

[22] See for example case 12 -1497 *U.S. v. Hatgen et al.*; Order No. 003830/42 g.Kdos. OKW/West, 18 October 1942; Editorial by Göbbels on the subject which appeared on 29 May 1944 in the Völkischer Beobachter; Himmler, Order RF/48/16/43 g , 10 August 1943; Keitel to the Supreme Commander of the Air Force, 14 June 1944. NARA, RG 338, Cases Tried Box 260.

[23] Yavnai, *Military Justice*, appendix, trials chart.

recognize these arguments as acceptable defense but did consider them as mitigating circumstances during sentencing.[24] Of the 533 accused found guilty, the court sentenced 196 to death, 92 to life in prison, and 245 to prison terms ranging from two months to 30 years.[25]

The second group of cases the army prosecuted at Dachau involved mass atrocities against allied nationals. The army prosecuted 232 mass atrocities trials against 1030 defendants. The accused committed war crimes in six main concentration camp rings including Dachau, Mauthausen, Buchenwald, Flossenburg, Nordhausen, and Müldorf, as well as at the Hadamar mental institution.[26] These unprecedented crimes were particularly difficult to prosecute because, as opposed to the downed flyer cases, their scope went beyond the traditional violations of the laws of war which the military courts had authority to handle.

The 1030 accused, including only three women, either held official positions at the camps as members of the Nazi Party, Allgemeine SS, SA, Waffen SS, Wehrmacht, Navy or Luftwaffe; were civilian employees of the Third Reich; or privileged concentration camp inmates including kapos and block elders. They included German, Austrian, Yugoslav, Czech, Romanian, Polish, Spanish, Latvian, Hungarian, and Dutch nationals and ranged in ages between 21 and 74 years old. In their defense, the accused argued that they executed legal orders; followed superior orders; suffered duress; mistaken identity; were the target of revenge by witnesses; or that they simply did not commit the crimes charged. The Dachau courts found 885 defendants guilty of war crimes and sentenced 233 accused to death, 106 to life in prison, and 546 to prison terms ranging from one to 20 years.[27]

Having to prosecute the mass atrocities cases within the narrow legal framework afforded by the laws of war affected the army's ability to present a coherent historical context for these crimes. For example, prosecutors could not introduce evidence on the Holocaust, as it was carried out in concentration camps, because genocide was not a recognized crime yet, and persecution based on religion was a crime against humanity, but not a violation of the laws of war.[28] Instead, prosecutors focused on the criminality of daily life at the camps. In the Mauthausen case, prosecutors illustrated the various forms of mistreatment, malnutrition, hard labor, executions, poison injections to the heart, and gassing, which caused the deaths of many inmates there. While this evidence did not explain the reasons or policies of persecution of certain groups in the camp, it did help the court to find that the camp was a criminal enterprise; that it was impossible for anyone to be present there without knowledge of the criminal practices; and that personnel connected with the camp, regardless of their capacity, could be found guilty of violating the laws of usages of war.[29]

In another example, the Hadamar case, prosecutors could not present evidence against the mental institution's staff for their role in killing thousands of Germans as part of Hitler's T4 euthanasia program, because this policy was a domestic matter outside the scope of international law.[30] Instead, prosecutors had to focus on the deportation to Hadamar and subsequent murder by the institution's staff of a few hundred eastern workers who were not mentally or otherwise handicapped.[31] As a result, the purpose of the Hadamar institution was never fully explained through the trial evidence, and staff involved in killing thousands of other victims could not be prosecuted.

---

[24] According to the U.S. Army's *Rules of Land Warfare* paragraph 347.1 as amended on 15 November 1944, superior orders do not absolve military personnel from responsibility for committing war crimes. However, the fact that the accused had committed war crimes pursuant to an order of a superior or government sanction "may be taken into consideration in determining culpability, either by way of defense or in mitigation of punishment. The person giving the orders may also be punished." "Report by the Deputy Judge Advocate for War Crimes", 16. NARA, RG 338, General Administration, Box 13.

[25] Yavnai, *Military Justice*, appendix, trials chart.

[26] Ibid.

[27] Ibid.

[28] The term genocide, coined by Raphael Lemkin in 1943, became officially recognize as a war crime in the 1948 by the United Nations in the *Convention on the Prevention and Punishment of the Crime of Genocide*.

[29] Case number 000-50-5, *U.S. vs. Hans Altfuldisch et al.*

[30] Patricia Heberer, *Exitus Heute in Hadamar: The Hadamar Facility and "Euthanasia" in Nazi Germany,* 481 (unpublished dissertation, 2001).

[31] Case number 12- 449, *U.S. vs. Alfons Klein et al.*

Prosecutors were very careful not to introduce evidence that was outside the legal scope of the court. Partly for this reason they built their prosecution strategy on carefully controlled witness testimonies supported by documentary evidence.[32] As was later the strategy of the Israeli prosecution in the Eichmann trial, and in marked contrast to the IMT where most of the evidence presented was documentary, at the Dachau mass atrocity cases prosecutors tried to link the evidence with the personal suffering of the victims. The witnesses were carefully selected based on the credibility they projected, namely, their ability to convey their experiences in an eloquent and convincing manner.[33] The witnesses could only testify about the daily working of the camps, the lower-ranking defendants only about their personal acts and observations. This allowed prosecutors to better control the history narrative they were presenting to the court and the public, even if it was a limited one.

In conclusion, as Martha Minow argues, war crimes trials by themselves cannot create "an international moral and legal order, prevent genocides, or forge the political transformation of previously oppressive regimes."[34] Whether war crimes trials are the correct forum for presenting historical narratives remains debatable. But as the U.S. Army trials at Dachau illustrate, when using war crimes trials to educate a nation about its criminal past, the choice of law is not less important than the development of evidence. At Dachau, legal limitations dictated the kind of evidence prosecutors could present, often limiting its scope. While the trials afforded the German public an opportunity to hear in open court directly from the perpetrators and their victims, the historical narrative presented was often incomplete or distorted. Nevertheless, the Dachau trials were able to provide accountability, closure for the victims, and offer *a starting point* in which the crimes of the Nazi regime could be discussed in the immediate aftermath of war.

---

[32] William Dowdel Denson, *Justice in Germany: Memories of the Chief Prosecutor* (New York, 1990). No pagination.
[33] Joshua M. Greene, *Justice at Dachau: The Trials of an American Prosecutor*, 55-56 (New York, 2003).
[34] Minow, *Between Vengeance and Forgiveness*, 49.

Lisa Yavnai

Militärjustiz: Kriegsverbrecherprozesse in der amerikanisch besetzen Zone in Deutschland, 1945-1947

Die Dachau-Prozesse umfassten 462 Prozesse mit insgesamt 1.676 Angeklagten. Dieser Beitrag befasst sich mit dem Einfluss des Rechts auf die von den Anklägern präsentierte historische Darstellung. Durch die öffentliche Präsentation der Beweise von Nazi-Taten beabsichtigte man, die Deutschen über die Verbrechen ihres vergangenen Regimes aufzuklären. Dieses didaktische Ziel der US-Armee wurde jedoch stark beeinträchtigt, weil die Angeklagten nur für Kriegsverbrechen für schuldig befunden werden konnten. Völkermord war zu dieser Zeit noch nicht als Straftat anerkannt. Aus diesem Grund war es der Anklage nicht erlaubt, die Beweise für den in den Konzentrationslagern durchgeführten Holocaust vorzulegen. Verfolgung aus religiösen Gründen galt als ein Verbrechen gegen die Menschlichkeit und fiel unter dieselbe Kategorie. Somit blieb der Anklage nur die Alternative, die Beschuldigten für Kriegsverbrechen anzuklagen.

Der Zwang, die Greueltaten innerhalb des engen, sich durch das *ius in bello* bietenden rechtlichen Rahmens anzuklagen, hatte Auswirkungen auf die Fähigkeit der Armee, einen einheitlichen historischen Kontext für diese Verbrechen zu präsentieren. Im Ergebnis mussten sich die Anklagen auf die Verbrechen des täglichen Lebens in den Konzentrationslagern, die verschiedenen Formen von Misshandlungen, ungenügende Ernährung, schwere Arbeit, Erschießungen, Giftspritzen und Vergasungen konzentrieren, die den Tod vieler Insassen verursacht hatten. Das Gericht befand, dass das Konzentrationslager ein kriminelles Unternehmen war und dass jeder dort Anwesenden von den kriminellen Praktiken gewusst haben musste. Deshalb konnte jegliches KZ-Personal, unabhängig von dem jeweiligen Aufgabenbereich, für schuldig befunden werden, die Gesetze und Gebräuche des Kriegs verletzt und sich damit strafbar gemacht zu haben. Doch die erzieherischen Bemühungen der Armee wurden stark behindert, weil der rechtliche Rahmen die Art der Beweisführung vorgab, und die Gründe für die Verfolgung gewisser Gruppen damit häufig im Dunkeln blieben. Gerade dieser Aspekt wäre jedoch für eine Aufklärung der Deutschen über die Verbrechen des Nazi-Regimes von großer Wichtigkeit gewesen. Somit stellt sich die Frage, ob – damals wie heute – die Durchführung von Kriegsverbrecherprozessen grundsätzlich zur Aufarbeitung vollständiger historischer Hintergründe geeignet ist, um eine Aufklärung über die Ursachen von Genozid und Unmenschlichkeit zu erreichen und die Bevölkerung über die Verbrechen ihrer Regierung aufzuklären.

V. National Prosecution in Germany, Israel, Australia and Other Nations/ Nationale Strafverfolgung in Deutschland, Israel, Australien und anderen Ländern

Hinrich Rüping

Zwischen Recht und Politik: Die Ahndung von NS-Taten in beiden deutschen Staaten nach 1945

1. Vorgaben der Alliierten

Seit der Moskauer Deklaration über die Verantwortlichkeit der Hitler-Anhänger für begangene Greueltaten (1943) kehrt 1945 in den Beschlüssen der Krim-Konferenz, der Erklärung von Potsdam und im Londoner Viermächteabkommen über die Verfolgung und Bestrafung der Hauptkriegsverbrecher, damit als zentraler Punkt in den Vorstellungen der Alliierten zur Neuordnung Deutschlands nach dem Krieg die Bestrafung der Schuldigen wieder. Was sich zunächst nur als politische Absichtserklärung darstellt, wird mit der Einsetzung des Internationalen Militärgerichtshofs in Nürnberg und den Verfahren zur Aburteilung der Hauptkriegsverbrecher rechtlich verfasst. Das Statut des Gerichtshofs deklariert Straftatbestände, insbesondere den neuen Begriff der Verbrechen gegen die Menschlichkeit (Art. 6 c) und schafft eine Verfahrensordnung als Ausdruck prozessualer Gerechtigkeit (Art. 16).[1]

Das KRG Nr. 10 (Kontrollratsgesetz) von 1945 baut auf den Regelungen des Statuts auf und ist gedacht als eine für alle vier Zonen einheitliche Grundlage, um bei zunehmender Delegation von Verfahren auf deutsche Stellen eine einheitliche Verfolgung von NS-Taten zu gewährleisten. Kernstück des materiellen Rechts wird die Ahndung von Verbrechen gegen die Menschlichkeit. Art. 2 Nr. 1 (c) nennt beispielhaft „Mord, Ausrottung, Versklavung, Zwangsverschleppung, Freiheitsberaubung, Folterung, Vergewaltigung oder andere an der Zivilbevölkerung begangene unmenschliche Handlungen; Verfolgung aus politischen, rassischen oder religiösen Gründen, ohne Rücksicht darauf, ob sie das nationale Recht des Landes, in welchem die Handlung begangen worden ist, verletzen".[2]

Hauptangriffspunkt wird in einer nicht nur rechtlich, sondern auch politisch geführten Diskussion ein darin liegender Verstoß gegen das Verbot der Rückwirkung. So wie bereits der Nürnberger Gerichtshof eine entsprechende Gesamteingabe der Verteidigung zurückgewiesen hat,[3] lässt auch die Militärregierung in den einzelnen Zonen keinen Zweifel an der Verbindlichkeit der Norm. Als der Celler Oberlandesgerichtspräsident einwendet, wer durch rückwirkende Anwendung von Normen einer „höheren Gerechtigkeit" zum Siege verhelfen wolle, gebe unter inhaltlich anderen Vorzeichen, aber methodisch wie im Nationalsozialismus einem „gesunden Rechtsgefühl der Volksgemeinschaft" Vorrang vor der Bindung des Richters an das Gesetz, wertet die Militärregierung diesen Vorstoß als Aufforderung zur Rechtsbeugung.[4]

Die deutsche Praxis setzt sich daher auch weitgehend über Bedenken gegen die Rechtsgültigkeit hinweg, indem sie, gerade wie kritisiert, aus dem „Wesen des Bösen" folgert, „daß ihm im Bereich des Sittlichen Strafe gebührt auch ohne besondere Strafdrohung"[5] oder sich unter den politischen Verhältnissen des Besatzungsrechts in der positivistischen Tradition des Gesetzesgehorsams mit dem Hinweis auf die Existenz des KRG begnügt.[6]

---

[1] Text in: Der Prozeß gegen die Hauptkriegsverbrecher vor dem Internationalen Militärgerichtshof Nürnberg [IMG], Amtlicher Text in deutscher Sprache, Nürnberg 1947-1949, Bd. 1, 10 ff.

[2] Text in Amtsblatt Kontrollrat, S. 50 ff.

[3] IMG Bd. 1, 187, 189 ff., 245.

[4] Zur Kontroverse um den Beitrag *v. Hodenbergs,* Süddeutsche Juristenzeitung [SJZ] 1947, Sp. 120 ff. vgl. *Rüping,* Staatsanwälte S. 80 f., *Buchholz-Schuster,* S. 53 ff.; beispielhaft stellt auch eine Berliner Verordnung v. 2. 7. 1945 in § 2 Nr. 4 für die Konfiskation bei früheren Nationalsozialisten darauf ab, dass sie „nach gesunder Volksanschauung" unangemessene Vorteile aus ihrer Stellung gezogen haben (Verordnungsblatt Berlin 1945, 45).

[5] OLG Köln, Justizministerialblatt für das Land Nordrhein-Westfalen [JMBlNW] 1947, 111, 113; zur Naturrechtsrenaissance *Radbruch,* SJZ 1947, Sp. 135 sowie bei der Eröffnung des Bundesgerichtshofes Bundespräsident *Heuß* und der Präsident des BGH *Weinkauff,* SJZ 1950, Sp. 854, 855.

[6] Z. B. OLG Köln, Monatsschrift für Deutsches Recht [MDR] 1947, 2, OLG Hamm, MDR 1947, 205 (gegen die Vorinstanz LG Siegen, MDR 1947, 203, 204, das sich auf *v. Hodenberg* [vgl. Fn. 4] berufen hatte), OLG Braunschweig, Neue Juristische Wochenschrift [NJW] 1947/48, 309, OLG Hamburg, MDR 1947, 241, 242 hält bereits wieder auch ein sittenwidriges Gesetz für verbindlich. Zum neu etablierten Positivismus Verordnung Nr. 165 v. 15. 9. 1948 über die

2. Ahndung in den westlichen Zonen

Was zunächst die Ahndung von Verbrechen gegen die Menschlichkeit in den westlichen Zonen – primär der Britischen und dann der Amerikanischen – angeht, bleiben die Resultate mager. Die im Vergleich zum hohen, auch moralischen Anspruch des KRG Nr. 10 geringe praktische Bedeutung bedarf der Erklärung. Rahmenbedingungen für die Tätigkeit der Justiz liegen in ihrer personellen Seite, wie sie sich nach dem Ergebnis der Entnazifizierung von Richtern und Staatsanwälten darstellt, sowie in der Haltung gegenüber der jüngsten Vergangenheit.

2.1. Rahmenbedingungen

Instruktiv erscheinen die Verhältnisse in der Britischen Zone. Mit der forcierten Verlagerung der Entnazifizierung auf deutsche Ausschüsse und weitgehender Verrechtlichung der Verfahren misslingt das ursprüngliche Ziel eines politischen Neuanfangs. Gestützt auf die rechtliche Konstruktion, wegen ihrer Belastung des Amtes enthobene Richter und Beamte seien nur vorläufig suspendiert, da sie abstrakt dem Staat unabhängig von seiner konkreten Staatsform dienten, kehren zwar nicht mehr überzeugte Nationalsozialisten, aber geringer Belastete und Mitläufer nach einer Wartezeit in ihre beruflichen Stellungen zurück.[7]

Dass Richter auch in zurückliegenden dunklen Zeiten als Ausdruck „stillen Heldentums" die „Flamme des Rechts" gehütet und als Opfer des Nationalsozialismus zu gelten hätten,[8] schafft zudem bereitwillig aufgenommene apologetische Mythen. Was die Entnazifizierung des Rechts angeht, gelten entsprechend auch Normen aus der Zeit zwischen 1933 und 1945 weiterhin, soweit sie nicht im Einzelfall aufgehoben oder als Ausdruck „typisch nationalsozialistischer" Vorstellungen obsolet sind, und selbst zeitgebunden dem „gesunden Volksempfinden" verpflichtete Novellierungen bleiben um ihres abstrakten Ordnungswertes Willen unverfänglich.[9] Derartige restaurative Züge der westdeutschen Nachkriegsjustiz lassen ihr das KRG Nr. 10 nach Anspruch wie Umsetzung als skeptisch betrachtetes Neuland, wenn nicht als Diktat der Alliierten und als Oktroy erscheinen.

2.2. Zur Praxis der Strafgerichte

Die politischen Erwartungen der Besatzungsmacht – im Folgenden beschränkt auf den am besten dokumentierten Bereich der Britischen Zone – an die Handhabung des KRG Nr. 10 sind hoch und äußern sich in zunehmendem Druck auf die deutsche Justizverwaltung. Obwohl die Militärregierung stets die Dringlichkeit der Verfahren betont und das Bewusstsein der Staatsanwaltschaft durch gesteigerte Berichtspflichten zu schärfen sucht,[10] kommen Verfahren, sofern sie nicht eingestellt werden, nur langsam voran, denn die Handhabung des KRG bereitet erhebliche dogmatische wie praktische Schwierigkeiten.

Probleme, dem Verbrechen gegen die Menschlichkeit Konturen zu verleihen, erwachsen aus der Fassung des Gesetzes, die dem *common law* verpflichtet und der kontinentalen Kodifikationstechnik fremd ist, sowie aus dem Ziel, strafrechtliche Schuld für Taten in einem totalitären System zuzumessen. Die allgemeine Voraussetzung des Art. 2 Nr. 1 (c), ein aus der nationalsozialistischen Gewalt- und Willkürherrschaft erwachsener Angriff auf die Humanität, das heißt die zivilisierte Menschheit als

---

Verwaltungsgerichtsbarkeit in der Britischen Zone, die eine Berufung auf Billigkeit oder „übergesetzliche Grundsätze" untersagt (Verordnungsblatt für die Britische Zone 1948, 263) § 1 II sowie *Rüping*, Justiz S. 987.

[7] *Rüping*, Staatsanwälte S. 88 f., 91; zur „Suspensionstheorie" BGH, Großer Zivilsenat, Entscheidungen des BGH in Zivilsachen [BGHZ] 13, 265, 296.

[8] Entgegenkommende Deutungen finden sich bei *Radbruch*, SJZ 1948, Sp. 64, *Eb. Schmidt*, MDR 1948, 378, Minister der Justiz *Sträter*, JMBlNW 1948, 197 (gegen ihn ausdrücklich die Grußadresse an den Chef der Deutschen Justizverwaltung [DJV] in der SBZ, *Fechner*, Neue Justiz [NJ] 1948, 201), *Versen*, MDR 1949, 580.

[9] Zu Einzelheiten, mit weiteren Nachweisen, *Rüping*, Justiz S. 987 f.

[10] Am Beispiel des Bezirks Celle mit Belegen aus den Generalakten des Generalstaatsanwalts *Rüping*, Staatsanwälte S. 78 f.

Trägerin des ideellen Menschenwertes, müsse sich kausal ausgewirkt haben und individuell zurechenbar sein, bereiten insbesondere Probleme bei der Ahndung von Denunziationen.

Denunziationen können sich als „Verfolgung" im Sinne der beispielhaft genannten Alt. 9 des Art. 2 darstellen. Handelt der Denunziant, wie häufig, ohne primär politisches Motiv, sondern etwa, um es einem privaten Konkurrenten „heimzuzahlen" und ihn kurzzeitig „auszuschalten", wird er sich darauf berufen, nicht seine Anzeige, sondern spätere Misshandlungen durch die Gestapo im Lager bzw. das Todesurteil durch die Justiz sei für den schließlichen Erfolg kausal geworden, und subjektiv habe er die konkret eingetretenen Folgen weder vorhergesehen noch gewollt. Soll die Ahndung in derartigen Fällen nicht scheitern, kann sie das nur um den Preis, von den allgemeinen Erfordernissen der objektiven Zurechnung bei der Kausalität und der subjektiven beim Vorsatz Abstriche zu machen.[11] Es genügt dann die bewusste Auslieferung des Denunzierten an ein System, das nach Willkür mit ihm verfährt.

Doch reicht die Problematik tiefer. Sie erwächst aus dem Grundproblem justizieller Vergangenheitsbewältigung nach politischen Systemwechseln, ein seinerzeit legales Verhalten nachträglich für illegal zu erklären: „Der mit dem jeweiligen Rechtssystem konform handelnde Denunziant hat keinen Richter. Wird dieses System nachträglich seiner Legitimationsgrundlagen beraubt, hat er schließlich deren zwei. Den ersten hat er benutzt, der zweite verurteilt ihn deswegen".[12] Die Rechtsabteilung der Britischen Militärregierung gibt dabei selbst die Schwierigkeiten zu, wenn die Handlungen nach deutschem Recht nicht strafbar sind, ihre Ahndung damit gegen den Grundsatz *nulla poena sine lege* verstößt.[13]

Am Beispiel der Tätigkeit des Obersten Gerichtshofes für die Britische Zone werden grundsätzliche Dimensionen der Nachkriegsjustiz deutlich. 1947 errichtet die Militärregierung der Britischen Zone mit ihren acht Oberlandesgerichten einen Obersten Gerichtshof, der in Strafsachen über Revisionen gegen Urteile der Landgerichte entscheidet.[14] Er sieht in der Formulierung eines prominenten Richters seine Aufgabe darin, „geleitet von dem Willen nach Gerechtigkeit und Rechtsstaatlichkeit", das Beste aus dem KRG Nr. 10 zu machen „und die Einheitlichkeit der Rechtsanwendung durch brauchbare Maßstäbe, wie sie unter deutschen Verhältnissen nur ein Gesetzestatbestand bietet, möglichst zu sichern".[15] Er tut das, ohne die Verbindlichkeit zu bezweifeln,[16] um den Preis rechtlicher Konstruktionen, die zunehmend den Widerstand der Instanzgerichte herausfordern.[17] Kennzeichnend für die Schärfe der Auseinandersetzungen, bezeichnet ein Schwurgericht die höchstrichterliche Rechtsprechung, den Vorsatz bei Denunziationen nicht auf die konkret eingetretenen Folgen zu beziehen, als „unerträglich".[18]

Die juristische Kontroverse besitzt einen politischen Hintergrund. Sämtliche Richter des OGH – als einzigem Gericht im westlichen Teil Deutschlands – haben nicht der NSDAP angehört, was die Strenge der Rechtsprechung und den Versuch erklärt, gegenüber Tätern die Strafzwecke der Sühne und Abschreckung durchzusetzen. Nach Abschluß der Entnazifizierung herrscht jedoch kurz darauf gesamtgesellschaftlich die Mentalität vor, die Vergangenheit zu verdrängen und sich mit den Tätern zu

---

[11] Zu Einzelheiten der strafrechtsdogmatischen Diskussion *Rüping,* Studien- und Quellenbuch S. 293 f.
[12] *Franßen,* NJ 1997, 170, z. B. bezogen auf das früher strafbare Abhören von „Feindsendern" OLG Gera, Regierungsblatt Thüringen [RegBl Thür.] 1947 II, 442; zur Frage, wieweit die Norm bzw. auch ihre Handhabung entscheidet, *Diestelkamp,* Zeitschrift für Neuere Rechtsgeschichte [ZNR] 1999, 433.
[13] Erlaß v. 21. 12. 1946, Nr. 4a, Hanseatisches Justizverwaltungsblatt [HansJVwBl] 1947, 17.
[14] Verordnung Nr. 98 v. 1. 9. 1947 (AmtsBl Militärregierung [MR] Deutschland, Britisches Kontrollgebiet, S. 572).
[15] Zum Konflikt für die Praxis im Selbstzeugnis eines Richters *Rüping,* Neue Zeitschrift für Strafrecht [NStZ] 2000, 357.
[16] Noch unter der Geltung des Art. 103 II GG: Oberster Gerichtshof [OGH], MDR 1950, 369.
[17] Zum Ausweg, statt auf den Vorsatz nur auf eine „inhumane Gesinnung" abzustellen, OLG Hamm, MDR 1948, 94.
[18] Grundlegend OGH, Entscheidungen in Strafsachen [OGHSt] 1, 11, 16, ebenso OLG Braunschweig, MDR 1948, 125, zur Kritik dagegen LG Göttingen, MDR 1951, 312; zu dieser Kontroverse *Rüping,* NStZ 2000, 358, weiter *Homann,* S. 32 f.

solidarisieren.[19] Im Schwurgericht können sechs Geschworene bei der Abstimmung drei Berufsrichter majorisieren und aufgrund Verständnisses für die „Verstrickung" von Tätern in ein Unrechtssystem Freisprüche bewirken.[20]

2.3. Spruchgerichtsverfahren

Wie die Resultate der ordentlichen Strafgerichte bleiben auch die der Spruchgerichte mager. Nur die Britische Militärregierung macht von der Vorgabe des Kontrollrats Gebrauch, Angehörige der in Nürnberg für verbrecherisch erklärten Organisationen wegen ihrer Zugehörigkeit strafrechtlich zu belangen. Über das Zentraljustizamt für die Britische Zone macht die Militärregierung auch das Programm „Old Lace" für die sechs, in der Nähe von Internierungslagern errichteten Spruchgerichte und den beim OLG Hamm gebildeten Obersten Spruchgerichtshof als Revisionsinstanz dringlich.[21]

Auch hier stößt die Durchführung auf rechtliche Einwände, einen auf die reine Zugehörigkeit zu einer Organisation beschränkten Tatbestand rückwirkend anzuwenden, und auf praktische Schwierigkeiten, Betroffenen die Kenntnis des verbrecherischen Charakters nachzuweisen.[22]

Wenn diese Bedenken zurücktreten vor „einer Aufgabe, die auf jeden Fall aus vaterländischen Gründen gemeistert werden muss", so, um den 27.000 Internierten die im Vergleich zu einer politischen Lösung Vorteile eines justizförmigen Verfahrens zukommen zu lassen. Als willkommene Resultate bleibt ein Drittel der Überprüften wegen Freispruchs oder Einstellung straflos und wird ein Großteil als Folge der Anrechnung von Internierungshaft entlassen.[23]

2.4. Deutung der Verfolgungspraxis

Die weiteren Etappen der Verfolgung von NS-Taten in der Bundesrepublik sind bekannt – von der Errichtung der Zentralen Stelle in Ludwigsburg 1958 über die Verlängerung der strafrechtlichen Verjährungsfrist für Mord bis zu einzelnen Großverfahren wie dem Frankfurter Auschwitz-Prozess.[24]

Wiederholt ist der Justiz Versagen und darüber hinaus vorgeworfen worden, auf Grund stillschweigenden Einverständnisses mit den Belasteten durch sachlich nicht gerechtfertigte Einstellungen wie Freisprüche eine wirkliche Ahndung verhindert zu haben.[25] Die Praxis verweist demgegenüber auf Schwierigkeiten, die sich der Ermittlung und Ahndung individueller Schuld in einem rechtsstaatlichen Strafverfahren in den Weg stellen: auf verhandlungsunfähige Angeklagte, auf Zeugen, die keine zuverlässige Erinnerung mehr besitzen, wie auf die Unmöglichkeit, mit den Mitteln des Prozessrechts die häufig erforderliche individuelle Beteiligung an Massenverbrechen nachzuweisen.[26]

---

[19] Kennzeichnend führt LG Weiden im Urteil v. 19. 2. 1948 für die Durchsetzung des Nationalsozialismus u. a. die hypnotische Wirkung des Führerkults und die Gehorsamsbereitschaft der Deutschen an (Justiz und NS-Verbrechen, Bd. 2, Nr. 45, S. 235, 311).

[20] Belege bei *Rüping,* Juristische Rundschau [JR] 1976, 271.

[21] Verordnung Nr. 69 v. 31. 12. 1946 (AmtsBl MR, Britisches Kontrollgebiet, S. 405 ff.), Verfahrensordnung v. 17. 2. 1947 (Justizblatt [JBl] für den OLG-Bezirk Düsseldorf 1947, 24 ff.).

[22] Z. B. hält der Oberste Spruchgerichtshof für allgemeinkundig, dass Häftlinge in Konzentrationslagern Schäden davontragen können (Die Spruchgerichte 1948, 25 f.); den Spruchgerichten auch rechtlich problematische Fälle von Denunziationen zu übertragen, gibt die MR auf (Schreiben der Rechtsabteilung v. 23. 5. 1947, HansJVwBl 1947, 17, Nr. 2).

[23] *Rüping,* Staatsanwälte S. 75 ff., als Beispiel, ohne auf Hintergründe einzugehen, das milde Urteil des Spruchgerichts Bielefeld gegen den Düsseldorfer Gauleiter *Florian* bei *Zimmermann,* S. 53 f. sowie zur Statistik S. 78. Dass Staatsanwälte (im Gegensatz zu Richtern) der NSDAP angehört haben dürfen, wird mit dem rechtlichen, nicht politischen Charakter der Verfahren begründet (dazu auch *Wember,* S. 286 ff.).

[24] Zur Diskussion der NSG-Verfahren in der Öffentlichkeit und den Wandlungen der Wahrnehmung vgl. das Standardwerk von *Steinbach,* zur Vergangenheitspolitik in den 60er Jahren *v. Miquel.*

[25] *Freudiger,* S. 407 ff., gegen den häufig anzutreffenden Schluß von Biographien beteiligter Richter auf ihre Spruchtätigkeit *Greve,* S. 403.

[26] Aus der Sicht eines früheren Generalstaatsanwalts *Hoffmann,* S. 276 ff.; dazu kritisch *Greve,* S. 80 ff. sowie zur Bilanz der Verfolgung von NS-Taten *Diestelkamp,* ZNR 1999, 429 f., *Zimmermann,* S. 195 ff.

Aus heutiger Sicht erscheinen Versuche, einzelnen Entscheidungen, insbesondere höchstrichterlichen Entscheidungen im Rechtsmittelverfahren Aussagen im Sinne eines stillschweigenden Paktes mit den Tätern zu entnehmen, nicht verifizierbar. Doch kann diese Feststellung die Beteiligten nicht exkulpieren. Der Vorwurf, aus einer Distanzierung zum Nationalsozialismus, soweit sie überhaupt, etwa in den Kategorien „gesetzlichen Unrechts" erfolgt ist, gerade bezüglich der Verantwortlichkeit richterlicher Kollegen nicht die notwendigen Konsequenzen im Sinne einer strafrechtlichen Verantwortlichkeit gezogen zu haben, lässt sich nicht entkräften. Auch haben strafrechtliche Konstruktionen, wie die Notwendigkeit eines direkten Vorsatzes bei der Rechtsbeugung oder die Annahme bloßer Beihilfe statt Täterschaft im Sinne subjektiver Kriterien, erkennbar die Handhabe gegeben, Täter zu begünstigen.[27]

2.5 Zwischenergebnis

Das Ethos strafrechtlicher Vergangenheitsbewältigung, unter dem das KRG Nr. 10 antritt, wird zermahlen im Alltag der Rechtspflege, – vordergründig als Folge rechtlicher Einwände und hintergründig wegen der politischen Haltung zur jüngsten Vergangenheit. Bezogen auf einen Oberlandesgerichtsbezirk und in der Tendenz verallgemeinerungsfähig für die Britische Zone kommen bis 1949 auf 64 Verurteilungen 40 Freisprüche. Einstellungen nach § 153 StPO wegen „Geringfügigkeit", die zunächst beim Vorwurf eines Verbrechens gegen die Menschlichkeit als undenkbar und als Verhöhnung der Opfer erscheinen, dienen der Staatsanwaltschaft auch dazu, einem als größeren Affront empfundenen Freispruch durch das Gericht zuvorzukommen. So erklärt sich ihre Quote im Bezirk von 133 Ermittlungsverfahren bis 1948 bei einer Gesamtzahl von 420 Verfahren.[28]

Was die Ahndung in den folgenden Jahren angeht, lässt sich ein pauschaler wie weitgehender Verdacht nicht erhärten, selbst durch ihre Tätigkeit im Nationalsozialismus belastete Richter hätten systematisch die wegen NS-Taten Angeklagten und vor allem richterlichen Kollegen der verdienten und nach dem gesetzlichen Rahmen möglichen Strafe entzogen. Doch fehlt eine wirkliche Distanzierung vom Nationalsozialismus, und wenn anders, werden aus ihr nicht die notwendigen Konsequenzen im Sinne einer strafrechtlichen Mitverantwortlichkeit gezogen.

3. Ahndung in der SBZ

Die Lage in der sowjetisch besetzten Zone zeigt zunächst eine in Teilen vergleichbare Ausgangslage für die Ahndung von NS-Taten, verfolgt dann jedoch andere Lösungen und mündet in einer politischen Justiz nach Vorgaben der Sowjetischen Militäradministration.

3.1. Verfolgung von Humanitätsverbrechen

Bereits erste Ansätze zur Ahndung von NS-Taten erscheinen rigoroser als im Westen. Das gilt für die kurzzeitig 1945 in Sachsen verwirklichte Schaffung eines als „Volksgericht" konstituierten außerordentlichen Gerichts zur Aburteilung politischer Verbrechen. Es gilt ebenso für den Entwurf des früheren Reichsjustizministers und 1945 zum Präsidenten der Deutschen Justizverwaltung berufenen *Schiffer*, Taten „aus nazistischer Gesinnung" zu ahnden und zu diesem Zweck das Rückwirkungsverbot ausdrücklich beiseite zu setzen.[29]

---

[27] Zur Begründung des unbedingten Vorsatzes bei der Rechtsbeugung BGH, Entscheidungen in Strafsachen [BGHSt] 10, 295, 298 sowie zur Anwendung der Kategorien von Täterschaft und Teilnahme auf NS-Taten BGHSt 8, 393, 397 f.; zur Kritik nur *Hoffmann*, S. 285, *Greve*, S. 186. Zur Annahme „gesetzlichen Unrechts" im Sinne der *Radbruchschen* Formel etwa das Urteil des BGH im *Huppenkothen*-Prozeß v. 12. 2. 1952 (Justiz und NS-Verbrechen, Bd. 13, Nr. 420, S. 325, 331 f.), weiter BGHSt 2, 234, 237; 3, 357, 362 (weitergeführt für DDR-Regierungskriminalität in BGHSt 40, 272, 276); BGH, NJW 1968, 1339, 1340 stellt im *Rehse*-Prozeß ausschließlich auf die normative Lage ab, die Richter seien auch damals nach § 1 GVG unabhängig gewesen.

[28] Zur Ahndung im OLG-Bezirk Celle *Rüping*, Staatsanwälte S. 79; für die Britische Zone *Broszat*, Vierteljahrshefte für Zeitgeschichte [VjZ] 1981, 516 ff., *Laage*, Kritische Justiz [KJ] 1989, 429 ff.

[29] *Meyer-Seitz*, S. 25, 23.

Im Osten herrscht von Anfang an eine andere Haltung zu normativen Vorgaben, die sich einer auch politisch wirkungsvollen Ahndung in den Weg stellen können. Rechtlichen Bedenken aus dem Westen hält der damalige Vizepräsident der DJV und spätere Generalstaatsanwalt der DDR *Melsheimer* auf dem letzten gemeinsamen Juristentag 1947 in Konstanz entgegen, das Gesetz, das die Verurteilung der Kriegsverbrecher fordere, sei seit Jahrtausenden geschrieben „in der Brust jedes anständigen Menschen"; in der Ostzone gebe es kein Problem mit der Anwendung des KRG, man habe dort „losgelegt". Für die angegriffene Position kontert *Güde*: „Wir möchten nicht, daß losgeschlagen wird. Wir möchten, daß Recht gesprochen wird. Das KRG 10 ist für uns kein Stock, sondern Recht".[30]

Seit 1946 werden Verfahren nach dem KRG in Einzelfällen von der SMAD auf deutsche Stellen übertragen, wobei Zwangssterilisationen als Anwendungsfall besondere Regelungen erfahren.[31] Als Beispiel für die Frühzeit der Ahndung verurteilt das Schwurgericht Dresden 1947 Ärzte im „Euthanasie-Prozess" wegen massenhafter Tötung von Kranken in Heilanstalten, hält das KRG als Ausnahmestrafrecht ohne weiteres für gültig und untersagt den Angeklagten die Berufung auf Normen, die den „für die gesamte Menschheit gültigen Grundsätzen der Humanität" widersprochen hätten. Dass es zu einem öffentlichen Verfahren kommt, beruht andererseits nur auf der ursprünglichen Annahme der SMAD, auch russische Zwangsarbeiter und Kriegsgefangene seien in sächsischen Anstalten getötet worden.[32]

Da sich das Interesse der Sowjetischen Besatzungsmacht darauf konzentriert, Taten, die sich gegen ihre Belange richten, durch eigene Militärtribunale zu ahnden, verzeichnet die Statistik bis Ende 1947 nur 518 Verurteilungen nach dem KRG.[33] Bereits in diesem Zusammenhang reduziert sich der Antifaschismus entgegen der Legende um seine grundlegende politische Bedeutung, wie sie dem Deutungsmonopol der KPD entspringt,[34] auf einen Antikommunismus.

Umso bemerkenswerter erscheint der methodische Weg, den die Praxis bei der Ahndung nach dem KRG Nr. 10 teilweise in der ausdrücklichen Konzeption eines Feindstrafrechts unter Berufung auf den Kampf gegen den Faschismus beschreitet. Als Vorkämpfer der fortschrittlichen Stoßrichtung versteht sich das OLG Dresden. Wie sich der Strafsenat über traditionelle Grenzen der Strafrechtsprechung mit ihrer Orientierung am Gesetz hinwegsetzt, bleibt in dieser Zuspitzung singulär.

Wegen des ersichtlich verbrecherischen Charakters der NS-Herrschaft wird dem Täter die Berufung auf die damalige Rechtslage versagt, wenn er z. B. einen jugendlichen Plünderer getötet oder einen „Arbeitsbummelanten" denunziert hat.[35] In der subjektiven Seite des Humanitätsverbrechens schneidet das Gericht Tätern „im Interesse energischer Ahndung" die Berufung auf einen Irrtum oder auf fehlendes Unrechtsbewusstsein ab,[36] wie es generell auch „im Dienste der Wahrung der Menschlichkeit eine gewisse Beherztheit" bei der Ahndung fordert und daher eine Berufung auf Notstand ausschließt.[37] Schließlich erscheint die Strafzumessung, damals ein Vorstoß in Neuland, revisibel, um auf die entscheidende „politische Schuld" angemessen reagieren zu können.[38]

Neben dem von vornherein als Strafnorm konzipierten KRG Nr. 10 steht die Kontrollratsdirektive Nr. 38, um weniger kriminelle Handlungen als vielmehr politisches Fehlverhalten zu sühnen. Die Direktive legitimiert in der Amerikanischen und Französischen Zone Spruchkammern zur politischen Säuberung, in der Britischen Zone Entnazifizierungsausschüsse. Nur in der Sowjetischen Zone wird sie

---

[30] Bericht über die Diskussion in Deutsche Rechtszeitschrift [DRZ] 1947, 231, 232.
[31] Z. B. bestraft die Verordnung für Brandenburg v. 10. 7. 1946 in § 1 beteiligte Richter und Ärzte mit Zuchthaus bis zu 10 Jahren (Verordnungsblatt der Provinzialverwaltung 1946, 179).
[32] Urteil v. 7. 7. 1947 bei *Hohmann*, S. 383, 422 f.; zum Anlass für die SMAD dort S. 3 und zum rechtsstaatlichen Charakter des Verfahrens *Wentker*, KJ 2002, 65.
[33] Zur Statistik sowie zur nicht überzeugenden Kritik der SMAD an der Ahndung *Meyer-Seitz*, S. 50, 48.
[34] Zum theoretischen Anspruch des Antifaschismus z. B. Befehl der SMAD Nr. 35 (Landesregierung Sachsen, Gesetze 1948, 134) und zur Entlarvung als Legende der von *Agethen* herausgegebene Sammelband; Belege zur Deutung der Ursachen und Erscheinungsform des Faschismus durch die KPD bei *Wolgast*, S. 29 ff.
[35] OLG Dresden, NJ 1947, 108, NJ 1948, 86, 87 und NJ 1948, 171 betr. eine Anzeige gegen eine Antifaschistin.
[36] OLG Dresden, JR 1948, 166, 167 sowie zur „naturrechtlichen" Rechtswidrigkeit einer Denunziation NJ 1948, 25 f.
[37] OLG Dresden, NJ 1947, 139.
[38] OLG Dresden, NJ 1948, 56, 26; dazu *Meyer-Seitz*, S. 108 f.

darüber hinaus als eigentliche Strafnorm gewertet und macht Strafgerichte für Aburteilungen zuständig.[39] Als Beispiele betrifft dies die Ankündigung, die als Befreier gekommenen Russen angreifen zu wollen, damit eine strafbare Propaganda für Nationalsozialismus und Militarismus, und ebenso die antisemitisch begründete Scheidung von der jüdischen Ehefrau, indem das erotische Motiv einen politischen Gehalt bekommt.[40]

3.2. Politische Justiz auf Grundlage des Befehls Nr. 201

Wenn die SMAD mit dem Befehl Nr. 201 von 1947 die Kontrollratsdirektive Nr. 38 für ihren Machtbereich umsetzt, schafft sie in Wirklichkeit – jetzt unter ihrer maßgeblichen Lenkung – ein Sonderverfahren politischer Justiz. Scheinbar noch in der Tradition, NS-Taten zu ahnden und Kriegsverbrecher nach ihrer Schuld zu bestrafen (vgl. unter Nr. 3 und 7 des Befehls) wird unter dem Vorwand, die Wiederkehr des Faschismus zu verhindern, nach sowjetischem Vorbild ein schlagkräftiges Verfahren geschaffen, um Angriffe auf den Kommunismus zu unterdrücken. Kennzeichen sind unter anderem die automatisch eintretende Haft (Ausführungsbestimmung 3, Nr. 7), die beherrschende Stellung der Polizei, die als Ergebnis ihrer Ermittlungen selbst die Anklageschrift verfasst (Nr. 9a) sowie die gezielte Inszenierung öffentlicher Hauptverhandlungen als Schauprozesse.[41] Höhepunkt und Abschluss bilden die Scheinverfahren der wiederholt behandelten „Waldheimer Prozesse" in vollständiger Abhängigkeit von der Regie der Partei.[42]

Die DDR übernimmt aus dem KRG Nr. 10 in ihr StGB von 1968 die bis zuletzt geltenden Bestimmungen über Verbrechen gegen die Menschlichkeit, über Kriegsverbrechen und ebenso den Ausschluss eines Befehlsnotstandes (§§ 91, 93, 95).[43] Dass sie das „Machbare" unternommen habe, um die Vergangenheit durch „ehrliche antifaschistische Prozesse" zu bewältigen, kann ebenso wenig überzeugen wie die Sichtweise, die Ahndung auf Grund des Befehls Nr. 201 der SMAD könne Vorbildfunktion auch für den Westen beanspruchen.[44]

Stattdessen folgen Selektion und Durchführung von Verfahren den politischen Vorgaben, den Kampf gegen den Neofaschismus im Westen in einen Kampf für den Kommunismus zu verwandeln und die Bundesrepublik in Misskredit zu bringen. Das zeigt sich z. B. an der Behandlung von Denunziationen zum Nachteil von Antifaschisten, von Justizverbrechen im besetzten Osteuropa wie an der Propagandaaktion des Obersten Gerichts, den Staatssekretär im Bundeskanzleramt *Globke* in Abwesenheit zu lebenslangem Zuchthaus zu verurteilen, weil er sich durch seine maßgebliche Beteiligung an verbrecherischen Normativakten „außerhalb der humanitären Prinzipien der zivilisierten Menschheit" gestellt habe.[45] Konsequent konzentriert sich in der DDR die Anerkennung als „Opfer des

---

[39] Text in Zentralverordnungsblatt [ZVOBl] SBZ 1947, 203 ff.; zur Praxis *Meyer-Seitz*, S. 155 ff., für die Britische Zone, wobei der Charakter einer Strafnorm offen bleibt, *Erdsiek*, DRZ 1947, 55 und Bekanntmachung des Oberlandesgerichtspräsidenten Celle, Hannoversche Rechtspflege 1946, 145, 146.

[40] OLG Gera, RegBl Thür. 1948 II, 131, OLG Dresden, NJ 1948, 88 f., zur Anwendung der Direktive in einem Denunziationsfall Bezirksgericht [BG] Neubrandenburg v. 22. 8. 1955 (DDR-Justiz und NS-Verbrechen, Bd. 3, Nr. 1102, S. 649 ff.).

[41] Text in ZVOBl SBZ 1947, 185 f. mit Ausführungsbestimmung 3, 188 ff.; zur Praxis in einem „rechtsfreien Raum" *Meyer-Seitz*, S. 236 ff., *Wentker*, KJ 2002, 67.

[42] Dazu in diesem Zusammenhang *Meyer-Seitz*, S. 232 ff. sowie der von *Haase* herausgegebene Sammelband.

[43] StGB v. 12. 1. 1968 in der Fassung v. 14. 12. 1988 (GBl DDR I 1989, 33 ff.).

[44] Entgegen *Wieland*, damals Staatsanwalt beim Generalstaatsanwalt der DDR, auf einer Tagung 1987 (nach dem Bericht von *Bücker*, Demokratie und Recht [DuR] 1987, 19); zur Wertung der Verfahren nach dem Befehl Nr. 201 *Meyer-Seitz*, S. 348.

[45] Zu Denunziationsfällen BG Neubrandenburg (wie Fn. 40) a.a.O. S. 651, BG Leipzig v. 30. 11. 1960 betr. die Denunziation von Antifaschisten (DDR-Justiz und NS-Verbrechen, Bd. 3, Nr. 1084, S. 415, 417), zur Verurteilung eines Staatsanwalts beim Sondergericht Graudenz (Polen) Stadtgericht Berlin v. 19. 10. 1981 (DDR-Justiz, Bd. 1, 2002, Nr. 1011, S. 315, 325), zum Prozeß gegen *Globke* OG v. 23. 7. 1963 (DDR-Justiz, Bd. 3, Nr. 1068, S. 75, 113); zur Analyse *Wentker*, KJ 2002, 71 f., 76, *Weinke*, S. 68 ff., 76 ff., 141 ff.

Faschismus" auf antifaschistischen Widerstand und schließt andere Opfergruppen, auch jüdische Verfolgte, aus.[46]

4. Recht und Politik in der Auseinandersetzung mit der Vergangenheit: ein Vergleich

Ost und West sehen sich nach 1945 vor die Aufgabe gestellt, auf der zunächst gemeinsamen Basis des KRG Nr. 10 politische Verantwortlichkeit in einem justiziellen Verfahren zu ermitteln und festzustellen. Die unterschiedlichen politischen Rahmenbedingungen in den Zonen führen zu unterschiedlichen Wegen der Justiz, ihren Auftrag zu erfüllen. Gemeinsam sind die mageren Resultate aller Versuche, nach Systemwechseln individuelle Schuld für Taten unter dem überwundenen System zuzumessen.

Mit der Einbindung der beiden deutschen Staaten in die gegensätzlichen politischen Lager zur Zeit des Kalten Krieges verliert das ursprüngliche Ziel juristischer Auseinandersetzung mit der Vergangenheit seine Überzeugungskraft und dann seine Existenzberechtigung. Das gilt nicht nur für die DDR, sondern auch die Bundesrepublik: die bis heute existente Strafvorschrift der politischen Verdächtigung (§ 241a StGB) wird 1951 geschaffen, um Verbrechen gegen die Menschlichkeit in der SBZ zu ahnden, auf Verfolgung unter der Herrschaft der SED bezogen und konsequent auch für Taten innerhalb der DDR angenommen.[47]

So liegen Kontinuitäten in der Instrumentalisierung des Rechts für politische Zwecke. Keine der beiden Alternativen nach 1945, sich der Vergangenheit in einer „Nacht der langen Messer" zu entledigen, die Schuldige wie Unschuldige getroffen hätte, oder auf dem Weg über Gerichtsverfahren, in denen die eigentliche politische Schuld nicht geahndet werden konnte, vermag zu überzeugen. Daher bleibt nur das Resümee: „Es gibt keine Bewältigung. Aber es gibt das bewusste Leben mit dem, was die Vergangenheit gegenwärtig an Fragen und Emotionen auslöst."[48]

Tabellarische Aufstellung ausgewählter Quellen bzgl. der Aufarbeitung der NS-Verbrechen in West- und Ostdeutschland nach 1945
A. Die Verfahren wegen NS-Verbrechen bis Ende 1950

Anzahl der Verfahren	Verurteilte Personen	Kriegsverbrecher	Hauptbeschuldigte	Belastete	Minderbelastete
201	8.321	5	2.045	5.638	273
	→100%	→0,06%	→24,5%	→67,7%	→3,28%
Strafzumessung bis Sept. 1950	1-3 Jahre Gefängnis 3.660	Gefängnis höher als 3 Jahre 699	Unter einem Jahr Freiheitsstrafe 1.674	Anderweitige Maßnahmen zur Sühnung 1.218	

Quelle: *Meyer-Seitz*, S. 143, 319.

---

[46] *Hölscher*, S. 226 ff.
[47] Zu Einzelheiten *Rüping*, Historical Social Research 26 (2001) Nr. 2/3, 38 f.
[48] *Schlink*, S. 153 und zur Situation nach 1945 S. 30 f.; zum Problem einer „Vergangenheitsbewältigung durch Strafverfahren" der gleichnamige Sammelband von *Weber/Steinbach* (1984) sowie der weitere von *König/Kohlsbruck/Wöll* (1988), wobei Einzeluntersuchungen (Nachweise bei *Sérant*, *Rüping*, Staatsanwälte S. 90 und für Italien *Woller*) zum Vergleich der Systeme einladen.

B. Urteile deutscher Gerichte innerhalb der sowjetischen als auch der westlichen Besatzungszone wegen Denunziantentums während der NS-Zeit

Besatzungszone	Urteile wg. Denunziantentums	Verfahren bis zum Außerkrafttreten des KRG 10 1951	Tatsächliche Verurteilungen im Zeitraum bis 1951
Westliche Besatzungszone	518 (bis Aug. 1947)	7.674	603
Sowjetische Besatzungszone	17.175 (bis Jan. 1947)	2.426	

Quelle: *Meyer-Seitz*, S. 50, 319.

C. Die Ahndung von NS-Verbrechen vor west- und ostdeutschen Gerichten

Ahndung in der BRD	Gesamte Verfahren	Verurteilte	Ermittlungsverfahren	Angeklagte	Frei-Spruch /Einstellung etc.	Rechtskräftig verurteilt	Lebenslängliche Freiheitsstrafe	Todesstrafe
bis 1958		267 in Nds. 703 in NRW 485 in Rhl-Pf.	4.954					
bis 1965 bzw. 1967	61.000 bis 1965	6.000 bis 1962 bzw. 6300 bis 1965	gegen 30.000 Personen bis 1969, 15.500 eingestellt	12.846	4027	5426	123 bis 31.12.1970	12 bis 1949 1949 abgeschafft
bis 1975		6.257	72.874			6.257		
bis 12.1985		6.479 6.494 bis 1996	- gegen 90.912 Personen - 4.853 erledigte Verfahren - 1996 noch 4.002 anhängig		83.140 →mehr als 90%			
Ab 31.12. 1985	noch 1.302 Verfahren anhängig bis 1996 106.496							
Ahndung in der DDR bis 1964		12.807					271	118 bis 1964 127 bis 1976
bis 1971		12.825						

Quellen: *Kröger, Ulrich*; Die Ahndung der NS-Verbrechen vor westdeutschen Gerichten, Diss. phil. Hamburg 1973, S. 53 f., 315, BT- Drucks. 10/6566 v. 21.11.1986, S. 3, 4, *Blanke* (Hg.), Die juristische Aufarbeitung des Unrechts-Staats, 1998, S. 295, *Greve*, S. 79, 398, *Wieland, Günther*, Die Ahndung von NS-Verbrechen in Ostdeutschland 1945 bis 1990, NJ 1991, 49 f., *Freudiger*, S. 31, 32, 33.

D. Gesamtübersicht über die Eckdaten der Verfahrenszahl, der Einstellungen und Verurteilungen in Ost- und Westdeutschland

	Verfahren	Einstellungen	Tatsächlich Verurteilte
Westdeutschland	106.496 1945 bis 1996	83.140 1945 bis 1996	6.494 1945 bis 1996
Ostdeutschland	-	-	12.881 1945 bis 1989

Quellen: *Freudiger*, S. 31-33, *Wieland, Günther*, Die Ahndung von NS-Verbrechen in Ostdeutschland 1945 bis 1990, NJ 1991, 49 f.

Hinrich Rüping

Between Law and Politics: The Prosecution of NS Criminals in the Two German States after 1945

After the IMT trial against the major Nazi war criminals in Nuremberg, it was Control Council Law No. 10, which provided the legal framework to prosecute crimes against humanity before national courts. The high moral expectations associated with this law could, however, never be fulfilled, neither in the Western nor in the Soviet Occupied Zones. In the Western Zones, it was mainly due to specific fundamental issues as illustrated by examples in the British Occupied Zone. The hope for a new beginning, both politically and with new judicial personnel failed because of former Nazi judges and civil servants, who rejected a resolute prosecution of NS criminals and considered Control Council Law No. 10 as an interference by the Allied Powers in Germany's internal affairs. At the same time as Denazification measures receded, a state of mind among the general public (East or West) refused to grapple with the Nazi legacy and showed an increased form of solidarity with the perpetrators.

In the Soviet Occupied Zone, at first the prosecution of NS-criminals appeared to be more resolute, as would be expected from the constantly emphasised anti-fascist attitude in the East. But rather soon these trials were misused by the Socialist Party (Sozialistische Einheitspartei – SED) to persecute opponents of the Socialist regime while claiming the trials were necessary to prevent a revival of Fascism.

Hence, neither in the East nor in the West enough was done to be able to speak of a comprehensive legal attempt to come to terms with National Socialist injustice.

Rebecca Wittmann

The Normalization of Nazi Crime in Postwar West German Trials

Although this conference has already shown us that both East and West Germany made attempts to deal with the Nazi past through the law, it is surprising to many to discover that in West-Germany an enormous number of Nazi defendants were brought to trial – over 6000, in fact. A great many more – about 100,000 – were investigated but never tried. They sat in court accused not of crimes against humanity, but regular murder, as defined by the German penal code in 1871. In this paper I would like to shed light on these trials, and particularly on the extraordinary difficulty prosecutors had in bringing former Nazis to trial, in getting them convicted, and then finally, in ensuring they served their time. Focusing on the period between 1960 and 1980, I will argue that there was a massive divide between the young and eager prosecutors and the older, more conservative, largely former Nazi judiciary. There is no clear cut picture of complicit jurists; in nearly every state in West-Germany there was evidence of a young, committed, and probing prosecution. But they had to work within a system that was defined by the generation of jurists who came before them and who still wielded extraordinary influence over the West German judicial system; in some states, 100% of Nazi judges had maintained or returned to their former posts. These judges sent a message to the public – through their interpretation of the laws – that the Nazi past was being dealt with properly. They developed the notion of the middleman as neutral, and therefore innocent; this representation of Nazi crime, reinforced time and again by trial verdicts, created a society in which there was no public will to deal with the Nazi past through the law, to punish Nazism fully. This is what Joachim Perels has called a normalization of the NS system from the elites. We have discussed here the legacy of Nuremberg, and I would like to explore the legacy of West German trials of Nazi perpetrators. Through an examination of the legal reforms in the 1960s, and by giving examples from 3 major investigations – The Auschwitz Trial, the RSHA investigation, and the Majdanek trial – I will show that changes to the law made it easier and easier for those who had the most power in the Nazi regime – the desktop murderers – to go free or escape trial, and in the end really only the most sadistic – and exceptional – of Nazi criminals, usually camp guards, were tried and convicted of murder. On the one hand, there were thousands of trials. On the other, the continuities in the jurist's personnel made the sentences and interpretation of the laws extremely favourable to the defendants.

In the past decade there has been an explosion of historical research about West German confrontation with the past; in their work, most historians point to an undeniable presence of former Nazis in all parts of public life: in the civil service, the government, academia, the press, and most especially, in the judiciary. According to Ingo Müller, despite the best efforts of the Allies to purge the judicial system of its Nazi members, this proved to be virtually impossible as it would have left the justice system without any functionaries. Therefore, during the reconstruction period of 1945-49, the Allies made more and more exceptions to their initial rule that anyone who had even nominally participated in the Hitler regime should lose their jobs. First, all those who had retired or been fired in 1933 were called back; next, anyone who joined the party after 1937 was given a clean slate; then, for every judge with a clean record, a tainted judge could be hired; and finally, all judges who had gone through the flimsy denazification process could be brought back. This meant that by 1949, for example, 93% of court officers in Westphalia had been affiliated with the Nazi party, in Schweinfurt 100%, and in the enormous state of Bavaria, 81% of judges were former Nazis.[1]

Astonishingly, as Joachim Perels has pointed out, historians have not been willing to make the connection between the jurists and the laws that they generated, arguing that the new laws of the Federal Republic were basically purged of any antidemocratic tendencies from the Nazi period. However, upon examination, it becomes clear that legal theorists actively introduced road blocks to the

---

[1] Ingo Müller, HITLER'S JUSTICE: THE COURTS OF THE THIRD REICH, 202-203, trans. by Deborah Lucas Schneider (Cambridge, MA: Harvard University Press, 1992).

conviction of former Nazis. This was an intentional act so that jurists could shield themselves from conviction as lawmakers and law enforcers during the Nazi period. The best proof of the lasting heritage of Nazi law on postwar law is the fact that there were only 2 judgments of lawyers or judges who instituted and carried out the Nazi program, and both were before 1949 (by the West German courts).[2] There was certainly a connection between the jurists creating and interpreting the law, and the law itself, as we shall see.

The perception of Nazi crime was very different in the early postwar period; according to Norbert Frei, during the Adenauer years there was "A widespread desire to see the purging project's circle of 'victims' narrowed to the smallest possible group of 'main offenders' corresponded to an increasingly prevalent theory limiting the blame for Nazi crimes to the narrow band of top Nazi leaders."[3] This perception of Nazi crime – that only the top leaders were guilty – was slowly eroded after the Nuremberg trials, whereby the prosecution of desktop murderers lost its urgency in West German courts and in turn in public consciousness as well. Tired of victor's justice, swayed by the perception that all the major Nazis had already been tried by the Allies, and wanting to move forward instead of continuing to shamefully look back, West Germans were ready and willing to accept the changes enforced by the judiciary which led to a very different kind of Nazi convict and, I would argue, a distorted perception of Nazi crime.

We have already seen that in 1949 the newly formed Justice Ministry rejected the incorporation of the international criminal charges into the West German penal code. What did this mean for Nazi trials? There were serious problems with using the West German penal code to prosecute crimes of mass murder. Prosecutors had to adhere to rigid interpretations of the murder statute and subjective definitions of perpetrators and accomplices that, in the end, condemned only those who had gone above and beyond ordered acts of murder. In effect, those who carried out the state-ordered genocide were convicted only – if they were convicted at all – as accomplices to murder; and after 1968, not even accomplices could be tried.

The reasons for this lie in the law that was used. First, the murder charge stipulated that the prosecution prove the subjective inner motivation of the defendant. Elements of intent in murder included sadism, lust for murder, sexual drive for killing, treachery, malicious intent, cruelty, and finally, base motives (which the post-war German courts defined as race-hatred for the Nazi trials). Second, the distinction between perpetrator and accomplice in the penal code specified that the primary perpetrator must show individual initiative and knowledge of the illegality of the act. This meant that the state had to prove beyond doubt that each defendant had acted individually and with personal initiative in order to be convicted of murder. In the case of bureaucratic or political entities of the Third Reich, where physical acts of murder did not take place, the only unquestioned perpetrators of murder – those with base motives – were the people who dreamt up the Final Solution: Hitler, Himmler, and Heydrich. All other state functionaries, no matter their rank, could (and usually did) claim that they were simply doing their jobs. Third, the statute of limitations prevented the courts from using the manslaughter charge, as any crimes with possible sentences of 15 years or less were statute barred 15 years after the crimes had been committed; in the case of Nazi crimes, this meant that manslaughter could not be charged after 1960. This made the state's task much more difficult as it was limited to proving murder or the far lesser charge of aiding and abetting.

The law is of course not inanimate, and there were important discussions within judicial circles that led to the constant redefining of the murder charge, the manslaughter charge, and the definition of perpetrator and accomplice. Specifically, in the 1950s and 1960s legal theoreticians fell into different camps regarding the definition of perpetration as an objective or subjective act. The objective definition saw the perpetrator as the one who pulled the trigger, and was generally considered too narrow a

---

[2] Joachim Perels, DAS JURISTISCHE ERBE DES "DRITTEN REICHES": BESCHÄDIGUNGEN DER DEMOKRATISCHEN RECHTSORDNUNG, 23 (Frankfurt am Main: Campus, 1999).

[3] Norbert Frei, ADENAUER'S GERMANY AND THE NAZI PAST: THE POLITICS OF AMNESTY AND INTEGRATION, 304, trans. by Joel Golb (New York: Columbia University Press, 2002).

definition. Ultimately more conservative scholars, and in turn the German High Court of Appeals, adopted an entirely subjective definition, which determined perpetration entirely by the presence of will, regardless of whether the defendant physically committed the act – thus allowing for the possibility that the person who committed the act not be guilty of murder. This was the standard adopted by most judges in Nazi trials, before 1968. In addition to this, German criminal law requires, uniquely, that the prosecution prove that the defendant possesses "Knowledge of the illegality of the act;" this means that, unlike Anglo-American law where it is assumed that citizens know the law, defendants can use the excuse that they did not know they were committing a crime. This leads, in Nazi trials, to a perverse result: the more a defendant claimed that he believed in and identified with the Nazi world view, the less likely he was to be convicted. In turn, the more doubt a defendant showed about the morality and legality of Nazi laws – i.e. the more remorse he showed – the more likely he was to be convicted.[4]

And so it was already difficult for prosecutors to convict anyone who did not show individual initiative. This becomes most obvious if we take the Auschwitz Trial as our example. This enormous and very public trial – probably the first and sadly the last major Nazi trial that either the newspapers or the public really cared about – had on its defendant's stand 20 Auschwitz perpetrators, from a kapo to two adjutants to the commander, representing a cross section of all the possible criminals at Auschwitz. The trial began in 1963, lasted two years and produced tens of thousands of pages of files, made use of over 400 witnesses, and made history in that it brought to light for the first time what Auschwitz really was, to a willfully uninformed German public. The prosecution was led by Fritz Bauer, attorney general of the state of Hesse, and his determined and dedicated state attorneys were very much devoted to putting the whole of the "Auschwitz complex" on trial. This was not to be, however. Because of the incredibly narrow interpretation of the laws, and because of a very conservative (and former Nazi) judge, only the most sadistic of defendants, who had murdered people drunkenly, wantonly, and without official orders, was convicted of perpetrating murder and sentenced to life in prison. The rest, the vast majority, got mild sentences that usually were reduced to time served at the end of the trial. They remained ordinary citizens who were basically decent and reluctant in their tasks, while the others, the sadists and "excess perpetrators," were monsters and animals and devils that in no way bore resemblance to the majority of society. The murder of millions in the gas chambers, or the creation and execution of laws that allowed for the murder of Jews, the handicapped and political prisoners, became a lesser crime, with a lighter sentence, than the murder of one person without orders from superiors. The German public learned to chastise and denounce the sadistic "excess perpetrators" of Auschwitz, and to forgive the order-followers whose crimes of complicity were never the true focus of the trial, the law, or the extensive press coverage from which people obtained their information about the trial and, I would argue, about Auschwitz.

The prosecution of desktop murderers and Nazi lawmakers became even more difficult with the introduction of an extremely controversial amendment to the criminal code in 1968. Arguably introduced in order to reduce the sentences of defendants convicted of traffic offenses, jurists began already in 1955, to discuss ways to amend the law and introduce more "humane" and "democratic" sentences for less serious offences. According to the old version of § 50 of the German Criminal Code, anyone who was convicted as an accomplice to a crime was subject to the same penalty as the perpetrator. This meant, ostensibly, that a Nazi defendant who was convicted as an accomplice to murder could be sentenced to life in prison. In 1968 the amendment to § 50 Section 2 Criminal Code was finally introduced:[5] Now, in order to sentence a convicted accomplice to life in prison, the prosecution had to show that the defendant possessed "base motives." Otherwise, the defendant had to be given a shorter sentence, which would be 15 years or less. You will recall that base motives, in the case of Nazi trials, meant racial hatred or anti-Semitism. In the case of desktop murderers – civil servants, bureaucrats, and jurists – base motives were virtually impossible to prove, as defendants could

---
[4] Perels, DAS JURISTISCHE ERBE, 27.
[5] This provision is to be found in § 28 Section 1 of the revised German Criminal Code.

always claim that they had no anti-Semitic motivation. So prosecutors were faced with the daunting task of somehow showing that a pen-pusher or a lawmaker had hatred as an inner motivation. If the prosecution could not do this, then the defendant had to be given a milder sentence. The problem here lies with the statute of limitations, mentioned earlier: all crimes carrying sentences of 15 years or less were no longer prosecutable after 1960, because they became statute barred 15 years after the crime was committed. Effectively, this amendment meant that no one could even be tried as an accomplice after 1968 unless their base motives can be proven.[6]

Historians and legal scholars disagree about the motivation behind the introduction of this amendment; Adalbert Rückerl, Joachim Perels, and Michael Wildt all argue that the change was brought in without regard for what it would mean for Nazi trials, and its disastrous effect on the prosecution of Nazis was the result of an oversight; Ingo Müller, a much more ferocious and often one-sided critic of the German legal system, contends that it was introduced precisely to make it impossible to try Nazi desktop killers. Müller may be imputing too much importance to the Nazi past for jurists in the 1960s, who had long repressed their own complicity and were much more preoccupied with immediate crimes against the state (not the least of which were the increasingly violent student protests of the New Left); however, it is also striking that the main jurist heading the commission for criminal law reform during the 1960s was a man named Eduard Dreher. Dreher was the former prosecutor at the "Sondergericht" –special courts set up by the Nazis that regularly sentenced people to death for the smallest of infractions – in Innsbruch during the Nazi period, and is presumed to be responsible for the execution of hundreds of innocent people.[7] He represents perhaps the most powerful of many former Nazi jurists in the postwar period, as he wrote the most widely used commentary on the criminal law during the 1960s. Surely Dreher's past, and that of so many jurists making reforms to the legal system, played a role their worldview.

Whatever the case, this amendment had devastating effects for a massive investigation that was going on in Berlin at this time. The Berlin Court of Appeal, in conjunction with East Berlin prosecutors, had opened an investigation of the high command of the RSHA, or Main Reich Security Office. Located in Berlin, the RSHA was responsible – on the bureaucratic level – for all aspects of state security, including the police, the Gestapo, the Einsatzgruppen, and the concentration camp administration. About 7,000 people worked for the RSHA (which was headed by Reinhard Heydrich), and so the prosecution had their work cut out for them. Prosecutors had high hopes for the investigation and divided the proposed proceedings into three groups: those who had been involved in the implementation of the Final Solution, those involved in the administration of the Einsatzgruppen and development of the mobile gas vans, and those in charge of POWs, slave labourers, political prisoners, and their eventual murder.[8] Unlike the Auschwitz trial, where prosecutors tried to prove the individual crimes of particularly sadistic people, in Berlin the state attorneys were faced with having to explain the whole world of the RSHA, its structure and hierarchy, as well as the acts of individuals. The RSHA was a political entity, and was therefore even more difficult to investigate than the world of hands-on murder that was Auschwitz. The main perpetrators in the RSHA were not physically involved killers; their motives would be very difficult to prove. And yet, before 1968, prosecutors were not concerned with this problem, and felt extremely optimistic about the prospects for this colossal trial.

When the 1968 amendment was introduced, the RSHA investigation fell apart. Defense lawyers for former Nazis who had already been indicted were the first to recognize this new loophole as advantageous for their clients. For example, in 1969, Otto Bovensiepen, former head of Gestapo in Berlin, found himself on the defendant's bench. He wrote to Werner Best, former head of Office 1 of the RSHA, later Reich's representative in Denmark, who after the war was one of the most active jurists in the largely successful movement to amnesty former Nazi civil servants. Best judiciously observed to

---

[6] Michael Wildt, GENERATION DES UNBEDINGTEN, 831 (Hamburg: HIS Verlag, 2002).
[7] See Norbert Podewin, ed., BRAUNBUCH: KRIEGS- UND NAZIVERBRECHER IN DER BUNDESREPUBLIK UND IN BERLIN (WEST), 128 (Berlin: Edition Ost, 3rd ed., 2002).
[8] Wildt, GENERATION, 825.

Bovensiepen, "if our interpretation is correct, nobody accused of aiding and abetting can be punished anymore, if base motives cannot be established."[9] This proved to be correct, and Bovensiepen's trial was suspended.

What is ironic about this loophole for Nazi defendants is that in practice, no defendant who was convicted of aiding and abetting was ever actually subjected to a life sentence – only perpetrators were. Mostly, judges were already lenient with accomplices, as is evidenced in the Auschwitz trial, where only six defendants were sentenced to life imprisonment (all for perpetrating murder), three were acquitted, and the eleven remaining all were convicted to less than 15 years as accomplices. So even though judges could mete out harsher punishment, in the case of Nazi defendants, they rarely did. After 1968, however, they no longer had to face this dilemma, as no prosecutor would be given the green light to indict anyone as an accomplice if his base motives were not provable.

The Berlin prosecution office scrambled to stop their investigation from falling apart; they argued, cleverly, that the base motives of racial hatred or anti-Semitism should, logically, apply to the crime itself, and not to the person who committed the crime. After all, the mass extermination of the Jews was clearly a crime with base motives and therefore all Nazi crimes should be exempt from the amendment that was otherwise being used to deal with individual crimes like traffic offenses. The Federal Court of Appeal, however, denied this motion and insisted that base motives had to be shown in the defendant himself, not just in his crime.[10]

The devastating result of this ruling was that the plan to try the whole administrative complex responsible for the mass murder of the Jews fell apart on a technicality. The prosecution's efforts to have the amendment overturned in the case of Nazi trials were wasted. According to Adalbert Rückerl, one of the harshest critics of the conservative legal community during the 1960s, "[i]t is too late…. The small men, who shot, will continue to be caught through their treachery or cruelty. But the big men, who didn't commit the murder with their own hands, can only be prosecuted for aiding and abetting murder with base motives. Since today it's virtually impossible to prove that they possessed these motives, they benefit the most."[11]

My preliminary research into later trials in West Germany confirms Rückerl's dismal projection. After 1968, only four RSHA members were ever tried, and only for crimes related to base motives and hands on murder. The largest trial of the 1970s, the Majdanek trial in Düsseldorf, was a trial of camp guards who were mainly charged with crimes of excess and gruesome cruelty. The trial lasted from 1975 to 1981 and was plagued by legal limitations: endless debates about eradicating the statute of limitations on murder; aging and dying defendants; survivors whose memories were fading and who were more and more reluctant to appear at yet another trial for fear of being branded "professional witnesses"; a disinterested press; and a public who felt that these senior citizens who had lived productive lives for the last 30 years were harmless in comparison to the "state enemies" on trial in Stuttgart at the same time, namely the Baader-Meinhof gang. After all, the Nazi defendants had been acting in the name of the state, had not shown individual initiative except in the most extreme and rare of cases, and had, for the last 30 years, been represented in legal language as mainly functionaries of a perverted state. Demonstrative of the priorities of the conservative judiciary and the frightened public was the fact that while over 100,000 Nazi were investigated and 6,000 tried in the postwar period, over 125,000 Communists were investigated and 6,500 tried.[12] By 1975, when the Stammheim trial of the RAF terrorists was in full swing, the state and the public was no longer very interested in the distant crimes of a few old men and women, despite the fact that their atrocities far outweighed the crimes of the RAF in magnitude. In the end, at the Majdanek trial, the press showed up only at the very beginning and the very end; while the Auschwitz trial had over 20,000 visitors and 900 press articles, the

---

[9] Werner Best in Ulrich Herbert, BEST. BIOGRAPHISCHE STUDIEN ÜBER RADIKALISMUS, WELTANSCHAUUNG UND VERNUNFT 1903-1989, 510 (Bonn: Dietz Verlag, 1996).
[10] Wildt, GENERATION, 834.
[11] Adalbert Rückerl in Der Spiegel, Jan 1 1969, in Wildt, GENERATION, 835.
[12] Müller, HITLER'S JUSTICE, 223.

Düsseldorf courtroom was mainly empty except for a new kind of spectator, the right wing extremist. Of the 15 indicted defendants, nine were men and six were women; the focus was entirely on the sadistic actions especially of the female guards, whose excessive cruelty was especially shocking and sensational because of their gender. Otherwise, the trial dragged on interminably; four defendants were acquitted at an early phase because of lack of evidence. Only 1 defendant, known as "Bloody Brigitte," was sentence to life in prison, and of the rest no one received more than twelve years.

Scholars have recently turned to the question of continuity between Nazi and postwar Germany. A handful of new books have demonstrated that there was a general willful failure among early postwar German journalists, scholars, politicians, and jurists, to earnestly face up to their roles in perpetuating the racist, persecutory policies of the Third Reich. Challenging the protestations of almost all professionals that they remained outside of Nazism as silent resistors, scholars of postwar Germany now agree that the most influential members of society readily complied with the demands of the regime, pursued professional programs that would please the state, and by their denial allowed the foundations of the new West German state to be built – at least partially – on the remnants of the Nazi political and social structure. However, just as these continuities are being recognized, there is still not enough examination of the continuities in the law, the legal personnel, and what this meant not only for Nazi trials but for the public perception of Nazi criminality. We know of course that the most heinous of Nazi laws were repealed: the Nuremberg laws, arbitrary death sentences, persecution on racial and religious grounds, or based on sexuality or mental capacity; all were removed from the penal code during the reconstruction period. However, many changes made in the Nazi period remained. Legal precedents set during the Nazi period, often by the same judges who would later work on Nazi trials, were judged wholly appropriate in the postwar setting. A good example of this continuity in legal interpretation was the so called "bathtub-case" of 1940[13], which went a long way towards defining perpetrator motivation: in a case where a woman drowned her sister's baby, it was determined that the mother of the child had willed the act and that therefore the actual killer of the child, the sister, was not guilty of perpetrating but aiding and abetting murder due to her lack of will. Precisely this interpretation was used again and again in postwar Nazi trials, in which hands on killers without individual initiative were convicted as accomplices.[14] Finally, it is astounding to note that the Volksgerichtshof was only recognized as a state operated instrument of terror in 1985, and the summary dismissal of all criminal judgments issued during the Nazi period occurred finally in 1998.[15] Such delays in historical justice are not surprising, considering the constituency of the postwar judiciary. The desire of former Nazi judges to protect themselves from possible prosecution led to a deeply conservative postwar legal system, whereby Nazi perpetrators, although valiantly pursued by state attorneys, mostly escaped punishment, and the public absorbed a largely distorted image of the Nazi criminal. The law was not the setting in which Germans would come to recognize the wholesale complicity of an entire generation: this would occur through left wing agitation, mainstream television broadcasts (like the Holocaust in 1979), and earnest historical inquiry which helped to erode prevailing myths about Nazi crime.

---

[13] Reports of the Reichsgericht in Criminal Matters, 74 RGSt 84.
[14] Rebecca Wittmann, BEYOND JUSTICE: THE AUSCHWITZ TRIAL, 39 (Cambridge, MA: Harvard University Press, 2005).
[15] Perels, DAS JURISTISCHE ERBE, 37.

Rebecca Wittmann

Die Normalisierung von NS-Kriegsverbrechen in den Nachkriegs-Prozessen der Bundesrepublik Deutschland

Dieser Beitrag beschäftigt sich mit den außerordentlichen Schwierigkeiten, mit denen Staatsanwälte bei der Anklage, Verurteilung und schließlich auch Vollstreckung der Strafe gegen frühere Nazis zu kämpfen hatten. Der Schwerpunkt liegt auf der Zeit zwischen 1960 und 1980. Es zeigt sich, dass es einen erheblichen Konflikt zwischen jungen und engagierten Staatsanwälten einerseits und der älteren und konservativen, oft vormals nationalsozialistischen Richterschaft andererseits gab. Die Strafverfolgung fand in einem System statt, das von einer Juristengeneration definiert und beherrscht wurde, die aus der Nazi-Richterschaft stammte; in manchen Bundesstaaten wurden 100% der Nazi-Richter übernommen oder wieder in ihre früheren Posten eingesetzt. Diese Richter riefen in der Öffentlichkeit durch ihre Gesetzesinterpretation den Eindruck hervor, dass die nationalsozialistische Vergangenheit sorgfältig aufgearbeitet wurde. Dazu wurde die Vorstellung von einem neutralen und daher unschuldigen Mittelsmann kreiert. Es war gerade diese immer wieder in Urteilen bestätigte Vorstellung vom Nazi-Verbrechen, die eine Stimmung entstehen ließ, in der kein öffentliches Interesse mehr an der rechtlichen Aufarbeitung der nationalsozialistischen Vergangenheit und der konsequenten Bestrafung von Nazismus bestand. Eine Analyse der Rechtsreformen der 1960er Jahre und die exemplarische Darstellung des Auschwitz-Prozesses, der RSHA-Ermittlungen und des Majdanek-Verfahrens werden zeigen, dass es den mächtigsten Vertretern des Nazi-Regimes, den Schreibtischtätern, durch diese Reformen immer leichter gemacht wurde, der Strafverfolgung zu entgehen. Am Ende waren es ausschließlich die sadistischen Nazi-Verbrecher, zumeist Lageraufseher, die angeklagt und wegen Mordes verurteilt wurden. Einerseits gab es Tausende von Verfahren; andererseits wurden gerade auf Grund der personellen Kontinuität in der Richterschaft die Gesetze sehr täterfreundlich ausgelegt und angewendet.

Gabriel Bach

Genocide (Holocaust) Trials in Israel

The acts of genocide perpetrated by Nazi Germany against the Jewish people, usually referred to as the Holocaust, had been mention by international tribunals before the Eichmann trial, and was referred to in the judgment of the International Military Tribunal rendered on October 1, 1946 at the Nuremberg trials. But it was only during the trial of Adolf Eichmann, held in Jerusalem in 1961 and 1962 that the Holocaust was presented in all its stages and in all its aspects, with the focus fully centred on this terrifying and unspeakable crime.

Eichmann was, during the whole period of the perpetration of the Holocaust, including the period of World War II, the head of the Jewish Department of the German Secret Police, the Gestapo, and as such he was in charge of all the steps taken to implement the demonic plan for the so-called "Final Solution of the Jewish Problem". After the War, he managed to escape to Argentina and lived there under an assumed name. In May 1960, he was abducted by Israeli agents, taken to Israel, and handed over to the Israeli Police. When, on May 23, 1960, the Prime Minister of Israel, David Ben-Gurion, announced in the Knesset (the Israeli Parliament); "Adolf Eichmann is under arrest in Israel and will shortly be put on trial," the impact throughout the country was electrifying. The police investigation, placed in the hands of a special unit established for this purpose, took about nine months to complete. I was at that time the Deputy State Attorney of Israel, and was asked by the Minister of Justice to be in charge of the investigation, and later to appear in the trial, together with the Attorney General of Israel, the late Gideon Hausner.

The crimes against the Jewish people with which the accused was charged consisted of all aspects of the persecution of millions of Jews, including their arrest and imprisonment in concentration camps, their deportation to extermination camps, their murder, and the theft of their property. The charges did not, however, confine themselves to Eichmann's participation in crimes against the Jewish people; they also included crimes against other peoples, such as the mass expulsions of Poles and Slovenes; the seizure, deportation to extermination camps, and murder of tens of thousands of Gypsies; and the deportation and murder of Borne one hundred children from the village of Lidice in Czechoslovakia, in revenge for the killing of Reinhard Heydrich, the notorious head of the SS Secret Police.

All the counts related to offences under the "Nazis and Nazi Collaborators (Punishment) law" of 1950, a law passed in Israel about ten years before Eichmann was caught and placed on trial. He was defended by two German lawyers of his and his family's choice. The leading defence counsel was Dr. Servatius, one of the advocates who had appeared for some of the defendants at the Nuremberg trials. Until the arrival of his lawyers in Israel, I was in fact the only contact Eichmann had with the outside world, and whenever he wanted to discuss any of his personal problems, he was brought before me.

I intend to share with you, during my lecture, some of my reminiscences and personal experiences at the early stages of the investigation and later during the trial itself.

By means of more than one hundred witnesses and some sixteen hundred documents – many of them bearing Eichmann's own signature – the prosecution presented to the court the full account of all the events related to the Holocaust of European Jewry, or the "Final Solution of the Jewish question", as the Nazis called it. In great detail the prosecution furnished the court with proof of the persecution of the Jews in all its stages: the anti-Jewish legislation; the incitement among the general population of hostility to the Jewish minority; the plunder of Jewish property; and, worst of all, the searching out of Jews in every European country under German occupation and in the satellite states, their imprisonment, under inhuman conditions, in ghettos and concentration camps, where they were harassed and humiliated, and finally, their systematic mass murder, with the aim of completely destroying the Jewish people. The prosecution demonstrated what had happened to the Jews of Europe, proved the personal involvement of Eichmann, as IV B 4 (the Gestapo section for Jewish affairs) the heinous operation.

It is rather surprising to me that, even now years after the trial, in many countries, and amongst members of the legal profession, the opinion prevails that the Israeli Court was not competent to try

Eichmann, that it was not a proper forum to do so. Needless to say, these arguments were brought forward by the defence during the trial itself.

First, we hear time and time again that Eichmann was charged on legislation – the above-mentioned Law against Nazi Collaborators – which was passed in 1950, i.e. after the commission of the alleged offences, and that it constituted ex post facto, retroactive legislation. This argument was rejected by the Court. The administration of justice is generally outraged by a person being charged with an act that was not illegal at the time it was committed. With regard to the offences that were being charged in this case, however, it was quite different: the Nazi and Nazi Collaborators Law (like similar laws enacted by various countries after the war) did not introduce new legal norms; all it did was to make it possible to bring persons to trial for committing offences that were known to be against the law at the time they were committed, in every place in the world, including Germany. Those persons themselves were well aware of the illegality of their acts. Owing to the illegal regime that was in power in Nazi Germany, the perpetrators of these crimes were not punished for them at the time; but it was precisely the sense of natural justice that called for the establishment of a forum where the persons suspected of these crimes could be brought to trial.

We can already read in the famous Blackstone Commentaries that "ex post facto laws were objectionable when, after an action indifferent in itself is committed, the legislator then, for the first time declares it to have been a crime and inflicts a punishment upon the person who committed it. Here it was impossible that the party could foresee that an action, innocent when it was done, should afterwards be converted to guilt by a subsequent law. He had, therefore, no cause to abstain from it and all punishment for not abstaining mast, in consequence, be cruel and unjust." As Kelsen wrote in his book. Peace Through Law 87 (1944): "There is no rule of general customary law forbidding the enactment of norms with retrospective force, so-called ex post facto laws." Julius Stone wrote similarly in Legal Controls of International Conflict 869 (1959): "There is clearly no principle of international law embodying the maxim against retroactivity of criminal law."

The Nazi regime created an arbitrary vacuum in the legal sphere, and justice demanded the institution of a procedure which would make the punishment of the offenders possible. As a matter of fact, the same argument, as to the retroactivity of the law and the charter under which they were charged, was advanced by the defendants in the Nuremberg trials, and was rejected by the International Military Tribunal.

A second charge against the propriety of the trial relates to the fact that the crimes in question were committed outside the territory of Israel and before the State was created. This fact was of no significance in the case. War crimes, crimes of genocide, and crimes against humanity have been recognized by the international community as universal crimes and every sovereign nation has the right – indeed, the duty – to bring the perpetrators of such crimes to justice. Such crimes have been likened to piracy and the slave trade. It has been held that a pirate is an outlaw, the enemy of all mankind (*a hostis humani generis*), whom every nation may in the interest of all capture and punish. The Israeli Law of 1960 under which Eichmann was indicted certainly did not contravene any concept of International Law.

A third argument that is sometimes put forward may be formulated as follows: How is it that an Israeli court, representing the Jewish people, which is the victim of the crimes attributed to the Nazis in general, and to Eichmann in particular, can sit in judgment over this defendant? Is this not contrary to the principle of justice, especially the principle that justice should manifestly be seen to be done? Intrinsically, there is of course no merit to this argument. The purpose and normative meaning of criminal law everywhere are that the society against whom a crime has been committed should defend itself against the offender, punish him, and try as far as possible to prevent similar offences in the future. Society – generally the sovereign state, through its Courts and other organs – is organized in part to prevent the injured victims of a crime or his family from taking the law into their own hands and punishing the offender in revenge by themselves. This is accomplished by ensuring that the offender is suitably punished by the organs of society as a whole. The fact that a crime is perpetrated against a certain society does not detract from the moral or other right of the courts of that society to judge a person who has tried to harm its interests. On the contention in the Eichmann trial that the judges of an Israeli court might be influenced by their emotions, the Court stated: "When a judge sits on a bench, he does not cease to be flesh and blood with human emotions; but he is bidden by law to overcome these emotions. If this were not so, no judge would ever be qualified to sit in judgment in a criminal case evoking strong disgust, such as a case of treason or murder or some other heinous offence." As Professor Helen Silving wrote in her article "In Re Eichmann: A Dilemma of Law and Morality" (1961) 55 Am. J. Int. L. 307: "Israel's special fitness to try Eichmann results from her mission as a haven of the survivors of the National Socialist Regime and as a country created for the very purpose that crimes against 'Jews' as a group may never be repeated". The fact that this was also the most convenient court, with the accused, the major part of the witnesses and the relevant documentation present in Israel, only added weight to these considerations.

In this context, I should like to relate an experience I had during the trial. A professor from a European University asked me about the propriety of the victim trying the offender. Before I could reply, however, he asked me to show him a copy of the indictment against Eichmann. After perusing it, he expressed his surprise that we had charged Eichmann, inter alias, also with the murder of Polish, non-Jewish citizens, the Czech children of Lidice, Russian Commissars and Gypsies. "What have these people to do with you?" he asked, "why do you not leave the adjudication of those matters to the Polish, Czech, and Russian courts?" I responded as follows: "Just five minutes ago, you said that according to your opinion, a nation or a people against whom offences have been committed should not be permitted to judge the perpetrators; but here you seem to find no fault with Polish, Czech, or Russian judges trying the accused for offences committed against their people. What therefore, is the basis for your opposition and shock when a court of a Jewish State tries a person for crimes committed against the Jewish People?" The learned professor had the decency to blush. He answered in all embarrassment that he would have to think about the matter again, and that off-hand, he could not justify his earlier distinction.

I shall never forget the first moment of the trial, when those judges came into the courtroom – with the Israeli flag and the Israeli emblem behind them – and this man, whose central purpose in life had been to bring about the total destruction of the Jewish People, jumped to attention before the Court. I felt at this moment, more than on any previous occasion, the importance and the impact of the creation of the State of Israel. Any state would have been a proper forum to try one accused of crimes against humanity. However, it was not only proper, but an act of justice, that this man should be tried – with all his rights scrupulously protected – before this Court.

A fourth challenge is sometimes voiced, regarding the abduction of Eichmann from Argentina by Israeli agents. It is argued that the abduction was an illegal act, which automatically invalidated the legality of his detention and the right to bring him to trial. When this point was raised by the defense, it was rejected; the judges held, basing themselves mainly on English and American judgments that the method whereby a suspected criminal is brought to trial is of no concern to the court that tries him. In the English case of *Ex parte* Elliott, 1 All E.R. 373, decided in 1949, the Court heard an application of a British soldier for *Habeas Corpus*. He had deserted from his unit in 1946, was arrested in Belgium in 1948 by two members of the British Military Police, accompanied by two Belgian gendarmes, and brought back to England where he was in custody awaiting trial by court martial for desertion. The applicant's counsel argued that the British authorities in Belgium had no power to arrest his client and that he was arrested contrary to Belgian law. The Lord Chief Justice dismissed the application and said, in his judgment, that if a person was arrested abroad and brought before a court in this country, charged with an offence which this court had jurisdiction to try, the court had no power to go into the question of the circumstances in which he may have been brought here. In this case, he said, the court martial had jurisdiction to deal with the applicant and the High Court would not interfere. Similar decisions were handed down by English Courts in other cases, and American Courts adhered to the same principle. The issue arose frequently in the United States, where suspects were apprehended in one State and brought forcibly into a neighbouring State where the suspect was wanted. The U.S. Supreme Court has consistently held that the illegal apprehension of such suspects was no bar to their being tried in the state to which they had been transferred. (See Ker v. Illinois, 199 U.S. 436.)

The contention that Eichmann as head of the Jewish Department of the Gestapo merely carried but "acts of State" and obeyed orders, and was therefore absolved from criminal responsibility was also rejected by the Israeli Judges. The idea that only the State could be held responsible for crimes of this nature and that its agents in performing such acts will go unpunished is untenable. As Professor Lauterpacht wrote: "The fact that the offender acts on behalf of the State is irrelevant. He is bound personally by rules of international law whether he is acting in his personal capacity, in order to satisfy private greed or lust, or as an organ of the State" (63 Law Quarterly Review 442-3 [1948]). This principle was applied in Article 7 of the Charter of the International Military Tribunal at Nuremberg (hereafter "I.M.T."), which declared: "The official position of the Defendants, whether as heads of State, or responsible officials in government departments, shall not be considered as freeing them from responsibility or mitigating punishment". The Israeli Courts therefore only reiterated what had already been laid down by experts on International Law and by the Charter of the I.M.T.

The same applies to the argument, that the accused merely carried out orders received from his superiors. The orders Eichmann received were manifestly unlawful orders, and as such could not establish a legal defence. Art. 8 of the Charter of the I.M.T. stipulates: "The fact that the defendant acted pursuant to orders of his government or of a superior shall not free him from responsibility, but may be considered in mitigation of punishment if the Tribunal determines that justice so requires". The possibility mentioned in the latter part of the article did not arise in the case of Adolf Eichmann, as the evidence clearly indicated that this accused performed his duty with a fanatical and obsessive zeal, which even surpassed that of his superiors, and became completely identified with the purposes of the criminal scheme, the carrying out of which was entrusted to him.

Now as to the trial itself: As I mentioned before, I shall try to let you share in some of my impressions and feelings during the traumatic experience of conducting the investigation into these matters, preparing the indictment and appearing as prosecutor, at the trial before the court of first instance and later at the appeal.

These reminiscences are difficult to reduce to words in cold print. I shall prefer to describe them orally. But some general remarks can also be included in this written outline. Strange as it may sound, at first it was rather difficult to find witnesses who were prepared to testify at the trial. The reason was, that most of the survivors of the Holocaust were reluctant to relate their terrible experiences because for all these many years they had attempted to suppress these memories and pass them into the realm of the subconscious. However, once we succeeded in persuading these people to testify, then one could not stop them and they wanted to tell all the details about what happened to their families and friends. We did not want the trial to go on for too long and therefore we often asked these witnesses to limit their testimony to a particular point that was not covered by the already existing evidence. Often we felt that we would be unable to curb the evidence of these witnesses, and with a heavy heart we had to strike some of them off the list of witnesses for this reason.

I am often asked: what sort of a man was this Eichmann, and "what made him tick?" As a general rule I object to defining any person, including an offender, by "pigeon holing" him as being only a murderer, a robot, a bureaucrat, a sadist or, in genocide cases – a typical Nazi. People are never only something. They are a combination of things and they pass through stages of development. This holds true for Eichmann as well. It seems that when he, as member of the SS, became an expert on Jewish affairs, and the head of the relevant department in the German Secret Police, the Gestapo, he did this because he thought that this would help him in his career. Then he carried out, efficiently, all parts of the plan concerning the persecution of the Jews and later their annihilation. Then you could trace through the oral evidence and the official documents how this gradually became a form of obsession with him. Maybe it is psychologically understandable, that when for years you deal only with the mass murder of innocent people, men, women and children, then you must either go mad, or by same defence mechanism become obsessed with the idea that yon do something which is justified and worth while. One can see how towards the end of the war he became even more fanatical than people like Hitler and Himmler. That does not mean that he was as guilty as those leaders. They were the originators of this hideous scheme, and as such the persons mainly responsible. But for them there were other areas of interest, like the political and military situation. For Hitler those problems were not less important than killing every last Jew, perhaps even more so. But for Eichmann, all his endeavours centred on this one purpose – the liquidation of the Jewish race. Here we had proof, that during the final stages of the war, when the German generals on the Eastern Front were clamouring for reinforcements and for ammunition, Eichmann, by all kind of tricks and trickery, managed to get priority for his death-trains, knowing that by doing so he was actually harming Germany's war-effort. He told his friends: "I know the war is lost, but I am still going to win my war". And then he went to Auschwitz in order to increase the rate of killings from 10,000 a day to 12,000.

When in the final stages of the war, in 1944, Admiral Horthy, the leader of Hungary, who fought on the side of Germany and Italy, wanted to make separate peace with the Allies, because he thought the war was lost, Hitler came to Budapest to meet him, in order to persuade him, by threats and promises, to continue the fight together with Germany. Horthy finally agreed, but attached some conditions to this, one of those being that the German should permit 8,000 Jewish families from Budapest to go to a neutral country, to Switzerland. Hitler agreed, because Hungary's continued support was more important for him then those 8,000 families. In this connection we found in the archives of the German Foreign Ministry a telegram from the German Ambassador, Von Veesenmayer to the Foreign Minister, Von Ribbentropp. He described in this telegram the agreement between Hitler and Horthy, including the condition concerning the 8,000 Jewish families, and then he added: "I have however to inform you, that the local representative of the SS Obersturmbannführer Eichmannn is very upset about this arrangement. He fears that those 8,000 families might constitute important biological material. They may come to Palestine and may cause there a new cell for the rebuilding of the Jewish race". Von Veesenmayer added that Eichmann has therefore given instructions to increase the speed of the deportation of the Jews from Budapest in such a way that until the visas can be arranged for the entry of these people to Switzerland no 8,000 Jewish families will remain in Budapest. Herr Eichmann was faced with a decision of the Führer Adolf Hitler himself, and he succeeded in thwarting even this order, because he wanted to prevent the saving of a small number of Jews. Documents like that and similar pieces of evidence helped us to explode the "small cog" theory of the defence, according to which Eichmann was an officer of relatively low rank who merely had to obey orders.

One of the striking features was his pre-occupation with killing Jewish children. Proof of that we found in the notes of the last commander of the Auschwitz camp, named Rudolf Höss. He was sentenced to death by a Polish Court and hanged in 1951, e.g. ten years before Eichmann's trial. Before be was executed he wrote his auto-biography, which was published in a book called "The last Commander of Auschwitz". There Höss relates how they sometimes carried out actions in which they put 1,000 children to death on one day. He described how some of the children begged for their lives, and wrote that when he had to push those children into the gas chambers, then his knees often got a bit shaky. But after that he adds: "I did however always feel ashamed of this weakness of mine after I talked to Obersturmbannführer Adolf Eichmann. Eichmann explained to me that it was especially the children who have to be killed first, because where was the logic in killing a generation of older people and leaving alive a generation of young people, who can be possible avengers of their parents and can constitute a new biological cell for the re-emerging of this people". This was not devoid of some macabre logic, but I must admit that when ten minutes after reading this I had to sit opposite Eichmann, who wanted to discuss something with me, it was not without difficulty to preserve a poker face.

During his testimony in Court, Eichmann said that he thought that this was the worst crime ever committed in history. I was asked by the Judges and others whether I believed that he honestly meant that. This point could have been important for the sentence which was finally imposed on him. My reply was that this was mere lip-service on his part. When asked, "what was the basis for this contention", my answer was as follows: "I could imagine that even a man like that could theoretically change his mind. His eyes could have been opened between the end of the war in 1945 and 1961 when his trial took place. But here we had proof that in 1956, when he was in Argentina, he was visited by a Dutch Fascist journalist called Sassen, who recorded his talks with him on tape. The idea was that he would publish this after Eichmann death. This was a kind of insurance policy for his family. When

Eichmann was caught the journalist sold this material to "Life" magazine and the transcripts, with Eichmann's handwritten corrections, were obtained by us and submitted to the Court as evidence. There Eichmann enthusiastically describes the trains that pulled towards the death camps almost in lyrical terms ("It was marvellous to watch these trains"). And when he was asked by Sassen whether he ever felt remorse and whether he was ever sorry for what he had done, he replied: "Yes, I am sorry for one thing, and that is that I was not hard enough, that I did not fight those damned interventionists enough, and now you see the result: The creation of the State of Israel and the re-emergence of the Jewish people there!" And I added, that if Eichmann said this in 1956, eleven years after the end of the war, and now in 1961, five years later, when he is fighting for his life, he suddenly speaks about "the worst crime in history", I think we are justified in being sceptical about the sincerity of such a remark.

Eichmann was sentenced to death, his appeal was dismissed by the Supreme Court, by a panel of five justices, and he was executed in 1962. He is the only person who was ever sentenced to death and executed in Israel.

The Eichmann trial achieved the following main purposes:

(a) First and foremost it was an act of real justice, that this man should be tried and convicted by an Israeli court, and received the severest punishment known in progressive and democratic societies.

(b) This trial triggered a chain-reaction, mainly in Germany, of investigation into Nazi crimes and the conduct of trials against those responsible for the murders and crimes against humanity committed. Also before that there were prosecutors and teachers in Germany, who wanted to put the guilty persons on trial and teach the facts about the Holocaust in the schools. But they never got the necessary encouragement and budgets to carry out their intentions. Those who were Nazis certainly did not want such r activities, but even those who did not approve of the Nazis and the persecution of the Jews did not want to be questioned by their children about those happenings and about the reasons for their not doing anything in opposition. But after the Eichmann trial, which brought the relevant facts into all the homes for hours every day, no one dared to stand any more in the way of the above mentioned prosecutors and teachers.

(c) Until the trial many people in Israel and especially our youth did not want to hear about the Holocaust. They felt in a way, ashamed about what had happened. A young Israeli can understand that you can be killed in action, or even lose a military battle. But he could not grasp how it was possible for millions of people to be slaughtered without offering active resistance.

As one of the by-products of this trial we proved that there was absolutely no ground for this feeling of shame. We depicted the devilish systems and plans that managed to mislead the victims and made resistance impossible. We showed how all victim of whatever I nationality or race were lured to their death by cruel designs and by trickery and deception. And, on the contrary, we also showed that when it became absolutely clear to the Jewish people that death was intended for all of them by the Nazis as the inevitable result, then there came the famous uprisings like the one in the Warsaw Ghetto, where the young Jewish defenders fought with incredible bravery until death, and this was a basis for respect towards the victims and for national pride. As a result, our young people in Israel began to take a greater interest in the history of European Jewry, in Jewish European culture, and in all details of the Holocaust.

I shall briefly mention some facts about the other internationally known genocide trial in Israel which took place recently – the trial against the Ukrainian citizen Demanjuk, who was extradited by the American judicial authorities to Israel, and charged before an Israeli Court for the mass-murder of Jews in the gas-chambers of the notorious Treblinka death-camp. It was alleged that the accused was the person known by the inmates of the camp as "Ivan the Terrible", on account of the unspeakable cruelty and sadism that he exhibited towards the victims.

Demanjuk was identified as being "Ivan the Terrible" by a number of survivors of Treblinka. His own evidence, denying all guilt, and denying that he was the Ivan of Treblinka, was rejected as not credible by the judges of the District Court. He was found guilty, and sentenced to death. The accused appealed to the Supreme Court. Actually I should have been one of the judges who sat on the panel of the Court of Appeal in this case, but I asked to be excused. I felt that I was so much associated with the prosecution in the Eichmann case that it would be undesirable for me to sit in judgment in this case. While the hearing of the appeal was in progress, the following development arose. As a result of the revolutionary changes in the Soviet Union, archives of documents from World War two were opened to the public for inspection. The Israeli State attorney, who acted as prosecutor in this case, visited the former Soviet Union and detected a large amount of written testimony by German and Ukrainian members of the SS, who were no longer alive. These people testified that they were active in Treblinka, and that there was a Ukrainian guard, known for his cruelty, who was called "Ivan the Terrible". Those witnesses also mentioned that the surname of this Ivan was Marchenko. This in itself did not sound very significant, because Demanjuk, when entering the U.S., had stated that his mother's maiden name was Marchenko. The assumption was therefore that Demanjuk and Marchenko were the same person. But then it transpired that those SS guardsmen had identified this Marchenko by pointing at a picture which was not that of Demanjuk. This gave rise a serious doubt about the real identity of "Ivan the Terrible". The Israeli State Attorney passed this information on to the defence attorney and also handed it to the Court of Appeal as additional evidence. This was clearly his duty, but I think it certainly goes to the credit of the prosecutor that he unhesitatingly did so, although he was of the opinion, that the accused had been active in one of the death camps. There was also no doubt that he was trained in a special camp to act as guard in one of the death camps.

On account of this new evidence, the Court of Appeal decided to give the accused the benefit of the doubt and acquitted him. Later a petition was brought to the Supreme Court, sitting as the High Court of Justice, in which we were asked to instruct the Attorney General to charge Demanjuk with criminal activities in another death camp, the Sobibor camp. There was same proof that the accused had been sent to that camp, I myself sat as one of the judges in this case. We rejected the petition. I based this decision on the following grounds:

First of all, the evidence connecting the accused with the Sobibor camp appeared very flimsy, and I did not see any justification for interfering with the decision of the Attorney General, who also based his conclusions in part an this ground. And secondly, as the prosecutor in the original case had asked the Court of Appeal to find Demanjuk guilty, in the alternative, for his activities in Sobibor, he had in fact been in jeopardy of such a conviction, and charging him again on account of those allegations would have put him in what is known as "double jeopardy", and this is not permitted under our accepted Rules.

Demanjuk was therefore freed, and he has returned to his home in America. Many people in Israel were very unhappy with this result. Of course it is rather disturbing to think that a man who voluntarily underwent training for such bestial crimes and probably was active in this field escaped punishment. But I think the rule of law and the reputation of our judicial system as one where justice is scrupulously applied are more important than that.

Let me close with one final remark as to the effect of these trials: People everywhere have to realize, that if they take part in crimes of genocide or in the commission of unspeakable crimes against humanity, then as long as they live they have to face the apprehension of being apprehended, interrogated, charged before a court of justice and punished for those acts.

Gabriel Bach

Völkermord (Holocaust)-Verfahren in Israel

Richter Bach berichtet über verschiedene Strafverfahren gegen Nazi-Verbrecher in Israel, insbesondere aber über den Prozess gegen Adolf Eichmann, bei dem er selbst neben dem Generalstaatsanwalt Gideon Hausner als Ankläger auftrat.

Eichmann war vor und während des 2. Weltkriegs Leiter der Abteilung für Judenfragen innerhalb der Geheimen Staatspolizei (Gestapo) der Nazis. In dieser Eigenschaft war er maßgeblich an der Planung und Durchführung der „Endlösung der Judenfrage" beteiligt. Nach dem Krieg gelang es ihm, sich nach Argentinien abzusetzen, wo er im Mai 1960 vom israelischen Geheimdienst aufgespürt und nach Israel verbracht wurde. In dem Strafverfahren gegen Eichmann stand der Holocaust wie in keinem anderen Verfahren davor im Mittelpunkt. Mit mehr als 100 Zeugen und über 1.600 Dokumenten wies die Staatsanwaltschaft die Mitwirkung Eichmanns an der systematischen Zerstörung des Europäischen Judentums nach.

Trotz dieser eindeutigen Beweislage wurde eine Reihe von rechtlichen Argumenten vorgebracht und die Legitimität des Strafverfahrens in Zweifel gezogen. So wurde auf das Erfordernis des nullum crimen sine lege-Satzes hingewiesen, die Zuständigkeit des Gerichts abgelehnt, weil der Staat Israel zum Zeitpunkt der Verbrechen noch nicht existierte, die Verhaftung Eichmanns für unrechtmäßig erachtet und die Unabhängigkeit der israelischen Justiz angezweifelt. All diese Punkte erwiesen sich als haltlos und wurden vom Strafgericht und später im Berufungsverfahren vom Obersten Gericht in Jerusalem widerlegt.

Bach berichtet davon, dass es zunächst nicht einfach war, Zeugen zur Aussage im Prozess gegen Eichmann zu bewegen. Das lag wohl vor allem daran, dass diese Menschen seit Ende der Naziherrschaft versuchten, ihre furchtbaren Erlebnisse zu verdrängen und zu vergessen. Eichmann selbst war wohl zunächst ein auf Karriere besessener Nazi, der sich den Machthabern anbiedern wollte. Später hat er sich allerdings das Ziel der Vernichtung der Juden zu Eigen gemacht. Er wollte wenigstens „seinen Krieg gewinnen", wenn schon der große Krieg verloren ging. Reuige Aussagen Eichmanns im Prozess sind für Bach unglaubwürdig, da er aus seinem Antisemitismus auch später keinen Hehl machte, was sich vor allem aus den mit dem holländischen Journalisten und ehemaligen SS-Offizier Willem Sassen zwischen 1956 und 1959 aufgenommenen Interviews ergibt. Eichmann wurde zum Tode verurteilt.

Der Eichmann-Prozess und andere Verfahren in Israel sollen ein Signal senden, dass kein Völkermörder sich sicher fühlen, sondern zu jeder Zeit, überall auf der Welt aufgegriffen und für seine grausamen Taten zur Verantwortung gezogen werden kann.

Greg James

A Summary of the History of Nazi War Crime Trials in Australia

Acknowledgements

I am grateful for the kind assistance of Mr Grant Niemann, of Flinders University, formerly Deputy Director of Public Prosecutions, my junior counsel in the Polyukhovich and Wagner prosecutions, later prosecution trial counsel at ICTY; His Honour Judge Michael David QC of the District Court of South Australia who acted for the accused and made available to me his paper on the defence perspective; Mr David Bevan of the Australian Broadcasting Commission, author of "A Case to Answer", Wakefield Press, South Australia 1994 in which he chronicled the prosecutions and particularly Mark Aarons, author of a number of valuable studies on the presence of war criminals in Australia, notably *War Criminals Welcome - Australia, a Sanctuary for Fugitive War Criminals since 1945* published by Black Inc, Melbourne 2001, which records the political history of the prosecutions.

This paper merely gives a summary overview of the proceedings brought against the three individuals to whom I refer from the point of view of a prosecutor. The prosecution of Polyukhovich has been the subject of a most detailed report by David Bevan in his text "A Case to Answer". That report was compiled both from the transcript and Mr Bevan's constant attendances at the committal and at the trial. The background and the more detailed political history underlying the investigations and prosecutions has been chronicled by Mr Mark Aarons in the book to which I have referred *War Criminals Welcome - Australia, a Sanctuary for Fugitive War Criminals since 1945*. I commend both of those to the researcher who might like to consider in far more detail that I can deal with in this paper the history and circumstances of the Australian Nazi war crimes prosecutions.

At the close of the Second World War the Australian government enacted the *War Crimes Act* 1945 to provide for the trial and punishment of war criminals. That Act provided for military courts for the trial of war crimes under military law, of persons who were at any time resident in Australia, in respect of war crimes, wherever committed. Military law so far as it related to field general courts martial was applied to the procedure of those courts. Persons convicted of such crimes were liable to the death penalty or any lesser penalty. After the disruption in Europe occasioned by the war Australia accepted a mass of immigrants. As is recorded in the text published by Mark Aarons to which I have referred in my acknowledgement, amongst those migrating to Australia were a number of persons who had been involved in their respective countries, in the commission of war crimes whether as principals themselves or in aid of Nazi occupying forces. In his book "War Criminals Welcome", Mark Aarons sets out in detail the political history of the amendment to the *War Crimes Act* 1945. The amended act prescribed for those arrested in Australia for war crimes and crimes against humanity as defined in that Act, a regime involving trials under Australian domestic criminal law in the courts of the States in which they resided in Australia.

That amendment had occurred because of a community awareness of the prospect that former Nazi war criminals were obtaining effective sanctuary in Australia which had been generated following Mark Aarons production of a television documentary put to air by the Australian Broadcasting Commission. Prior to that community awareness being aroused, there had been a number of Commonwealth police investigations that had identified persons reasonably suspected of having been such war criminals. In addition a number of reports had been received from the Soviet Union in particular, referring to such persons and in some cases seeking extradition.

Until that community awareness was aroused, the post war Australian coalition governments had refused to prosecute such persons, it being considered that the 1945 *War Crimes Act* was unsuitable and had refused extradition requests. However during the 1960's and 70's, various immigrants to Australia with a possible history of involvement in war crimes had been identified by investigators.

In 1979 the United States announced intensified efforts to deport accused war criminals from that country, and established the Office of Special Investigations to conduct enquiries. Simon Weisenthal and the Australian group, Research Services, had disclosed to appropriate Australian Security instrumentalities and various bureaucrats, persons who might be suspected of war crimes. In April 1985 the United States Justice Department drew attention to the lack of action against suspected Nazi war criminals in Australia. In May 1986 the documentary series to which I have referred "Nazi's in Australia" was broadcast on ABC Radio National. Following that in early June 1986, the newly elected Labor Government decided to hold an "informal inquiry into Nazi war criminals". A senior bureaucrat, Andrew Menzies was appointed to conduct a review of material relating to the entry of suspected war criminals into Australia. Much material was provided by Mr Aarons and other investigators to him. On 28 November 1986 he reported to the Hawke Government that it appeared that "it is more likely than not that a significant number of persons who committed serious war crimes in World War II entered Australia; certainly the likelihood of this is such that some action needs to be taken."

Notwithstanding that, in 1961 the then Attorney-General Barwick had announced that Australia had officially closed investigations into whether suspected war criminals had emigrated to Australia, the new government in 1987 determined to amend the 1945 *War Crimes Act* to provide for the new legislative regime to which I have referred and to set up investigatory and prosecution agencies. The purpose of the amendment was set out in the Act.

"WAR CRIMES ACT 1945
Reprinted as at 30 April 1990
An Act to provide for the Trial and Punishment of War Criminals

Preamble
WHEREAS:
(a) *concern has arisen that a significant number of persons who committed serious war crimes in Europe during World War II may since have entered Australia and became Australian citizens or residents;*
(b) *it is appropriate that persons accused of such war crimes be brought to trial in the ordinary criminal courts in Australia; and*
(c) *it is also essential in the interests of justice that persons so accused be given a fair trial with all the safeguards for accused persons in trials in those courts, having particular regard to matters such as the gravity of the allegations and the lapse of time since the alleged crimes."*

In February of 1987 the Special Investigations Unit within the Attorney-General's Department was set up to investigate and recommend possible prosecutions to the Director of Public Prosecutions. The Unit was headed by the late Robert Greenwood QC and Graham Blewitt, who later, after replacing Greenwood as the head of that Unit, on the cessation of Australian War Crimes prosecutions became the Deputy Prosecutor at the ICTY.

Mr Grant Niemann, one of the Deputy Directors and I were retained by the Director of Public Prosecutions to advise on and prosecute charges against persons referred to the Director by the Special Investigation Unit and in particular to prosecute the charges against Ivan Polyukhovich and Heinrich Wagner. A third person Mikolay Berezowsky was charged but the committing Magistrate did not commit him for trial. Legal aid was granted by the government to allow all three accused the highest level of legal representation.

Under the amended *War Crimes Act* the ambit of matters that might be brought before the Australian courts as war crimes was narrowly defined. The Act only applied to the War in Europe between 1 September 1939 and 8 May 1945. War crimes were defined as serious crimes as defined in section 6 having the further features required by section 7.

"Serious crimes
6. (1) *An act is a serious crime if it was done in a part of Australia and was, under the law when in force in that part, an offence, being:*
(a) *murder;*
(b) *manslaughter;*
(c) *causing grievous bodily harm;*

(d) wounding;
(e) rape;
(f) indecent assault;
(g) abduction, or procuring, for immoral purposes;
(h) an offence (in this paragraph called the "variant offence") that would be referred to in a preceding paragraph if that paragraph contained a reference to:
(i) a particular intention or state of mind on the offender's part; or
(ii) particular circumstances of aggravation; necessary to constitute the variant offence;
(j) an offence whose elements are substantially the same as the elements of an offence referred to in any of paragraphs (a) to (h), inclusive; or
(k) an offence of:
(i) attempting or conspiring to commit;
(ii) aiding, abetting, counselling or procuring the commission of; or
(iii) being, by act or omission, in any way, directly or indirectly, knowingly concerned in, or party to, the commission of; an offence referred to in any of paragraphs (a) to (j), inclusive.

(2) In determining for the purposes of subsection (1) whether or not an act was, under the law in force at a particular time in a part of Australia, an offence of a particular kind, regard shall be had to any defence under that law that could have been established in a proceeding for the offence.

(3) An act is a serious crime if:
(a) it was done at a particular time outside Australia; and
(b) the law in force at that time in some part of Australia was such that the act would, had it been done at that time in that part, be a serious crime by virtue of subsection (1).

(4) The deportation of a person to, or the internment of a person in, a death camp, a slave labour camp, or a place where persons are subjected to treatment similar to that undergone in a death camp or slave labour camp, is a serious crime.

(5) Each of the following is a serious crime:
(a) attempting or conspiring to deport or intern a person as mentioned in subsection (4);
(b) aiding, abetting, counselling or procuring the deportation or internment of a person as so mentioned;
(c) being, by act or omission, in any way, directly or indirectly, knowingly concerned in, or party to, the deportation or internment of a person as so mentioned.

(6) For the purposes of subsections (3), (4) and (5), the fact that the doing of an act was required or permitted by the law in force when and where the act was done shall be disregarded.

War crimes

7. (1) A serious crime is a war crime if it was committed:
(a) in the course of hostilities in a war;
(b) in the course of an occupation;
(c) in pursuing a policy associated with the conduct of a war or with an occupation; or
(d) on behalf of, or in the interests of, a power conducting a war or engaged in an occupation.

(2) For the purposes of subsection (1), a serious crime was not committed:
(a) in the course of hostilities in a war; OR
(b) in the course of an occupation;
merely because the serious crime had with the hostilities or occupation a connection (whether in time, in time and place, or otherwise) that was only incidental or remote.

(3) A serious crime is a war crime if it was:
(a) committed:
(i) in the course of political, racial or religious persecution; or
(ii) with intent to destroy in whole or in part a national, ethnic, racial or religious group, as such; and

(b) committed in the territory of a country when the country was involved in a war or when territory of the country was subject to an occupation.
(4) Two or more serious crimes together constitute a war crime if:
(a) they are of the same or a similar character ;
(b) they form, or are part of, a single transaction or event; and
(c) each of them is also a war crime by virtue of either or both of subsections (1) and (3)."

The Act provided that such crimes might be prosecuted whenever they had been committed. The Act provided similarly to the Nuremberg Charter that superior orders did not constitute a defence but that if the doing by the defendant of the relevant act was permitted by the laws, customs and usages of war and was not under international law a crime against humanity that would amount to a defence. The Act in addition limited the circumstances in which persons accused of war crimes might be extradited.

The intent of the Act was to provide a trial regime at least as fair as that for criminal trials generally in Australia, with special protections for the accused. On 25 January 1990 Ivan Polyukhovich was arrested and charged the following morning in the Adelaide Magistrates Court with a number of counts, including having been party to the murder of 24 people and having taken part in the mass killing of about 850 people in the village of Serniki, now located in modern Ukraine, formally in an area of the former Poland subject initially to Soviet-, and then later, to Nazi-occupation.

The following chronology is of assistance:

- **27 June 1990** after service on his lawyers of the mass of prosecution material, Polyukhovich withdrew consent for the committal proceedings to take evidence outside Australia.
- **29 July 1990**, Mr Polyukhovich shot himself, not fatally. His committal hearing had been set to begin the following morning.
- **3 September 1990** the High Court of Australia commenced hearing a challenge brought by him against the constitutional validity of the war crimes legislation. Pending the determination of that challenge, the proceedings against him were deferred.
- **14 August 1991** the High Court upheld substantially the validity of the war crimes legislation.
- **5 September 1991** Mikolay Berezowsky and Heinrich Wagner were charged with various war crimes.
- **28 October** the committal proceedings against Polyukhovich commenced and were resumed for two weeks in November. Thereafter they continued in March 1992 until on 5 June 1992 the Magistrate committed Polyukhovich for trial on charges of six murders, dismissing the balance of the charges. Notwithstanding and in accordance with Australian law, the Director of Public Prosecutions decided to charge Polyukhovich himself with involvement in the mass execution.
- **19 July 1992** the Magistrate held that there was insufficient evidence to warrant Berezowsky being put on trial.
- **22 December 1992** as a result of a pre-trial application in the Supreme Court of South Australia an attempt to have the proceedings against Polyukhovich permanently stayed as an abuse of process because of the long lapse of time since the events, was dismissed. Numerous other substantially unsuccessful similar applications were later made to stop the trial.
- The trial of Polyukhovich began on 18 March 1993 and three months later on 18 June 1993 he was acquitted of all charges.
- **10 December 1993** the Director of Public Prosecutions withdrew the proceedings against Heinrich Wagner due to his ill health.

It is useful to set out some history by way of background to the three cases. All related to allegations of war crimes committed in the European summers of 1942 and 1943 in various parts of Ukraine. In June of 1941 in Operation Barbarossa, Germany invaded Russia. The Ukraine was conquered very quickly. With and behind the German army special extermination squads operated killing the Jewish population. In 1942, in particular, a more systematic policy of extermination was implemented. All three of the cases involved similar techniques applied in particular areas to implement that policy. The local men were required to dig large pits outside a particular town or village to assist with the logistics of rounding up the Jewish inhabitants; they were marched to the pits and shot by a German execution squad. The locals were again enlisted to fill in the pit.

In all three cases the accused were charged with being persons who assisted in the carrying out of those executions. Polyukhovich and Berezowsky were alleged to be persons who had enrolled in the Schutzmannschaft or were Helfer, ie. helpers. It was alleged by the prosecution that both Polyukhovich and Berezowsky assisted extermination on the days of the killing or themselves participated in certain killings incidental to the mass executions. Wagner was an ethnic German who became a member of the Gendarmarie. In particular it was alleged against him that following the mass killing he and others in a unit of the Gendarmarie killed a number of babies who had not been killed during the earlier mass execution.

The Polyukhovich Trial

Ivan Polyukhovich had lived in the village of Serniki which is in the vicinity of the Pripjet Marshes in Ukraine. Under the Nazi regime, he became one of the local police and a forester. It was alleged against him that he had participated in partisan war against those partisans, who had taken refuge in the Marshes, and had assisted in the extermination of the Jewish population of Serniki. Following the Nazi occupation, the Jews of that village were placed in a ghetto and the adult men killed in an early action. Subsequently in September 1942, a number of local Ukrainians were ordered to dig a pit on the outskirts of the village, the Jews of the village rounded up, marched to the pit and executed.

The night prior to that execution a number of local Ukrainians assisted a large number of the Jews to escape. Those persons eventually went to live in Canada, the United States and Israel and gave evidence at the committal and trial.

From the chronology that I have given it can be seen that not only before charge, but after charge there was a considerable lapse of time. Due to that many witnesses had died and some had become unfit to give evidence, it was remarkable that the Special Investigation Unit was able to locate and obtain the testimony of as many witnesses as it did.

A number of the charges at committal could not be sustained due to those effects of that lapse of time particularly the death of witnesses. At trial the charges included that relating to Polyukhovich's involvement with the pit killing and his escorting three people to the pit and shooting them personally. Eyewitness evidence was called as to Polyukhovich's presence at the pit. However, by the time of trial only one eyewitness was left alive able to testify to Polyukhovich's actions at the pit.

The important issue that arose at trial was whether the eye witness had accurately identified Polyukhovich at the time as having been the person who performed those actions. There was no doubt on both the prosecution and defence case that the man charged, Ivan Polyukhovich, who had emigrated to Adelaide in 1949, was the man who had lived in Serniki and had been a forester. The witnesses brought to Australia to give evidence from the village clearly knew him and indeed some were related to him. The Special Investigation Unit had not only interviewed the witnesses to whom I had referred but in addition had exhumed the execution site and obtained scientific and ballistic evidence to establish the precise time and nature of the mass killing and the pathological evidence of the cause of death in the case of a large number of the deceased.

Historians gave evidence at the committal and the trial in particular as to the circumstances of the Nazi onslaught against the Jews and the implementation of Nazi policy in Serniki, in order to prove that the killings had been committed in pursuance of a policy associated with the conduct of the war or with the occupation, a necessary requisite under section 7 of the *War Crimes Act*.

Further, historical evidence was called as to the role of members of the Schutzmannschaft and the foresters. A mass of archival and documentary material was put into evidence through experts who could explain the significance of that documentation as relating to the Nazi policy and Mr Polyukhovich personally.

Under Australian law, Polyukhovich had, and exercised the right to give no evidence. He remained mute. He had originally on his arrest denied to police that he had committed any offences.

The defence relied upon the evidence of Polyukhovich's first wife who still lived in the village. She was unable to come to Australia. She was prepared to give evidence that Polyukhovich had not assisted the Germans as one of the witnesses most important to the prosecution case, had said that he had. In order that her evidence might properly be taken, the court, that is counsel and the judge went to Serniki, recorded her evidence, including full examination in chief and cross examination on video, which video was played in evidence to the jury when the court returned from Serniki. As pointed out by Judge Michael David QC who appeared for the accused, the case threw up very difficult problems. He refers to these problems as follows:

1. *The first problem was the difficulty of time. Half a century was really just too long. In saying that, I must admit that many of the witnesses were very good and their memories of these events were very good. However, just the effect on the jury that a person was thinking back fifty years caused its own difficulties.*

2. *Another problem was the Ukrainian witnesses' total unfamiliarity with our system. This really caused the greatest problems. This, combined with the difficulty of language and interpreting, made cross-examination, for instance, very difficult. It also made it difficult for the witnesses to tell their story. Let me give you some examples. When the Ukrainian witnesses were first interviewed by the Australian authorities who went over to the Ukraine, the statements were in fact video taped and the defence were provided with those video tapes before trial. Trying to cross-examine them about an inconsistent statement from those video tapes, bearing in mind there was an interpreter at the video taping and an interpreter in Court, was almost impossible.*

3. *Another problem was that some of the Ukrainian witnesses, before the Australian authorities spoke to them, had spoken to Russian procurators about the allegations. These statements, of course, were provided to the defence. The Russian procurators, not knowing our system, often took statements which did not have the necessary accuracy that was needed in such an investigation. Consequently, there were many exaggerations and, indeed, some statements came close to being mere policy statements. Cross-examination on these original statements allowed the defence to dent the credibility of these witnesses.*

4. *Of course, the Ukrainian witnesses were also totally unused to the experience of cross-examination. I suppose what I am saying in setting out those difficulties is that our present system, in certain areas, struggled to cope with this type of trial. However, it was thought that, despite those difficulties, it was better off to have the safeguards of our criminal system and the strict rules of evidence rather than another system.*

The Case against Heinrich Wagner

It was alleged against Wagner that in the summer of 1942 he had helped escort adult Jews to a pit killing near the village of Ustinovka, near Kirovograd. It was alleged that 20 children of Jewish fathers and Ukrainian mothers who had not been caught up in the original execution, coming from the town of Isralyovka, had been, in the presence of their mothers, put into a cart driven by a Mr Davyborsch, taken to the site of the earlier execution and were there shot by Wagner and others. At this time Wagner was a 19 year old Volksdeutscher. His German background had permitted him to join the Gendarmarie.

Witnesses against him included a fellow member of the Gendarmarie, Ivan Zhilun who gave evidence that he had accompanied Wagner in escorting the adult Jews to the execution scene and gave evidence of the rounding up and execution of the 20 children. He had been found guilty by a Russian court, sentenced to 25 years in Siberia and released after eight years. The cart driver, Davyborsch who had been press-ganged to taking the children to the pit also gave video evidence. Certain of the survivors of the mothers were available to give evidence.

Heinrich Wagner was committed for trial to the Supreme Court of South Australia. Prior to the trial an application was made to the Trial Judge to stay the proceedings. Counsel and the judge went to the Ukraine to take evidence on that application. Zhilun had given evidence in person at the committal but when cross examined some inconsistencies appeared between his testimony and the statements made by him to the Russian court in 1947. Zhilun denied that the record of the Russian court was accurate.

However the interrogators and members of the Russian court had died during the interim. In order to ascertain whether the record was likely to be accurate and to examine its integrity, evidence was taken in Russian from the person in charge of the district and of the court proceedings in 1947. That evidence was videotaped to be used at the trial.

The defence relying on that evidence contended that it was almost impossible to exploit any inconsistent statements that had been made some 50 years earlier. However the application for stay was not successful.

After he had been indicted but prior to the trial commencing, on 10 December 1993, Wagner suffered a heart attack. Evidence was given that a trial would put his life at risk. It was determined by the then Director of Public Prosecutions having had him examined by an independent medical specialist, that the proceedings against him would be withdrawn. Consequently, the allegations against him were never publicly aired at trial.

Mikolay Berezowsky

It was asserted against Berezowsky that he had been one of the leaders of the Schutzmannschaft in Gnivan near Vinnitsa in the Ukraine who had taken part in a pit killing in which some 100 people had been executed. There were a number of eye witnesses who had claimed to identify him as having assisted in the round up of the Jews and marching them to execution. However it became apparent on committal that Berezowsky's case was that he was not there. Contemporary documentation became available from Russian archives during the proceedings including a day-to-day list of the personnel of the Schutzmannschaft at Gnivan which did not show him as present, but did indicate that he was one of the people scheduled at that time to be at a training course at another town far away. The eyewitness evidence was entirely unsatisfactory and in the light of this the committing Magistrate ruled the case was not of sufficient strength to warrant Berezowsky being put to trial.

Although there remained at that time a number of other matters that might have warranted prosecution including of persons suspected of involvement in open air shootings and gas van operations in and around Minsk and in mass killings in Latvia, the Commonwealth government determined to commit no further resources to the trials and prosecutions and terminated the investigations then underway, notwithstanding that, throughout the 1990's successful Nazi war crimes trials had been brought in the United States, Britain, France, Italy and Croatia. Even then however Australian concerns did not entirely die.

In 1944 Kommrads Kalejs was deported to Australia from the United States. Publicity given to that matter resulted in a reconsideration of the prospects of his being prosecuted. Concern was also aroused concerning another person who had been under investigation prior to the withdrawal of resources, one Karlis Ozols who later died in 2001. The cases of both men were referred back to the Australian Federal Police who drew attention to the cost of further investigating and determined not to continue any inquiries. Kalejs died in Melbourne in 2003 during a bitter legal contest over an attempt to extradite him for trial in Latvia.

There was a deal of media interest when the likelihood of extradition of Kommrad Kalejs was raised, and there remains current in Australia, media interest about the proposed extradition from Australia of a man alleged by the Wiesenthal Centre to have been involved in a murder in Hungary as a member of the then Nazi aligned Hungarian Army, but no further action has been taken or proposed in Australia to prosecute alleged war criminals here.

Unfortunately the acquittal of Polyukhovich, the failure of attempts to prosecute Wagner and Berezowsky resulted in a failure of government will and the termination of any further action.

It is apparent that the attempt to use the standards and requirements of Australian domestic laws was unsuccessful particularly due to the age and death of necessary witnesses. It is clear that the delays were substantially due to original government opposition to prosecuting war criminals so that the later government commitment proved ineffectual. The failure of Australian governments to take action earlier is with hindsight deplorable.

Greg James

Eine Zusammenfassung der Geschichte der Nazi-Kriegsverbrecherprozesse in Australien

Die Nazi-Kriegsverbrecherprozesse in den 1990er Jahren resultierten aus der durch eine Fernsehdokumentation über die Rolle Australiens als Immigrationsziel für Kriegsverbrecher entstandenen öffentlichen Beunruhigung. Nach dem Ende des Zweiten Weltkrieges hatte die australische Regierung das Kriegsverbrechergesetz 1945 verabschiedet und Kriegsgerichte im Feld etabliert. Dieses Gesetz fand aber nur im pazifischen Raum Anwendung. Von Europa nach Australien setzte eine Einwanderungswelle ein.

Unter den Immigranten, die sich in Australien niedergelassen hatten, befanden sich auch eine Reihe von Nazis und deren Anhänger. Die Ermittlungen der Commonwealth Polizei sowie die Beschwerden der Sowjetunion hatten zu ihrer Aufdeckung geführt, wobei die Fernsehdokumentation nun einige dieser Personen bekannt gab.

Im Gegensatz zur öffentlichen Haltung der australischen Regierung gegen Kriegsverbrechen, hatte im Jahr 1961 der australische Generalstaatsanwalt alle Ermittlungen gegen Verdächtige abgeschlossen. 1986 ergab eine Untersuchung der Regierung, dass sich mit hoher Wahrscheinlichkeit eine bedeutende Anzahl von Kriegesverbrechern in Australien aufhielt.

Obwohl frühere Regierungen keinerlei Ermittlungen oder Anklagen eingeleitet hatten, wurde nun eine spezielle Untersuchungskommission berufen mit dem Ergebnis, dass fünfzig Jahre nach dem Ende des Zweiten Weltkrieges ein Gesetz verabschiedet wurde, wodurch vor australischen Gerichtshöfen auf der Grundlage australischen Rechts die Verfolgung von Kriegsverbrechen möglich wurde. In der Folge wurden gegen einige angebliche Kriegsverbrecher Ermittlungen eingeleitet, die zu drei Anklagen führten. Allerdings verzögerten eine verfassungsrechtliche Streitfrage und der Selbstmord eines Angeklagten die Durchführung der Prozesse für einige Jahre. Die Gesetzgebung wurde zwar als verfassungsgemäß eingestuft, jedoch scheiterten die Prozesse primär an dem hohen Alter der Zeugen, die alle während der Verfahren starben. Danach verweigerte die australische Regierung die für eine Weiterführung der restlichen Ermittlungen und Anklagen notwendigen Ressourcen. Ein Verfahren hatte mit einem Freispruch geendet, weil zur Zeit des Prozesses nur noch ein einziger Augenzeuge mit zweifelhafter Glaubwürdigkeit zur Verfügung stand, einer der Angeklagten eine schwere Herzerkrankung entwickelt hatte und in einer dritten Angelegenheit sich die Beweise als unglaubwürdig erwiesen. Obwohl andere Untersuchungen verlässliche Beweise versprachen, mangelte es an behördlicher Unterstützung; dies ungeachtet der Tatsache, dass andere Länder Ermittlungen und Anklagen gegen potentielle Kriegsverbrecher fortsetzten. Von Zeit zu Zeit jedoch wurden verschiedene Personen in Australien als ehemalige Nazi-Kriegsverbrecher identifiziert, die in der Folge auslieferungsrechtlich behandelt wurden.

VI. Germany's Attitude towards International Criminal Law/ Deutschlands Haltung zum Völkerstrafrecht

Claus Kress

Germany and International Criminal Law: Continuity or Change?

"Comedy, scandal and parody of justice!" – These are the words used by the French Prime Minister *Briand* in 1921 during the National Assembly on the Leipzig Trials concerning German war crimes against the French.

"What lesson can we learn from Versailles and Leipzig? – First, the United Nations must not again trust the Germans to do justice in the case of German war criminals. For them they are heroes." – This is *Sheldon Glueck*'s evaluation of the Leipzig trials as contained in his monograph on "War Criminals" from 1944.

In 1953 the American State Department came to a very similar conclusion – now with regard to the German attitude to the Nuremberg trials: "The German position on the trials of war criminals is a problem which has continued to trouble us ever since the trials were held. The Germans have failed to accept the principles on which the trials were based and do not believe that those convicted were guilty. Their attitude is very much sentimental and can not be influenced by arguments or an objective statement of the facts. They adhere to the view that the majority of the war criminals were soldiers who were punished for doing what all soldiers do in war, or indeed were ordered do."

45 years later, in 1998, *Bill Pace*, the American convenor of the global coalition of non-governmental organisations for an international criminal court, passed the following verdict on Germany's international criminal law policy:

"No country can be prouder than Germany of their participation and support for the ICC [the International Criminal Court]. The German refusal to accept what they called 'an alibi court', and their resistance to the highly publicised threats from the United States to the German leaders during the Rome conference deserves great appreciation by the world community".

These four citations demonstrate that it is indeed fascinating to reflect on the German position on international criminal law over the past 100 years. For this reason I can only express my gratitude to the organisers of this most interesting and informative conference for intending me for this topic. I do, of course hope that you are not expecting me to deal with this topic exhaustively, as it is far too extensive for that and, in particular, my competence in the field of legal history is too limited. What follows instead is firstly a very brief and almost certainly very selective review of the German position on international criminal law, from Leipzig and Nuremberg through to the early stages of Germany's membership of the United Nations. I would then like to contrast this first phase with the more recent development in the German position since the 1990s including, in particular, the Rome negotiations on the ICC Statute.

Leipzig

Following *Prof. Reginbogin's* lecture I need say little about the German position on international criminal law *before* Nuremberg. His report on the *Leipzig* trials makes *Briand's* angry statement from 1921, which I quoted at the beginning of my lecture, easily understandable. The trials concerning war crimes against English soldiers are, though, perhaps deserving of a somewhat less severe verdict overall. After all, in the famous *Llandovery Castle* case the *Reichsgericht* rejected the defence of superior orders because of the order's manifest illegality. In 1944 this principle of "manifest illegality" was incorporated into the leading English treatise on international law by *Lauterpacht,* with an explicit reference to the judgment of the *Reichsgericht*. This led to a corresponding amendment to the British "Manual of Military Law" in the same year. However, even in the light of more recent research, little changes in the overall evaluation: The Leipzig trials are a prime example of the lack of will of the nation to undertake a serious, or to employ a term from the modern international criminal law, a "genuine" prosecution of crimes under international law. Suggestions as to why this will was lacking can be seen in a passage taken from memoirs of the then chief *Reich* public prosecutor, *Ebermayer*:

"Even today I still find it hard to understand that we took on the obligation in the Versailles treaty to have these war crimes [...] prosecuted in Germany and in the German courts. We had lost the war, we had to submit to the harsh conditions of the enemy, dictated by hate and revenge, and we suffered losses, both of land and money, something which was unavoidable. We should, however, have never ever allowed ourselves to submit to the condition of prosecuting our own people for these so-called war crimes, when no other country involved in the war took it upon **them** to undertake such an obligation. Such a concession went against our honour."

Nuremberg

The sense of a damaged national honour in the case of the prosecution of crimes under international law comes up also in respect of the German reaction to the Nuremberg trials, and here particularly as regards the Nuremberg follow-up trials. In a judgment from 1958, the *Bundesgerichtshof* quoted German Member of Parliament *Dr. von Merkatz* as saying that the German government's unwillingness to recognise the Nuremberg judgments reflected "a part of our German dignity".

After what we heard yesterday from *Benjamin Ferencz*, *Louise Harmon* and *Harry Reicher* about the *Einsatzgruppen*, the *Medical*, and the *Justice* trial, the citation of the German parliamentarian must seem profoundly strange, and yet it is precisely the more recent research findings of *Ulrich Brochhagen* and *Norbert Frei* which confirm that a widespread belief among the German population is reflected in the words of that member of parliament. The contemporary historians share the belief contained in the evaluation of the American State Department from 1953 cited at the beginning of my talk, according to which the legal objections to the Nuremberg trials raised by the Germans – particularly the argument of *nullum crimen* and that against the death penalty – were not the main reasons for their rejection. Indeed the convictions of many defendants in the follow-up trials were ultimately viewed as being unjust. On this point let us consider two original statements. The Foreign Relations Committee of the *Bundestag* (the German parliament) unanimously declared the following on January 5, 1951:

"Those concerned have been sentenced to death for acts committed in connection with the war. If an execution were now to take place, the recollections of suffering which the war left in its wake across the country would once again be brought to mind. The justice, which has been dispensed in Nuremberg and Dachau, was solely against Germans. This fact has done serious damage to the sense of justice of the German people and has at no time and in no place been approved of by them."

Perhaps even more unpleasant than this resolution is the pompous demonstration of solidarity with the Landsberg prisoners by the Bavarian protestant bishop *Meiser*:

"These brothers, who to a large extent must suffer on behalf of our people, can now be more certain than before that they hadn't been forgotten out there."

The official Germany of the time formulated its objection against Nuremberg in legal terms and placed it on record when acceding to the European Convention on Human Rights: A so-called reservation was made to the "international criminal law qualification" of the *nullum crimen* principle as contained in Article 7, paragraph 2 of the latter instrument.

As is well known, in the time which followed, the victorious powers made Germany considerable concessions. These concessions, incidentally, went somewhat further than those granted to Japan. In particular in the 1950's the three western occupying powers accepted the non-recognition of the Nuremberg judgments by Germany in the *Convention on the Settlement of Matters arising out of the War and the Occupation*. At the time the British Foreign Office justified these concessions laconically by stating that, in contrast to Japan, an army was expected from Germany. This led journalist *Jörg Friedrich*, who has been concerned with our topic to some considerable extent, to draw the following, certainly somewhat critical conclusion:

"Nuremberg, as a precedent, which the international law optimists maintain as a positive example, was wrecked by its organisers in just a short time. This served, quite successfully, as a triumph for the free world and a defeat for the law."

The early years of Germany's membership in the United Nations

Starting from here it is interesting to see at what point Germany has articulated a future-orientated policy position on international criminal law. An opportunity to take such a position at the international level came in 1978 when the 6th Committee of the General Assembly of the United Nations recommenced its work on the codification of international criminal law, a task it had abandoned in 1954. Germany, however, spoke out *against* the continuation of the codification efforts. The German attitude in 1978 may be seen as a "Post-Nuremberg reflex". On the other hand, "Nuremberg" was the past and, as we have seen, Germany had done what could be done to dissociate itself with its legal effects. Against this background and with a view to Germany's foreign policy emphasis on multilateralism and the rule of law in international relations, one could have expected Germany to formulate a more favourable position on international criminal law. Perhaps the main reason for the, initially still negative German attitude towards international criminal law was not so much their own belief, but rather that of the major Western Powers. In 1978, not only Germany, but also the USA, Canada, the United Kingdom, Italy and Japan voted against continuing the codification of international criminal law.

The early position of Germany's academics

Before I turn to the more recent evolution of the official German international criminal law policy, I would just like to add that Germany's academics, in their vast majority, did not take a position which would have countered the government's policy. Among criminal lawyers, the exception confirming the rule was *Hans-Heinrich Jescheck* who, in 1952, published a landmark study on the Nuremberg trials. But even *Jescheck* was full of scepticism in 1965 as to whether in fact there was a future for international criminal justice. His words were:

"Both drafts (produced by the International Law Commission on the codification of the international criminal law and on the establishment of an international criminal court) seem today to be the result of a very promising, yet unsuccessful attempt at creating a legal system truly reflecting the idea of the international community."

In the years following 1965, *Otto Triffterer*, a disciple of *Jescheck*, remained for a while the only German criminal lawyer who took an interest in the further development of the international criminal law and participated in the respective academic discussion with a degree of optimism.

As regards Germany's public international lawyers, the picture is essentially the same: International criminal law commanded at best a very peripheral interest at this time. To the extent that this topic was at all touched upon, the reactions were a mixture of scepticism and rejection. Characteristic of this situation is the plain negative assessment made by the renowned international legal historian, *Wilhelm Grewe*, in 1989:

"The criminal prosecution of leading individuals for escaping a war of aggression was, as far as the past is concerned, a miscarriage of justice (a victim of which was Rudolf Hess, who, whatever one cares to think about his role in the Third Reich, was jailed for 40 years). As for the future, this was the wrong path to take. In so far as the other crimes listed in the London Statute are concerned, it seems to make little sense to continue to cling to the failed attempts and abandon oneself to the hope that one day there would indeed be a comprehensive international criminal law applied by an international criminal court."

As we know, the turbulent development since the 1990s caused the realist, *Grewe*, to be disproved by reality. The fact that this development also led to a notable reorientation of the German position is something I would now like to touch on briefly.

The International Criminal Tribunal for the former Yugoslavia

When it came to the establishment of the two international criminal courts for the former Yugoslavia and Rwanda, Germany took a moderately positive attitude, perhaps one which comes close to some sort of acquiescence, to use this public international law category: Germany may not have been one of the driving forces behind establishing those tribunals, while the United States of America was in both cases the key player, Germany has supported the work of both courts from the very beginning, particularly as regards the Yugoslavia criminal court, the ICTY. In particular it was Germany that made the groundbreaking international criminal trial against the Serb *Dusko Tadic* possible in the first place. The Bavarian criminal justice authorities had pursued a case against Tadic up to the point when it was ready to go to trial, when Germany received a request from the Yugoslav Tribunal to hand the case over to it. Germany fulfilled the unusual "vertical" request for cooperation based on the primacy of the international criminal jurisdiction and sent the case to the international level. The relevance of this step must not be underestimated. Let us think back to what route the history of international criminal law would have taken, had the Netherlands not denied the victorious powers' request in the First World War for the extradition of the former German Kaiser.

At the same time, in the light of the German attitude to the Nuremberg trials, Germany's position in the *Tadic* case is everything but a natural consequence: In the early 1950s, the German Minister of Justice had rejected the Nuremberg Tribunals on the basis of their exceptional nature which was said to run counter to a basic principle enshrined in the new German constitution. Following the logic of this argument, it would not seem to have been far-fetched to also criticise the ICTY which had been established *ad hoc* (and partly *ex post facto*). What is perhaps even more remarkable in the historical perspective is the German reaction to the jurisdiction of the ICTY in exactly this *Tadic* case: Even if *Tadic's* position *within* the Serbian regime does not come close to the role of the Nuremberg defendants, the judgments pronounced in the *Tadic* case most certainly had far-reaching consequences, which come close to those in Nuremberg: With the *Tadic* judgments, the ICTY paved the way for what I call the "the second generation of international criminal law", an international criminal law whose field of application extends to crimes in *non*-international armed conflicts and – moving away from the so-called Nuremberg *Junktim* clause – to crimes against humanity irrespective of the existence of an armed conflict. In the historical perspective it is particularly remarkable that the Secretary of State of the Federal Ministry of Justice, *Hans-Jörg Geiger*, has mentioned the *Tadic* judgment as a positive achievement in his greeting note to this conference. Why is this so remarkable? Because the recognition of war crimes in non-international armed conflicts and their application in the *Tadic* case could have been challenged for precisely the same reasons that Germany criticised the convictions of the German defendants in Nuremberg, in particular for a war of aggression, namely for reason of an infringement of the prohibition of retroactivity. If we read the case made by the ICTY for recognizing "civil war crimes" as crimes under (customary) international law in its landmark decision of October 2, 1995, the parallels to Nuremberg are particularly evident. Indeed the ICTY expressly establishes them by relying on the Nuremberg precedent at a crucial juncture of its reasoning. An even more critical comparison can be drawn: By looking more closely at the efforts of the Nuremberg tribunal in light of the underlying conduct at the time to establish that each defendant could be held criminally responsibile under international law for waging a war of aggression was almost more sensational than the decision by the ICTY in affirming the customary nature of "civil war crimes" in the early 1990s. It is thus hard for a State not to question the *Tadic* decision, if that State wishes to insist on the prohibition of retroactivity to be applied to the fullest extent to crimes under international law. As already stated, Germany did not raise any objections. This implied a distancing from the *ex post facto* objection which – as we have seen – Germany officially raised against some parts of the Nuremberg judgments.

The International Criminal Court

From there, let us move to the latest phase of the development in international criminal law, or rather the German position on it. In that phase, Germany's attitude has evolved towards proactivity – in short: Germany has become a driving force behind what can be called the emerging system of international criminal justice. This can be seen in the particular dedication and commitment shown by Germany when the Rome Statute on the ICC, first permanent criminal court in legal history was being drawn up. The new proactive trait of German international criminal law policy is also shown by the timely passing of an innovative law on the country's cooperation with the ICC and by the parallel enactment of the *Völkerstrafgesetzbuch*, the German codification of international criminal law by which the country's legal framework to deal with crimes under international law on a national level has been completely revised to allow Germany to effectively play its complementary role in the global endeavours to end impunity.

The question now is, how did we get to this final step in German international criminal law policy? In this final phase, Germany's position on international criminal law was in no way predestined by previous events. It was more a case of it needing a decisive push in the right direction by an active individual. It may surprise you, but I cannot name one single German politician, who is responsible for this decisive push although it is clear that the move would not have been possible without the very positive actions taken by the then acting Foreign Minister *Klaus Kinkel* and Justice Minister *Edzard Schmidt-Jortzig* including German parliamentarians from all other mainstream political parties. As far as I am concerned the person most responsible for shaping Germany's new approach towards international criminal law is sitting among us: Judge *Hans-Peter Kaul*.

Judge *Kaul*'s contribution consists, in my view, of essentially three things: He *firstly* realised very early on that, contrary to *Wilhelm Grewe*'s powerful prediction, a window of opportunity for a breakthrough for a permanent international criminal jurisdiction would soon emerge. *Secondly*, he then came up with a coherent vision of how the ICC should ideally appear. This enabled the German delegation to not only sit on the sidelines while western delegations negotiated as it had so often been the case in the past, but to actually take on an active and decisive role. *Thirdly*, *Kaul* worked tirelessly behind the scenes to build up a broad and strong consensus among Germany's decision makers for the support of such a decisive role. This consensus was of particular relevance because it would soon turn out that Germany would also have to defend positions not supported by its closest friends. I am by no means thinking only of the USA. You may well remember that France's early position was not especially supportive of the court, and that it was only under *Tony Blair*, just before the Rome Conference, that England adopted a favourable position towards the establishment of the court.

What then were the key points of the German position during the negotiations? Basically, Germany was in favour of strictly confining the Court's substantive jurisdiction to crimes under customary international law and it insisted on stringent requirements for the individual responsibility for such crimes. With this rather narrow concept of international criminal law as a starting point, Germany has then argued for the establishment of a collective criminal justice system that fully reflects the peculiarities of crimes under international law, including, in particular, universal jurisdiction, non-immunity up to the position of Heads of States and a stringent regime of vertical cooperation. Of course, Germany was not successful on all those points in the Rome negotiations. It is probably fair to say, though, that Germany has significantly contributed in shaping the final compromises in all those areas of international criminal law.

According to Germany, it was also essential to ensure equality before the international criminal law. This precluded the creation of the ICC as a "permanent *ad-hoc* tribunal" of the Security Council of the United Nations by making the Court's exercise of jurisdiction dependent on the referral of a situation or case by the Security Council. Instead, Germany supported the idea of a *proprio motu* power of the International Prosecutor to trigger international criminal proceedings. At this point, incidentally, with all this change you might well recognise an element of continuity in the German position from Versailles to Rome. The idea of equality before the international criminal law encompasses the demand that even soldiers fighting their aggressor in self-defence must also be subject to a criminal prosecution, if they commit war crimes. Yet, it does perhaps make a difference whether Germany, looking to the future, advocates an international criminal jurisdiction, which does not lend itself to criticisms of a victors' justice or whether, as in the case of Versailles and Nuremberg, it brings the objection of victors' justice into play emotively, to discredit the criminal prosecution of the most abject of German crimes by the allies.

Concluding note

Be that as it may, it has certainly been a long way from the times of *Briand*'s verdict over the Leipzig trials to Germany's contribution to the establishment of the ICC during the Rome Conference.

On October 5, 2001, Germany has chosen to manifest its changed position by way of a symbolic act: It has formally withdrawn its so-called reservation to Article 7, paragraph 2, of the European Convention on Human Rights. Hereby, Germany has formally joined the international community in its recognition that the evolution of international criminal law is marked by certain points of crystallization, which do not meet the most stringent standards of the principle of non-retroactivity. At the same time, the withdrawal signals that Germany has made its peace with Nuremberg.

Selective Bibliography

Brochhagen, Ulrich, Nach Nürnberg: Vergangenheitsbewältigung und Westintegration in der Ära Adenauer, Hamburg 1994.
Frei, Norbert, 1945 und wir, München 2005.
Glueck, Sheldon, War Criminals. Their Prosecution & Punishment, New York 1944.
Grewe, Wilhelm, Rückblick auf Nürnberg, in: Hailbronner *et al.*, eds., Staat und Völkerrechtsordnung, Festschrift für Karl Doehring, Berlin/Heidelberg/New York/London/Paris/Tokio/Hong Kong 1989, p. 229.
Jescheck, Hans-Heinrich, Die Verantwortlichkeit der Staatsorgane nach Völkerstrafrecht, Bonn 1952.
Jescheck, Hans-Heinrich, Gegenwärtiger Stand und Zukunftsaussichten des Völkerstrafrechts, in: H. Kaufmann *et al.*, ed., Erinnerungsgabe für Max Grünhut, Marburg 1965, p. 47.
Kaul, Hans-Peter/Kreß, Claus, Jurisdiction and Cooperation in the Statute of the International Criminal Court, in: Yearbook on International Humanitarian Law (1999), p. 143.
Pace, William R., The Relationship between the International Criminal Court and Non-Governmental Organizations, in: von Hebel *et al.*, eds., Reflections on the International Criminal Court. Essays in Honour of Adriaan Bos, The Hague 1999, p. 189.
Safferling, Christoph J.M., Germany's Adoption of an International Criminal Code, 1 Annual of German & European Law (2003), p. 365.
Selle, Dirk von, Prolog zu Nürnberg – Die Leipziger Kriegsverbrecherprozesse vor dem Reichsgericht, in: Zeitschrift für Neuere Rechtsgeschichte (1997), p. 193.
Triffterer, Otto, Hans-Heinrich Jeschecks Einfluss auf die Entwicklung des Völkerstrafrechts und auf dessen Durchsetzung, 116 Zeitschrift für die gesamte Strafrechtswissenschaft (2004), p. 959.
Wilkitzki, Peter, The German law on co-operation with the ICC, International Criminal Law Review (2002), p. 195.

Claus Kress

Deutschland und das Völkerstrafrecht: Kontinuität oder Wandel?

„Deutschland kann nicht mit der strafrechtlichen Aufarbeitung von Kriegsverbrechen betraut werden" – das entsprach der internationalen Meinung nach den Leipziger Prozessen und nach den juristischen Aufarbeitungsversuchen der NS-Verbrechen in Deutschland. Ende der 1990er Jahre hatte sich die Einstellung gründlich verändert, da Deutschland in der ersten Reihe der Staaten stand, die für die Schaffung eines Internationalen Strafgerichtshofs eintraten. In diesem Beitrag wird dieser Weg Deutschlands nachvollzogen.

Die Leipziger Prozesse sind ein Beispiel für politischen Unwillen, Kriegverbrecher zu verfolgen, auch wenn im Einzelfall, namentlich hinsichtlich der Frage des Handelns auf Befehl, internationales Recht durch das Reichsgericht weiterentwickelt wurde. Die Nürnberger Prozesse wurden in der Nachkriegszeit nie wirklich akzeptiert, gelegentlich gab es eher Sympathiebekundungen für die verurteilten Kriegsverbrecher. Bei der Nichtanerkennung der Nürnberger Urteile durch die Bundesregierung gehe es um „ein Stück unserer deutschen Würde". Die politische Ablehnung der Nürnberger Prozesse zeigt sich vor allem auch darin, dass die Bundesregierung die Ausnahme zur *nullum crimen*-Vorschrift in Art. 7 Abs. 2 EMRK mit einem Vorbehalt versah. In der Rechtswissenschaft herrschte ebenfalls Skepsis sowohl unter den strafrechtlichen wie den völkerrechtlichen Vertretern. Zugleich wurde Deutschland von den westlichen Alliierten wieder stark gemacht.

Die Situation änderte sich mit der Etablierung des Internationalen Straftribunals für das ehemalige Jugoslawien durch den Sicherheitsrat der Vereinten Nationen. Die Bundesregierung kooperierte mit dem Internationalen Tribunal und in der Tat wäre der erste und überaus wichtige Prozess gegen Tadic nicht möglich gewesen, ohne dass dieser von München nach Den Haag ausgeliefert worden wäre. Die positive Reaktion der Bundesregierung auf die durchaus umstrittene Weiterentwicklung des Völkerstrafrechts durch das Jugoslawien-Tribunal zu einem „Völkerstrafrecht der zweiten Generation" zeugt davon, dass sich zwischenzeitlich auch die Einstellung zu den Nürnberger Verfahren gewandelt haben muss.

Hinsichtlich der Schaffung des Internationalen Strafgerichtshofs ging von Deutschland ein enormes Engagement aus. Ohne dass eine einzelne Person oder ein einzelnes Ereignis dafür verantwortlich gemacht werden kann, nahm die deutsche Regierung in diesem Prozess eine proaktive Rolle ein und war bereit, diese auch gegen Widerstände der engsten Verbündeten – und solche gab es durchaus nicht nur in den USA, sondern auch Frankreich und England waren zunächst einem Internationalen Strafgerichtshof skeptisch gegenüber eingestellt – aufrecht zu erhalten. Deutschland favorisierte in dem Prozess eine Zuständigkeit des ICC nur für Aggression, Völkermord, Kriegsverbrechen und Menschlichkeitsverbrechen, zugleich aber eine größtmögliche Unabhängigkeit und Selbständigkeit des internationalen Anklägers.

Zwischenzeitlich hat Deutschland den Vorbehalt zu Art. 7 Abs. 2 EMRK zurückgezogen und damit implizit die Nürnberger Prozesse anerkannt.

VII. The Legacy of Nuremberg/Das Vermächtnis von Nürnberg

Hans-Peter Kaul

The International Criminal Court: Key Features and Current Challenges

At the outset, let me express the hope that my German countrymen will not take it unkindly, if I hold my presentation in English.[1] It is a sign of respect and sympathy acknowledging the many distinguished participants from abroad especially the American guests, co-organizers, and Touro College. I would like to express my personal appreciation that Touro-College under the farsighted leadership of its distinguished President, Dr. Bernhard Lander, is making such an important contribution in seeking a better understanding between Jews and a 'New Germany.' As I am still moved by Justice Bach's (Israel) impressive speech this morning, may I take the liberty in mentioning that in the course of my career, I have devoted more than ten years of my work to promote German-Israeli relations and German-U.S. Jewish relations in Tel Aviv, Washington D.C. and in my own country.

On Sunday evening as we heard a gripping and mesmerizing key-note address by Whitney Harris, we jointly witnessed a very special return to Courtroom 600. In a much more modest sense, it was also for me a return to Courtroom 600. Why? Well, shortly after taking up my work as a full-time judge at the International Criminal Court in The Hague, I had the opportunity to speak on 21 October 2003 in the very same Courtroom 600 about the International Criminal Court, a conference organized by its distinguished Director, Prof. William Sheldon of the German-American Institute in Nuremberg. The title which I gave to my lecture may be of interest to you. I had thought about it quite a while. In the end, I concluded that the title should be: "The International Criminal Court – The Legacy of Nuremberg."[2]

The title mirrors an obvious truth. Members of the German delegation, which were together with me at the Rome Conference, – among them Claus Kress, who spoke this morning and Andreas Zimmermann, whom we will hear this afternoon – are all aware of this: Without the International Military Tribunal of Nuremberg, there would be no International Criminal Court. I am, therefore, very pleased to have been invited to make a presentation at this important conference. I am touched especially by the presence of two American friends, former Nuremberg Prosecutors, Messrs Whitney Harris[3] and Benjamin Ferencz[4]. Those who know the story of the Rome Conference will also know that both of them were, time and again, a source of encouragement and inspiration to the German delegation – you might even say that sometimes they acted as informal advisers to my delegation. Benjamin Ferencz advised us primarily on issues related to the crime of aggression[5] – and jointly we somehow managed in getting at least the crime of aggression recognized as an international crime of major concern to the whole world as referred to Art. 5 of the Rome Statutes. Having Whitney Harris on your side was an invaluable source of encouragement to the German delegation not to resign, not to give up in our quest for a credible International Criminal Court.

In my remarks I will deal with three questions:
– What are some noteworthy key features of the ICC?
– What are current tasks and challenges?
– Where does the Court stand today?

---

[1] For editing purposes the original oral presentation given on 19 July 2005 has been generally maintained throughout the text.

[2] Hans-Peter Kaul, *Der Internationale Strafgerichtshof – Das Vermächtnis von Nürnberg*, in: Deutschland und die internationale Gerichtsbarkeit, (A. Zimmermann ed., 2004), pp. 71 et seq.

[3] Whitney A. Harris, *Tyranny on Trial – The Trial of the Major German War Criminals After the End of World War II At Nuremberg, Germany 1945-1946* (rev. edition, 1999), with an introduction by Robert H. Jackson.

[4] Benjamin Ferencz, *The Nuremberg Precedent of the Prosecution of State-sponsored Mass Murder*, New York Law School Journal of International and Comparative Law, vol. 3 (1990), pp. 325 et seq.

[5] Benjamin Ferencz, *Defining International Aggression: The Search for World Peace* (1975).

I. Features of the Court

Before I summarize some key features of the Court, please permit me to make a brief announcement: In the latest edition of the American Journal of International Law, which appeared at the beginning of July 2005, you can find an article of mine entitled: "Construction site for more Justice – The International Criminal Court after two years"[6]. This is the first article ever published by an active ICC judge in the American Journal of International Law. Obviously I am pleased that the AJIL accepted it so graciously, despite the well-known fact that the current U.S. Government does not have a very high regard for the International Criminal Court.

Now, what are some of the most noteworthy key features guaranteeing that the ICC will indeed remain an impartial, non-political and independent judicial institution engaged in fair proceedings? It is not possible in this short time to review all of the many detailed safeguards built into the Court.[7] But allow me at least to highlight some different aspects:

The jurisdiction of the International Criminal Court is limited to the most serious crimes of concern to the international community as a whole, namely, genocide, crimes against humanity and war crimes, pursuant to Art. 6-8 of the Statute of Rome. It is worthwhile to take a personal look at the long list of five different forms of genocide, 15 forms of crimes against humanity and more than 50 different war crimes. You will indeed discover that all of the crimes – and more – were prosecuted at the Nuremberg trials.

The Court's jurisdiction[8] is not universal. It is clearly limited to the well-recognized forms of jurisdiction. The Court has jurisdiction over:
– Nationals of States Parties; or
– Offences committed on the territory of a State Party.
– In addition, the Security Council can refer cases to the ICC independent of the nationality of the accused or the location of the crime.
– The Security Council also has the power to defer an investigation or prosecution up to one year in the interest of maintaining international peace and security.

The ICC is a court of last resort. This is known as the principle of complementarity:
– In normal circumstances, States will investigate or prosecute offences.
– The Court can only act when States are unwilling or unable genuinely to investigate or prosecute offences. The primary responsibility to investigate and prosecute crimes remains a matter of the State.
– Furthermore, cases will only be admissible, if they are of such sufficient gravity to justify the Court's involvement.
– The principle of complementarity was one of the many constructive inputs of U.S. negotiators at the Rome Conference. In passing, let me mention that other and more fingerprints of the able and competent U.S. delegation[9] can be found all over the Statute.

The ICC is an independent institution, created by a treaty open to any state to join voluntarily. The Court is not part of the United Nations, or any other political body. It exercises a purely judicial function. All cases are handled judicially, in accordance with its Statute. Numerous safeguards in the Statute also ensure that politically-motivated prosecutions will not take place. The Pre-Trial Chamber is one example of an important innovation in this regard. As I was just re-elected as President of the Pre-

---

[6] Hans-Peter Kaul, *Developments at the International Criminal Court – Construction Site for More Justice: The International Criminal Court After Two Years*, American Journal of International Law, vol. 99 (2005), pp. 370 et seq.

[7] Monroe Leigh, *The United States and the Statute of Rome*, American Journal of International Law, vol. 95 (2001), pp. 124 et seq.

[8] Michael P. Scharf, *The ICC's Jurisdiction Over the Nationals of Non-Party States: A Critique of the U.S. Position*, Law and Contemporary Problems, vol. 64 (2001), pp. 67 et seq.

[9] David Scheffer, *Staying the Course with the International Criminal Court*, Cornell International Law Journal, vol. 35 (2001/02), pp. 47 et seq; id., *Article 98 (2) of the Rome Statute: America's Original Intent*, Journal of International Criminal Justice, vol. 3 (2005), pp. 333 et seq.

Trial Division with three Pre-Trial Chambers, I feel obliged to explain this safeguard. Generally the Prosecutor is under the control of the Pre-Trial judges. Before launching an investigation on his own initiative, the Prosecutor must first obtain authorization from the Pre-Trial Chamber. This ensures that investigations comply with the strict legal standards set forth in the Statute. These include the obligation upon the Prosecutor to consider whether there are reasonable grounds to believe that a crime within the jurisdiction of the Court has been committed and whether the case is admissible. The Pre-Trial Chamber also holds a hearing to confirm the charges against the accused, determining for itself that substantial grounds and sufficient evidence exist to proceed to trial. Only if the Pre-Trial Chamber is clearly satisfied may the prosecution go forward.

The guarantee of a fair trial and protection of the rights of the accused have paramount importance before the ICC. The Statute incorporates the fundamental provisions regarding the rights of the accused and due process common to national and international legal systems.

Another novelty in the Rome Statute is: Subject to the requirements of the rights of the accused and the guarantee of a fair trial, victims are substantially integrated into the Court's proceedings – and this embraces both an acknowledged right to actively participate in the proceedings against the accused as well as a procedure to regain redress.

II. Current tasks and challenges

Since the start of my work in The Hague, I had the chance to follow, sometimes as an observer, sometimes as chairman of a working group, sometimes as a driving force, sometimes concerned or somewhat impatient, the manner in which the ICC continues to be confronted with at least four essential tasks. All of them have to be tackled concurrently under pressure and visible expectations of the international community while new difficulties arise on a daily basis:

First, the ICC must consolidate its ongoing effort to be an efficient and professional international organization while remaining a fully-functioning international court. Secondly, the Office of the Prosecutor needs to develop procedures, which are effective in the prosecuting war crimes, genocide, and other crimes against humanity. At the same time – and this is particularly difficult – the Office of the Prosecutor must successfully coordinate investigations in countries thousands of kilometers away from The Hague such as Congo, Uganda and in Darfur. I will return to this challenge in a moment. Thirdly, as the ICC is 100% dependent on the support of Member States, the Court must increasingly build up a new network of international criminal cooperation by winning over more State Parties so that it can work effectively.

Lastly – and this point is particularly difficult as it concerns an organizational weakness of the ICC as indicated in Chapter 9[10] of the Rome Statute – the States Parties and the Court must in a foreseeable future develop a system of best practices of effective criminal cooperation: direct, flexible, without bureaucracy, fast flow of information and supportive measures. This system must fully take into account that the ICC can only be as strong as the States Parties themselves. This concerns the

---

[10] For a discussion of the cooperation regime in the Rome Statute, see Bruce Broomhall, *The International Criminal Court: Overview and Cooperation with States,* in ICC Ratification and National Implementing Legislation (Nouvelles Études Pénales, 1999), pp. 45 et seq; Annalisa Ciampi, *Other Forms of Cooperation,* in The Rome Statute of the International Criminal Court, A Commentary (A. Cassesse, Paola Gaeta & John R.W.D. Jones, eds., 2002), pp. 1705 et seq; Frederik Harhoff & Phakiso Mochochoko, *International Cooperation and Judicial Assistance,* in The International Criminal Court: Elements of Crimes and Rules of Procedure and Evidence (Roy S. Lee ed., 2001), pp. 637 et seq; Hans-Peter Kaul & Claus Kreß, *Jurisdiction and Cooperation in the Statute of the International Criminal Court: Principles and Compromises,* Yearbook of International Humanitarian Law, vol. 2 (1999), pp 143 et seq; Claus Kreß et al., *International Cooperation and Judicial Assistance: Preliminary Remarks,* in Commentary on the Rome Statute of the International Criminal Court (O. Triffterer ed., 1999) pp. 1045 et seq; Phakiso Mochochoko, *International Cooperation and Judicial Assistance,* in The International Criminal Court: The Making of the Rome Statute – Issues, Negotiations, Results (Roy S. Lee ed., 1999) pp. 305 et seq; Valerie Oosterveld, Mike Perry & John McManus, *The Cooperation of States with the International Criminal Court,* Fordham International Law Journal, vol. 25 (2002) pp. 767 et seq; Bert Swart & Göran Sluiter, *The International Criminal Court and International Criminal Co-operation,* in Reflections on the International Criminal Court (H. von Hebel et al eds., 1999) pp. 91 et seq.

unresolved question about servicing arrest warrants and transferring suspected criminals to The Hague. It is obvious that the States Parties and all forces that support the ICC cannot allow the ICC lose its authority by other nations not carrying out arrest warrants with the result that an attitude prevails: "We have given you the money for the first budgets – now see yourselves, how you get the perpetrators before your Court ...". This will not work. One must hope that this is clear to all concerned. In the former Yugoslavia, most arrests by NATO and coalition forces have been for the International Criminal Tribunal. Likewise, States Parties and Security Council members must now find ways and means to support the ICC regarding the decisive issue of making arrests and transferring suspected criminals to The Hague.

III. The Court Today

Today the Court functions. The four bodies of the ICC, the Presidency, the Chambers, the Office of the Prosecutor and the Registry, are now working effectively in well organized parameters. We have currently a staff of around 450, most of them highly motivated, often working evenings and on the weekends. The Court's daily workload and judicial proceedings are functioning better and better. Indeed, we are more and more in the critical transition from the organizational to the judicial phase of the Court's operations: Four cases have been referred to the Prosecutor; three States Parties have referred cases by virtue of Article 14 of the Rome Statute. As you are undoubtedly aware, on 31 March 2005, the Security Council referred the situation in Darfur, Sudan to the ICC. The President of the ICC has assigned each case to one of the Pre-Trial Division chambers of which I am the President. Meanwhile, the Office of the Prosecutor is carrying out investigations in three other parts of the world: Uganda; the Democratic Republic of Congo; and, as announced by the Prosecutor on 6 June 2005, the situation in Darfur. Many investigative missions have been carried out by The Office of the Prosecution requiring that it conclude agreements necessary to complete its work, and participate in pre-trial hearings. Pre-Trial Chamber I, which has the responsibility for the situation in the Democratic Republic of Congo, has held the first hearings and issued several rulings. Our Public Information Office promptly disseminates information about these proceedings and the status of all situations. Apart from that, the judges have held a plenary session in which they adopted the Code of Judicial Ethics, which you can find on the ICC website.[11] The Court's Registry has undertaken a range of activities to support the Court in its field operations. The Kampala field office in Uganda is fully operational as will soon be the field office in Kinshasa in the Democratic Republic of Congo. Networks have been established with local counterparts to support the Court in carrying out its mandate and efforts are underway to provide information to affected communities about the work of the Court.

From a long-term perspective – as Chairman of the ICC Committee dealing with the future permanent location of the International Criminal Court –, the ICC is currently preparing a public solicitation to build a new court. We hope that among the international architects competing for the bid will also be the finest architects of the United States.

IV. Conclusion

In concluding let me note that the Court is one ratification away from having 100 members, Mexico probably being number 100 and more to come. It took the international community more than half a century after the Nuremberg Tribunal to establish a permanent international criminal court. Many obstacles still lie between the Court and the effective enforcement of international justice. Over time, however, with international cooperation, we can work together to fight against the depressing phenomena of impunity and build a culture of accountability.

---

[11] www.icc-cip.int.

Finally, let me reaffirm one point – which I have already made quite often, also before American audiences, in New York[12] and elsewhere – and I continue to draw some encouragement from a personal letter of congratulations and good wishes dated 18 February 2003 from Jimmy Carter, which I received after my election as an ICC judge – the point is: The Court needs the support of the United States of America, this great country, which time and again had a decisive role in bringing about the fall of tyranny and in re-establishing the rule of law. Especially here in Nuremberg I need not elaborate on this. It remains our hope that the U.S. government will eventually make its peace with the ICC to which Americans have contributed so much. The Court needs American support morally, politically, materially and in other ways. It also needs American prosecutors and other U.S. staff working for the Court.

It remains also our hope that one day the judges may have an American colleague on the bench, maybe somebody with the stature of Justice Jackson or Whitney Harris whom they may elect as the first American President of the International Criminal Court.

This day shall come. It will.

---

[12] See statement by Hans-Peter Kaul in New York on 27 November 2000 before the Preparatory Commission of the United Nations for the International Criminal Court on the occasion of the ratification of the Rome Statute by Germany.

Hans-Peter Kaul

Der Internationale Strafgerichtshof – Hauptmerkmale und künftige Herausforderungen

In diesem Beitrag werden zunächst die wichtigsten Merkmale und Sicherungen des Römischen Statutes des Internationalen Strafgerichtshofs (IStGH) genannt, die garantieren sollen, dass der IStGH eine unparteiische, nicht-politische und unabhängige gerichtliche Institution ist und bleiben wird, die mit allen rechtsstaatlichen Garantien für ein faires Verfahren ausgestattet ist. Dies findet seinen Ausdruck etwa in der beschränkten Gerichtsbarkeit des IStGH, dem Prinzip der Komplementarität, der Einschaltung der Vorverfahrenskammer, die den Chefankläger kontrolliert und die im Rom-Statut verankerten Rechte des Angeklagten.

Um den IStGH zu einem effizienten und funktionierenden internationalen Gericht zu machen, haben sich der Gerichtshof und sein wachsender internationaler Mitarbeiterstab weiterhin zahlreichen Aufgaben und Herausforderungen zu stellen. Der IStGH hängt seinerseits von wirksamer strafrechtlicher Zusammenarbeit durch die Vertragsparteien und der internationalen Gemeinschaft ab. So müssen etwa die Gerichtsdienste weiter aufgebaut werden, während die Anklagebehörde gleichzeitig die ersten Ermittlungen einleiten muss. Im Lichte dieser Schwierigkeiten erscheint es bemerkenswert, dass der Internationale Strafgerichtshof in seiner noch jungen Existenz seit 2002 Fortschritte erreicht hat, sowohl bei seiner eigenen Konsolidierung wie auch bei der Sicherung seiner Position in der internationalen Gemeinschaft: bereits vier Situationen wurden dem Gerichtshof überwiesen, der Chefankläger führt in drei Situationen Ermittlungen vor Ort durch und einige Vorverfahrenskammern haben ihre ersten Entscheidungen gefällt.

Der Autor schließt mit dem erneuten Ausdruck der Hoffnung, dass die Regierung der Vereinigten Staaten eines Tages ihren Frieden mit dem neuen Weltstrafgericht schließen wird, zumal Amerika und die Amerikaner zur internationalen Strafgerichtsbarkeit bereits so viel beigetragen haben.

Anne Bayefsky

The Legacy of Nuremberg

My paper asks, what are Nuremberg's lessons and what has become of them? My response is that the legacy of Nuremberg has largely been squandered and the only chance of recovery lies in an honest, though uncomfortable assessment of the unfortunate state of international human rights law today.

The legacy of Nuremberg is often understood to be primarily the lesson of international individual responsibility for violations of human rights. On this line of thinking the Rwandan and Yugoslav tribunals, and now the ICC, are the major extensions of a movement that began in Nuremberg.

Nuremberg, however, had a more primordial message – the definition of a human right itself. The evidence of the Holocaust presented at Nuremberg, ought therefore to be a bulwark against the scepticism and cynicism of each new generation. And yet sixty years later the moral compass that was then missing in millions of people in this country, and others, is matched by the moral relativism of our time.

Nuremberg was intended to define and apply universal human rights, to all people, for all time. But today, the concept of universality is challenged once again. The Universal Declaration of Human Rights, the 1948 centerpiece of the UN's human rights framework, could no longer be adopted by consensus.

The core lesson of Nuremberg – of universal rights – lies at the foundation of any international system for the protection of human rights. Nevertheless, it has been corroded by international actors, both non-democratic and democratic. Most believed that the end of the Cold War would mean a giant leap forward for international law, and in particular, for the international protection of human rights. Instead, the assault on universality gained credence in the June 1993 UN world conference on human rights held in Vienna, which produced the Vienna Declaration and Programme of Action. It reads in part "while the significance of national and regional particularities and various historical, cultural and religious backgrounds must be borne in mind, it is the duty of states ... to promote and protect all human rights...". This move to modify the commitment to universality by historical or cultural or religious particularities was further entrenched in three more UN world conferences in the 1990's – on population, development and women's rights in Cairo, Copenhagen and Beijing respectively. So-called particularities are not benign reminders of contextual considerations, or appeals for sensitivity or accommodation of difference. The same states that push such particularities also insist on non-interference in domestic affairs and the insulation of national legal systems from international rebuke.

Liberal democracies also bear responsibility for these developments. For example, liberal democratic states in Vienna accepted limitations on freedom from religious intolerance and a free media based on peculiarities of any national legal system. For all the criticism of a monolithic, pathological, western ideological imperialism, in international fora, liberal democratic state actors are often confused and defensive. Their behaviour manifests deep moral scepticism. On a philosophical level, such relativism claims that even in similar situations what is right or good for one individual or society is not necessarily right or good for another. The standpoint of relativism permits no common critique of the substance of legal or moral rules.

This is not an abstraction: Only a few months ago, Amnesty International, the world's largest international human rights NGO, released its 2005 annual report. It begins with a message from Irene Khan, Amnesty's Secretary-General. She writes: "The leadership challenge for the UN and its member states is clear: Listen to the voices of the victims..." These are the same words she used at the 2001 UN World Conference Against Racism in Durban, South Africa. The final NGO document adopted at Durban said "Zionism is racism," accused Israel of crimes against humanity and genocide, and called for the total isolation of the Jewish state. Though asked specifically to vote against it, Ms. Khan encouraged the caucus of international NGOs as a group to abstain. The only voices which were deleted from that final document were those of the Jewish caucus, representing Jewish NGOs from all over the world. They had proposed a statement objecting to a new form of anti-Semitism directed at Jews because of their support of Israel. When it came time to vote on the motion to delete the voices of

Jewish victims, Amnesty, along with all other international NGOs, again abstained. And yet at a news conference held two days later, Ms. Khan said: "this document is a collection of the voices of the victims. We don't believe it was appropriate to vote... The angry voices of the victims at this conference have been heard." Anti-Semitism was everywhere at Durban, where handouts read "what if Hitler had won? The good things: there would be no Israel." But instead of judging voices against universal standards, the world's leading human rights NGOs encouraged and supported what amounts to mob rule.

The particular legacy of Nuremberg – the equal rights of the Jewish people – has also been subverted by what is supposed to be the centerpiece of international law, the UN. Since the creation of the UN in 1945 there has never been a single resolution of the General Assembly dedicated to anti-Semitism. At the moment there are three minor references to the subject buried in resolutions, divorced from any concrete requirement of producing a report or taking action on this still lethal and widespread phenomenon. There has also never been a single report devoted to anti-Semitism mandated by a UN body in UN history. By contrast, the UN Commission on Human Rights adopts annual resolutions which focus on the defamation of Islam, and mandates an annual report on discrimination against Moslems and Arabs. This year the UN Special Rapporteur on racism, Doudou Diène from Senegal, produced on his own initiative, a report which among other things considered anti-Semitism. He used the occasion to maintain that anti-Zionism need not be considered a form of anti-Semitism. On the contrary, while anti-Semitism is discrimination against individual Jews, anti-Zionism is discrimination against the Jewish people by seeking to deny Jews an equal right to self-determination. Far from contributing to the fight against anti-Semitism, the UN rapporteur fueled it.

Failing to combat anti-Semitism is not the only manner in which the Nuremberg legacy of recognizing human rights for Jews has been frustrated by the UN. The UN Charter, in its words, was founded on the equality of men and women and of all nations large and small. But nowhere is the inequality of nations so manifest than in the UN's treatment of the member state of Israel. To name just a few examples: Only Israel is refused full admission to one of the UN's five regional groups, which determine electoral slates for UN bodies and conduct vital information-sharing or negotiating sessions during various UN meetings, such as those of the UN Commission on Human Rights. Six of the ten emergency sessions ever held by the General Assembly have been on Israel. The 10th emergency session is actually a permanent tribunal on Israel – reconvened 13 times since 1997. By contrast, no emergency session was ever held on the Rwandan genocide, estimated to have killed a million people, or the ethnic cleansing of tens of thousands in the former Yugoslavia, or the death of millions over the past two decades of atrocities in Sudan. The basis of the International Court of Justice decision declaring Israel's security fence to be a violation of international law was a November 2003 report of Secretary-General Kofi Annan. It detailed the alleged harm to Palestinians from the fence without describing one terrorist act against Israelis which preceded the fence's construction. When Israel successfully targets Hamas terrorists – even with no civilian casualties, such as was the case with mastermind Abdel Aziz Rantissi, the secretary-general denounced Israel for an "extrajudicial" killing. But when faced with the 2004 report of the UN Special Rapporteur on extrajudicial executions detailing the murder of more than 3,000 Brazilian civilians shot at close range by police, Mr. Annan said nothing. In fact, Brazil along with three other states including Germany, apparently believes it is entitled to a permanent seat on the UN Security Council. More than one quarter of the resolutions condemning a state's human rights violations adopted by the UN Commission on Human Rights over 40 years have been directed at Israel. But there has never been a single resolution about the decades-long repression of the civil and political rights of 1.3 billion people in China, or the million female migrant workers in Saudi Arabia kept as virtual slaves, or the virulent racism which has brought hundreds of thousands to the brink of starvation in Zimbabwe. Every year, UN bodies are required to produce at least 25 reports on alleged human rights violations by Israel, but not one on an Iranian criminal justice system which mandates punishments like crucifixion, stoning and cross-amputation of right hand and left foot. At last fall's General Assembly there were eight resolutions adopted condemning Israel on the very same day that an attempt to adopt a single resolution on Sudan was defeated. This is not legitimate critique of states with equal or worse human rights records. It is demonization of the Jewish state.

The real perversion of the legacy of Nuremberg is that this egregious discrimination takes place in the name of human rights. This is the face of modern anti-Semitism and it indicates how profoundly astray the international community has gone from the recognition of Jew-hatred so essential to the proceedings and outcome of Nuremberg.

Nevertheless, it is not a condition that is beyond repair. And it is Germany that can and should play a leadership role in taking back the language and the intent of international human rights. Germany, for example, is ideally suited to table a resolution on anti-Semitism at the forthcoming General Assembly – which would be a first in UN history. Last year, Germany demurred from taking such an action because the 56 members of the Organization of the Islamic Conference threatened to work against Germany's campaign to obtain a permanent seat on the UN Security Council. But the moral responsibility ought to outweigh the exigencies of the blackmail. Secondly, it is the European Union that is standing in the way of Israel's full membership in the Western European and Others regional group – in violation of the UN Charter. Germany can and should insist that the EU immediately accept Israel's full admission into the Western regional group.

There is one other major front in which the Nuremberg vision has sadly been undermined – in the name of justice. It is the International Criminal Court. The United States and Israel are deeply opposed to the International Criminal Court in its current form. In the case of Israel, this is despite the state having been a leading advocate of international legal accountability. In Europe in particular, US and Israeli opposition is cast as one of arrogance, double-standards and isolationism. In fact, however, the ICC statute as it is currently formulated was clearly intended to trump the legitimate interests of the US and Israel – and not merely by puritanical notions of justice.

The definition of war crimes, for example, includes "the transfer, directly or indirectly, by the Occupying Power of parts of its own civilian population into the territory it occupies..." Obviously, those words were meant for Israel. The ICC statute is therefore a global treaty of general application with a central provision written for a party of one. Such a tactic is incompatible with the rule of law. Furthermore, as a matter of substance the transfer of a civilian population to occupied – in Israel's case 'disputed' – territories does not belong in the company of heinous offences, like actual attacks on civilian population centres or mass murder, which the statute was intended to address. The insertion of an inappropriate substantive provision in the midst of a purported statement of principle about what offends the conscience of mankind, or "the most serious crimes of concern to the international community as a whole", undercuts the stature of the statement and the document as a whole.

There is no doubt that the creation of a Palestinian state will one day mean the use of the ICC as a vehicle to threaten Israel and any of its citizens who venture beyond its borders. European states will likely be drawn into the attempted detention and trial of Israelis of all kinds – since every young Israeli man and woman is bound to participate in the defense of the country from enemies sworn to its destruction. The ICC Prosecutor has indicated he has already received communications concerning the Israeli-Palestinian conflict, although jurisdictional considerations preclude investigation at this time. There is a long list of those threatening to make as early possible use of the ICC in relation to Israel, including UN delegates from the Palestinian Authority, Syria, Lebanon and Egypt. The potential for ad-hoc jurisdiction through some of these actors cannot be dismissed.

There are various other elements of the ICC statute that bear the scars of politicization. The crime of aggression was included but left undefined, in the context of various General Assembly resolutions which condemn Israel for aggression, (while ignoring the existential threat the country has faced since 1948). Although unlikely to succeed, there is now pressure to define elements of the crime of aggression written for an Israeli defendant.

In contrast, definitional issues precluded the statute from including terrorism, though it purports to include the most serious crimes of concern to the international community as a whole. The UN has no definition of terrorism and the definitional impasse has prevented the UN from adopting a comprehensive convention against terrorism. The roadblock is the effort of the Organization of the Islamic Conference to repeat the substance of the Arab Terrorism Convention, namely, that "all cases of struggle by whatever means" for various approved causes should be exempt. Consequently, Israeli acts of self-defense against terrorism will be covered by the ICC statute, while the terrorism itself may not.

In the context of the politicization of the substantive elements of the statute, and attempts to increase it even further, certain procedural elements of the statute become of greater concern. For example, the ability of the Prosecutor and the Court to act in relation to nationals of states not party to the statute. The statute conceptually adds another dimension to the realm of international jurisdiction since it empowers an international body to assume jurisdiction over a state's nationals without that state's consent in certain circumstances. The statute's creation of a network of state parties with reciprocal and collective obligations also means that the implications of perpetrating an offence outside one's state are much greater. The ad-hoc provisions also undercut traditional notions of reciprocity through extradition treaties by permitting a state to accept the jurisdiction of the court where its national is the victim, but refuse jurisdiction where its national is the perpetrator.

Secondly, of particular concern are the extensive powers of the Prosecutor to initiate proceedings. It is naive to believe that the prosecutors, whoever they may be, live in a vacuum and that the double-standard now applied to Israel in contrast to other nations in global human rights fora might not have an impact. Bear in mind, that the misinformation is of such proportions that a 2004 EU poll found that a majority of the Europeans surveyed believed that the state which is the greatest threat to world peace is Israel. Though Israel is a democratic state with all the checks and balances of an independent judiciary, active parliament and flourishing conditions for freedom of expression, the poll results placed Israel above Iran or Syria, totalitarian states which fund and sponsor international terrorism. To suggest that one should simply assume that the prosecutor will prove wiser or insulated from the pressures (or ignorance) of popular opinion, does not inspire confidence. Such concern is magnified by the fact that even the process of requesting an investigation from the Pre-Trial Chamber, with its possible representation of victims, can have serious political consequences.

The irony involved in the ICC laying claim to be the ideal progeny of Nuremberg is also evident from the early case of Sudan. Reports estimate that more than two million people have been killed in Sudan over two decades of conflict, 200,000 have been murdered in the Darfur region in the past two years, and another 1.85 million persons are currently displaced. The toll from disease and malnutrition is now over 200,000 with a mortality rate estimated to be 15,000 per month. Instead of holding an emergency session of the General Assembly, last fall the UN sent a commission of inquiry to Sudan to "determine whether or not acts of genocide have occurred or are still occurring." Four months later the commission reported in January that it could not figure out whether genocide had occurred. A commission, in which the executive director from the Office of the UN High Commissioner for Human Rights was Palestinian, claimed it was impossible to tell whether Darfur was an ethnically-motivated conflict perpetrated by Moslem Arabs against Moslem Africans. But they did have in mind a strategy which would simultaneously avoid actually stopping the atrocities while embarrassing the United States – the UN state at the forefront of efforts to label Darfur events as genocide: Sending the subject to the ICC.

Here we are, another seven months later, claiming criminal law – an ex post facto tool – is the leading preventative mechanism of international human rights law. Says the Prosecutor in his first report to the Security Council at the end of June: "...we are...vigilant to the on-going commission of serious crimes in Darfur and the devastating impact they have on the civilian population. The Office will closely monitor these ongoing crimes... The commencement of investigation marks an opportunity for all parties to take all possible steps to prevent the continuation of such offences." Closer to reality, the investigation is an opportunity for the perpetrators and their allies to insist that potential interveners keep their distance.

Current trends in international law also stress universal criminal jurisdiction, alongside the ICC, as primary implementation tools. Under this banner there have already been attempts to prosecute Israel Prime Minister Ariel Sharon in Belgium and Minister of Defense Shaul Mofaz in the United Kingdom – a strategy which will continue to gather steam in various forms across Europe.

In the 21st century international criminal law, a key legacy of Nuremberg rooted in bringing to justice those who sought to destroy the Jewish people, has been turned against those responsible for the defence of the Jewish state. Israel, as a democracy with a vibrant independent judiciary, is committed to ensuring that none is above the law. But it is disingenuous to claim that such international manoeuvres are motivated by the same spirit or proffer the same guarantees of independence, fairness and non-discrimination.

The resources and attention devoted to international criminal law, has also had a broader impact on the implementation of international human rights standards generally. Seven major international human rights treaties have been adopted over the past four decades, one or more of which has been ratified by all 191 UN members. Four of those treaties permit individuals to complain to independent treaty bodies of violations of a wide range of rights – from the right to life, to non-discrimination on any ground. The potential remedies for violations include changing or repealing laws and practices, and hence can affect very large numbers of people. At the moment almost two and a half billion people live in the 121 states which have agreed to this power of international petition. But the cases sent to the UN human rights treaty bodies are handled by a staff of less than a dozen, from a handful of countries, and little is done to educate or encourage victims and their advocates to bring forward many more cases than the 200 currently registered each year. By contrast, the ICC, with 99 states parties, has 311 staff members from 57 countries.

The comparison is indicative of another general trend in international law, in which criminal law is saddled with preventative expectations beyond its capacity, manipulated to target unpopular rather than the most deserved of acts or actors, and used to direct attention from the implementation of a vast array of international standards that apply to all 191 UN members and their governments.

The message of Nuremberg was unqualified universality of human rights, equality of the Jew, the responsibility to prevent genocide, and the paramountcy of turning human rights standards from hollow phrases to political imperatives. On each of these counts, the Nuremberg legacy is under siege. We have an obligation to redeem it.

Anne Bayefsky

Das Vermächtnis von Nürnberg

Für viele besteht die wichtigste Erkenntnis aus den Nürnberger Prozessen in der internationalen Verantwortung für Menschenrechtsverletzungen und in den internationalen Gerichtshöfen für Ruanda und Jugoslawien einschließlich des IStGH als die wohl bedeutsamste Weiterführung einer Entwicklung, die in Nürnberg ihren Ursprung fand.

Doch das IStGH-Statut in seiner derzeitigen Fassung zielt eindeutig darauf ab, die legitimen Interessen der Vereinigten Staaten und Israels zu attackieren, indem kultureller Relativismus die Universalität der Menschenrechte in Frage stellt. Das Vermächtnis von Nürnberg ist unter Beschuss.

Nürnberg hatte eine viel grundsätzlichere Botschaft – die Definition eines Menschenrechts an sich. Diese Kernlehre von Nürnberg – universale Rechte –, die jedem internationalen System zum Schutz der Menschenrechte zu Grunde liegt, ist durch internationale Akteure sowohl demokratischer als auch nicht-demokratischer Provenienz untergraben worden. Durch ständige Kritik eines angeblich monolithischen, pathologischen und ideologischen Imperialismus des Westens verhalten sich Vertreter demokratischer Staaten oft konfus und defensiv. Ihr Verhalten offenbart eine tiefe moralische Skepsis. Auf einer philosophischen Ebene betrachtet, behauptet ein derartiger Relativismus, dass selbst in gleichartigen Situationen das, was richtig oder gut für ein Individuum oder eine Gesellschaft ist, nicht notwendigerweise richtig oder gut für eine andere ist. Der relativistische Standpunkt erlaubt keine allgemeingültige substantielle Kritik an rechtlichen oder moralischen Regeln.

Die einzige Chance auf Rettung für die Lehren und damit das Erbe von Nürnberg liegt in der Formulierung und Anwendung universaler Menschenrechte für alle Menschen, für alle Zeit. Der Angriff auf die Universalität der Menschenrechte gewann bereits nach dem Ende des Kalten Krieges an Akzeptanz. Im Juni 1993 wurde auf der Wiener Menschenrechtskonferenz der UN die Wiener Deklaration und das Aktionsprogramm verabschiedet. Dadurch wurde die Verantwortung für den Schutz nationaler und regionaler Besonderheiten und verschiedener historischer, kultureller und religiöser Umstände den Staaten anheim gestellt, während diese gleichzeitig propagierten, sich für die Aufrechterhaltung und den Schutz der Menschenrechte einzusetzen. Dieser Schritt, das Bekenntnis zur Universalität durch historische oder kulturelle oder religiöse Relativität auszuhöhlen, wurde in den 1990er Jahren noch in drei weiteren UN-Weltkonferenzen verankert – in Bezug auf Bevölkerungswachstum, Entwicklung und Frauenrechte in Kairo, Kopenhagen und Peking.

Die so genannten Besonderheiten sind nicht als freundliche Erinnerung an kontextuelle Umstände, als Appelle für größere Feinfühligkeit oder als Ausgleich unterschiedlicher Meinungen gemeint. Dieselben Staaten, die solche Sonderwünsche fordern, bestehen auch auf Nicht-Einmischung in innenpolitische Angelegenheiten und auf Immunität des nationalen Rechtssystems gegenüber internationaler Kritik.

Wanda M. Akin

Nuremberg, Justice and the Beast of Impunity

I have listened carefully to the powerful and varied voices that have spoken so eloquently during this Conference about the Nuremberg trials. If I was requested to elicit a consensus from amongst these voices about the most important aspect of Nuremberg's legacy, I would expect to hear the phrase "a challenge to impunity" echo from Courtroom 600. This idea is so powerful that if the question were posed to a conference evaluating the specific impact Nuremberg has had on the Ad Hoc Tribunals for Rwanda and the Former Yugoslavia, the Special Court for Sierra Leone and the fledgling ICC, the echo would be the same, "a challenge to impunity!" A similar response would doubtlessly arise concerning Nuremberg's impact on municipal efforts to try violators of human rights and humanitarian law since World War II. However, with respect to these post-Nuremberg proceedings, there arises the question of whether adequate concern has been devoted to the defense function to justify the claim that impunity has been fairly challenged.

The Beast of Impunity

This Nuremberg "impunity" has been so powerful that many of its champions in the international human rights community have come to lose sight of Robert Jackson's pre-Nuremberg warning about the highest principle of justice:

"The ultimate principle is that you must put no man on trial under the forms of judicial proceedings if you are not willing to see him freed if not proven guilty. If you are determined to execute a man in any case, there is no occasion for a trial; the world yields no respect to courts that are merely organized to convict."[1]

My own experience with the Special Court for Sierra Leone has led me to believe that the establishment of that Court did not involve a careful examination of the costs of challenging impunity or of the consequences of not having adequate resources to ensure that the international court solution was the preferable answer to the post war challenges facing that nation.

The civil war in Sierra Leone consumed the decade before 2000, as well as 50.000 lives, tens of thousands of human limbs and the homes of 500.000 refugees. The fighting was part of a larger armed conflict in West Africa that engulfed Sierra Leone, Cote d'Ivoire, Liberia and parts of Guinea. The entire conflict was characterized by significant violations of humanitarian law. In 2000, after a period of disarmament the Special Court for Sierra Leone was established by agreement between the UN and Sierra Leone.[2] A Truth and Reconciliation Commission was established in 2002. There is little evidence of coordination in the decision to launch these two bodies or of significant appreciation of the true "costs" of the Special Court.[3] Nonetheless, the banner "a challenge to impunity" was raised often and sometimes inappropriately during the early stages of trials before the Special Court. During the first trial session of the RUF[4], in which I served as Co-counsel, prosecutor David Crane[5] began his opening statement with talk of impunity:

---

[1] Rule of Law Among Nations Speech, April 13, 1945 http://www.roberthjackson.org/Man/theman2-7-7-1/.

[2] Statute of the Special Court for Sierra Leone, pursuant to S.C. Res. 1315 (2000) of 14 August 2000, at arts. 2, 3, & 5, available at http://www.sc-sl.org/.

[3] See for an early optimistic assessment of the two institutions which concedes the lack of planning Elizabeth M. Evenson, *NOTE: Truth and Justice in Sierra Leone: Coordination Between Commission and Court*, 104 COLUM. L. REV. 730 (2004) and Report from the Freetown Conference on Accountability Mechanisms for Violations of International Humanitarian Law in Sierra Leone (Feb. 20-22, 2001), available at http://www.sierra-leone.org/npwj0200.html.

[4] The principle forces in the Sierra Leonean civil war were: the regular Sierra Leonean Army (SLA), the Revolutionary United Front (RUF), who was the earliest rebel group, the AFRC composed of military factions that mutinied during the Civil War, and a civilian militia, which fought for the government (CDF). Witnesses frequently called the AFRC personnel "junta" members, the CDF "Kamajors" for the traditional hunters that comprised much of its personnel. Other terms like "rebels" were used without clear distinctions. Because relatively few personnel outside of the SLA wore complete uniforms ("combat") efforts to visually distinguish the groups were less than precise. As trials commenced there were nine detainees

"May it please the Court; this is a tale of horror, beyond the gothic into the realm of Dante's inferno. They came across the border, dark shadows, on a warm spring day, 23 March of 1991. Hardened rebels trained by outside actors from Liberia, Libya and Burkino Faso. These dogs of war, these hounds from hell, unleashed by cynical –

MR. BROWN: *I object. Objection. I object, your Honour.*"[6]

Crane frequently used the phrase "beasts of impunity", employing it to link the accused on trial with others whose guilt may be manifest but who are likely to never face a court:

"Throughout this war crimes trial against Sesay, Kallon and Gbao, the phantoms of the deceased indictees, Foday Sankoh and Samuel Bockarie, will be ever present in this hall of justice. Additionally, Charles Taylor would be sitting next to these accused war criminals today had he been turned over to this tribunal for a fair trial. Their alleged crimes against humanity cannot justly or practically be ignored, as they were the handmaidens to the beast, the beast of impunity that walked this burnt and pillaged land."[7]

Counsel for Morris Kallon gave an opening statement in which he offered a response to the "impunity" notion.

"...[T]here is something troubling about talking about impunity by itself because it invites us to say, 'Well there clearly were,' and this Court is judicially noticed 'wide-scale humanitarian violations in Sierra Leone during the period of this conflict and someone must pay,' and the phrase 'beast of impunity' invites us to say, 'Well we must find someone who can pay from among these Accused,' ... when in fact the nature of impunity does not revolve [sic] such sacrifices, but rather a continued adherence to the rule of law and the burden of this Prosecution ...to prove a case against Morris Kallon.... The evidence about Morris Kallon will not demonstrate or even come close to suggesting that he is a hand-maiden of evil as has been suggested in this hall."[8]

This colloquy squarely puts the question of whether the accused should be tried on the basis of the evidence against him, or on the basis of society's resentment of historical "impunity" for humanitarian and human rights law violations. As my husband and co-counsel argued, "this beast of impunity ought not to be satiated by feeding him – Morris Kollon – in the absence of evidence of proof beyond a reasonable doubt."[9]

An Ironic Smuggling Incident

The question which disturbed me was whether the need for resources for the defense severely prejudiced the defense function in disregard of Robert Jackson's warning. In seeking an answer to these questions, I have been continually haunted by an ironic smuggling episode long after leaving West Africa. The incident occurred during the first trial session whose opening statements I have already touched upon. The narrative's unwillingness to retreat from my consciousness reflects its symbolic connection to important questions surrounding the Special Court.

---

in the Special Court Detention Facility. (No accused had been granted bail). Each of the main military forces other than the SLA was represented. Three accused were from the RUF, three from the CDF, and three from the AFRC. Although prosecutors originally sought a joint trial, the Special Court severed the accused into three different trials conforming to their group identification. The three RUF accused were Issa Sesay, Augustine Gbao, and Morris Kallon. They faced indictment SCSL-04-15-T. I was co-counsel to Morris Kallon.

[5] David Crane, an American, was Chief Prosecutor at the Special Court for Sierra Leone until the summer of 2005. He shared responsibility for delivering the Opening Statement in the RUF case with a Sierra Leonean in the Office of The Prosecutor, Abdul Tejan Cole.

[6] Tr. Page 19 Lines 17 – 22. Brown's objection "The reference to dogs of war, my client – that may be a metaphor – I find that objectionable" was sustained at Page 20 Line 2. [Videotapes of this and other relevant portions of the opening statements were played during my presentation at the Nuremberg Conference].

[7] Tr. Page 22 Lines 17 – 22. An objection to this passage was overruled.

[8] Tr Page 72.

[9] Tr.76 Lines 7-9.

On July 22, 2004, Counsel to Issa Sesay, regarded as the senior ranking accused, informed the Court that on the previous day an incident had arisen which was "of great concern to the defense." Counsel said that when the families of the accused, including women, had terminated their visits, "[T]he accused [sic] families were then taken to the old courtroom wherein a search took place of the females which involved the removal of clothes and the insertion of fingers into the vaginas of the women."[10] The Court appropriately directed that the Registrar and the head of the Detention Facility report to the Court on this event as soon as possible.[11] Because this exchange took place in open session, the *Sierra Leonean Press*, which can resemble tabloids on steroids, provided headlines such as, "Sexual Harassment at Special Court."[12] Readers had to explore the smaller print to find suggestions that these were mere allegations.

Consumers of the Sierra Leone Fourth Estate did not have long to wait to learn of further developments. On July 25, 2004, the headline in the *Salome Times* declared "No Private Parts Were Searched,"[13] while the *Concord Times* took a stab at legal journalism with the lead "Judge Itoe Rules Against Private Parts."[14] These reports were based on a hearing at which Barry Wallace, the Chief of Detention for the Special Court, reported that there had been a proper search, conducted by Sierra Leonean personnel, under the supervision of his international staff. Furthermore, Wallace testified that, "at no time was any person asked to remove clothing or subject to an intimate internal search."[15]

More importantly, Wallace said the investigation revealed that family members, were smuggling "medication, cigarettes, and bars of soap" *out of the detention facility*. In the world of criminal justice and incarceration, it is extremely rare for contraband to flow *out* of a prison. The normal laws of supply and demand usually direct the flow of forbidden items from the world outside in to the incarcerated. However, the poverty of Sierra Leone, in particular that of demobilized former combatants, meant that the tiny, thriving sub-economy in the comparatively well-appointed detention facility behind the walls of the Special Court Compound, provided more basic necessities than even the former leaders of the RUF, AFRC and CDF could muster. Consequently, a logical resource for the accused's families to explore was the rations available to their detained breadwinners.[16]

As if to reemphasize the depth of the continuing economic depression in Sierra Leone, this "reverse smuggling" episode took place six days after the United Nations Development Programme (UNDP) released its annual Human Development Index[17] which ranked Sierra Leone last *in the world*.[18] War obviously takes a toll on developing countries.[19] However, governments like those of Sierra Leone, which continuously fail to meet the economic needs of their people also contribute to this effect.[20]

---

[10] Trial Transcript, Special Court Sierra Leone, Trial Chamber I, Thursday, 22 July 2004, Page 1, Lines 27-29.

[11] I have been visiting detention facilities, prisons, and jails in the United States for over 20 years and the general conditions in the Special Court Detention Facility compare favorably, if not indeed better, than in the United States.

[12] www.BrownAkin.com.

[13] www.BrownAkin.com.

[14] www.BrownAkin.com.

[15] Transcript Of Hearing, Special Court Sierra Leone, Trial Chamber I, Thursday, 23 July 2004.

[16] Wallace had testified at the Special Court hearing that he had ordered the searches because the detainees had been consuming more malaria diarrhea medication than was reasonable for their number.

[17] The Index is published as part of UNDP's Annual Development Report, entitled in 2004, Cultural Literacy in Today's Diverse World, available at http://hdr.undp.org/reports/global/2004/pdf/hdr04_HDI.pdf (last visited June 5, 2004).

[18] Sierra Leone ranked 177th out of the 177 ranked nations. The ranking is based on UNDP's Human Development Index Value which is a function of *inter alia* GDP, per capita GDP Education Index, Life Expectancy Index, and Literacy Index.

[19] Afghanistan ranked 173rd in the 2004 Human Development Index.

[20] The Sierra Leone Truth and Reconciliation Commission found that "even before the war public service delivery had ground to a halt". SLTRC VOL 2.3 paragraph 249. It noted further that even after the war, and with UNAMSIL still present the government continued to spend more on the military than on education. SLTRC VOL 2.3 paragraph 249.

The refusal of this strange episode to leave my mind as I anticipated participating in this Conference[21] led me to wonder if the reverse smuggling tale had importance beyond illustrating a Sierra Leonean nuance to the laws of prison economy. My exploration of this possibility raised two questions requiring further examination:

1. Is the Special Court for Sierra Leone part of a broader international effort that is likely to help produce social justice for Sierra Leone?

2. What is the "Quality of Justice" likely to be dispensed with by the Special Court? Is the court likely to achieve significant advances in international humanitarian law? Are the Court's resources adequate to explore these issues in the context of a fair trial? (These are the criteria by which any international judicial effort is evaluated.)

Justice in Sierra Leone

I shall explore both of these questions briefly, hoping in the future to examine them in greater depth. Is the Special Court for Sierra Leone part of a broader international effort that is likely to help produce social justice for Sierra Leone?

I whole heartedly embrace the movement against impunity described in the first section of this paper for those guilty of serious violations of international humanitarian law. The movement has existed since Nuremberg, and gained momentum since the Cold War with the advent of the ad hoc-Tribunals,[22] a series of "hybrid" courts,[23] and the International Criminal Court. However, in the aftermath of a specific conflict, one of the questions posed about the effectiveness of a special court or tribunal is whether the institution can contribute to social justice and whether nations can insure adequate resources so that the challenge to impunity involves fair proceedings.

The particulars of the Special Court for Sierra Leone suggest the need for close examination of our "special lesson" in prison economics. The international community will spend $50 to $100 million dollars[24] on this Court, which will try nine men while suffering from the "big fish" syndrome.[25] Charles Taylor, viewed by many as the prime moving force in the series of civil wars in West Africa and under indictment at the Special Court, currently is sheltered in Nigeria. RUF leaders Foday Sankoh, acknowledged as the leader of the RUF during the war, and Sam "Mosquito" Bockarie, an RUF leader regarded as perhaps the most egregious violator of humanitarian laws during the ten year Sierra Leone civil war, died before they could be tried. Also indicted by the Special Court, is former AFRC leader, Johnny Paul Koroma, who is at large or deceased.

According to the statute of the Special Court for Sierra Leone the Court has jurisdiction over those "who bear the greatest responsibility for serious violations of international humanitarian law...".[26] Although it could be argued that it is still too early for final judgment, it can easily be maintained that eight of the nine accused[27] fall outside of this description. In fact, the negotiators of the statute specifically rejected language proposed by UN officials which would have broadened the Court's

---

[21] Law and the Humanities' Representation of the Holocaust, Genocide and Other Human Rights Violations, presented by Thomas Jefferson School of Law and the Law and Humanities Institute, January 16-17, 2005 at Congregation Beth Israel and Thomas Jefferson School of Law.

[22] The International Criminal Tribunal for Rwanda and the International Criminal Tribunal for the Former Yugoslavia.

[23] These include *inter alia*: Special Panels for Serious Crimes in East Timor, Regulation 64 Courts in Kosovo, Extraordinary Chambers in the Courts of Cambodia for the Prosecution of Crimes Committed during the Period of Democratic Kampuchea, and the Special Court for Sierra Leone.

[24] '*Bringing Justice*': *The Special Court for Sierra Leone Accomplishments, Shortcomings and Needed Support*, 16 HUMAN RIGHTS WATCH 1, 4 (2004).

[25] *Id*. at 10 (Human Rights Watch, which generally supports the Special Court's mission, concedes that some of the "biggest fish" are absent).

[26] Statute of the Special Court for Sierra Leone, Art 1.1 (2000).

[27] Sam Hinga Norman, the former Minister of Internal Affairs and National Security of Sierra Leone and a leader of the Kamajors, by virtue of his former government high office might be said to be one of those accused encompassed by the statute.

mandate to include those who bore "most" responsibility.[28] This suggests that the Court's activities may ultimately be found wanting when the final assessment is made of the balance between deterrence, retribution, judicial economy, and the economic prospects of most Sierra Leoneans. Resources expended in prosecuting major alleged violators, like Charles Taylor, could produce a more favorable evaluation of the Court's performance than when used to try nine accused, eight of whom clearly do not bear the greatest responsibility.

The large shadow cast by Taylor over Sierra Leone's bloody decade raises an even more profound question. Are there times when economic and social justice requires security and stability rather than judicial process? In Liberia itself, the international community opted to support Nigeria's grant of "asylum" to Taylor, even in the face of an outstanding indictment at the Special Court for Sierra Leone and quite possibly in lieu of any future prosecution of Taylor in Liberia. In defending Taylor's continued presence in Nigeria, President Olusegun Obasanjo recalled the reached solution with then US Secretary of State, Colin Powell, and stated, "[w]e put our heads together and decided that Charles Taylor must be eased out because if we fail to ease him out, he would dig in and there would have been a tremendous destruction of lives and property. In coming to that decision to ease him out, we were mindful of our duty and responsibility to humanity, the people of Liberia and West Africa."[29]

This same analysis of the importance of social and economic justice in the Sierra Leonean context leads to the question of whether any resources expended on any trials of any persons can be justified in light of the economic plight facing most Sierra Leoneans in the post-war economy. As I have already noted, the TRC concluded that bad governance was a primary cause of the civil war. A renewed focus on the problem of bad governance and the related issue of economic development may be seen one day in retrospect to have been a wiser channeling of resources than any trials.

While avoiding a comparative analysis of expenditures on criminal justice versus an attack on bad governance and poverty, a variety of voices have noted *that because of bad governance* Sierra Leone missed the latest wave of economic assistance and debt relief to poor countries.

"Sierra Leone this month [June 2005] received a double blow. First, a meeting between prospective donors in Paris to discuss the World Bank's poverty-reduction strategy was called *off and the* country was left off the G 8's list of 18 nations marked down as the first beneficiaries of its debt-cancellation plan. In both cases Sierra Leone's government failed to convince donor and creditor countries that it is truly tackling corruption."[30]

Sierra Leonean journalist Rod MacJohnson observed that, "[t]he European Union has withheld two million euros that were to be used to fund local elections set for May 22, citing among its reasons the fact that the electoral commission has not accounted for how it disbursed funds for the 2002 presidential and general elections. The EU is also sending audit teams this month to the capital Freetown to see just how the millions it has contributed to help rebuild the country have been spent."[31] He also quoted former British MP from Bridgend, Winston James Griffiths, who led a November 2003 Parliamentary corruption investigation into Sierra Leone as warning, "[t]he government of Sierra Leone must do

---

[28] In a Sep. 25, 2000 press briefing by UN Assistant Secretary-General Office of Legal Affairs, Ralph Zacklin stated, "In terms of those who bear the greatest responsibility for the crimes, in our report we will be suggesting a slightly different variation of this formula. That would be 'those most responsible'. The reason for this is that we feel that the formula 'greatest responsibility' probably pitches the personal jurisdiction very narrowly and probably too high to capture all of those who bear some degree of command or leadership responsibility may have committed crimes. And so we will be proposing in our report that the personal jurisdiction should extend to those who are most responsible. This is intended to cover those who were in leadership positions, either politically or militarily." Press Release, UN Assistant Secretary-General Office of Legal Affairs, Ralph Zacklin, (Sept. 25, 2004) (on file with the Thomas Jefferson Law Review).

[29] *The Heat Is On: Just when he thought he could breathe easy, exiled former Liberian president, Charles Taylor finds himself facing an uncertain future as pressure mounts on his hosts Nigeria to hand him over to the International War Crimes Tribunal.* By Martin Luther King, VOL. 11 No. 6 AFRICA TODAY, June 2005.

[30] Sierra Leone Still in intensive care: Despite British and UN help, Sierra Leone remains too fragile to go it alone, THE ECONOMIST, June 25, 2005.

[31] Spotlight falls on corruption in Sierra Leone, by Rod MacJohnson/South African Press Association-Agence France-Presse, Independent Online, May 6, 2004, available at http://www.odiousdebts.org.

everything within its power to stop corruption." Other sources have noted similar warnings from Gordon Brown, the UK's finance minister.[32]

The Special Court compound may serve as a tangible metaphor for the failure to assess accurately the need for justice expenditures versus anti-corruption and economic development activities. The Special Court's physical courthouse has been touted as a state-of-the-art facility, outfitted with the latest advances in architecture, design and technology.[33] Justification for these expenditures on bricks, mortar, and wire for an international tribunal in poverty stricken Sierra Leone, as opposed to bread, butter, and books has been questioned. Advocates for the SCSL have argued that perhaps, the Special Court could be a legacy for the country, as a permanent locale for a regional or even international tribunal once the Special Court has outlived its usefulness under the Statute.

The ten-year Sierra Leone civil war left a government with its economy in tatters, still influenced by corruption, and susceptible to charges of bad governance. At the same time, its citizens continue to be denied basic human rights. There is at least an entire generation of the population left uneducated, tens-of-thousands in the population in need of health care, thousands of amputees in camps in Freetown, and a country with a cobbled together infrastructure – without a "Marshall Plan" to rebuild it. The ultimate assessment of the value of the Special Court will have to acknowledge the economic plight of most ordinary Sierra Leoneans.

The question about the quality of justice requires an examination about whether the Special Court has the appropriate structure and adequate resources in order to significantly improve international humanitarian law. The international community has lauded the Special Court for the opinion of its Appeals Chamber finding that its Rule 4(c)[34] permits the accused to be tried for the recruitment of child soldiers. While this is the first ruling on this subject by an international criminal tribunal, the only real issue in dispute in the Appeals Chamber was whether this duty flows from the Geneva Conventions and the Convention On The Rights Of The Child, which would establish a pre-war duty, or from the Rome Statute for the International Criminal Court which would establish a duty as of 1998.

Within the framework of the fight over funding for the Special Court, the share of the resource pie for the defense is insufficient, arguably an afterthought, in marked contrast to careful planning for the outfitting of judicial chambers, the Office of the Prosecutor, and the Registry.[35] The debate over insufficient funding for the defense of the accused at the SCSL is well documented.[36]

I have experienced firsthand the limitations that a lack of resources places on developing a defense and preparing for trial. I was responsible for amassing the statistical data and anecdotal facts to support the defense's theory respecting the child soldier and forced marriage issues. The defense to the charge of conscription of child soldiers can be profoundly affected by the determination of exactly who was a child. Obtaining age information for all of the disarmed "children" was impossible in Sierra Leone, a

---

[32] *Sierra Leone Misses Out on Debt Relief This Time Out: Corruption and Poor Democratic Governance the cause?*, Article available at http://www.cocorioko.com.

[33] See photo of the author, Wanda M. Akin, with husband and co-counsel, Raymond M. Brown, outside of the newly constructed courthouse at the Special Court of Sierra Leone, July 20, 2004. The courthouse is by far the best structure *in the entire country*. www.BrownAkin.com.

[34] DECISION ON PRELIMINARY MOTION BASED ON LACK OF JURISDICTION (CHILD RECRUITMENT) PROSECUTOR V SAM HINGA NORMAN (Moinina Fofana intervening) Case Number SCSL-2003-14-AR72(E) May 31, 2004.

[35] Rupert Skilbeck, *'Building the Fourth Pillar: Defence Rights at the Special Court for Sierra Leone'*, 1 ESSEX HUMAN RIGHTS REVIEW, 66, 69 (2004).

[36] Even Human Rights Watch which has given the Special Court high marks overall concedes that "the lack of resources available to defense teams paid for by the court, which relates at least in part to under funding of the court more generally by donors, could constrain their ability to mount a defense". *Bringing Justice: The Special Court for Sierra Leone Accomplishments, Shortcomings and Needed Support*, *supra* note 25, at 6. My experience with the UN version of the British VHCC system which requires lawyers to guess at their own, or the client's peril how much they will require for fees and costs is unworkable in international trials. (For a detailed description of this system see Skilbeck, *supra* note 36.).

country having a birth registration rate of less than 10%.[37] Additionally, adult males frequently visually appear to be significantly younger than their stated age. Further complicating matters, many witnesses were uncertain of their actual ages and had to guess. UNICEF noted in its report on *The Progress of Nations 1998* that, "[a] birth certificate is a ticket to citizenship. Without one, an individual does not officially exist and therefore lacks legal access to the privileges and protections of a nation."[38] Pursuit of this birth registry aspect of the defense was particularly daunting, requiring interviews with dozens of government officials, and many hours on the ground "gum shoeing" the facts and chasing down statistical data in a multitude of cyber locations.

The indictment of the RUF accused on the forced marriage-charge is the first in international humanitarian law.[39] The defense to the charge of forced marriage is profoundly affected by the various defense teams' ability to conduct research and line up witnesses to expound upon Sierra Leone's customary family law. Presented with this challenge, it was only through a serendipitous confluence of events and circumstantial meetings, taking place all over the world that I was able to speak with a Sierra Leonean jurist and legal scholar, H.M. Joko Smart, B.A., LL.M, Ph.D, who authored a long out of print authoritative text[40] on this question. Extensive interviews with the "bush wives" and their families and in-depth exploration of their circumstances and motives for their involvement with the accused were required. *Sierra Leone Customary Family Law* had to be read and fully digested to explore the evolution of family law in Sierra Leone and to trace its tribal origins. A collective of brilliant interns was needed to break down these tribal notions of traditional marriage into the relevant facts in order to organize this aspect of the defense. As in municipal law,[41] unraveling the social relationship and legal history of any couple in the context of family law litigation can be extremely complicated. Add to this the component of international criminal prosecution of an accused, in a war crimes-tribunal where the defense has limited resources, and this task can be characterized as extraordinarily daunting.

Without resources to develop fully these issues and to unveil them to the international legal community at trial, the SCSL's contribution to any "advance" in international humanitarian law may prove one-sided and lack credibility. Simply put, the prosecution of these charges has not been tested in a fair fight. The Special Court was created as a model for other regional tribunals and heralded as a viable option for the resolution of other "African conflicts". The failure to fund fully the defense efforts could give rise to the charge that the prosecutions were unjust, and that the "advance" in international law that the prosecutions ushered in may be discredited as soundly achieved precedent.

Conclusion

I began this paper with an exploration of the challenge to impunity. The question which is dramatized by my experience in Sierra Leone is whether the rush to challenge impunity causes us to undermine the integrity of the institutions we build for this purpose. Someday, historians will evaluate the impact of "completion strategies" on the Special Court and even perhaps the ad hoc-Tribunals. These fiscal, administrative and politically driven requirements that the task of administering justice be completed within financial and time constraints are necessary but risky. If these constraints are developed without adequate consideration for their impact on the quality of justice, then the legacy of Nuremberg is seriously jeopardized.

The London Charter negotiations were full of spirited debates involving Robert Jackson and General I.T. Nikitchenko, the Soviet representative, about the need for speedy trials for the accused Nazi war criminals. The Soviets were so committed to a rapid trial process that they sought to bypass the

---

[37] UNICEF, Child protection, available at http://www.unicef.org/infobycountry/sierraleone_statistics.html (last visited June 8, 2005).
[38] The Progress of Nations 1998 Civil Rights: Commentary, available at http://www.unicef.org/pon98/civil1.htm (last visited June 8, 2005).
[39] RUF Case No. SCSL-204-15-PT Amended Consolidated Indictment, so amended to charge forced marriage.
[40] H.M. Joko Smart, SIERRA LEONE CUSTOMARY FAMILY LAW (Freetown: Atlantic Printers Ltd. 1983).
[41] Municipal Law: the law of nation states as opposed to international law.

determination of guilt altogether and proceed to the question of sentencing. The Soviet delegate said, "[t]he whole idea is to secure quick and just punishment for the crime."[42] Robert Jackson was equally convinced of both the culpability of the accused and of the need for speed but sought to resolve those dilemmas in the context of a complete and fair trial.[43] Jackson's sensitivity to competing concerns about speed and justice was reflected in his opening statement:

"Before I discuss the particulars of the evidence we are about to offer, some general considerations which may affect the credibility of this trial in the eyes of the world should be candidly faced. There is a dramatic disparity in circumstances between the accusers and the accused that might discredit our work if we should falter in even minor matters of being fair and temperate. Unfortunately the nature of these crimes is such that both prosecution and judgment must be by victor nations over vanquished foes. The world wide scope of the aggressions carried out by these men has left but few real neutrals. Either the victor must judge the vanquished or we must leave the defeated to judge themselves. After the First World War we learned the futility of the latter course."

One could argue that Jackson partially skirted the dilemma himself by invoking the specter of the failed Leipzig trials. Nonetheless, the London Charter negotiations and the trial itself reflected a continuous effort to struggle with this question and arrive at a balance between expedition and resources that has caused so many divergent voices at this conference to articulate confidence that Nuremberg stands in large part for the principle of challenging impunity. I remain concerned that efforts at the Special Court to wrap that tribunal's efforts in the mantle of Nuremberg may ultimately fail because the forces shaping that court have not shown comparable concern for the functional needs of the defense.

---

[42] Whitney R. Harris, TYRANNY ON TRIAL, THE TRIAL OF THE MAJOR GERMAN WAR CRIMINALS AT THE END OF WORLD WAR II AT NUREMBERG, GERMANY, 1945-1946, 17 (Dallas 1999).
[43] Id., at 18.

Wanda M. Akin

Nürnberg, Gerechtigkeit und das Schreckgespenst der Straflosigkeit

Straflosigkeit für Verbrechen gegen die Menschlichkeit ist in der Folgezeit von Nürnberg zu einer Horrorvision geworden. Bei den *ad hoc*-Tribunalen für das ehemalige Jugoslawien und Ruanda, beim Internationalen Strafgerichtshof ebenso wie vor dem Sondergericht für Sierra Leone wird die Straffreiheit von den Verteidigern der Angeklagten immer wieder gefordert. Die Autorin dieses Beitrags erinnert als ehemalige Strafverteidigerin vor dem Sondergericht für Sierra Leone an den Ausspruch des Nürnberger Chefanklägers Robert Jackson, dass ein Strafverfahren nur dann eröffnet werden soll, wenn die Bereitschaft besteht, die Angeklagten freizusprechen, falls ihre Schuld nicht bewiesen werden kann. Darüber hinaus wird die Gerechtigkeit insgesamt in Frage gestellt, wenn in einem der ärmsten Länder der Welt, wie in Sierra Leone, vor einem finanziell bestens ausgestatteten Sondergericht (dem Gericht stehen mehr als 50 Millionen Dollar zur Verfügung) einigen wenigen Angeklagten (lediglich neun in Sierra Leone) der Prozess gemacht wird, deren Angehörige anlässlich von Besuchen im Gefängnis versuchen, Lebens- und Genussmittel aus dem Gefängnis zu schmuggeln. Untersuchungshäftlinge werden zu Ernährern ihrer Angehörigen. Zugleich fehlt eine angemessene Unterstützung zur Finanzierung einer effektiven Verteidigung vor Gericht. Am Beispiel der Kindersoldaten und von Zwangsheirat wird aufgezeigt, dass Strafverteidigung auch bei berüchtigten Bürgerkriegsverbrechern notwendig ist und erfolgreich sein kann. Die Autorin kommt zu dem Ergebnis, dass am Sondergericht von Sierra Leone die von Jackson in Nürnberg feinfühlig erkannte Spannung zwischen Beschleunigung der Verfahren und Gerechtigkeit für die Angeklagten zu Lasten Letzterer entschieden wurde und so das Erbe von Nürnberg in Gefahr geraten ist.

Andreas Zimmermann

Das juristische Erbe von Nürnberg – Das Statut des Nürnberger Internationalen Militärtribunals und der Internationale Strafgerichtshof

I. Einleitung

Im Jahr 2005 jährt sich zum 60. Mal der Beginn der Nürnberger Prozesse gegen die Hauptverantwortlichen für die im Kontext mit dem Zweiten Weltkrieg begangenen Verbrechen gegen den Frieden, Verbrechen gehen die Menschlichkeit und Kriegsverbrechen. Anlass genug der Frage nachzugehen, welche Folgen die Verfahren für die weitere Entwicklung des Völkerstrafrechts und dabei namentlich für das im Jahr 2002 in Kraft getretene Römische Statut des Ständigen Internationalen Strafgerichtshofes (ICC)[1] hatten.

Nach dem fehlgeschlagenen Versuch, Kaiser Wilhelm II. nach dem Ersten Weltkrieg – wie im Versailler Friedensvertrag vorgesehen – wegen Bruchs der internationalen Moral und der Heiligkeit der Verträge – vor ein alliiertes Militärgericht zu stellen,[2] und den Leipziger Prozessen vor dem deutschen Reichsgericht, die bekanntermaßen entweder zu Freisprüchen oder aber nur zu geringen Freiheitsstrafen führten, die zudem in nur wenigen Fällen wirklich verbüßt wurden,[3] aber auch angesichts der Einzigartigkeit hinsichtlich der Art und des Umfangs der begangenen Verbrechen, hatten sich die Alliierten bereits in ihrer Moskauer Erklärung aus dem Jahre 1943 dazu entschlossen, sowohl für die in Europa durch Deutsche als auch für die japanischen Hauptverantwortlichen jeweils ein eigenes Militärtribunal einzusetzen, deren Rechtsgrundlagen aber im Wesentlichen identisch waren.

Es war dieser Präzedenzfall, welcher für die Errichtung einer internationalen, auf einer völkerrechtlichen Grundlage beruhenden Strafgerichtsbarkeit für individuelle Täter – wenn auch mit einer jahrzehntelangen Verzögerung – bahnbrechend war, wenngleich der ausbrechende Ost-Westkonflikt und die mit ihm einhergehenden ideologischen Konflikte verhinderten, dass es bereits in der unmittelbaren Nachkriegszeit zu einem ernsthaften Versuch kam eine ständige internationale Strafgerichtsbarkeit zu etablieren.

Vielmehr bedurfte es erst der tragischen Ereignisse im ehemaligem Jugoslawien und in Ruanda und der seinerseits bahnbrechenden Initiative des Sicherheitsrates der Vereinten Nationen, für die juristische Aufarbeitung der Konflikte jeweils *ad hoc* ein Tribunal zu errichten,[4] um den Gedanken an einen ständigen internationalen Strafgerichtshof wiederzubeleben und ihm zugleich neue Schubkraft zu verleihen. Gleichzeitig lassen sich aber vielfältige Einflüsse des Nürnberger Statuts und der Rechtsprechung des Internationalen Militärtribunals (IMT) auf das Statut von Rom nachweisen.

II. Nürnberg und die Grundlagen der Völkerstrafgerichtsbarkeit

1) Nürnberg und der Einwand des unzulässigen Vertrags zu Lasten Dritter

Rechtsgrundlage für die Errichtung des Nürnberger Militärtribunals war das von den Hauptsiegermächten in der Londoner Charta konzipierte und schließlich von insgesamt 23 Staaten ratifizierte Statut, mithin also ein völkerrechtlicher Vertrag. Anders als die beiden *ad hoc*-Tribunale für das ehemalige Jugoslawien (ICTY) und für Ruanda (ICTR) basierten die Nürnberger Prozesse also weder auf einem Beschluss des formal noch existierenden Völkerbundes,[5] noch gar auf einer

---

[1] Rome Statute of the International Criminal Court, adopted by the United Nations Diplomatic Conference of Plenipotentiaries on the Establishment of an International Criminal Court on 17 July 1998, A/CONF.183/9 (17. Juli 1998); die Bundesrepublik Deutschland hat das Statut am 10. Dez. 2000 ratifiziert, vgl. BGBl. 2000, Teil II, 1394.

[2] Vgl. insoweit Art. 227 des Versailler Friedensvertrages, abgedruckt in RGBl. 1919 II, S. 687-1349; näher zu den Hintergründen der niederländischen Weigerung, Wilhelm II. an die Alliierten auszuliefern H. Ahlbrecht, Geschichte der völkerrechtlichen Strafgerichtsbarkeit im 20. Jahrhundert: unter besonderer Berücksichtigung der völkerrechtlichen Straftatbestände und der Bemühungen um einen ständigen Internationalen Strafgerichtshof, 1999, S. 37 f.

[3] Näher zu diesen sogenannten „Leipziger Verfahren" H. Ahlbrecht, *supra* Fn. 2, S. 41 ff.

[4] Vgl. insoweit Sicherheitsresolution 827 vom 25. Mai 1993 bzw. Sicherheitsresolution 955 vom 8. Nov. 1994.

[5] Der Völkerbund wurde erst durch eine Entscheidung des Völkerbundsrates vom 18. April 1946 aufgelöst.

Entscheidung der Organe der neu gegründeten Organisation der Vereinten Nationen, noch anders als das Militärtribunal für den Fernen Osten auf einer Anordnung der Besatzungsmächte.[6] Damit stellte sich für das Nürnberger Militärtribunal die Grundsatzfrage, wie sich die entsprechende Ausübung strafrechtlicher Jurisdiktion gegenüber dem *de jure* fortbestehenden Deutschen Reich[7] im Lichte der *pacta-tertiis*-Regel rechtfertigen lassen konnte, zumal Gegenstand der Strafverfahren ja nicht nur Taten zu Lasten von Staatsangehörigen der Vertragsparteien des Statuts des IMT, sondern auch solche zu Lasten von Staatsangehörigen von Drittstaaten, sowie solche zu Lasten von deutschen Staatsangehörigen, und dabei namentlich solche jüdischen Glaubens, waren.

Vor diesem Hintergrund gewinnt die Aussage des Nürnberger Gerichtshofes besondere Bedeutung, dass die Siegermächte gemeinsam das getan haben, was jeder Einzelne von ihnen hätte tun können,[8] nämlich Strafgerichtsbarkeit für die im Nürnberger Statut umschriebenen Delikte auszuüben. Mithin lag also dem Nürnberger Verfahren der Grundgedanke einer gebündelten Ausübung delegierter nationaler Strafgewalt zugrunde.

Und es ist genau diese Überlegung, die im Zusammenhang mit dem Statut des Internationalen Strafgerichtshofes den US-amerikanischen Einwand widerlegt, bei diesem handele es sich um einen nach Art. 34 des ‚Wiener Übereinkommens über das Recht der Verträge' verbotenen Vertrag zu Lasten Dritter.[9] Denn auch im Fall des Rom-Statuts tun die Vertragsparteien nichts Anderes als – um mit den Worten des Nürnberger Gerichtshofes zu sprechen – das, was jeder von ihnen allen allein hätte tun können. Anders als im Fall des IMT haben die Vertragsparteien des Rom-Statuts zudem im Hinblick auf Drittstaatsangehörige nach Art. 12 des Statuts die Jurisdiktion des ICC auf solche Taten beschränkt, die auf ihrem Staatsgebiet oder durch ihre Staatsangehörigen begangen werden, obwohl sie mit guten Gründen – wie denn auch von der Bundesrepublik Deutschland während der diplomatischen Konferenz in Rom vertreten[10] – dessen Jurisdiktion nach dem Weltrechtsprinzip auch in völkerrechtlich zulässiger Weise hätte weiter gezogen werden können.[11]

Am Rande sei noch darauf hingewiesen, dass sich auch das Jugoslawientribunal im *Milutonovic*-Verfahren – wenn auch nur indirekt – der Auffassung angeschlossen hat, dass die Vereinten Nationen auch zu Lasten eines Drittstaates Strafgewalt ausüben können.[12]

2) Nürnberg und der Einwand der ex post facto-Strafbarkeit

Der wohl gewichtigste juristische Einwand gegen die Errichtung des IMT konnte sich – jedenfalls was die Verbrechen gegen den Frieden und die Verbrechen gegen die Menschheit anbelangte – auf den *nulla poena*-Grundsatz stützen. Konnte man diesen Einwand nach meiner Auffassung im Kontext des Nürnberger Gerichtshofes allenfalls mit grundsätzlichen Überlegungen entkräften, die dahingehen, dass die Bestrafung der fraglichen schlimmsten Menschheitsverbrechen, die wir heute zweifellos als *jus*

---

[6] Vgl. im Hinblick auf das International Military Tribunal for the Far East die entsprechende Anordnung des US-amerikanischen Oberkommandierenden MacArthur vom 19. Januar 1946, Wortlaut u.a. bei http://www.yale.edu/lawweb/avalon/imtfech.htm.

[7] Vgl. insoweit nur etwa grundlegend BVerfGE 36, 1, 16.

[8] Urteil des Internationalen Militärgerichtshofes im Prozeß gegen die Hauptkriegsverbrecher, Urteil vom 1.10.1946, Bd. 1, 244.

[9] Der insoweit einschlägige Art. 34 des Wiener Übereinkommens über das Recht der Verträge lautet: „Ein Vertrag begründet für einen Drittstaat ohne dessen Zustimmung weder Pflichten noch Rechte." Näher zu diesem Einwand D. Scheffer, The United States and the International Criminal Court, AJIL 93 (1999), 12, 17 ff.; vgl. andererseits aber auch G. Hafner, An Attempt to Explain the Position of the USA Towards the ICC, JICJ 3 (2005), 323 ff., sowie A. Zimmermann/ H. Scheel, Zwischen Konfrontation und Kooperation – die Vereinigten Staaten und der Internationale Gerichtshof, VN 50 (2002), 137 f.

[10] H.-P. Kaul, Der Internationale Strafgerichtshof: Das Ringen um seine Zuständigkeit und Reichweite, Humanitäres Völkerrecht 11 (1998), 138, 140f.

[11] Dazu näher A. Zimmermann, Die Schaffung eines ständigen Internationalen Strafgerichtshofes. Perspektiven und Probleme vor der Staatenkonferenz in Rom, ZaöRV 58 (1998), 45, 84.

[12] *The Prosecutor v. Milutinovic et al.*, Decision on motion challenging jurisdiction (Case No. IT-99-37-PT), 6. Mai 2003, Ziff. 45-63, Text verfügbar unter: http://www.un.org/icty/milutinovic/trialc/decision-e/030506.htm.

cogens-Verstöße qualifizieren würden,[13] auch eine Abweichung vom Verbot des *nulla-poena*-Satzes rechtfertigen, stellt es einen wesentlichen rechtsstaatlichen Fortschritt dar, dass mit der Schaffung des ICC nunmehr *ex ante* sowohl die materiell-rechtlichen Tatbestände kodifiziert worden sind, als auch die Grenzen der Jurisdiktion *ratione temporis* des Gerichtshofes umschrieben wurden.

Darüber hinaus dürften, anders als im Fall des IMT, aber parallel zum Statut des ICTY, auch keine Zweifel (mehr) bestehen, dass die im Rom-Statut niedergelegten Straftatbestände lediglich bestehende völkergewohnheitsrechtliche Normen kodifiziert haben,[14] die bereits *ex ante* eine individuelle Strafbarkeit begründet hatten oder spätestens heute begründen.[15]

Selbst im Falle einer „rückwirkenden" Überweisung einer Situation an den Gerichtshof durch den Sicherheitsrat nach Maßgabe von Kapitel VII der UN-Charta, mit der dieser – wie im Falle Darfur durch Resolution 1593 (2005) geschehen – die Gerichtsbarkeit des ICC nachträglich für Taten begründet, für die dieser ansonsten nicht zuständig wäre,[16] handelt es sich nicht um eine nachträgliche Begründung der materiellen Strafbarkeit. Zudem sind etwaige Täter auch deshalb nicht schutzbedürftig, weil sie ja jederzeit damit rechnen mussten, dass der Sicherheitsrat von der ihm durch Kapitel VII in Verbindung mit Art. 13 des Römischen Statuts eingeräumten Befugnis für eine solche Überweisung[17] Gebrauch machen würde.

3) Verhältnis zur Ausübung nationaler Jurisdiktion

Ein erster wesentlicher Unterschied zwischen Nürnberg, Den Haag und Arusha einerseits und Rom andererseits besteht aber im Hinblick auf das Verhältnis zur Ausübung nationaler Jurisdiktion,[18] räumten doch die Mütter und Väter der drei erstgenannten Instrumente ausdrücklich oder – wie im Falle Nürnbergs – implizit der Ausübung völkerrechtlich begründeter Strafgewalt einen Vorrang ein, während der Internationale Strafgerichtshof nur dann und nur insoweit zuständig ist, als der oder die betroffenen Staaten nicht willens oder in der Lage sind, selbst ernsthaft (*genuinely*) die fraglichen Straftaten selbst zu verfolgen.

Neben dem Umstand, dass im Falle der drei *ad hoc* gegründeten Tribunale, Nürnberg, Den Haag und Arusha, die das Projekt tragenden Staaten erwarten konnten, dass ihre eigenen Staatsangehörigen *de jure* oder zumindest *de facto* nicht selbst Verfahren vor dem jeweiligen Gericht ausgesetzt werden würden, kann man die Gründungsinstrumente aber auch als Ausdruck einer dahinter stehenden Überzeugung interpretieren, dass die betroffenen Staaten, also Deutschland beziehungsweise die Nachfolgestaaten des ehemaligen Jugoslawien, von vorne herein nicht willens sein würden, die Mitglieder der eigenen Führungselite oder Angehörige der eigenen Streitkräfte selbst zu bestrafen.

---

[13] Näher zum Konzept des *jus cogens* und dessen inhaltlicher Umschreibung L. Hannikainen, Peremptory Norms (*jus cogens*) in International Law: Historical Developement, Criteria, Present Status, 1988, *passim*; S. Kadelbach, Zwingende Normen des humanitären Völkerrechts, Humanitäres Völkerrecht 5 (1992), 118 ff., sowie *ders*., Zwingendes Völkerrecht, 1992, *passim*.

[14] Kritisch insoweit aber W. Heintschel v. Heinegg, Criminal International Law and Customary International Law, in: A. Zimmermann (Hrsg.), International Criminal Law and the Current Development of Public International Law, 2003, 27, 35 ff.

[15] Vgl. im Einzelnen zum Verhältnis zwischen individueller Strafbarkeit einerseits und den für Zwecke der Staatenverantwortlichkeit geltenden Regeln des humanitären Völkerrechts, A. Zimmermann, Responsibility for Violations of International Humanitarian Law, International Criminal Law and Human Rights Law – Synergy and Conflict?, in: W. Heintschel v. Heinegg *et al.* (Hrsg.), Symposium in Honour of Knut Ipsen on the Occasion of his 70th Birthday (erscheint in Kürze).

[16] Dazu näher A. Zimmermann, Two steps forward, one step backwards? – Security Resolution 1593 (2005) and the Council's Power to Refer Situations to the International Criminal Court, in: P.-M. Dupuy *et al.* (Hrsg.), Festschrift für Christian Tomuschat zum 70. Geburtstag (erscheint 2006).

[17] Zu Umfang und Grenzen solcher Überweisungen näher S. Williams in: O. Triffterer (Hrsg.), Commentary on the Rome Statute of the International Criminal Court, 1999, Art. 13 Rn. 13.

[18] Vgl. einerseits zur ‚primacy' der beiden *ad hoc*-Tribunale gegenüber der Ausübung nationaler Gerichtsbarkeit Art. 9 des Statuts des Jugoslawien-Tribunals und Art. 8 des Statuts des Ruanda-Tribunals, und andererseits zur Komplementarität des Internationalen Strafgerichtshofes nach Art. 17 des Rom-Statuts, sowie näher dazu Williams in: Triffterer, *supra* Fn. 17, Art. 17, *passim*.

Immerhin ist aber darauf hinzuweisen, dass anders als im Falle des ICTR, dessen Jurisdiktion von vorne herein auf Staatsangehörige von Ruanda beschränkt war, die Jurisdiktion des ICTY lediglich *rationae materiae* und geographisch beschränkt war[19] und ist, nicht jedoch *rationae personae*. Dementsprechend hatte denn auch die Ermittlungsbehörde des Jugoslawientribunals wegen etwaiger Kriegsverbrechen von Staatsangehörigen von NATO-Staaten während des Kosovo-Krieges Vorermittlungen eingeleitet,[20] diese dann jedoch wieder eingestellt. In diesem Ansatz des Grundsatzes einer „equal justice under the law", die auch bereits in dem berühmten Satz des US-amerikanischen Anklägers Jackson zum Ausdruck kam, wonach

"we must never forget that the record on which we judge these defendants today is the record on which history will judge us tomorrow"[21]

als ein großer zivilisatorischer Fortschritt zu sehen ist.

Um so bedauerlicher ist es, dass der Sicherheitsrat der Vereinten Nationen auf Druck der USA in seiner bisherigen Praxis immer wieder Versuche unternommen hat, einzelne Personengruppen *per se* von der Jurisdiktion des Internationalen Strafgerichtshofes auszunehmen, sei es wie in den Resolutionen 1422 (2002)[22] und 1487 (2003)[23] geschehen durch den – zudem völkerrechtlich mehr als problematischen – Versuch einer generalisierenden Freistellung, sei es wie im Fall der Resolution 1497 (2003) im Rahmen einer konkreten friedenserhaltenden Maßnahme[24] oder sei es schließlich wie im Falle von Resolution 1593 (2005)[25] im Rahmen der Überweisung einer bestimmten Situation an den internationalen Strafgerichtshof.

Ansätze für den im Rom-Statut verankerten Grundgedanken der Komplementarität, also des Vorrangs nationaler Strafverfolgung, sofern die betroffenen Staaten ihrerseits willens und in der Lage sind, die entsprechenden Straftaten selbst ernsthaft zu verfolgen, finden sich aber in der Praxis der Alliierten, nach Abschluss des Nürnberger Verfahrens und der Nachfolgeverfahren vor Militärgerichten der einzelnen Besatzungsmächte die Strafkompetenz nach Kontrollratsgesetz Nr. 10 auf deutsche Gerichte zu übertragen.[26] Dementsprechend haben denn auch westdeutsche Gerichte bis in die 50er Jahre des letzten Jahrhunderts hinein[27] und Gerichte der DDR gar bis noch weit in die 80er Jahre[28] auf der Grundlage dieses Gesetzes Personen unter anderem wegen Verbrechen gegen die Menschlichkeit bestraft.

Eine ähnliche Tendenz lässt sich heute auch in der Praxis der beiden *ad hoc*-Tribunale nachweisen, drängen diese doch zunehmend darauf, dass die entsprechenden Territorialstaaten der ihnen nach allgemeinem Völkerrecht zukommenden Pflicht zur Bestrafung der schlimmsten Völkerrechtsverbrechen in vollem Umfang nachkommen.

---

[19] Vgl. insoweit Art. 1 des Statuts des ICTY.

[20] Wortlaut des entsprechenden Berichts in: HRLJ 21 (2000), 257 ff., dazu näher P. Benvenuti, The ICTY Prosecutor and the Review of the NATO Bombing Campaign Against the Federal Republic of Yugoslavia, EJIL 12 (2001), 503 ff.

[21] Justice Jackson's Opening Address for the United States of America, by Justice Robert N. Jackson, Chief of Counsel for the United States, before the Tribunal on 21 November 1945, abgedruckt in: Nazi Conspiracy and Aggression, Volume I, United States Government Printing Office, Washington, 1946, 114, 116.

[22] Dazu näher A. Zimmermann, 'Acting under chapter VII (...)' – Resolution 1422 and Possible Limits of the Powers of the Security Council, in: J. A. Frowein *et al.* (Hrsg.) – Verhandeln für den Frieden – Festschrift für Tono Eitel, 2003, 253ff.

[23] Allerdings war eine erneute Verlängerung der Resolutionen 1422 und 1487 durch den Sicherheitsrat im Jahre 2004 angesichts der Ereignisse im irakischen Abu-Grahib-Gefängnis gescheitert.

[24] *In concreto* war Gegenstand der Resolution die Mandatierung einer friedenserhaltenden Maßnahme durch den Sicherheitsrat in Liberia.

[25] Dazu näher Zimmermann, *supra* Fn. 16, *passim*.

[26] Vgl. insoweit Art. III, Abs. 1, lit. d), S. 2 des Kontrollratsgesetzes Nr. 10 vom 20. Dezember 1945: „d) (...) Für die Aburteilung von Verbrechen, die deutsche Staatsbürger oder Staatsangehörige gegen andere deutsche Staatsbürger oder Staatsangehörige oder gegen Staatenlose begangen haben, können die Besatzungsbehörden deutsche Gerichte für zuständig erklären."

[27] Dazu näher H.-J. Papier/J. Möller, Die rechtsstaatliche Bewältigung von Regime-Unrecht nach 1945 und nach 1989, NJW 1999, 3289 ff.

[28] Zur (allerdings nicht selten politisch gesteuerten) Verfolgung von Verbrechen gegen die Menschlichkeit durch Gerichte der DDR näher Papier/Möller, *supra* Fn. 27, 3289 ff.

4) Nürnberg v. Rom: generell-abstrakt v. konfliktbezogen

Ein wesentlicher Unterschied zwischen „Nürnberg" und „Rom" liegt jedoch in dem Umstand, dass die Schaffung des Nürnberger Militärtribunals neben der Beschränkung auf einzelne Tätergruppen ähnlich wie im Falle des Tokioer Tribunals, aber auch noch parallel zu den beiden *ad hoc*-Tribunalen oder den in den letzten Jahren eingerichteten internationalisierten Gerichten für Ost-Timor, Sierra Leone oder Kambodscha, von vorne herein nur der juristischen Bewältigung der in einem bestimmten Konflikt begangenen Verbrechen dienen sollte. Dementsprechend sah beziehungsweise sieht sich jedes dieser Gerichte zumindest in einigen Staaten dem politischen Verdacht ausgesetzt, es handele sich jeweils nur um bloße *ex post-facto*-Siegerjustiz.

Mag man diesen Vorwurf auch für ungerechtfertigt halten, bleibt doch festzuhalten, dass ein solcher rein spezifisch auf einen einzelnen Konflikt bezogener Ansatz von vorne herein nicht geeignet ist, generalpräventive Überlegungen zum Tragen zu bringen. Vielmehr mussten und konnten daher in einer solchen Konstellation vor allem Sühneüberlegungen und allenfalls spezialpräventive Überlegungen zum Tragen kommen, wobei die letzteren im konkreten Fall der vollständigen Umgestaltung der politischen Ordnung Deutschlands nach dem Zweiten Weltkrieg von keiner wesentlichen Bedeutung gewesen sein dürften.

Die wesentliche kriminalpolitische Bedeutung des Nürnberger Verfahrens dürfte daher meines Erachtens in der Bestätigung beziehungsweise Weiterentwicklung der zugrundeliegenden völkerrechtlichen Verbotsnormen zu sehen sein – darauf wird im Einzelnen nachfolgend noch näher einzugehen sein.

5) Nürnberg und die Frage der compétence de la compétence

Schließlich ist noch auf die für das Selbstverständnis der internationalen Strafgerichtsbarkeit wesentliche Frage der sogenannten *compétence de la compétence* einzugehen. Sowohl die Angeklagten in Nürnberg als auch *Dusko Tadic* vor dem ICTY,[29] als auch einzelne Angeklagte vor dem ICTR[30] und dem Sondertribunal für Sierra Leone[31] haben jeweils die Rechtmäßigkeit der Errichtung der jeweiligen Strafinstanz bestritten. Und in jedem dieser Fälle hat das jeweilige Gericht beginnend mit dem Nürnberger Gerichtshof nicht nur – vielleicht wenig überraschend – die Legalität der eigenen Existenz bestätigt, sondern auch – anders als noch die erstinstanzlich zuständige Trial Chamber des ICTY im *Tadic*-Fall – für sich selbst zumindest implizit, teilweise aber auch *expressis verbis*, die Kompetenz in Anspruch genommen, die Rechtmäßigkeit der eigenen Einsetzung zu beurteilen, sowie darüber hinaus aber auch die Grenzen der eigenen Jurisdiktion zu definieren.

Damit haben die einzelnen Gerichte und zwar jenseits des Völkerstrafrechts im engeren Sinne einen nicht unwesentlichen Schritt zur Verrechtlichung der internationalen Beziehungen insgesamt geleistet. Auch der ICC dürfte zu gegebener Zeit diesen Schritt tun, sei es im Kontext der Frage der Rechtmäßigkeit der bereits erwähnten, für seine Jurisdiktionsausübung relevanten Sicherheitsratsresolution, sei es im Zusammenhang mit der Frage der Ausübung von Jurisdiktion zu Lasten von Drittstaatsangehörigen.

III. Nürnberg und das materielle Völkerstrafrecht

A. Bestimmtheit völkerstrafrechtlicher Tatbestände[32]

Einzelne Staaten, insbesondere aber die USA, haben während der Verhandlungen die Auffassung vertreten, die im Römischen Statut verankerten Tatbestände seien zu unpräzise und bedürften einer

---

[29] *The Prosecutor v. Dusko Tadic a/k/a „Dule"*, Decision on the Defence motion for Interlocutory Appeal for Jurisdiction (Case No. IT-94-1), 2. Oktober 1995, Ziff. 2 and 4-6, Text siehe unter: http://www.un.org/icty/tadic/ appeal/decision-e/51002.htm.

[30] ICTR (trial Chamber II), Decision on the Defence Motion on Jurisdiction of 18 June 1997, case no. ICTR-96-15-T.

[31] *The Prosecutor v. Moinina Fofana*, Decision on preliminary motion on lack of Jurisdiction Materiae: Illegal Delegation of Powers by the United Nations (Case No. SCSL-2004-14-AR72(E)), Text siehe unter: http://www.sc-sl.org/Documents/SCSL-04-14-PT-100-6836.pdf.

[32] Näher zur Auseinandersetzung mit diesem Einwand A. Zimmermann/H. Scheel, *supra* Fn. 9, S. 141.

weiteren Ausdifferenzierung durch sogenannte „elements of crimes" – einem Anliegen welches das Römische Statut, wenn auch nur bedingt, in seinem Art. 9 nachkommt.[33] Insoweit mag man sich fragen, ob diese These, sollte sie denn zu Recht vorgetragen worden sein, was ich bezweifle, dann nicht auch in gleichem Umfang für das Nürnberger Statut sowie die Statuten aller anderen modernen internationalen Strafgerichte bis hin zu dem von den Besatzungsmächten im Irak eingerichteten Sondergericht für den Irak zutreffen würde.[34] In all diesen Fällen ist jedoch jeweils einvernehmlich davon ausgegangen worden, dass schon aufgrund der dahinter stehenden Staatenpraxis, insbesondere aber auch aufgrund der gefestigten Rechtsprechung der beiden *ad hoc*-Tribunale, keine Zweifel bezüglich der hinreichenden Bestimmtheit der fraglichen Straftatbestände mehr bestehen dürften. Diese unterschiedliche Herangehensweise wird auch dadurch deutlich, dass – wie die Formulierung „namely (...) but not be limited to" in dessen Art. 6 lit. b) belegt – die Liste der Kriegsverbrechen im Nürnberger Statut nicht abschließend war, sondern auch die Bestrafung aufgrund anderer, nicht aufgeführter Kriegsverbrechenstatbestände in Betracht kommen konnte. Demgegenüber zeigt etwa Art. 8 Abs. 2 lit. b) (xx) des Römischen Statuts, wonach eine ausdrückliche Vertragsänderung notwendig ist, um weitere Waffenarten in den Kanon der verbotenen Kampfmittel aufzunehmen,[35] aber auch Art. 7 Abs. 1 lit. (k) mit seinem Erfordernis der Vergleichbarkeit mit anderen Deliktsformen der Verbrechen gegen die Menschlichkeit,[36] dass das Rom-Statut hier – auch ohne die Konkretisierung durch die „elements of crimes" – ausreichende Anforderungen an die Bestimmtheit völkerstrafrechtlicher Tatbestände stellt.

B. Einzelne Delikte
1) Völkermord
Evidenterweise war der Holocaust, also der Völkermord an den europäischen Juden, einer der wesentlichen, wenn nicht der wesentliche Grund für die Errichtung des Nürnberger Militärtribunals. Gleichwohl fand sich bekanntlich im Gründungsstatut des IMT noch keine entsprechende Strafnorm, sollte das entsprechende Delikt doch erst durch und in der Völkermordkonvention des Jahres 1948 kodifiziert werden. Dies ist demnach sicher ein Punkt, bei dem das IMT-Statut die weitere Entwicklung des Völkerstrafrechts *nicht* mit geprägt hat. Ganz anders demgegenüber im Bereich der Verbrechen gegen die Menschlichkeit.

2) Verbrechen gegen die Menschlichkeit
Der erste, allerdings gescheiterte, Versuch, das Konzept der Verbrechen gegen die Menschlichkeit in ein völkerrechtliches Instrument zu verankern, bildete bekanntlich der wegen des türkischen Widerstands nie in Kraft getretene Vertrag von Sèvres[37] – und bekanntlich weigert sich die offizielle Türkei bis heute, sich mit dem Völkermord an den Armeniern in angemessener Form auseinander zu setzen.[38]

Um so bedeutsamer war es, dass das Nürnberger Statut erstmals ein umfassendes Konzept der Verbrechen gegen die Menschlichkeit entwickelte und das IMT in seiner Rechtsprechung erste rote Linien zur näheren Umschreibung des fraglichen Tatbestandes zog. Dies gilt zunächst für die Frage der Notwendigkeit eines sachlichen Zusammenhangs mit einem bewaffneten Konflikt, sprach Art. 6 lit. c des IMT-Statuts doch davon, dass die fraglichen Taten „vor oder während des Krieges" begangen

---

[33] Der Kompromisscharakter des Art. 9 des Römischen Statuts ist darin zu sehen, dass die Verbrechenselemente dem Gerichtshof bei der Auslegung und Anwendung der Artikel 6, 7 und 8 nur empfehlenden Charakter besitzen und den Gerichtshof nicht binden, wird doch in Art. 9 nur von einem „shall assist" gesprochen, dazu näher auch E. Gadirov in: Triffterer, *supra* Fn. 17, Art. 9 Rn. 30.

[34] Der Wortlaut des Statuts findet sich u.a. unter http://www.cpa-iraq.org/human_rights/Statute.htm.

[35] Dazu näher M. Cottier in: Triffterer, *supra* Fn. 17, Art. 8 para 2 (b) (xx).

[36] Dazu näher M. Boot in: Triffterer, *supra* Fn. 17, Art. 7 para 1 (k).

[37] Artikel 230 lautete: "The Turkish Government undertakes to hand over to the Allied powers the persons whose surrender may be required by the latter as being responsible for the massacres committed during the continuance of the state of war on territory which formed part of the Turkish Empire on August 1, 1914."
Wortlaut des Vertrages u.a. in: 15 AJIL 197 (1921) (Suppl.).

[38] Kritisch dazu etwa nur V. N. Dadrian, Genocide as a Problem of National and International Law: the World War I Armenian Case and Its Contemporary Legal Ramifications, Yale J. Int'l L. 14 (1989), S. 221 ff. (278 ff.).

worden sein mussten. Hieraus hat das Tribunal in seiner Rechtsprechung bekanntlich den Schluss gezogen, dass Verbrechen gegen die Menschlichkeit zwingend einen sachlichen Nexus zu einem bewaffneten Konflikt haben müssten,[39] obwohl dann bereits das Kontrollratsgesetz Nr. 10 dieses Erfordernis nicht mehr enthielt.[40]

Bekanntlich ging auch die gewohnheitsrechtliche Entwicklung – zunächst angestoßen durch die grundlegenden Arbeiten der International Law Commission[41] – in diese Richtung. Dessen ungeachtet enthielt aber wieder das vom Legal Counsel der Vereinten Nationen erarbeitete und vom Sicherheitsrat der Vereinten Nationen beschlossene Statut des ICTY genau dieses Erfordernis.[42] Nur wenig später besann sich der Sicherheitsrat dann aber doch wieder eines Besseren, als er im Statut des Ruanda-Tribunals das Erfordernis eines bewaffneten Konflikts nicht erneut aufnahm.[43] Dementsprechend vertrat denn auch das Jugoslawien-Tribunal in seiner Rechtsprechung zutreffend die Auffassung, der Sicherheitsrat sei mit der Aufnahme dieses Nexus-Erfordernisses trotz des Nürnberger Vorbildes hinter geltendem Völkergewohnheitsrecht zurückgeblieben.[44] Auch das Rom-Statut ist dieser Auffassung – trotz eines deutlichen Widerstands der VR China, der Russischen Föderation und der meisten arabischen Staaten – gefolgt.[45]

Sehr viel stärker hat der Nürnberger Präzedenzfall demgegenüber bis heute die weitere Entwicklung bei der Frage eines Angriffs auf eine Zivilbevölkerung als konstituierendes Element aller *crimes against humanity* geprägt. Dies gilt namentlich auch für die Aussage, dass die Gegenwart vereinzelter Soldaten

---

[39] Dazu näher R. Dixon in: Triffterer, *supra* Fn. 17, Art. 7, Rn. 9.

[40] In Art. 11 des Kontrollratsgesetzes Nr. 10 hieß es lediglich ohne Bezugnahme auf einen bewaffneten Konflikt: „1. Jeder der folgenden Tatbestände stellt ein Verbrechen dar: (...) c) *Verbrechen gegen die Menschlichkeit*. Gewalttaten und Vergehen, einschließlich der folgenden den obigen Tatbestand jedoch nicht erschöpfenden Beispiele: Mord, Ausrottung, Versklavung, Zwangsverschleppung, Freiheitsberaubung, Folterung, Vergewaltigung oder andere an der Zivilbevölkerung begangene unmenschliche Handlungen; Verfolgung aus politischen, rassischen oder religiösen Gründen, ohne Rücksicht darauf, ob sie das nationale Recht des Landes, in welchem die Handlung begangen worden ist, verletzen."

[41] ILC Code of Crimes against the Peace and Security of Mankind 1954 Art. 2; ILC Code of Crimes against the Peace and Security of Mankind 1996 Art. 18.

[42] Artikel 5 - Verbrechen gegen die Menschlichkeit
„Der Gerichtshof ist befugt, Personen strafrechtlich zu verfolgen, die für folgende Verbrechen verantwortlich sind, wenn diese in einem, ob internationalen oder internen, bewaffneten Konflikt begangen werden und gegen die Zivilbevölkerung gerichtet sind:
a) Mord;
b) Ausrottung;
c) Versklavung;
d) Deportierung;
e) Freiheitsentziehung;
f) Folter;
g) Vergewaltigung;
h) Verfolgung aus politischen, rassischen und religiösen Gründen;
i) andere unmenschliche Handlungen."

[43] Artikel 3 - Verbrechen gegen die Menschlichkeit
„Der Internationale Strafgerichtshof für Ruanda ist befugt, Personen strafrechtlich zu verfolgen, die für folgende Verbrechen verantwortlich sind, wenn diese im Rahmen eines breit angelegten und systematischen Angriffs gegen die Zivilbevölkerung aus nationalen, politischen, ethnischen, rassischen oder religiösen Gründen begangen werden:
a) Mord;
b) Ausrottung;
c) Versklavung;
d) Deportierung;
e) Freiheitsentziehung;
f) Folter;
g) Vergewaltigung;
h) Verfolgung aus politischen, rassischen und religiösen Gründen;
i) andere unmenschliche Handlungen."

[44] The Prosecutor v. Dusko Tadic a/k/a „Dule", Decision on the Defence motion for Interlocutory Appeal for Jurisdiction (Case No.IT-94-1-AR 72), 2. Oktober 1995, *supra* Fn. 29.

[45] Näher zur Auseinandersetzung während der Verhandlungen A. Zimmermann, *supra* Fn. 11, S. 54f.

innerhalb einer größeren Menge von Zivilisten nicht dazu führt, dass diese damit ihren Charakter als Zivilbevölkerung verliert.[46]

Aber auch die Einzelausprägungen der Verbrechen gegen die Menschlichkeit, so wie sie sich bereits im Nürnberger Statut fanden, also Mord[47], Ausrottung[48], Versklavung[49] und Deportation[50] haben – um bildlich zu sprechen – ihren Weg über Den Haag und Arusha praktisch wortgleich nach Rom gefunden. Hinzugekommen sind lediglich definitorische Präzisierungen, sowie neue Formen der Verbrechen gegen die Menschlichkeit, die auf nachfolgenden Unrechtserfahrungen in verschiedenen Regionen dieser Erde beruhen, so wie dies insbesondere für das Verschwindenlassen von Personen,[51] Verbrechen gegen das sexuelle Selbstbestimmungsrecht von Frauen,[52] sowie das Apartheidsverbrechen[53] gilt. Eine ähnlich weitreichende Rezeption des Nürnberger Statuts wie im Bereich der Verbrechen gegen die Menschlichkeit lässt sich auch bei den Kriegsverbrechenstatbeständen nachweisen.

3) Kriegsverbrechen

Die Zuständigkeit des Nürnberger Tribunals beschränkte sich schon angesichts des historischen Hintergrunds auf in internationalen bewaffneten Konflikten begangene Kriegsverbrechen. Es sollte erst mit der bahnbrechenden Entscheidung des Jugoslawien-Tribunals im *Tadic*-Fall gelingen, auch Bürgerkriegsverbrechen zu pönalisieren.[54] Anders demgegenüber die Situation für internationale bewaffnete Konflikte. Insbesondere im Bereich des traditionell als ‚Genfer Recht' bezeichneten Komplexes des Schutzes bestimmter Personengruppen lassen sich hier – vermittelt über die Genfer Konventionen des Jahres 1949 mit ihrem Konzept von „grave breaches" – deutliche Entwicklungslinien nachweisen, zumal das Römische Statut in seinem Art. 8 Abs. 2 b) ja regelmäßig nicht zuletzt wegen des Widerstands der USA, die bekanntlich bis heute nicht Vertragspartei des Ersten Zusatzprotokolls aus dem Jahre 1977 sind,[55] regelmäßig auf Formulierungen aus der Haager Landkriegsordnung und nicht auf solche aus dem Ersten Zusatzprotokoll rekurriert hat, obwohl dieses in nicht wenigen Fällen modernere, und zugleich auch spezifischere Tatbestandsformulierungen enthält.

4) Verbrechen des Angriffskrieges[56]

Nach Art. 6 lit. a des Nürnberger Statuts war das IMT nicht zuletzt auch für Verbrechen gegen den Frieden zuständig. Demgegenüber konnte im Kontext des Rom-Statuts – vielleicht wenig überraschend – bislang keine Einigung über diesen Straftatbestand sowie die weiteren Voraussetzungen für die Ausübung von Jurisdiktion durch den ICC im Hinblick auf dieses Verbrechen erzielt werden – ja es scheint mir, dass dies bis auf unabsehbare Zeit dabei bleiben wird.[57]

In der Tat würde ich mittlerweile davon ausgehen, dass es eine Überforderung des Gerichtshofes darstellen würde, wollte man ihm die implizite Beantwortung elementarer Fragen hinsichtlich der Legalität des Einsatzes militärischer Gewalt – angefangen von der Frage der Zulässigkeit einer, meines Erachtens völkerrechtlich unzulässigen sogenannten „präemptiven" Selbstverteidigung,[58] über Fragen

---

[46] R. Dixon in: Triffterer, *supra* Fn. 17, Art. 7 Rn. 13.
[47] C. Hall in: Triffterer, *supra* Fn. 17, Art. 7 Rn. 19 ff.
[48] *Supra* Fn. 47, Rn. 24 f.
[49] *Supra* Fn. 47, Rn. 26 ff.
[50] *Supra* Fn. 47, Rn. 31 ff.
[51] *Supra* Fn. 47, Rn. 73.
[52] *Supra* Fn. 47, Rn. 41 ff.
[53] *Supra* Fn. 47, Rn. 76 ff.
[54] Grundlegend dazu die Entscheidung im *Tadic*-Fall, näher dazu C. Kreß, Friedenssicherungs- und Konfliktvölkerrecht auf der Schwelle zur Postmoderne: Das Urteil des Internationalen Straftribunals für das ehemalige Jugoslawien (Appeals Chamber) im Fall *Tadic* vom 2. Oktober 1995 (HRLJ 1995, 437), EuGRZ 23 (1996), 638 ff.
[55] Zu den Gründen der Nichtratifikation des Ersten Zusatzprotokolls zu den Genfer Konventionen aus dem Jahre 1977 durch die USA näher G. Aldrich, Prospects for United States Ratification of Additional Protocol I to the 1949 Geneva Conventions, AJIL 85 (1991), 1 ff.
[56] Näher zum Verbrechen des Angriffskrieges B. Clemens, Der Begriff des Angriffskrieges und die Funktion seiner Strafbarkeit, 2005, *passim*.
[57] Vgl. zu den Voraussetzungen einer entsprechenden Vertragsänderung näher Art. 121 des Römischen Statuts.
[58] Kritisch dazu auch R. Hofmann, International Law and the Use of Military Force Against Iraq, GYIL 45 (2002), 9 ff.

humanitärer Interventionen,[59] bis hin zur Auslegung von Sicherheitsratsresolutionen, die aus der Sicht einzelner Staaten ein implizites Mandat zur Gewaltanwendung umfassen sollen, übertragen.

Würde es jedoch zu einer entsprechenden Ergänzung von Art. 5 des Römischen Statuts kommen, würde die enge Formulierung des Art. 6 lit. a) des IMT-Statuts richtigerweise als nach wie vor für das geltende Völkergewohnheitsrecht angesehen werden,[60] so wie dies etwa auch durch Art. 5 von Generalversammlungsresolution 3314 bestätigt wird.[61] Zudem müsste – darauf sei nur am Rande hingewiesen – natürlich auch der Rolle des Sicherheitsrates nach Kapitel VII der Charta in ausreichendem Maße Rechnung getragen werden. Allenfalls wäre zu überlegen, ob nicht der Sicherheitsrat in einem ähnlich evidenten Fall eines Verstoßes gegen das völkerrechtliche Gewaltverbot wie dem des Überfall Deutschlands auf Polen im Jahre 1939 auf der Grundlage seiner Kapitel VII-Befugnisse die Jurisdiktion des ICC entsprechend um das Aggressionsverbrechen erweitern könnte.

C. Ausgewählte Fragen des allgemeinen Teil des Völkerstrafrechts

Anders als das Statut von Rom enthält das Nürnberger Statut so gut wie keine ausdifferenzierten Regelungen im Bereich des Allgemeinen Teils des Völkerstrafrechts. Dessen ungeachtet lassen sich hier aber zumindest in Teilbereichen Querverbindungen nachweisen.

1) Täterschaft und Teilnahme/Kriminelle Verantwortlichkeit von Organisationen

Im Bereich von Täterschaft und Teilnahme war insbesondere das im kontinentaleuropäischen Recht unbekannte, aber in Art. 6 des Nürnberger Statuts sowie in der Rechtsprechung der *ad hoc*-Tribunale rezipierte Konzept des „common plan or conspiracy" umstritten. Letztlich hat man hier – so glaube ich – mit Art. 25 Abs. 3 lit. d) des Rom-Statuts einen gangbaren Kompromiss gefunden.[62]

Auch der nunmehr in Art. 28 des Rom-Statuts kodifizierte Grundsatz der „command responsibility"[63] war bereits Gegenstand sowohl der Tokioer als auch der Nürnberger Rechtsprechung. Als zu begrüßende Klarstellung ist demgegenüber Art. 28 insoweit anzusehen, als nunmehr eindeutig auch zivile Vorgesetze sich wegen Handlungen ihrer Untergebenen strafbar machen können.

Schließlich ist noch darauf hinzuweisen, dass sich die in Art. 9 des Nürnberger Statuts angelegte Strafbarkeit von Organisationen oder juristischen Personen trotz entsprechender französischer Vorschläge letztlich nicht durchsetzen konnte.

2) Irrelevanz der Innehabung offizieller Positionen

Bereits Art. 7 des Nürnberger Statuts hatte deutlich gemacht, dass die Innehabung einer offiziellen Position für die Zwecke der Strafverfolgung wegen Kriegsverbrechen, Verbrechen gegen die Menschlichkeit, Verbrechen gegen den Frieden und Völkermord irrelevant ist. Art. 27 des Römischen Statuts nimmt diesen Gedanken wieder auf und bestätigt damit zugleich dessen gewohnheitsrechtliche Geltung. Das Urteil des Internationalen Gerichtshofes im Arrest Warrant-Fall zwischen der Demokratischen Republik Kongo und dem Königreich Belgien[64] hat die Geltung dieses Grundsatzes jedoch in Frage gestellt. Auch Art. 98 Abs. 1 des Römischen Statuts scheint diese eher restriktive Sicht zu bestätigen.[65] Immerhin hatte der Internationale Gerichtshof jedoch ausdrücklich offen gelassen, ob für internationale Strafgerichtshöfe wie den ICC etwas anderes gelten kann.[66] Letztlich wird sich insoweit wohl Folgendes sagen lassen:

---

[59] Vgl. dazu statt aller nur etwa M. Wellhausen, Malte, Humanitäre Intervention - Probleme der Anerkennung des Rechtsinstituts unter besonderer Berücksichtigung des Kosovo-Konflikts, 2002, *passim*.

[60] Dazu bereits näher Zimmermann, *supra* Fn. 11, S. 73 ff.

[61] Art. 5, Abs. 2 von GV-Res. 3314 lautet: "(…) A war of aggression is a crime against international peace."

[62] K. Ambos in: Triffterer, *supra* Fn. 17, Art. 25 Rn 20 ff.

[63] W. J. Fenrick in: Triffterer, *supra* Fn. 17, Art. 28 Rn 4.

[64] Case concerning the Arrest Warrant of 11 April 2000, ICJ Reports (2002), 3 ff.

[65] Die Bestimmung lautet in der deutschen Übersetzung: „Der Gerichtshof darf kein Überstellungs- oder Rechtshilfeersuchen stellen, das vom ersuchten Staat verlangen würde, in Bezug auf die Staatenimmunität oder die diplomatische Immunität einer Person oder des Eigentums eines Drittstaates entgegen seinen völkerrechtlichen Verpflichtungen zu handeln, sofern der Gerichtshof nicht zuvor die Zusammenarbeit des Drittstaates im Hinblick auf den Verzicht auf Immunität erreichen kann."

[66] Case concerning the Arrest Warrant of 11 April 2000, *supra* Fn. 64, S. 24 f., Ziff. 57-59.

Zum einen ist in Art. 27 des Rom-Statuts zunächst ein Verzicht der Vertragsparteien auf ansonsten möglicherweise bestehende Immunitäten zu sehen. Weiterhin greifen Immunitäten jedenfalls im Falle einer Sicherheitsratsüberweisung wegen der Vorrangwirkung der UN-Charta von vorne herein nicht ein. Im Übrigen, also gegenüber Drittstaaten, ist entweder davon auszugehen, dass nach Völkergewohnheitsrecht für die in Art. 5 des ICC-Statuts genannten Delikte *ipso facto* keine Immunität zu gewähren ist, oder aber, den fraglichen Personen, insbesondere also amtierenden Staats- und Regierungschefs sowie Außenministern, ist auch im Verhältnis zum ICC Immunität zu gewähren.

3) Handeln auf Befehl[67]

Eine weitere Frage, bei der das Rom-Statut – wenn auch nur teilweise – von dem Statut von Nürnberg abweicht, betrifft die Frage der rechtfertigenden Wirkung eines Handelns auf Befehl. Insoweit hatte Art. 8 des IMT-Statuts und ihm folgend die Statuten der beiden *ad hoc*-Tribunale jeweils eindeutig vorgesehen, dass ein Handeln auf Befehl in keinem Fall als Strafausschließungsgrund zu werten sei. Demgegenüber trifft Art. 33 des Rom-Statuts insoweit eine nuancierende Lösung, als unter bestimmten Umständen, nämlich dann, wenn der Täter verpflichtet war, dem Befehl zu folgen, er nicht wusste, dass der Befehl rechtswidrig war und der fragliche Befehl nicht offensichtlich rechtswidrig war. Dabei wird unwiderleglich vermutet, dass Befehle zur Begehung von Völkermord oder Verbrechen gegen die Menschlichkeit *per se* offensichtlich rechtswidrig sind. Dieser jedenfalls völkerrechts*politisch* zu bedauernde Rückschritt, der sich jedoch auf eine nicht unerhebliche Praxis nationaler Gerichte stützen konnte, dürfte wohl damit zu erklären sein, dass die Staaten im Hinblick auf ein generell-abstraktes Statut, welches zumindest potentiell auch auf ihre eigenen Staatsangehörigen und namentlich ihre eigenen Soldaten Anwendung finden kann, anders als im Falle des Nürnberger Statuts bei der Gewährung von Straffreistellung eher großzügig verfahren wollten.

D. Kooperation mit dem Gerichtshof

Ein wesentlicher Unterschied zwischen dem Nürnberger und dem Römischen Statut ist schließlich in dem Umstand zu sehen, dass in dem Fall der Verfahren gegen die deutschen Kriegsverbrecher die Alliierten durch die Berliner Erklärung vom 5. Juni 1945 die oberste Regierungsgewalt in Deutschland übernommen hatten.[68] Dementsprechend waren sie von vorne herein nicht auf die Kooperation des betroffenen Territorialstaates angewiesen. Strukturell ist demgegenüber die Lage im Hinblick auf den Internationalen Strafgerichtshof völlig anders, ist dieser doch auf die Zusammenarbeit durch die Vertragsparteien beziehungsweise im Falle einer Sicherheitsratsüberweisung auch sonstiger Staaten angewiesen. Insofern ist auch nur in den ganz engen Grenzen des Art. 57 Abs. 3 lit. d) ein Tätigwerden des Gerichtshofes ohne Zustimmung des betroffenen Territorialstaates zulässig.[69]

E. Strafen und Strafvollstreckung

Wesentliche strukturelle Unterschiede zwischen Internationalem Strafgerichtshof und Nürnberger Militärtribunal lassen sich auch im Hinblick auf die zu verhängenden Strafen und die Strafvollstreckung feststellen. So ist es als wesentlicher Fortschritt zu verstehen, der auch, und zwar ungeachtet der Unberührtheitsklausel des Art. 80, als Beleg einer sich allmählich abzeichnenden gewohnheitsrechtlichen Entwicklung angesehen werden kann, dass das Römische Statut, anders als Art. 27 des IMT-Statuts, auf die Verhängung der Todesstrafe verzichtet.[70] Es ist darüber hinaus auch zu begrüßen, dass die Vollstreckung nunmehr der Kontrolle des Gerichtshofes selbst, also einem unabhängigen Gericht unterliegt, und nicht mehr wie im Falle des Nürnberger Statuts einem von den Vertragsparteien

---

[67] Dazu näher O. Triffterer in: Triffterer, *supra* Fn. 17, Art. 33 Rn. 14; A. Zimmermann, Superior Orders, in A. Cassese (Hrsg.), The Rome Statute of the International Criminal Court – a commentary, Vol. I, 2002, 957 ff.

[68] Die Erklärung lautete: „Die Regierungen des Vereinigten Königreichs, der Vereinigten Staaten von Amerika, der Union der Sozialistischen Sowjet-Republiken und die Provisorische Regierung der Französischen Republik übernehmen hiermit die oberste Regierungsgewalt in Deutschland, einschließlich aller Befugnisse der deutschen Regierung, des Oberkommandos der Wehrmacht und der Regierungen, Verwaltungen oder Behörden der Länder, Städte und Gemeinden."

[69] F. Guariglia/K. Harris in: Triffterer, *supra* Fn. 17, Art. 57 Rn. 16 ff.

[70] R. E. Fife in: Triffterer, *supra* Fn. 17, Art. 80 Rn. 4 ff.

errichten Organ, *in concreto* damals dem Alliierten Kontrollrat für Deutschland. Schließlich ist noch auf den Umstand hinzuweisen, dass die Vertragsparteien des Rom-Statuts die eigentliche Strafvollstreckung nunmehr einzelnen Vertragsparteien übertragen und nicht mehr wie im Falle des Spandauer Gefängnisses hierfür ein gemeinsames Organ schaffen.

F. Zusammenfassende Würdigung

Lässt man das oben Gesagte noch einmal gedanklich Revue passieren, so kann man den Einfluss des Nürnberger Statuts sowie der Rechtsprechung des IMT auf die Entwicklung des Völkerstrafrechts wohl kaum groß genug einschätzen. Gleichzeitig ist es zu bedauern, dass die Nürnberger Prozesse in Deutschland über lange Zeit hinweg, und zwar durchaus auch in der rechtswissenschaftlichen Diskussion, eher kritisch gesehen wurden. Umso positiver ist es zu werten, dass die Bundesregierung die vor diesem Hintergrund zu Art. 7 Abs. 2 der Europäischen Menschenrechtskonvention abgegebene Erklärung im Jahr 2001 zurückgezogen hatte. Ferner ist es auch zu begrüßen, dass die Bundesrepublik Deutschland während der Verhandlungen die zum Römischen Statut führten, eine aktive Rolle spielte und auch mit dem deutschen Völkerstrafgesetzbuch nunmehr eine entsprechende innerstaatliche Umsetzung erfolgt ist.

Umso bedauerlicher ist es, dass einer der Staaten, die maßgeblich zur Entstehung des Nürnberger Tribunals beigetragen haben, nämlich die Russische Föderation, bislang das Statut nur gezeichnet und nicht ratifiziert hat, und dass die US-amerikanische Regierung sich gar veranlasst sah, die zuvor abgegebene Unterschrift zurückzuziehen,[71] ja dass die USA zumindest derzeit gar eine deutlich ablehnende Haltung einnehmen. Umso bemerkenswerter ist, dass der Sicherheitsrat der Vereinten Nationen mit Resolution 1593 (2005) vor kurzem erstmals auf der Grundlage von Kapitel VII der UN Charta eine bestimmte Situation bei vier Enthaltungen, darunter die der USA, an den ICC überwiesen hat. Damit hat der Sicherheitsrat – wie zuvor die Alliierten Siegermächte im Falle des Nürnberger Militärtribunals – deutlich gemacht, dass er die Begehung von Völkermord, Verbrechen gegen die Menschlichkeit und Kriegsverbrechen als Bedrohung des Weltfriedens und der internationalen Sicherheit ansieht. Bedauerlicher ist es zugleich, dass dies um den Preis geschah, dass Staatsangehörige von Drittstaaten weitgehend von der Jurisdiktion des Gerichtshofes ausgenommen wurden und dass eine Finanzierung durch den UN-Haushalt ungeachtet der Überweisung der Situation durch den Sicherheitsrat ausgeschlossen wurde.

Während der Verhandlungen von Rom und in deren Vorfeld bestanden Bestrebungen seitens der Stadt Nürnberg, die durch den Freistaat Bayern unterstützt wurden, die Bundesrepublik Deutschland möge eine Kandidatur Nürnbergs als Sitz des künftigen Internationalen Strafgerichtshofes ins Spiel bringen. Eine solche Kandidatur wurde aber seitens der Bundesregierung nicht weiterverfolgt, weil man ungeachtet der historischen Bedeutung eines solchen Standorts wenig Chancen sah, gegen Den Haag zu gewinnen, zumal die Bundesrepublik Deutschland mit der Freien und Hansestadt Hamburg ja nur wenige Jahre zuvor Sitzstaat des Internationalen Seegerichtshofes geworden war und ferner Den Haag mit seinen Botschaften und angesichts seiner Lage gegenüber Nürnberg vielfältige praktische Vorteile bot. Gleichwohl hätte ein Sitz Nürnberg die aufgezeigten historischen Verbindungslinien zwischen dem IMT und dem ICC geradezu augenfällig gemacht.

---

[71] Näher zur rechtlichen Bedeutung dieses Vorgehens A. Zimmermann/H. Scheel, *supra* Fn. 9, S. 142 f.

Andreas Zimmermann

The Judicial Legacy of Nuremberg – The Statute of the International Military Tribunal of Nuremberg and the International Criminal Court

The implementation of international criminal law by the International Military Tribunal (IMT) in Nuremberg after World War II was a ground-breaking measure. Although it was only after the massacres in the former Yugoslavia and Rwanda that criminal responsibility was again executed internationally by the Yugoslav-tribunal (ICTY) and the Rwanda-tribunal (ICTR), the Nuremberg trial against the major German war criminals serves as precedent. This paper takes issue with the trial at Nuremberg and the foundation of international criminal law in particular as it is to be found at the International Criminal Court (ICC).

At the beginning of the presentation general objections against international criminal trials are discussed. The IMT was at the time criticised, as is the ICC today, for violating the *pacta tertiis*-rule, because it was established by an international agreement without participation of the "German Reich", which formally still existed at the time. This plea can be overruled by referring to the Nuremberg Judgment, which states that the allied nations simply combined the right to prosecute war criminals, which each nation could have exercised individually by virtue of the principle of universality. Similarly the member states of the ICC have bundled their individual jurisdictional powers into one institution. Likewise the claim of a violation of the *nullum crimen*-principle, which has some value at least with regard to the IMT, can be responded to because the Rome Statute comprises only crimes which are clearly part of international customary law. A major difference between the IMT, the ICTY and the ICTR on the one side and the ICC on the other is the relationship to national jurisdictions. In contrast to the earlier tribunals the ICC gives prevalence to national courts (so-called principle of complementarity, Art. 17 ICC).

The author then addresses several issues concerning substantive law. As concerns the question of certainty under the law, the Rome Statute is comprehensive compared to the IMT-Statute. Not only is the wording much more precise, Art. 9 ICC refers to further "elements of crimes". Concerning individual norms, the concept of crimes against humanity was further influenced by the IMT (the crime of genocide was only established in 1948 in the Genocide Convention). Likewise war crimes were influenced by the IMT. However, the IMT presupposed a link between the crime and an international armed conflict. It was only in the *Tadic* Case in 1995 when the ICTY terminated this connection and applied the concept of war crimes also to national armed conflicts. The crime of aggression, however, remains problematic. It is questionable whether the ICC should have the power to rule on the legality of the use of force in difficult matters like pre-emptive self-defence, humanitarian intervention, or the interpretation of Security Council Resolutions.

The general part of criminal law was practically nonexistent in the IMT Statute. The ICC has taken heed to the developments in international criminal law since then, so that the Rome Statute comprises a whole set of general principles. Nevertheless, conspiracy (Art. 25 § 3 lit. d ICC) and command responsibility (Art. 28 ICC) originate from the IMT. Immunities for head of states are still debatable under the Rome Statute, but are inapplicable with a view to member states or UN SC referrals to the ICC (Art. 27 ICC). The relevance of superior orders as a defence has grown at the ICC, but is not applicable, if the order is blatantly unlawful (Art. 33 ICC). As concerns possible sanctions it is to be seen as a sign of a growing customary international law that the death-penalty is ruled out by Art. 80 ICC.

The cooperation of the German government with the ICC is a strong sign of support for international criminal justice. The reluctance of the US government to ratify the ICC Statute as former initiators of the IMT is disappointing. Nevertheless, the UN Security Council has clarified that genocide, crimes against humanity and war crimes constitute a threat to international peace and security as in the case of Dafur by referring the situation to the Prosecutor of the ICC by Resolution 1593 of March 13, 2005 acting under Chapter VII of the UN Charter.

Dan Derby

Enforcement of Nuremberg Norms: The Role for Mechanisms other than the ICC

In this courtroom 60 years ago it seemed as if the wrath of the world community descended upon the authors of aggressive war and unprecedented atrocities. This was because the Allies controlled Europe and they were united in their resolve to find perpetrators and evidence for the trials here.

One of the early tasks of the United Nations was to create a permanent international criminal tribunal to continue the role of the Nuremberg and Tokyo International Military Tribunals, bringing justice to international crimes for which national legal systems were inadequate. By 1954 the International Law Commission reported a draft statute for such a tribunal, but that was shelved pending completion of a draft code of offenses against the peace and security of mankind – and that draft code project dragged on for decades. In the early 1990s, the shocking events in former Yugoslavia, and then those in Rwanda, provoked the creation of ad hoc international criminal tribunals by the United Nations Security Council. Finally, rather than continuing to rely on the Security Council's ad hoc approaches, the international community created a permanent International Criminal Court, a replica of the Nuremberg tribunal.

However, even after the end of the Cold War, the world is not united in the same way it was six decades ago, and bringing the wrath of the world community to bear on international crimes is more complex and no longer seamless. As a result, the powers of the new ICC are quite limited.

First, unlike the IMT, the ICC cannot deal with crimes against peace because nations could not agree on a durable definition of aggression. Second, it can only deal with crimes committed after its creation. Third, the Security Council can suspend the ICC's power to deal with a particular situation for a year at a time. Fourth, while its jurisdiction over genocide is global, for other crimes against humanity and for war crimes its jurisdiction is limited to crimes committed within the territory of nations that are parties to the ICC statute or committed by citizens of parties[1], unless the U.N. Security Council deems otherwise for a particular situation. Finally, the ICC is authorized to deal only with the most serious crimes within its subject matter competence, and it cannot deal with a particular alleged crime if any nation having jurisdiction has shown that it is willing and able to genuinely complete investigation and prosecution of that crime.

All of the above restrictions have the effect of leaving punishment of a great many "Nuremberg crimes" to national legal systems. Critics of the ICC, particularly the United States, would like to see more restrictions, but many supporters of the ICC would like to remove some restrictions, or see its competence widened to include additional crimes. However, the ICC statute was the result of years of negotiations and numerous compromises for the sake of consensus. It is unlikely that major proposals to expand its power will be successful in the near future.

One burning question about the adequacy of the ICC is whether it can deal with the scourge of international terrorism. Aren't attacks like 9/11, Bali, Madrid and London war crimes or crimes against humanity? In truth, such attacks probably do not fit the definition of war crimes because an armed conflict is required for war crimes and the violence perpetrated by Al Qaeda and its affiliates is not part of an armed conflict – and this determination is not one that is favorable to terrorists. If such attacks were deemed to be part of an armed conflict, captured perpetrators might have a claim to favorable prisoner of war treatment under the Geneva Conventions, or at least a basis to invoke the exhortation in

---

[1] Jurisdiction of the ICC is governed by Art. 12 of the Rome Statute, which means in general jurisdiction of the ICC is limited to the territoriality and personality-principle. However, I maintain that ICC jurisdiction over genocide is virtually universal because Art. IV of the Genocide Convention (1948) obligates parties to cooperate with an international criminal jurisdiction. Nearly every nation in the world is a party to the Convention. Since the genocide prohibition unquestionably belongs to a body of higher law, "jus cogens", in my estimation the duty to extradite or prosecute in other words "aut dedere, aut judicare" applies, meaning that if nations cannot or will not prosecute a case, then ICC complementarily would apply – though only to crimes since the Statute went into effect (Art. 11 Rome Statute). At the very least, it would seem that the ability of parties to the Genocide Convention to oppose ICC action would be impaired by Article VI.

Protocol I of 1977 that the broadest possible amnesty be granted to combatants after cessation of the conflict.

There is a good argument that attacks like those mentioned above constitute crimes against humanity because they are perpetrated by an organization against a civilian population. However, the natural construction of the term "organization" in the definition of crimes against humanity in the ICC Statute is either governmental organizations or rebel structures resembling those of a government. Because Al Qaeda is not a government and does not aspire to become the government of any of the victim nations mentioned above, it is unlikely to qualify as an organization for these purposes.

It is therefore not surprising that the ICC prosecutor has shown little if any inclination to try to deal with Al Qaeda terrorism. Accordingly, it is likely that the task of dealing with terrorism will remain with national courts, along with Nuremberg crimes that escape the grasp of the ICC due to the many restrictions described above.

National legal systems

While national prosecutions have their disadvantages, they also have surprising advantages. The main advantages come from the normality of national criminal process. This begins with the rules of procedure in any given national system. The mere fact that these procedures have been in place for a long time gives them advantages.

Procedural strengths

First, national procedures are not open to attack as *ad hominem* the way that ICC procedures are. Normal national procedures are used for a wide range of suspects, not just for persons suspected of Nuremberg crimes. Second, national procedures have been tested for effectiveness and found adequate, while the ICC's procedures are untested and are a unique hybrid of adversarial and inquisitorial approaches. Third, there are numerous prosecutors, judges, and defense attorneys who are highly experienced with national procedures. For ICC cases, all legal actors will be learning the ICC's procedures year by year, and for many years there will be a shortage of experienced defense counsel. It is worth noting that the first case heard by the ICTY, the *Tadic* case, was actually developed by the Bavarian state prosecutor, and was chosen partly because it was a nearly completed package that would be easier for an untested prosecutorial team to handle. Fourth, national procedures are apt to be more efficient, not only because the legal actors are more experienced but also because standards of relevance for evidence are rather narrow. In contrast, the ICC procedures are designed to permit the prosecutor to turn the proceedings into a show trial, and under the principle of equality of arms, this means that the defendant can do the same. The current trial of *Slobodan Milosevic* before the ad hoc International Criminal Tribunal for Former Yugoslavia is an excellent example. The case is entering its third year, and its crucial messages have been obscured by the sheer volume of tedious evidence. Moreover, the defendant has been able to propagandize his version of the history surrounding the alleged crimes, causing many in Serbia to believe that the government of Serbia was not responsible for crimes in Bosnia against Moslems. In contrast, a recently discovered videotape of Serbian auxiliary police participating in the slaughter of captives at Srebrenica has created an opportunity for trials in Serbian courts, and many observers expect that national trials of minor perpetrators will do more the teach the Serb populace about their government's culpability than the ICC's trials of higher-ranking defendants.

Substantive strengths

Normal national substantive law can also have advantages. In a national proceeding the prosecutor can prosecute persons suspected of Nuremberg crimes simply for conspiracy to commit murder, etc. This can make the likelihood of success greater because there is no need to prove beyond a reasonable doubt certain attending circumstances. In the ICC, the attending circumstances are part of the definition of substantive offenses, meaning the more must be proved to obtain a conviction.[2] There is reason to believe that such circumstances should have been treated as grounds for ICC jurisdiction rather than elements of substantive crimes.

One result of the strain of using jurisdictional factors as elements of substantive crimes is that for unusual crimes against humanity an ICC prosecutor might have to rely on Article 7(1)(k) of the ICC Statute, which states that crimes against humanity include, "Other inhumane acts of a similar character intentionally causing great suffering, or serious injury to body or to mental or physical health." This involves "crime by analogy", and some may argue that it is justified because innovation by creative perpetrators should not prevent their punishment when they cause harm to society but do not use the particular methods encompassed by the penal law. One argument in favor of crime by analogy was stated as follows: "…wrong may be committed…even in cases where there is no law against what is being done…What is right can be learned not only from the law, but also from the concept of justice which lies behind the law and may not have found perfect expression in the law."

Some may find such a natural law argument persuasive, but it was offered to justify the use of crime by analogy in Nazi Germany by Reich Minister of Justice Franz Gurtner. Actually, all modern legal systems reject crime by analogy, and a prohibition against crime by analogy even appears in the ICC Statute in Article 22(2). A prosecutor in a national legal system would not have to resort to crime by analogy to charge defendants who behaved in that general way because conduct of that kind will readily fit one or more of the many national criminal proscriptions, such as assault.

Having a complete set of national criminal proscriptions to work with can also put things in useful perspective. For example, some argue that the ICC should be empowered to deal with the international crime of torture, which is defined in relevant part as infliction of "severe" mental or physical suffering. However, if the ICC were so empowered and it heard a case of alleged torture, if it determined that the suffering inflicted fell short of "severe," the ICC could not mandate any punishment for the underlying conduct. The defendant would have to be acquitted or the case would have to be dismissed for lack of jurisdiction. In contrast, a national legal system would have a crime of assault that would apply to lesser unjustified inflictions of suffering.

Ironically, some of the authors of the infamous memoranda submitted to the U.S. President concerning permissible interrogation techniques made the mistake of focusing only on the international crime of torture. They cited the Convention Against Torture and the U.S. statute implementing it, and the Geneva Convention requirement that parties punish "grave breaches" of that Convention and leapt to the conclusion that it would be permissible to inflict a considerable amount of pain on interrogation subjects. They overlooked the prohibition of assault in the Uniform Code of Military Justice, which applies to military personnel "everywhere".

Hopefully, legal advisors and prosecutors in most nations would not overlook ordinary criminal law that would apply to reprehensible conduct that falls short of the criteria for an international crime.

Jurisdictional reach

One might worry that relying on national legal systems to deal with crimes like those punished at Nuremberg would permit many offenders to escape punishment because of gaps in the web of national jurisdiction. For example, when crimes of that kind are committed by persons in government positions, such governments would prevent their legal systems from punishing them. However, the nation within whose territory a crime is committed is not the only one whose legal system may have jurisdiction over a crime. Nations have quite a range of traditional, non-controversial bases for criminal jurisdiction:

---

[2] Regarding standard of proof, Common Law nations speak of degrees of proof but elsewhere matters are either proved or not. The framers of the ICC statute were persuaded to use the common law phrase in Article 66, and it may mean something even when handled by civil law personnel. However, I see little reason to push it onto systems that have considered degrees of proof too subtle to be meaningful and I think there would be considerable resistance to such an effort.

Territorial jurisdiction extends not only to ships and aircraft registered in a given nation, but also to inbound aircraft and cruise ships using ports of that nation. Also, nations use "local effects" jurisdiction to deal with events outside of their territory that may produce effects within their territory – the U.S. uses such jurisdiction for conspiracies abroad that result in antitrust violations in the U.S. economy.

Jurisdiction can also be based on nationality. When based on the nationality of the perpetrator, it is called active nationality jurisdiction. This is used by civil law nations to apply their criminal law to their citizens everywhere, and used by common law nations for military offenses and a few other offenses. There is also passive nationality jurisdiction, based on the nationality of the victim, and it is used by many nations – including the U.S. – for a variety of international crimes.

As a result, a crime in one nation may fall under the jurisdiction of one or more other nations. Of course, obtaining custody of a perpetrator can be challenging. While most nations have extradition treaties with scores of other nations, a government whose agents are committing Nuremberg crimes is unlikely to honor requests for their extradition. However, crimes of this character are often committed in a situation of conflict and instability, meaning that there is a chance that the perpetrators will be forced to flee to another country. That is what happened in the *Tadic* case – the bully who ran a prison camp had migrated to Munich, and was identified by victims who had also migrated there.

Thus, there is a web of national jurisdiction that may trap perpetrators of Nuremberg crimes. There is also a web of evidence sharing through mutual legal assistance treaties. This means that witnesses and documents that are found in various nations can be brought to bear on a criminal prosecution in a distant nation, and the sum of this evidence may be sufficient to produce a conviction without cooperation from the nation where the crimes occurred. This kind of cooperation was found in the *Demjanuk* and *Sawoniuk* cases. The former involved deportation from the U.S. of a suspected war criminal for trial in Israel, and witnesses and documents were garnered from several nations, including the Soviet Union. The latter case was prosecuted in the United Kingdom and featured a trip by the entire court to the Eastern Europe site of the crimes.

The web is not without some gaps and technicalities of cooperation can be formidable, but the web is wider and more complete than one might have thought. It should be noted, however, that this web of cooperation applies when the criminal case is being heard in a normal court. When cases are to be heard by special courts or military courts cooperation is far less likely.

Universal jurisdiction

Some think that the web of cooperation against serious international crimes can be enhanced by the use of universal jurisdiction. A group of scholars gathered at Princeton a few years ago to promulgate "principles" regarding universal jurisdiction for serious international crimes, such as Nuremberg crimes. Their principles declared that nations should exercise universal jurisdiction in order to prevent impunity of perpetrators, and that other nations should cooperate with such exercises of jurisdiction, extraditing suspects and providing evidence.

At about the same time, in Belgium, where a law authorized courts to use universal jurisdiction, the first results were arrest warrants for Mr. Abdulaye Yerodia Ndombasi (Yerodia), who at that time was the Minister for Foreign Affairs of The Democratic Republic of the Congo, and the Prime Minister of Israel, Ariel Sharon, for acts they allegedly committed before assuming those positions. The Democratic Republic of the Congo challenged the warrant for its foreign minister in the International Court of Justice and obtained a ruling that issuance of the warrant was improper because it mandated the arrest of someone whose presence in Belgium would involve a diplomatic visit. The same reasoning would apply to the warrant for Sharon because as head of government any visit by him to Belgium would be diplomatic in nature. In addition to the rebuff from the ICJ, the Belgian law was criticized by some nations, particularly the U.S. Ultimately it was revised to limit use of universal jurisdiction to cases that had a strong link to Belgium.

Meanwhile, universal jurisdiction has been in use in Spain where Judge Balthazar Garzon issued an extradition request for General Augusto Pinochet when he was visiting the U.K. Because the U.K. would not apply universal jurisdiction to the crimes in question it would not recognize Spain's claim to universal jurisdiction. However, a decision by the Law Committee of the House of Lords indicated that the U.K. would recognize Spanish passive nationality jurisdiction for the crime of torture for the time period in which the U.K. adopted such jurisdiction for that crime. However, that would have led to extradition only for a few cases of torture of Spanish citizens that occurred late in the period of military rule in Chile. That has not deterred Judge Garzon from issuing various warrants for other individuals based on universal jurisdiction.

Several nations, including Canada and the U.K. used universal jurisdiction for war crimes and crimes against humanity that occurred in World War II. The results were uninspiring because the difficulty of prosecuting decades-old crimes was aggravated by the distance between the trials and the evidence and witnesses.

In principle, universal jurisdiction for Nuremberg crimes is well established. However, there is no consensus about use of such jurisdiction by nations that do not have the individual in their custody. Use of universal jurisdiction by nations that do not have the individual in custody could lead to multiple simultaneous prosecutions and conflicting requests for cooperation. Moreover, the nation where the individual is found will insist that its action – prosecution or a decision not to prosecute – should be dispositive.

In any event, there is a dramatic practical limit on the workability of universal jurisdiction. When a prosecution is commenced in a nation that has little relation to the crime, evidence from other nations may be crucial, but those nations may not choose to cooperate. This can thwart a trial if a defendant has a credible claim that there is exculpatory evidence in a nation that refuses to cooperate. Under such circumstances it would be inappropriate to convict, but a dismissal of the case might be seen by some as an indication that the accused in innocent.

The U.S. never used universal jurisdiction even as to Nuremberg crimes from World War II. Instead, when a suspect was found inside the U.S. he would be deported, after being denaturalized if he was a citizen, based on lies on his application for citizenship. That is how Demjanuk was delivered to Israel. However, such an approach raised questions about the suitability of particular national legal systems for particular cases, especially during the Cold War.

Bias

Obviously, one great concern about relying on national legal systems to deal with serious international crimes is potential bias based on political factors. One way to deal with this is to add internationally-appointed judges to a national court, as has been done in Sierra Leone and is planned in Cambodia. This approach was proposed for crimes by Indonesian forces in East Timor, but Indonesia did not accept it. It will not be taken for the trials of major Iraqi leaders including Saddam Hussein, and those cases will suffer credibility deficits that could have been reduced by using international judges.

The ICC has a cure for bias in one situation. Where a nation tries its own agents for genocide, crimes against humanity or war crimes and acquits them, if the ICC regards the action as a white-wash, it can act like an appellate court, treating the acquittal as void and starting its own prosecution.

If delegating such appellate power to the ICC is acceptable when nations acquit their friends, it seems that such a delegation should be acceptable when a nation tries its enemies and convicts them, but there has been no active consideration of assigning such a role to the ICC or creating another court to perform that role. In contrast, when nations convict their own agents or acquit their enemies, the risk of bias is lower and so is the need for international oversight.

Creativity may produce other ways to limit potential bias in national prosecutions. For example, to deal with the Pan American Flight 103 bombing extended negotiations finally settled on a trial of Libyan suspects before a jury-less Scottish court sitting in the Netherlands.

Accordingly, the use of national legal systems – indirect enforcement – to deal with serious international crimes like those punished at Nuremberg can be quite effective, but there are still potential gaps in the web of cooperation against such crimes and some bias issues have not been seriously addressed.

Dan Derby

Durchsetzung der Normen von Nürnberg: Strafverfolgungsmechanismen jenseits des Internationalen Strafgerichtshofs

Schon bald nach Abschluss der Verfahren gegen die Hauptkriegsverbrecher vor dem Internationalen Militärtribunal in Nürnberg wurde unter dem Dach der UN an der Schaffung eines ständigen Internationalen Strafgerichtshofs gearbeitet. In den politischen Wirren des Kalten Kriegs war es nicht möglich, sich auf einen Kodex internationaler Verbrechen und die Errichtung eines internationalen Gerichts zu deren Durchsetzung zu verständigen. Erst durch die Initiative des UN-Sicherheitsrats Anfang der 1990er Jahre als Reaktion auf die schockierenden Vorgänge im ehemaligen Jugoslawien und in Ruanda mit internationalen *ad hoc*-Tribunalen zu reagieren, war es möglich, den Internationalen Strafgerichtshof (ICC) zu installieren. Fast sechzig Jahre nach Nürnberg war die Einigkeit in der Weltgemeinschaft jedoch weit weniger groß als damals, so dass die Kompetenzen des ICC limitiert sind. Hinsichtlich des Verbrechens der Aggression konnte noch keine Formulierung gefunden werden; die Zuständigkeit ist auf die Ahndung schwerster Völkerverbrechen beschränkt, der UN-Sicherheitsrat kann die Strafverfolgung vor dem ICC suspendieren, das Universalitätsprinzip konnte nicht durchgesetzt werden und das Prinzip der Komplementarität räumt den Nationalstaaten Vorrang bei der Strafverfolgung ein. Unklar ist außerdem, ob der ICC gegen Akte des internationalen Terrorismus tätig werden kann.

Die nationale Verfolgung internationaler Verbrechen hat, und das mag überraschen, dagegen einige Vorteile. Die Kompetenz ist nicht auf Akte schwerster Kriminalität beschränkt, so dass die fließende Grenze zwischen gewöhnlichen und schwersten internationalen Verbrechen kein Verfolgungshindernis darstellt. Die nationalen Verfolgungsbehörden sind erfahren und eingespielt und müssen sich nicht auf ein unbekanntes, neues internationales Verfahrensrecht einstellen. Die dadurch entstehenden Reibungsverluste und zeitlichen Verzögerungen zeigen sich in dramatischer Weise im Verfahren gegen Milosevic vor dem Jugoslawientribunal. Im nationalen Verfahren kann außerdem das Weltrechtspflegeprinzip für die in Nürnberg aufgestellten Verbrechenstatbestände angewendet werden. Dieses gerade in den USA nicht unumstrittene Prinzip vermag aber aus praktischen Gründen selten zur Anwendung kommen. Die internationale Kooperation in Strafsachen ist noch weit unterentwickelt, so dass für einen auf der Grundlage dieser Kompetenz ermittelnden Staat unüberwindbare Schwierigkeiten bei der Beweissicherung bestehen. Fehlende transnationale Kooperation ist der große Nachteil der nationalen, d.h. indirekten Durchsetzung von Völkerstrafrecht.

Roger P. Alford

War Reparations, the Holocaust, and the ICC

I would like to focus my discussion on the International Criminal Court in the context of war reparations generally, both past, present, and future. I should begin by emphasizing that while international law is exceptionally good at dealing with certain issues relating to international wrongs, but it is exceptionally bad at dealing with others. International law can deal with revolutions, catastrophes, and lesser evils we euphemistically call acts of God. But when the fury of hell is unleashed on earth, international law quakes. The great irony of war is that the more catastrophic and widespread its destructive consequences, the less likely that those caught in its path will ever be repaid for their injury.

I. Revolutions Are Easy for International Law

We should begin with a minor thesis: revolutions are easy. International law is now well positioned to respond to revolutions. Mechanisms for enforcing international rights have been established and international law itself has blossomed through a network of bilateral investment treaties and judicial decisions protecting foreign investment. Now we know the drill when a revolution occurs: immediately freeze the country's assets, invoke investment treaties, waive sovereign immunity for acts of expropriation, establish a dispute resolution mechanism, and honor that mechanism's awards through frozen assets, lump-sum settlements, or assets chased under the New York Convention. We can credibly state, as international courts like the Iran-United States Claims Tribunal regularly do, that in the aftermath of a revolution, foreign investors whose property has been expropriated must receive prompt, adequate, and effective compensation representing the full value of their losses.

II. Wars Are Hard for International Law

But what about wars? Wars are hard because the suffering is so great and reparations so onerous that often there is no mutuality of interest between the victorious governments and their own constituent victims. Wars force victorious States to make hard choices between looking backward to repair the harm caused to constituent victims and looking forward to a relationship with a potential strong and strategic ally. Just as "the conduct of [w]ar, in its great features, is ... policy itself,"[1] so too it often appears that war reparation schemes have almost everything to do with international relations, and very little to do with international law. The victorious States must choose to either (1) wholly embrace the past harms of the victims and ignore a future with the vanquished, or (2) wholly embrace a future with the vanquished and ignore the painful past of the victims, or (3) strike a balance of both that will satisfy neither the victims nor the vanquished. To turn an old maxim on its head, failure to address war reparations properly may result in a bad peace after a good war.

(1) <u>Embrace the Victims at the Expense of the Vanquished.</u> An example of the first approach is the Treaty of Versailles. Article 232 of the Treaty of Versailles required Germany to "make compensation for all damage done to the civilian population of the Allied Powers ... and to their property ... and in general all damage." Shortly thereafter, John Maynard Keynes wrote that reparations are "preach[ed] ... in the name of Justice," but such justice is not so simple "[i]n the great events of man's history, in the unwinding of the complex fates of nations." He famously predicted that the reparations scheme established at Versailles would reduce Germany "to servitude for a generation ..., degrad[e] the lives of millions of human beings, and ... depriv[e] a whole nation of happiness."[2]

---

[1] Carl von Clausewitz, 3 *On War* 130 (Routledge 7 kegan Paul 1962).
[2] John Maynard Keynes, *The Economic Consequences of the Peace* 225 (Harcourt, Brace & Howe 1920).

Adolf Hitler built his early career railing against the Treaty. In *Mein Kampf*, "the shameless and monstrous word 'reparations' was able to make itself at home in Germany." In speeches attacking the "inhuman cruelty" of the Treaty of Versailles, Hitler wrote that he was "struck by the glances of [thousands of] hostile eyes" and the "surging mass full of the holiest indignation and boundless wrath." He said that he repeated this theme "dozens of times ... until ... a certain clear and unified conception became current among the people from among whom the [Nazi] movement gathered its first members."[3] Many historians of course have argued that the seeds of discontent were sown at Versailles and bore devastating fruit in the Second World War.

(2) Embracing the Vanquished at the Expense of the Victims. If the Treaty of Versailles illustrates the problems of the first approach, the Peace Treaty with Japan illustrates the problems of the second approach, which embraces the vanquished at the expense of the victims.

Following the Second World War, the United States and Japan signed a peace-treaty, the purpose of which the United States asserts was to limit the exposure of Japan only to those amounts claimed by the Allied Powers and to preclude the rights of victims of the war to claim directly against Japan and her nationals. In furtherance of this treaty, the United States waived its claim to war reparations. This policy and subsequent nurturing of the US-Japan relationship has transformed Japan from one of our greatest enemies into one of our strongest allies.

But the soft underbelly of this policy is that it was undertaken at the expense of United States constituent victims. Under United States legislation, each prisoner of war was authorized to receive $ 1.50 for each day he was held as a prisoner-of-war and was subjected to forced labor and inhuman treatment. The unspoken deficiency in the policy toward Japan has festered for fifty years and now US prisoners of war and other victims are attempting to challenge the wisdom of that policy employed at their expense. Had Japan taken the courageous approach of Germany and provided compensation when it later had the ability to pay, matters would have been different. But Japan has hidden behind the legal protections of the peace treaties, and victims of the war in the Pacific remain bitter at the burdens they have been forced to bear in the name of a strong alliance with Japan.

(3) Embrace Both But Satisfy Neither. An example of the third approach, one that embraces both the vanquished and the victims but satisfied neither, can be found with the United Nations Compensation Commission. Despite the noble efforts of the United Nations, many Gulf War victims remain unsatisfied with the results because the UNCC has awarded only partial compensation to individual victims and has disingenuously denied compensation to many meritorious corporate and government claims. Under the UNCC regime, individual claimants are denied full recovery for the extent of their injuries, with the UNCC providing a fixed fee of $ 2,500 for serious personal injury and $ 10,000 per family in the event of death, and in some cases more if the claimant can provide adequate proof. Fixing the amount of loss to such a relatively low amount will ensure that the families of the victims will not feel that the full extent of their injuries has been compensated. Likewise, corporate and government claimants are often denied compensation based on strained interpretations of what constitutes evidence of a direct loss or an offsetting gain.

But the UNCC approach was likewise unsatisfactory to the vanquished Iraq. Presumably these measures were undertaken not only in recognition of the limited resources of Iraq, but also to limit the overall exposure of Iraq to Gulf War reparation claims. Today of course the new government in Iraq faces a major problem as it seeks forgiveness of its debt obligations. Unlike the Peace Treaty between Japan and the United States, which provided a measure of certainty to Japan regarding its long-term exposure to war reparations, the Gulf War approach offers no such security for Iraq. The UNCC is supplemental to other avenues of compensation, permitting claimants to pursue any other avenue that may be available to them, including contractual arbitration clauses and litigation in foreign courts. To put another way, Iraq secure no legal peace in the UNCC compensation scheme.

---

[3] Adolf Hitler, *Mein Kampf* 468 (Houghton Mifflin 1999).

One wonders in analyzing these different models where international law is in this picture. Are these choices in any way circumscribed by general principles of international law? Does international law require some balance of interests between the victims and the vanquished?

One also wonders where international law was in the Holocaust restitution movement. Was it yet another example of international relations devoid of international law? Of course as you all know, there were a variety of Holocaust reparation claims involving numerous countries – Germany, France, Switzerland, Austria, Japan – and a range of subjects, ranging from art, slave labor, bank accounts, and insurance policies.

III. War Reparations and the Holocaust

If one analyzes the Holocaust restitution movement, as I have in great depth, one finds parallels with these historic choices regarding war reparations.

(1) <u>Embracing the Victims: The Case Against Switzerland.</u> The initial wave of litigation involving the Holocaust was focused on Switzerland. A number of steps were taken that established a predominant emphasis on victim compensation without significant regard to the foreign policy implications of future relations with the Swiss government. First, there were the congressional hearings in 1996 led by Alfonse D'Amato, followed by Clinton Administration investigations of U.S. archives for the trail of Nazi assets.

This led to a four-fold strategy against the Swiss banks, in which local officials in New York threatened sanctions against the banks, state regulators threatened to refuse approval of a proposed merger between the two largest Swiss banks, fractured Jewish interests initiated major public relations campaign against the Swiss banks, and scores of class action lawyers threatened billions of dollars in lawsuits. As the Swiss banks' top lawyer put in our forthcoming book, these groups "focused on what pressures they might bring to bear on the banks here, they generally gave scant attention to, and lacked a sufficient understanding of, the Swiss domestic pressures that constrained the banks' conduct."[4] Moreover, the Swiss Government took a hands-off approach and passing the responsibility to the banks, viewing it as their problem, and generally avoiding any significant involvement in brokering an acceptable global solution to the problem. The U.S. was left to mediate a private settlement between American lawyers and the Swiss banks.

In the end, the banks settled the dispute with a $ 1.25 billion settlement under the supervision of a district court judge in New York. The broad consensus was that the settlement was extraordinarily favorable to the victims. The goal of the Swiss settlement is to make individual account holders completely whole. That is, if a Holocaust victim is entitled to an account, he or she is entitled to the full value of the account, backing out over forty years of interest payments and adding from 1945 over forty years of compound interest that would have accrued. The Swiss settlement illustrates an example in which private party litigation seeks to achieve full compensation for claimants, reflecting an unrelentingly focused on victims concerns, not foreign relations implications.

(2) <u>Embracing the Vanquished: The Case Against Japan.</u> When Holocaust litigation turned to Japan, and more specifically Japanese corporations, the focus was radically different. Japan had the law on their side, and Japanese corporations invoked the Peace Treaty to argue that the claims of Holocaust victims should be dismissed. The United States Government intervened on the side of the Japanese, submitting statements of interest. The Japanese government refused to succumb to the various pressures and refused to consider any settlement. Indeed, when I was asked to consult on these Japanese POW cases, I read the briefs, examined the treaty provisions, considered the political calculus of the Japanese, and politely declined the invitation. It was just too obvious the victims were getting nowhere in this

---

[4] Roger Witten, *How Swiss Banks and German Companies Came to Terms with the Wrenching Legacies of the Holocaust and World War II: A Defense Perspective*, in MICHAEL BAZYLER & ROGER ALFORD, HOLOCAUST RESTITUTION: PERSPECTIVES ON THE LITIGATION AND ITS AFTERMATH (NYU Press 2005).

litigation. And of course, in the end the Japanese were victorious in the courts. The continued perception in the United States, however, is that Japan has failed to live up to its responsibility for grave human rights violations during the Second World War, and that unlike Germany, it has ignored its moral, if not legal, burdens as a civilized, developed country that is more than capable of redressing its past transgressions.

(3) Embracing Both: The Case Against Germany. Germany was radically different. It exemplifies an approach to Holocaust restitution that embraced both victim and government concerns. While Germany had paid significant reparations in the immediate aftermath of the War, these reparations expressly excluded slave labor. This left it vulnerable to Holocaust restitution litigation in the 1990s. Germany and in particular German corporations were faced with an onslaught of private lawsuits in the wake of the successful Swiss settlement. In 1998 German corporations appealed to the German government to intervene and treat it as a national problem. Recognized the foreign policy implications, the Germany government was quick to intervene. The remarkable thing was that after the Germans won a handful of initial lawsuits filed against them, they then resolved to broker a settlement with the victims. Through the intervention of German and U.S. negotiators, the Germans established a German Foundation in which $ 5 billion were paid to distribute to Holocaust victim slave laborers. The negotiations addressed not simply slave labor, but also certain other outstanding issues. It is also combined public and private compensations schemes in a joint effort between German corporate and government interests. And it included the plaintiff lawyers in the bilateral government negotiations.

The result is a balance of victim and state concerns. It does not attempt to offer full compensation. Each slave laborer in a concentration camp is to receive around $ 7,000 dollars, while slave laborers in less severe conditions are to receive around $ 2,500 dollars. This is a far cry from what one survivor who contributed to our book argued he was entitled, which was around $ 70,000 for his slave labor. In exchange for this, the Germans secured a commitment of legal peace from future litigation. This peace not only meant the lawyers dropping all of the outstanding cases, but also a binding commitment from the United States to intervene to request dismissal of any future litigation. Thus, the victims' and the governments' interests were both satisfied.

IV. Three Models for War Reparations

So with the Holocaust, we again see different examples of reparation schemes that highlight different concerns. Which raises the much broader question of the future of war reparations. Whither war reparations? I would suggest that there are at least three models for the future of war reparations.

(1) The Human Rights Litigation Model. The first is private human rights litigation model. This approach will focus on victim interests and diminish the role or importance of foreign relations concerns. This is the approach currently being taken with September 11th litigation in the Multi-District Litigation in New York. These plaintiffs are seeking billions, if not trillions of dollars in compensation from defendant countries including Iran, Iraq, and Saudi-Arabia. The plaintiffs involved in that litigation care very little about foreign relations concerns, except to the extent it will undermine their case. A degree of foreign relations concerns are built into the system, as with foreign sovereign immunity defenses, but generally this approach will emphasize victim compensation. One should expect that with the success of the Holocaust litigation, future war reparations will be litigated in U.S. courts as human rights litigation.

(2) Classic Interstate Negotiation Model. A second approach is focused on interstate negotiations using a classic state responsibility model. Under this approach, a state can broker with another state to resolve claims at an interstate level, without predominant regard to the interests of their constituent victims. This approach will focus on questions such as (i) the establishment of principles for determining appropriate compensation for acts of war; (ii) the relevance of the vanquished country's present or future ability to pay; and (iii) the responsibility of states for war-like conduct undertaken by

non-state actors. As you all know, the German Foundation slave labour scheme in many ways fits this model.

(3) <u>Victim Compensation Fund</u>. A third model is focused on both state interests and victim compensation through the establishment of compensation funds using resources other than the unlawful nations' assets. One modern example of this is the twin effort of the United States to compensate the victims of September 11 out of a special Compensation Fund funded by U.S. taxpayers, while at the same time spending billions to rebuild Afghanistan, which of course was the country most culpable for the September 11 attacks. Another modern example is the International Criminal Court. Two key provisions address victim compensation. Article 75 provides that the Court may require a "convicted person" to make "appropriate reparations to … victims including restitution, compensation, and rehabilitation." In addition, Article 79 provides a trust fund and states that the assembly of state parties may establish a trust fund "for the benefit of victims of crimes … and of the families of such victims" and "may order money and other property collected through fines or forfeiture to be transferred … to the Trust Fund." A significant portion of this trust fund will be paid by member states, corporations and other philanthropic organizations.[5] It should be noted, however, that the ICC does not contemplate a scheme of state responsibility for reparations to the victims. It is either the individual perpetrators of war crimes or humanitarian aid through the Trust Fund that will seek a measure of compensation. This approach will mean that victims will rarely if ever secure full compensation. But it will also mean that States will not be saddled with crippling war reparation obligations in the aftermath of unlawful conduct. This third model has been described by Desmond Tutu, who serves on the Board of Directors of the Victim Trust Fund, as "perhaps the most innovative aspect of an innovative institution…" recognizing that a "judicial process concentrating only on perpetrators has not usually been able to make the crucial contribution to reconciliation and peace."[6] The great advantage of this model is that by sourcing the funds from both through fines and forfeiture imposed on the wrongdoer, as well as voluntary contributions from public and private sources, the victims receive a measure of compensation and the future relationship with the vanquished is not compromised. This third model is innovative because it frees states to avoid the hard choice of choosing between the victims and the victimizing state.

---

[5] *See* Report of the Assembly of States Parties on the Activities and Projects of the Board of Directors of the Trust Fund for Victims, 2003-2004, ICC-ASP/3/14/Rev.1 (26 August 2004) available at http://www.icc-cpi.int/library/asp/ICC-ASP-3-14-Rev.1-English.pdf.

[6] Statement of His Eminence Archbishop Desmond Tutu, on behalf of the Board of Directors of the Trust Fund for Victims, April 22, 2004, available at http://www.icc-cpi.int/press/video.html.

Roger P. Alford

Kriegsentschädigung, der Holocaust und der ICC

Völkerrecht tut sich schwer mit der Abwicklung von Kriegen und der Entschädigung von Kriegsopfern. Das liegt vor allem daran, dass der Siegerstaat eine Wahl zu treffen hat. Er kann (1.) sich allein auf die Opfer konzentrieren und dafür Sorge tragen, dass ihnen Gerechtigkeit widerfährt, muss dabei jedoch eine Zukunft mit dem Täter vernachlässigen. Er kann (2.) die zukünftige Kooperation mit dem eigentlichen Täterstaat in den Mittelpunkt rücken und muss dafür die Opferinteressen hintanstellen, und er kann (3.) versuchen zwischen diesen beiden Extrempositionen einen Mittelweg zu finden. Für alle drei Modelle gibt es historische Beispiele. Modell (1) wurde im Versailler Vertrag verwirklicht, in dem nach dem 1. Weltkrieg Deutschland die gesamte Kriegsreparation aufgebürdet wurde. Das (2.) Modell lässt sich im Friedensvertrag mit Japan nach dem 2. Weltkrieg finden, der sämtliche Individualansprüche ausschloss. Das Modell (3.) kann man in der UN Compensation Commission beobachten, durch die individuelle Ansprüche bezogen auf Schäden, die von der Besetzung Kuwaits durch den Irak herrühren, befriedigt werden, aber nur bis zu einer relativ geringen Höchstgrenze.

Auch im Umgang mit dem Holocaust lassen sich alle drei Modelle finden. Während die Vereinbarung mit der Schweiz die Opfer bevorzugte, wurde eine Opferbeteiligung beim Friedensvertrag mit Japan ausgeschlossen. Im Falle Deutschlands wurde ein Mittelweg beschritten, was sich vor allem an der symbolischen Entschädigung von Zwangsarbeitern durch die Errichtung der Stiftung „Erinnerung, Verantwortung, Zukunft" zeigt.

Aus diesen Erfahrungen lassen sich drei grundsätzliche Wege zum Kriegsopferausgleich feststellen. Der Weg zur Entschädigung über die so genannten Human Rights Litigation hilft den Opfern am meisten, der Weg über einen bilateralen Friedensvertrag kann zum Ausschluss der Individualansprüche führen und die Lösung durch die Errichtung eines Opferfonds, wie nun auch im ICC Statut vorgesehen, versucht einen Kompromiss zwischen den Opferinteressen und den staatlichen Interessen zu ermöglichen.

VIII. Totalitarianism and German Resistance/Totalitarismus und deutsche Widerstandsbewegungen

Winfried Heinemann

Das Attentat auf Hitler: 20. Juli 1944 und die Geschichte des deutschen Widerstands

1. Der Staatsstreich als militärische Operation

Lage:
„I. Der Führer Adolf Hitler ist tot!
[Feindlage:] Eine gewissenlose Clique frontfremder Parteiführer hat es unter Ausnutzung dieser Lage versucht, der schwerringenden Front in den Rücken zu fallen und die Macht zu eigennützigen Zwecken an sich zu reißen.
[Auftrag:]
II. In dieser Stunde höchster Gefahr hat die Reichsregierung zur Aufrechterhaltung von Recht und Ordnung den militärischen Ausnahmezustand verhängt und mir zugleich mit dem Oberbefehl über die Wehrmacht die vollziehende Gewalt übertragen.
[Durchführung:]
III. Hierzu befehle ich:
Ich übertrage die vollziehende Gewalt [...] auf den Befehlshaber des Ersatzheeres unter gleichzeitiger Ernennung zum Oberbefehlshaber im Heimatkriegsgebiet [...]
Die gesamte Waffen-SS ist mit sofortiger Wirkung in das Heer eingegliedert. [...]

Der Oberbefehlshaber der Wehrmacht
gez. v. Witzleben – Generalfeldmarschall[1]"

Im Einzelnen:
Es kommt darauf an, die Schaltstellen der Macht, vorrangig den Hauptgefechtsstand des Umsturzes beim Befehlshaber des Ersatzheeres, sodann die Ministerien des Großdeutschen Reiches gegen Angriffe feindlicher, also systemtreuer Kräfte zu sichern.

Feind:
- Bodentruppen der Luftwaffe in unbekannter Stärke und Kampfkraft in der General-Göring-Kaserne am Feldflugplatz Tegel.
- Ersatztruppenteile der Leibstandarte SS „Adolf Hitler" in vermutlich größerer Stärke, Beweglichkeit und Kampfkraft in der ehemaligen Hauptkadettenanstalt in Berlin Lichterfelde, dort feindlicher Schwerpunkt.

Eigene Kräfte, nach Verfügbarkeit:
- Wachbataillon in Moabit, motorisierte Infanterie, ausweislich des Übungsalarms vom 15. Juli sofort verfügbar, geführt von dem absolut systemtreuen Major Remer, auf den aber so lange Verlass ist, wie er der ausgegebenen Lage glaubt, untersteht Stadtkommandantur Berlin unter Generalmajor von Hase.
- Infanterieschule Döberitz, drei Bataillone stark, verfügbar erst nach Mobilisierung und Anmarsch über rund 25 km, untersteht Wehrkreiskommando III. Auftrag: Verstärkung der zur Sicherung des Regierungsviertels eingesetzten Kräfte, Besetzung des Rundfunks an der Masurenallee, der Sender Tegel und Nauen (letzterer außerhalb des Kartenausschnitts).
- Panzertruppenschule II in Krampnitz, zwei gepanzerte Bataillone, ebenfalls erst verfügbar nach Mobilisierung und Anmarsch über rund 30 km, ebenfalls Wehrkreis III. Auftrag: leicht gepanzerte Kräfte fahren Aufklärung und überwachen SS-Kräfte in Lichterfelde, ansonsten gepanzerte Reserve in Verfügungsraum Tiergarten in unmittelbarer Nähe des Bendlerblocks.
- Heeresfeuerwerkerschule und Heereswaffenmeisterschule in Treptow: Feldwebel in der Ausbildung, fronterfahren, aber nicht beweglich (Anmarsch per Straßenbahn?) und von geringer Stärke, unterstehen

---

[1] Spiegelbild einer Verschwörung, S. 20 f. (24. Juli 1944).

Standortkommandantur. Auftrag: Sicherung des Berliner Stadtschlosses und der daneben liegenden Standortkommandantur.
- Pionierschule in Karlshorst: Stärke unbekannt, daher zu vernachlässigen, ebenso wie Garnison Spandau mit nicht mobilen Landesschützenbataillonen unbekannter Stärke.
Unter Führung Wehrkreiskommando III und erst nach längerem Anmarsch, vermutlich am Tage X+1 verfügbar:
- Panzertruppenschule I Wünsdorf, ebenfalls in unbekannter Stärke; wird bei weiteren Planungen nicht berücksichtigt.
- Ersatzbrigade Großdeutschland in Cottbus, rund 7 000-8 000 Man; Einsatzbereitschaft ebenfalls am 15. Juli überprüft, kann innerhalb von 12 Stunden den Sender Herzberg, den Sender Königs Wusterhausen, den Flugplatz Rangsdorf bei Zossen sichern und von Süden nach Berlin hinein vorgehen. Dabei Auftrag: SS-Kräfte in Lichterfelde von hinten binden und Flughafen Tempelhof für eigene Verstärkungen sichern.

Führung und Fernmeldewesen:
Es wird darauf ankommen, die Fiktion, der Führer sei einem Anschlag der SS zum Opfer gefallen, möglichst lange aufrecht zu erhalten. Anders als 1938 beruht diese Planung nicht darauf, solche Verbände einzusetzen, deren Führer vorher in die Verschwörung eingeweiht sind, sondern darauf, mittels einer plausiblen Notfallplanung alle verfügbaren Heeresverbände gegen die verhasste SS und Luftwaffe anzusetzen.
Chef Wehrmachtnachrichtenwesen, General Fellgiebel, blockiert dazu alle militärischen Verbindungssysteme und lässt allein den eigenen Fernmeldeverkehr zu.
Zugleich wird es darauf ankommen, das feindlich kontrollierte Medium des Rundfunks auszuschalten, dazu stellt Truppe entsprechende Stoßtrupps zum Funkhaus und zu allen Sendern im Wehrkreis III ab, die Chef Wehrmachtnachrichtenwesen unterstützt durch Abstellung von Fernmeldeoffizieren[2].

2. Fragestellung: „Gemeinsame Zivilität"?

Meine Damen und Herren, was ich Ihnen hier in militärisch-knappen Worten vorgetragen habe, ist ein klassischer Militärputsch. Da sollen Panzer rollen, da sollen Minister verhaftet und Behörden dem Heer unterstellt werden. Was Sie hier sehen, steht in der Tradition des preußischen Belagerungszustands; es geht darum, an die Stelle des für den Nationalsozialismus charakteristischen Kompetenzenwirrwarrs eine einheitliche, eben militärische Führung des Reiches im Inneren wie nach Außen zu setzen. Als Vorbild dienen die Zustände im Ersten Weltkrieg, als die vollziehende Gewalt im Inneren bei den Generalkommandos der Wehrkreise gelegen hatte, und gewisse Anleihen an den Kapp-Putsch von 1920 sind unverkennbar[3].

Das ist der Kern des Aufstandsversuchs vom 20. Juli, dessen wir hier in Deutschland heute gedenken. Auftakt war – gegen Mittag – das Attentat des Oberst Claus Graf Stauffenberg, jene Bombe, die unter Hitlers Lagetisch explodierte, die aber den Diktator nicht getötet hatte. Deutschland gedenkt heute jener Menschen, die Hitler töten, das NS-Regime stürzen und – ja, was wollten sie danach tun?
Bei dem Karlsruher Politikwissenschaftler Peter Steinbach finden Sie die Aussage: „Die Frage nach dem Verhältnis zwischen militärischem und zivilem Widerstand stellte sich für sie nicht, weil sie im Kern einer gemeinsamen Zivilität übereinstimmten."[4] Wenn militärischer und ziviler Widerstand in einer „gemeinsamen Zivilität" übereinstimmen, wenn also der militärische Widerstand sich lediglich als

---

[2] Zur Planung für den Umsturz im Großraum Berlin nach wie vor einschlägig: Hoffmann, Widerstand – Staatsstreich – Attentat; Hoffmann, Stauffenberg; auch Kopp, Hase. Weitgehend irrig und ungenau Dirks/Janßen, Krieg der Generäle, S. 172-176.

[3] Hierzu und zum folgenden Deist, Kriegszustand, S. XXXI-XXXIV, ähnlich ders., Voraussetzungen innenpolitischen Handelns.

[4] Steinbach, Peter: Zum Verhältnis der Ziele, S. 992.

Unterabteilung einer größeren, zivil konzipierten und geführten Verschwörung verstand, gibt es dann ein Spezifikum der Soldaten im Widerstand?

Ich glaube das mit der „gemeinsamen Zivilität" nicht. Ich möchte Ihnen heute die wesentliche Entwicklung hin zum Staatsstreichversuch und damit auch die wesentlichen Motive der Verschwörer darlegen – und dabei auch aufzeigen, dass die meisten unter ihnen von einer parlamentarischen Demokratie nach unserem Verständnis weit entfernt waren.

3. Militärische Motive für den Umsturz

Ein wesentliches, immer wiederkehrendes Motiv von Soldaten für den Entschluss zum Widerstand war die Forderung nach einer Änderung der militärischen Spitzengliederung. Hinter diesem eher technischen Begriff verbarg sich während der Kriegszeit allerdings nichts weniger als das Nachdenken über den Rücktritt Hitlers vom Oberkommando der Wehrmacht, seit 1942 zumindest vom Oberkommando des Heeres. Das galt insbesondere seit Hitlers Übernahme des Oberbefehls über das Heer am 19. Dezember 1941[5].

Der Major i.G. Claus Graf Stauffenberg von der Organisationsabteilung des Oberkommandos des Heeres pflegte Vorträge über dieses Thema mit der Bemerkung einzuleiten, „die Kriegsspitzengliederung der deutschen Wehrmacht sei noch blöder, als die befähigsten Generalstabsoffiziere sie erfinden könnten, wenn sie den Auftrag bekämen, die unsinnigste Kriegsspitzengliederung zu erfinden[6]".

Die Folgen, die sich aus Hitlers fehlender Fachkompetenz für die militärische Führung des Reiches ergaben, standen ja nur zu deutlich vor Augen. Sogar in der akademischen Jugend war man sich bewusst, dass Hitlers Dilettantismus spätestens mit Stalingrad in die Katastrophe geführt hatte. Sarkastisch beginnt das letzte Flugblatt der Münchener Studenten, die sich unter dem Namen „Weiße Rose" zusammengefunden haben: „Dreihundertdreißigtausend deutsche Männer hat die geniale Strategie des Weltkriegsgefreiten sinn- und verantwortungslos in Tod und Verderben gehetzt. Führer, wir danken dir!"[7] Fachleute sahen es noch präziser: ein Major i.G., den man an die Ostfront geschickt hatte, um sich den Stab der SS-Division Leibstandarte SS Adolf Hitler näher anzusehen, berichtete später: „Daß durch hochmütige Vernachlässigung solider Ausbildung und Tollkühnheit tapfere und ideologisch verführte junge Männer sinnlos geopfert wurden, das schien den Führern dieser Waffen-SS-Division kaum bewußt zu werden. Der Glaube an den Führer war ihnen wichtiger als professionelles Können. Betroffen und ernüchtert kehrte ich ins Hauptquartier zurück, wo ich Gelegenheit erhielt, dem Chef des Generalstabes meine Eindrücke vorzutragen."[8]

Hitlers ablehnende Reaktion auf alle Alternativvorschläge ließ erkennen, dass der Diktator auch unter dem Eindruck der militärischen Krise nicht gewillt sein würde, sachgerechten Lösungen im Sinne einer zweckrationalen Kriegführung zuzustimmen. Hitler war nicht, wie sich mancher bisher eingeredet haben mochte, schlecht beraten, sondern selbst der Kern des Unheils. Stauffenberg urteilte im Winter 1942/43: „Letzte Ursache liegt, darüber bin ich mir nun vollkommen im klaren, in der Person des Führers und im Nationalsozialismus."[9] Der brillante Generalstabsoffizier zog daraus die Konsequenz: „Es kommt nicht darauf an, ihm die Wahrheit zu sagen, sondern es kommt darauf an, ihn umzubringen."[10]

Hitlers Politik wurde in zivilen wie militärischen nationalkonservativen Kreisen als Verbrechen am deutschen Volk empfunden. Stauffenberg sagte schon 1942, zu seiner Zeit in der

---

[5] Spiegelbild einer Verschwörung, S. 334 f.
[6] Hoffmann, Stauffenberg, S. 239.
[7] Gedenkstätte Deutscher Widerstand. Ausstellung Widerstand gegen den Nationalsozialismus; http://www.dhm.de/lemo/html/nazi/widerstand/weisserose/index.html.
[8] Maizière, In der Pflicht, S. 78.
[9] Stauffenberg im Gespräch mit Kuhn im August 1942 in Winniza: Chavkin/Kalganov, Neue Quellen, S. 378.
[10] Kramarz, Stauffenberg, S. 113, auch zitiert bei Fest, Staatsstreich, S. 221.

Organisationsabteilung des Generalstabs des Heeres, über Hitler: „Er ist ein Narr und ein Verbrecher"[11] – die Gleichsetzung ist bezeichnend. Die Erkenntnis, dass die Fortführung der Kriegspolitik ein „großes Verbrechen gegen das eigene Volk (Wette)"[12] war, ließ aus der fachlichen Motivation allmählich einen moralischen Antrieb werden.

Neben die Erkenntnis des „Verbrechens am eigenen Volk" trat dann aber in unterschiedlicher Intensität das Wissen darum, dass die Kriegführung des Reiches dazu diente, Verbrechen im Weltmaßstab an den Menschen in den von der Wehrmacht besetzten Gebieten zu begehen. Besonders deutlich musste der Unrechtscharakter des Krieges gegen die Sowjetunion hervortreten, als der Truppe die verbrecherischen Befehle zum Unternehmen „Barbarossa", also zum Angriff auf die Sowjetunion bekannt wurden[13].

Aus Hitlers Sicht kam es letztlich nicht darauf an, ob der Krieg professionell oder dilettantisch geführt wurde, sondern darauf, dass er die Voraussetzung für die Umwälzung Europas im nationalsozialistischen Sinne schuf. Keiner, der an diesem Krieg beteiligt war, konnte für sich in Anspruch nehmen, ohne jede Schuld daraus hervorgegangen zu sein. Im Gegenteil: Generalmajor Stieff, später Beteiligter am 20. Juli, hatte seiner Frau schon Anfang 1942 geschrieben: „Wir alle haben so viel Schuld auf uns geladen – denn wir sind ja mitverantwortlich –, daß ich in diesem angehenden Strafgericht nur eine gerechte Sühne für alle die Schandtaten sehe, die wir Deutschen in den letzten Jahren begangen bzw. geduldet haben."[14]

Mancher Offizier war durchaus gewillt, das Verbrecherische des Regimes zuzugestehen, aber angesichts der Lage an der Front könne man im Moment nichts dagegen unternehmen. Nach dem Krieg dagegen werde man die braune Brut davonjagen. Umgekehrt verschob aber auch das Regime die Lösung so mancher Frage auf die Zeit nach Kriegsende: die Kirchenfrage etwa, aber auch die Machtfrage zwischen den konservativen Eliten im Heer und der sich sozialrevolutionär gebenden Partei. Stauffenberg und seine Freunde sahen jedoch, wie eine immer deutlicher werdende Bevorzugung der Waffen-SS die Gewichte für einen solchen Endkampf nach innen immer mehr zu verschieben drohte[15].

Dem nationalkonservativen Widerstand ging es darum, gegen diese schleichende Entmachtung des Heeres und gegen die immer stärker werdenden militärischen Potentiale des Parteiapparates vorzugehen, so lange die eigenen Kräfte noch hinreichten. Daher galt es, das Heer in seinem Kern zu erhalten – oder, wenn dies nicht mehr lange möglich sein würde, rechtzeitig loszuschlagen. Die „Rettung der Armee" sollte so auch dazu dienen, „daß insbesondere die Wehrmacht in der Hand ihrer Führer ein verwendbares Instrument bleibe"[16].

Manchmal werde ich gefragt, warum Menschen wie Stauffenberg Widerstand geleistet haben, obwohl sie doch so national dachten. Meine Antwort ist: Sie hatten erkannt, dass Hitler in seiner sozialdarwinistischen Verblendung Deutschland in den Untergang führte, führen wollte. Aus dieser Erkenntnis heraus leisteten sie Widerstand nicht obwohl, sondern gerade weil sie national und konservativ dachten.

4. Das Verhältnis Goerdeler-Stauffenberg

Wie war nun das Verhältnis zwischen dem zivilen Kopf der Verschwörung, Carl Goerdeler, und ihrem militärischen Führer, Stauffenberg? Stauffenberg war klar, dass sich der bisherige Honoratiorenwiderstand um eine größere Massenbasis bemühen musste, sollte er nicht wie 1920 der Kapp-Putsch an einem Generalstreik der Arbeiterschaft scheitern. Stauffenberg suchte daher den

---

[11] Institut für Zeitgeschichte München, ED 88: Sammlung Zeller, Band 2, S. 353.
[12] Wette, Untergangspathos, S. 13.
[13] Heinemann, Widerstand gegen das NS-Regime; abwegig dagegen Gerlach, Männer des 20. Juli, sowie ders., Hitlergegner.
[14] Brief an seine Frau vom 10.01.1942, abgedruckt in: Stieff, Ausgewählte Briefe.
[15] Hierzu neuerdings Kroener, Fromm, Kapitel V und VI.
[16] Spiegelbild einer Verschwörung, S. 34; Interpretation bei Mommsen, Stellung der Militäropposition, S. 125.

Kontakt mit dem Sozialdemokraten Julius Leber, während er Goerdelers Politik als eine „Revolution der Greise" verächtlich machte[17].

Das alles verstärkte die Entfremdung zwischen dem Kopf der militärischen Verschwörung und Goerdeler. Stauffenberg hatte eigene Verbindungen zu den Westmächten – sein Vertrauensmann in Madrid verschaffte ihm über seine britischen Kontakte ein sehr viel realistischeres Bild über die außenpolitische Situation des Reiches, als es Goerdelers Verbindungsmann zum amerikanischen Geheimdienst in Zürich vermochte[18]. Daraus resultierten Unterschiede in den außenpolitischen Zielsetzungen, und die waren ein wesentlicher Streitpunkt zwischen den beiden höchst unterschiedlichen Charakteren. Dass Stauffenberg zudem Kapitulationsverhandlungen „von Militär zu Militär" führen, also doch Goerdeler und seine Freunde ausschalten wollte, hatte diesen nachhaltig verstimmt. Als „hochgesinnten, in Afrika schwer verwundeten Generalstabsoffizier, der sich später als Querkopf erwies, der auch Politik machen wollte"[19] bezeichnete Goerdeler Stauffenberg später.

Ein wichtiger Streitpunkt zwischen den beiden war die Frage, ob ein Attentat auf Hitler notwendig, ja, ob es moralisch zu rechtfertigen sei. Goerdeler wollte die „Majestät des Rechts" wieder aufrichten[20], und dazu passte es aus seiner Sicht nicht recht, mit einem politischen Mord zu beginnen. Goerdeler wollte Hitler von im Sinne der Verschwörung loyalen Truppen verhaften und vor ein deutsches Gericht stellen lassen – wie wir in den letzten Tagen gehört haben, eine im Sommer 1944 völlig abwegige Vorstellung[21].

Stauffenberg dagegen wusste, wie sehr sich auch das Heer in seinem Inneren verändert hatte, und dass es keine Truppen mehr gab, die zu einem Vorgehen gegen einen noch lebenden Hitler bereit waren. Ihm ging es um den Staatsstreich, den Umsturz, das Kriegsende – und ohne das gelungene Attentat war das alles illusorisch. Stauffenberg war Realist, Generalstabsoffizier eben. Deutschland gedenkt heute des gescheiterten Umsturzversuchs; das Attentat in Hitlers Hauptquartier in Ostpreußen ist nur ein Teilaspekt davon[22].

Oft heißt es, nicht um einen Militärputsch sei es Stauffenberg gegangen, sondern um die Wiederherstellung des Rechts. Meine Damen und Herren, das ist eine falsche Alternative, geboren aus der Annahme, dass Militär und Rechtsstaat sich ausschließen. Juristen wie Sie wissen, dass das nicht der Fall ist, und uns kann daher die Einsicht nicht überraschen, dass Stauffenberg einen Militärputsch zur Wiederherstellung des Rechtsstaats plante[23].

5. Und doch: Aufstand des Gewissens

Bleibt also vom „Aufstand des Gewissens" nichts anderes über als ein Putsch systemnaher Offiziere? Ich hatte schon erwähnt, dass Stauffenberg innen- wie außenpolitisch viel realistischer dachte als etwa Goerdeler. Ihm war völlig klar, dass auch eine Umsturzregierung an bedingungsloser Kapitulation und Besetzung des Reichsgebiets nicht mehr würde vorbeikommen können. „Es ist Zeit, daß jetzt etwas getan wird. Derjenige allerdings, der etwas zu tun wagt, muß sich bewußt sein, daß er wohl als Verräter in die deutsche Geschichte eingehen wird. Unterläßt er jedoch die Tat, dann wäre er ein Verräter vor seinem eigenen Gewissen." Und, ebenfalls kurz vor dem 20. Juli: „Das Furchtbarste ist, zu wissen, daß es nicht gelingen kann und daß man es dennoch für unser Land und unsere Kinder tun muß."[24] Sie hören hier eine grundsätzlichere, ethisch-moralische Dimension heraus, die über die bloße

---

[17] Zeller, Geist der Freiheit, S. 296.
[18] Stöver, Otto John, S. 167.
[19] Denkschrift „Unsere Idee" (nach 09.11.1944), zitiert nach Politische Schriften und Briefe, Band 1, S. liii.
[20] Beck und Goerdeler, S. 233.
[21] Spiegelbild einer Verschwörung, S. 101 (30. Juli 1944).
[22] Mühleisen, Patrioten, S. 453 f.
[23] Ich unterscheide mich in dieser Interpretation von Autoren wie etwa Peter Steinbach (vor allem Zum Verhältnis der Ziele, S. 980, 987, 989). Steinbach geht von einer „gemeinsamen Zivilität" aller Gruppen des Widerstands aus – eine Auffassung, die die spezifisch militärischen Antriebe zu sehr übersieht. Für Einzelheiten siehe Heinemann, Der Widerstand und der Krieg, S. 821 f.
[24] Beide Zitate nach der Version in Hoffmann, Stauffenberg, S. 395.

Nützlichkeit hinausgeht. Ähnliches gilt für Henning von Tresckow, der die Notwendigkeit des Umsturzes so begründet hatte: „Das Attentat auf Hitler muß erfolgen, coûte que coûte. Sollte es nicht gelingen, so muß trotzdem der Staatsstreich versucht werden. Denn es kommt nicht mehr auf den praktischen Zweck an, sondern darauf, daß die deutsche Widerstandsbewegung vor der Welt und vor der Geschichte unter Einsatz des Lebens den entscheidenden Wurf gewagt hat. Alles andere ist daneben gleichgültig."[25] Nach dem Scheitern des Umsturzversuches äußerte er: „Jetzt wird die ganze Welt über uns herfallen und uns beschimpfen. Aber ich bin nach wie vor der felsenfesten Überzeugung, daß wir recht gehandelt haben. Ich halte Hitler nicht nur für den Erzfeind Deutschlands, sondern auch für den Erzfeind der Welt. Wenn ich in wenigen Stunden vor den Richterstuhl Gottes treten werde, um Rechenschaft abzulegen über mein Tun und mein Unterlassen, so glaube ich mit gutem Gewissen das vertreten zu können, was ich im Kampf gegen Hitler getan habe. Wenn Gott einst Abraham verheißen hat, er werde Sodom nicht verderben, wenn auch nur zehn Gerechte darin seien, so hoffe ich, daß Gott auch Deutschland um unsertwillen nicht vernichten wird. Niemand von uns kann über seinen Tod Klage führen. Wer in unseren Kreis getreten ist, hat damit das Nessushemd angezogen. Der sittliche Wert eines Menschen beginnt erst dort, wo er bereit ist, für seine Überzeugung sein Leben hinzugeben."[26] Sie hören hier auch ein religiöses Element heraus, eine Vertrautheit mit der Schrift, die heute Vielen schon fremd geworden ist.

Die Feststellung, dass die Angehörigen des militärischen Widerstands als verantwortungsbewusste Offiziere gehandelt haben, dass sie politisch und militärisch über die bloße Geste hinaus noch etwas verändern und gestalten wollten, das alles wird uns nicht an der menschlichen Hochachtung dafür hindern, dass diese Frauen und Männer als wenige unter vielen das menschlich Anständige, das moralisch Richtige getan haben.

Solange wir den Widerstand als eine im wesentlichen moralische Größe betrachten, so lange wird er angreifbar bleiben für Vorwürfe, die Verschwörer seien keine Demokraten, seien Antisemiten oder an Kriegsverbrechen beteiligt gewesen. Widerstand stellt sich vielmehr dar als „zeitbedingte Alternative zum Faschismus"[27]. Ihn heute vordergründig-moralisierend an dem Kriterium seiner Nähe oder Ferne zur Werteordnung des Grundgesetzes zu messen, wird dem Opfer der wenigen nicht gerecht, die unter Einsatz ihres Lebens gegen das Unrecht aufgestanden sind.

Literatur

Beck und Goerdeler. Gemeinschaftsdokumente für den Frieden 1941-1944, hg. von Wilhelm Ritter von Schramm, München: G. Müller 1965.
Chavkin, Boris L., und Aleksandr Kalganov: Neue Quellen zur Geschichte des 20. Juli 1944 aus dem Archiv des Föderalen Sicherheitsdienstes der Russischen Föderation (FSB). „Eigenhändige Aussagen" von Major i.G. Joachim Kuhn, in: Forum für osteuropäische Ideen- und Zeitgeschichte 5 (2001), S. 355-402.
Deist, Wilhelm: Der Kriegszustand nach Art. 68 der Reichsverfassung. Ausführungsbestimmungen der militärischen Führung, in: Militär und Innenpolitik im Weltkrieg 1914-1918, bearb. von Wilhelm Deist, 2 Teile, Düsseldorf: Droste 1970 (=Quellen zur Geschichte des Parlamentarismus und der politischen Parteien. Zweite Reihe: Militär und Politik, 1), S. XXXI-LI.
Ders.: Die Aufrüstung der Wehrmacht, in: Das Deutsche Reich und der Zweite Weltkrieg, hg. vom Militärgeschichtlichen Forschungsamt, Band 1: Ursachen und Voraussetzungen der deutschen Kriegspolitik, Stuttgart: dva 1979, S. 371-532.
Dirks, Carl, und Karl-Heinz Janßen: Der Krieg der Generäle. Hitler als Werkzeug der Wehrmacht, Berlin: Propyläen 1999.
Fest, Joachim: Staatsstreich. Der lange Weg zum 20. Juli, Berlin: Siedler 1994.
Gerlach, Christian: Hitlergegner bei der Heeresgruppe Mitte und die „verbrecherischen Befehle", in: NS-Verbrechen und der militärische Widerstand gegen Hitler, hg. von Gerd R. Ueberschär, Darmstadt: wbg 2000, S. 62-76.
Ders.: Männer des 20. Juli und der Krieg gegen die Sowjetunion, in: Vernichtungskrieg. Verbrechen der Wehrmacht 1941-1944, hg. von Hannes Heer und Klaus Naumann, Hamburg: HIS 1995, S. 427-446.
Heinemann, Winfried: Der militärische Widerstand und der Krieg, in: Das Deutsche Reich und der Zweite Weltkrieg, Band 9/1: Die deutsche Kriegsgesellschaft 1939-1945. Politisierung, Vernichtung, Überleben, Stuttgart: dva 2004, S. 743-892.
Ders.: Der Widerstand gegen das NS-Regime und der Krieg an der Ostfront, in: Militärgeschichte 8 (1998), S. 49-55.

---

[25] Schlabrendorff, Offiziere gegen Hitler, S. 109.
[26] Ebd. S. 129.
[27] Mommsen, Die moralische Wiederherstellung., S. 15.

Hoffmann, Peter: Claus Schenk Graf von Stauffenberg und seine Brüder. Das Geheime Deutschland, Stuttgart: dva 1992.
Ders.: Widerstand – Staatsstreich – Attentat. Der Kampf der Opposition gegen Hitler, München: Piper 1969.
Kopp, Roland: Paul von Hase. Von der Alexander-Kaserne nach Plötzensee. Eine deutsche Soldatenbiographie 1885-1944, Münster: Lit 2001.
Kramarz, Joachim: Claus Graf Stauffenberg. 15. November 1907-20. Juli 1944. Das Leben eines Offiziers, Frankfurt: Bernard & Graefe 1965.
Kroener, Bernhard R.: „Der starke Mann im Heimatkriegsgebiet". Generaloberst Friedrich Fromm. Eine Biographie, Paderborn: Schöningh 2005.
Maizière, Ulrich de: In der Pflicht. Lebensbericht eines deutschen Soldaten im 20. Jahrhundert, Herford: Mittler 1989.
Mommsen, Hans: Die moralische Wiederherstellung der Nation, in: Süddeutsche Zeitung, 21. Juli 1999, S. 15
Ders.: Die Stellung der Militäropposition im Rahmen der deutschen Widerstandsbewegung gegen Hitler, in: NS-Verbrechen und der militärische Widerstand gegen Hitler, hg. von Gerd R. Ueberschär, Darmstadt: wbg 2000, S. 119-134.
Mühleisen, Horst: Patrioten im Widerstand. Carl-Hans Graf Hardenbergs Erlebnisbericht. Dokumentation, in: Vierteljahrshefte für Zeitgeschichte 41 (1993), S. 419-477.
Politische Schriften und Briefe Carl Friedrich Goerdelers, hg. von Hans Mommsen und Sabine Gillmann, 2 Bände, München: Saur 2003.
Schlabrendorff, Fabian von: Offiziere gegen Hitler, Berlin: Siedler 1984.
Spiegelbild einer Verschwörung. Die Opposition gegen Hitler und der Staatsstreich vom 20. Juli 1944. Geheime Dokumente aus dem ehemaligen Reichssicherheitshauptamt, hg. von Hans-Adolf Jacobsen, 2 Bände, Stuttgart: Seewald 1984.
Steinbach, Peter: Zum Verhältnis der Ziele der militärischen und zivilen Widerstandsgruppen, in: Der Widerstand gegen den Nationalsozialismus. Die deutsche Gesellschaft und der Widerstand gegen Hitler, hg. von Jürgen Schmädeke und Peter Steinbach, München: Piper 1985, S. 977-1002.
Stieff, Helmuth: Ausgewählte Briefe von Helmuth Stieff (hingerichtet am 8. August 1944), hg. von Hans Rothfels, in: Vierteljahrshefte für Zeitgeschichte 2 (1954), S. 291-305.
Stöver, Bernd: Otto John (1909-1997). Ein Widerstandskämpfer als Verfassungsschutzchef, in: Konspiration als Beruf. Deutsche Geheimdienstchefs im Kalten Krieg, hg. von Dieter Krüger und Armin Wagner, Berlin: Links 2003, S. 160-178.
Wette, Wolfram: Zwischen Untergangspathos und Überlebenswillen. Die Deutschen im letzten halben Kriegsjahr 1944/45, in: Das letzte halbe Jahr. Stimmungsberichte der Wehrmachtspropaganda 1944/45, hg. von dems., Ricarda Bremer und Detlef Vogel, Essen: Lit 2001 (= Schriften der Bibliothek für Zeitgeschichte, N.F. 13), S. 9-37.

Winfried Heinemann

The Plot to Kill Hitler: July 20, 1944, and the Story of the German Resistance Movement

All during 1943 and 1944, a group of nationalist conservatives, both civilians and officers, planned to overthrow the Nazi regime. They came from the only group which still had access to the levers of power, and that made it hard to distinguish between loyal alternative concepts, and fundamental resistance. Actually, in many instances the latter developed out of the former. The national and conservative resistance hoped to cleanse Germany of Nazi rule after it had become clear that Hitler's intention was to destroy Germany entirely, but also to obtain concessions from the Western Allies. As policy options narrowed, the general, religious and moral motives of the members of the resistance group became more apparent.

The author's interpretation of the German Resistance Movement of July 20, 1944 is distinctively different from the ideas expressed by Peter Steinbach, Head of Academic Research at 'Widerstand gegen den Nationalsozialismus. Ständige Ausstellung' (Resistance to National Socialism. Permanent Exhibition) and the 'Gedenkstätte Deutscher Widerstand' (German Resistance Memorial Centre) both located in Berlin, especially about the goals of the resistance movement. Steinbach refers to a "gemeinsamen Zivilität" – common civility – shared by everyone in the resistance movement, which according to Winfried Heinemann overlooks specific motives that led members of the German Armed Forces to plot to kill Hitler.

Joachim Gauck

Totalitarismus im 3. Reich und in der DDR – eine vergleichende Analyse

Verehrte Damen und Herren,

dass Sie zum Abschluss Ihrer Konferenz einen Blick auf den deutschen Widerstand werfen und mir Gelegenheit geben, über die deutsche Nachkriegsdiktatur zu sprechen, begrüße ich ausdrücklich. Nun, ich bin weder Politikwissenschaftler noch Historiker noch Völkerrechtler oder Staatsrechtler und deshalb werde ich Ihnen nicht die im Programmheft angekündigte Analyse geben. Als ein Zeitzeuge, der Beobachtung und Erfahrung mitteilt, wird es sich bei meinen Ausführungen eher um eine vergleichende Perspektive als um eine wissenschaftliche Analyse handeln. Ich möchte Ihnen zunächst ein wenig von mir erzählen und werde Ihnen in diesem ersten Teil gleichzeitig die Möglichkeit bieten, sich in das Lebensgefühl einer Diktatur nach dem Kriege einzuleben.

Ich bin im Jahr 1940 in Rostock an der Ostsee geboren, also im östlichen Teil Deutschlands, der nach dem Krieg zur Beute der Sowjetarmee und des sowjetischen Systems geworden ist. An den Krieg habe ich naturgemäß kaum Erinnerungen, an das Kriegsende sehr wohl. Ich erinnere mich an die Angst der Frauen, die massenhaft Beute der sowjetischen Soldateska wurden. Ich erinnere mich an Not und Hunger und Unsicherheit. Und dann sollte etwas passieren, dass dazuführte, dass ich schon mit zehn/elf Jahren ein politischer Mensch wurde. Denn kaum war mein erstes Lebensjahrzehnt in Mecklenburg vergangen, griff die kommunistische Staatsmacht verändernd auch ganz konkret in meine Familie ein. Eines Tages kam mein Vater nicht nach Hause. Mein Vater war ein Seemann, ein Kapitän bei der Handelsmarine. Er war verschwunden. „Abgeholt" nannte man das, diese Vokabel bezeichnete sowohl in der Nazi- wie auch in der kommunistischen Zeit den Vorgang, dass eine Person durch die Staatsmacht abgeholt, weggebracht wurde und verschwand. Unsere Familie, die nun aus meiner Mutter, mir als Ältestem und drei weiteren Kindern bestand, sollte zweieinhalb Jahre nicht erfahren, wo der Vater und Ehemann war. Er war nicht mehr da und man konnte weder von der Polizei, einer staatlichen Dienststelle oder einer sowjetischen Autorität, eine Auskunft über den Verbleib derart verschwundener Menschen erhalten. Es schien, als wären diese Leute vom Erdboden verschluckt worden. So geriet ich schon als Kind in den Einflussbereich der Politik. In der Schule lernte ich antifaschistische Lieder und Themen und ich wuchs mit dem staatlich erzeugten Gefühl auf: Wir leben in einer neuen, antikapitalistischen Gesellschaft und mit dem Sozialismus kommt eine neue Zeit der Gerechtigkeit auf uns zu. Gleichzeitig lebte ich jedoch in dem sicheren Gefühl, in einem Unrechtsregime zu leben, wo über Jedermann jederzeit ein Urteil gefällt werden konnte, an dem niemand etwas zu ändern vermochte. Man könnte sagen, dass ich schon als Kind mit dem Gefühl, fester staatlich organisierter Ohnmacht aufgewachsen bin.

Tatsächlich war es so, dass mein Vater ohne unser Wissen vor ein sowjetisches Militärtribunal gebracht worden war. Zwar existierte in Ostdeutschland seit 1949 ein eigener, selbständiger Staat aber noch bis Anfang der 50er Jahre waren in diesem Staat insgeheim sowjetische Militärtribunale tätig. Das ‚Gericht', welches meinen Vater verurteilt hatte, residierte in Schwerin in einem Gebäude, in dem sich der NKGP niedergelassen hatte, dasselbe Gebäude in dem sich zuvor das Hauptquartier der Gestapo befunden hatte. Mein Vater wurde in einem Geheimverfahren zu zweimal 25 Jahren Zwangsarbeit verurteilt. Meine Damen und Herren, dieses Urteil wurde aus reiner Willkür und ohne jeden Grund gefällt. Einer der Seemannskollegen meines Vaters war nach Westberlin geflohen und man hat drei der engeren Mitarbeiter dieses Mannes automatisch festgenommen und hat dann Gründe gesucht, mit denen man sie verurteilen konnte. Zugespitzt formuliert könnte man sagen, wenn man damals eine Person festgenommen hatte, so fand sich auch das Delikt. Dies war die Art der stalinistischen Verfahren, Urteile zu bilden. Ich kann vorausschicken, dass mein Vater überlebt hat. Nach Stalins Tod kamen die letzten deutschen Kriegsgefangenen im Jahre 1955 aus der Sowjetunion zurück und mit ihnen die euphemistisch ‚Zivilinternierte' genannten Personen, die ein ähnliches Schicksal wie mein Vater erlitten hatten. Dabei handelte es sich nicht um Wenige, sondern um Abertausende, die nach Sibirien oder auch nach Bautzen, Waldheim oder Brandenburg kamen. In meiner Heimatstadt Rostock, wo ich Theologie studiert habe – ich bin später evangelischer Pfarrer geworden – gab es einen jungen Mann, dem es in der Nachkriegszeit ähnlich ergangen ist wie meinem Vater. Arno Esch war sein Name. Er konnte sein Leben nicht retten. Er war wegen seiner Aktivitäten an der Uni, wo er für liberale Hochschulpolitik eintrat, verhaftet worden, obwohl die liberale Partei im Rahmen des demokratischen, so genannten demokratischen Blocks, ein erlaubtes Element der Politikgestaltung war. Arno Esch war mit anderen zusammen tätig und wurde dann in einem der vorher beschriebenen stalinistischen Verfahren zum Tode verurteilt. Er hat sein junges Leben vor einem Erschießungskommando in Moskau ausgehaucht. Sein Schicksal und das seiner Freunde – es wurden damals noch mehr verurteilt – erinnert mich ein wenig an die schon zitierte Gruppe aus München während der Nazi-Zeit, an die weiße Rose der Geschwister Scholl, Christoph Probst und ihrer Freunde.

Die Bewohner in Ostdeutschland hatten sich schon unmittelbar nach dem Kriegsende daran gewöhnen müssen, dass es eigentlich eine neue Zeit der Freiheit nicht gab. Zwar feierten wir jährlich am 8. Mai den Tag der Befreiung, der im Osten lange staatlicher Feiertag war. Aber wir erlebten den Einmarsch der Befreier als den gleichzeitigen Beginn neuer Unfreiheit. Insofern, meine Damen und Herren aus den Vereinigten Staaten, werden sie Deutschland nur dann richtig kennen lernen, wenn sie die ostdeutsche und die westdeutsche Mentalität berücksichtigen. Das sind völlig unterschiedliche Prägungen, die wir in diesem einen, wieder vereinigten Lande haben. Dabei handelt es sich nicht darum, dass die Ostdeutschen charakterlich schwächer wären, aber sie haben nicht eine langjährige, jahrzehntelange Einübung in Demokratie, sondern sie haben eine 12 plus 44-jährige Ohnmachtsgeschichte hinter sich. Und das bewirkte bis heute noch maßgebliche Unterschiede in der Mentalität.

Ich hatte bereits erwähnt, dass die Ostdeutschen sehr früh feststellen mussten, dass sie in einer besonderen Weise befreit worden waren, nämlich befreit zu Unfreiheit. Viele junge Menschen im Alter zwischen 13 und 16 Jahren landeten durch Denunziation zum Beispiel in den von den Sowjets weitergeführten Konzentrationslagern Sachsenhausen und Buchenwald. Vordergründig sollten darin Nazis konzentriert werden. Tatsächlich aber fanden sich dort innerhalb kürzester Zeit riesenhafte Mengen von jugendlichen Oppositionellen oder ganz normalen Menschen, die in Folge einer Denunziation in einem solchen Lager gelandet waren. Es war eine schlimme Zeit der Rechtlosigkeit. Es gibt Beispiele dafür, dass etwa drei Viertel einer Schulklasse durch Denunziation in diesen Lagern verschwunden sind. Ein Drittel der Menschen, die in diesen Lagern inhaftiert waren, ist gestorben. Es war außerordentlich brutal. Wenn man sich mit einer gewissen Nostalgie an die DDR erinnert, vergisst man sehr oft diese brutale Anfangsphase der kommunistischen Herrschaft im Osten Deutschlands. Für einige unserer verwirrten Linken, besonders im Bereich der Intellektuellen in Westeuropa, in Westdeutschland aber auch sonst wo auf der Welt, gelten ja die Anfangsjahre der DDR als sozusagen antifaschistische Unschuldsjahre. Dies ist eine schlimme politische Lüge und eine arge Legende, denn von Anfang an war der Antifaschismus der dortigen Staatsführung alles andere als glaubwürdig. Da der neuen Staatsform eine natürliche Legitimation und Legitimität fehlte, wurde der Antifaschismus als Legitimationsersatz in Form einer Gründungslegende eingesetzt. Ich komme später auf die Elemente der Legitimation zu sprechen. Wie schade, dass eine so wichtige Haltung wie die des Antifaschismus im Osten auf diese Weise von Anfang an unglaubwürdig war. Nie hat es eine Mehrheit in Ostdeutschland gegeben, die dieser Gründungslegende geglaubt hatte. Immer war die Mehrheit auf der Seite etwa von Eugen Kogon, der mit seinem berühmten Buch: ‚Der SS-Staat', die erste grundlegende Abrechnung mit dem Nationalsozialismus vorgelegt hatte, die unmittelbar nach dem Krieg erschien. Er hat sich in der 2. Auflage dieses Buches 1949 ausdrücklich an seine ehemaligen kommunistischen Mitgefangenen, die jetzt zum Teil im Osten regieren, gewandt und gefragt: Macht ihr nicht dasselbe, was wir erlitten haben mit euren Gegnern? Und er hat gemeint, einige hätten das ruhig zugegeben. Sie meinten ja, einem guten Zweck zu dienen. Kogon legt dann in diesem Vorwort zur 2. Auflage seines Buches, ‚Der SS-Staat', ein Glaubensbekenntnis ab, wo er die Grundzüge der parlamentarischen Demokratie beschreibt und sie lobt. Dies ist übrigens einer der Gründe, warum dieses Buch in der späteren 68er Bewegung in Westdeutschland nicht mehr die Rolle gespielt hat, die es hätte spielen müssen, da die 68er ihrerseits den freiheitlichen Rechtsstaat in Frage zu stellen trachteten.

Ich habe Ihnen die Anfangsjahre der DDR beschrieben. Wenn wir nun aus der unmittelbaren Anfangssituation heraus gehen, kommen wir auf ein interessantes Datum. Es ist der 17. Juni 1953. An diesem Tag beginnt mit Streiks in Berlin und Sachsen ein Volksaufstand, der bald in über 800 Orten der DDR Aktivitäten nach sich zieht. Zum ersten Mal im besetzten europäischen Ostblock sprechen breite Teile der Bevölkerung, angeführt von Arbeitergruppierungen, dem Sozialismus als Staatsform ihr Misstrauen aus. Sie fordern freie Wahlen, Demokratie insgesamt und bessere Lebensbedingungen. Dieser Aufstand wird blutig niedergeschlagen. Nicht nur von Kräften der eigenen Polizeitruppen, sondern von sowjetischen Panzern. Hier beginnt das Lösungsmodell, das Problemlösungsmodell des Sowjetimperiums, das den Sozialismus immer nur mit Hilfe von Panzern als wirkmächtig am Leben erhalten konnte. Diese blutige Verfolgung, die nach der Niederschlagung beginnt, kostet zahlreichen Menschen nicht nur die Karriere, sondern vielen auch das Leben. Wenn wir die Geschichte des Herrschaftskommunismus betrachten, so will ich hier nur wenige Punkte nennen, die Ihnen bei der Betrachtung der Geschichte selbstverständlich selber im Bewusstsein sind. Ich erinnere daran, dass drei Jahre nach dieser Niederlage des Volkes 1956 in Ungarn eine schon erfolgreiche Revolution gegen den Kommunismus wiederum von Sowjet-Panzern niedergeschlagen worden ist. Die nächste Niederlage des Volkes ist 1961 der Bau der Berliner Mauer. Für uns Deutsche im Osten, bedeutet dieses Datum die eigentliche Staatsgründung der DDR, denn vor 1961 hatte noch jedermann die Freiheit, in den Westen zu reisen. Ich habe zum Beispiel 1958 Abitur gemacht und viele meiner Klassenkameraden haben sich für die Freiheit des Westens entschieden. Ich blieb im Osten, weil ich nicht wollte, dass die Kommunisten alleine in unserem Landesteil übrig blieben und auch, weil mein Vater, der meinte, die Kommunisten würden ihm nichts mehr tun, das Land nicht verlassen wollte. Also entschloss auch ich mich, zu bleiben. Allerdings konnte ich meine eigentlichen Berufswünsche nicht erfüllen und habe dann Theologie studiert und bin Pastor geworden. Aber viele anderen hofften immer auf eine Veränderung und diese Kette von Niederlagen ist es, die unsere Hoffnung arg gestutzt hat. 1961 also, da hatten sie uns, da konnten wir noch so oppositionell sein, wir konnten nicht mehr weglaufen. Wir hatten keine Alternative, denn die Sache mit dem Aufstand, das hatten wir 1953 und 1956 gelernt, das bringt nichts. Das ist keine wirkliche Variante. Aber vielleicht geht es mit einer inneren Demokratisierung. Diese Hoffnung gab es, aber sie zerschlug sich 1968. Der nächste Einsatz der Sowjet-Panzer, diesmal gegen ein System, man nennt es Veränderungsprogramm. Dubcek in Prag wollte Demokratie und Sozialismus verbinden und ist mit diesem Ansatz kläglich gescheitert. 1970/1971 Solidarnosc beginnt in Polen mit der Arbeit, es gibt die Kriegsrechtsphase. 1980 erneut in Polen heftige Proteste und immer noch spüren wir: der Staat ist stärker. So sind die Geschichte der Ostblockstaaten und auch des östlichen Teils Deutschlands, eine Geschichte scheinbar perpetuierter Ohnmacht.

Es gibt eine Macht, Ohnmachtrelation, die für die Betroffenen nicht zu brechen scheint. Das ist eigentlich das Thema meiner langjährigen Arbeiten und meiner ganzen Überlegungen nach der Zeit meiner Tätigkeit als Bundesbeauftragter für die Stasiakten. Es ist eben zu besichtigen, dass Menschen, die in einer ununterbrochenen, Generationen dauernden Kultur der Ohnmacht aufwachsen, eine mentale Prägung annehmen, die wir eigentlich nur vergleichen können mit der Prägung der Gemeinwesen in vormodernen Gesellschaften. Wir könnten sagen, in Deutschland Ost hat sich der alte Typus des deutschen Untertanen neu in der Moderne dargestellt. Die Untertanenexistenz ist eben nicht nur die Existenzform von Bürgern im Gemeinwesen der Vormoderne, sondern das andere Gesicht der Moderne, der politischen Moderne ist im 20. Jahrhundert gerade in Deutschland zweimal präsent mit bitteren Diktaturen, die eine absolute Macht, Ohnmachtrelation darstellen und den Menschen im Grunde zurück transponiert in eine eigentlich schon überwundene Daseinsgeschichte. Der Citoyen wird zurückgenommen in diesen Systemen, und anstelle des Citoyens tritt erneut so etwas wie ein Untertan. Nun bedeutet das Wort Untertan in der deutschen Sprache, die Person, die in einer Adelsgesellschaft zum Volk gehört. Aber uns fehlt der Begriff einer Person, die keine Bürgerrechte hat und in einem Staat lebt, ich habe früher gesagt Staatsbewohner, aber Staatsbewohner erscheint mir noch zu euphemistisch für die Lebenssituation der Menschen, die in den modernen Diktaturen leben. Ich bin dann auf den Begriff Staatsinsasse gekommen. Der Insasse ist eine Person, die in einer Anstalt, einem Gefängnis lebt und nicht eigenständig über Hinein- oder Hinausgehen bestimmen kann. Und die Situation über die ich spreche, also aus Ostdeutschland, gleicht genau dieser Insassensituation in der über Gehen und Bleiben eine Obrigkeit entscheidet, die nicht durch das rationale Argument oder Gewissen zu beeinflussen ist. Dieser Typus ist es nun, der uns bis heute ein Riesenproblem schafft. Wir haben an der Entwicklung der westdeutschen Demokratie gesehen, dass es eine gewisse Zeit dauert, bis Menschen den Wechsel aus dem Status des Gläubigen, in den Status eines Citoyen vollziehen. Wir könnten sagen, dass etwa die Hälfte der Zeit, die die Diktatur gedauert hat, etwa sechs/sieben Jahre, bis in Westdeutschland diese Bindung an die Nazizeit vorüber gegangen ist. Noch lange danach aber war in vielen Familien zu hören, es sei auch nicht alles schlecht gewesen beim Führer und dann kamen die Erinnerungsgüter des selektiven Gedächtnisses und die Menschen erinnerten sich an das so genannte ‚Gute' aus der Nazibarbarei: Der Führer hat die Autobahn gebaut, es gab Vollbeschäftigung und keine Kriminalität. In unendlich vielen Familien beim Kaffeeklatsch und an unendlich vielen Stammtischen wurde so gesprochen. Es ist doch sehr interessant, dass man sich nicht daran erinnern wollte, was in der Nazidiktatur verschwunden war, nämlich Menschenrechte, Herrschaft des Rechtes, Gerechtigkeit und Freiheit. Nostalgie meine Damen und Herren kennen wir auch jetzt wieder, sie deshalb so beliebt, weil sie nicht schmerzt. Die wirkliche Aufarbeitung der Vergangenheit löst Zorn, Verlassenheitsgefühle und Trauer aus. Das sind dunkle Gefühle, die die Menschen nicht suchen und darum neigen die Übergangsgesellschaften regelmäßig zu einer Selektion der Erinnerung zu einer Beschäftigung mit der Vergangenheit ohne Trauer, d.h. dann aber leider auch ohne wirklichen Abschied.

Ich hatte über diese Prägung gesprochen und will noch einmal in einer vergleichenden Perspektive diese beiden Systeme der deutschen Diktaturen miteinander vergleichen. Wobei die zweite Diktatur eigentlich weniger eine deutsche als eine Moskauer ist, aber von den Deutschen hinlänglich großartig übernommen und ausgestaltet wurde. Am Ende der Phase des ostdeutschen Kommunismus versucht der Staatssicherheitsminister der DDR, Erich Mielke, seinen sowjetischen Kollegen noch einmal zu erklären, wie man den Sozialismus richtig macht. Unter Gorbatschow sind die entscheidenden stalinistischen Elemente des Staatssozialismus in Frage gestellt bzw. abgeschafft. Typen wie Erich Mielke und Erich Honecker missfällt das und man versucht nochmals mit deutscher Gründlichkeit, den Russen richtig beizubringen, was Sozialismus ist. Ich hatte über Ohnmacht gesprochen. Es ist wichtig zu wissen, dass die Menschen tatsächlich ohnmächtig waren, aber sich in den Systemen nicht selbst so bezeichnet hätten, und der Staat hat es schon gar nicht getan. Sowohl die braune wie die rote Diktatur legte Wert darauf, denen, die sie gewinnen wollten oder gewonnen hatten, einzuhämmern, ihr seid keineswegs ohnmächtig, sondern ihr seid Vertreter einer neuen Zeit. Im Kommunismus hieß das so: wir sind Vertreter einer wissenschaftlichen Weltanschauung. Unser System ist eine ganze historische Epoche weiter als das verfaulende kapitalistische System. Ähnlich wie die Nationalsozialisten zuvor, die ein 1000-jähriges Reich herauf ziehen sahen, wussten auch die Kommunisten, dass sie das Ziel der Geschichte waren und pflegten diese elitäre Überzeugung, die auch einen gewissen Stolz hervorbrachte. Nach dem Motto, wir, die führende Kraft die Kommunisten, wir bestimmen dieses Ziel. Und alle die daran mitwirken, gehören zum fortschrittlichen Teil der Menschheit. In aller Kürze analysiert bedeutet dies, dass Ideologie den Menschen erlaubt, ihre tatsächliche Ohnmacht als Einbezogensein in einen historischen Plan von weltgeschichtlicher Bedeutung misszudeuten. Dieses Elitebewusstsein kontrastierte nun in der zweiten Diktatur kräftig mit dem normalen Empfinden. Die erste deutsche Diktatur war getragen von Mehrheiten in der Bevölkerung, für die zweite jedoch traf dies niemals zu. Es ist interessant und wir können uns damit beruhigen, dass die Leute im Grunde mehrheitlich eigentlich anders denkend waren. Das Schlimme ist, dass die Diktatur sehr lange leben konnte, weil sie sich mit einem unüberzeugten Minimalkonsens der Mehrheit in der Bevölkerung begnügen konnte. Dies zeigt wiederum, dass sich eine Gesellschaft ohne ein Potenzial an Widerständigkeit und ohne Handlungen des Widerstandes nicht verändert. Nicht-Überzeugtsein alleine bringt ein System nicht zum Einsturz. Ich bin sicher, dass etwa in der Diktatur Kubas, um nur ein Beispiel zu nennen, die Mehrheit der Menschen keineswegs von dem Castro-Sozialismus überzeugt ist. Aber auch dort gibt es bis jetzt nicht dieses kritische Potential von Widerstand, und daraus resultierenden Handlungen, um den Staat tatsächlich zu verändern. Schauen wir auf beide Staaten und fragen uns, wo die Unterschiede sind. Einen habe ich genannt. Die erste Diktatur war getragen von Mehrheiten, die zweite nicht. Ich könnte einen zweiten nennen. Die erste Diktatur war zumindest in Deutschland hundertmal verbrecherischer. Für uns Deutsche besteht das schwarze Loch der Geschichte im Holocaust, in der systematischen

Aussonderung und Ermordung unserer jüdischen Mitbürger. Vorher haben wir es im Kleinen trainiert mit unseren Behinderten, die man in so genannten Aktionen des Gnadentodes vom Leben zum Tode führte. Die Selektion bestimmter Bevölkerungsgruppen und ihre systematische Bezeichnung als todeswürdig und dann die Umsetzung in einer hoch technisierten Weise, hat für uns Deutsche diesen Teil unserer Geschichte zu dem schwarzen Loch der Weltgeschichte gemacht. Wir sind uns dessen bewusst und besprechen dies zumindest seit 1970 offen miteinander. Was uns bei diesem "Ja" zu unserer eigenen Schuld verloren ging, ist die Fähigkeit, in gleicher Weise gegenüber ähnlichen Systemen kritisch zu sein, die die politische Moderne in anderer Weise manchmal gleich verbrecherisch auch zurückgenommen haben. Ich spreche dabei vom Herrschaftskommunismus des sowjetischen und chinesischen Vorbildes. Wenn wir uns einmal bestimmte Elemente totalitärer Herrschaft vor Augen führen, dann könnten wir nennen:

Die Auflösung des Prinzips der Gewaltenteilung, in beiden Staaten gibt es sie nicht;

die Auflösung des Prinzips der freien Wahlen zugunsten akklamatorischer Bestätigungsrituale, gleich in beiden Systemen;

die Auflösung der Rolle des Rechtes, keine rule of law mehr, sondern immer ist Recht ein dienstbarer Markt der staatlichen Macht geworden; und schließlich

die Auflösung der Grundrechtegarantie für die Bürger.

Mit diesen vier Elementen einer zurückgenommenen demokratischen Staatsform beheben sich beide Systeme auch grundsätzlich ihrer Legitimation. Sie haben sich durch ihre Form der Staatspraxis selber delegitimiert und deshalb bedürfen beide Elemente irgendwelcher Surrogate, die ihnen eine Ersatzlegitimation geben. Ich habe bereits darauf hingewiesen, für die zweite Diktatur war es die Ideologie des Antifaschismus, die als konstitutives Element hervorgenommen wurde. Der späte Einblick in die geöffneten Archive der Staatssicherheit und der Partei hat ergeben, dass der Antifaschismus der DDR durchaus selektiv war. Es gab in Westdeutschland und Ostdeutschland keine einzige Partei, die mehr Mitglieder der NSDAP in ihrer Reihen gehabt hätte als die SED, die kommunistische Partei in Ostdeutschland, weil alsbald galt, wer Faschist ist, das bestimmen wir. Wer Antifaschist ist, übrigens auch. KZ-Opfer und Zuchthausopfer wie Robert Havemann galten, als sie in der DDR oppositionell wurden, nicht mehr als Antifaschisten. Es ist also interessant zu beobachten, dass man alles ruinieren kann. Eben auch eine vernünftige und gute Haltung wie die des Antifaschismus.

Wir könnten uns jetzt noch andere stützende Elemente dieser Grundprinzipien, die beide Diktaturen verleugnet haben, vor Augen führen und würden weitere Ähnlichkeiten bei totaler Unterschiedlichkeit der Ideologie finden. Und das ist ja das Paradoxe, meine Damen und Herren, dass auf dem Gebiete der Ideologie die sozialistisch-marxistische Ideologie Riesenvorteile hat gegenüber der nationalsozialistischen, faschistischen Ideologie. Ich stehe nicht an zu bezeugen, dass es viel schöner ist, ein gläubiger Marxist zu sein als ein gläubiger Nationalsozialist. Nur die staatliche Praxis, die Entkernung des Politischen, die Entrechtung und Entkernung der Autonomie der Person, die Zurücknahme der Rolle des Citoyen, die Zurücknahme der Rolle des Rechtes in einem Gemeinwesen, all dies schafft so eklatante Ähnlichkeiten, dass man sich nur wundern kann, wenn man die Unterschiedlichkeit der Ideologien anschaut. Deshalb sind diejenigen immer auf dem Holzweg, die abgesehen von der Praxis durch einen ideologischen Vergleich der Systeme den Sozialismus immer noch hell und klar strahlen lassen. Man kann nur die armen Verwirrten, die nach wie vor gläubige Anhänger des Staatssozialismus sind, zutiefst bedauern und muss ein neues Zeitalter der Aufklärung über sie herabrufen und vor allen Dingen diesen Blick der Gelassenheit bestimmter linksliberaler Eliten gegenüber der kommunistischen Herrschaftsform als etwas Verschriemeltes, Untaugliches angreifen. Eine antihumane Gesellschaft zu delegitimieren, so wie es ihr gebührt.

Ich hatte gesagt, dass es noch einen Blick auf weitere Elemente geben muss, die die Vergleichbarkeit so unterschiedlicher Ideologien aus der Praxis heraus dartut. Das ist die Kaderpolitik, die Personalpolitik. Wenn in einem Staat in allen Gebieten bis hinein in die Wirtschaft staatliche Instanzen dafür sorgen, dass Karrieren gemacht oder verhindert werden, wenn in der Schule bestimmt wird, wer die Oberschule besuchen kann und wer nicht; meine Kinder zum Beispiel durften die Oberschule nicht besuchen, sie waren nicht Mitglied der staatlichen Jugendorganisation. Ich kenne viele

Christen, die mit dem Leistungsdurchschnitt 1,0 nicht zum Abitur oder auch zum Studium zugelassen wurden. Also wenn von der Ausbildung bis über die Karrieremuster der Staat eingreift in die Karrierewege, in die Kaderplanung, dann haben wir einen Grad von Abhängigkeit der Einzelnen erreicht, die es niemals in einer feudalen Adelsgesellschaft gegeben hat. Und insofern sind die Herrschaftstechniken, ist die Durchherrschung der Systeme im Grunde etwas Neues. Wir könnten sagen, nicht das Mittelalter, sondern die politische Moderne ist der eigentliche Ort, wo die Ohnmacht der Masse der Bevölkerung am eklatantesten zu besichtigen ist. Es ist das zweite Gesicht der Moderne. Nicht Aufklärung, nicht Herrschaft des Rechtes, sondern immerfort das Gegenteil dieser Elemente der politischen Aufklärung. Und es ist schon einigermaßen deprimierend, dass in einem eigentlich emanzipatorischen Ansatz, wie dem des Marxismus, eine derartige Leugnung und Durchstreichung der Möglichkeiten des Humanum der Politik zu besichtigen ist. Ich sprach von der Kaderpolitik und ich muss das natürlich ergänzen durch eine nie gekannte Stärke von Einwirkung polizeilicher und geheimpolizeilicher Instanzen in alle Bereiche des Lebens. Jawohl, in alle. Der deutsche Autor Rainer Kunze beschreibt in einem Erinnerungsbuch – er stammt aus Ostdeutschland und ist später in den Westen gegangen – wie die Staatssicherheit, die ostdeutsche Geheimpolizei, bei den Nachbarn vorstellig wird und versucht und es auch erreicht, bei der Nachbarin die Erlaubnis zu erhalten, ein Loch in die Wand zu bohren, damit eine Wanze im Schlafzimmer des Ehepaars Kunze platziert werden kann. Man hat diesen Menschen erklärt, es sei für den Aufbau des Sozialismus wichtig, auch das Privatleben dieser gefährlichen Staatsfeinde völlig zu überwachen. Dies ist nur ein kleines Beispiel für das dreiste Eindringen der Staatsmacht in die privatesten Bereiche des Menschen. Herrschaft nennen wir das in der politikwissenschaftlichen Sprache.

Die ostdeutsche Geheimpolizei war natürlich nicht so brutal und verbrecherisch wie die Gestapo. Das gebe ich gerne zu. Aber man fragt sich doch, warum für so wenig Volk (im Osten 16,56 Millionen Menschen) eine Geheimpolizei in der Stärke von 90.000 hauptamtlichen plus 175.000 ehrenamtlichen, inoffiziellen Mitarbeitern gehalten wurde. Hier in Westdeutschland hat das personenstärkste Bundesland Nordrhein-Westfalen etwa 17 Millionen Menschen. Kein Bewohner dieses Bundeslandes könnte sich vorstellen, dass die Landesregierung 90.000 überbezahlte Staatsdiener hält, nur um die Macht der regierenden Partei zu sichern. Das wäre völlig neurotisch und nicht vorstellbar. Wir Ostdeutschen aber lebten in einem derartigen System. Und wenn wir uns nach den Gründen fragen, warum ein solches System soviel Geheimpolizei benötigt, gelangt man zu der Antwort, dass Systeme, denen eine echte Sicherheit durch Rechtssicherheit, Gewaltenteilung und Grundrechte fehlt, einen Sicherheitsersatz benötigen. Dieser wird dann in die Gesellschaft eingezogen, um einem brüchigen System Stabilität zu verleihen.

Ganz zum Schluss möchte ich noch den individuellen Teil betrachten. Solche Systeme neigen dazu, die Rechte und die Rolle des Einzelnen systematisch herunter zu deklinieren. Sie werden im Kindergarten und in der Schule Verformungsvorgänge erleben, die die Würde der Person, das Recht des autonomen Ich und eine Gewissensentscheidung ganz systematisch hintanstellen und den Einzelnen als Rolle in einer Gruppe, in einem Gesamtsystem, fortwährend vorführen. Das wird eintrainiert. Deshalb wird in der schulischen Ausbildung ständig darauf geachtet, dass eben nicht das kritische Hinterfragen, die eigene Urteilsbildung gefördert wird, sondern das Sich-Einfügen in ein System der staatlichen Ordnung, die nicht hinterfragt werden darf. Wenn dies dann fortgesetzt wird an der Universität, durch Personalentscheidung, durch ständige ideologische Beeinflussung, wenn es gleichzeitig kein Verfassungsgericht gibt, das dir deine Bürgerrechte garantiert, ja nicht einmal Verwaltungsgerichte, um sich staatlicher Willkür zu erwehren, wenn es nicht eine Medienwelt gibt, in der man unterschiedliche Meinungen über die Welt hört, dann können Sie sich vielleicht vorstellen, in welchem Grad das Individuum schablonisiert und zu einem abhängigen Element, einem Staatsinsassen wird. Diktatur, so lernten wir es von beiden Formen illegitimer Herrschaft, Diktatur macht krank. Sie zerstört, um von Hanna Arendt zu sprechen, nicht nur die Strukturen des Politischen, sondern sie greift in den Personenbereich der einzelnen Individuen ein, entkernt sie, beraubt sie ihrer Fähigkeit, des eigenverantwortlichen Handelns und lässt sie im Grunde zurück als eine Verfügungsmasse derer, die gerade was zu sagen haben.

Nie, und das ist unser Trost, trifft das alle, und immer gibt es Hoffnungspotentiale, die Minderheiten in oppositionellen Vierteln in Widerstandsgruppen wach werden lassen und es gibt Anständige, die sich nicht völlig fügen, immer noch an die glauben, auch wenn sie Jahrzehnte in Unfreiheit leben. Und dass aus so konditionierten Menschen 1989 eine Freiheitsrevolution hervorbricht, in Sachsen zunächst und dann im gesamten Ostdeutschland, grenzt für uns Deutsche fast an ein Wunder. Und wir würden uns immerfort freuen, wenn in Deutschland nicht ein Grundgesetz gelten würde, das heißt: Fühle dich nie wohl, sondern preise dein Unbehagen. Wenn wir anders wären, wenn wir etwas von ihnen hätten oder von unseren französischen Nachbarn, wir würden nicht aufhören, uns darüber zu freuen, dass wir trotz der Gewöhnung an Ohnmacht mit dem Slogan „Wir sind das Volk" den Citoyen zurückgebracht haben, auf die Handlungsebene, auf die Bühne des Politischen. Irgendwann werden die Deutschen das auch haben. Werden sich freuen können darüber, dass es uns nach einem blutigen Terrorjahrzehnt in 50/60 Jahren gelungen ist, eine lebendige Zivilgesellschaft hier im Westen und eine Freiheitsrevolution im Osten geschaffen zu haben, wie dies in der deutschen Geschichte vorher niemals stattgefunden hat. Irgendwann, wenn der tiefe, dunkle Schatten unserer jüngsten Geschichte und die Erinnerung an jene, die für die Tötungsmaschinerien verantwortlich waren, ein wenig weiter verblasst sein werden, werden wir auch daran glauben, dass wir über das Können verfügen, unsere Wünsche auch Wirklichkeit werden zu lassen. Das wünschen wir uns und irgendwann werden wir daran glauben, dass wir das auch können. Genau das ist es nämlich, was uns die Diktaturen beider Arten versucht haben, abzugewöhnen.

Ich danke Ihnen für Ihre Aufmerksamkeit und wünsche mir, dass Sie gelegentlich in einem Feldversuch durch einen Besuch in Ostdeutschland meine Erklärungen verifizieren können.

Danke für Ihre Aufmerksamkeit!

Joachim Gauck

Under Totalitarian Regimes: A Comparative Analysis of National Socialism And the German Democratic Republic

This is an eye-witness account of life in the German Democratic Republic under a totalitarian regime. The starting point is the recollection of a young boy at the age of ten living in an oppressive Soviet dominated East-German system, whose father 'wurde abgeholt', was abducted by the socialist authorities in 1950 and sentenced to 50 years forced labour by a secret Soviet military court because one of his colleagues at work had fled the GDR to live in the West. As to his whereabouts, the family had no idea and no information was released by the government. Not until his return after two and half years later following his release did the family learn of the circumstances surrounding his abduction. The socialist regime propagated that a new era of freedom had been born, which was nothing else than a bunch of lies. Instead of the official propaganda that the former Nazi concentration camps Sachsenhausen and Buchenwald continued to operate under the Soviet military to imprison former Nazis; in truth they were soon full of young people who were opposed to the socialist system. For the population living in East Germany there was a continuous feeling of powerlessness against an oppressive state. The governments of the Eastern Block were totally controlled and governed by the Soviet Union and its tanks. In 1961 East Germans were held confined by the building of the Berlin Wall, which again enhanced a feeling of helplessness against the power of the state.

Despite the differences, there were many similarities between National Socialism and the communist system evolving in the Soviet-occupied zone after World War II. People were deprived of their status as active citizens – in other words of being a 'citoyen'. They were turned into mere subjects through the Party of Socialist Unity (SED) whose primary interest was to remain in power. Both totalitarian systems have four elements in common: (1) disbanding a separation of power (2) the abolition of free elections and the raise of acclamatory rituals of self-preservation, (3) the abolition of the rule of law and (4) the abolition of basic rights for citizens.

Antifascism served as a myth to justify the birth of a repressive system directed by the SED Party, which had the most former Nazis amongst its members in all of Germany. In order to totally control the population, a secret police (Stasi) was created consisting of 90,000 full-time and 175,000 part-time staff, for an overall population of 17 million people living in East Germany. Obeying rules was systematically trained from nursery school onwards. However, there were people in East Germany, who opposed such indoctrination and stood up for the return of the 'citoyen' through a unique and peaceful revolution, which led to the fall of the Berlin Wall in 1989.

IX. A Different Story/Eine andere Geschichte

Robert Wolfson

Liberating Perspectives

We see through a lens. It can be a mental lens that determines our point of view. It can be an actual lens in the eye that can only capture bits and pieces of the complex reality before us. It can be the lens of a camera that captures light and preserves for us an image, frozen in time that can carry with it power and meaning.

It is a great honor for me to be able to share with you a story of one photograph taken over 60 years ago that has changed forever my own sense of our lenses and the power of an image to change the way we view a particular event in history.

We must pause to remember that the words we use reflect the complexity of our respective lenses. The Americans who were there at Dachau, April 29, 1945 call it "Liberation". From the point of view of the soldiers and the prisoners of Dachau and many other camps- there is no question that this day reflected the road back to life having survived unimaginable suffering. For many, out of respect for the sacrifice and memory of those who fought to stop the Nazi regime, there is no question or challenge in using such a powerful word. And it should be understood in the context of the whole war experience. However, "liberation" did not come at the hands of a policy to find, locate and "liberate" camps from the Nazis. It was more of an accidental discovery. Although the discoveries at the camps were difficult, gruesome and complex, there was the focused lens toward the military defeat of the Third Reich and the capture of Berlin, which would close this European war.

I come to this discussion with experience in the modern manifestations of the "Nazi" philosophy- an idea not yet eliminated from the human heart. In Omaha, Nebraska, we were able to address the challenges and opportunities of Holocaust education several years ago by recruiting an incredible professional Beth Seldin Dotan. Beth worked at the Ghetto Fighters House Museum in Israel for several years before returning to Omaha. We have been blessed to benefit from her perspective of having worked at a museum founded by survivors of the Warsaw Ghetto. These incredible teachers and models have never viewed the history of the Shoa through the lens of victimhood but from a lens of strength and survival in spite of the suffering.

Beth came into possession of the photo album of a man from Omaha, Lt. Col. Williams, who was there the days Dachau was discovered by American troops, April 29-30, 1945. Americans moving towards Berlin discover a camp, a very large camp called Dachau, a place we will visit this afternoon. Williams had a camera with him and as he had been doing since landing in Normandy, he recorded the trail of his personal journey through the war with photos. When he returned from the war, like so many others, he rarely spoke of this journey to family and friends. Through this one man's story we see that grasping huge chunks of history is difficult and that individual stories provide a powerful lens through which we can connect to the deeper messages of history. "Testimonial portals" are the most common road into the stories of the dark of the Shoah.

The only recording we have of this one man's experience of the day of "Liberation" is a moving letter he wrote the evening after. A letter written to his wife back home. It is a moving and a once in his lifetime written testimony of this day. I would like to read a selection from that letter.

Monday
30 April 45.

My Honey,

Had a new experience today that I will never forget as long as I live. I had read a lot about concentration camps and the brutal treatment given the prisoners but often wondered if it were all true. Now I can vouch for it. The camp covered an area of probably ten square blocks and much of it was surrounded by high cement walls with barbed wire on top and electric wires over those. A railroad runs through the camp and we saw an entire train of boxcars with dead human bodies that they had no time to dispose of. Several press photographers were there so if you see any pictures in the newspapers or Life Magazine I would appreciate your letting me know and saving them for me. Some of our medics are in the pictures and they may even be shown in the movies as there was one movie camera there.

Inside the camp was one building used as a crematory rather it was built especially for that purpose. It had one room for showers which the prisoners could get wet and open up the pores of their skin then into the gas chamber. Here they were killed, removed and stacked like cardwood until they could be shoved in the ovens. They were stacked in four rooms and the boys estimated around 700 – 800 bodies awaiting cremating. Those laying in the box cars were nothing but skin and bone and on many, the thighs of their legs weren't as big as my forearm. Inside the camp they had factories, machine shops, hospital, and foundries where they used the slave labor guarded by SS Troops to make the tools of war etc. In the largest single section of the camp was several thousand prisoners from every country in Europe and even some Americans. They were now displaying all their national flags and it was very colorful. We talked with one prisoner from Yugoslavia (formerly a bank vice-president) who had been there 20 months. His neighbor had reported him listening to BBC and American news broadcasts. He was well educated and spoke English very well. Around this section was barbed wire entanglements and cement pill boxes for the guards every few yards. There was also a deep ditch surrounding the section inside the wire. Outside there was a moat running around the section. They told us the men on the train had been riding without food for 18 days and the prisoners told us they worked 7 days a week from 5:00 AM until 8:00 PM. There were several guards still laying around the ground where they had been killed. Most of them they didn't bother to shoot but merely beat them to death with rifle butts when our troops took over. Thousands of our troops visited the camp today and I doubt very much if there will be another SS Trooper taken prisoner. It is almost unbelievable that anyone could be hardened to the point of doing the brutal things they did and it certainly gives me a different viewpoint toward the German people. This is all probably boring to you but you just can't picture such sights without seeing them with your own eyes.

Well darling guess that will be all for today except to tell you again I love you worlds.

Always Yours
Clarence.

One letter found in a shoe box stuffed with correspondence to his wife. On loan from Dr. Tom Williams, son of Staff Sergeant Clarence Williams of the 42nd Rainbow Infantry Division.

His photos and the letter, neatly collected and labeled were discovered by his family after his death and the family graciously shared these with us as a testimonial and honor to his war story.

In the many photos taken that day, one in particular strikes deeply. It reminds responsible people of the power of images, the care we must take not to minimize the death of so many unidentifiable souls. The sheer size of the events and the loss of life are so large it may tend to harden us to the reality and depth of the meaning for us. This one photo may help to illuminate the many facets, the multiple lenses that must be at work as we continue the hard task of peeling away the fog of war to find history and meaning and hopefully lessons.

We began to explore the one disturbing photo out of a need to triangulate the story of Lt. Col. Williams with the recorded and known events of that day. We discovered that two American military groups had entered Dachau on that day. The 42nd Infantry Rainbow Division of the Seventh Army and the 45th Thunderbird Division of the Third Army came from two sides of the camp. Much discussion and dispute about who "liberated" the camp and the timeline of the events of that day have taken up many pages and hours. The people who fought Hitler's regime are deeply passionate about their role in this historic fight. It is beyond the scope of this discussion but a worthwhile subject to explore. The varied accounts of eyewitnesses on these two days helps magnify the reality of our lens analogy. No one can know for sure the events surrounding these days. There remains no question that these two military groups were in and around when the camp surrendered at 4:50 p.m. on April 29, 1945. The surrender was from SS Lieutenant Wickert, a low ranking Nazi whose boss had fled, to Brigadier General Henning Linden, Assistant Commander of the 42nd Rainbow Infantry Division. Linden had arrived at the camp with a contingent that included a female journalist, dressed as a man to avoid difficulties in the war zone. The camp itself displays notices that acknowledge the role of both of these military groups in the discovery of the camp.

As American approached the camp, almost all who have written and spoken of that day talk about the smell. Another Omaha man, Bob Perelman relates, "The smell of death, the stink, the stench – it stays with you all your life – you can't forget it." The stench came from the camp itself and from the "Death train", parked outside the fence of Dachau behind the SS encampment. The train had 39 railcars. The train had been on a three week attempt to relocate those on the train to other locations. The train had left Weimar, Germany on April 5, 1945 with over 80 prisoners in each car. They had come from a wide variety of places all being moved away from the front in attempt to hide from the oncoming Allied forces. They came from Langensalza a satellite camp of Buchenwald, mostly in good condition reflecting the situation in that particular camp. They came from the Dora V-2 rocket plants were conditions were much worse. The train came to Buchenwald and that camp was filled beyond capacity and the commandant refused to take more inmates. It was to travel for three days and rations for the three days were distributed at the start of this horrible journey. But the train went to Leipzig, to Dresden to the Protectorate of Bohemia and on to Passau, at each stop, more people were shoved onto the train with no provisions or facilities provided. The train eventually made its way to Dachau on April 27. Of the original over 5,000 people on the train, approximately 1,300 were alive when the train arrived at Dachau and entered the camp. Thousand had died on route, were removed at various stops and others added. Some had been shot at the arrival in Dachau. The train, when discovered by the advancing Americans, was filled with bodies – 2,310 bodies in all.

The actual takeover of the camp is a story of its own. But the "Death Train" became a symbol of the Nazi brutality, of the nature of the Nazi regime. For many American soldiers who viewed this site, it explained the emotions of long battles and finally put into focus the lens that explained why they were there fighting the Nazi regime. Eisenhower himself ordered that the train be left intact until May 13. Every available soldier and reporter was brought to this place. The bodies were only removed after these viewings. And of course many of the witnesses were taking photos. At the end of this gruesome display of death, the townspeople of Dachau removed the bodies and put them in a mass grave on Leitenberg Hill – forever overlooking the area.

Over the next few months, we learned what we could of these historical events, consulting books and memoirs, news accounts and original documents when we could find them. To our surprise, another photo was delivered to us even though we had not gone public with our discovery. It shook us deeply when we realized that these photos were of the same place – the same rail car – the same man – so disturbingly lying with eyes open on the pile of bodies.

Then we noticed that the two photos were not exactly the same. They were taken of the same scene but from slightly different angles – different camera – different photographers. We then realized the metaphor. Not only were we struggling to find the history of these days but to find the stories and the meanings. We were struck that so many who were there related their stories only very late in life and were also moved by how many must have seen this site or similar sites and never spoken of it. We were shaken by the realities of so many having important stories to tell dying without ever sharing what had happened to them.

This journey has led to discovering over 49 individual images of this same railcar. An 8 millimeter film of the same car was discovered.

Beth Seldin Dotan assembled a team that began work on a preliminary exhibit which we mounted in Omaha called "Liberating Perspectives". This display of the photos and the accompanying discoveries illuminates that each G.I. took his own lens – actual or virtual – and captured this horrific scene. Each image taken from a slightly different angle – each person with his own reactions and histories, and each who survived – returning to life to somehow cope and integrate all that comes with war and with these particularly horrifying images emblazoned on their memories.

We wondered about the impact of those who returned and had to bury the memories to create a new reality in the civilian world. Today there is a reported explosion of Post traumatic Stress Disorder cases from Korean and World War II veterans. They returned to American soil and rarely told of the emotions and power of the images they saw and how those memories have impacted their lives. Many became like the survivors of the Holocaust – reluctant or unable to talk or to adequately process their experiences. There are those who wrote or spoke of their experiences. But for the thousands who must have seen these images there are but a few who have spoken of them. For those whose lives live on many continue to suffer from untold effects from war.

The images we have collected tell us that at sometime, someone closed the eyes of the dead as the bodies were viewed. It touches the soul deeply thinking of the sensitivity of a person, forced to view this incomprehensible situation, taking a hand to the dead to give whatever small portion of dignity was possible. Our lenses were even further challenged upon the discovery that shortly after these events; the Seventh Army ordered a formal investigation of alleged mistreatment of German Guards on May 2, 1945.

The investigation was conducted by Lt. Col. Joseph M. Whitaker as the investigating officer. There remains some disputed facts about what occurred and why. But here are a few of the conclusions from the Whitaker report.

Four German soldiers surrendered and were made to climb into one of the boxcars filled with bodies and these men were killed by American soldiers. SS soldiers were round up and put into a separate enclosure. There is no dispute that 17 of these prisoners were shot and killed by machine gun and carbine fire. Others were wounded. A number of presumed SS men were captured around the camp tower and were summarily killed.

The report of the Investigating Officer Whitaker came to the conclusion that there were actions take at Dachau that were beyond the pale and should be followed up. His report was reviewed at a higher level and was followed up with a report from Wade H. Haislip, Lieutenant General, USA Command. This is from the summary paragraph of his report.

"This investigation indicates an apparent lack of comprehension on the part of the investigating officer of the normal disorganization of small unit combat action and of the unbalancing effects of the horrors and shock of Dachau on combat troops already fatigued with more than 30 days continuous combat action."

In the opinion of the undersigned the investigation indicates further an apparent attempt to accentuate testimony unfavorable to the participants rather than to develop the investigation impartially. Since it is not felt that the foregoing investigation conducted by the Inspector General, this headquarters, gives a true and unbiased conclusion after considering all factors, including the extenuating circumstances, it is recommended that circumstances surrounding the alleged mistreatment and shooting of German guards at the concentration camp at Dachau, Germany, be re-investigated.

As we look back on the many ways in which the participants have characterized the trials and the motivations behind the trials, it is impossible not to wonder what must the child of an SS officer summarily killed after the surrender at Dachau feel like when he or she reads of our lofty discussions on how war crimes and crimes against humanity would be treated differently in accordance with the new Nuremburg proceedings? How do we all deal with a history when once exposed shows that in war – many things occur – and the notions of justice are challenged in ways that history alone cannot help us untangle? The lens we bring – like the lens of those American soldiers – each taking mental and actual photos of the horror of war – each lens leads us to new information, new thoughts and new challenges to consider. The processes of trying to find a new way to end a war and assign responsibility for crimes may not help untangle all the different perspectives hindsight provides us. The power and complexity of each situation we uncover, each new story we hear, each new layer of history that comes into the awareness of those who care, challenges our understandings of history and our ability to see the totality of each historical moment.

The power of a few photographs:
They remind us of the horror of war,
Of the difficulty of ever comprehending the totality of history,
And of the human need to continue to dig for kernels of truth.

Robert Wolfson

Perspektiven der Befreiung

Als amerikanische Truppen am 29./30. April 1945 gegen Berlin vorrückten, entdeckten sie in der Nähe von München ein großes Lager mit Namen Dachau. Unter den Soldaten war auch Oberstleutnant Williams, der mit seiner Kamera Aufnahmen von dem Lager machte. Unter seinen Fotos befand sich ein Bild des bekannten „Todeszuges" mit 39 Waggons, der in Dachau entdeckt wurde.

Der Zug hatte Weimar am 5. April 1945 mit Verpflegung für eine dreitägige Reise und über 80 Gefangenen in jedem Waggon verlassen. Er fuhr allerdings noch andere Orte an, und immer mehr Menschen wurden ohne Verpflegung in die Waggons geschichtet, bevor er schließlich am 27. April Dachau erreichte. Von den ursprünglich über 5.000 im Zug befindlichen Menschen waren bei seiner Ankunft in Dachau noch etwa 1.300 am Leben. Als die anrückenden Amerikaner den Zug entdeckten, fanden sie Waggons gefüllt mit toten Körpern vor – insgesamt 2.310.

Untersuchungen amerikanischer Militärbehörden zeigten Bilder, wie deutsche Soldaten in Dachau gezwungen worden waren, in einen mit Leichen gefüllten Waggon zu steigen, wo sie dann von amerikanischen Soldaten erschossen wurden; andere Bilder zeigten die Tötung von siebzehn gefangenen deutschen Soldaten – offensichtlich der SS angehörige Männer – mit Maschinengewehren, die ebenfalls kurzerhand exekutiert wurden.

Als verschiedene Redner im Laufe der Konferenz die Nürnberger Prozesse und die dahinterstehenden Motivationen beschrieben, tauchten Fragen auf wie jene, ob es möglich ist sich vorzustellen, was das Kind eines SS-Offiziers von Dachau, der nach der Niederlegung seiner Waffen von amerikanischen Soldaten standrechtlich erschossen wurde, wohl fühlt, wenn es heute unsere hochtrabenden Diskussionen liest, wie Kriegsverbrechen und Verbrechen gegen die Menschlichkeit nun in Übereinstimmung mit den in Nürnberg abgehaltenen Verfahren anders gehandhabt werden?

Wie wird Geschichte dargestellt, die – einmal aufgedeckt – zeigt, dass im Krieg die Vorstellungen von Gerechtigkeit in einer Art herausgefordert werden, wie sie durch Geschichte allein nicht entwirrt werden können? Die Macht und Komplexität jeder Situation, die wir aufdecken, jede neue Geschichte, die wir hören, jede neue geschichtliche Erkenntnis für jene, die daran interessiert sind, fordert unser Verständnis der Geschichte und unsere Fähigkeit, jeden historischen Moment in seiner Gesamtheit zu sehen, immer wieder heraus.

List of Authors/Autorenverzeichnis

Autorenverzeichnis/List of Authors

Akin, Wanda M.	Adjunct Professor at Seton Hall Law School. Co-counsel to an accused at the UN backed Special Court for Sierra Leone
Alford, Roger	Professor of Law at Pepperdine School of Law
Ascensio, Hervé	Professor of Law at the University of Paris I (Panthéon-Sorbonne)
Bach, Gabriel	Judge of the Israeli Supreme Court (ret.)
Bank, Dr. Roland	Legal Officer at the Branch Office of the UNCHR in Berlin, former principal legal adviser of the Foundation "Remembrance, Responsibility and Future", Berlin
Barrett, John Q.	Professor of Law, St. John's University School of Law, New York City, and Elizabeth S. Lenna Fellow, Robert H. Jackson Center, Jamestown, NY
Bayefsky, Anne	Visiting Professor at Touro College, Visiting Scholar at Metropolitan College of New York, Senior Fellow with the Hudson Institute
Bazyler, Michael	Professor of Law and the "1939" Club Law Scholar in Holocaust and Human Rights Studies at Whittier Law School, California, research fellow at the Holocaust Education Trust in London
Bloxham, Dr. Donald	Lecturer in History at the University of Edinburgh, UK
Brown, Raymond M.	Professor of Law at Seton Hall University School of Law and Seton Hall's Diplomacy School, former Co-Lead Defense Counsel at the Special Court for Sierra Leone
Cesarani, David	Research Professor in History at Royal Holloway, University of London, UK
Citron, Rodger	Assistant Professor of Law at Touro Law Center
Derby, Daniel H.	Professor and Director of international programs at Touro College Jacob D. Fuchsberg Law Center
Douglas, Lawrence	Professor of Law, Jurisprudence & Social Thought, at Amherst College
Eser, Dr. Dr. h.c. mult. Albin	Professor or Law, Director of the Max Planck Institute for Foreign and International Criminal Law, Freiburg, Germany (ret.). Judge ad litem at the International Criminal Tribunal for the former Yugoslavia in The Hague
Ferencz, Dr. Benjamin B.	Chief Prosecutor in the subsequent Nuremberg "SS-Einsatzgruppen"-Trial
Garkawe, Sam	Professor at the School of Law and Justice at Southern Cross University, NSW, Australia
Gauck, Dr. h.c. Joachim	President of the association "Gegen Vergessen Für Demokratie e.V." (Against Forgetting For Democracy), former Special Attaché of the Federal Government for the Personal Files of the Former State Security Service
Harmon, Louise	Professor of Law at Touro Law School

Harris, Whitney	Member of the prosecuting team at the International Military Tribunal at Nuremberg
Heinemann, Dr. Winfried	Colonel, German Armed Forces' Center of Military History (MGFA), Potsdam, East German military history
James, Greg, Q.C.	former NSW Supreme Court and Court of Criminal Appeal Judge in Australia
Kastner, Dr. Klaus	President of the Regional Court Nürnberg-Fürth (ret.); honorary Professor at the Friedrich-Alexander-Universität Erlangen-Nürnberg
Kaul, Hans-Peter	Judge and the President of the Pre-Trial Division at the International Criminal Trial in The Hague
Kress, Dr. Claus	Professor of Law; Director of the Institute for Criminal Law and Criminal Procedure at Cologne University
Marrus, Michael	Chancellor Rose and Ray Wolfe Professor of Holocaust Studies at the University of Toronto
Reginbogin, Herbert	Professor of Law and History at Touro College, Potsdam Germany Law Program, University of Potsdam, and Bogazici University Istanbul
Reicher, Harry	Professor at the University of Pennsylvania Law School, former Director of International Affairs and Representative to the United Nations of Agudath Israel World Organization
Rüping, Dr. Hinrich	Professor for Criminal Law, Criminal Procedure and History of Criminal Law in Hannover, Judge in the Upper Regional Court in Celle, Germany
Safferling, Dr. Christoph J.M.	Assistant professor at the Institute for Criminal Law of the Friedrich-Alexander-Universität Erlangen-Nürnberg, Germany, and the Whitney R. Harris International Law Scholar, Jackson Center, Jamestown, NY
Wittmann, Rebecca	Assistant Professor of History at the University of Toronto (Mississauga)
Wolfson, Robert	Regional Director of the Anti-Defamation League
Yavnai, Elisabeth	Director of Visiting Scholars Programs at the Center for Advanced Holocaust Studies, United States Holocaust Memorial Museum in Washington, DC
Zimmermann, Dr. Andreas	Professor of Constitutional and International Law and Director of the Walther-Schücking Institute for International Law at University of Kiel